DIMENSIONS OF DEVELOPMENT

VOLUME—ONE : AGRICULTURE

Dimensions of Development Series
Analysis of An Underdeveloped State

Vol. I : Agriculture
Vol. II : Industry
Vol. III : Mining, Decentralised Industry and Infrastructure
Vol. IV : Resources : Financial and Human

About the Author

Prof. Dr. K.N. Prasad was educated at Patna University and Cambridge University culminating in the Ph.D. degree in Economics from the latter in 1960. He attended in 1955 the Advanced Refresher Course in Economics, organised jointly by the International Economic Association and the Indian Economic Association in Poona. Dr. Prasad joined the Bihar Education Service as Lecturer in Economics in 1949. He was appointed Reader in Economics in 1962 and University Professor of Economics in 1964. He was Head of the Economics Department, Patna College (Bihar's oldest and premier college) for about 12 years. He was Principal of the college for four years. He was Head of the Department of Economics of Patna University during 1979-89. He was also Dean of the Faculty of Social Sciences of Patna University. He was Vice-Chancellor of the university twice, first in 1979 and then in 1985. He retired as University Professor and Head of the Department of Economics of Patna University in 1989. After retirement, he was Member of the Bihar State Planning Board and Member of the Second Bihar Irrigation Commission till August 1994. Professor Prasad is an author of several well-known books and research papers and has produced a large number of Ph.D.'s under his supervision. He was associated with a number of State-level and a few national committees and commissions as well as the academic and the administrative bodies of several universities. He has travelled widely abroad and lectured in several foreign universities.

DIMENSIONS OF DEVELOPMENT
Analysis of An Underdeveloped State

VOLUME-ONE

AGRICULTURE

Prof. (Dr.) K.N. PRASAD

CONCEPT PUBLISHING COMPANY, NEW DELHI-110059

ISBN 81-7022-741-0 (Vol. 1)
ISBN 81-7022-740-2 (Series)

First Published 1998

Published and Printed by
Ashok Kumar Mittal
Concept Publishing Company
A/15-16, Commercial Block, Mohan Garden
NEW DELHI-110059 (India)

Phones : 5648039, 5649024
Fax : 091-11-5648053

PREFACE

This book is intended to be a standard reference for the students who have to prepare for the examinations, college/university/competitive, for the interviews, for writing dissertations/essays/articles for journals, as also for those who are involved in the decision-making process and execution of the plan programmes, etc. It may be useful even to the general reader interested in the problems of India from the regional point of view.

Bihar agriculture is taught at all levels in the academic institutions, particularly those concerned with higher education, either as part of the Indian Economics/Economy/Economic Problems paper or as an independent paper or, again, as one of the two-paper special group at the Honours/Master stage. Besides the Economics, the Commerce, Geography and Sociology courses of studies incorporate topics on Bihar agriculture. The competitive tests held at the State-level for recruitment to the various services invariably have in their question-papers questions on Bihar agriculture. At any time there are numerous research students in Bihar and other States who work on some topic or other relating to Bihar agriculture for composing their dissertation for the Master, Master of Philosophy or Ph.D./D.Litt. degree of a particular university.

A glance at the Contents and the List of Tables would show that this treatise is cast in the same mould as any standard treatise on Indian Economics/Economy/Economic Problems. Alternatively, this work on Bihar Agriculture is on all fours with any standard work on Indian Agriculture, which is taught in colleges and university departments and is referred to by the researchers in their research work on any subject dealing with agriculture.

Very few books on Indian Agriculture contain information on the agriculture of the States. But this book makes a comparative study of Bihar and All-India in each and every aspect of agriculture. This was necessitated by the urge on our part to know at length how Bihar stands in relation to/*vis-a-vis* All-India, and this for the entire period of the present study. In other words, it is a comparative study of Bihar and All-India based on comparative statics/dynamics. That Bihar should not remain below the national average in the years to come and moves up is the motive-force guiding the production of this volume. References are made to other States wherever required but the focus is on Punjab, which remains the ideal in respect of agriculture. The present position of Punjab agriculture is summarised in a short write-up placed at the end of the book.

As the tempo of development in Bihar is below that in All-India, agriculture continues to be more important to the State economy than to the national economy. Whichever of the two, contribution to the aggregate income or contribution to the total employment, is the acid-test, agriculture remains very important in Bihar. Also, in the horizon of the future, Bihar's fortune would depend more critically on how its agriculture fares. If the backwardness of an economy is, in the ultimate, resolvable into its low productivity, then a thrust/break-through in the productivity of agriculture must occur so as to become the fulcrum for the uplift of industry and, through their interaction, of the economy as a whole. That is to say, to make out why Bihar is poor and backward, we have to first understand why Bihar agriculture is poor and backward.

Agriculture can be a help or a hindrance to development at a time or through time. There is a school of thought in Bihar/India that agriculture in Bihar is a drag on the economy in the sense that it is over-crowded and its performance has been unsatisfactory on many counts; it has not met the food requirement of the State and the raw materials requirement of the industry in Bihar nor has it contributed directly to the State finances. Since some years past the country side has become a storehouse of tensions. Another school holds that the potentials of agriculture are very great, provided that structure and the institutions which encompass it are remodelled and refashioned. Our work addresses itself to the critical examination of these conflicting views.

In the concluding chapter we have outlined the situation facing Bihar agriculture on the eve of Independence. Juxtaposing the present situation with that situation, we can arrive at certain facts which may throw a flood of light on how and to what extent the hypotheses of growth economics stand the test so far as Bihar agriculture is concerned.

All agricultural problems and issues have been analysed carefully and illustrated with adequate statistics and other information and remedies have been suggested as far as feasible.

The last chapter pertains to be an over-all estimate/stock-taking of Bihar agriculture. One salient feature of that chapter lies in its trying to enunciate the political economy of Bihar with special reference to its agriculture. As far as it has been possible, a detached, dispassionate stand has been taken, by eschewing and shunning all bias and prejudice; there is no attempt to grind one's axe, so to say.

The data and other information embodied in this book are for fifty years, from 1947 to 1997. This work is the product of the author's association with the subject in his capacity as a student, teacher and researcher for about 55 years. The language used in it is simple and lucid, chiselled and chaste as far as possible.

The author hopes that this book would be of value to a wide range of readers, student or non-student, in Bihar and other States as well as serve as a model for the study of the development of a low-income State.

The author has the satisfaction that with his very meagre resources he could dedicate his life of shunt and isolation (which retired life represents in the case of people with very few contacts and practically no political patronage in this country) to the completion of this study which he started while he was still in his own State which he was obliged to leave in December 1994. He knew that there were institutions/councils/commissions which helped retired university teachers with funds in their research studies/publications but he had no heart left to approach any of them for the sole reason that in the early 1970s when he had submitted a project to a particular council, he was, after some time, treated with a note containing the observations of the critic of his project, which made him think that he did not know Economics at all and all his studentship and teaching experience had been sheer waste, and hence he would have to learn Economics again by becoming a student of that great economist. Since then the author could not muster courage enough to repeat the act. Criticism or review should be balanced; it should not become a vehicle of display of one's superior knowledge or ideological or regional prejudice or a mere caricature.

My thanks are due to Mr S.N. Mishra (Sanskrit Department, Patna University for doing some typing), Dr. Sharat Kumar, Dr. Krishna Kumar and Mr Vikaram Sarin (for procuring some data), Md Shan Alam and Mr Sanjiv Verma of Cyber Space, NOIDA (for help in getting some photocopying done), Mrs Usha Prasad and Mrs Meena Verma (for some help in classifying the typescripts), Mr Sachin Verma (for buying some books for my use), Prof. Dr. Kamta Prasad, a very distinguished past pupil of mine (for inviting me to his workshop at which I could meet my equally eminent old students like Prof. Dr. Kamal N. Kabra, Prof. Dr. Vikas Mishra, etc.), Prof. Muchkund Dubey, I.F.S. Retd., an internationally renowned old pupil of mine (for his kind words), Engineer

Mr V.B. Bhagat (for help in tackling some pending matters in Patna), Dr. R.C. Paul (for his medical advice as and when sought), Dr. I.B. Sinha, Dr. P.K. Verma, Dr. T. Prasad, Mr K.N. Yadav, Mr Vimal Rastogi, Mr Binda Sah, Diwakar, Dr. T.N. Chaudhary, Dr. H.K. Sahay, Dr. N.K. Chaudhary, Dr. Jagdish Prasad, Mr R.P. Sinha, Dr. Rama Raman Behari, Dr. B.S. Prasad, Mr R.P. Mishra and Mr Lalit Rajpal (the last eighteen, all in Patna, for maintaining contact with me in varying degrees). Last but not the least, I am obliged to Mr P.K. Lahiri, I.A.S. (Retd.), my neighbour, for his kind help in connection with the review of an earlier book of mine.

The author dedicates this book to Mother Ganga in all humility. His place of work for 45 years was located on her bank. For several years he had his residence too on or near her bank, with the result that he could see her almost everyday. Mother Ganga is the source of all knowledge. I, therefore, seek her kind blessings through this work. I also wish to pray to her to be so pleased as to purify the hearts and minds of those people in Bihar who are steeped in rank/rabid casteism, communalism, corruption and narrow-mindedness, evils which besmirch the State and keep it stuck up in the morass of poverty and backwardness in order that it regains its lost past glories some recounted towards the end, with the democratic repuplic of the Lichhavis added to the list.

The Reader to Please Note

Unless otherwise indicated, throughout the book the figures in the brackets in the tables indicate the All-India figures, aggregates, averages, percentages, and so on.

339, Sector 15A, NOIDA (201301) K.N. PRASAD

CONTENTS

LIST OF TABLES

1

LAND IN BIHAR
Its Physical Problems

Bihar is one of the twenty-five States of India. It has a total geographical area of 1.74 lakh sq. km., about 5.3 per cent of the total land area of India. It falls partly in the Gangetic plain which accounts for nearly 2.86 per cent of the country's total geographical area. Its plain part has a width ranging from less than 200 km. to 500 km. (as in Punjab and Rajasthan). It comprises the raised Bhangar and Khadar areas, deferred junctions, the Bhabars and Terais. It represents a sag or depression in the earth's crust which has been filled up with alluvium brought down by the rivers. It is drained by the Ganga and its tributaries.

Bihar is divided into three physiographic regions, namely, North Bihar, South Bihar and Chotanagpur, accounting for 31, 23 and 46 per cent respectively of the State's geographical area. Its geographical and natural boundaries have remained the same. Chotanagpur claims almost half of its total area and consists of hills and plateaus, while the remaining half is an alluvial plain, divided into two unequal parts, North and South, by the river Ganga. Chotanagpur and North Bihar are isolated from each other. The cultural and economic pattern of Chotanagpur is absolutely distinct from that of North Bihar.

In 1991 the Chotanagpur plateau had an area of 0.80 lakh sq. km. and a population of 21.8 million, giving a density of 273 persons per sq. km.; North Bihar an area of 0.54 lakh sq. km., a population of 40.1 million and a density of 761 per sq. km.; and finally, South Bihar an area of 0.40 lakh sq. km., a population of 24.4 million and a density of 609 persons per sq. km.

Land represents, in general, nature and natural resources that are used in production. It represents the free gifts of nature, upon which man works. It represents the materials and forces given by nature to man for his aid. It furnishes standing room for the productive purposes as well as raw materials for production. It is equated with the soil the powers of which are original to the extent that they were derived from nature. *Soil* is the end-product of the parent material resulting from the consistent influence of climate, topography and the natural vegetation over a long period of time.

The very low-levelled middle Ganga plain comprises the plains, north and south, of Bihar, which are very fertile with the rich alluvium soil, perhaps among the most fertile agricultural tracts in India. The rivers carry the rich soil with them and leave it behind at the places they pass through. As a result, the farmers get very luxuriant crops on their fields.

The Gangetic plains account for nearly 77 per cent of the total sown area. Their alluvial soil is being cultivated from time immemorial and shows little signs of exhaustion. Its composition favours the cultivation of almost every crop that can be produced on semi-tropical low-lands. North Bihar is more fertile of the two plains. Land in the plateau region is less fertile than that in the two plains, North and South Bihar. Soil fertility is the prime determinant of agricultural productivity.

There are areas in Bihar which have faced serious soil problems for ages, such as erosion, acidity and deficiency in organic and nitrogenous content. Soil erosion is removal of the topsoil cover either as single particles or *en masse* by water, wind and human activities. It has gone on for long in the hilly and laterite areas in the plateau region of Chotanagpur, where the soil conditions and moisture retention are poorer by comparison despite heavy rainfall as well in some districts of South Bihar. This has rendered the inhabitants of these areas economically worst-off.

Estimates made of the degraded/problem land in Bihar are not accurate and hence not reliable but they give a rough, broad idea of the seriousness of the situation. In the 1950s 23.48 lakh ha. land area was reported to be suffering from soil erosion. In 1960-61 soil erosion affected 7.28 lakh ha. In 1977-78, 23 lakh ha. land area, 19 lakh ha. agricultural land and 4 lakh ha. forest land areas were subject to severe soil erosion during the rains. In 1984-85 a sumtotal of 3.8 per cent of the all-India aggregate land was affected partly by water erosion, and partly by soil erosion. The latest estimate of degraded/problem land is 26.6 lakh ha., of which 10 per cent is due to floods.

Among the affected areas are the catchments of the major and medium irrigation projects, *e.g.*, Kosi and parts of South Bihar and areas with heavy rainfall and improper land management, as in the plateau region.

Soil erosion is caused by a combination of rainfall and topography, as in parts of South Bihar and the Chotanagpur plateau region; infertile sand and dense grass, as in the Kosi region; salinity, especially in North Bihar; and increased deforestation, which has destroyed the defences/ powers of the soil, as in the Chotanagpur plateau region.

The effect of soil erosion is: Impoverishment of the pastures in the plateau region, depletion of soil fertility, enhanced frequency and coverage of floods, silting of the streams, and lowering of the sub-soil water level. In a word, the agricultural land under the plough diminishes in area.

In several parts of the Bihar plains the soils are highly deficient in organic matter and nitrogenous content. In the plateau region the red soil is poor in nitrogen, phosphorus and humus, though rich in potash.

To fight the soil erosion menace what is called for is soil improvement by means of adequate adjustments and conditioning, soil management including suitable conservation measures, afforestation to replenish the powers of the soil, pasture development and social forestry, and irrigation which is indispensable for the red soils.

The anti-soil erosion drive would hinge on factors like vegetation, climate, topography of the region and the parent material for its effectiveness and success.

While the fight against soil erosion would definitely improve the fertility of land, allowing the cultivable land rest for a time would also serve the same purpose by reducing the strain on the soil, other things being equal.

Climate denotes the average *weather* conditions over a large area and a long period of time. In other words, the aggregation of weather over a period constitutes the climate. Climate is the net product of a variety of factors, the most important of them being temperature, precipitation, humidity, atmospheric pressure, wind, sunshine and clouds.

Agriculture is consigned to precariousness because of its vulnerability to adverse weather conditions. The economic development of a region is affected profoundly by climate via its great bearing on the social and cultural activities of the people. Intermittent, dry spells during July to August are good for kharif in Bihar. Blowing of the Western wind during March is bad for rabi, whereas adequate and opportune cold weather improves it. In the areas dotted with forests, for example, in Chotanagpur and Western Champaran the climate is not quite healthy and causes malaria but the higher parts of Chotanagpur have a healthy and pleasant climate.

Average annual rainfall in Bihar is estimated at 1270 mm (approx.), the national average being 1100 mm. Another estimate is 1500 mm for the plateau and 1360 mm for the plain regions. Twenty-four districts are in the high rainfall region, having 68.72 lakh ha., and seven in the low and medium rainfall region, having 11.65 lakh ha. Eighty per cent of the annual rainfall is received from the south-west monsoon during June-September in most parts of the State. More rainfall is associated with a humid atmosphere.

One feature of the monsoon is that there are large variations in rainfall within the season. To illustrate, Bihar had sub-optimal rainfall between 1960-61 and 1970-71. 1983-84 and 1987-88 were years of inadequate rainfall. Another feature is that the monsoon rains are unevenly distributed from week to week. A third feature is that the monsoon has an erratic nature. The rainy season may close abruptly and early on account of failure of the *Hathia Nakshatra* showers. During 1910 to 1960 the *Hathia* rains generally failed once in every three years in South Bihar, once in every 4 years in North Bihar and once in every 5 years in Chotanagpur. The materialisation and failure of the *Hathia* rains made all the difference between plenty and scarcity.

Because of the peculiar nature of the monsoon intensive agriculture is not practicable during the main crop (rice/paddy) season. In the rainfed areas, the available moisture in the soil, in the winter and summer months is not adequate to support multiple cropping. Let us develop this a bit more with reference to paddy/rice cultivation.

The main crop in Bihar is the winter paddy and this crop not merely requires rainfall in adequate quantity but also demands that the rainfall should be distributed evenly over the season of the crop. Late monsoon rain leads to late preparation of land, delayed raising of paddy seedlings and their delayed transplantation. Delayed transplantation exposes the paddy crop to the maximum incidence of pests and diseases. The plough-bullock-manpower combine available in the rural areas is just below the optimum required to bring all the land available into a condition fit for the transplantation of the paddy plants in time. Even when the monsoon is on time, 5 to 6 per cent of the land is planted late due to the inadequate and untimely supply of power. To sum up, the intermittent, long dry spells or inadequate rainfall in the crucial months of transplantation and plant growth adversely affects rice production. At least 173.1 mm of the monsoon rainfall during June and July is required for sowing the rice seedlings. The extent of variation between a year of good rainfall and a year of intermittent rainfall is quite large, showing the insecurity of rice production under present conditions.

Despite the fact that 94 per cent of total net sown area in Bihar has a reasonably assured supply of rain-water (100-150 cm per year), a high percentage, the average for the country being 51 per cent per annum only, that is, despite the fact that Bihar is in the eastern wet region, as also in spite of increased irrigation since independence, the rural economy of the State continues to be controlled by the monsoon rainfall, for 64 per cent of the areas rely on it.

On the whole, the agriculture in Bihar is still a hostage to the vagaries of the monsoon. Agricultural activities are at their peak when the rains are timely; otherwise not.

The continued dependence of the peasantry, in general, on monsoon rainfall in most parts of the State is a distressing matter. Agricultural instability is the outcome.

In so far as Bihar agriculture is directly dependent on the rains, the monsoon is the single largest factor influencing the Bihar economy.

We may suggest contingency planning against the uncertainty of the monsoon rainfall in the areas encompassed by it.

The River System

The river system of Bihar is composed, in the main, of the Ganga, the Sone, the Gandak, the Kosi, the Damodar and the Subarnarekha. The Ganga, being the principal river, determines Bihar's river system. All other streams of the plain region join it from north and south. The rivers flowing through the plains are snow-fed, active during the rainy season and carry enormous detritus load. The supplies of water in the rivers fall from October onwards and are low in winter. The Sone drains the northern edge of the peninsula and flows into the Ganga system. There are numerous other rivers and rivulets in which water is available for utilisation, mostly on an intermittent basis during the rainy season.

Bihar is richly endowed with *water resources*, having abundant water supply from the rivers which flow within its territory. It is rich in hydro reserves. Apart from the rivers, underground water in which also the State is rich, being in the Gangetic alluvial region, forms an important source of water supply for domestic and agricultural purposes. Sub-surface/underground water is water that occurs below the surface of the earth. Surface water, not underground water, is replete with turbidity, objectionable colours and pathogenic organisms and thus requires very little treatment. Wells have been constructed through the ages in all parts of the State for domestic supply of water and they are still in vogue.

Bihar has got 8 million ha. of the ultimate water resources, ranking third in this respect, after Uttar Pradesh and Andhra Pradesh. In the early 1950s the Ganga's estimated average annual flow was 400 million acre-feet. Currently India's groundwater resources are estimated at about 45.32 m ha. of total replenishable groundwater resources every year, 38.38 m ha. for irrigation and 6.94 m ha. for industrial and domestic consumption, etc. Bihar's share would be proportionally higher, compared to States other than Uttar Pradesh and Andhra Pradesh. Groundwater is replenishable. The percentage of rainfall tending to infiltrate down to groundwater may be between 7 to 9 per cent of annual rainfall in the plateau region and 20 to 23 per cent of annual rainfall in the flat alluvial region. The total annually replenishable groundwater resource may be put at 3.38 m ha.

Bihar had one of the earliest civilisations owing to the presence in it of the Ganga and its tributaries. The Ganga has influenced the civilisation of North Bihar most. Alongwith other rivers it has had a mighty impact on the life pattern of the people in the plain region. The rivers contribute immensely to irrigation, domestic and industrial water supply, hydroelectricity generation and inland water transport. Use of river water has made possible successful agriculture in Bihar down the ages.

On the other hand, during the rains the *Tal* lands, found primarily on the backwater of the Ganga and Sone rivers, remain inundated, with the result that there is no kharif crop; only rabi crop is raised on them.

Water availability turns on place and time. The extent to which the river supplies could be put to further use is governed largely by the extent to which the monsoon flows could be restored. Oddly, everywhere the natural resources, river water being one, came to be developed within a comparatively short and recent period of history, a brute fact, and so in Bihar too, notwithstanding its relative àdvantage over several other States, water conservation measures are called for. To be faced squarely is the problem of conserving surface flows and their optimal allocation between agriculture, industry and rural and urban domestic uses. To crown all, the best possible use of the available irrigation water resource ought to be made with a view to augmenting agricultural production.

Bihar is struck every year by flood and often by drought, besides hailstorm and blight, which are ignored. (Gandhiji identified this with Nature's avenge upon Man for his unbridled greed : Nature was capable of meeting Man's need, but not his greed.) Between 1946-47 and 1960-61 there was hardly a year when Bihar was not exposed to the vagaries of these *natural calamities*; only two years, viz., 1953-54 and 1954-55 were free from the incidence of drought.

At times a paradoxical situation has prevailed—in one and the same division there was flood in some parts and also drought in others, let alone some parts of the State being ravaged by drought, while other parts being devastated by flood. Here the reference is to the Tirhut division—in 1993-94 while Vaishali and parts of Muzaffarpur were drought-affected, Sitamarhi was in the grip of flood.

During 1969-70 to 1970-71 the loss on account of the natural calamities equalled Rs. 159.39 crore per year, on an average.

The natural calamities have a serious repercussion on the Bihar economy. They make heavy inroads into the slender resources of the State. The total loss adds up to about 4.3 to 5.8 per cent of the SDP—2.9 to 3.9 per cent due to floods and 1.4 to 1.9 per cent from droughts. Since the growth rate of agriculture is affected adversely by the natural calamities, the growth rate of the SDP is also affected, income from agriculture being its major component. The natural calamities subject vast areas and their activities to constant insecurity and instability as well, which, in its turn, foil the farmer's best efforts directed towards saving and investment. Bad harvests stimulate unproductive consumption and indebtedness, besides disrupting law and order and inciting crimes. Distress migration to other States is another consequence. Development work is on sufferance because the administrative machinery is geared to execute relief operations. The relief operations represent unproductive expenditure. They provide enough room for bungling and politicisation. Misappropriation of funds earmarked for relief operations is reported. But worse than that, while the State reels under the natural calamities, the State legislators, including former chief ministers, are provided with a rise in their perks and emoluments (see *Hindustan Times*, 25 August, 1993).

The National Commission on Flood (1980) identified Bihar as one of the most flood-affected states in India. Bihar accounts for 56.6 per cent of the total flood-affected area in the country. Sixteen per cent of total land area of the State is flood-prone. This amounts to about 64 lakh ha. Per 100 ha. of agricultural land 37 ha. is flood-prone. In several parts of North Bihar *flood* is a normal annual feature. North Bihar has 5.85 m ha. land, of which 4.5 m ha. is flood-prone; Kosi tributaries 1.0 m ha., Burhi Gandak 0.8 m ha., Mahananda 0.5 ha., Gandak, Kamla and Ghagra 0.3 m ha. and Ganga 0.8 m ha. Approximately 17 lakh ha. land is affected by flood, according to another estimate.

Twenty-five per cent of the land area in South Bihar is flood-prone. But flood is less frequent in this region, besides being of a shorter duration.

The flood-proneness of the twin plain regions is attributable to heavy seasonal rainfall as well as the irregularity of the monsoon.

Nearly one-third of the gross cropped area in the districts of Saharsa, Darbhanga, Sitamarhi, Samastipur, Muzaffarpur and East Champaran in North Bihar remains flooded during the kharif seasons. That is to say, about 34.40 lakh ha. land is prone to waterlogging, and the result is no kharif crop production.

The different river projects in Bihar condemn 4 to 6 lakh ha. of land in the kharif and 2.4 to 3.6 lakh ha. in the rabi season to perennial waterlogging. 1.82 lakh ha. is always submerged because of waterlogging by the Kosi alone, which has altered its course several times in the last 100-odd years. These shifts have destroyed large cultivable areas. This excludes 1.052 lakh ha. which comes between the embankments of the Kosi. Siltation in parts of the Kosi project area is responsible for waterlogging and salinity. In 1987-88 the Kosi caused colossal damage.

In 1981-82 about 8 lakh ha. of the fertile paddy-growing land in North Bihar had remained waterlogged.

Parts of South Bihar are also affected by waterlogging due to flood during the kharif season.

From waterlogging originate a number of diseases affecting human beings and cattle.

Nearly 1.5 lakh ha. in the Gandak and Kosi Command Areas have been freed through flood control and drainage methods. Construction of drainage works is the only remedy of waterlogging and salinity.

Twenty-seven per cent of the total damage caused by floods in India is sustained by Bihar alone. Average annual loss from floods since 1947 has been estimated at Rs. 70.5 crore. In some years the loss from them in North Bihar alone was of the order of Rs. 250 crore, excluding the costs of rehabilitation and repair. Not all damages from them are quantifiable and those which are quantifiable are so only imprecisely. The loss due to the death of human beings is quantifiable only roughly. Destroyed are the standing crops and swept away are the expensive HYV seeds, assets (private and public) and impaired are the roads and uprooted are the electric and telephone poles. The soil is partly robbed of its fertility consequent upon the deposit of sand and owing to salinity. Areas remain flooded from a few weeks to 3 to 4 months, depending on the physiographic situation. People are obliged to quit their homes during the period, only to return at its end. This is a yearly phenomenon.

The shattering effect of the flood on the local economy is taken as providential. The insecurity and instability factor is soon forgotten. The old pattern of life and activity reasserts itself, giving an impression as if no calamity had ever hit the area(s), a unique case of resignation to fate with ample fortitude. Settlements have expanded in the flood-protected areas. However, some of these areas have been still vulnerable to floods in the event of a breach in the embankments. This has made people doubt the integrity of the engineers and politicians. Cultivation of marginal lands in the river beds has progressed in recent years. Districts like Kathar are accustomed to harvest a relief crop almost every year during the flood. The deposit of fresh silt revamps the impaired powers of the soil so much so that the next crop, rabi is bumper, richer and more luxuriant.

Prior to 1951, 285 miles of embankments protecting 24.87 lakh acres existed. In the First Plan 350 miles of them costing Rs. 5.60 crore were constructed, which protected 5.75 lakh acres from flood. In the first two plans the flood control programme was executed in great measure by popular support in which the non-official agencies like Bharat Sevak Samaj and local Gram Panchayats lent a great hand in the construction of the embankments. The local people displayed tremendous enthusiasm.

The Kosi was sought to be tamed by the Kosi dam, and the Damodar by the DVC. Whereas the Kosi dam was chiefly to give protection to 2.26 lakh ha., the DVC was designed to primarily supply electricity.

Among the flood-protection measures barrages and embankments provide temporary protection against flood. Flood forecasting systems have been set up at Buxar and Patna on the bank of the Ganga.

In sptie of all measures taken so far, control of flood has not been satisfactory. As protection was given to some areas against flood through the construction of embankments, new areas became liable to flood. Embankments like the Burhi Gandak, Adhwara Karch, Bhutahi Balan, Bagamati, Kamla Balan, Mahananda, etc. remain vulnerable to heavy rains. North Bihar has to drain off its own heavy rainfall water, the melted snow water and rain water of about 60,000 sq. miles of the Himalayas, which is a causative factor.

The rehabilitation programme of the Kosi flood-affected people as well as the area within the two embankments of the Kosi being executed by the State Government suffers from the resource crunch. Flood control and drainage call for a massive investment which Bihar cannot afford by itself. A body of public opinion favours the idea that this investment should be a charge on the Centre.

The Government effort is constrained by the fact that the catchments of most rivers and their tributaries which flood the Bihar plains are located outside Bihar, as they arise from outside the State and hence their management is beyond the competence of the Government. Long-term flood-control measures like afforestation of the catchment areas, construction of reservoirs on tributaries, mitigating floods by depleting groundwater storage through large-capacity artesian wells in the Terai areas, operating in the dry season and allowing for recharge during the monsoon, and so on presuppose the cooperation of the Nepal Government.

Parts of Bihar are drought-prone. 9.2 per cent of the total number of blocks are prone to drought. These fall in South Bihar and Chotanagpur. The Seventh Plan listed Monghyr, Nawadah, Palamau, Rohtas and Santhal Parganas among the drought-prone districts. Palamau and Rohtas receive lowest monsoon rain, less than 125 mm a year. They are most drought-prone. It cannot for certain be said as to what the total area of the drought-prone districts is, for it is the nature of the monsoon on which this area depends.

As for the frequency of drought, one year in five years is expected to be a dry year, and one in ten years a year of severe drought. In 1950-51, 1951-52 and 1957-58 were years of drought. In 1963-64 there was a drought at the beginning of the monsoon. During the latter part of October 1963 there was a hailstorm in certain parts of Bihar. In 1964 the monsoon failed. Near-famine conditions obtained during 1965-66. 1966-67 was another year of drought. Similarly, the year 1973, 1991 and 1992-93 faced an acute drought situation. During 1993-94 the months of July and August were confronted with a drought-like situation. 10.7 lakh ha. land could not be cultivated. Erraticity of the monsoon is said to be the root cause—unusual delay in the commencement of the monsoon and long dry spells during the monsoon seasons.

Due to drought the HYV seeds die, there is no kharif outturn, drinking water becomes scarce because the water table goes down, so also cattle fodder, the employment level sags and with it the earnings of the labouring classes, there is distress sales and malnutrition and migration of labourers and people and cattle to other places. The carry-over effect of drought on the succeeding rabi crops is unwholesome because of the absence of moisture in the soil and in operativeness of the tubewells and pumpsets.

Under the 1971 Central Government Scheme each drought-affected block obtains 15 lakhs from the Centre and an equivalent amount from the State Government, which are spent on minor irrigation schemes. There is in addition to this the Drought-Prone Areas Programme. But in actual operation these schemes have been fraught with flaws. The success achieved in this direction is limited. Whenever the State is hit by drought, there is a clamour for more and more funds by manipulating and thereby exaggerating the area affected.

A view is gaining ground rapidly that where irrigation can be arranged for, whatever its magnitude, short-duration crops like various pulses, mustard, maize, millets and groundnuts could be raised, besides fodder, extensive pasture or social forestry. Research may suggest other kinds of crops. Where irrigation is not possible, short-duration, drought-resistant pulses and oilseeds can grow, assuming necessary agronomical manipulations.

2

LAND USE/UTILISATION IN BIHAR

Land use/utilisation refers to reporting area, which, in turn, refers to the area maintained by the village revenue agency. Bihar's share in land area has been 5.2 per cent of all-India, equal to 1.74 lakh sq. km., whereas its share in population in 1991 was 10.2 per cent of all-India, equal to 84.34 million.

We have given in Table 2.1 the land use/utilisation pattern in Bihar in 1991. Total reported area was 17.33 million ha. Of this, 44.52 per cent was net sown area (NSA). This gave 0.91 ha. per capita. Between 1966-67 and 1975-76 NSA increased by 14.1 per cent. NSA increased by 2.1 per cent in 1983-84 and 14.9 per cent in 1978-79, as compared to the preceding year in each case. It fell in 1972-73, 1981-82 and 1983-84. Between 1950-51 and 1986-87 NSA declined by 13.5 per cent. Between 1955-56 (year of reorganisation of the States) and

TABLE 2.1 : Land Use/Utilisation Pattern : 1991

Use	*Area (Lakh ha.)*	*As Percentage of total Reported Area in the State*
Net area sown	77.15	44.52
Current fallow	16.90	9.75
Other fallow	10.30	5.94
Cultivable/Cultural waste land	3.98	2.30
Miscellaneous tree crops and groves	2.76	1.59
Permanent pasture and other grazing land	1.30	0.75
Land put to non-agricultural uses	21.26	12.27
Barren and uncultivable land	10.16	5.86
Forests	29.49	17.02
Total	173.30	100.00

Note : ha. = hectare, throughout.
In 1992-93 total geographical area was 173.30 lakh ha., total cropped area 93.58 lakh ha., net cropped area 71.63 lakh ha., double-cropped area 21.94 lakh ha. and intensity of cropping 1.31.

1987-88 NSA declined by 2.92 per cent. Area-wise this meant 3.80 lakh ha. In NSA fluctuations are the regular feature. Reclamation of the barren and uncultivable lands caused its increase in the earlier years.

A glance at Table 2.2 would show that in absolute terms NSA increased from 7.86 to 8.51 m ha. between 1955-56 and 1990-91, though as percentage of total reported area (TRA) it remained almost static. During 1950-51 to 1986-87 it declined by 13.5 per cent. Bihar's percentage share in all-India NSA has continuously declined. Increase in the percentage of NSA to gross cropped area (GCA) over the years connotes decline in cropping intensity.

TABLE 2.2 : Net Sown/Cropped Area

Year	*Area (M ha.)*	*As Percentage of*		
		Total Reported Area	*All-India Total*	*Total/Gross Sown/Cropped Area*
1944-45 to 1950-51 (Average)		5 49.5	8.2	60.7
1950-51	8.72	48.4		
1955-56	7.86	44.8 (44.7)	6.7	
1960-61	8.19	46.3		
1962-65 (Av.)	8.47	6.19	5.94	
1966-67		42.7		
1968-69	5.91			
1970-71	8.36	48.8 (46.2)		
1970-73 (Av.)	8.26			
1980-81	8.08	48.1 (46.0)		49.0 (46.0)
1980-83 (Av.)	7.90		5.60	
1983-84		43.6		
1986-87	7.54		5.4	
1990-91		44.4 (46.6)		
1990-91	8.51	44.5		73.2
1992-93	7.16			
1995-96	7.695		5.23	
1990-95 (Av.)	7.43		5.02	

Note : M/m = million, throughout.

During 1955-56 to 1995 GCA rose only slightly, from 10.12 to 10.56 m ha. (Table 2.3). As proportion to all-India total, it has tended to fall off, whereas as proportion of TRA, it has tended to move up. Fluctuations in GCA occurred absolutely or relatively. Between 1950-51 and 1960-61 it underwent a 3.1 per cent increase. But over a longer run of years, that is, between 1950-51 and 1986-87 it underwent a 3.8 per cent decrease. During 1966-67 to 1977-78 it increased by 25.4 per cent. The trend rate of growth of GCA during 1971-72 to 1983-84 was (–) 0.954 per cent per year; and during 1979-80 to 1985-86, (–) 1.07 per cent per annum. The years showing a fall were 1971-72, 1972-73, 1978-79, 1979-80, 1981-82, 1982-83 and 1986-87. GCA has tended to cluster around 10.0 m ha. While multiple cropping abetted by an extension of the cultivable land area in the wake of increased irrigation facility and short-harvesting based on improved seeds have provided an impetus to the expansion of GCA, inadequacy of irrigation and finance has played the part of a detractor. This apart, the upward trend in NSA and GCA over the years is to the credit of Bihar, considering adverse factors, floods and droughts encountered.

TABLE 2.3 : Gross/Total Sown/Cropped Area

Year	*Area (M ha.)*	*As Percentage of All-India (Total (per cent)*	*As Percentage of Total Reported Area (per cent)*	*As Percentage of Total Geo-graphical Area (per cent)*
1950-51	10.93	7.9		
1955-56	10.12	6.7	56.8	
1960-61		7.1		
1962-65 (Av.)	10.69	7.06		
1966-67	9.21			
1970-71	10.81			
1970-73 (Av.)	10.72	6.84		
1978-79	11.38			
1980-81	10.88	6.4		
1980-83 (Av.)	10.19	6.15		
1983-84	9.10			59.5
1985-86	10.51			
1986-87	10.32/10.43	6.2		
1987-88	10.32	5.45	60.2	
1990-91	10.41/10.48			
1992-95 (Av.)	9.30			
1994-95	10.80			
1995-96	105.71			

Between 1971-72 and 1990-91 NSA fell to the extent of 574 thousand ha. and rose to the extent of 2513 thousands ha. GCA fell by 199 thousand ha. and rose by 20291 thousand ha. Whereas in the State half of the land is cultivated, in Chotanagpur and Santhal Parganas the percentage is 31 to 32 per cent. In the plains the percentage is higher, 69 to 70 per cent. In Chotanagpur average annual area under shifting cultivation was 16.2 thousand ha., which came to 1.5 per cent of the all-India total.

Fallow land (Table 2.4) refers to uncultivated land. Ihe plain regions have 9 to 10 per cent fallow. In Chotanagpur most land is cultivated after remaining fallow for 2 to 4 years. In other parts land is ready after a year of fallowing. Although the total fallow land in Bihar fell from 34.98 lakh ha. in 1958-59 to 27.20 lakh ha. in 1990-91, the fallow land area that can still be brought under cultivation is not large for the reason that much of it in the plateau region is marginal and submarginal and is more suited to forestry, horticulture and pasture than for farming. Inadequate water supply, malarious climate, silting of the rivers and canals, unremunerative nature of farming or due to the cultivators being too poor to continue cultivation. Not all fallow land for rest deserved rest but part of the land in cultivation deserves rest, subject to the proviso that the post-rest yield is higher.

TABLE 2.4 : Fallow Land

Year	*Current Fallow*		*Other Fallow*		*Total Fallow*	
	Lakh ha.	*As Percentage of Total Reported Area*	*Lakh ha.*	*As Percentage of Total Reported Area*	*Lakh ha.*	*As percentage of Total Reported Area*
1958-59					34.98	20.2 (21.7)
1970-71						14.1 (6.5)
1987-88	10.82	11.42	19.02	6.24		15.9 (7.7)
1988-89		10.05	6.03			
1990-91	16.90	9.75	10.30	5.94	27.20	

The term 'current fallow' denotes one thing in the plateau and another thing in the plain regions. Putting out of use more land results in increase in the area of current fallow. Increase in current fallow is caused by uncertainty of rain, labour shortage, flood, inadequate supply of inputs, etc. The recent trend is towards a rise in the area of current fallow, as between 1987-88 and 1990-91.

The area under other fallow land rose in Bihar during 1958-59 and 1988-89 owing to the fear of the Bataidari Act. This can be sown if reclaimed.

Land use is determined by a variety of factors, viz., physical (e.g., topography, climate and soil), human (e.g., population pressure, technical awareness of the farmer, his health, his economic condition, etc.), economic (e.g., credit and inputs supply, technical and marketing assistance, etc.) and institutional (tenurial and tenancy reforms, etc.). It varies from region to region, depending upon soil fertility and volume and distribution of rainfall, availability of irrigation facility, cultivation practices, etc. North Bihar is marked by an unbalanced picture of land use where the forests, orchards and pastures occupy negligible areas, and almost all available land has been cultivated. Prior to 1950-51 the area under cultivation had fluctuated from year to year on account of variations in rainfall and weather conditions. Subsequent to 1950-51 and upto 1966-67 the factors responsible for acreage fluctuations remained more or less the same but after 1966-67, with the advent of the new agrarian technology (NAT) more factors came to influence the acreage.

The rate of growth of acreage between 1970-71 and 1988-89 was negative, –0.66 per cent per annum.

Cultural wasteland is that land which is not put to any use or not cultivated for five years in succession. Its suitability is in doubt. Between 1955-56 and 1987-88 its area had dwindled by about 5.10 lakh ha. On the other hand, between 1987-88 and 1990-91 there has been a niggling increase in its area in the State (Table 2.5). There was proportionally less of such land in Bihar than in most other States. And Bihar's share in all-India total diminished in recent years.

TABLE 2.5 : Cultivable/Cultural Waste Land

Year	*Area (Lakh ha.)*	*As Percentage of Total reported Area (per cent)*	*Bihar's Share in All-India Total (per cent)*
1950-51		5.8	
1958-59	9.00	5.2	
1960-61	12.95	11.6	
1980-81	4.47	2.6	
1984			4.20
1986-87			2.54
1987-88	3.88		2.24
1988-89			2.30
1990-91	3.98		2.30

Cultural waste has existed in a high percentage in Saharsa district where the Kosi has kept throwing large areas out of cultivation, in Dhanbad district where mining activities have caused a similar damage to cultivation and, finally, in the wooded districts of Chotanagpur.

Waste land is reclaimed through afforestation with the people's participation because much of it and a fair proportion of cultivated marginal land are more suited to afforestation than for arable farming. Their cultivation is tantamount to an outrage of Nature. In Bihar some land has been put under the plough which should have been left for afforestation and soil conservation.

In dire need cultural waste as well as fallow land ought to be cultivated, subject to surmounting soil erosion and good land management.

The land area under tree crops and groves (Table 2.6) has expanded due to the plantation programmes executed by the Government. In the early 1950s in most parts of Bihar the entire countryside used to be turned into grazing ground after the harvesting of paddy, with the result that even if a cultivator was enterprising enough to attempt to grow the same broadcast catch crop or to take to regular arable cultivation of his isolated field, he could not do so if the fields all around were open to grazing. Table 2.7 casts light on the paucity of land meant for pasture and other grazing ground, and underscores the case for earmarking more land for the purpose. The reclamation schemes hampered increase in the percentage of pastures.

TABLE 2.6 : Miscellaneous Tree Crops and Groves

Year	*Area (Lakh ha.)*	*As Percentage of Total Reported Area (per cent)*
1958-59	—	0.09
1987-88	2.67	1.54
1988-89	—	1.05

TABLE 2.7 : Permanent Pastures and Other Grazing Land

Year	*Area (Lakh ha.)*	*As Percentage of Total Reported Area (per cent)*
1958-59	—	1.02
1987-88	1.37	0.79
1988-89	—	0.07
1990-91	1.30	0.75

The percentage of land put to non-agricultural uses has constantly increased and is likely to increase further on account of the growth of industry and population (Table 2.8). There is a slight increase in the absolute area of land which is barren and uncultivable, though in percentage terms there is no apparent rise (Table 2.9). Coal mining has converted vast areas into barren tracts. Table 2.10 indicates that area sown more than once has been most unstable. Between 1950-51 and 1986-87 it increased in Bihar at a faster rate than elsewhere in India but subsequently the rate slowed down.

The increase in cropping intensity (Table 2.11) has been influenced by irrigation and short-duration HYVs. Cropping intensity at different stages of cultivation may be pitched at different levels with reference to any particular crop. Where single-cropping prevails, the deficit, when it occurs, precipitates a crisis. Between 1950-51 and 1994-95 the difference of cropping intensity was of 16 to 17 percentage points. Double-cropping is low in all districts of the Chotanagpur region, as it is in Santhal Parganas too. Lands on which multiple cropping is possible are the best land. Multiple cropping denotes not only intensive farming and higher annual aggregate production but also lesser risks and a larger volume of well-distributed rural employment than does the single-cropping system.

TABLE 2.8 : Area Put to Non-Agricultural Uses

Year	*Area (Lakh ha.)*	*As Percentage of Total Reported Area (per cent)*	*Bihar's Share in All-India Total (per cent)*
1955-56	—	7.3	
1958-59	—	7.9	
1970-71	—	8.9 (5.4)	
1980-81	—	9.9	
1986-87	—	—	9.61
1987-88	20.57	11.8	
1988-89	—	11.9	
1990-91	21.26	12.27 (7.0)	

TABLE 2.9 : Barren and Unculturable Land

Year	*Area (Lakh ha.)*	*As Percentage of Total Reported Area (per cent)*
1958-59	—	5.0
1970-71	—	6.1 (9.3)
1987-88	10.16	5.86
1988-89	—	5.8
1990-91	10.66	5.86 (6.4)

Furthermore, there is no need to maintain a large reserve or carry-over of foodgrains between harvests under the multiple-cropping system. A single crop, kharif, is grown in a number of districts in South Bihar, as also is the case in Chotanagpur and Santhal Parganas, districts inhabited mostly by scheduled castes and scheduled tribes and other poor farmers.

TABLE 2.10 : Area Sown More than Once

Year	*Area (M. ha.)*	*As Percentage of*		
		Gross Cropped Area (per cent)	*Net Sown Area (per cent)*	*Total Reported Area (per cent)*
1944-45 to 1950-51 (Average)	—	—	29.6	—
1950-51	—	10.9	—	—
1955-56	2.43	13.4	—	—
1956-57	—	—	—	30.3 (14.3)
1978-79	2.85 (32.24)	—	—	—
1990-91	2.90	—	—	—
1991	2.43	—	—	—

TABLE 2.11 : Cropping Intensity/Gross Cropped Area divided by Net Sown Area/ Indicator of Improved Cultural Practice

Year	*Percentage*
1950-51	123.6
1956-57	130.3 (114.3)
1960-61	135.7
1966-67	123.0
1970-71	130.1
1977-78	134.8
1980-81	134.6
1985-86	136.6 (125.7)
1990-91	139.0
1994-95	140.0
1995-96	138.0

Total cultivable land (Table 2.12) seems to have stabilised at a figure between 10 and 12 million ha. being between 57 and 70 per cent of the total reported area (TRA), as brought out by Table 2.13. TRA has remained nearly constant. During 1971 to 1991 cultivated area fell by 4.30 per cent. It is forecast that in 10 to 20 years to come 5 per cent agricultural land would be diverted to non-agricultural uses, which would necessitate cultivation of 90.21 lakh ha. land to raise the required foodgrains.

TABLE 2.12 : Total Cultivable Area

Year	*Area (Million ha.)*	
1955-56	10.57	
1956-57	12.40	
1990-91	7.07	
1994-95	11.74	(State Planning Board)
1994-95	11.26	(State Agricultural Department)
1994-95	10.08	(State Irrigation Department)

Note : According to an estimate, total culturable area in Bihar is 108.28 lakh ha., whereas total gross area is 173 lakh ha.

Reclamation has been executed in the lands of marginal fertility or waterlogged areas or grassy wastes of the Kosi basin. Through deep ploughing or levelling and copious use of water and fertilisers even cultivable wastes have been brought under cultivation. The extension of the farm land through reclamation reached a point of saturation much earlier, particularly in the densely settled plain areas. At the outset of the reclamation programme in Bihar subsidies were given to private persons to encourage them but this could benefit only the big farmers. In the process uplands were converted into paddy fields. Instead allotment of the land-to-be-reclaimed to the small farmers on an ownership basis would have achieved the goal through their normal labour.

TABLE 2.13 : Total Reported Area

Year	*Area (M. ha.)*	*As Percentage of Total Geographical Area (per cent)*	*Bihar's Share in All-India Total (per cent)*
1955-56	17.32	—	—
1980-81	17.32	—	—
1986-87	—	52.8	5.68
1987-88	17.35	—	—
1990-91	17.33	—	—

'Other uncultivable land' as percentage of TRA increased from 2.2 in 1970-71 to 2.4 per cent in 1990-91, the all-India figures being 5.8 and 5.1 per cent respectively.

About 27.06 lakh ha. of degraded land can be brought under stable agriculture alongwith pasture development and social forestry with suitable soil and water conservation measures. Eighteen lakh ha. current fallow and 4 lakh ha. culturable waste, that is, a sumtotal of 22 lakh ha. can be developed for cultivation. The *diara* lands (waste lands near the river margin), the weed-infested lands and the *chaurs* and *tars,* lands which are waterlogged and marshy lands, after draining, can be reclaimed and rice-and-fish culture can be developed in those areas. Change of routes by the rivers creates *diaras, chaurs* and *tars.* All these are fertile lands. This is with regard to the plains. So far as the plateau region is concerned, there is some scope for extending cultivation. Terracing of the milder slopes of the hills would afford a method of land reclamation. But land reclamation in the plateau region is an extremely slow and costly affair. The quality of the land to be reclaimed is inferior. Water for irrigation is a serious barrier after a point.

To conclude, the land use/utilisation pattern in Bihar, which remained more or less stable during 1960-61 to 1980-81, has altered only insignificantly in the years that have followed. To crown all, the pattern of land use does not appear to allow much room for change.

3

FORESTS IN BIHAR

Forests signify the biosphere and are formed biotic. They are a localised natural resource since they occur in particular places. They are a renewable natural resource and symbolise natural vegetation.

The gum-bearing trees, the seeds and flowers of the *sal* trees, *kendu* leaves for *bidi*-making and *babul* grass for coir are the forti of the forests in Bihar. *Sabai* grass is the staple material for paper.

Forests contribute substantially to the State economy by making available a number of useful products. They are of utmost importance in the ecological system of Chotanagpur and parts of Bihar. The rural areas in Chotanagpur have a mixed arable economy based on agriculture and forests. There are in the State quite a number of forest-based industries—tanning, catechu, essential oils, gums, Ayurvedic medicines, etc. In the last few years have come up plywood factories at Hajipur and Chakulia, and saw mills in Singhbhum and Patna. Bihar is the largest producer of lac, a good earner of foreign exchange. In addition to Chotanagpur, lac growers abound in Gaya and Aurangabad.

Lac, a forest product, has an important place in the Bihar economy for three reasons: (1) Export value—shellac, seed lac and processed stick lac are exported but their exports have been facing a sagging demand. (2) Uses in different industries. (3) Subsidiary income to the tribals as a good cash crop, which is low because of the malpractices of the indigenous middlemen.

The Government has been promoting the lac industry by taking different measures under its various departments : (1) The Forest Department, (2) The Bihar Cooperative Lac Marketing Society, (3) The Directorate of Lac Development, set up by the Central Government of Ranchi, (4) The Lac Research Institute at Nankum, which is concerned with marketing, and (5) The Lac Development Council of the Central Government.

Sal is the most important tree in the forests of Chotanagpur and other forests of Bihar. It is hard, strong and durable. Formerly it was in great demand for railway sleepers, beams, rafters, etc. but today it is used mainly for making furniture, doors and windows and in the construction of train coaches, etc.

Between 1953 (value 18 million rupees) and 1989 (value 1254 million rupees) there occurred a 70-fold increase in the monetary value of the forest produce in Bihar. At 1970-71 prices, income from forestry and logging in 1970-71 was 0.99 per cent of SDP (Rs. 22.34 versus Rs. 2245.44 crore); in 1975-76, 1.42 per cent (Rs. 35.95 versus Rs. 2533.36 crore); in 1980-81, 0.84 per cent (Rs. 24.87 versus Rs. 2941.35 crore); and at current prices, in 1989-90, 0.65 per cent (Table 3.1).

TABLE 3.1 : Income from Forestry and Logging

Year	*As Percentage of SDP*
At 1970-71 Prices	
1970-71	0.99
1975-76	1.42
1980-81	0.84
At Current Prices	
1989-90	0.65

Note : Forestry grew at the rate of 29.7 per cent (all-India 1.6%) during 1990-91 and (-) 2.1 per cent (all-India 2.0%) during 1991-92.

Bulk of the State revenue from the forests comes from the felling of trees. The revenue from the sale of timber itself was Rs. 35 crore in 1986-87, which rose to Rs. 38 crore in 1987-88, then fell to Rs. 35 crore in 1988-89 and had risen to Rs. 50 crore by 1992-93.

The forest cover in Bihar has been destroyed/degraded/rendered open more than elsewhere in India. Total forest area had fallen from about 32.15 lakh ha. in 1955-56 to about 29.23 lakh ha. in 1992-93 (Table 3.2). As percentage of total reporting area in the State forest area in Bihar had decreased from nearly 19.3 per cent in 1955-56 to nearly 16.8 per cent in 1992-93 (Table 3.3). Per capita forest resource had declined from about 0.08 ha. in 1955-56 to about 0.03 ha. in 1992-93 (Table 3.4). Bihar's share in the country's total forest area had diminished from nearly 5.1 per cent in 1955-56 to nearly 3.8 per cent in 1992-93 (Table 3.5). Seen against the norm of 33 per cent of total reporting area in an economy to be under forests, Bihar had only about half of it in 1991. So far as forest area with good tree cover as percentage of total reporting area is concerned, Bihar had during 1987-89, on an average, 7.7 per cent, the all-India share being 10.9 per cent.

TABLE 3.2 : Total Forest Area in Bihar

(*Lakh ha.*)

Year	*Area*
1955-56	32.15
1960-61	31.97
1970-71	29.28
1974-75	29.23
1980-81	28.26
1992-93	29.23

Note : In 1993 area under forests was 29.2 thousand km., 3.79 per cent of all-India total. Total forest covered area was 26.6 thousand km., 15.3 per cent of total geographical area of the State. Dense forest with crown density above 40 per cent was 13.2 thousand km., 7.6 per cent of total geographical area.

TABLE 3.3 : Forest Area as Percentage of Total Reporting Area

Year	*Percentage*
1956-57	19.3
1960-61	21.3
1970-71	16.9
1974-75	16.8
1980-81	16.8
1984-85	16.9
1992-93	16.8

TABLE 3.4 : Per Capita Forest Area (ha.)

Year	*Area*
1955-56	0.08
1960-61	0.06
1971-72	0.05
1980-81	0.05
1992-93	0.03

TABLE 3.5 : Bihar's Percentage Share in All-India Forest Area

Year	*Share (per cent)*
1950-51	5.1
1960-61	3.4
1992-93	3.8

The forest cover in the State was unevenly distributed as between the three regions : North Bihar 3.3 per cent in 1955-56 and 1.6 per cent in 1992-93 (a fall of 1.7 per cent), South Bihar 14.8 and 11.7 per cent respectively (a fall of 3.1 per cent), and Chotanagpur and Santhal Parganas 81.8 and 27.5 per cent respectively (a fall of 54.3 per cent). Here the percentage is to total reporting area in the region concerned. That Chotanagpur was the worst sufferer is obvious from these statistics. In the plains Rohtas topped in forest wealth, 24.5 per cent and in the plateau Hazaribagh, 48.3 per cent.

Remote sensing has brought to light the fact that half of the existing forests in Bihar are degraded, i.e., the open forests and blanks. These have, over the past four decades or more, suffered from a severe biotic pressure, resulting in destruction of the forest cover, loss of top-soil, ecological imbalance, and so forth. Areas which were considered stable a few decades ago have now become ecologically fragile with large chunks of erstwhile richly forested areas turned into barren overburns and mining spoils. The rate of deforestation and soil erosion has been the highest in Chotanagpur and Santhal Parganas. The verdant forests of Chotanagpur are a mere apology for the vegetal cover.

The decline of forest wealth has been caused by a multiplicity of factors : One, increasing pressure of population on forest resource for sustenance—an inverse relationship between population density and forest cover percentage has been discernible. Two, indiscriminate felling of trees—unplanned, unrestricted, repeated cutting, excessive commercial exploitation and denudation of the existing forests. Three, replacement of forests by fruit orchards in numerous places in North Bihar. Four, conspiring of both agriculture and industry to lower the forest area—mining activities have caused degradation of the forests to an alarming extent—large areas of the protected and reserved forests have become barren due to the mine spoils—excessive soil erosion caused by mining overburns—the ore belts lie in areas where we have the best forests. Five, overgrazing of forests by cattle. Six, depletion of forests through fires—resulting in land erosion—destruction of ground flora. Seven, recurrent annual hot season. Eight, washing away of the rich fertile top-soil in subsequent rains in the absence of ground cover—results? Regeneration is obtrusively difficult to retrieve. Nine, reckless utilisation of the forest products for fuel and charcoal. Ten, thieving of timber by anti-social elements.

To the above list we may add the constraints on account of the Government policy and action : Firstly, lip service to the national forest policies of 1952 and 1988—Government apathy and neglect in the earlier years. Secondly, delay in the release of funds. Thirdly, inadequacy of all-weather roads, staff and research. Fourthly, slashing of outlays on forests due to the financial crunch.

There are three types of schemes for the forests : (1) totally financed by the State Government; (2) on 50 : 50 basis between the Union and the State Government; and (3) 100 per cent financed by the Centre.

The State forests are characterised by low productivity. Against their capacity of producing 3 cubic metres of timber per ha., they produce only 1.2 cubic metres of timber per ha.

The people are not involved in the development of the State forests. There is lack of awareness of the need to develop and conserve forests.

The gap between demand and supply of not only timber but also fuel wood has been widening continuously. While there is a cogent case for developing the forests, there is an urgent need to explore alternative sources of fuel for cooking purposes in rural areas, keeping in mind the uneven distribution of fuel wood between North and South Bihar and between North Bihar and Chotanagpur.

Deforestation over the years has disturbed the ecological balance and the cultural life of the forest-based society. In addition, the climatic pattern of the plateau region has been affected as the magnitude of rainfall has been reduced. Land has been degraded. The impoverished forests have failed to fulfil the task of conservation of soil and moisture.

Let us now review the Government role since Independence : in 1950-51 the Government took over the ownership and control of private forests, comprising 85 per cent of all forests. After a few years, the kendu leaf trade was taken over by the State Government. *Van-Mahotsava* was launched to counter deforestation. Increasing soil moisture near the river water storage reservoirs led to some expansion in the forest area of the State. Horticulture has been integrated with agriculture. The State Forest Department laid stress on the growth and development of eucalyptus, a raw material for the paper mills. The lac culture has been promoted. Degraded forests are rehabilitated. Forests are protected against biotic interference. The sal tree regeneration is receiving special attention. The Government has helped opening of saw mills. The forestry programme has been strengthened. Afforestation is being executed with an eye to making good deforestation. This is enshrined in the Jawahar Rajgar Yojna (JRY) and similar other rural development programmes. Social forestry initiated in the Sixth Plan and farm forestry emphasised in the Seventh Plan and aimed at meeting the requirements of fruits, fuel and timber of the local people are given due place in the forestry development programme. Soil conservation extends to the forests. Forests are being protected against the anti-social elements and fires. All-weather roads are being constructed in the forest area. The forest administration is being reorganised. Increase, preservation and maintenance of the forest cover is the central aim and object of the Government policy. Waste land, previously rich with forest, is being reclaimed and turned into social forestry afresh. The efforts made by the Government in this direction are bearing fruit.

All the same, the Government is blamed for its failure to exploit the forest wealth of the State properly and suitably. It is pointed out that in the Chotanagpur region the illegal timber trade amounts to over Rs. 10 crore a year. This racket is stated to have become widespread since 1977 when the Janata Government interpreted the Chotanagpur Tenancy Act to imply that the ryots could utilise the trees on their lands not only for meeting their own needs but also for commercial disposal. Unscrupulous entrepreneurs, abetted by some forest and revenue officials and even social workers, in times of hardship, allegedly induced the ryots to sell timber at nominal prices and had it illegally transported out of the area. Reports of the revenue officials in Chotanagpur blatantly indulging in the open loot of forest property by giving clearance on fake applications for transit permits from the Forest Department, without any action being taken by the Government, with the booty shared by all, from the Circle Officer upto the Minister have piled up continuously.

Public opinion would desire that the user agencies should compensate for the lost forest area and provide adequate funds for its afforestation. In North Bihar care should be exercised in order that social forestry does not encroach upon the roads and embankments. There is already plenty of land area in the belts of foothills in the plateau region which can be covered up under vegetation by afforestation in lieu of being subjected to the erosive action of wind and rain due to cultivation. The *sal* culture should be given treatment for its proper growth and development. The plateau region is suitable for timber development. At the same time, the output of minor forest products should be stimulated. Forest-based industries have a bright prospect in Chotanagpur and other parts where forests form a good proportion of the reported land area. In so far as the Chotanagpur forests have a multidimensional character in providing the basic needs of the tribal people, it is further suggested that the poverty-alleviation programme in the plateau region should be interwoven with the forest development programme, considering that there is a close connection between tribal development and forest development. The rural and tribal people should be supplied with their requirement of the forest products like fuel wood and fodder.

To conclude, were man and animal to stop interfering with the natural wealth of forests, the Bihar plains, in course of time, would be replaced by woodlands and ultimately by dense forests with no chance of grass to grow. On the contrary, were they to go on exploiting it, as they are doing in the plateau region, without striving to recompense the loss, there would grow weeds only, and nothing else.

4

CROPPING PATTERN IN BIHAR AGRICULTURE

Cropping pattern stands for the proportional distribution of cultivated land area among the crops. It is intimately identified with the three principal seasons in Bihar, namely, summer (March to May), rainy (June to October) and winter (November to February). Accordingly, we have three harvests, viz., *Bhadai* (autumn) crops, *Agahani* (winter) crops and Rabi (spring) crops. The northern and eastern parts of the Bihar plain where the early rain is relatively heavy are sown with the *Bhadai* crops, the most important ones. But they are also grown in the plateau region. They are sown in May and June and are ready in July and August.

The *Agahani* crops are sown in July and August and are ready in November and December.

The *Rabi* crops are sown in November and December and ready in March and April. They are grown only in the plains. They are dependent on irrigation. They are less prevalent in the plateau region.

The *Garma* crops are sown in April and are ready in June. They are rice, maize, pulses and onion. They have a restricted acreage.

Kharif subsumes Bhadai and Agahani. The principal Bhadai crops are : Rice, maize, *marua* (ragi), bajra, urhad and jute. Rice is the leading Agahani crop. This crop calls for an equitable distribution of rain throughout the season. The Chotanagpur plateau is basically a monoculture area and *kharif* is the main crop of the year.

The Bhadai harvest is less uncertain than the Agahani but the Rabi is the least uncertain. The Rabi crops are wheat, gram, khesari, mustard and potato.

The Agahani crops are more time-consuming than the Bhadai crops, with the result that the former are followed by a second crop only, whereas the latter are invariably followed by a full Rabi crop.

The Rabi harvest is a 'mosaic of mixed crops', such as wheat and gram, wheat and mustard, gram and linseed. The Rabi crops are largely unirrigated, whereas the Bhadai and Agahani crops are rainfed. The Rabi harvest is becoming increasingly important because it lowers the reliance of the farmers on the temperamental monsoon. It is sensitive to irrigation. With extension of irrigation, the Rabi crops have increased in acreage. In many cases the Rabi harvest is comprised of inferior catch crops. Rabi is the chief crop in the *Tal* area and marshy lands of North Bihar.

An upland is suited to the production of dry crops; a lowland, wet crops. Rice and jute are wet crops. Millets and oilseeds are dry crops. Rice, maize, jute and millets are quick-maturing crops.

In 1950-51, according to the 1951 Census, in Bihar there were four crops, namely, *Garma, Bhadai, Agahani* and *Rabi* and the acreage diverted to them in percentage terms were : 3, 17, 43 and 37. In 1955-56 the corresponding figures were : 3, 17, 53 and 27.

In the Government publications, gradually, in place of the four divisions of the crops only two divisions, viz., kharif and rabi have found acceptance. As Table 4.1 shows, over 33 (approx.) years the distribution of land as between kharif and rabi has remained more or less unchanged in percentage terms. During 1970-71 to 1989-90 the acreage under the kharif crops declined by 6.35 per cent (all-India : 10.23 per cent), from 70.4 to 64.1 lakh ha. By comparison, the area under the rabi crops improved by 1.43 per cent (all-India 32.09 per cent), from 28.7 to 30.1 lakh ha. During the same period the compound annual rate of growth of acreage under kharif was –0.50 per cent (all-India –.07) and under rabi 0.20 per cent (all-India 0.39).

TABLE 4.1 : Allocation of GCA between Kharif and Rabi

(*Percentage*)

Year	*Kharif*	*Rabi*
1966-67	67.8	32.2
1970-71	71.0 (66.2)	29.0 (33.8)
1989-90	68.0 (64.3)	32.0 (35.7)

Note : In the 1996-97 Annual Plan the ratio of the Kharif target to the Rabi target was 0.93.

The dependence of Bihar on kharif has been so far very heavy. It has become heavier with the passage of time. This may not be advisable from the point of view of gaining stability of agricultural production, notwithstanding the fact that from the point of view of meeting the staple food requirements of the people this may be a decidedly good thing. Since kharif comprises cash crops the level of development in Bihar has had a close relationship/affinity with the level of commercialisation.

The cropping pattern in Bihar is overwhelmingly food crops-oriented. Between 1950-51 and 1990-91, as Table 4.2 would indicate, there has taken place a marginal change of 4 per cent approximately. During the 1980s food crops acreage was nearly 90 per cent of Gross Cropped Area (GCA), doubtlessly lop-sided and skewed. Bihar's relative share in all-India food crops acreage during 1970-71 to 1990-91 was reduced marginally (Table 4.3). In the case of non-food crops the position had worsened more acutely. In Bihar agriculture has not been commercialised as much as in the country. Bihar has not done equally well in the production of non-food crops, though the pace in that direction definitely gathered momentum during the 1980s.

TABLE 4.2 : Allocation of GCA between Food and Non-Food Crops

(Percentage)

Year	*Food Crops*	*Non-Food Crops*
1950-51	94.1 (73.3)	5.9 (26.3)
1955-56	95.6	4.4
1960-61	88.3	11.7
1960-61	89.3	10.7
1970-71	92.8 (78.7)	7.2 (21.3)
1970-71	86.3	13.7
1980-81	90.0	10.0
1980-81	84.6	15.4
1984-85	89.5	10.5
1989-90	90.2 (69.5)	9.8 (30.5)
1990-91	89.9 (69.0)	10.1 (31.0)
1990-91	89.1 (69.0)	10.1 (31.0)

Note: The underlined data are our estimates.

TABLE 4.3 : Bihar's Percentage Share in All-India Acreage

Year	*Food Crops (per cent)*	*Non-Food Crops (per cent)*	*Total (lakh ha.)*
1950-51	9.70	—	—
1955-56	8.30	—	—
1961-62	8.40	—	97.4 (1146.2)
1970-71	6.76	0.17	106.7 (1578.0)
1988-89	7.50	—	—
1989-90	7.30		
1990-91	5.65/7.2	(–) 0.34	104.9 (1854.8)

Note : In 1992-93 area under food crops was 83.53 lakh ha.

Growth of population and purchasing power and consequential increase in the demand for foodgrains, the slow increase in the yield (relatively to non-food crops) and relatively more price and non-price incentives to the producers of staple foodgrains are the reasons why land has not been diverted from food to non-food crops in any marked manner. It is only in an insignificant degree that medium and large holdings have been switched over to the production of non-food crops. Small and marginal holdings have clung to the production of food crops.

With reference to Table 4.4 we can say that the acreage under food crops fell by about 5.5 per cent during 1955-56 to 1990-91 and that under non-food crops rose by about that percentage. The range of fluctuations in total acreage, i.e., GCA has been wide, almost 29 per cent. GCA has fluctuated steeply at times, leaving its imprint on the acreages devoted to the different groups of crops, food and non-food. The acreage devoted to cereals fell by 6 per cent during the period, while that devoted to pulses rose by about 0.5 per cent. This is as good as remaining static. With increased irrigation facility land allocated to oilseeds has nominally increased. In 1951 the acreage under oilseeds, nuts, sugarcane, cotton and vegetables was deficient. Between 1952-53 and 1964-65 the rate of growth of cereals acreage was 1.67 simple/0.41 compound per cent per annum, that of pulses acreage 1.4 simple/1.64 compound per cent per annum, and all foodgrains acreage 1.53 simple/ 1.064 compound. The predominance of cereals acreage was enhanced

TABLE 4.4 : Allocation of Acreage : Principal Crops : Group-wise

(Percentage)

Year	*Cereals*	*Pulses*	*Foodgrains*	*Non-food Crops Oilseeds*	*Other Non-food Crops*	*Total Acreage (Lakh. ha.)*
1955-56	84.73	10.80	95.53	negligible	4.47	92.15
1960-61	68.32	20.98	89.30	8.04**	3.66	111.12
1970-71	71.98	14.33	86.31	2.07	11.62	114.80
1980-81	72.27	12.27	84.54	2.32	13.14	111.48
1989-90	78.6	11.6	90.2	2.3	—	—
	(56.6)*	(12.9)	(69.5)	(12.8)		
1990-91	78.70	11.21	89.91	1.99/2.3	4.76	104.85
	(55.6)*	(13.4)	(69.0)	(13.5)	—	—
Range of Variation	16.41	10.18	10.99	—	—	9.95

* Including millets.

** Including other crops.

during 1955-56 to 1970-71. Between 1950-51 and 1980-81 food crops acreage fluctuated to the extent of 22.2 per cent (all-India 24.9).

The range of variation was maximum in the case of cereals during 1955-56 to 1990-91. In Table 4.5 an attempt has been made to depict the relative shares of five principal crops raised in Bihar over a span of 45 years (1955-56 to 1990-91) in total acreage. The least affected crop is sugarcane, and the most affected wheat. Whereas the acreage under the former moved down by 0.29 per cent, that under wheat moved up by 12.02 per cent. The decline in gram acreage is maximum (3.99 per cent). Maize acreage fell by 0.94 per cent, and rice acreage by 2.60 per cent. The degree of instability of allocated acreage was the highest in the case of rice and the lowest in that of sugarcane.

TABLE 4.5 : Acreage under Certain Principal Crops

(*As percentage of GCA*)

Year	*Rice*	*Wheat*	*Maize*	*Gram*	*Sugarcane*
1955-56	58.78	6.72	7.28	5.59	1.71
1960-61	47.17	5.86	7.24	4.87	1.66
1970-71	42.43	10.94	8.63	2.12	1.41
1980-81	48.89	16.17	7.91	1.75	0.99
1989-90	50.60	19.10	6.70	—	1.20
	(23.1)	(12.9)	(3.2)		(1.9)
1990-91	51.4/56.18	18.74/18.8	6.34/6.4	1.60	1.42
	(23.0)	(13.0)	(3.2)		(2.0)
Change (Rise/Fall)	2.60	12.02	0.94	3.99	0.29
Range of Variation	16.35	12.88	2.29	3.99	0.72

Note : Estimates made by us.

Between 1960-61 and 1980-81 cereals acreage varied upto 23.4 per cent. In 1986-87 per capita cereals acreage was 0.13 ha. The area sown with minor, coarse cereals exhibited a progressive decline during 1960-61 to 1983-84 on account of persistent neglect of and lack of support by the government. The demand for them has fallen over the years because the food habits of the people have changed and the demand for finer cereals has risen proportionally more instead. The Food-For-Work Programme, the rising ratio of money wage payment to payment in kind and the Public Distribution System (PDS) in which wheat has been the main grain, have all contributed to a situation in which the farmer has had no alternative, except to transfer his land from the coarse cereals to the superior grains. The coarse cereals are the poor man's great ally. They are the safety-valve against the truancy of the monsoon. They are ubiquitous and amenable to mixed cropping.

Rice acreage has dwindled, as evident from Table 4.6, but still claims half of the total cropped area, i.e., GCA. As percentage of total foodgrains acreage, rice acreage has slid down sharply. Yet it claims a little over half of it. As percentage of all-India rice acreage, rice acreage in Bihar has declined perceptibly. Besides, its rank in all-India has gone down. Acreage variation during 1950-51 to 1988-89 was 24 per cent. The decline in rice acreage has been absolute as well as relative. Between 1966-67 (a drought year) and 1985-86 rice acreage, as percentage of GCA, was maximum (51.3 per cent) in 1983-84 and minimum (46.7 per cent) in 1972-73.

TABLE 4.6 : Rice Acreage

Year	*Acreage (lakh ha.)*	*As Percentage of GCA*	*As Percentage of Foodgrains Acreage*	*Growth Rate Simple*	*Growth Rate Compound (Per cent per annum)*	*Rank in All-India*	*As Percentage of All-India*
1950-51	58.11	55.6	59.08 (48.0)				18.8
1955-56	52.56	53.0	57.03				15.0
1960-61	52.42	47.1	52.80				14.3
1952-53 to 1964-65	—	—	—	(–) 6.82	(–) 0.23		—
1970-71	48.71	42.43	49.20				13.4
1974-75	52.28	50.5	53.83			2nd	—
1980-81	54.51	50.5	54.37			1st	182
1986-87 to 1988-89	52.57	51.4	—				11.0
1955-56 to 1988-89	—	—	—				—
1989-90	52.90		56.09		(–) 1.6	3rd	8.6/12.2
1990-91	53.90	51.4	57.09			3rd	11.7/12.7
1993-94	52.70	—	—				—

Range of variation : 1950-51 to 1988-89 24 per cent

Note: Estimates made by others.

In some areas all the three varieties of rice, viz., Bhadai, Agahani and Garma grow. Agahani rice grows in all regions. But the plain areas are most suited. In the north-east districts it is grown without irrigation on the strength of good rainfall. In the north-west, southern and middle-west districts irrigation is inevitable because the monsoon is uncertain and the rainfall is inadequate. Bhadai rice grows mostly in the northern and eastern districts. Agahani rice is next to be grown on the same lands. Bhadai rice is more uncertain and more expensive to grow. Most farmers grow it by allocating more or less land.

Rice occupies half of the cropped land area in the delta of the Ganga. In the 1980s rice acreage was distributed among the three regions as under : North 54 per cent, South and Chotanagpur each 23 per cent. Within Chotanagpur itself, one-third of GCA is sown with rice. In addition to eating, rice is used for brewing and paper-making. Its bran is also used. Many small farmers in Chotanagpur find it difficult to sow paddy and in many cases land remains uncultivated. The owners, mostly *Adivasis*, either work as farm labourers or pull *rickshaws.* They also sow maize or coarse grains in their small holdings.

Rice-growing lands are the best of all. Bhadai rice is sown in May-June and harvested in September. Agahani rice is sown during May-June, transplanted from the seed-bed in June-July and harvested in October-November. Rice cultivation requires not only that rainfall is in adequate quantity but also that the rainfall is distributed evenly over the season of the crop. In areas where the labour supply is relatively less scarce and hence more elastic and is steady in character rice acreage has an edge over wheat.

If rice is Number One crop, wheat is Number Two crop, in Bihar. Table 4.7 purports to inform that wheat acreage in the State has multiplied more than three-fold in the last forty years. Share of wheat acreage in total foodgrains acreage has increased nearly three-fold, and in GCA a little over three-fold. Bihar's wheat acreage share in all-India wheat acreage has risen, though not in any remarkable manner. The year-to-year fluctuations have been within the limits of about 13 per cent of GCA.

In acreage wheat has been encroaching upon barley. During 1951-52 to 1977-78 area under barley increasingly shifted to area under wheat. Wheat has been the prime vying crop for rabi pulses so far as acreage was concerned. The earliest Government Intensive Agricultural District Programme had resulted in the replacement of khesari by wheat, as for example in Shahabad.

As of late, wheat has emerged as an important crop with an average profit of Rs. 3767 per ha. and 240 per cent rate of profit. The GCA has declined by one per cent but as a result of technological changes the area under wheat has increased. Wheat has proved to be more profitable than maize. Wheat has been competing more fiercely with sugarcane. During 1967-68 to 1984-85 wheat acreage as percentage of GCA was maximum (18.1 per cent) in 1984-85 and minimum (10.2 per cent) in 1955-56. Acreage grew with extension of the irrigation facility and increased consumption of wheat by Biharis.

TABLE 4.7 : Wheat Acreage

(Percentage)

Year	*Acreage (Lakh ha.)*	*Share in Food-grains Acreage*	*Share in GCA*	*Growth Rate (Per cent per annum)*	*Share in All-India Acreage*	*Rank in All-India*	*Range of Varia-tion*
1950-51	5.89	5.98 (14.9)	5.6		6.0		
1952-53 to 1964-65	—	—		Simple 3.34 Compound 0.98			
1950s (Early)						4th	
1955-56	6.02	6.53	5.8		4.8		
1956-59 (Av.)	—	—	6.0		—		
1960-61	6.52	6.56	5.8		5.0		
1965-66	6.75	7.03	6.2		—		
1967-68	10.56	9.27	NA		—	2nd	
1970-71	12.16	12.28	10.6		6.6		
1974-77 (Av.)	—	—	16.0		—		
1975-76	18.15	17.98	16.0		—		
1980-81	18.03	17.98	16.0		8.1		
1986-87 to 1988-89 (Av.)	20.22	21.44	17.6		8.1		
1989-90	19.90	21.10			8.4/8.5	4th	
1955-56 to 1990-91	—	—			—		12.88
1990-91	19.70	20.86			8.2/8.3	4th	
1993-94	21.00	—			—		

The prime acreage of wheat falls in the Gandak and Sone Command Areas. Sixty-two per cent of wheat acreage lies in North Bihar. The plateau districts raise wheat on an acreage that is two per cent of the aggregate wheat acreage in the State.

Owing to the late harvesting of paddy, most of the sowing of wheat is generally done towards the latter half of November and the first fortnight of December. Harvesting is done in March-April. Wheat acreage is largely contingent upon irrigation.

Maize is a poor Bihari's food in the form of *sattu* or *atta.* Its area has displayed an upward but not a downward trend. The same observation holds good with regard to the maize acreage as percentage of GCA. From its second position among the food crops, next to rice, it was pushed back to the third, with wheat seizing its second position. But precedent to that the maize area declined in favour of the rice area (Table 4.8). Between 1966-67 and 1984-85 maize acreage, as percentage of GCA, was maximum (9.5 per cent) in 1967-68 and minimum (5.5 per cent) in 1984-85. Rice, wheat and maize claimed 86.3 per cent of GCA in 1955-56, which rose to 91.27 per cent in 1970-71.

TABLE 4.8 : Maize Acreage

Year	*Acreage (Lakh ha.)*	*As Percentage of*			*Rank in All-India*	*Grwoth Rate (Per cent)*
		GCA (Per cent)	*Foodgrains Acreage (Per cent)*	*All-India (Per cent)*		
1950-51	6.13	5.81	6.23	19.4		—
1952-53 to 1964-65	—	—	—	—		Simple 3.91 Compound 1.48
1955-56	6.51	6.56	7.06	17.6		—
1960-61	8.05	7.24	8.10	18.3		—
1970-71	9.91	8.63	10.01	16.9		—
1974-75	8.81	8.10	9.07	—	2nd	—
1980-81	8.82	7.91	8.79	14.6	3rd	—
1986-87	6.44	6.20	6.84	—		—
1989-90	—	—	—	11.5		—
1990-91	6.65	6.34	7.05	11.1/11.5	4th	—

Maize is popular in both the plains and the plateau. North Bihar has the lion's share, 81.6 per cent, followed by Chotanagpur 10.8 per cent and South Bihar 7.6 per cent. Bhadai maize grows in *Diara* lands and flood-affected areas, whereas Agahani maize grows in the northern and western parts of the State. Bhadai maize is popular among the Scheduled Tribes and the poorer farmers. With increased use of the HYVs all the three crops—Bhadai, Agahani and Rabi—are grown. The rising water-table in some North Bihar districts has gradually resulted in partial shift of maize from the kharif to the rabi season.

Many kinds of pulses grow in Bihar. In spite of his poverty, an average Bihari is fastidious/conscious about pluses as being an essential part of his meals and so gives them a special place in his food as well as in his farming. However, we can notice from Table 4.9 the sad tale of decline in pulses acreage and Bihar's place among the pulses-growing States. Between 1967-68 and 1985-86 pulses acreage was maximum (16.3 per cent) in 1967-68 and minimum (11.1 per cent) in 1985-86. Pulses can be raised on rainfed as well as dryland areas. They are proof against the failure of the monsoon.

TABLE 4.9 : Total Pulses Acreage

Year	*Area (Lakh ha.)*	*As Percentage of*			*Rank in All-India*	*Range of Variation (Per cent)*
		GCA	*Foodgrains Acreage*	*All-India Total Pulses Acreage*		
1955-56	—	—	—	5.4		—
1960-61	23.22	20.89	23.38	9.8		—
1960-61 to 1980-81	—	—	—	—		46.5
1965-66	21.56	20.03	22.47	—		—
1970-71	16.45	14.33	16.61	7.2		—
1974-75	—	—	—	—	5th	—
1980-81	13.68	12.27	13.64	5.9	8th	—
1986-87	12.10	11.60	13.10	—		—
1986-87 to 1988-89 (Av)	11.90	—	—	—		—
1988-89	—	—	11.90	—		—
1990-91	11.90	11.35	12.62	—	8th	—

Oilseeds are among the leading non-food crops grown in Bihar. An average cultivator regards them as cash crops rather than food crops. In the early 1950s they were consumed largely by the oil-mills in the State but part of the total outturn was exported to other parts of the country. From Table 4.10 it can be gathered that the area under oilseeds has slid down, also as percentage of GCA. As percentage of all-India oilseeds acreage, it has tapered off, but the rank remains constant. Between 1975-76 and 1983-84 oilseeds acreage in Bihar was maximum in 1975-76 and minimum in 1981-82. The range of variation was 25 per cent. Where the monsoon was too late for sowing rice, rice was substituted by millets or pulses or oilseeds because their water requirement was far lower.

Bihar was the pioneer in launching sugarcane cultivation in India. The self-sufficient farmers grow one staple food crop and one non-food, that is, cash crop, for example, sugarcane or jute, which they sell to the sugar-mill or the trader merchant. Sugarcane acreage has been unstable and has declined over the years as percentage of both GCA in the State and all-India sugarcane acreage, as revealed by Table 4.11. During 1950-51 to 1982-83 the year of maximum acreage was 1976-77 (1.47 lakh ha.) and that of minimum 1955-56 (0.43 lakh ha.). The factors responsible for this fluctuation were : sugarcane price policy of the Government and hence competition of sugarcane with other crops like maize and wheat for the given land, depending on labour supply (if assured, sugarcane has an edge over maize) and technological progress (which has favoured wheat), condition of transport facility from farm to mill, regular payment to the farmers, price of sugar vis-a-vis prices of *gur* and *khandsari,* distribution of sugar, weather, pests and diseases, etc.

TABLE 4.10 : Oilseeds Acreage

Year	*Area (Lakh ha.)*	*As Percentage of*		*Rank in All-India*	*Range of Variation (Per cent)*
		GCA in the State	*All-India Oilseeds Acreage*		
1950-51	3.46	3.31	3.44	8th	—
1956-57	2.63	2.65	1.85		—
1960-61 to 1980-81	—	—	—		25
1970-71	2.50	2.17	1.50		—
1975-76	3.14	2.78	1.85		—
1980-81	2.59	2.32	1.47		—
1986-87	2.26	2.22	0.96		—
1989-90	—	—	1.0		—
1990-91	2.09	1.99	0.9/1.18	8th	—

Sugarcane acreage rose from 1955-56 (0.43 lakh ha.) to 1968-69 (1.11 lakh ha.)/1973-74 (1.06 lakh ha.) to 1976-77 (1.47 lakh ha.) and fell from 1969-70 (1.02 lakh ha.) to 1971-72 (1.05 lakh ha.) and again from 1977-78 (1.42 lakh ha.) to 1979-80 (1.30 lakh ha.). In other words, the rise was by 138 and 258 per cent in the first two cases and the fall by 103 and 109 per cent in the latter two cases. The magnitude of variation/ fluctuation between the first rise and the first fall was 155 per cent and that of variation/fluctuation between the second rise and the second fall was 29 per cent.

TABLE 4.11 : Sugarcane Acreage

Year	*Area (Lakh ha.)*	*As Percentage of*			*Rank in All-India*	*Range of Variation (Per cent)*
		GCA in the State	*Non-food-grains Acreage*	*All-India Sugarcane Acreage*		
1952-53 to 1964-65						**1.92 (Compound rate of growth)**
1955-56	1.53	1.46	21.76	8.28		
1960-61	1.85	1.66	15.63	7.66		
1961-62	1.97	2.54	—	—		
1965-66	1.70	1.58	14.54	5.99		
1966-67	1.49	2.01	—	—		
1970-71	1.62	1.62	10.25	6.20		
1974-75					4th	
1975-76	1.34	1.19	11.06	4.85	5th	
1980-81	1.11	0.99/1.00	9.88	4.16	7th	
1986-87	1.12	1.5 (1.8)	—	3.44		
1989-90	—	—	—	3.8		
1990-91	0.15	0.11	1.42	3.8/4.10	6th	
1994-95	0.12	—	—	3.15	7th	

* Other rates of growth of acreage were : All non-foodgrains 1.75, All crops 0.71, Jute 2.17, Potate 7.81 and Foodgrains 0.64.

Jute cultivation is, by and large, a characteristic of North Bihar, where it has supremacy over wheat as the second crop. As Table 4.12 discloses, jute acreage has managed to expand over time, though fluctuating, and its proportion to all-India acreage tending to fall off, though Bihar's rank has remained undisturbed at the second. During 1967-68 to 1985-86 both sugarcane and jute acreages had their maxima and minima in percentage terms equal at 1.5 and 0.9 per cent, but in different years, the former in 1969-70 and 1980-81 and the latter in 1967-68 and 1968-69. The time-spread was longer in the case of sugarcane acreage. In the case of jute, the decline in acreage was in the very next year.

Spices like *chillies* (red pepper) and turmeric, potato, onion, garlic and tobacco are other cash crops that are grown in Bihar, besides horticultural products like mango, *lichi*, banana and guava.

At present the cropping pattern is dominated by low-value, inferior-quality crops. The high-value cash/money crops count far less. While it cannot be denied that no significant changes have taken place in the cropping pattern since the early 1960s, some changes which have occurred cannot be overlooked. In North Bihar abandonment of oilseeds, pulses and fibres has taken place to an extent. Some high-value crops such as soyabean, sunflower and groundnut are new comers in South Bihar and Chotanagpur, in particular. With increased resort to the HYVs and fertilisers wheat acreage has made a long stride. Authorities are of the opinion that unless productivity increases more and sufficiently, there is scarcely any room for further alteration of the given cropping pattern, poised to meeting the State's food requirement, though without a breakthrough so far.

TABLE 4.12 : Jute Acreage

Year	*Area (Lakh ha.)*	*As Percentage of*	
		GCA	*All-India Acreage*
1950-51	1.10	0.96	22.6
1955-56	1.54	1.55	16.3
1960-61	1.46	1.31	16.2
1965-66	1.53	1.41	20.1
1970-71	1.42	1.23	13.1
1975-76	0.99	0.87	16.9
1980-81	1.35	1.71	10.3
1986-87	1.75	1.67	16.4
1989-90	—	—	17.2
1990-91	1.60	1.52	15.7/17.6

Let us now bring this topic to a close by trying to locate the factors or influences behind the cropping pattern in Bihar. At the beginning it would be proper to point out that the cropping pattern is the outcome of the long process of historical evolution. The existing cropping pattern in the State is a continuation of the past. We have enlisted above rainfall and weather conditions as the prime determinants in the period prior to 1966-67 and added more factors to the list in the period subsequent to that year. In areas prone to either flood or drought the cropping is different in view of the insecurity and instability elements. 'Survival First' is the maxim in such areas. Individual cultivators seek to ensure themselves against the natural vagaries by sowing broadcast some combination of rice, maize, arhar, urad, sesamum, moong, and so on. Intercropping is practised to eliminate the risk of rice crop failure—rice with pulses/oilseeds. This is widely in vogue in rainfed uplands. In Samastipur district rice is grown with tobacco, and *chillies* with vegetables; in Ranchi and Jamshedpur districts rice is grown with vegetables. Mixed farming has good prospects in Chotanagpur. However, as human effort and ingenuity is trying to contain the natural calamities, these areas are coming to have cropping patterns conforming to those in other areas.

Innovations made by the peasants themselves have led to the cultivation of the rainy season potato in Ranchi and winter rice in the Kosi belt.

Areas within the reach of the urban and industrial centres have different cropping patterns from areas that are inferior and isolated.

A number of farmers cultivate land to earn maximum profit, generally cash/money crops.

In several parts of Bihar the cultivators are content with merely growing a single rice or rabi crop, even under quite wholesome soil and climatic conditions for more intensive farming. In limited parts the land is continuously under a succession of crops throughout the year with very short and regulated rest for the soil. The cultivation of jute, potato, etc. fits well with this system. There are certain cultivating castes which practise highly intensive farming wherever they are.

The subsidiary crops are very responsive to the intensity of manual work and are less dependent on the favours of Nature. They were once upon a time highly crucial as reserve food resources in anticipation of a foodgrains deficit. Through special efforts their sowing was stimulated, intensified and encouraged. Provided irrigation facility exists, they can be raised anywhere in the State.

The 'Survival First' motto has made the tribals adopt the self-sufficiency principle in tilling land. Irrigation facility has been extended and soil protection has progressed in Chotanagpur. These are influences which herald a modicum of change in the cropping pattern of the plateau region.

There is plenty of scope for reinforcing physical and monetary resources in the areas of crop selection and rotation, including fodder crops, development of pasture, silviculture and animal husbandry in the three regions of Bihar.

5

AGRICULTURAL PRODUCTION IN BIHAR

In this chapter we shall discuss production in agriculture in two parts—one, foodgrains production and non-foodgrains production, which are a component of the primary sector, its other components being forestry and logging (this we have already discussed), fishing, animal husbandry (which two components we discuss separately) and mining and quarrying (which alongwith industry would compose another book). Food and non-food crops may be either kharif or rabi, their relative significance may vary spatially, i.e., region-wise as well as temporally, i.e., over and through time. In our study we have limited our purview to rice, wheat, maize, pulses and oilseeds among the food crops and sugarcane and jute among the non-food crops. In 1950-51 kharif crops were nearly two-thirds of the aggregate outturn, rabi crops being one-third of it. In 1991-92 the ratio had become 46 : 54.

As we proceed, we shall notice how agriculture in Bihar now contributes more to the economy in real terms as well as monetary, a remark which holds true in the case also of per unit of land and per unit of labour employed, crop-wise, besides the remarkable fact that food production, despite its slow growth, has taken population growth in its stride, without letting the situation turn uncontrollable. The composite index has indicated a secular trend of improvement in spite of the fluctuations staring the agricultural sector in its face.

The twin determinants of agricultural production, viz., area and yield have played their respective parts in varying proportions, depending upon the crop concerned and in close proximity with the sub-determinants. Performance of agriculture has turned consistently on man's effort and new agrarian technology (which two have jointly countered stagnancy and staticism), assuming that nature has remained benevolent.

Those who dissent from the foregoing maintain that the situation facing agriculture in Bihar in the early years of the 1990s was not decidedly different from that facing it in the 1950s, marked by depression, a shaky base betraying inadequacy of food production, a growing food deficit, and a violently oscillating agricultural output. The situation in the early 1990s was not only slow but also unstable. Agricultural production was low, as compared to the needs of the State.

In the last 42 years agriculture in Bihar has not been in a position to realise a rate of growth which is in accord with its universally admitted potential.

Instability of agricultural production is a salient feature of the agricultural sector of Bihar. The rainfed areas in the State, which predominate particularly in the plateau region, are subject to uncertain rains, on which they rely in a big way, with the result that they face uncertainty as to agricultural output and experience large variations in their agricultural production. The materialisation or failure of the *Hathia* rains in the winter causes all the difference between plenty and scarcity. The cropping pattern which is a map of the relative importance enjoyed by the different crops (Table 5.1) is an additional factor which governs the degree of stability of agricultural production. The manner in which the harvests, namely, kharif and rabi and the major crops, food and non-food, react to the natural and man-made factors is specific to them and defies generalisation. The kharif crops are more susceptible to the vagaries of nature than the rabi ones. Waterlogging as well as underwatering is injurious to the former. Coarse cereals are comparatively more thick-skinned to bear the brunt of Nature, so are oilseeds as compared to pulses.

TABLE 5.1 : Production of Principal Agricultural Commodities : 1950-51 *Versus* 1990-91

Commodities	*Quantity ('000 tonnes)*			*Percentage Distribution*		
	1950-51	*1990-91*	*Difference (per cent)*	*1950-51*	*1990-91*	*Difference*
(1)	(2)	(3)	(4)	(5)	(6)	(7)
Rice	2554	6,564	256.6	65.4	30.1	(–) 35.3
Wheat	245	3,560	1,453.0	6.2	16.3	10.1
Barley	134	52	(–) 61.2	3.4	0.23	(–) 3.2
Jowar	—	2	—	—	0.01	—
Bajra	2	4	200.0	0.05	0.02	(–) 0.03
Maize	313	1,038	331.6	8.0	4.76	(–) 3.3
Ragi (Marua)	—	88	—	—	0.40	—
Small millets	—	35	—	—	0.16	—

(*Contd.*)

TABLE 5.1 (*Contd.*)

(1)	(2)	(3)	(4)	(5)	(6)	(7)
Gram	156	158	101.2	3.9	0.72	(–) 3.2
Tur (Arhar)	—	82	—	—	0.37	—
Other Pulses	—	676	—	—	3.10	—
Total Foodgrains	3,304	12,259	371.0	84.63	56.28	(–) 28.35
Sugarcane	309	7,805	2,525	7.9	35.83	27.9
Tea	1.063	—	—	0.02	—	—
Groundnut	—	5	—	—	0.02	—
Linseed	23	40	173.9	0.59	0.18	(–) 0.41
Sesamum	4	5	125.0	0.10	0.02	(–) 0.08
Rape & Mustard	30	83	276.6	0.76	0.38	(–) 0.38
Castor	3	—	—	0.06	—	—
Cotton	2.45	—	—	0.06	—	—
Jute & Mesta	117.5	81.32	(–) 30.8	3.01	0.37	(–) 2.64
Tobacco	10	13	130.0	0.25	0.06	(–) 0.19
Potato	—	1,482	—	—	6.80	—
Others	—	10	—	—	0.04	—

Table 5.1 obliges us to hedge our preceding statement with the qualification that even in absolute terms the production of barley, jute and mesta has declined. Cultivation of tea, castor and cotton has dwindled so much so that they have become statistically irrelevant. On the other hand, ragi, tur, groundnut and potato have become statistically important with their increased output.

From the table it is also evident that in the last forty years in terms of their percentage shares in total agricultural production the sufferers are rice, maize, barley, gram and jute and mesta. Sugarcane and wheat are gainers by comparison.

Droughts, more than floods, have acted as depressants, leading to sharp dips in their output figures. We have listed elsewhere 1950-51, 1951-52, 1954-55, 1957-58, 1965-66, 1966-67, 1969-70, 1973-74, 1979-80, 1982-83, 1987-88, 1989-90 and 1991-92 as bad harvest years. The period 1961-62 to 1966-67 was one of the worstever periods. With exceptions, the 1970s and, more so, the 1980s were glorious periods, for the plain reason that the growth rate of value of agricultural produce at constant prices exceeded the growth rate of agricultural labour force.

Variations in the supply side factors like power, irrigation (these two are interconnected), fertilisers and improved HYV seeds result in similar declines. The uncertainty of the monsoon is compounded by the uncertainty of the behaviour of the governmental organisations as well as by that of the peasants' behaviour itself. Were we to apportion the responsibility among these factors, we would do most of it to the monsoon and next to it, to the shortage of power and diesel and fertilisers, both being exogenous in nature.

Bihar's performance in the agricultural sector has been unsatisfactory, more so when compared with the performance of agriculture in Punjab. Whereas in Bihar foodgrains production increased by 258 per cent during 1950-51 to 1991-92, in Punjab it increased by 686 per cent during the same period. During 1950-51 to 1987-88 foodgrains yield rose by 330 to 350 per cent in Bihar and by 530 to 570 per cent in Punjab. In value productivity of land Bihar remains inferior to Punjab. So far as improvement in value productivity of land is concerned, Bihar is on heels close to Punjab. When compared to Punjab, labour productivity in agriculture in Bihar deteriorated considerably during 1960-61 to 1984-85. Underutilised potential of Bihar agriculture exceeds that of Punjab. Floods and droughts and pests and wild animals have done greater harm to Bihar agriculture than to Punjab agriculture. Return over operating cost per hectare in 1985-86 in the case of irrigated wheat was Rs. 4326 in Bihar and Rs. 5974 in Punjab. In respect of irrigated paddy the figures were Rs. 5132 and Rs. 6949 respectively. Cost per quintal of rice produced in 1987-88 was Rs. 175.63 in the case of Bihar and Rs. 149.19 in that of Punjab. In commercialisation of agriculture, dry farming and land utilisation Punjab was far ahead of Bihar.

That fluctuations in the quantity of agricultural production persist cannot be denied, the amplitude or range of the fluctuations is smaller now because the capability of the economy to resist, that is, its resiliency, has risen, in the sense that it recovers more speedily from any setback wrought by any natural calamity. Whereas the spurts in agricultural production have been fewer and less frequent and of smaller dimensions, the dips have been more numerous and more frequent and of larger magnitudes. In agriculture man's greed is curbed by nature's stinginess. That holds the clue to the element of instability faced by agriculture everywhere, more so in Bihar.

Foodgrains Production in Bihar

Foodgrains production in Bihar increased from 44.42 lakh tonnes in 1950-51 to 122.59 lakh tonnes in 1990-91, that is, by 276 per cent. During the same period the increase in all-India was from 508 to 1762 lakh tonnes, that is, by 346 per cent (Table 5.2). The increase in foodgrains production in Bihar between 1950-51 and 1965-66 was of the order of 27.93 lakh tonnes. On the other hand, in all-India it was to the extent of 215.3 lakh tonnes. As percentage to the all-India increase, the increase in Bihar was 12.9 per cent. Between 1980-81 and 1990-91 the rise in Bihar was to the tune of 23.84 lakh tonnes; in all-India to the extent of 466.12 lakh tonnes. The rise in Bihar as percentage of that in all-India was 5.03 per cent. This is proof of Bihar's bad performance with the passage of time.

TABLE 5.2 : Foodgrains Production

Year/Period	*Production (lakh tonnes)*	*Share in All-India (per cent)*	*Rank in All-India*
(1)	(2)	(3)	(4)
1950-51	44.42 (508)	8.1	4th
Quinquennium ending 1950-51 (Av.)	49.17		
1955-56	56.21	8.4	
Quinquennium ending 1955-56 (Av.)	45.00		
1960-61	74.19	9.0	3rd
Triennium ending 1961 (Av.)	70.15		
1965-66	72.35	10.0	
1966-67	36.21	4.8	
1970-71	78.65	7.2	
Quinquennium ending 1970-71 (Av.)	71.82		
Triennium ending 1971 (Av.)	80.99		
1975-76	91.77	7.5	
1980-81	99.11	7.6	
Triennium ending 1981 (Av.)	89.99		
1985-86	109.55	7.2	
Quinquennium ending 1987-88 (Av.)	102.3		
1990-91	122.59 (1762)	6.9	5th
1949-50 to 1953-54 (Av.)		9.1	
1967-68		9.0	
1962-63			3rd
1949-50 to 1953-54 (Av.)		9.4	
1958-59 to 1962-63 (Av.)		9.1	3rd
1959-60			5th
1960-61 to 1964-65 (Av.)		9.0	
1967-68			3rd

(Contd.)

TABLE 5.2 (*Contd.*)

(1)	(2)	(3)	(4)
1969-70	83.5 (961.8)	8.6	
1974-75		9.4	4th
1974-77 (Av.)		8.3	
1982-83		5.4	7th
1982-83 to 1986-87 (Av.)		6.7	
1984-85 to 1986-87 (Av.)		7.3	
1985-86 to 1989-90 (Av.)		5.7	
1987-90 (Av.)		6.9	
1989-90	118.34 (1603.0)	6.7/6.9	7th
1990-91		6.1	
1993-94	127.33 (Provisional)	6.9	
Average at the end of			
First Plan (1951-56)	51.40 (631.78)	8.1	
Second Plan (1956-61)	58.38 (including bad years) (740.00)	60.75 (excluding bad years) 7.8/8.2	
Third Plan (1961-66)	72.52 (810.42)	8.9	
Fourth Plan (1969-74)	81.60 (1029.58)	7.9	
Fifth Plan (1974-79)	90.61 (1180.68)	7.6	
Sixth Plan (1980-85)	89.85 (1380.64)	6.5	
Seventh Plan (1985-90)	110.53 (1550.58)	7.1	

Note : Av. = Average.

The First Plan had a target of 7.22 lakh tonnes of additional foodgrains production, and the Second Plan of 15 lakh tonnes. In 1960-61 foodgrains production was of the order of 74.19 lakh tonnes. This was in excess of the target. No clear headway was made during the Third Plan. During the Fourth Plan the shortfall in comparison with the target was to the extent of 15 lakh tonnes. The Fifth Plan was not any the better. The Sixth Plan showed no distinct improvement. The Seventh Plan was the best part of the latter half of the period under study. We base these remarks on the percentage shares of Bihar in all-India foodgrains production, plan-wise (Table 5.2), which we have taken as the measuring-rod of the State's performance on the foodgrains production front.

The unsatisfactory performance of Bihar in this area has been ascribed generally to unfavourable weather conditions, difficult supply position of chemical fertilisers, delay in the establishment of seed multiplication farms, absence of a suitable agency for an effective exchange of improved seeds (the cooperative system existing in the State being unable to cope with the task), the ineffectiveness of the minor irrigation schemes when confronted with a subnormal monsoon in both quantity and distribution, the ineffectiveness of the chemical fertilisers when faced with bad rain or fickle and intermittent supply of irrigation water, inadequacy of the extension facility, discrimination of the State in allotment of agrarian credit by the national financial institutions, and so on.

It would not be out of place to note here that the uncertainty as to total foodgrains production was mainly attributable to the instability of rice production which exceeded wheat production. Fluctuations/variations in foodgrains outturn were caused principally by the natural factors. In the 1970s the range of fluctuations was 28 per cent; in the 1980s, 41 per cent. In the earlier periods it was still higher; in the later, lower. The degree of instability during 1960-61 to 1984-85 was 23.4 per cent; during 1985-86 to 1993-94, 15.9 per cent. But in absolute terms, the quantum involved was larger in the later than in the earlier period (Table 5.3). This apart, the trend was definitely towards an absolute increase in foodgrains output.

TABLE 5.3 : Foodgrains Production : Trends

During 1965-66 to 1982-83 (excluding 1966-67, the worst year)	During 1980-81 to 1993-94
Number of Years of :	Number of Years of :
Rise : 11	Rise : 7
Fall : 7	Fall : 5
	Constant (more or less) : 2

Note : Fall was at times for two years in succession at most, while rise was at times for five years in succession.

Range of fluctuations/Variations in Foodgrains Production

Between 1950-51 and 1982-83 : 54.69 lakh tonnes.
During 1965-66 to 1982-83 : 63.56 lakh tonnes.
Between 1967-68 and 1982-83 : 31.25 lakh tonnes.
Between 1973-74 and 1982-83 : 29.46 lakh tonnes.
Between 1980-81 and 1989-90 : 45.34 lakh tonnes.
Between 1982-83 and 1990-91 : 52.94 lakh tonnes.
Between 1984-85 and 1993-94 : 31.06 lakh tonnes.

Amplitude of Fluctuations in Foodgrain Production

During 1950-51 to 1980-81 : Decreased.
During 1956-57 to 1972-73 : More pronounced.
During 1982-83 to 1990-91 : Increased.

It had been claimed that since 1960-61 foodgrains production in Bihar had developed a modicum of stability despite the recurrence of flood and drought but in 1966-67 when an unprecedented drought struck the State this claim proved to be unfounded in so far as the foodgrains output reached an all-time low of merely 36.21 lakh tonnes. Subsequently the extended use of the modern inputs resulted into a situation which could undoubtedly be held as stable, judging by the non-recurrence of the 1966-67 situation at any time in the years that followed. Bihar did quite well in the opening and closing years of the period 1951-85.

Notwithstanding the magnitude implicit in any up or down, we find that during 1965-66 to 1982-83 the rise in foodgrains production was in 11 years, whereas the fall in it was in 7 years. While the fall was at times for two years in succession, the rise was at times for five years in succession. Again, during the period 1980-81 to 1993-94 the number of years in which foodgrains output increased was 7, whereas that of the years in which it decreased was 5, outturn being more or less constant during the two successive years, viz., 1985-86 and 1986-87.

In between the opening and closing years of the period 1951-85 foodgrains production in Bihar experienced spells of improvement in its growth rate (Table 5.4). By and large, foodgrains production has grown at a rate slightly faster than the rate at which agricultural production has grown. To exemplify, during the 1980s the rate of growth of agricultural production was 3.2 per cent per annum; for foodgrains production it was 3.6 per cent per annum. In most years the growth rate of foodgrains production in Bihar has been below the all-India rate. To amplify, between 1951 and 1978 the rates were 1.39 and 2.59 per cent per year respectively and between 1977-78 and 1988-89 they were 2.68 and 3.52 per cent per annum respectively.

TABLE 5.4 : Rate of Growth of Foodgrains Production

(per cent per annum)

Year/ Period	*Growth Rate*
(1)	(2)
1950-51 to 1965-66	3.04
1950-51 to 1970-71	2.9
1950-51 to 1983-84	3.6
1950-51 to 1988-89	3.14
1950-51 to 1990-91	3.5
1951-78	1.39 (2.59) (C)

(Contd.)

TABLE 5.4 (*Contd.*)

(1)	(2)
1952-53 to 1964-65	3.05 (2.50)
Quinquennium ending 1953-54 to quinquennium ending 1964-65	3.2
1961-62 to 1978-79	1.8
1961-62 to 1982-83	0.4 (2.4)
1961-62 to 1983-84	0.7
1961-71	1.5 (C)
1961-81	1.2 (C)
1962-65 to 1970-73	1.55
1962-65 to 1971-81	2.33
1964-65 to 1983-84	0.6
1966-67 to 1983-84	0.7 (2.5)
1967-68 to 1977-78	1.1 (2.31), both (C)
1969-70 to 1989-90	1.4/1.5 (2.6)
1970-73 to 1978-81	3.14
1970-71 to 1979-80	0.33
1970-71 to 1984-85	0.55 (when not adjusted for weather)/ 1.25 (when adjusted for weather) : all-India figures being 2.66 and 2.77 respectively
1970-71 to 1988-89	1.24 (1.31)
1970-71 to 1988-91	1.77 (Kharif : 1.87 and Rabi : 1.60) : (C)
1971-81	1.1 (C)
1972-73 to 1979-80	0.7
1977-78 to 1988-89	2.68 (3.52) : both (C)
1979-80 to 1988-89	2.1
1980-81 to 1988-89	3.45 (2.7)
1980s	3.6
1982-83 to 1984-85	1.0
1985-86 to 1987-88	1.4
1949-50 to 1990-91	(2.68 = 0.58 × 2.10)
1949-50 to 1964-65	(2.93 = 1.41 × 1.52)
1967-68 to 1990-91	(2.80 = 0.20 × 2.60)
Plan-Wise	
Third Plan	(–2.2)
Fourth Plan	(2.5)
Fifth Plan	6.1 (C) (5.3)
Sixth Plan	5.6 (C) (6.3)
Seventh Plan	(3.6)

Note : C = Compound.

Per capita per annum foodgrains production is regarded as a better index of agricultural production. We have elucidated this in the preceding chapter. Here we would like to add that during 1969-70 to 1989-90 the growth rate (compound) of per capita foodgrains production was negative,

(–)0.7 per cent per annum. This testifies to the fact that for most part of the period Bihar's performance on the foodgrains front has been far from satisfactory.

Increase in foodgrains output so far has originated from both area expansion and yield improvement, the part played by the latter has been twice that played by the former. From 1950-51 to 1965-66 the ratio between the two was 0.23 to 2.60. From 1967-68 to 1977-78 the ratio was 0.93 to 2.09. Between 1980-81 and 1988-89 the contribution of yield improvement exceeded that of area expansion. Actually, the contribution of area expansion was negative. This contrasts with the period 1970-71 to 1979-80 immediately precedent, during which the contribution of area was much ahead of that of yield.

During 1950-51 to 1990-91, while population increased by 242 per cent (from 36.10 million to 86.37 million), foodgrains production increased by 276 per cent. Average annual rate of increase of foodgrains production during the period was 3.5 (simple)/2.9 (compound) per cent per annum, whereas that of population was 3.2 (simple)/2.2 (compound) per cent per annum. In relative terms Bihar did not face the food problem on account of population growth. But during this long period there were short periods during which the converse held good. However, the periods during which population growth rate was short of foodgrains growth rate outnumbered periods which were of the opposite kind, the average rural dweller ate slightly better than before, for example, in the late 1970s, compared to the late 1960s. That was so because primarily the income level of the rural people depended on the state of production of principal food crops, e.g., rice, wheat and maize. Moreover, increased foodgrains outturn implied general betterment in rural areas and was reflected *ipso facto* in increased consumption in these areas.

In some of the Five-Year Plans of Bihar the dose or combination or package of the inputs required to raise one additional tonne of foodgrains was as brought out in Table 5.5. One common feature of those packages was the emphasis laid on irrigation. Other inputs were complementary to it. With increased recourse to the modern inputs the importance of credit requirement had become self-evident.

Rice

Rice production was 26.44 tonnes in 1950-51 and 65.63 lakh tonnes in 1990-91, a 246 per cent increase, as against a 362 per cent increase in all-India, from 205.8 to 745.9 lakh tonnes. In 1993-94 rice production

TABLE 5.5 : More Inputs Requirement per Additional Tonne of Foodgrains

Inputs	*Third Plan (Share in Package) (per cent)*	*Fourth Plan (More Land Coverage/More Quantity)*	*Seventh Plan (More land Coverage/More Quantity)*
Irrigation			
Major & Medium	14.4	1.62 ha.	0.82 ha.
Minor	14.9		0.28 ha.
Nutrients			
Chemical fertilisers	29.1	1.5 tonnes	0.01 tonne
Compost :			
Rural		0.03 tonne	
Urban		0.025 tonne	
Land Development/ Soil Conservation	1.8	8.1 ha.	0.002 ha.
Reclamation of Waste-Land		1.21 ha.	
Improved Seeds/ HYVs	14.3	0.81	0.03 ha.
Cultural Practices/ Multiple Cropping	15.5	1.21 ha.	
Co-operative Credit			525 Rs.
	100.0		

was 60.63 lakh tonnes (provisionally estimated), as against 790.48 lakh tonnes in all-India. Although the general trend has been towards increase, rice production has varied from year to year (Table 5.6). Rice production in Bihar was 12.8 per cent of all-India in 1950-51, which fell to 8.8 per cent in 1990-91, and further to 7.67 per cent in 1993-94. Between 1965-66 and 1982-83 maximum rice production was 56.35 lakh tonnes in 1980-81 and minimum, 30.60 lakh tonnes in 1982-83, a difference of 25.75 lakh tonnes, which meant a range of fluctuation of 45 per cent. During 1984-85 to 1993-94, the maximum was 65.63 lakh tonnes in 1990-91, and the minimum, 46.74 lakh tonnes in 1987-88, a difference of 18.89 lakh tonnes, which implied a range of fluctuation of 29 per cent (Table 5.7). The number of years of rise in production and that of fall in it equalled in both periods. Only in exceptional years in rice production Bihar had the second or third rank in all-India, otherwise at the beginning of the four at decade period (1950-51 to 1990-91) as well as its end Bihar's place was the fourth. In 1993-94 its rank had declined to the seventh, a rank which it had in the year 1982-83. The rate of growth of rice production in Bihar was maximum during 1979-80 to 1988-89 (Table 5.8).

TABLE 5.6 : Rice Production

Year	*Production (Lakh tonnes)*	*As Percentage of*		*Rank in All-India*
		All-India Production	*Foodgrains Production in the State*	
1950-51	26.44	12.08	58.5	
1955-56	27.29	9.90	48.5	4th
1960-61	45.45	13.01	61.2	
1965-66	42.63	13.09	63.0	
1966-67	14.73	4.84	40.6	
1970-71	41.54	9.83	52.8	
1975-76	48.55	9.09	52.9	4th
1980-81	56.35	10.05	56.8	3rd
1985-86	60.63	9.05	55.2	4th
1990-91	65.63	8.08	53.4	4th
1962-63	42.13	13.04	58.2	2nd
1964-65	55.04	14.00	—	3rd
1967-68	39.24	10.43	53.28	2nd
1974-75	45.40	11.47	55.02	3rd
1982-83	30.60	6.58	43.93	7th
1983-86 (Av.)	54.67	9.00	—	
1986-87	60.44	9.98	55.39	4th
1989-90	—	7.08	—	
1990-91	—	6.07	—	
1993-94 (P)	60.63	7.67	47.61	7th

TABLE 5.7 : Rice Production : Trends

During 1965-66 to 1982-83 (excluding 1966-67, the worst year)	*During 1984-85 to 1993-94*
Number of Years of : Rise : 9 Fall : 9	*Number of Years of* : Rise : 5 Fall : 5

Note : Rice production in 1985-86 and 1986-87 was more or less constant.
Range of Fluctuations/Variations in Rice Production :
Between 1965-66 and 1982-83 : 25.75 lakh tonnes, 45 per cent.
Between 1984-85 and 1993-94 : 18.89 lakh tonnes, 29 per cent.

Rice has dominated the food scene in Bihar. It has occupied the foremost place among the foodgrains, the percentage varying from about 44 in 1982-83 to 63 in 1965-66 (Table 5.6). The entire pressure for food supply has fallen on it.

In 1955-56 winter rice formed 94 per cent of total rice production in Bihar, in 1964-65 it formed 75 per cent, which rose to 79 per cent in

1982-83. The percentage of kharif rice was 6, 5 and 11 per cent respectively in these years. Dominance of winter or Agahani rice connoted greater security and risk. Kharif or Bhadai rice production belonged to the hot and humid months. Rabi rice existed with the other two rice crops having increased security and immunity from natural calamities and hence under greater density of population than the normal. Dominance of the Rabi crop accompanied a lower population density.

The output trends of rice exhibited considerable fluctuation from year to year. The rice-dominated economy was often a precariously balanced economy so much so that the failure of the rice crop in a single year (for example, in 1966-67 when rice output was 14.73 lakh tonnes) brought about in its train a sudden scarcity or famine-like condition and forced migration of the poor and unemployed from the affected areas.

In the last four years of the period of our study (1987-88 to 1990-91) performance of Bihar in rice production has been a shade better than that of all-India. Whereas in all-India rice production increased by about 30 per cent (568.62 versus 742.91 lakh tonnes), in Bihar it increased by 38 per cent (46.74 versus 65.63 lakh tonnes). Rice yield rose in all-India during the same span of time by nearly 18 per cent, in Bihar it did so by nearly 31 per cent. It is on the basis of this that the authorities talk of the signs of the firstever breakthrough in rice output in Bihar. Summer rice yield, most of which was covered by the HYV, reflected a significant improvement, contrasted with kharif rice yield which manifested only a modest increase.

Some estimates of rice production in Bihar during 1952-53 to 1982-83, with 1964-65 as the year of bifurcation or partition, credit it with high growth in both periods—in the first period growth is accounted for with reference to area expansion and yield improvement, and in the second it is explained in terms of productivity so far as winter rice is concerned and in terms of area expansion as well as yield improvement so far as autumn rice is concerned (Table 5.8).

Other estimates appertaining to the period 1950-51 to 1977-78, with 1966-67, the drought year as the watershed or buffer, lead us to the inference that in the first period in growth of winter rice production yield had a greater influence than area, as it had in the second period too. During 1961-81 yield was the causative factor, whereas area expansion a negligibly associative factor. During 1970-71 to 1988-89, according to another study, area expansion proved a negative factor and yield improvement had therefore, the whiphand in rice production growth. D. Ahluwalia's study for 1970-73 to 1986-89 allots 13 points out of 100 to area, 85 to yield and 2 to a mix of area and yield in throwing light on the growth of rice production in Bihar. In another study for the period 1970-73 to 1986-89, in the positive rice production growth in Bihar, yield had a contribution 6.5 times higher than area. Finally, according to yet another study for the periods 1970-71 to 1979-80 and 1979-80 to 1989-90, in the case of kharif rice area had a positive role, while yield a negative one during the former period and yield a greater part than area during the latter period. In the case of rabi rice, both area and yield had negative influences, area more than yield during the first period, and yield a greater influence than area during the second period.

TABLE 5.8 : Rate of Growth of Rice Production

(Per cent per annum)

Year	*Growth Rate*
1950-51 to 1985-86	3.54 (5.82)
1950-51 to 1965-66	3.04 (C) for winter rice
1950-51 to 1990-91	3.70
1952-53 to 1964-65 (Av.)	3.20
1961-62 to 1980-81	0.7
1964-65 to 1983-84	0.3
1967-68 to 1977-78	2.80 (C)
1970-71 to 1979-80	0.30 (C)—(Rabi (-) 8.85 (C), kharif 0.45 (C)
1970-71 to 1988-89	1.06 (C)—Rabi (-) 1.65 (C), kharif 1.11 (C)
1970-71 to 1980-81	1.0 (Constant)
1979-80 to 1988-89	3.67

Note : C = Compound.

The districts where the percentages of rice production are high as are the yields of rice have tended to become areas of excellence and pursue rice cultivation intensively. A second rice crop during February to June with the help of the HYVs is being tried in some of them. Research in rice has received a reinforcement as a high priority item in all regions of Bihar. But the expenditure on research on rice in the irrigated areas has until quite recently equalled 0.035 per cent of the value of the rice crop. There is thus a clear case for the reinforcement of the public expenditure on rice research.

The districts which have shown better results are those which have had an advantage over others in irrigation which has enabled them to tide over the vagaries of rainfall in the State and thereby stabilise the outturn of rice, the mainstay of the farmers everywhere in Bihar.

In discussing rice cultivation in Bihar, we are reminded of the Japanese method of rice cultivation. This method, first tried at Kosbad Agricultural School and Agricultural Research Station, Karjat, was introduced in Bihar during the First Plan. By this method, the yield of paddy was stepped up more than twice or even thrice the yield that obtained then under local practices. In this method more emphasis was laid on higher doses of fertilisers, though only in areas where adequate moisture supply was assured. The main items of the Japanaese method of rice cultivation were : Growing seedling on a raised seed-bed with the help of organic bulky measures and inorganic fertilisers, instead of rabbing (that is, burning the seed-bed) which was the local practice in Bombay; using less seed per unit area to get healthy and vigorous seedlings, instead of the high seed rate used locally; grading of seeds and treating them with perenox as a precaution against the blast disease; green manuring wherever possible with San (*Crotolaria juneea*) in fields at the higher levels and Dhaineha (*Seshania aculeats*) in low-lying fields; application of bulky organic manures like compost or F.Y.M. up to 24.7 cartloads per hectare, i.e., 24,700 lbs; planting the seedlings straight while transplanting and planting them in lines to facilitate after-cultivation; using only 3 or 4 seedlings per bunch considering their health and vigour; applying heavy doses of fertilisers at proper time in instalments, as recommended for the region; weeding the field twice and interculturing three or four times by a hand-hoe as and when required; taking proper precautions against diseases and pests as well as treating them with fungicides and pesticides, as and when required; typing strings as support to the standing crop to prevent damage by lodging at the advanced stage of crop growth; and taking a crop of legume, if possible, in the rabi season after harvesting rice. This enriched the soil and gave some additional returns. In a word, the Japanese method epitomised a more obsessed way of farming, akin to a way of living.

Wheat

Wheat production in Bihar rose from 2.57 lakh tonnes in 1950-51 to 35.60 lakh tonnes in 1990-91, a 1385 per cent rise. During the same period the rise in all-India wheat production was from 64.6 lakh tonnes to 545.2 lakh tonnes, by 844 per cent. In 1993-94 wheat production in Bihar was 43.23 lakh tonnes (provisionally estimated), as against 591.31 lakh tonnes in all-India. Although the general trend has been towards increase, production has varied from year to year (Table 5.9). Wheat production was 3.8 per cent of the national total in 1950-51, which increased to 6.5 per cent in 1990-91 and further to 7.3 per cent in 1993-94. This was just the obverse of the rice case (discussed above). Between

1965-66 and 1982-83 wheat outturn was maximum in 1980-81, 28.25 lakh tonnes and minimum in 1965-66, 4.78 lakh tonnes, the two extremes giving a difference of 23.47 lakh tonnes. The range of fluctuation was 83 per cent. During 1984-85 to 1993-94, the maximum, 43.23 lakh tonnes, was attained in 1993-94 and the minimum, 28.61 lakh tonnes, in 1986-87, giving a difference of 14.62 lakh tonnes. The range of fluctuation was 34 per cent (Table 5.10). A comparison between these two periods would bring out that the amplitude of fluctuation, absolutely as well as proportionally, had become less with the passage of time. This implied a modicum of stability. The year 1967-68 marks the beginning of the wheat revolution, which is equated with the Green Revolution for all practical purposes in Bihar. During the earlier period the number of years of rise was proportionally higher, as compared to that in the later period. Bihar has had the sixth rank among the wheat-producing States in the majority of the years studied, including the beginning and the last; only in the exceptional years, very few in number, had it the fifth position. The rate of growth of wheat production has been much faster than the rate of growth of rice production (Table 5.9). During the first quinquennium of the Green Revolution wheat production recorded a quantum jump of the order of 142 per cent. In 1950-51 wheat was Number 4 crop in Bihar. In 1968-69 it was Number 2 crop, a position that has remained unaltered since then.

TABLE 5.9 : Wheat Production

Year	*Production (Lakh tonnes)*	*As Percentage of*		*Rank in All-India*	*Growth Rate (Per cent per annum)*
		Foodgrains Production in the State	*All-India Production*		
(1)	(2)	(3)	(4)	(5)	(6)
1950-51	2.57	5.7	3.8	6th	
1950-51 to 1964-65					3.28
1950-51 to 1985-86					3.54
1955-56	3.57	6.3	4.0	5th	
1952-53 to 1964-65					2.52 (C)
1960-61	4.43	5.9	4.6		
1961-71					11.6
1962-63 to 1977-78					11.7

(Contd.)

TABLE 5.9 (*Contd.*)

(1)	(2)	(3)	(4)	(5)	(6)
1961-81					8.8
1964-65	4.90		4.0		
1964-65 to 1983-84					8.8
1965-66	4.78	6.6	4.6		
1966-67	3.65	10.0	3.2		
1967-68	9.14	12.4	5.5		
1967-68 to 1977-78					11.17
1967-68 to 1988-89				?	
1969-70 to 1978-79					
1969-70 to 1989-90					5.6 (C)
1970-71	12.59	16.0	4.6		
1975-76	22.97	25.0	7.9	5th	
1971-81					6.1
1974-75				4th	
1980-81	28.25	28.5	7.78	6th	
1980-91					2.6
1982-83	22.02	31.61	5.14	6th	
1984-85	30.32	34.06	6.88		
1985-86	30.55	38.11	6.5		
1984-85 to 1986-87	29.82	32.80	6.5		
1986-87	28.61	26.22	6.6		
1987-88	32.57	33.38	7.05		
1988-89	35.57	30.41	8.6		
1989-90	32.70	27.63	6.56		
1990-91	35.60	28.9	6.3/6.5	6th	
1991-92	35.94	33.78	6.45		
1992-93	34.49	37.97	6.02		
1993-94	43.23	33.95	7.31		
1984-94					4.2

Note : C = Compound.

The modest growth rate of wheat production in Bihar during 1950-51 to 1965-66 owed itself more to the continuance of the trend of yield improvement than to area expansion, though both played their respective parts in it. The high growth rate of wheat production during 1967-68 to 1977-78 owed itself to both area expansion and yield improvement in rather equal measure. The substantial difference in the growth rates of wheat production in these two periods is attributed to the difference in the growth rates of the twin determinants. During 1970-73 to 1986-89 the influence of yield improvement was 1.3 times that of area expansion. During the same period, according to another study, area scored 39 points, while yield improvement scored 52 points and the mix of the dual influences 9 points, in contributing their respective shares to the progress made by wheat production.

TABLE 5.10 : Wheat Production : Trends

During 1965-66 to 1982-83 (Excluding 1966-67, the worst year)	*(During 1984-85 to 1993-94*
Number of Years of: Rise : 13 Fall : 5	*Number of Years of:* Rise : 6 Fall : 4

Note : Wheat production in 1984-85 and 1985-86, as also in 1990-91 and 1991-92, was more or less constant.
Range of Fluctuations/Variations in Wheat Production :
Between 1965-66 and 1982-83 : 23.47 lakh tonnes, 83 per cent.
Between 1984-85 and 1993-94 : 14.62 lakh tonnes, 34 per cent.

Based on field experience, it has been pointed out that timely sowing of seeds, increased use of the HYVs, prevailing of low temperature for a longer period, absence of the westerly dry wind, the *Hathia* rains and alertness of the farmers have, when they have materialised, produced a positively favourable impact on wheat production in the State.

In comparison with rice production wheat production in Bihar has achieved a greater degree of stability. Also, incomes have risen more speedily in the wheat-growing districts than in the rice-growing ones.

It would amount to a misunderstanding were we to surmise that wheat production in Bihar has been problem-free. In the south-west alluvial plain districts sowing of wheat has quite often been late owing to the non-use of the short-duration HYVs of rice, with the result that the yields of both wheat and rice have been low, lowering their outputs. In the early years much wheat produce was lost an account of rust.

Maize

Maize production in Bihar increased from 3.31 lakh tonnes in 1950-51 to 10.60 lakh tonnes in 1990-91, that is, by 320 per cent. During the same period maize production in the country went up from 17.29 lakh tonnes to 90.70 lakh tonnes, that is, by 524 per cent. Maize output in Bihar as a proportion of total foodgrains output was 7.4 per cent in

1950-51. In the worst year, i.e., 1966-67 it was a record, that is, 19.4 per cent (Table 5.11). Since then the production trend has been towards a decline, though at the end of the period studied here it exceeded the figure at the beginning. But in the year 1950-51 maize was Number Two crop in the State. In the best production year it had slid to Number Three (wheat had come in as Number Two crop), to which position it seems to have been stuck up till today. On the other hand, in the country its rank was second in 1950-51, third in 1974-75 and finally, fourth in 1990-91. During 1965-66 to 1982-83 the maximum outturn was 11.13 lakh tonnes in 1970-71, and the minimum, 1.33 lakh tonnes in 1971-72, giving a difference of 9.80 lakh tonnes, which means a range of 88 per cent. During the same period maize output fell in seven and rose in eleven years.

TABLE 5.11 : Maize Production

Year	*Production (Lakh tonnes)*	*As Percentage of*		*Rank in All-India*	*Growth Rate (Per cent per annum)*
		Foodgrains Production in the State	*All-India Production*		
1950-51	3.31	7.4	19.1	2nd	
1955-56	2.98	5.3	11.4	2nd	
1960-61	8.21	11.0	20.1	2nd	
1965-66	7.57	10.4	15.7		
1966-67	9.49	19.4	19.4		
1970-71	11.13	14.1	14.8		
1974-75				3rd	
1975-76	9.39	10.2	12.9	2nd	
1980-81	8.69	8.7	12.4	2nd	
1982-83				3rd	
1985-86	8.77	8.0	13.2		
1989-90			13.0		
1990-91	10.60	8.6	11.6/13.2	4th	
1950-51 to 1965-66					2.80 (C)
1950-51 to 1985-86					4.58 (7.87)
1950-51 to 1990-91					5.5 (8.5)
1952-53 to 1964-65					3.17 (C)
1964-65 to 1983-84					0.4
1967-68 to 1977-78					(–) 250 (C)

Note : C = Compound.

Over time, autumn maize has become less important, whereas summer maize has become more important, winter maize remaining as important as before.

The growth rate of maize production in Bihar has been slower than that in the country as a whole. It was reasonable in the first three Plans but extremely unfavourable in the later Plans, and really bad in the years of the Plan Holiday and the Fourth Plan (Table 5.11).

Enquiries made affirm the view that during 1950-51 to 1965-66 the low growth rate of maize production in Bihar was due to the decline in the area diverted to maize, neutralised, however, by the yield improvement factor, to an extent. The retrogression during 1967-68 to 1977-78 is accounted for by referring to the negative growth rates of the dual factors during the period. The divergence between the twin growth rates, considered moderate by a number of enquirers, is attributed to the disparity in the area expansion as between the two periods. In some other studies the difference is explained with reference to the area decline factor alone.

D. Ahluwalia accords 231 percentage points to yield but subtracts 73 percentage points for area decline and 58 percentage points for the area-yield mix in accounting for the performance of maize production during 1970-73 to 1986-89. Whereas yield improvement added one positive percentage point, area decline siphoned off 0.3 percentage point.

Pulses

Production of pulses in Bihar was 10.16 lakh tonnes in 1950-51, which was about 12 per cent of all-India total production of pulses and about 23 per cent of total foodgrains production in the State. In 1990-91 it was 9.20 lakh tonnes, which was 6.5 per cent of all-India total and 7.5 per cent of total foodgrains production in the State in that year. Thus in the last four years pulses production in Bihar had declined by 9.5 per cent, whereas in the country it had gone up by 67 per cent (Table 5.12). The percentage shares in both senses had suffered a serious setback. Pulses production has varied from one year to another. Between 1965-66 and 1982-83 the difference between maximum and minimum production was 6.27 lakh tonnes, 49 per cent being the magnitude of variation. Between 1984-85 and 1993-94 the range of fluctuation was 2.22 lakh tonnes, 25 per cent. Both the amount and percentage of variation of pulses production had become lower. There was some gain in stability. During the first period the number of years of rise was 8 and that of fall

10, while during the second period the corresponding numbers were 6 and 4. Bihar's relative position among the pulses-producing States deteriorated from the fifth at the beginning of the period to the sixth at its end. A marked decline in the pulses production took place during 1977-78 to 1982-83 on account of a steep decli.. in the growth rate.

TABLE 5.12 : Pulses Production

Year	*Production (Lakh tonnes)*	*As Percentage of*		*Rank in All-India*	*Growth Rate (Per cent per annum)*
		Foodgrains Production in the State	*All-India Production*		
1950-51	10.16	22.8	12.08	5th	
1955-56					
1960-61	11.70	15.7	9.21	5th	
1965-66	12.62	17.4	12.7		
1966-67	5.38	14.8	6.44		
1970-71	9.87	12.5	8.35		
1975-76	8.22	8.95	6.30	5th	
1980-81	8.33	8.4	7.83	5th	
1985-86	9.02	8.2	6.75		
1990-91	9.20	7.5	6.54	6th	
1993-94	7.54	6.0	5.75		
1950-51 to 1965-66					3.51(C)
1950-53 to					2.13
1963-66					(–) 1.80 (C)
1950-53 to 1978-81					2.13 (C)
1950-53 to 1963-66					2.13
1952-53 to 1964-65					2.89
1963-66 to 1978-81					(–) 3.78
1961-81					(–) 2.1
1961-71					(–) 0.6
1963-66					(–) 3.78
1971-81					(–) 3.5
1978-81					(–) 1.80
1967-68 to 1977-78					(–) 2.13

Note : C= Compound.

Bihar is largely in the rabi pulses region. In the light of contribution to total pulses output, the individual pulses are listed in the following order : khesari, masoor, gram, moong, *arhar* (tur) and peas.

Oilseeds

Oilseeds production in Bihar increased from 1.14 lakh tonnes in 1970-71 to 1.19 lakh tonnes in 1988-89, a bare 4.3 per cent rise. During the same period oilseeds production in all-India increased from 96.30 lakh tonnes to 180.30 lakh tonnes in 1988-89, 87 per cent rise. As percentage of all-India oilseeds production, oilseeds production in Bihar in 1970-71 was 1.18 per cent and in 1988-89, this was 0.66 per cent. During 1970-71 to 1982-83 maximum oilseeds output in Bihar was attained in 1974-75 at 1.48 lakh tonnes and minimum in 1971-72 at 0.94 lakh tonnes, a difference of 0.54 lakh tonnes—36 per cent fluctuation. During this period production fell six times and rose seven times. During 1984-85 to 1986-87 Bihar's relative share was 1.1 per cent. In the early 1960s Bihar's relative position in the country among oilseeds-producing States was tenth, in 1979-80 it was thirteenth, and in 1982-83 fourteenth. In 1975-76 oilseeds production was 1.48 lakh tonnes and in 1980-81, 1.10 lakh tonnes. During 1950-51 to 1965-66 the rate of growth of oilseeds production in Bihar was 1.16 per cent per annum (compound) and during 1967-68 to 1977-78, 3.04 (compound) per cent per annum. Whereas in the former period yield improvement proved a greater influence than area expansion, in the latter period the role of the two factors was reversed. Another estimate puts the growth rate during 1961-71 at 3.7, during 1971-81 at (–) 0.1 and during 1961-81 at 1.8 per cent per annum.

In the late 1980s the Oilseeds Production Programme, development of sunflower farming, development of commercial crops, and the like had a wholesome impact on the production of oilseeds in Bihar, though not so much as in some other States.

By 1990-91 the output had risen as had Bihar's percentage share but its relative position has not improved (Table 5.13).

Non-foodgrains Production in Bihar

In 1950-51 in Bihar non-foodgrains production was, roughly speaking, 22.91 lakh tonnes. In 1988-89 it was about 85.21 lakh tonnes. Over the period the increase was 3.72 times. The principal crops were oilseeds (discussed above) and cash crops, of which sugarcane, jute, potato, tobacco and cotton were the main ones. The growth rate of non-foodgrains production was 2.80 per cent per annum (compound) during 1950-51 to 1965-66 and 0.69 per cent per annum (compound) during 1967-68 to 1977-78. In the first period yield was a greater augmenting factor than area, while in the second period the reverse was the case, although area had proportionally a greater influence in the first rather than the second period. The ratio between yield and area was 1.39 : 1.16 in the first period and 0.23 : 0.46 in the second period. The emphasis on increased production of foodgrians via area expansion diluted the effort to divert more area to non-foodgrains. In the late 1980s the Oilseeds Production Programme, development of sunflower farming, development of commercial crops, and the like had a wholesome impact on the production of non-foodgrains in Bihar too, though not so much as in some other States.

TABLE 5.13 : Oilseeds Production

Year	*Production (Lakh tonnes)*	*As Percentage of All-India*	*Rank in All-India*
1961-62	0.91	1.33	10th
1962-63	0.96	1.42	10th
1970-71	1.14	1.18	
1975-76	1.48	1.40	
1980-81	1.10	1.17	13th
1986-87	1.24	1.10	
1988-89	1.19	0.66	
1989-90	—	0.80	
1990-91	1.49	0.80	
1992-93	1.19	0.59	
1994-95	1.50	0.70	14th

The part which capitalist/gentlemen farmers have played in promoting this segment of Bihar agriculture through their entrepreneurship cannot be gainsaid. This class is guided by the pure commercial profit motive. They strive to exact maximum yield from their land. Their production is market-oriented. In such commercialisation of agriculture the key variables have been capital formation, technical progress and research and development. Apart from this class, we have also the other class of farmers who have carried on the heritage of producing cash crops during the slack season when both land and labour are idle, resulting in diversification of farming/mixed farming. Where improved methods are used, part of land and part of labour engaged in the production of staple crops are released for raising commercial crops. Bulk of the produce is sold. In giving this account we premise that the needed incentives, including price protection, and opportunities exist.

Notwithstanding what has been stated above, the fact remains that in Bihar agriculture has not been commercialised as much as in the country, on an average and Bihar had not done equally well in the production of non-foodgrains, though the pace had definitely gathered momentum during the 1980s.

Sugarcane

Sugarcane production in Bihar increased from 22.65 lakh tonnes in 1949-50 to 78.1 lakh tonnes in 1990-91, that is, by 344 per cent. On the other hand, in all-India the increase was by 479 per cent from 501.7 to 2402.9 lakh tonnes during the same period. In some intervening years sugarcane production in Bihar was 29.19 lakh tonnes in 1955-56, 69.27 lakh tonnes in 1960-61, 59.49 lakh tonnes in 1965-66, 62.09 lakh tonnes in 1970-71, 49.07 lakh tonnes in 1975-76 and 34.80 lakh tonnes in 1980-81. As percentage of all-India sugarcane production, sugarcane production in Bihar was 4.5 per cent in 1949-50, 4.8 per cent in 1955-56, 6.3 per cent in 1960-61, 4.8 per cent in 1965-66, 4.9 per cent in 1970-71, 3.5 per cent in 1975-76, 2.2 per cent in 1980-81, 2.2 per cent during 1984-85 to 1986-87 and 3.3 per cent in 1990-91. Between 1965-66 and 1982-83 the maximum sugarcane output in Bihar was 65.63 lakh tonnes in 1969-70 and the minimum 34.80 lakh tonnes in 1980-81, the difference being 30.83 lakh tonnes—47 per cent oscillation. During that period sugarcane production fell in eight years and rose in ten years. In the early 1960s Bihar held the seventh place among sugarcane-producing States, which had deteriorated to the eighth place in 1974-75, which continued till 1982-83, but further worsened to the ninth in 1990-91. Table 5.14 casts light on this.

TABLE 5.14 : Sugarcane Production

Year	*Production (Lakh tonnes)*	*As Percentage of All-India*	*Rank in All-India*
1955-56	29.19	4.80	
1960-61	69.27	6.30	
1961-62	62.31	6.24	
1962-63	48.01	5.20	
1965-66	59.49	4.80	
1970-71	62.09	4.91	
1975-76	49.07	3.49	8th
1980-81	34.80	2.26	8th
1986-87	37.29	2.01	
1988-89	54.83	2.68	
1989-90	—	3.00	
1990-91	78.11	2.9/3.31	9th
1994-95	56.71	2.11	8th

The rate of growth of sugarcane production in Bihar during 1950-51 to 1965-66 was 1.39 per cent per annum (compound) and (–) 0.92 per cent per annum (compound) during 1967-68 to 1977-78. The first period was characterised by stagnant production and an erratic pattern, area expansion exerting a positive influence, while the yield factor proving a negative factor. In the second period the same trend persisted, with the area factor having a negative effect and the yield factor remaining constant. Another estimate for 1952-53 to 1964-65 arrived at 0.69 as the rate of growth. Yet another estimate disclosed a negative rate, (–) 0.7 per cent per annum for 1961-71, (–) 5.2 for 1971-81 and (–) 3.0 per cent per annum for 1961-81. A fourth estimate for 1964-65 to 1983-84 came out with a figure equal to 2.2 per cent per annum. A fifth estimate for the Fifth Plan in Bihar was 4.71 per cent per annum (compound). A sixth estimate for 1970-73 to 1986-89 gave a negative rate of growth. During this period if yield contributed one percentage point, fall in area took away two. For the same period Ahluwalia allots 83 points to yield, (–) 168 points to area and (–) 15 points to the mix of area and yield.

To develop the decline episode, sugarcane production decline has been caused also by the diversion of water and fertilisers in many areas from it to foodgrains, as well as by a less favourable price policy, non-fixation of a profitable price for sugarcane much in advance of the sowing season, and on payment of dues by the sugar mills to the cultivators in time.

In the early 1950s Champaran (22 per cent of total sugarcane production in the State) and Saran (19 per cent of it) between the two accounted for nearly 41 per cent of total sugarcane production in Bihar. The relative share of Darbhanga and Shahabad each was 9.9 per cent and that of Muzaffarpur 7.2 per cent. In 1955-56 the top five sugarcane-growing districts were Champaran 35.7 per cent, Saran 15 per cent, Muzaffarpur 14.7 per cent, Gaya 9.6 per cent and Shahabad 8.0 per cent. In 1961-62 these places were enlisted by Champaran (30.4 per cent), Saran (18.2 per cent), Darbhanga (12.1 per cent), Muzaffarpur (12.0 per cent) and Gaya and Shahabad (bracketed, each 6.3 per cent). In 1982-83 the five top districts were Champaran West 30.3 per cent, Siwan 6.5 per cent, Samastipur 4.4 per cent, Gaya 3.8 per cent and Sitamarhi 3.3 per cent. The smaller districts had their relative shares adjusted according to their geographical areas. Finally, in 1989-90 Champaran East (10 per cent) and West (45.60 per cent) had the monopoly of sugarcane production, followed by Gopalganj 13.2 per cent, Siwan fourth place 5.73 per cent and Sitamarhi fifth place 5.64 per cent.

Jute

Jute production in Bihar fell from 14.47 lakh bales (each bale weighs 180 kgs.) in 1950-51 to 11.90 lakh bales in 1990-91, a fall by 18 per cent. On the other hand, in the country jute production increased from 33.09 lakh bales to 91.0 lakh bales in the country, 175 per cent increase, during the same period. In Bihar in some interim years jute output was 5.87 lakh bales in 1955-56, 7.50 lakh bales in 1960-61, 7.84 lakh bales in 1965-66, 7.73 lakh bales in 1970-71 and 6.99 lakh bales in 1980-81. As percentage of all-India jute production, jute production in Bihar came to 43.7 per cent in 1950-51, 19.9 per cent in 1961-62, 12.2 per cent in 1974-75, 14.5 per cent during 1984-85 to 1986-87 and 13.0 per cent in 1990-91. Between 1965-66 and 1982-83 maximum jute output occurred in 1979-80 at 9.33 lakh bales and minimum in 1968-69 at 4.00 lakh bales, the difference being 5.33 lakh tonnes—57 per cent fluctuation. During that period the fall in jute production was in six years, and rise in twelve. In the early 1960s Bihar's rank among the jute-growing States was the second, in 1974-75 it was third, which lasted till 1982-83, and in 1990-91 it was second. The rate of growth of jute production in Bihar during 1950-51 to 1965-66 was (–) 1.37 (compound), with area helping but yield sagging faster. During 1967-68 to 1977-78 it was 0.69 (compound), with yield helping but area constant. Both periods disclosed an erratic pattern with stagnant growth, yield turning out to be the more destabilising factor. Another estimate for a shorter period, 1952-53 to 1964-65, was (–) 0.91 per cent per annum (compound). A third study (RBI's 1984 report) reveals (–) 4.7 per cent per annum for 1961-71, 3.0 per cent for 1971-81 and (–) 0.9 per cent per annum for 1961-81. Production tapered off during 1961-71 but curled upwards thereafter but despite this revival jute production reached in 1981-82 was lower than that in the triennium ending 1960-61. In 1970-73 to 1986-89 the growth rate was estimated at a positive figure by Ahluwalia and in this if yield improvement contributed one per cent, area increase contributed only 0.05 per cent. Alternatively, yield claimed 93 per cent, area five per cent and their mix two per cent. Table 5.15 throws light on this.

Inducement to jute production has come from entitlement of jute to minimum support price. But in spite of this total sale of jute in Bihar to the Jute Corporation declined both absolutely and relatively to those in some other States during the 1980s. Subsidy has been provided to individuals or groups or village bodies for the construction of jute resting tanks of various dimensions and sizes.

TABLE 5.15 : Jute Production

Year	*Production (Lakh bales : One bale = 180 kgs.)*	*As Percentage of All-India*	*Rank in All-India*
1950-51	14.47	43.70	
1955-56	5.87	13.87	
1960-61	7.50	18.19	
1961-62	12.63	19.90	2nd
1962-63	10.24	19.08	2nd
1965-66	7.84	17.52	
1970-71	7.73	15.65	
1975-76	6.12	13.78	3rd
1980-81	6.99	10.74	3rd
1986-87	12.60	14.61	
1988-89	11.81	15.33	
1989-90	—	13.00	
1990-91	11.90/11.94	12.94/13.4	2nd
1992-93	11.99	13.34	
1994-95	11.61	12.31	2nd

On the other hand, the importance of jute as a commercial crop has declined in Bihar because of a steady pull exercised by food crops. Unscientific and improper resting undertaken by the jute growers has resulted in poor quality produce. The share of Bihar in line sowing has not been commensurate with jute acreage. The consumption of chemical fertilisers in the State has been less than proportionate to acreage. Deficiency of inputs supply and uncertain market conditions have been other detractors.

In the early 1950s Purnea had the virtual monopoly of jute production, 80 per cent; Bhagalpur's share was 14 per cent. Champaran, Saran, Muzaffarpur and Santhal Parganas had each around one per cent as their share. In 1989-90 Purnea, Katihar, Madhepura, Kishanganj, Araria, Saharsa, Madhubani and Darbhanga led in producing jute.

6

FOOD DEFICIT IN BIHAR
The Achilles Heel of the Bihar Economy

We have elsewhere termed the Bihar economy as a clay-footed economy. We consider the persistent food deficit in Bihar as the Achilles Heel of the Bihar Economy. With these facts in mind we propose to make our inquiry into the State's food problem prefaced by certain excerpts from the Budgets, the Census reports, the State Plans, etc.

In his 1950-51 Budget speech Bihar's Finance Minister remarked, "We have decided to reduce the size of the mechanised farm from thirty thousand acres to ten thousand acres (through waste land reclamation). This is part of our intensive Grow More Food Campaign (GMFC) for marking the State self-sufficient in food by 1951.

The Agricultural Department is required to meet the deficit of foodgrains to the extent of 125 thousand tonnes. . . ."

The Census of 1951 report noted, "There was a recrudescence of cholera epidemic during 1941-50 due largely to chronic food shortage and breakdown of normal administrative arrangements between 1942 and 1947. Determined efforts have since been made for increasing food production and for tightening administrative control, particularly in respect of measures for control of epidemics and with a popular Government at the helm of affairs now, it seems unlikely that a situation would arise in which large sections of people have to suffer for want of food for a prolonged period, even if there is failure of crop in any particular year."

In 1952-53 Budget the State's Finance Minister regretted that "the food problem continued to cause extreme anxiety throughout the year 1951. Again, in his 1953-54 Budget speech he observed, "While these measures (GMFC) are absolutely essential, it does not follow that the food deficit would be made up by these activities alone. . . . A considerable part of any increased production is immediately swallowed up by increased consumption and is thus not reflected in increased marketable surpluses".

The Second Five-Year Plan of Bihar continued further the emphasis on agricultural production, taking care to see that production of more foodgrains did not hamper the effort needed for the production of industrial raw materials.

The NCAER techno-economic survey, released in 1959, commented thus, "The central weakness of Bihar's economy lies in its poor agricultural base, which produces neither enough food for its rapidly growing population nor raw materials for its industry".

From 1952-53 to 1964-65 in Bihar agricultural production increased at the annual rate of 2.97 per cent, area under crops increased at the annual rate of 0.71 per cent, the rate of increase in productivity worked out to 2.25 per cent per year. Productivity gain contributed 75.7 per cent to the increase in output.

Let us investigate how population and food have grown over the years relatively to each other, from different angles. One of the angles to review them is to compare Bihar's percentage share in all-India population with its percentage share in all-India foodgrains production in the first years of the Plans or in years close to them and in the years of the census, as attempted in Table 6.1. It can be seen from the data presented in it that the adverse ratio between population share and foodgrains share diminished in its adversity during the period 1950-51 to 1965-66, increased in its adversity in the subsequent years upto 1970-71, again diminished in its adversity after that, which lasted upto 1980-81, and, finally, increased in its adversity subsequent to it, which trend became pronounced from the year 1985-86 onwards and persisted till 1990-91. It became more difficult for Bihar to feed its population with its foodgrains share dwindling in the latter half of the 1980s. With a few exceptions, the food-population ratio in Bihar has been to its real, genuine disadvantage, in the last four decades or so. The country became self-sufficient in food way back around the late 1970s. Had Bihar been in a position to raise on its soil about ten per cent of the national food output, we could have, on its very face, held that Bihar was similarly self-sufficient in food. In other words a one to one ratio between food and population shares is, according to our proposition, the ideal situation for a State, ignoring inter-State trade and the futility of self-sufficiency in food for a State richer enough to meet its food gap by purchase from other States, without compounding its indebtedness, internal or external. In our case it is the underutilised portion of agricultural poverty which reduces a positive account to a negative finale.

TABLE 6.1 : Bihar's Shares in Population and Foodgrains Production

(Percentage)

Year		*Population Share*	*Foodgrains Production Share*	*Difference between (2) and (3)*
For (2)	*For (3)*			
(1A)	(1B)	(2)	(3)	(4)
				(All minus)
1951	1950-51	10.74	8.1	2.6
1956	1955-56	10.66	8.4	2.2
1961	1960-61	10.57	9.0	1.5
1966	1965-66	10.43	10.0	0.4
1971	1970-71	10.28	7.2	3.0
1976	1975-76	10.25	7.5	2.7
1981	1980-81	10.22	7.6	2.6
1986	1985-86	10.21	7.2	3.0
1991	1990-91	10.21	6.9	3.3

When we descend from the State level to the regional level in Bihar (Table 6.2), we find that South Bihar had a favourable food-population ratio, its percentage varying from 0.64 to 3.50, throughout the period; except for 1961/1961-62 when North Bihar was in an identical position, with a relatively better ratio; and except for 1961-62/1961 when the Chotanagpur and Santhal Parganas (SP) region had, on the whole, an adverse ratio all along.

At the district level, during the period (1955-91), we have selected the years 1955-56, 1961-62, 1970-71, 1980-81 and 1991 (five in number) for analysis, in each case food has been assumed to be represented by the sumtotal of three leading cereals, namely, rice, wheat and maize and the percentage shares of the districts (17 in number in the first three years, 31 in number in the fourth year and 39 in number in 1991 in the aggregate population and aggregate food outturn estimated approximately. In 1955-56, 7 districts had each an excess of their food shares over their population shares. They were Champaran, Saran, Saharsa, Purnea, Santhal Parganas (SP), Ranchi and Dhanbad. The excess figure ranged between 0.34 and 16.05 per cent, and the shortage figure in the case of the remaining 10 districts between 0.05 and 5.20 per cent. The year 1961-62 was an exceptional year for five out of seven districts, the two exceptions being Saran and Santhal Parganas. The surplus distinction of Saharsa was limited to only one year, that is, 1955-56. Purnea was deficit in one more year, i.e., 1970-71; Santhal Parganas in two years, viz., 1970-71 and 1991; Ranchi in two more years, namely, 1970-71 and 1991; and, lastly, Dhanbad also in two more

TABLE 6.2 : Population *Versus* Food : Regional Variations Share in Population

(Percentage)

Region	*Share in Population Per cent*					*Share in Foodgrains Production Per cent*					*Difference in Two Shares*				
	1951	*1961*	*1971*	*1981*	*1991*	*1949-50*	*1961-62*	*1970-71*	*1980-81*	*1989-90*	*1949-50/1951 (3A) – (2A)*	*1961-62/1961 (3B) – (2B)*	*1970-71/1971 (3C) – (2C)*	*1980-81/1981 (3D) – (2D)*	*1989-90/1991 (3E) – (2E)*
(1)	(2A)	(2B)	(2C)	(2D)	(2E)	(3A)	(3B)	(3C)	(3D)	(3E)	(4A)	(4B)	(4C)	(4D)	(4E)
North Bihar	50.32	.61.10	53.50	53.47	55.20	54.60	56.42	56.30	59.90	60.82	4.28	(–) 4.68	2.80	6.43	5.62
South Bihar	21.36	21.11	21.30	21.29	24.73	22.00	24.16	24.80	22.80	25.42	0.64	3.05	3.50	1.51	0.69
Chotanagpur & Santhal Parganas	28.32	17.79	25.20	25.24	20.07	23.40	19.42	18.90	17.30	13.76	(–) 4.92	1.63	(–) 6.30	(–) 7.94	(–) 6.31

years, that is, 1970-71 and 1980-81. Hazaribagh, which existed as a district in 1955-56, had a surplus position first in 1961-62 and then in 1991. Monghyr existed as a district in 1955-56 but its surplus label was achieved in the last three years. The surplus districts in 1961-62 were 5, with surplus figures varying between 0.44 and 4.06 per cent; and the deficit districts were 12, with deficit figures varying between 0.06 and 2.47 per cent. For other years the figures were : 1970-71 (4—1.2 to 4.4 per cent and 11—0.4 to 2.0 per cent, two districts being neither surplus nor deficit—Patna and Palamau); 1980-81 (17—01. to 3.0 per cent and 14—0.1 to 2.4 per cent); and 1991 (22—0.04 to 6.44 per cent and 17—0.08 to 2.03 per cent). Table 6.3 contains these data :

TABLE 6.3 : Food : Population Ratio in Bihar : District-wise

District	*Number of Years in which Ratio was favourable*	*Years in which Ratio was adverse*
Champaran (East & West)	4	1961-62
Saran	5	
Saharsa	1	1961-62, 1970-71, 1980-81, 1991
Purnea	3	1961-62, 1970-71
Santhal Parganas	3	1970-71, 1991
Ranchi	2	1961-62, 1970-71, 1991
Dhanbad	2	1961-62, 1970-71, 1980-81
Hazaribagh	2	1955-56, 1970-71, 1980-81
Monghyr	3	1955-56, 1961-62

With reference to Table 6.4 we can controvert the observation made by the RBI 1984 Committee that since 1961 population in Bihar has risen at a rate higher than that at which foodgrains output in the State has risen, thereby causing a growing deficit in foodgrains supply. During 1951-61 population grew at the rate of 1.97 per cent per annum (the all-India rate was higher at 2.17 per cent per annum). On the other hand, during 1952-53 to 1964-65 foodgrains production increased at the rate of 3.05 per cent, which was above the national average of 2.50 per cent per annum. During 1961-71 population growth rate was 2.13 per cent per annum (all-India 2.48), whereas foodgrains growth rate was 1.5 per cent per annum (all-India about 3.2 per cent per annum). Population growth pressed against foodgrains growth. During 1971-81 whereas population grew at the rate of 2.41 per cent per annum (all-India rate 2.48), foodgrains production grew at the rate of (–)0.31 (compound) during 1970-73 to 1980-83 (all-India rate 2.30). Population had assumed a more serious proportion relatively to food. The Green Revolution appears to have bypassed Bihar, except for its impact in some pockets, which failed to turn the overall picture into a positive one. During 1981-91 while population increased at the rate of 2.35 per cent per year (all-India average 2.38), foodgrains outturn during 1980-83 to 1990-93 increased at the rate of 2.33 per cent per annum (the national figure being 2.84), with the result that the two variables were pitted against each other almost neck-to-neck, though the bleak part had become a bygone thing, thanks to the special attention paid to rice cultivation in the agricultural programmes of the eastern States. For the entire period, whereas population grew at the simple rate of 1.9 per cent per annum (all-India rate being 2.2) during 1951-91, foodgrains production progressed at the rate of 3.5 per cent per year during 1950-51 to 1990-91. To conclude, the RBI version has to be taken with a pinch of salt, the situation having improved slightly since.

TABLE 6.4 : Rate of Growth of Population/Foodgrains Production in Bihar

(Per cent per year)

Year/Period	*Rate of Growth of Population*	*Rate of Growth of Foodgrains*	
		Simple Average	*Compound*
1949-50 to 1964-65			(2.9)
1949-50 to 1986-87			(2.7)
1950-51 to 1990-91		3.5	
1950-51 to 1991-92		(40.02)	
1951-61	1.97 (2.17)		
1951-91	1.9 (2.2)	(2.2)	
1952-53 to 1964-65			3.05 (2.50)
1961-66			
1961-71	2.13 (2.008)	1.5 (3.2)	
1961-81		1.2	
1966-67 to 1983-84		0.7	
1967-68 to 1986-87			(2.8)
1969-74		3.5 (2.5)	
1969-70 to 1989-90		(-) 0.43	1.4/1.5
1970-73 to 1980-83			(-) 0.31 (2.36)
1970-73 to 1988-89			1.77
1970-73 to 1990-93		1.00 (2.60)	
1971-81	2.41 (2.48)	1.1	
1974-79		(5.3)	
1980-83 to 1990-93			2.33
1980-85		6.3 (2.84)	
1981-91	2.35 (2.38)		
1985-86 to 1987-88		1.4	
1985-90		(3.6)	

Between 1950-51 and 1990-91 the increase in foodgrains production in Bihar was 276 per cent, as against the all-India average of 347 per cent. On the other hand, the absolute increase in Bihar's population was 223 per cent, the all-India figure being 234 per cent. During 1950-51 to 1994-95 the percentage increase in foodgrains output in Bihar was by 289 per cent, as compared to 376 per cent in the country's foodgrains output during the period. The bulk of increase in foodgrains outturn was concentrated in a few districts, which had relatively more fertile lands as well as more resourceful and exposed farmers.

Were we to review the progress made on the foodgrains production front at a 15-year space during the period, we would find that during 1950-65 the increase in foodgrains output was to the extent of 26.10 lakh tonnes, during 1965-80 there was a decrease of the order of 1.30 lakh tonnes and during 1980-95 there was another increase to the tune of 57.47 lakh tonnes. From this it could be deduced that the trend was towards a smaller dip and a much bigger jump—a happy augury.

The worstever year after the two earliest years during the period outlined here was 1966-67 caused by an unprecedented drought. In the remaining years, grouped for every five years (1960-65, 1970-75, 1980-85 and 1990-95), the limits of fluctuation, given by the maximum and the minimum quantities of foodgrains production, indicate that the magnitude of increase exceeds that of decrease in it and that the magnitude of decrease has declined over the years and that the range of variation/ fluctuation has become narrover.

The preceding outline of foodgrains production in Bihar would not be complete without a reference to the diminishing share of the State in all-India foodgrains production. Between 1950-51 and 1990-91 the fall was from 8.74 to 6.95 per cent, i.e., 1.79 per cent; between 1950-51 and 1994-95 the fall was from 8.74 to 6.69 per cent, i.e., 0.05 per cent; from 1950-51 to 1966, the fall was 1.26 per cent; from 1967-68 to 1981-82, the fall was 2.5 per cent (9.00 minus 6.49 per cent); and, finally, from 1981-82 to 1994-95, the rise was 0.2 per cent (6.5 versus 6.7 per cent). Except for the last period, which showed a slight improvement, because of the special attention paid to the eastern States in rice cropping during the period, all the previous periods showed a decline (Table 6.5).

The pattern and pace of foodgrains production in Bihar related above is intended to emphasise that the economic lot of the three-fourths of the State's population is largely influenced by it. The falling foodgrains production, both absolutely and relatively, is an aggravator of the population problem confronted by the State, and *vice-versa.* At a lower level of analysis, it is the fluctuations in specific cereals, e.g., rice,

TABLE 6.5 : Foodgrains Production, Requirement and Deficit/Gap in Bihar

(Percentage)

Year/Period	*Production (lakh tonnes)*	*Share in All-India (per cent)*	*Change : Increase in*		
			(1) (lakh tonnes)	*(3) (per cent)*	*(2) (per cent)*
(1)	(2)	(3)	(4)	(5)	(6)
1949-50 to 1964-65				8.7	
1950-51	44.42	8.05			
1950-51 to 1989-90					260 (360)
1950-51 to 1991-92		(-) 1.38	70.1		258
1950-51 to 1993-94					408
1950-65			24.28/27.93		124
1951-56		8.1			
1955-56	56.21	8.40			
1956-61		7.8/8.2			
1958-59 to 1962-63		9.15			
1960-61	74.19	9.13			
1961-62	72.88	9.13			
1961-66		8.9			
1962-63	73.49	8.45			
1964-65					
1965-66	72.35	10.00			
1966-67	36.2	4.87			
1967-68		9.0			
1969-70	64.37				
1969-74		7.9			
1969-70 to 1989-90			27.42	4.3	
1969-89				4.27	104
1970-71	78.65	7.25			
1970-73	87.56	8.46			
1970-73	77.65	7.41			
1970-73 to 1980-83				1.97	
1974-79		7.6			
1975-76	91.77	7.58			
1980-81	99.1	7.64			
1980-83	84.89	6.49			
1980-95			57.47		
1980-83 to 1989-90				(–) 0.19	
1980-85		6.5			

(Contd.)

TABLE 6.5 (*Contd.*)

(1)	(2)	(3)	(4)	(5)	(6)
1981-82	82.39				
1982-83 to 1986-87		8.0		(-) 0.19	
1982-83	69.65	5.11			
1983-84 to 1985-86		6.9			
1984-85	103.38	6.67			
1984-85 to 1988-89		6.9			
1985-86	109.71	7.1/7.3			
1985-86 to 1989-90		6.8			
1987-88	88.41				
1988-89	130/135	7.3			
1989-90	118.34	6.92			
1989-92	114.49	6.67			
1990-91	122.59 (1763.90)	6.96			
1990-93	106.88	6.17			
1991-92	106.33 (1683.73)	6.31			
	121.21 (estimate by 2nd Irrig. Coms.)				
1992-93	90.82	5.06			
1993-94	127.76 (1794.83)	6.93			
1994-95	128.52 (1910.03)	6.69			
	174.90 (State Planning Board)				
	194.50 (State Agr. Deptt.)				
1950-51 to 1990-91					275 (347)
1950-51 to 1994-95					289 (376)

wheat and maize, which go to demonstrate the ups and downs in the levels of material well-being enjoyed by specific classes—to the very rich and the very poor fine and coarse rice respectively, to the middle class people wheat, and, lastly, to the poor maize are the staple food, the mainstay, and hence the fluctuations in their production, both absolutely and relatively, affect their day-to-day happiness intensely. This would follow from a perusal of the statistics compiled in Table 6.6. Ignoring

1966-67, an abnormal year, we find that wheat output had the highest percentage of increase, 1385 per cent, followed by maize output, 320 per cent, second, whereas rice output was third, 249 per cent increase. The absolute range of fluctuation of output was maximum in the case of rice, 39.19 lakh tonnes and minimum in that of maize, 8.15 lakh tonnes, wheat output being in between, 33.03 lakh tonnes. As proportion of total foodgrains production, the range of variation (that is, the difference between maximum and minimum percentages) was maximum in the case of wheat production, 23.31 per cent, minimum in that of rice, 12.71 per cent, and in between in that of maize, 20.91 per cent. In the drought year of 1966-67 maize output was higher than ever before. This brought succour/relief to the poor sections. In so far as altogether three harvests are raised, rice output in its totality surmounts the element of instability

TABLE 6.6 : Rice, Wheat and Maize Production

(Lakh tonnes)

Year Period	*Rice*		*Wheat*		*Maize*	
	Quantity	*As Percentage of Total Foodgrains Production in the State*	*Quantity*	*As Percentage of Total Foodgrains Production in the State*	*Quantity*	*As Percentage of Total Foodgrains Production in the State*
1950-51	26.44	59.52	2.57	5.78	3.31	7.45
1955-56	27.29	48.55	3.57	6.35	2.98	5.30
1960-61	45.45	61.26	4.43	5.97	8.21	11.06
1965-66	42.63	58.92	4.78	6.60	7.57	10.46
1966-67	14.73	40.69	3.65	10.08	9.48	26.21
1967-68	39.24	53.28	9.13	12.39	9.98	12.88
1969-70	36.76	57.10	9.66	15.00	8.76	13.62
1970-71	41.54	52.81	12.59	16.00	11.13	14.15
1974-75	45.40	55.02	20.00	24.24	5.72	6.93
1975-76	48.55	52.90	22.97	25.03	9.39	10.23
1980-81	56.35	56.86	28.25	28.50	8.69	8.76
1985-86	60.16	54.83	29.36	26.76	8.77	7.99
1990-91	65.63	53.53	35.60	29.09	10.6	8.64

Note : Bihar's rice deficit in 1947 = 3.70 lakh tonnes, basis : per head per day rice availability from 1949-50 to 1955-56 = 167.0 gms. In 1950-51 = 7.25 lakh tonnes. In 1951 = 315 lakh tonnes. In 1960-61 = 250.52 gms. In 1965-66 = 222.68 gms. In 1969-70 = 194.85 gms. In 1974-75 = 202.68 gms. This continued upto 1987-88. In 1988-89 = 199.18 gms. Wheat availability per capita per day 1970-71 = 55.67 gms. In 1975-76 = 111.34 gms. This continued upto 1985-86. In 1988-89 = 126.93 gms. Cereals availability per capita per day during 1961-63 was 11.9 ounces. Availability is equated with production, an assumption made here.

to a large extent, and the percentage share of rice in total foodgrains production has the lowest degree of variation. Failure of the *Hathia* rains quite often affects *rabi* (wheat) output and its percentage share is subject to maximum degree of fluctuation. The range of variation of maize output in relative terms is extremely high, considering its absolute volume of output, and with increase in this, the plight of the poorer sections dependent on maize is far worse.

Those who base upon the absolute amount of production, regret the instability of rice production from year to year, relatively to wheat production, considering the fact that rice has always dominated the food scene in Bihar, enlisting the first place among the foodgrains, and trying to bear the brunt of the entire pressure of food demand. It has been elevated to the position of the king of foodgrains in Bihar, being the staple foodgrains, the mainstay of the Bihar farmer everywhere. Per capita consumption of rice varies from region to region as well as district to district and turns largely on the pattern of production and the availability of rice in the region.

During 1987-88 to 1990-91 rice production performance in Bihar was a shade better than that in all-India (138 versus 130 per cent increase—31 versus 18 per cent increase in the yield). This made experts speak of the signs of the firstever breakthrough in rice output in the State. Summer rice yield far exceeded kharif rice yield.

Table 6.7 is an endeavour in the direction of encapsuling the seminal facets of Bihar's food problem since 1951. From it we arrive at the following conclusions : One, unanimity of the per capita per day (and from it per annum) foodgrains requirement norm has been conspicuous by its absence. The norm has been unstable. While the FAO norm was fixed at 160.60 kgs. a year, the State Government and others had laid down a norm which was appropriate to a particular situation and as soon as the situation altered, the norm was recast to match the new situation. In addition, the norm at the State level was not beyond the influence of the norm adopted at the Centre. As a result, the norm varied within the two limits of 164.25 and 186.25 kgs., a divergence of 22 kgs. In working out the consumption units 1.25 persons were taken to be equivalent to one consumption unit.

The Table 6.7 contains data on per head per year foodgrains production, which was assumed to be coordinate with availability. Not full reliance can be placed on these data, for the reason that except for the years in which population census was carried out, in other years the figures of population adjusted for the purpose were approximate, thus

TABLE 6.7 : Production, Norm of Consumption Requirement and Gap/Deficit of Foodgrains in Bihar

Year/ Period	*Per Capita Per Year Foodgrains Requirement Norm (kgs.)*	*Per Capita Per Year Foodgrains Production (kgs.)*	*Approximate Foodgrains Gap for Total Population Per Year (lakh tonnes)*	*Approximate Foodgrains Required for Total Population Per Year (lakh tonnes)*
(1)	(2)	(3)	(4)	(5)
1947			25.00	
1949-50	165.11		11.00	
1950-51	164.25	116.37	18.27	
1951				62.69
1955-56		110.7+		
1956				65.02/71.58
1956-57			31.00*	
1961				71.68/78.85
1960-61		159.73		
1961-62		122.1+		
1961-66	186.25			
1965-66		140.75	8.36	86.26
1966				78.83/86.71
1967-68		140.02		
1969-70		124.74		
1970-71		115.0+		
1971-72		161.04		
1970-73 (Average)		155 (189)		
1973-74		130.59		
1980			10.00	
1977-78		153.40		
1980-81	175	123.2+	15 to 20	
1983		95.15	9.32	
1984			6.00	
1984-85	183	150.00	24.72*	
1985			6.33	
1985-86	183	111.76 (169.72)		
1986			7.88	
1987			12.20	
1987-90			58.05*	
1987-90 (Av.)	73	134	32.55*	146.47
1988			18.43	
1988-89	164.25	182.89	24.8*	152.0
1989-90	182.89	125.8+	16.23 20 to 22	
1990-91	164.25	142.4	6.25	2nd IIIrd. Com., 255.78 FAO : 129.50
1991	164.25 /160.60 (FAO)	142.4		
1990-93 (Av.)		121 (201)		

(*Contd.*)

TABLE 6.7 (*Contd.*)

(1)	(2)	(3)	(4)	(5)
1992-93			20.00	
1992-93				155.5
				178.85 Agr. Deptt.
			160.00	
				Pl. Bd. 232.50
				215.22
				200.0 independent
1994-95			58.06*	

Note : + In these cases foodgrains signifies rice, wheat and maize.

* Our estimate.

1949-50 : The gap was estimated on the basis of nutritional needs at 18 per cent of the combined cereals and pulses outputs.

1950-51 : At the rate of 309.48 gms cereals per head per day, including 18 per cent for conversion wastage, driage, seeds and cattle feed. Some writers have estimated the deficit at higher figures. Other estimates were 7/12.50/16.23 lakh tonnes—7 lakh tonnes, provided the harvest was normal, i.e., 18 to 20 per cent of the normal harvest—another 10 to 16 per cent. Still another 28.1 per cent.

1951 : In November 1951, Bihar's annual requirement was : rice 24 lakh tonnes, wheat 12 lakh tonnes and millets 3.60 lakh tonnes. Average annual foodgrains production per rural household was 19.9 maunds (mds) and average annual foodgrains consumption 26.4 mds, leaving a gap/deficit per rural household of 6.5 mds—1 md = 37.3242 kgs.

1956 : 15 ounces of cereals and 3 ounces of pulses per head per day. Annual gap was 65.02 lakh tonnes without livestock feed requirement, and 71.58 lakh tonnes with it.

1961 : 71.68 lakh tonnes without livestock feed requirement and 78.85 lakh tonnes with it.

1961-66 : Per head per day 14 ounces of cereals and 3 ounces of pulses.

1966 : 78.83 lakh tonnes without livestock feed requirement and 86.71 lakh tonnes with it.

1978-79 : The food deficit was estimated at 35 per cent, in spite of the year being a bumper food output year.

1980 : The food deficit was 6.7 per cent of the total foodgrains output.

1988 : 4.6 per cent of total foodgrains production.

1988-89 : 13 to 25 per cent of production.

1991 : The Second Bihar Irrigation Commission estimated a deficit of 255.78 lakh tonnes (188.57 + 35.75 per cent of 188.57), 15 to 20 per cent of output. State Planning Board : 13 per cent. An independent estimate was 67.40 lakh tonnes. Another : 35.75 lakh tonnes. An independent study : 18.56 lakh tonnes. On the FAO criterion, the deficit would be 2.3 per cent less, say, 18.41 lakh tonnes.

1990-91 : 440 gms. foodgrains per head per day. Between 1950-51 and 1990-91 the foodgrains deficit was overcome to the extent of 22 per cent. For the same year the Irrigation Commission estimated the food gap at 67.21 lakh tonnes. Other estimates were 18.14 and 18.56 lakh tonnes. The deficit was 5.09 per cent of production.

1992-93 : 14 per cent of outturn.

1994-95 : 490 gms. foodgrains per head per day. Agri. Deptt. 637 gms., Other estimates : 74.90/213/215.23 lakh tonnes.

giving approximate figures of per capita per annum production and hence availability of foodgrains. The average varied between 110.7 kgs. (here too only three staple foodgrains, namely, rice, wheat and maize, were taken into consideration) and 155 kgs. (the national average was 189 kgs.), a disparity of 44 kgs.—a big figure. It would not be out of place to mention here that per capita availability of foodgrains is one of the macrolevel indicators of the standard of living of a community. During 1950-93 the improvement in this direct measure in Bihar was about 4 per cent (*Note :* The reader should bear in mind that this figure excludes supplements to and leakages from the realised production), with, of course, some technological advance made in the course of the years—not a gain to be proud of, considering the length of time and the sumtotal of planned efforts made on this front.

Total foodgrains requirement on the basis of the norm from period to period is given in this table. This also reflects lack of unanimity because of the same with regard to the norm. In 1950-51 the State's total food requirement was 62.69 lakh tonnes, which, in consequence of population growth, rose to a figure ranging between 160.00 and 255.78 lakh tonnes in 1990-91, say, an average of 208 lakh tonnes. In other words, the economic betterment of the people had increased the foodgrains demand almost one and a half times more than the population increase (330 *versus* 222 per cent).

The extent of the foodgrains gap/deficit estimated from the difference between foodgrains requirement and foodgrains production, in 1991, according to two estimates was akin to the extent of the foodgrains gap/deficit faced by the State in 1950-51. The third estimate for 1991 was over thrice the 1950-51 figure. For the year 1994-95 the State Agricultural Department estimated the deficit at 40.32 lakh tonnes. This sounds realistic, seen in the perspective of the breakthrough achieved in the early 1990s.

To conclude, food self-sufficiency has eluded Bihar. Bihar is even today far from achieving self-sufficiency in food. This is a stigma on the performance of Bihar agriculture during the last 40 to 45 years. Bihar has to depend on other States and the Centre to feed its people. The State Government's claim of self-sufficiency in food and the reported FCI's approval in 1994-95 to buy 5 lakh tonnes of foodgrains from the open market appears to be a make-believe, far too much to be quietly stomached.

For an average annual addition to population in Bihar to the extent of 20 lakhs, additional foodgrains required during 1991-2000 would be 2.99 to 3.63 lakh tonnes.

Bihar faced the firstever food crisis in 1943, which has dogged the State since in the shape of its food problem. In 1943, 77 thousand tonnes of foodgrains went outside Bihar in exchange of cloth. With the cessation of food imports in 1949 from Nepal the problem persisted with the State all the more. Both 1950-51 and 1951-52 were years of near famine because the problem caused extreme anxiety. Relief operations had to be launched. In 1951 North Bihar alone was short of nearly 60 lakh tonnes of foodgrains. The urban population of 2.7 million required another 11 million mds., i.e., about 40 lakh tonnes of cereals and pulses.

On the eve of the First Plan families in Bihar with no land practically starved, almost famished. Those with land up to 5 acres could afford less than adequate food intake. Only those with at least 15 acres of land could afford two square meals a day. They formed 20 to 22 per cent of the rural population. Worse still, most people ate an unbalanced diet, lacking in life-protecting elements. Almost 25 per cent had a balanced diet, 41 per cent an ordinary diet, and almost half the population a nominal diet. The calorie intake of over 30 per cent of the population was sub-normal. It was this underfed, undernourished section of the population which raised the entire foodgrains from the soil which fed and nourished the other half at different levels of consumption.

The food situation was grave in 1964 and graver in 1965 and the gravest during 1966-67, the drought year—the drought of an unprecedented intensity and rigour. The famine—like situation was averted only by taking well-organised relief and preventive measures.

Around 1971 Bihar fell in the low calorie and protein intake group of the States, between 1498 and 2044 in the calorie and 36 to 63 protein group per capita per day.

Of late, food intake has risen strikingly and the numbers and percentages of those below the weighted average of the recommended intakes are now far less/lower respectively than before. Nevertheless, class and caste differentials are observable in one and the same district together with seasonal variations among the same class and the same caste in one and the same place.

Roughly, a higher food consumption in Bihar rests primarily on the ratio between land and population and does not, of necessity, mirror the standard of consumption of other resources and amenities of life.

Writing in his June 15, 1995 report Farzand Ahmed rued that Bihar nourished hunger more than anything else. In 1991, according to him, of every thousand people, about 270 went without food every day. To quote, "Tales of adversity in Bihar, as poignant as they may be, seem trite and banal and rarely stir the public conscience."

In Bihar, in rural areas 730 persons out of 1000 persons get bread for two times a day. Rs. 41 out of Rs. 100 is spent on foodgrains in rural areas, as against the all-India figure of Rs. 24. A large percentage of the population, mothers included, are malnourished. Most people eat an unbalanced diet even now. The intake of protein and fats is much lower than essential.

Achieving self-sufficiency in food was considered an acute problem in the earlier Plans, which continued, with varying degrees of emphasis, right till the end of the period studied. For every additional tonne of foodgrains raised during 1950-51 to 1989-90 the State Government had to spend Rs. 9782 (all-India average being Rs. 15728) by way of direct investment in foodgrains production-augmenting projects and indirectly through the credit-lending institutions operating in agriculture.

Market intervention has been the key strategy to manage the food problem from the very outset. This has assumed various forms—State Government has purchased foodgrains from other States, it has been allotted quotas by the Centre on monthly/periodic basis for distribution through fair price shops, it has taken recourse to food levy and procurement, etc. The private individuals had also taken their own measures to tide over the deficit/gap encountered by them.

In 1951-52 the Centre allotted 1.26 lakh tonnes of rice and wheat to Bihar to be distributed among the needy people through the ration shops. Wheat allotment was 90 per cent and rice 10 per cent. In 1991 the Central allotment of cereals amounted to 6.72 lakh tonnes. A fluctuating trend in the Centre's food supply releases has been discernible from the very beginning. The maximum quantity so far allotted is 14.5 lakh tonnes and the minimum 1.26 lakh tonnes (Table 6.8).

As we have noted earlier, wheat production and consumption were insignificant in Bihar upto 1969. However, around Independence the typical rice-eating character of the people who collected their ration from the Government controlled shops was eroded and with the increase in wheat production in the State since 1969 rice and wheat are the two top cereals of the people in Bihar, accompanied by maize in the third place. The Public Distribution System (PDS) is based mostly on Central pool quotas, in which wheat supply is over 80 per cent and other cereals about 20 per cent. Rice is supplied by the Centre to Bihar in consideration of the people's first preference for rice, which in supply is less than demand in most places in Bihar.

Part of the Central supply of foodgrains has to be diverted to flood and scarcity/drought relief purposes as well. The PDS is handicapped to that extent when this takes place.

TABLE 6.8 : Foodgrains Imports in Bihar for Bridging the Foodgrains Deficit/Gap

Year/Period	*Foodgrains Receipts from the Central Pool*	*Purchases from Open Market & Other States*	*Total Imports (2) + (3)*
(1)	(2)	(3)	(4)
1945-46 to 1949-50			1.35 lakh tonnes
1951-52			Worth Rs. 32.5 crores
1951-52	1.15 lakh tonnes wheat + 0.11 lakh tonnes rice		
In certain years of the 1950s			4 to over 5 lakh tonnes per year but in some years 4 to 7 lakh tonnes
In the quinquennium ending 1954-55			Average annual 3.50 lakh tonnes
1957-59			Total : 46.7 lakh tonnes
1962-63	280250 tonnes (22600 tonnes wheat + 5420 tonnes rice) for PDS		
1963-64	2733257 tonnes (230400 tonnes wheat + 42857 tonnes rice)		
1964	7.65 lakh tonnes		
1965	7.00 lakh tonnes		
1965-66			5.58 lakh tonnes
1969-70			824500 tonnes
1969-70 to 1970-71			12.80 per cent of production Average annual : worth Rs. 65.27 crores
1970-71		10.48 lakh tonnes cereals 9.57, wheat 8.212 and maize 1.36 lakh tonnes	14.52 per cent of food production
1986			10.00 lakh tonnes
1987-88	14.5 lakh tonnes (25 per cent of the deficit)	5025 thousand tonnes	
1989-90	1.80 lakh tonnes	10.48 lakh tonnes	12.28 lakh tonnes
1991	6.72 lakh tonnes		

The Central supply is not adequate to meet the food deficit of the State. So the State Government is obliged to purchase foodgrains from other States. The volume of purchase is closely related to the volume of Central allotment. As Table 6.9 brings out, in 1947 the food deficit was 25 lakh tonnes; in 1949-50, 11 lakh tonnes; and in 1950-51, 18.27 lakh tonnes. In 1951 the State Government decided to import 10 lakh tonnes of foodgrains. On the other hand, the supply of foodgrains from the Centre in 1951-52 was 1.26 lakh tonnes. From this stands in bold relief the imperativeness of purchase of additional foodgrains by the State Government from outside. From 1945-46 to 1949-50 imports of foodgrains averaged 1.35 lakh tonnes a year. In 1989-90 the food requirement of the PDS was of the order of 18 lakh tonnes, while the release from the Centre was 1.80 lakh tonnes only—the State Government had to purchase 10.48 lakh tonnes from outside. The gap remained unbridged to the tune of 5.72 lakh tonnes. During 1989-90 to 1990-91 the Central allotment was 6.72 lakh tonnes per annum to the PDS, 84 per cent wheat and 16 per cent rice. Nearly 35 per cent of Bihar's cereals requirement was met by purchase from other States.

Some cardinal aspects of the PDS for the entire period in Bihar are arranged in Table 6.10. The quantity of foodgrains handled by the system increased from 2.08 lakh tonnes in 1953 to 8.43 lakh tonnes in 1988. As percentage to all-India, the increase was from 3.81 to 4.60 per cent during the same period. The number of fair price shops as proportion of the all-India number has remained stable but the absolute number increased by 396 per cent. The coverage of the PDS shrank during the 1980s but expanded afterwards. Lately, per capita monthly supply of foodgrains from the PDS has been 0.7 kg.

Summing up, Bihar has still to import foodgrains to feed its mounting population. Bihar is a net importer of foodgrains. The present situation is not far different from what prevailed on the eve of the First Plan when approximately 75 per cent of the people in the State had to rely on others for their foodgrains—others here meaning within the State, outside the State, in other States and outside the country. This posed the question of the marketed/marketable surplus in the hands of the private individuals. We propose to throw some light on this aspect of the food problem faced by Bihar over the period.

On the eve of the First Plan those with land above 5 acres had some surplus of produce over their subsistence level of consumption. During 1950-65, in a year of normal produce of rice, the marketable surplus of the rice-producing farmers was estimated to be about one-third of the total rice output, the rest being retained by the farmers themselves for self-consumption, seed, payment in kind to agricultural labour and for

TABLE 6.9 : Some Aspects of the Public Distribution System (PDS) in Bihar

Year/Period	*Number of Ration Shops (Fair Price Shops)*	*Percentage of Population served by (2)*	*Central Food Subsidy*	*Buffer-Stock*	*Quantity of Foodgrains handled*
(1)	(2)	(3)	(4)	(5)	(6)
1951 Oct.	11177 (11.5 per cent of all-India)				
1951 end		16.4 (= 256000) (0.54 per cent of all-India)			
1951-52			11 (Rs. Lakhs) (0.23 per cent of all-India)		
1953		5.90 (= 49.25 lakh)			2.08 lakh tonnes (3.81 per cent of all-India) (off-take 1.69 lakh tonnes, 3.73 per cent of all-India)
1951 Nov.				2.10 lakh tonnes	
1980					10.06 lakh tonnes (6.71 per cent of all-India)
1983					9.32 lakh tonnes
1984					6.00 lakh tonnes
1985	39030 (12.2 per cent of all-India)				6.33 lakh tonnes (4.00 per cent of all-India)
1986					7.88 lakh tonnes
1987 end	39627 (11.5 per cent of all-India)				10.20 lakh tonnes
1987-88					7.81 lakh tonnes
1988					8.43 lakh tonnes (4.60 per cent of all-India)
1992	44250 (11.07 per cent of all-India				

payment of rent for land. This amount of the marketable surplus was not sufficient to meet the requirement of the masses living in urban areas, having an inelastic demand, and for those farmers who did not grow rice. Unless their unmet demand was met partly by their own effort and partly by the Government management of it, serious administrative and political problems were created. In 1950-51 marketable surplus was about 25 per cent of the total foodgrains produce.

TABLE 6.10 : Movement of Agriculture Produce in Bihar

Item	*Proportion Sent Outside*		*Proportion received from outside*	
	March 1987	*March 1989*	*March 1987*	*March 1989*
Rice crop	14	16	86	84
Wheat crop	24	10	76	90
Wheat flour	5	29	95	71
Maize	11	30	89	70
Gram & gram products	13	5	87	95
Other pulses	37	45	63	55
Other millets	nominal	nominal		

In 1970-71, 1974-75 and 1980-81 market arrivals of rice were estimated at 24.8, 20.2 and 15.8 per cent, and those of wheat at 11.6, 16.5 and 12.2 per cent, of the aggregate produce in each case. Market arrivals of foodgrains as percentage of foodgrains production were, in general, lower in Bihar than in States such as Punjab, Haryana and Maharashtra, for the reason that the producers in Bihar themselves consumed a larger proportion of their produce.

In describing the pace and pattern of the marketable surplus, it is advisable to recognise that rural population growth is a drag on marketable surplus growth. As compared to the total, per capita foodgrains production is a more satisfactory index of the marketable surplus. Again, the rate of growth of the marketable surplus is faster than that of growth of foodgrains output because of the proportionally more share of the bigger farmers in its supply. Investigations disclose that farmers with landholdings upto 2 ha. are deficient in foodgrains and have to purchase them from other farmers having bigger landholdings. Landholders with holdings in size above 10 ha. supply 66.9 per cent of the total marketable surplus at the rate of 6.7 quintals per ha.; those with holdings between 6.01 and 9.99 ha.; 26.6 per cent of total marketable surplus at the rate of 4.9 quintals per ha., those with holdings between 4.01 and 6.00 ha.,

7.8 per cent of the same at the rate of 4.1 quintals per ha.; and finally, those with 2.01 and 4.00 ha., 7.5 per cent of it at the rate of 2.6 quintals per ha. (a study by J. Prasad). Augmenting of the purchasing power of nearly one-third of the rural population which has been suffering from deprivation and penury by launching a number of programmes and schemes in the last few decades has cut into the marketable surplus which has gone over to urban areas by making it consume more of the food produce. Increased urbanisation has meant increased dependence of the urban population on the rural suppliers of foodgrains. The falling rate of infant mortality has synchronised with a higher percentage of the adolescent and adult in the total population, with the result that at any given level of income food consumption per head of population has registered a rise. The increased longevity of the people too has had the same effect.

The foregoing account of the marketable surplus would be incomplete without the remaining finding that the marketable surplus of foodgrains varies crop-wise and region-wise.

Finally, were we to raise 0.22 tonne more of foodgrains on every hectare of land cultivated in Bihar, Bihar's food problem would be remedied, with the State reaching self-sufficiency in food.

7

AGRICULTURAL PRODUCTIVITY IN BIHAR

Growth is synonymous with productivity improvement, that is, more output per unit of a factor of production or all factors of production. Alternatively, the same output at reduced cost is also a reflex of improved productivity. This turns on allocational/allocative efficiency, scale economies and innovations.

By and large, in terms of land, agricultural productivity in Bihar is on the increase, and by comparison with the all-India position is generally a bit above, though not by comparison with some other States, such as Punjab and Haryana. (Table 7.1). In 1957 the value of crops per ha. in Bihar was 34.5 to 49.4 per cent less than that in all-India. Bihar produced a high proportion of low-value and a low proportion of high value crops. In 1984, gross value of agricultural produce in Bihar was higher by 10 per cent (in terms of GCA) and 29 per cent (in terms of NSA), when compared to Orissa. It was 19 per cent (in terms of GCA), when compared to Eastern Uttar Pradesh. It was 41 per cent lower than that in West Bengal in terms of GCA and 26 per cent lower in terms of NSA. Between 1960-61 and 1984-85 net value added in agriculture fell by 584 per cent. Bihar's superiority over all-India was of a lower order in 1955-56. It became very pronounced towards the end of the 1980s and then became less marked by the mid-1980s but again improved by the latter half of the 1980s. Apart from the drawback of the statistics from which these findings have been arrived at, the distortion caused by the price factor is a serious detractor to the derivation of an accurate conclusion. The same remark applies to agricultural productivity measured in terms of labour (Table 7.2). By and large, labour productivity in agricultural in all-India is distinctly above that in Bihar, in whatever form we calculate it. The productivity differential has increased over the period. In 1986-87, one rupee spent on labour engaged in agriculture yielded an output worth 56 paise (99 paise in the case of Punjab). In

1991 income of an average agricultural worker in Bihar was about one-fifth of that an average non-agricultural worker. During 1971-72 to 1983-84 labour productivity in Bihar retrograded at the rate of 0.68 per cent per annum.

TABLE 7.1 : Agricultural Productivity : Land-wise

(Rupees)

Year	*Gross Value Per ha. of* *GCA*	*NSA*	*Net Value Per ha.*
1955-56			399 (396)
1960-61	454.06	(462.40)	
1962-63	461.47	511.29	
1962-65 (Av.)+	3679.55 (3738.19)		
1970-73 (Av.)+	4009.73 (4256.79)		
1975-76 to 1979-80 (Av.)	1170 (1198)	1863 (1468)	Another estimate 2500 (2153)
1979-80 to 1981-82 (Av.)	2570		
1980-83 (Av.)+	4048.56 (5090.42)		
1984-85	3030 (2638)		
1984-85 to 1986-87 (Av.)	2993 (irrigated)		
1986-87			6785 (6792)
1986-87 to 1988-89 (Av.)		6785 (4646)	
1987-88 to 1989-90 (Av.)			6827 (5234)
1988-89	1092.60		
1992-93 (Av.)+	5678.08 (7388.05)		

\+ Average value of yield has been estimated at 1990-93 prices.

So far as the distortion caused by the price factor, stated above, is concerned, it may be added here that prices of agricultural commodities have increased more or less continuously, except during the First Plan period, when they actually fell. From 1962-63 they have risen continuously. In 1971-72 they were double those in 1961-62. In 1981-82 they were more than double those in 1971-72. In 1992-93 they were more than 2.5 times those in 1981-82. Wide fluctuations have characterised prices of certain commodities, e.g., rice, wheat, pulses and raw jute in a single year.

TABLE 7.2 : Agricultural Productivity : Labour-wise

(Rupees)

Year	*Net Value Per Agricultural Worker/ Cultivator from all Crops*	*Gross Income Per Agricultural Worker+*	*Gross Income Per Rural Worker+*	*Per Capita Gross Income from Agriculture (Rural Population only)*	*Per Capita Gross Income from Agriculture*
1950-51	118.90 (104.00) (Per Agriculturist)				
1951				68.90	
1955-56	88.30 (90.40) (Per Agriculturist)				156 (268)
1958-59			302 (477)	82.60 (102.00)	826
1960-61	396 (778.25)	590 (778.25)		113	
1961					
1960-61 to 1962-63 (Av.)				136.39	
1962-63	282.20				
1970-71	1190		895 (at 1970-71 prices)		
1970-73 (Av.)				278 (384)	
1971				195	
1975-76 to 1979-80 (Av.)	746				
1979-80		812 (1430)		450 (710)	
1979-80 to 1981-82 (Av.)				450 (710)	
1982-83	816 (1041) (Per Agriculturist)				
1983-86 (Av.)				739 (1171)	
1984-85	4362 (5973)				
1985-86			1077 (at 1970-71 prices)		
1986-87				1156 (1564)	809 (1449)
1986-87 to 1988-89 (Av.)				943/1156 (1320/1564)	
1987-90 (Av.)			933 (1325)	948 (1522)	
1988-89			302 (477)		

+ Part of his income may be from sources other than agriculture.

When we move from the value measure of productivity to its physical measure, we gain evidently in concreteness and objectivity. A look at Table 7.3 would show that land productivity, i.e., yield of foodgrains per hectare of land increased 2.87 times in Bihar and 2.64 times in all-India between 1950-51 and 1990-91. Whereas in all-India foodgrains yield rose continuously in Bihar , it rose between 1950-51 and 1980-81 but fell in 1981-82 and further fell in 1982-83. During 1960-61 to 1974-75 there were some years, such as 1960-61, 1965-66 and 1974-75, when foodgrains yield in Bihar exceeded that in all-India, otherwise, except for the year 1986-87, the converse was the case. In the best years foodgrains yield per ha. was about 1200 kgs in Bihar. The gap between foodgrains yield in all-India and foodgrains yield in Bihar, which was 70 kgs in 1950-51, widened to 84 kgs. in 1990-91. The year-to-year fluctuations were of lower amplitudes in the succeeding decades than in the preceding ones. Between 1950-51 and 1982-83 the range of fluctuation in foodgrains yield was 119 per cent, which had fallen to 67 per cent during 1967-68 to 1990-91. The diminution was ascribable most to the progress of irrigation and consequential reduced dependence on the monsoon. Another notable feature was that the decline in foodgrains yield as between years was of a lower dimension in all-India than in Bihar, and likewise for the improvement in it, which was of a higher order in the case of all-India, as compared to that in Bihar.

TABLE 7.3 : Agricultural Productivity : Yield-Wise

Year	*Land Productivity of Foodgrains (Yield/Per ha. in kgs.)*	*Labour Productivity (Per Capita Per Annum Foodgrains Production in kgs.)*	*Rate of growth of Yield of Foodgrains (Per Cent Per Annum)*
(1)	(2)	(3)	(4)
1950-51	452 (522)	116.3 (142.9) 133.5	
1950-51 to 1965-66	754 (629)		2.60*
1960-61		150.9	
1951-79			1.1*
1951-91			4.55*
1952-53 to 1961-62			2.16* 1.76**
1952-53 to 1964-65			2.25* 1.77**
1949-50 to 1964-65			0.99
1952-79			1.13 (1.72)

(*Contd.*)

TABLE 7.3 (*Contd.*)

(1)	(2)	(3)	(4)
1955-56	606 (605)	131.9	
1960-61	747 (710)	159.7 (189.7)	
1961-62	503 (705)		
1961-81			1.2*
1962-63	510 (680)		
1965-66	754 (629)	140.7	
1967-68 to 1990-91			2.27
1969-70 to 1989-90			1.7
1970-71	795 (872)	139.5 (200.9)	
1970-92		130.2	1.55* 2.50**
1970-73 (Av.)	882 (848)	155 (189)	
1974-75	850 (824)		
1975-76	907 (944)	149.6 (165.0)	
1979-80 to 1985-86 (Av.)			
Triennium ending 1980-81		1298	3.83 (3.21)
1980-81	989 (1023)	141.7 (192.2)	
1980-83 (Av.)	901 (1030)	121 (191)	
1981		141.5 (144.04)	
1981-82	862 (1032)		
1982-83	816 (1041)		
1982-87 (Av.)	1064 (1433)		
1984-87 (Av.)		138 (193)	
1986		147.63	
1985-86	1157 (1175)	142.2	
1985-86 to 1987-88 (Av.)		132.0 (186)	
1986-87	1159 (1128)		
1987-90	1182	134.0	
1988-89	1253 (1331)	127.7	
1988-91 (Av.)		139 (204)	
1989-90	1255 (1349)	133.8	
1989-92 (Av.)	1243 (1368)	133 (203)	
1990-91	1298/1300 (1380/1382)	142.4 (211.7)	
1990-93 (Av.)	1199		
1991-92	1171 (1371)		
1992-93	1110 (1440)		
1993-94	1060		
1949-50 to 1990-91			(1.69)

Note : * Compound.
** All-India.

Between 1951 and 1991 the increase in foodgrains yield was 408 per cent; between 1950-51 and 1987-88, 350 per cent (all-India 220 to 240 per cent); between 1960-61 to 1988-89, 1602 per cent; and between 1970-71 and 1991-92, 41 per cent. In other words, the percentage increase in foodgrains yield was higher in the earlier than in the later years.

Another finding of significance is that the gain becomes proportionally smaller as we estimate it for longer periods, as compared to shorter ones, more particularly when those periods fell before the mid-1960s. Thus the rate of growth of foodgrains yield was maximum during 1979-80 to 1985-86 for Bihar as well as all-India, 3.83 per cent per annum for the former and 3.21 per cent per annum for the latter. The rate was minimum for Bihar, 1.1 per cent per annum, during 1951-79, and for all-India, 0.99 per cent per annum, during 1949-50 to 1964-65.

Turning to labour productivity measured by per capita foodgrains production per year, we find that whereas the rise in it was 122.4 per cent between 1950-51 and 1990-91 in Bihar, in all-India the rise was 148.1, by a higher percentage, during the same period. When these percentage increments in labour productivity are juxtaposed against the percentage increments in land productivity, the period being the above, we find that population growth had swamped away the gain more in Bihar than in all-India, notwithstanding the fact that the rate of population growth was slightly lower in Bihar then that in all-India during certain inter-census periods.

The gap between per capita per year foodgrains production in all-India and that in Bihar became wider from 26.6 kgs. in 1950-51 to 69.3 kgs. in 1990-91.

Between 1969-70 and 1989-90 the compound annual growth rate of per capita foodgrains production in Bihar was (–) 0.7 per cent. There were year-to-year fluctuations in per capita per year foodgrains production in Bihar as well as all-India, though they were less relevant to our enquiry than the fluctuations as between the first years of the decades. To substantiate, the difference between 1950-51 and 1960-61 was 43.2 kgs. in the case of Bihar and 36.8 kgs. in that of all-India; the same between 1960-61 and 1970-71 was (–) 20.2 kgs. in the case of Bihar and 11.2 kgs. in that of all-India; the same between 1970-71 and 1980-81 was 2.2 kgs. in the case of Bihar and (–) 8.7 kgs. in that of all-India; and the same between 1980-81 and 1990-91 was 0.7 kg. in the case of Bihar and 19.5 kgs. in that of all-India. That is to say, the magnitude of fluctuations, decennial, had a downward trend in the case of both Bihar and all-India, largely because of the extension of irrigation, though the decline in the fluctuations was smaller in Bihar by comparison with all-India, which was a blessing in disguise for Bihar. This disclosure speaks volumes for Bihar, for its poverty is often accounted for with reference to the low productivity of its agriculture. The Fifth Plan of the State had rightly stated that per capita income could be raised and savings and capital formation generated on a significant scale only if agriculture yields could be raised substantially from their abysmally low levels. Only if Bihar, which is essentially rooted in agriculture, could optimise productivity of labour as well as land engaged in it, would it have picked up the necessary competence to shake off the shackles of poverty.

Fertility-wise lands in Bihar are divided into three classes, viz., class I, which claims half of all lands in the State; class II, 20 per cent of all lands; and class III, 30 per cent.

As a rule, up to a point the quantity of labour is helpful to the growth of its productivity but beyond that point any increase in it becomes an encumbrance. Throughout the quality of labour is an asset and it is a product of a number of factors, the chief among which are health, longevity, education and training, determining ability and willingness to work. The deficiency of productivity-augmenting assets is made up by harder and more disciplined work which excels other attributes when judged by the results produced. And this is subsumed under *X*-efficiency.

Bihar's rice yield is low. In the absence of area expansion, increased yield was the only means left to bring about a rise in rice output. Ten States were above Bihar in 1990-91 from the point of view of rice yield. The gap between rice yield in all-India and rice yield in Bihar was 140 per cent. The all-India average of rice yield was throughout above the average rice yield in Bihar (Table 7.4). The improvements in rice yield in the last forty years in the two cases were more or less equal (267 *versus* 262 per cent). Enquiries reveal that till 1982-83 there was marked improvement in rice yield in Bihar. According to them, during 1950-51 to 1987-88 the increase in rice yield was 230 per cent, all-India increase being 220 per cent. The post-Green Revolution period increase (during 1969-70 to 1989-90) in rice yield was 130 per cent, the national figure being 150 per cent. The rate of growth of rice yield during this period was a measly 0.3 per cent per annum (compound) (Table 7.5). Finally, there have taken place violent ups and downs in rice yield and hence in costs of production of rice per unit of output.

TABLE 7.4 : Yields of Certain Principal Crops

(Per ha. in kgs.)

Year	Rice	Wheat	Maize	Pulses	Oilseeds	Sugarcane	Jute
1950-51	455 (668)	437 (663)	538 (547)		520 (481)	14958 (33422)	
1950-53 (Av.)				452 (450)			
1955-56	707 (874)	610 (708)	467 (704)			19078 (32779)	686 (1038)
1956-59 (Av.)				438 (486)			
1960-61	867 (1013)	679 (851)	1020 (926)	502 (539)		37443 (45549)	925 (1183)
1963-66 (Av.)				472 (458)			
1965-66	813 (862)	709 (827)	1018 (1005)	585 (438)		34994 (43713)	922 (1062)
1970-71	852 (1123)	1035 (1307)	1124 (1279)	600 (524)	458 (579)	38753 (48322)	982 (1186)
1974-77 (Av.)				597 (494)			
1975-76	923 (1235)	1265 (1410)	1004 (1203)	537 (533)	472 (627)	36698 (50903)	1110 (1367)
1978-81 (Av.)				514 (457)			
1980-81	1036 (1336)	1567 (1630)	985 (1159)		413 (532)	31412 (57844)	812 (1245)
1983-84 to 1987-88 (Av.)	1043 (1474)	1552 (1934)			553 (813)	33759 (58767)	
1985-86	1120 (1482)	1556 (1998)		725 (508)	553 (813)	32260 (59730)	
1990-91	1215/ 1218 (1740/ 1751)	1801/ 1812 (2274/ 2281)	1597 (1524)	773/ 779 (576)	530/ 730 (533/ 720)	52490/ 52590 (65269/ 65395)	1306 (1602)
1992-93	810 (1740)	1750 (2320)		730 (570)	560 (790)	45390 (63810)	
Increase (per cent) 1950-51 to 1990-91	267 (262)	412 (343)	296 (278)	171 (128)	140 (66)	351 (195)	190 (64)

In 1990-91, so far as wheat yield was concerned, Bihar held the seventh rank among the wheat-producing States. Except for very few years, wheat yield in Bihar was below the all-India average. Improvement in wheat yield in the last four decades was of a higher percentage in

Bihar than that in all-India. Studies bear out that the increase in wheat yield in Bihar has been one of the lowest in the country. Between 1950-51 and 1987-88 it was 230 per cent in Bihar, as compared to 290 per cent in all-India. The post-Green Revolution period increase in wheat yield in Bihar was 150 per cent, as against 120 per cent in all-India. At any rate, the increase in wheat yield exceeded that in rice yield in the State. Also, the growth rate of wheat yield, 2.3 per cent per annum, was above that of rice yield during that period. According to a different study, during 1951-91 wheat yield increased at the rate of 7.75 per cent per annum.

TABLE 7.5 : Growth Rate of Yields of Certain Principal Crops

(Per cent per annum)

Year	*Rice*	*Wheat*	*Maize*	*Pulses*	*Oilseeds*	*Sugarcane*
1950-51 to 1965-66			1.40*	2.60*	(–) 2.95	(–) 0.46
1951-53 (Av.)				1.83		
1951-91	4.17					
1963-66 (Av.)				(–) 0.69		
1967-68 to 1977-78			(–) 0.46	(–) 1.14*	3.8	0.00
1969-70 to 1989-90	0.3*	2.3*				
1978-81 (Av.)				0.71		

Note : * Compound.

In 1952 Bhadai maize yield in Bihar was the highest in India (5415 kgs. per ha.). Bihar was awarded a prize for this. Till 1982-83 Bihar's place was third among the maize-producing States. In 1990-91 it slid down to the fifth position. Between 1950-51 and 1990-91 the gain in maize yield was 296 per cent in Bihar, which was higher than that in all-India, 278 per cent. It would appear from Table 7.4 that 1965-66 and 1990-91 were the twin exceptional years when maize yield in Bihar was above that in all-India, otherwise throughout it was below the average for the country. Maize yield increased at the rate of 4.9 per cent per annum during 1951-91. During the post-Green Revolution period the growth rate of maize yield remained negative.

Between 1950-51 and 1990-91 Bihar surpassed India in pulses yield improvement, 171 *versus* 127 per cent. In recent years Bihar has improved its relative position from the third to the second. In most years pulses yield in the State has been above that in all-India. Besides, improvement in pulses yield has been of a higher degree in Bihar than in the country. During 1963-66 and again during 1967-68 to 1977-78, the post-Green Revolution period, the growth rate of pulses yield in Bihar was negative.

At the beginning as well as at the end of our period oilseeds yield was higher in Bihar than in India as a whole; in other years it was lower. Improvement in oilseeds yield in Bihar was more than that in all-India. Till the mid-1980s the growth rate of oilseeds yield was negative. The years that followed witnessed an increase in the yield rate such that for the period 1950-51 to 1987-88 the increase was 230 per cent in the State, which was far above the all-India figure of 170 per cent.

All along the period of our review sugarcane yield in Bihar has been lower than the national average. On the other hand, improvement in sugarcane yield in Bihar has exceeded that in all-India—351 *versus* 195 per cent. Bihar's relative place in sugarcane yield deteriorated to the 10th by 1960-61. Only recently it has improved marginally to the ninth. During 1950-51 to 1987-88 increase in sugarcane yield in Bihar was 180 per cent, as against 170 per cent in all-India. In 1961 *gur* production was between 37 and 39 quintals per ha. By 1971 it had fallen to 30 quintals. During 1970-71 to 1982-83 sugarcane yield declined by 11.9 per cent. During 1950-51 to 1965-66 the growth rate of sugarcane yield was negative.

Lastly, we have jute. Its yield rate too has been lower throughout but the improvement in jute yield has exceeded the all-India average as in the case of sugarcane. Between 1955-56 and 1990-91 the increase in jute yield in Bihar was 190 per cent, while in India it was 154 per cent. The relative position of Bihar has improved recently—in 1960-61 it was fifth, in 1990-91, it was fourth. Between 1960-61 and 1980-81 the decline in jute yield was to the extent of 130 kgs. per ha.

To conclude, not only have the yield improvements in respect of the principal crops discussed above been on the low side, but also the rates of growth of the yields have been extremely low and fluctuating like the yields themselves. Compared to the range of improvement in the yield levels of rice, wheat and sugarcane between 23 and 55 per cent in the country, in Bihar it was between 4.2 and 4.1 per cent from 1970-71 onwards. And similarly for the range of rate of growth of the yield levels. A substantial gap exists at present between the potential and the actual farm yields, the potential yields range from 2.0 to 2.5 times the existing yields. In some cases, say, rice, the gap is one of the highest in India. Were this gap to be plugged, say, by such methods as increased irrigation and drainage, the given productivity levels would be raised significantly.

Let us at this stage summarise the factors which are responsible for low agricultural productivity. First of all, we have the inadequacies of irrigation, the first component of the package (inclusive of drainage). Coupled with these we have those of the other two components of the package on which the New Agrarian Technology (NAT) is based, namely, the *HYVs/improved seeds* and the *chemical fertilisers*. Mechanisation (pre-eminently, tractorisation) is an extension of this new technology. The success of the water-seeds-fertilisers package is contingent upon the provision of credit and an efficient extension service, inclusive of research. This is further connected with the existence of facilities such as transport, communications, marketing and co-operation. The smallness of the farms/holdings and their fragmented character are factors which too keep down productivity. The land tenancy and tenureship systems are also to blame. At the heart of all these is the human factor, the psychology of which is crucial to productivity. The part played by Nature cannot be disregarded in any attempt at explaining why productivity of agriculture in Bihar is so low. Productivity here is the collective product of land and labour and other non-land and non-labour factors and as such all those influences which prevent the productivities of these three categories of agents of production from becoming maximum have to be delineated in this context. In some of the chapters which follow we have attempted to elucidate these influences, severally and collectively.

8

BIHAR AGRICULTURE
Slow and Halting Progress

Let us begin this chapter with a summary of the main points contained in the last three chapters: From what has been said before, it can be concluded here that the cropping pattern in Bihar is dominated by foodgrains. Given the NSA and GCA, cropping intensity has indicated a swing, upward or downward. The past production trends in agriculture disclose considerable years to year fluctuations, depending on incidence of natural calamities like drought and flood. The expansion of area under rice was negligible for two decades (1961 to 1981). Rice production has been influenced immensely by the vagaries of rainfall. Bihar has not made any notable breakthrough in improving rice yield rates, which continue to be low. As the scope for area expansion is limited, an increase in rice output is possible only through increasing yield rates.

A cardinal feature of Bihar's cropping pattern is the impressive performance of wheat. Both area expansion and increase in productivity have contributed to the high growth rates of wheat production in an almost equal measure. The substantial improvement in wheat yield rates reveals that Bihar farmers are not unresponsive to technical innovation.

After rice and wheat, the next important crop in Bihar is maize. There has not been any significant improvement in maize output. The area devoted to the other minor cereals has remained negligible. Both area and production of these crops have recorded a progressive decline over the years. Identical has been the case with pulses, though their yield rates have demonstrated some improvement. But for this, the fall in pulses outturn would have been larger.

The area under oilseeds has remained more or less steady. Sugarcane yields have been lower in Bihar when compared with those in the other sugarcane-producing States. The cultivation of vegetables has registered a rising trend, particularly in the periphery of the urban areas. Potato, tobacco, onion, chillies, turmeric, banana, etc., are also grown in the State.

Jute and mesta are the major cash crops of Bihar. The State ranks second in the country, next to West Bengal, in the production of these two crops. Deterioration of input supply and uncertain market conditions account for the fluctuating levels in the yield of jute. There has been a steady improvement in the yield rates of the twin crops in recent years.

The foregoing review shows that the performance of the agricultural sector has been rather poor in Bihar. Bihar is deficient in foodgrains production. The situation is no better in respect of the cash crops. About half of the area under non-foodgrain crops is sown with jute and mesta, sugarcane and oilseeds. Yield levels of sugarcane and jute are extremely low. Superimposed as are the adverse effects of the downswings in production of foodgrains incorporating the gradual decline in coarse cereals (the so-called buffer crops) output, on a stagnant/slowly growing sector, their incidence is greatly magnified.

The principal constraints/limits to agricultural growth are :

(1) Social and Structural :
- (i) Agrarian structure.
- (ii) erratic rainfall.
- (iii) natural calamities.
- (iv) tal lands.
- (v) problem soil areas.

(2) Organisational :
- (i) inputs.
- (ii) credit.
- (iii) electric power.
- (iv) extension.
- (v) marketing facility.
- (vi) co-ordination.

(3) Technological :
- (i) water management, i.e., irrigation and drainage.
- (ii) machinery and implements.
- (iii) problems of agriculture in tribal area.
- (iv) research.
- (v) specific problems of agro-climatic zones.

Policy measures to release these constraints and accelerating agricultural development would fall primarily in the following areas :

(i) land management.
(ii) irrigation and drainage.
(iii) farm policy.
(iv) inputs supply.
(v) credit delivery.
(vi) community services.
(vii) rural industries.
(viii) ancillary activities.
(ix) transport and marketing arrangements.
(x) development of tribal agriculture.
(xi) management and organisational reforms.

We have noted above that productivity per agricultural worker is low in Bihar in most respects, as compared to the all-India average. His brawn power is low. His stamina is low. He lacks in nutrition. He is illiterate and unskilled. He is capable of hard work, no doubt, but he can also be unruly at times. There are spells during the peak seasons when the requisite and wayward dose of labour is not forthcoming or not forthcoming on time.

Ideally, labour without capital is inefficient. Investment per agricultural worker is low. The natural calamities have a deterring influence. The precariousness of Bihar agriculture makes heavy inroads into the thriftiness and prudence of the farming community. Crime against public property is exacerbated by bad harvests. The smallness of the middle class is an obstacle to investment.

The preponderance of the small and marginal farms in Bihar renders their proper management and organisation extremely difficult. They are not economic holdings. They cannot be operated in an optimum manner. The capital (including the livestock) invested in them is underutilised. Inputs like tractors, pumpsets, threshers and some agricultural implements are not scale-neutral; they are amenable to the scale economies. Likewise, the medium and large holdings are managed poorly. The hired labour adds much less to the total product. Often an inverse relationship exists between size of a holding and use of modern inputs as a result of disinterested and absentee ownership and management. These are the reasons which make consolidation of holdings a catalyst of agricultural transformation.

Excessive pressure of the growing population on the given land area in relation to other means of production accounts for the prevalent phenomenon in which agriculture is in the throes of diminishing returns.

In Bihar the people's attachment to land was encouraged and perpetuated by the erstwhile *zamindari* system. Land is a symbol or mark of social and political status of an average Bihari. Owing to the prevalent phenomenon the mobility of land as a resource is limited, and this is a check upon economic growth.

Take some data : Between 1971 and 1987-88 in Bihar net sown area as percentage of reporting area declined from 49 per cent to 43.2 per cent. In all-India this decline was by a lower percentage : from 46 to 44.6 per cent. Bihar's share in GCA in all-India in 1956-57 was 6.7 per cent, which fell to 6.5 per cent in 1981-82 and 5.8 per cent in 1984-85. On the other hand, population in Bihar was 10.74 per cent around 1956-57 and 10.21 per cent around 1984-85. The fall in the former exceeded that in the latter. In 1951 NSA per head of population in Bihar was 0.23 ha. (all-India average : 0.30 ha.); in 1991 it had become 0.08 ha. (all-India average : 0.16 ha.). GCA per head of population in Bihar was 0.75 ha. (all-India : 0.83 ha.) in 1950-51 and 0.40 ha. (all-India : 0.25 ha.) in 1984-85. ASMO was 0.59 ha. (all-India : 0.73 ha.) in 1950-51 and 0.10 ha. (all-India: 0.20 ha.) in 1984-85. Population density per ha. of GCA was 133 (all-India : 128) in 1950-51 and 678 (all-India : 390) in 1984-85. Average size of holdings in Bihar was 1.11 ha. in 1970-71 (all-India : 1.84 ha.) and 0.87 ha. in 1985-86 (all-India : 1.68 ha.). Of the total working population, 81 per cent was engaged in agriculture in Bihar in 1951 (all-India figure : 69.8 per cent) and 80.6 per cent in 1991 (all-India figure: 64.9 per cent). In 1961 in Bihar the percentage of agricultural labourers to total working population was 22.9 per cent (all-India : 16.7 per cent) and in 1991, 37.2 per cent (all-India : 26.2 per cent). The corresponding figures for cultivators were 54.2 per cent (all-India : 52.8 per cent) and 43.4 per cent (all-India : 38.7 per cent). The percentage of earners in the working population was 35.4 per cent in Bihar in 1951 (all-India : 39.1 per cent) and 29.6 per cent in 1981 (all-India : 33.4 per cent). These data go to show that Bihar's agricultural base has been poor right from the outset of planning.

Fertility of land is a prime determinant of agricultural productivity. North Bihar and parts of South Bihar are fortunate in that their lands are originally fertile but the plateau region and some other areas are not so blessed by nature because the level of their soil fertility is low. Besides, there are pockets in the State that face serious soil problems—of erosion, acidity and deficiency. In order to step up agricultural production the depleted/destroyed powers of the soil have to be replenished alongwith other measures pertinent to the goal. Afforestation would be an efficacious remedy. Bihar has suffered severely from deforestation which has upset the ecological balance which agriculture ought to have. In 1949 Bihar's share in all-India forest area was 8.4 per cent, in 1984-85 this had fallen to 4.3 per cent. Forest area in the State as percentage of total reported area of the State was 19.3 per cent in 1956 (all-India figure being 22.3 per cent) and in 1984-85 it was 16.7 per cent (all-India figure being 22.0 per cent). Per capita forest area in Bihar was 0.08 ha. in 1949-50 (all-India average being 0.09 ha.) and 0.04 ha. in 1984-85 (all-India average being 0.09 ha.).

In so far as *productivity of agriculture* is a compound of area and yield, while explaining its lowness, we have to allude to the problems associated with both area and yield. Parts of the cultivated area which are affected by flood or drought display low productivity, which is but natural. Similarly, parts of the crops that are afflicted with diseases and damaged by insects, pests and bacteria have poor yields. On the fields and *en route* storage and during storage there are additional losses. There are losses from the hailstorm and blight. All these are minuses to the quantum of agricultural output. Were they to be taken into account, productivity would not be as low as it is at present. But consideration of these ravages would be nonsensical as would be that of the Acts of God and those of the enemies of society.

Then there is the Nature-Against-Man explanation—pathetic dependence of nearly two-thirds of the cultivators on the monsoon rainfall which is uncertain, erratic and uneven in the absence of assured, effective, adequate and timely supply of irrigation, on the one hand and their vulnerability to adverse weather conditions, on the other; together they consign agriculture to precariousness. Intermittent, dry spells during July to August and blowing of Western wind during March are typical of Bihar, both are bad, one for Kharif and the other for Rabi. Late monsoon rain leads to late preparation of land, delayed raising of paddy seedlings, and their delayed transplantation. Delayed transplantation also exposes the paddy crop to the maximum incidence of pests and diseases. The end result is a steep fall in output. The plough-bullock-manpower available in rural areas is just below the optimum required to bring all the land available into a condition fit for the transplantation of the paddy plants in time. Even when the monsoon is on time, five to six per cent of the land is planted late because of the inadequate and untimely supply of power. In the dark picture painted of the monsoon there is one bright spot—the situation created by the temperamental monsoon is relieved, in part, by adequate and opportune cold weather showers, thereby improving the Rabi crops.

We know that technology and production interact in any field. Low productivity in agriculture is closely associated with the low level of technology employed in it. It is widely believed that technological innovations have not made any significant headway in Bihar. Bihar agriculture is replete with inefficient, inferior and outmoded techniques of cultivation. There is technological stagnation in Bihar agriculture, of the maximum extent in the country together with the lack of an appropriate alternative technology, farmers' ignorance of better methods, farmers' lack of motivation and barriers to adoption of the appropriate technology due to other market failures. Let us elaborate this :

Productivity depends, among other factors, on the acumen of the farmer, his knowledge of the arts of cultivation (even if traditional, not all farmers are seasoned, a certain attitude of the mind—or mentality, for many farmers are rooted in the primitive ideas and practices). Todaro is quite relevant here : In the case of an average Bihari farmer, his bare physical survival defines the concept of his life even today but even this is made difficult by the three real fears, fear of flood and drought, fear of the landlord and fear of the moneylender, in so far as he faces near starvation in bad years. Production of his staple foodgrain is the hall-mark of his entire effort and he jealously guards his static, though, stable equilibrium. The risk-averting farmer is apt to prefer a technology of food production that combines a low mean per hectare yield with a low variance to alternative technologies and crops that may promise a higher mean yield but also avert the risk of a greater variance. This accounts for his apathy for the new agrarian technology. On the other hand, Foland finds the farmer's existing techniques rationally scaled to his level of disposable capital. This also leaves the cake of his habit intact, i.e., uncut.

Inadequacy of research is no less to blame for low agricultural productivity. It is reported that the two agricultural universities in Bihar have suffered from the financial squeeze imposed on them and felt starved of research funds and were hence forced to rely heavily on the *ad hoc* ICAR projects and financial support. Moreover, agricultural research has not touched all the crops, except a few. In addition, the area of agricultural research is beset with several gaps—soil analysis, water management, drought-resistant varieties of wheat for unirrigated lands, red-rot resistant varieties of sugarcane, the needed varieties of rape-seed and mustard and pulses, and so on, have not been evolved so far.

Oddly, the improved techniques of production (including machines and tools and implements) that are supposed to improve labour efficiency have not been demonstrated (to see is to believe) in many places and where they have been demonstrated they are not conveniently available in the number required.

Transfer of the new agrarian technology from the laboratory to the farm has posed problems that could be surmounted only partially. This has been attributed to the inadequate, ineffective and inefficient extension staff. The Village Level Workers (VLWs) have been deployed by the politicians for purposes other than those for which they are meant. The old parrots cannot learn a new song if the teacher is not dutiful. Also, the desired change over is not without its real cost.

The organisational set-up with its paraphernalia and network is accused of bad delivery—its failure to deliver the goods. Also, the different departments engaged in agricultural development bristle with lack of co-ordination.

The disincentive effect of the existing market practices on the psychology and hence productivity of the farmer deserves special mention. In many matters he has to bank upon the market forces in order to know the market trends and counter them, if adverse. Among the post-harvest problems, lack of marketing facilities has a prominent place. Wholesale assembly markets are least developed in Bihar than elsewhere. Regulated markets are more developed than wholesale assembly markets. The average farmer in Bihar has to part with his produce at a very low price to the rapacious moneylender to whom he is eternally indebted ('Debt rather than profit is the normal fate of the average farmer',—Francis Foland writes). Where he is assured of working capital from a public institution or where he is assured of a reasonable price for his produce, he is a symbol of hard work, and is articulately disposed towards the new agrarian technology—he is a risk-taker and invests in its adoption.

The farmers' marketing problem is aggravated by the inadequacies and inefficiencies and imperfections of the transport and communications in rural areas as well as warehousing and storage facilities. In so far as externalities are implicit in the process farm and approach roads cannot be constructed where small holdings preponderate in the same manner as irrigation and drainage channels cannot be constructed. For these are scale-conscious agricultural activities.

The new agrarian technology is capital-using. Where institutional credit is not available in the requisite amount, whatever be the reason, the modern inputs which are expensive cannot be applied in the proportions desired for maximising output, no matter that they are scale-neutral, and hence usable by small landholders as well. It is immaterial to add here that Bihar agriculture is starved of institutional credit.

There are complaints of other kinds with regard to the modern inputs in use in Bihar agriculture. One relates to supply of inferior seeds by the government and private agencies. There is another side to this. The effectiveness of the improved seeds turns on careful soil analysis. Another is that the improved seeds can increase production only in a good year of rains or in areas of assured irrigation (thus the efficiency or quality of irrigation becomes important); in a lean year, they are not able to ensure a known minimum level of production. A third is that farmers living near the margin of subsistence are extremely reluctant to give up the seeds they have been using since they simply cannot run the risk that the new seeds may fail and reduce them to starvation condition.

Fertilisers augment yield of the land. In Bihar we have two outstanding features characterising them. One, general absence of fertilising practices in many areas old habits die hard. Two, consumption of fertilisers per hectare which is much below the all-India average. In 1990-91 per ha. of GCA it was in Bihar 56.8 kgs., the all-India average being 72.4 kgs. There had occurred a rise in this consumption over time. For example, in 1982-83 the two figures were 18.5 and 36.6 kgs. respectively. Per capita consumption of fertilisers in 1990-91 was 6.80 kgs. in Bihar, as against 14.84 kgs. in all-India. The effectiveness of the fertilisers on many fields was lower because they were used without soil analysis or, alternatively, because the base of irrigation was low (this was the greatest eroder/dampener of the zeal and enthusiasm of those who wanted to renounce their dependence on the monsoon rains).

Pesticides have been in short supply in Bihar. The State's share in GCA in 1986-87 was 5.9 per cent, whereas its share in total pesticides consumption was around 4.5 per cent.

Agricultural productivity is determined not only by physical, technical and organisational factors but also by institutional ones. The agrarian structure may be having either the incentive or the disincentive effect of the farmer's ability and willingness to work and save and invest. With a very high percentage of *Bataidars* (sharecroppers) in Bihar, not assured of the produce of their effort, the degree of agricultural productivity has to be low. The *zamindari* system had its quietus in law but the *zamindars* are still there. The conditions in which the agricultural labourers live and work are not very conducive to a higher level of productivity. Last but not the least, forces trying to accelerate the pace of reform and forces trying to resist it are at war with each other, entailing a situation of internal strife, which keeps agriculture in Bihar perpetually tense.

At this stage we propose to take stock of the factors that have assisted agriculture in augmenting its productivity (total product). As stated before, the area and the factors bearing on it, on the one hand and the yield of land and the factors bearing on it, on the other, have been the chief engines of growth of agricultural productivity as well as the rate of this growth period-wise. In short, extension of area cultivated through reclamation of land, land development including soil conservation, double or multiple cropping, topological factors, etc., are the principal factors that have acted on the side of area. On the side of yield, the factors in the vanguard have comprised irrigation—which has played the key role, water has virtually led the way—measured by the percentage of GIA to GCA, the new agrarian technology, improved implements, improved knowledge and information, improved agricultural practices, reorientation of the cropping pattern, commercialisation and modernisation of agriculture here and there, extension services, price and non-price support by the Government—factors that have contributed to the efficiency of the work-force occupied in agriculture—and, on top, the provision of working capital and technical and marketing expertise. Let us substantiate this with statistics :

In the rise in productivity of agriculture recorded by the index number the part played by the rise in yield has been bigger than the part played by the rise in area. In Bihar the ratio of growth rate of yield to that of area is estimated at 2.0. During 1950-51 to 1965-66 area contributed 0.46, while yield 2.33 per cent per annum. During 1967-68 to 1977-78 their respective contributions were 0.69 and 1.86 per cent per annum. Growth rate of agriculture was faster during 1950-51 to 1965-66 than during 1967-68 to 1977-78 by 5 per cent. Contribution of yield was over 5 times that of area in the first period, and 2.7 times in the second period. Compound growth rate of agricultural productivity in the first period was 3.04 per cent per annum and 2.80 per cent per annum in the second period. In both periods the contribution of yield exceeded that of area.

The relative share of Bihar in total population of India was 10.7 per cent in 1951, 10.2 per cent in 1981 and 10.2 per cent again in 1991, which showed a degree of stability on the population front.

The percentage of owner cultivators to total working population engaged in Bihar agriculture is higher today, compared to what it was in

1951, as a result of land redistribution and tenancy reform measures implemented by the Government during the period, and this has had its incentive effect on agricultural productivity.

The will to work of the farmer, which is the core of the land problem, is greater now. He devotes long, arduous Jays to the cultivation of his field.

The agrarian structure underwent far-reaching changes in the wake of zamindari abolition. The Bihar Land Reforms Act, 1950 was put into force with effect from September 25, 1950. *Zamindari* abolition went in favour of the hardworking peasant càstes like the *Kurmis*, the *Koeris* and the Yadavas. 4.5 lakh *zamindars* were brought within the ambit of the law. Up to March 1992 surplus land distributed as percentage of surplus land accounted for 69.3 per cent.

In certain districts the *Bataidari* system provided a more stable source of employment to the landless than mere casual wage work. The *Batai* (lease)-holder enjoyed a higher social status than the mere landless labourer and he was really the pick of the class. The system introduced a selective and flexible principle in the agrarian system by which the landless families with a higher sense of responsibility and willingness for hard work might improve their economic and social status.

Irrigation and short-duration HYVs have accounted for an increased cropping intensity in Bihar from 123.6 in 1950-51 (the all-India average being 120) to 137.0 in 1986-87 (as against 125 in all-India).

The literacy rate increased from 12.2 per cent in 1951 to 38.5 per cent in 1991 in Bihar, a three-fold increase. The ratio of urban population to total population increased from 7.5 per cent in 1951 to 13.2 per cent in 1991 in Bihar, a 1.76 times increase, as against a 1.48 times increase in all-India from 17.3 to 25.7 per cent. In consequence, the general outlook of the agriculturists had changed for the better. In this the dissemination of knowledge by the newspapers, the radio and the television, each, had a part. The channels of information between the rural and urban sectors had advanced rapidly with improved means of transport and communications. In 1956 road mileage per one lakh population in Bihar was 64.38 kms. By 1981 it had risen to 119.23 kms. Total number of motor vehicles in 1956 in Bihar was 17.8 thousands; in 1981, it was 1887 thousand. Population served by one post office in Bihar in 1955-56 was 7312; in 1988, it was 6374. Bihar's share in total radios in the country in 1955-56 was 2.68 per cent; in January 1982, it was 3.90 per cent. Bihar's share in newspapers in 1949-95 was 1.4 per cent and in total circulation in 1989, 3.8 per cent. In total number of the

T.V. sets in 1989 Bihar's share was 4.2 per cent. All these were indications of improvement.

Experience shows that the small and marginal farmers who are in an overwhelming percentage in Bihar too are impelled by a desire for modernisation of agriculture. A modicum of ability on their part to adapt and meet their technological needs is no more in doubt. Most peasants now know that it is just as good to use the money to improve the land they have already as to use it to buy still more land.

The Government has taken considerable interest in meeting the country's food requirements by enabling agriculture through a variety of policies and measures to produce increasingly more. This has cost the Government a great deal. In Bihar every additional tonne of agricultural output raised at the end of the Seventh Plan carried over its head a hidden tag—an average Plan outlay of Rs. 4419, two-thirds in the public sector and one-third in the private sector. That is to say, for Re. 1 worth rise in agricultural output in Bihar Rs. 4.42 had to be spent by the two sectors in that ratio. The fact that agriculture in Bihar was mostly in the hands of the small and marginal farmers who lacked initiative, individually and collectively (with notable exceptions), the entry of the Government in agriculture in numerous ways was essential for its integrated growth in consonance with the prerequisites of the new agrarian technology. This is a theme which would call for much space. In this chapter we shall confine ourselves to general remarks.

The Intensified Agricultural Districts Production Programme, i.e., the Package Programme was initiated in the Shahabad district during the Third Plan. Under it technical help was provided. Inputs were supplied through cooperatives. Extensive service on an integrated basis was geared up for the purpose. Seeds multiplication farms were set up.

Large areas which suffered from repeated failures of rainfall have received irrigation. Irrigation-cum-drainage acted as the spearhead of the agricultural prosperity in most parts of the State. The Second Bihar Irrigation Commission estimated the present average yields of paddy and wheat on the irrigated lands at 22 and 17.72 quintals per ha. respectively. It imputed the overall average increase in the yield of paddy at 3.77 quintals per ha. and of wheat at 2.81 quintals per ha. on account of irrigation. GIA as percentage of GCA increased from 14.0 per cent in 1949-50 (all-India figure being 13.0 per cent) to 39.3 per cent in 1987-88 (all-India figure being 32.5 per cent). NIA as percentage of NSA increased from 19.0 per cent to 42.1 per cent during the same period, the corresponding all-India figures being 18 and 31.6 per cent.

In 1949-50 acreage under rice in Bihar was irrigated to the extent of 30.1 per cent (all-India 31.3 per cent), wheat 29.9 per cent (all-India 30.8 per cent) and foodgrains 9.6 per cent (all-India 18.5 per cent). In 1984-85 the percentages had risen to 34.6, 71.0 and 36.2 respectively, all-India figures being 42.9, 74.0 and 31.5 per cent respectively. Irrigation had imparted some amount of security to Bihar agriculture.

Bihar agriculture consumed in 1965, 1.5 per cent of total electricity consumed in the State; in 1986-87, the percentage had risen to 16.5 per cent. In 1985, 49.4 per cent of all villages in Bihar were electrified; in 1992, 70 per cent.

Consumption of fertilisers increased in Bihar agriculture consistently. In 1950-51 it was about 22800 tonnes; in 1989-90, 564 lakh tonnes. Per ha. fertilisers consumption in Bihar in 1950-51 was 18.5 kgs., in 1989-90, 54.1 kgs. (all-India average being around 60.9 kgs.). In 1976-77 Bihar's share in all-India fertilisers consumption was 4.6 per cent, in 1989-90, 6.6 per cent. Fertilisers application per ha. has been regarded as a surrogate for the extension of the new agrarian technology. Rice production has looked up as a result of increased fertilisers consumption. Fertilisers have proved fully effective only in the good rain or under condition of assured irrigation. Irrigation held the key.

Improved seeds, including the HYVs, were another agent to step up agricultural productivity in Bihar. In 1974-75, on an average, 2.20 million ha. were under the HYV foodgrains, in 1988-89, 5.99 million ha.

Modernisation of agriculture has been equated with tractorisation in the bulk of the literature on the subject. In 1956 Bihar's relative share in total number of tractors in the country was 5.8 per cent, in 1989-90, it was 5.1 per cent (registered ones only). In 1972 the number of tractors per 100 ha. of GCA was 0.5 in Bihar, in 1981, it was 1.7. Bihar's share in total number of energised pumpsets/tubewells was 2.83 in 1991.

The credit support to agriculturists by public financial institutions had gone up. In 1959-60 cooperative loan per ha. of GCA in Bihar was Re. 0.19. In 1985-86 the credit support to agriculture by all agencies in Bihar was Rs. 59.

What has prevented Bihar agriculture from optimising its productivity in spite of the strides made? This is the question which we shall now try to answer as far as possible. Diminution in area expansion, whenever it has taken place, has caused a slump in the growth of agricultural productivity in Bihar. This happened during 1971-72 to 1983-84, when the trend rate of growth of GCA was a minus figure—(–) 0.954 per cent per annum. Rate of growth of area during 1979-80 to 1985-86 was

(–) 1.07 in Bihar, as against the positive all-India figure of 0.14 per cent per annum.

The farmers' best efforts are neutralised by the natural calamities and a far lower output is the end-result. 4 to 5 per cent of Bihar's annual produce is thus lost, let alone the deterring effect the loss has on the morale of the farmers. Instability of agricultural production is partly the outcome of the 'acts of God'. The lack of proper control of flood and drought which was felt in 1951 is still there despite the measures taken in the last four decades. This is one glaring area where Nature avenges upon Man for his unbridled greed (Gandhiji said that "Nature was capable of meeting Man's need, but not his greed").

The ratio of SDP from agriculture to working population, that is, agricultural labour productivity in Bihar has declined over the years, from 0.72 in 1950-51/1955-56 to 0.70 in 1970-71 to 0.62 in 1980-81 to 0.56 in 1986-87. According to an estimate, during 1971-72 to 1983-84 the trend rate of growth of labour productivity in Bihar was a negative/minus 0.68 per cent per annum.

Fight for land is one factor which deserves consideration here. Absentee management of land has grown. Large landholders let their lands to tenants for rent rather than cultivate them by hiring agricultural workers. They obtain more this way, since the wages they would have to pay to the labourers are more than what is left to the tenants after the rents have been extracted from them. Secondly, the Minimum Wages Act in agriculture has reduced its remunerativeness and dispirited a large number of landholders. Thirdly, during the seasons in many areas scarcity of labour supply is experienced acutely. Farm labour has been migrating from low-growth pockets to high-growth pockets in the State and outside it. The volume of emigration has tended to correspond to the condition of the harvests. If the harvests have been good, it has fallen, and vice-versa. Fourthly, the growing assertiveness of the labouring class bordering on violence in an organised form has further aggravated the situation.

Increased recourse to chemical fertilisers and farm mechanisation are reflected in the decline in the relative shares of Bihar in livestock from 8.9 per cent in 1951 to 8.4 per cent in 1982 as well as in working cattle from 11.1 per cent to 7.9 per cent during the same period. These dents had mixed effects, not easily quantifiable.

In irrigation Bihar is a shade above the all-India average but even in this regard Bihar's failures are glaring. Not all of the created potential has been utilised. This underutilisation is a butt of universal criticism, though it is not without genuine reasons. A satisfactory distribution-cum-drainage system could not be developed so far. The adequacy, timeliness and equity of canal irrigation are in serious doubt. The public tubewells and lift irrigation schemes have not been functioning properly due to mechanical faults, erratic power supply, burnt transformers, etc. Irrigation management is weak-kneed.

The Government has failed to diversify the use of the developed, improved and certified seeds and HYVs, resulting in a low seed replacement rate. Delay in the establishment of seed multiplication farms, inadequate systematic multiplication of the improved seeds, the riskiness of substituting improved seeds for the prevalent ones, allegation of adulteration of the new seeds with the old, difficulties of storage and distribution of the new seeds, the bottleneck created by inadequate supply of institutional credit to the willing farmers, etc. account for the slow pace of adoption of this input in Bihar. In 1990-91 the HYVs claimed 35.6 per cent of the cultivated rice land and 74.5 per cent of the cultivated wheat land in Bihar.

In Bihar fertilisers consumption has not grown proportionately with available irrigation. Inadequate credit supply has been one of the major impediments to it. The prevalent terms of credit, both the rate of interest and the repayment procedures, have not taken into account the special types of risks borne by the fertilisers users. The period of the repayment of the loans is insinuated to be inflexible. Even when the harvest was poor, repayments were insisted upon by the credit agencies. Nearly one-third and one-fourth of their total chemical fertilisers requirement is available on credit to the medium and marginal farmers respectively. Fertilisers consumption per ha. in Bihar remains below the all-India average. Per capita fertilisers consumption in Bihar is about 50 per cent less than that of the rest of the country taken together. Bihar is discriminated against in the allotment of fertilisers. In 1984-85 it got less than one-third of even its allotted share. In 1993-94 its urea requirement was 8.43 lakh tonnes but the quantity actually supplied was 3.50 lakh tonnes. In Bihar fertilisers consumption is lower in kharif than in rabi crops, and more so in the flood-prone areas, because the farmers do not reap good returns in the absence of controlled irrigation. In 1981-82 fertilisers use was in the ratio of 1 : 3 as between kharif and rabi.

Marked irrationalities characterise the distribution of fertilisers supplies between areas and over different periods of time. Accumulation is partly ascribable to the inability of administration to arrange supply on time. In March 1990 Bihar's share in fertilisers sales points was 4.1

per cent of the total number (equal to 2,31,170) in the country, its consumption share being 4.7 per cent (total equal to 1,25,46,182 tonnes).

Although huge losses are caused by various types of pests, diseases and weeds, yet the consumption of chemicals is very low in Bihar. Compared to the position in 1976-77, when pesticides consumption was 0.96 kg. per ha. of all holdings, in 1987-88 it was 0.28 kg. per ha., which meant a dent in the level of consumption. Besides, there were complaints that pesticides were adulterated.

In view of the fact that the supply of rural power is inadequate and erratic and hence unreliable (the bulbs burn merely as dim red coils) the rural electrification schemes in Bihar are a big fraud on the villages. Many of them were executed on paper alone.

Credit support to Bihar agriculture by the financial institutions is far from adequate. In 1988-89 Bihar's share in cooperative credit was 4.5 per cent (aggregate amount being Rs. 4944.40 crores). In 1992-93 the commercial banks had advanced Rs. 15 crores only towards kharif, as against the target of Rs. 100 crores and Rs. 14 crores only towards rabi, as against the target of Rs. 100 crores.

As against the all-India figure of 59 per cent, in Bihar in 1987-88, 65 per cent of all villages were unconnected by all-weather roads. This hampered the efficiency of those engaged in agricultural marketing.

The extension services in Bihar are not in a position to meet the felt and emerging needs of the farming community. The vast differentials of soil, rainfall and climate revealed by the different zones of the State, on the one hand, and the paucity of funds at the disposal of the two agricultural universities in the State for research purposes, on the other, have combined to frustrate their efforts to evolve improved technologies having extensive application.

To conclude, the new agrarian technology has not taken a firm root in Bihar's agriculture.

Institutional reform has created more problems than it has solved in Bihar because of the attitudes of the politicians, bureaucrats and zamindars associated with the campaign. Bihar's record has been both poor and slow in all ramifications of the reform. The land ceiling law has been enforced tardily and so has been the distribution of the surplus lands. Semi-feudal production relations continue to plague parts of Bihar. Forty per cent of the rural farming households in the Bihar plains still rely on sharecropping and oral leases. This renders extremely difficult assignment of water rights, management of tubewells, obtaining of bank loan, embarking on land development, and so forth. The farmers concerned face insecure tenancy conditions.

The awakening for higher levels of living, for representation in the services and in the legislative and other bodies proportionate to the numerical strength of communities/tribes/castes/classes (in *Whither India*, published in 1933, Pandit Nehru had called the caste system as a petrified form of class division), etc. has turned into a violent movement in Bihar. As a result, the even and calm tenor/ethos of the rural economy has been upset and its readjustment would take time. Harvest looting and land grabbing started in Bihar several years ago in pockets of glaringly iniquitous land relations. The *bagees* (rebels) dream of establishing a power base of their own and are working towards this end.

The growth performance of the different regions and different districts in Bihar in terms of rate of growth of agricultural productivity during the period has been different. According to one study, during 1950-51 to 1980-81, agricultural productivity growth rate ranged between 0.03 (Saran) and 1.01 per cent per annum (Champaran) in North Bihar region between 1.17 (Patna) and 3.08 per cent per annum (Gaya) in South Bihar region, and between 1.2 (Dhanbad) and 4.2 per cent per annum (Palamau) in Chotanagpur and Santhal Parganas region. Those districts which laid emphasis on the combination of irrigation and fertilisers use attained a higher rate of growth of agricultural productivity in contrast to others which relied on irrigation alone.

Another study covers the same period (1950-51 to 1980-81) but arrives at different estimates. Districts where agriculture grew at rates from 1.3 to 3.86 per cent per annum were Patna, Gaya, Shahabad, Muzaffarpur, Darbhanga, Monghyr, Bhagalpur, Purnea, Santhal Parganas, Hazaribagh, Ranchi and Singhbhum. The second group of districts, viz., Saharsa, Saran, Palamau and Champaran revealed 4.21 to 5.75 per cent per annum growth rates of their agriculture. Dhanbad was the isolated case of a district with a negative growth rate of its agriculture, minus 5.2 per cent per annum. Of the four high growth districts, Champaran and Saran were benefited by growth of GCA and Saharsa and Palamau by both area and yield. The remaining thirteen districts were low-growth. Of them, while yield was crucial in the case of Dhanbad, both area and yield were critical to Darbhanga, Ranchi and Singhbhum. In the remaining districts yield variations constituted the explanation.

A third study, which has a shorter period, i.e., 1950-51 to 1977-78, as its time-frame, has reached conclusions that are identical with the above.

A fourth study, which is also for a shorter period, that is, 1952-53 to 1961-62, deduces that districts showing higher rates of agricultural growth were, by and large, districts showing higher rates of growth of yield.

A fifth study for the period 1962-65 (average) to 1970-73 (average) and for fifteen districts has no district in the category of high growth, which implies above 4.5 per cent per annum growth rate. Five districts fall into the moderate growth category 1.5 to 4.5 per cent per annum, three districts in the low growth category below 1.5 per cent per annum growth rate, and seven districts in the negative growth category 0.0 per cent per annum growth rate.

Finally, the RBI Sen Committee 1984 report brought out that during 1980-82 (average) about nine districts in Bihar operated under low productivity (value of output per ha. being Rs. 1150), about six under medium productivity (Rs. 1150 to Rs. 1650 value of output per ha.) and the remaining two under high productivity (Rs. 1650 or more value of output per ha.). Five districts experienced negative growth rates, eight low growth rates (0.0 to 1.5), four medium growth rates (1.5 to 3.0) and none high growth rates (above 3 per cent per annum). Nearly three-quarters of the cultivated area of Bihar was operated under conditions of negative and very low growth rates. Gaya, Patna, Monghyr, Shahabad, Bhagalpur and Saran registered poor growth rates.

Planning for a faster rate of growth of agriculture under conditions obtaining in Bihar would necessitate a proficient management of the shocks, endogenous and exogenous, which the sector faces, by a dexterous dovetailing of the data, known as well as unknown, at a time and over a period of time.

9

AGRICULTURAL INCOME IN BIHAR

Agricultural income is agricultural production multiplied by prices of the various agricultural products. In Bihar between 1953 and 1993-94 agricultural income at current prices increased from Rs. 408/549 (average Rs. 478) crores to Rs. 14601.54 crores, that is, 30.5 times (Table 9.1). At 1960-61 prices it rose from Rs. 428.15 crores in 1960-61 to Rs. 1638.04 crores in 1985-86, that is, 3.82 times. At 1970-71 prices the increase was 7.35 times from Rs. 238.44 crores in 1949-50 to Rs. 1753.84 crores in 1988-89. At 1980-81 prices the rise was 1.5-fold between 1980-83 and 1993-94 from Rs. 2843 crores to Rs. 4280.34 crores.

In Chapter 7, Table 7.2, we have shown how between 1950-51 and 1983-86 net value per agricultural worker/agriculturist increased from Rs. 118.90 to Rs. 818, that is, by 688 per cent in Bihar, as against 1001 per cent in all-India from Rs. 104 to Rs. 1041 during the same period. Gross income per rural worker (including some income from non-agricultural sources) increased by 309 per cent, from Rs. 302 to Rs. 933 between 1958-59 and 1987-90 in Bihar, as compared to 278 per cent in all-India from Rs. 477 to Rs. 1325 during the same period. Per capita gross income from agricultural sources to a rural inhabitant rose from Rs. 68.90 in 1951 to Rs. 948 in 1987-90 in Bihar, as against from about Rs. 80 to Rs. 1522 in all-India during the same period. The increase was by 1376 per cent in Bihar, while in all-India it was by 1902 per cent. Lastly, per capita gross income from agriculture was Rs. 156 in 1955-56 in Bihar and Rs. 268 in all-India. In 1985-86 the corresponding figures were Rs. 809 and Rs. 1449. The increase amounted to 518 per cent in Bihar and 540 per cent in all-India. All in all, the increase, on an average in the four cases cited, was to the extent of 723 per cent in Bihar and 930 per cent in all-India during 1950-90. The average agriculturist in Bihar was definitely worse off than his all-India counterpart.

Table 9.1 brings out that during 1950-51 to 1989-90 Bihar's agricultural income as a proportion to all-India's agricultural income hovered around 7.6 per cent, showing a small decrease from 7.8 to 7.4 per cent. Agricultural income was unsteady. It fluctuated. The range of fluctuation was wide. It was the lowest 4.8 per cent of all-India total in 1973-74 and the highest 8.4 per cent twice—first in 1965 and next in 1984-85.

TABLE 9.1 : Growth of Agricultural Income in Bihar

(Rs. crores)

Year	*At Current Prices*	*At 1960-61 Prices*	*At 1970-71 Prices*	*At 1980-81 Prices*	*Bihar's Agri. Income as Percentage of all-India Agri. Income*
(1)	(2)	(3)	(4)	(5)	(6)
1946-47					8.7
1949-50				238.44	
1950-51	(4590)				
1951				387.89	7.8
1953	408/549				8.0
Av. value of output during 1960s	3933.22				6.95
1960-61	(6314)	428.15			7.2
1962-65 (Av.)	3933.22				6.95
1965-66	488.52 (9551)/ 761.18	433.78			8.4
1970-73 (Av.)	4299.29				6.45
1970-71	1132/1265.16 (16190)	535.04		1132/1265.16	6.7
1970-71 to 1979-80					7.6
1971-72				1304.08	7.7
1972-73				1265.20	
1973-74				1199.00	4.8
1974-75				1250.48	8.3
1975-76	2136.92 (25404)			1325.68	
1976-77				1347.25	
1977-78				1435.69	
1978-79				1426.85	
1979-80				1187.95	7.6
1980-81	3048.83 (39875.05)				
1980-81 to 1986-87 (Av.)	30791.63 (400.56)			1411.33/ 1418	7.4
1980-83 (Av.)		2843 (44060)			6.4

(*Contd.*)

TABLE 9.1 (*Contd.*)

(1)	(2)	(3)	(4)	(5)	(6)
1980-85 (Av.)					
1981-82	(44971)				
1982-83	(47476)				
1983-84	(57729)				
1984-85	4858.51 (61210)			4931.87	8.0
1985-86	7113 (94807)	1638.04		65348	
1984-87 (Av.)					8.0
1985-89 (Av.)					8.4
1986-87					6.2
1987-88	6557.85			1591.68	
1987-90 (Av.)			3292 (52237)		
1988-89	8158.60		1753.84	37862	8.1
1989-93 (Av.)	4127.59				4.89
1989-90					7.4
1991-92	(152907)				
1992-93 (Prov.)	12337.87 (173913)			3230.02	
1993-94 (Quick)	14601.54			4280.34	

In concrete, physical terms foodgrains production increased by 276 per cent in Bihar and by 346 per cent in all-India. On the other hand, agricultural income in Bihar increased by 30.5 times at current prices during an approximate period. When these two facts are juxtaposed, we find an eleven-fold rise in prices of agricultural products. In Table 9.2, we have prepared, giving the index number of primary products during 1950-95, indicates a 12.34 times rise in the prices of primary products. In so far as prices of agricultural products move up or down slightly less than those of other primary products, e.g., forestry, fishery, animal husbandry, etc. our findings are not unrealistic and hence not untenable.

During 1950-51 to 1991-92 net SDP in Bihar increased 4.12 times from Rs. 1165.80 crores to Rs. 4801.26 crores. At current prices agricultural income in the State was estimated at Rs. 387.89 crores in 1950-51. At constant (1970-71) prices it was Rs. 1265.16 crores in 1970-71.

Between 1960-61 and 1970-71, with 1960-61 as base, agricultural income increased by 127.21 percentage points at current prices and 124.97 percentage points at 1960-61 prices. Between 1970-71 and

1975-76 at current prices agricultural income rose by 59.55 percentage points, base being 1970-71, and at 1960-61 prices, the base becoming 1970-71, by 4.78 per cent and at current prices by 59.55 per cent, between 1970-71 and 1975-76. Net value added in agriculture of Bihar rose by 24 per cent at 1980-81 prices during 1980-81 to 1988-89, that is, from Rs. 3048.8 crores to Rs. 3786.2 crores.

TABLE 9.2 : Index Number of Primary Products

(Base 1950-51 = 100)

Year	*Percentage Points*
1950-51	100
1955-56	80.1
1960-61	112.5
1965-66	128.8
1970-71	183.0
1971-72	184.6
1975-76	303.3
1980-81	434.6
1981-82	460.8
1982-83	463.0
1985-86	549.5
1990-91	806.8
1994-95	1234.1

Note : This is a running index number, based on reducing of the index numbers based on 1970-71 and 1981-82 prices to 1950-51 prices base.

At 1970-71 prices agricultural income increased 4.52 times in Bihar between 1951 (Rs. 387.89 crores) and 1988-89 (Rs. 1753.84 crores). Between 1950-51 and 1990-91 the increase in Bihar's agricultural income was by 276 per cent at current prices.

As Table 9.3 would show, agricultural income, as percentage of primary sector income, kept on increasing, from 56.34 per cent in 1951 to 86 per cent in 1993-94, and from 90 per cent in 1970-71 to 84 per cent in 1988-89, in both cases at current prices. At current prices this percentage was stationary at around 89 per cent during 1965-66 to 1976-77. At 1970-71 prices too the position was more or less the same, static for over a decade, except for a couple of years, namely, 1977-78 and 1978-79. During 1970-71 to 1988-89 the percentage share of agriculture was highest in 1971-72, 90.01 per cent and lowest, 79 per cent in 1985-86. The range of variation was 11 per cent.

Agricultural income as a proportion of Bihar's State Domestic Product (SDP) was 62.76 per cent in 1951 and 42.48 per cent in

1993-94, a divergency of over 20 per cent if calculated at current prices. Calculated at 1970-71 prices, the relative share of agriculture was of the order of about 32 per cent between 1950-51 to 1991-92, from 64.30 to 32.92 per cent. The decline of Bihar's agricultural income in the SDP, at 1970-71 prices, was continuous, from 1955-56 to 1974-75 the percentage share was concentrated in 50s, from 1975-76 to 1988-89 in 40s, and from 1989-90 to the present day in 30s. During the 1980s agriculture's share was about 44 to 45 per cent.

TABLE 9.3 : Agricultural Income in Bihar during the Plan Period in relation to the State's Primary Sector Income and SDP

Year	*Agricultural Income as Percentage of Primary Sector Income (PSI)*			*Agricultural Income as Percentage of SDP*		
	At Current Prices	*At 1970-71 Prices*	*At 1980-81 Prices*	*At Current Prices*	*At 1970-71 Prices*	*At 1980-81 Prices*
(1)	(2A)	(2B)	(2C)	(3A)	(3B)	(3C)
1950-51				(53.8)	64.30	(50.4)
1951	56.34			62.76		
1955-56				58.76/58.0		
1960-61	80.49			43.11/43.3	56.6	(47.4)
				56.1 (44.4)		
1965-66	88.74			52.61	53.37	
1970-71	89.76	80.31/89.76		44.00/47.78/	56.34/56.30	41.5
1970-71 to 1979-80				58.00/56.35/ 53.8/55.8	50.41/62.80	
1970-71 to 1970-73 (Av.)				57.3 (46.4)		
1971-72		90.01		51.90	56.47	
1970-71 to 1972-73				57.3		
1972-73		89.35			55.01	
1973-74		88.60			53.04	
1974-75		88.96/84.35		58.63	52.61	
1975-76	87.93	87.93		53.32		
1976-77	89.39			53.18		
1977-78		50.00		90.75		
1978-79		50.00		90.10		
1979-80		88.17			43.00/44.80	
1979-80 to 1981-82				44.5		
1980-81	85.61	88.98		40.37/41.02/ 43.30/47.0 49.6/36.3	47.98/45.78	(36.3)

(Contd.)

TABLE 9.3 (*Contd.*)

(1)	(2A)	(2B)	(2C)	(3A)	(3B)	(3C)
1980-83						
1980-81 to 1986-87				44.71		44.77
1981-82				134.9		(36.4)
1984-87 (Av.)					45.3 (34.5)	
1985-86	79.49	89.14		41.34	43.58	
1985-86 to 1989-90				43.0 (32.0)		
1986-87				44.6		
1986-89 (Av.)				44.4 (30.5)		
1987-88	82.04	87.26	42.82	41.92		
1988-89	83.66	88.17	43.54/50.46	42.03/43.62	39.75	
1989-90					36.76	
1991-92 (Av.)				(31.3)	32.92	(29.4)
1992-93	85.59		79.35	42.05/(31.3)		33.09 (29.9)
1993-94	86.04		82.95	42.48/(29.7)		37.87 (29.4)

As percentage of the SDP, the primary sector income in Bihar dwindled from 61.54 per cent (average) in 1955-56 to 43.81 per cent (average) in 1989-90, a fall by nearly 17 to 16 per cent. By comparison, during the same period, the fall in respect of all-India was slightly higher, by about 18.5 per cent, from 54.5 to 33.6 per cent. During the same period, the share of Bihar's agricultural income in its SDP declined from 58.8 per cent, a bit above the all-India average of 58.3 per cent, to 36.7 per cent in 1989-90, the all-India figure being nearly 29.3 per cent, a difference of over 7 per cent (Table 9.4). Whereas the overall decline in agriculture's share was by about 20 per cent in the case of Bihar, in the case of all-India it was by nearly 29 per cent. During 1980-81 to 1989-90 the share of the primary sector in SDP in Bihar suffered a dent by about 22 per cent (52.63 *versus* 30.16 per cent); in all-India by nearly 13 per cent (44.35 *versus* 30.16 per cent).

TABLE 9.4 : Relative Shares of Primary Sector and Agriculture in SDP in Bihar

(Percentage)

Year	*Share of Primary Sector in SDP*	*Share of Agriculture* in SDP*
(1)	(2)	(3)
1955-56	64.3/58.78 (54.5)	58.8 (58.3)
1960-61	56.6 (52.1)	49.77

(*Contd.*)

TABLE 9.4 (*Contd.*)

(1)	(2)	(3)
1968-69	57.7	
1970-71	53.8/55.8/58.0/ 56.35/62.76/62.80 (44.67/49.5/48.2)	(45.9)56.30 (46.7)
1970-71 to 1972-73	57.3	
1970-73	57.5 (42.3)	57.3 (46.4)
1970-71 to 1979-80	51.90	
1974-75	58.63	
1975-76	59.50	
1979-80	43.90	43.00
1980-81	51.22/54.27/ 54.42/55.10 (41.6/47.1)	47.60/49.60 (36.3)
1980-81 to 1986-87	44.71	
1984-87	45.3 (34.5)	
1985-86 to 1988-89	43.0 (32.0)	
1986-89	44.0 (30.5)	
1986-87	44.6	
1987-90	42.7 (30.4)	39.20 (29.4)
1988-89	49.6/45.35 (34.39)	43.62 (48 per cent of NSDP at current prices)
1989-90	41.64/44.26/45.53 (33.60)	36.76 (29.3)
1990-91	—	36.4 (31.0)
1991-92	40.84	32.92 (30.2)

* Based on averages of the figures given in Table 9.3.

The reliability of the data being limited, what we write here on the rate of growth is to be accepted by the reader after due discount. From 1950-51 to 1966-67 (the pre-Green Revolution period) the rate of growth of agricultural income in Bihar was 3.04 per cent per annum. During 1969-70 to 1983-84 it was 0.5/-0.6 per cent per year. Between 1984-85 and 1989-90 it was 3.5 per cent per annum. Decade-wise the rates were: 1950s, 3.40 (all-India 3.23), 1960s, 0.54/0.9/(–) 1.18 per cent (all-India 1.95), 1970s, 0.72 (all-India 1.81) and 1990s, 3.15/3.97 (all-India 1.81). Here the reference is to Table 9.5.

Table 9.5 bears out that primary sector income is essentially influenced by agriculture and SDP is similarly influenced by primary sector income, which is practically agricultural income in sum and substance in most parts of the country.

TABLE 9.5 : Rate of Growth of SDP, Primary Sector Income and Agricultural Income in Bihar*

(Per cent per annum)

Year	*SDP*	*Primary Sector Income*	*Agricultural Income*
(1)	(2)	(3)	(4)
1950-70			0.7 (3.1)
1950-82	3.31 (3.51)		
1950-87	3.31 (2.51)		
1950-91	1.15 (1.9)		4.49
1950-51/1959-60			3.40
1950-51/1960-61	3.95/5.50 (3.30)		
1950-51/1965-66			3.04
1950-51/1976-77			2.22
1950-51/1977-78	2.54 (3.32)		
1950-51/1987-88	6.29		
1960-51/1988-89	3.30 (3.50)		
1951-52/1955-56	3.06 (3.60)		
1951-81	3.40/3.14 (3.31)	2.08/2.83/2.04 (net) (2.32)	0.9 (1.9)
1952-53/1954-55			3.40 (3.23)
1952-53/1960-61			3.40 (3.23)
1952-53/1961-62			3.40
1952-53/1964-65			2.97 (3.01)
1952-79			1.13/1.67 (1.72)
1953-54/1963-64			2.59
1955-56/1960-61	6.33/7.6	7.83/9.4	
1956-57/1960-61	5.92 (4.00)		
1960-70			0.9 (1.9)
1960-87			1.4 (2.3)
1960-61/1970-71	6.8/2.42/0.68 (3.17/7.5)		0.82 (net)
1960-61/1976-77	0.68/2.20 (3.17/3.70)		
1960-81			1.4 (2.3)
1960-61/1970-71	6.8		
1960-61/1977-78	2.50 (3.48)		
1960-61/1980-81			1.38
1960-61/1984-85	0.33 (1.31)		
1961-70	0.68	(–) 1.12	(–) 1.18
1961-87	2.50 (3.48)		1.4
1961-62/1966-67	2.40 (2.20)		
1962-65/1971-73			0.54 (1.95)
1962-65/1971-74			1.67

(Contd.)

TABLE 9.5 (*Contd.*)

(1)	(2)	(3)	(4)
1963-64/1977-78			1.66
1966-69			0.03
1967-68/1977-78			2.80
1969-70/1973-74	2.61 (3.40)		
1969-70/1983-84			0.5/0.6 (3.0 value added)
1970s			0.72 (1.81)
1970-80	3.00	0.96	0.80
1970-86		1.8 (1.8)	
1970-87			2.06/2.35
1970-71/1975-76			2.09/4.78
1970-71/1977-78	2.11/2.99 (3.50/3.32)		2.11
1970-71/1979-80			0.72/1.25 (1.81)
1970-71/1980-81	2.20/3.1/3.51/3.70 5.4/(3.70/4.5)		1.1 (value added)
1970-71/1981-82	3.11 (3.48)		
1970-71/1983-84			2.31
1970-71/1986-87			1.54 (2.01)
1971-80	2.75/3.00	0.72/0.96	0.67/0.80 (2.35)
1971-90			0.67
1971-72/1983-84			0.40 (3.92)
1972-73/1989-92			1.33 (C) Kharif 158 (Ditto) Rabi
1974-75/1978-79	4.8/4.97/(5.8)		3.09
1975-82			0.16
1975-76/1980-81	3.75		1.05/2.07
1976-87			1.05/2.3 (2.7)
1978-79/1988-89	4.66		
1980s			3.15/3.97 (1.81)
1980-82		1.40	
1980-85	4.05 (3.57)		
1980-88			2.13/2.25
1980-89		2.72	2.35
1980-90	2.3/4.85		0.6 (2.21)
1980-91			2.34
1980-92		0.76/1.40	
1980-94	4.53	3.02	2.70
1980-81/1983-84			3.95
1980-81/1984-85	6.4		
1980-81/1985-86	4.1 (5.0)		3.3 (value added)
1980-81/1986-87	3.52		3.97 (−1.81)
1980-81/1988-89	3.90		3.6
1980-81/1989-90	12.3 (11.3)		3.5
1980-81/1990-91	5.38 (5.36)		4.49

(*Contd.*)

TABLE 9.5 (*Contd.*)

(1)	(2)	(3)	(4)
1981-82/1986-87	4.26		
1981-89		4.54	
1984-85/1989-90			3.5
1985-86/1989-90	5.60		
1985-89	4.39		3.26
1985-90	2.8		2.60 (3.10)
1987-88/1988-89			2.72
1987-88/1991-92	1.9/3.1 (5.2/5.4)		
1990-91	23.9 (5.1)		21.8 (5.0)
1991-92	(-) 1.9 (0.7)		(-) 11.4 (- 2.0)

Note : * We have assembled and tabulated all available data, of which some are linear rates, others compound, estimated at current or constant prices (1960-61, or 1970-71 or 1980-81). The lower rates are compound.

C = Compound.

In India primary sector income increased by 2.88 times during 1950-51 to 1990-91 at 1980-81 prices from Rs. 24204 crores to Rs. 69860 crores, while national income rose by 4.95 times during the same period, from Rs. 42871 crores to Rs. 212276 crores. At current prices the increase in national income was 53.21 times. In the case of Bihar between 1953 and 1990-91 the increase was, at current prices, 26.69 times (Rs. 8979 crores *versus* Rs. 477814 crores in the case of India and Rs. 850 crores *versus* Rs. 22691 crores in Bihar). At any rate the increase in Bihar's primary sector during the period must have been far less than that in all-India.

Data available for shorter periods show that between 1960-61 and 1970-71 (with 1960-61 as base) in Bihar primary sector income rose by 128.31 percentage points at current prices and by 125.57 percentage points at 1960-61 prices. Between 1970-71 and 1975-76 the rise at current prices was to the extent of 70.87 per cent, and at 1960-61 prices 66.96 per cent, the base year being 1970-71 in either case.

During 1970-71 to 1980-81 the compound annual rate of growth of net SDP in Bihar was 3.12 per cent per annum, which fell short of the national average of 3.21 per cent per annum. For the period 1981-82 to 1991-92 the rate was 4.21 per cent per year in Bihar, which lagged behind the national average rate of 5.09 per cent per year.

The scenario of agricultural development in Bihar has been at once changing and mixed. A redeeming feature of this has been that the bulk of increased production has come primarily from improvement in productivity, though for most periods it has been below the national average. Where small and marginal farmers have been helped avowedly and consistently agriculture has progressed unquestionably and rural income has escalated. In Bihar in 1951 those with land upto 5 acres had less than adequate food intake. The same people since the mid-1960s have lived a comfortable existence. Increased agricultural productivity has been a gain in the wake of the new agrarian technology, which has been heralded by the management of water resources and watershed as well as conservation of water and soil. Improved agricultural implements and equipment, plant protection, fertilisers, insecticides and pesticides, improved seeds and extension services have, each and all of them, contributed their shares towards this. More output and stabler output being the outcome, a new era has gradually unfolded itself, marked by robust optimism in landowning sections and other sections of the agrarian community, even if without land, closely connected with the former sections.

But for the majority of the tillers in Bihar Nature has been unusually benevolent in the last few years in a row. We mean the monsoon which has been favourable in the last six years in most parts of the State successively. The years that have borne the scare of the vagaries of Nature have been 1962-63, 1965-66, 1966-67 (worsoever), 1969-70, 1973-74, 1979-80, 1981-82, 1982-83, 1987-88, 1991-92 and 1992-93, though they have been faced valiantly. Numerous families have suffered because of them but numerous other families have not, for except for a few, the calamities have not been State-wide.

Rural prosperity caused by increased agricultural productivity has reaped a by-product of the same causative factor, namely, enhanced intensity of agricultural employment.

In Bihar government effort has been focussed on the attainment of self-sufficiency in food from the very outset of planning. In recent years execution of the crop production-oriented programmes has paid rich dividends. Increasing population, increasing purchasing power and high income elasticity of demand for food have stimulated the growth of demand and hence widening of the market.

Scale-neutrality of the new agrarian technology has been an inducement to its increased employment. Improved agricultural marketing conditions, e.g., better roads, better communications, extension of storage and warehousing facilities, artificially reduced costs of inputs and related goods lumped with their improved delivery, which has acted as a great incentive, added emphasis on cooperative and other types of institutional credit, more attention to agricultural research and education, and the like have arrested costs from rising and encouraged the use of venture capital.

The market mechanism was interfered with by the planners in an area that held the key to agrarian production. Although this was largely a Central subject, the State Government had the freedom to make further concessions in response to regional pressures. The regime of a sound agricultural price policy allowed a reasonable return to the peasantry by not allowing the prices to fall below a reasonable minimum. The incentive prices were either support prices or procurement prices. In a food deficit State like Bihar wholesale prices of wheat and rice and their farm prices have generally remained somewhat above their procurement prices.

Altogether terms of trade have not unnecessarily embarrassed the agriculturists, who have uniquely cashed in on the price and non-price incentives devised by the Government, their exemption from income tax, and non-governmental initiatives.

Above all, agricultural development has been sustained. The downs have been amply moderated by the ups and the agricultural production/income graph has revealed a secular upward trend. The rate has not been as high as in some other States but certainly it has surpassed quite a number of States in this regard. As a signal of alarm has appeared imminent on account of persistent stagnation or even a retrogression, abruptly a revival has started off, snowballing into an advance not to be underestimated. Several factors have combined and the spectrum which has emerged has been too intricate to yield to over-simplification. The net result so far has been this that not only rural society has prospered but also rural inequalities have been less pronounced than urban.

The foregoing account presented by taking into account the bewildering variety of estimates is beset with a glaring gap in the sense that no reference has so far been made to the inter-regional and intra-regional dimensions, which when made would in all logic qualify the conclusions arrived at, though tangentially. First we have the increased degree of inter-regional inequality in agricultural growth in the years subsequent to the advent of the Green Revolution as compared to the years precedent to it. This deepening dichotomy in development of one and the same economy is a matter of grave concern.

The other qualification with which our generalisation has to be hedged is the intra-State disparities in growth. In Bihar twenty-six districts fall in the middle Gangetic plains and have almost 78 per cent of the State's total population concentrated in them, with the result that they have lower levels of development. Twelve districts are in the eastern plateau and hill region and manifest a great deal of imbalances in their levels of development. Dhanbad is highly developed. Palamau and Santhal Parganas are very backward. In the mining and industrial areas agriculture and land use have declined owing to a multiplicity of reasons.

At the end of the present chapter it is incumbent upon us to allude to the diversification of the economy and the structural transformation of the economy which have taken place during the last four decades and a half. Ordinarily, the economy is looked at in any one of the two ways: Either as composed of the goods-producing and the services sectors or as comprising three sectors—the primary, the secondary and the tertiary. The diversification of the economy follows the ever-expanding spectrum or structure of human wants but, with passage of time, tastes or preferences of the people undergo changes, mild or sharp and the structure of wants alters in its composition, with the exit of some extinct wants and the entry of some new, novel wants. A variety of factors lie at the root of these changes. The structural transformation of the economy is concerned with the relative sharing of the three sectors in total produce and total employment of the total economy. But this is not an invariate.

It is needless to state here that development is invariably accompanied by a structural change in the economy such that the share of the primary sector in aggregate product is reduced *vis-a-vis* the shares of the secondary and tertiary sectors. At the same time, the percentage of the work-force occupied in the primary sector becomes lower and its percentages in the other two sectors become increased, in consequence of transfer of manpower from the former to the latter.

Applying this theory to the Bihar case, we discover that the sectoral composition of its SDP does express what is happening on its structural front. But the tragic part of this is that it is only a half-hearted change. This is explained largely by the sluggish pace of agricultural growth in the State, which, in turn, is due to an insufficient step-up in productivity in agriculture. Modernisation has affected agriculture in a limited measure. This has kept the structural shift at a low level. The new agrarian technology has been adopted in a diffused and fragmented manner and in most places not in the package as a whole but in terms of its individual components. The total impact is therefore much less than the ideal. The manpower allocative effect has been frustrating because of the unsuccess on the agricultural productivity front. The secondary sector has not expanded itself to the extent and at a rate to provide employment to all those who are able and willing to work. As a result, the incidence of unemployment has fallen on either the primary or the tertiary sector, the percentage of sharing turning on the principle 'what the traffic will bear'. In so far as economic development has not made a satisfactory headway in Bihar, the tertiary/services sector per head of the population is far from being adequate, let alone its quality and efficiency. In a nutshell, the structural change has revealed itself to an extent in the primary sector diversification in both secondary and tertiary sectors. A complex of demographic and growth factors specific to Bihar has retarded the structural change of its economy in its dual sense—decline in the relative share of the primary sector in terms of SDP as well as total employment provided (in the latter sense it is not perceptible in Bihar). The preponderance of agriculture in the primary sector income epitomises the absence of diversification in it and furnishes a sad comment on the succour and support which activities allied to agriculture afford by way of income and employment to a sizable chunk of population connected directly or indirectly with agriculture in Bihar. Let it be noted that diversification is an index/a measure of the level/ stage of progress made.

10

ACTIVITIES ALLIED TO AGRICULTURE IN BIHAR+

As Table 10.1 indicates, over the years in Bihar the relative shares in primary sector income of agriculture, animal husbandry and fishery have declined, whereas the relative share of forestry and logging in it has moved up. During 1951 to 1991 the percentage of working population occupied in activities allied to agriculture in the State fell from about 3.9 per cent to nearly 0.3 per cent. There were 15.12 lakh people engaged in activities allied to agriculture in Bihar in 1951; in 1991 the number was 2.58 lakhs. In other words, the total employment in activities allied to agriculture had fallen by some 83 per cent during the period in question.

TABLE 10.1 : Subsectoral Composition of Primary Sector Net Income in Bihar

(Percentage)

Year	*Agriculture*	*Forestry and Logging*	*Animal Husbandry*	*Fishery*
1946-47	67.26	1.04	13.3	1.64
1960-61	43.30	0.50	12.3	0.50
1970-71	56.30	1.00	—	0.70
1975-76	49.70	1.58	—	1.06
1980-81	47.60	2.40	—	1.00
1985-86	41.34	1.15	—	1.30
1991-92	32.92	2.23	7.28*	1.30

* Our estimate.

Note : According to a study (*The Bihar Journal of Agricultural Marketing*, Vol. V, No. 1), proportion of livestock income to agricultural income of Bihar was 22.85 in 1980-81 and 34.58 per cent in 1992-93.

+ Forestry, one activity allied to agriculture, in Bihar is discussed in Chapter 3.

Animal Husbandry

Animal husbandry in Bihar is a leading subsector of the primary sector of the State.* It plays a significant part in the rural economy. It is an integral part, a bulwork, of the agriculture-dominated rural economy. It is firmly interwoven with the socio-economic matrix of the rural folk. The cattle are pivotal to agriculture in Bihar. Let us substantiate this :

Animal husbandry provides gainful, economically profitable farm self-employment, particularly to women and growing children in rural families, especially in those of the small and marginal farmers, agricultural labourers, chiefly the landless, who are accustomed to sheep, goat and pig-rearing, for it is these classes which dominate the agrarian economy of Bihar. Cattle rearing and tending is done on *Batai* basis. In some areas claves are reared for being sold as bullocks at the appropriate age. Arable animal farming is pursued as investment to enhance income incidentally and boost/buttress creditworthiness.

Animal husbandry is socially useful as it provides a variety of animal products consumed as food—milk, milk products such as ghee, curd/yogurt, butter, cheese, eggs, meat, wool, by-products of the slaughter-houses such as hides and skins, bones, hooves, horns, etc., which are used in food processing, leather, box, button, etc. making industries. These articles improve the nutritional standard of the food taken by practically all sections of the people and balance their diet. Even the poor who rear and tend the cattle/livestock partake of the products, which makes up the deficiencies of their food intake. The demand for livestock products is continuously rising consequent upon increasing urbanisation and rising income levels in the State, with the old and new industries closely linked with the process, though indirectly through their demand for raw materials. The city people want a change in the meat they eat and this is a fillip to the growth of poultry and fowl-raising in the countryside.

In the context of Bihar's food deficit and hence reliance on external sources for meeting that deficit, animal husbandry acquired a special significance not only because it brought in nutrition but also because certain varieties of cheap meat admirably substituted the staple cereals in the case of the lower strata of the people, society-wise as well as income-wise (game forming a sizeable part).

---

* In SDP computation animal husbandry is incorporated in agriculture and mining and quarrying are a component of the primary sector. The evident gaps in the data are on account of this method of computation.

The social usefulness of animal husbandry was the State's lot in a stupendous manner where the cattle provided drought/motive power and where the pack animals contributed richly to commerce and transport. The village oil industry based on the *Kolhu*, the gur-making industry, lift irrigation, water-drawing from the wells, are numerous examples of what inestimable service the animal kingdom renders to the human kingdom. The bullock-cart is still the backbone of rural transport.

Another valuable function of enormous social utility discharged by animal husbandry is the provision of bulk of energy and heat used in rural areas. Use of cattle dung for generating bio-gas (let us not forget that use of dung cakes as fuel for cooking food is not only a characteristic of rural life but also of urban, for those who inhabit the *Khatals, Raen Baseras*, etc., and pass their nights in the hovels, can think of no other substitute of cooking fuel than the dung cakes, which are within the reach of their petty earnings , as also quick in action) has ushered in an era not only of an amenity of life but also of its quality/tone.

Organic manure/compost, a product of animal husbandry, is productivity-augmenting. Combined with the chemical fertilisers in proper proportions it works wonders. It is also an adjunct of the recycling process which is a compound of Man-and-Nature conjunction/combine in agricultural production.

This brings us, in passing, to the Land-Man-Animal-Plant nexus but here we would limit ourselves to the delineation of the ramifications of the interaction between the two kingdoms, namely, the human and the animal.

Livestock

Livestock comprises cattle (which, in turn, comprises, in the main, cows, buffaloes—male and female and oxen), sheep, goats, pigs, horses and ponies, camels, and other livestock. As Table 10.2 shows, between 1951 and 1987 the livestock population increased by about 164 per cent in Bihar (from 264.5 lakhs to 434.49 lakhs) and by about 166 per cent in all-India (from 2684 lakhs to 4453 lakhs). Bihar's percentage share in all-India livestock number which was 9.85 per cent at the beginning of this period came down to 9.75 per cent at its end. This has to be viewed against Bihar's share in the total land area of the country, which has remained fixed at 5.29 per cent as well as its share in the decennial population of India, which continues to be above 10 but under 11 per cent.

Table 10.2 is a testimony to the fact that the pressure of livestock, like that of the human resource, has increased on the soil/land resource,

TABLE 10.2 : Livestock in Bihar

Characteristics	*1951*	*1956*	*1961*	*1966*	*1972*	*1977*	*1981-82*	*1982*	*1987*	*1989-90*
Number (in lakhs)	264.5 (2684.0)	259.58 (3670.83)	306.1/ 305.8 (3364.3)	286.55	279.4	317.57 (3695.40)		358.1	434.49 (4452.88)	
Percentage share in All-India	9.85	8.45	9.10	8.32	7.87	8.50		8.53	9.75	
Rank/Place in All-India	3rd	6th	5th					5th	4th	
Per eapita of Population	0.68		0.66		0.48			0.49	0.53	
Per ha. of NSA	3.09		3.80		3.33	3.80		4.51	5.70	
Per ha. of GCA	2.53		2.75		2.59	2.80		3.34	4.16	
Density (Per sq. km.)	1520		1605					2040	2494	
Per ha. of permanent pasturing and grazing land		165	138		170	204		253	297	
Forest area per head of livestock (ha.)							0.276			
Livestock vaccination (lakhs)										78.64

Note : A source gives 205.93 lakhs as Bihar's livestock population in 1952.

per capita-wise by 12 per cent, per hectare-wise, if NSA, then by 184.4 per cent; if GCA, then by 164.4 per cent, density of the livestock has mounted by 164 per cent, and the pressure of the livestock wealth has increased on the pastures and grazing lands by 180 per cent during the same period.

Cattle Population

Cattle (Table 10.3), in this study, comprises cows and oxen. Buffaloes are treated as a separate entity. Cattle are the cream, so to say, of the livestock, that is, animals kept for use or profit. Male catle (in our case the oxen), which are working, that is, put to work in the tasks of cultivation, for example, put to the plough, or are used, alternatively, as pack animals and female cattle (in our study, the cows) which are meant for yielding milk and raising the stock, are the two divisions based on sex. The Bachaur breed draught cattle is common in districts like Biharsharif, Bhagalpur, Muzaffarpur and Champaran.

Between 1951 and 1990 the cattle population in Bihar rose by 12 per cent. Between 1951 and 1987 it rose by 33 per cent in Bihar, as compared to 29 per cent in all-India. Bihar's share in the country's cattle population increased from 9.85 per cent in 1951 to 10.18 per cent in 1987. In ranking Bihar has consistently occupied the third place in terms of its cattle possession.

During 1951-82 per capita availability of cattle in Bihar declined from 0.39 to 0.25, a 36 per cent decline; in all-India the decline was steeper, from 0.43 to 0.23 per capita, during the same period, a 47 per cent decline.

The pressure of cattle on land has continuously increased. Between 1951 and 1987 the number of heads of cattle per hectare of NSA rose by about 150 per cent, and per hectare of GCA by about 133 per cent in Bihar. Density (per sq. km.) of cattle deepened by 133 per cent in the State. On the eve of the Third Plan about 90 per cent of agricultural production in Bihar was dependent on bullock-power. Since then there has taken place a tangible increase in the draft/draught ability of the bullocks in the State. Even today in many an area in Bihar most of the link roads between villages and main roads can only be negotiated by the bullock-carts. The bullock-driven Rahat continues to be more popular than the power-driven pump. The improved-tyre bullock-carts are generally used in the long-distance haul of the non-perishable goods, such as grains, potato, spices, onion and coal. Proportionally less bullock-carts are used in villages at present, thus lowering the number of bullocks

TABLE 10.3 : Cattle in Bihar

Characteristics	*1951*	*1959*	*1961*	*1966*	*1972*	*1977*	*1982*	*1987*	*1990 (Projected)*	*1995*
Number (lakhs)	152.9/153 (1550.9)		161.0 (1755.6)	151.6 (1760.6)	149.1 (1788.7)	151.6 (1840.5)	163.6 1910.0)	203.39 (1996.95)	171.07	
Percentage share in All-India	9.85		9.17				9.58	10.18		
Rank in All-India	3rd		3rd					3rd		
Heads of cattle per capita of population	0.39	0.36 (0.26)	0.34		0.26		0.18	0.25		0.46
Number of cows over 3 years (lakhs)				38		39				
The above as percentage of total cattle							26.51			
Number of young stock				115.56						
Number of cows (lakhs)							42.99			
Number of male cattle over 3 years (lakhs)				69.30		72.83 (749.07)				
Number of female cattle (lakhs)	5.48							197.66		
Number of female cattle over 3 years (lakhs)				41.04						
Heads of cattle per ha. of NSA	1.78		2.00		1.78	1.81	2.06	2.67		
Heads of cattle per ha. of GCA	1.46		1.45		0.72	0.74	1.52	1.95		
Density of cattle (Per sq. km.)	879		925		856		931	1169		

against the sown area without indicating any decrease in the draft ability. There is another factor responsible for this, the increasing mechanisation of agricultural operations. If, therefore, the cattle-land ratio has risen, other kinds of cattle, not bullocks, have increased their proportions in the aggregate. The excess of bullocks relatively to sown land, as alleged in the past, is not a valid issue according to our analysis.

There is a much larger number of farm animals in those districts which have large forest and waste land areas than in the densely cultivated districts.

The number of farm animals varies in Bihar in accordance with the dearth of family labour. The size of farm livestock has adjusted itself to the availability of the family labour force. Empirically, an average family land holding has been the product of the tripartite partnership between land, the farming family and the farm livestock. The family serves the land and the livestock. The livestock and the family are nourished by the land. The livestock provides power and nature for the farm as well as some cash income for the family. The normal minimum size of the farm livestock is a pair of bullocks. But if the family is without an adult male head, the widow may just manage with one bullock. A larger family acquires a pair of stronger bullocks suitable for bullock-carts also, and by adding one or more cows and she-buffaloes to the stock so as to husband its farm unit comfortably.

The average ploughing capacity of a pair of bullocks in Bihar is between 3 and 4 hectares. By comparison, one tractor equals 7 animals in terms of draught power. But more of this a little while afterwards.

Working Cattle

Table 10.4 bears out that the working cattle population decreased in Bihar by nearly 24-25 per cent, whereas in all-India it increased by about 255 per cent. As percentage of the national aggregate, Bihar's working cattle was 11.12 per cent in 1951 and 3.32 per cent in 1987. Bihar's rank had also declined from the third to the fourth position during that period. As proportion of the total cattle population, Bihar's working cattle fell from 49.21 to 28.64 per cent. Male working cattle in 1987 was about one-tenth of total cattle. Bihar's percentage share with regard to working male cattle in that year stood at a meagre 1.11 per cent, while its place in all-India was fourteenth.

A positive correlation has been found to exist between the number of working cattle and the degree of agricultural mechanisation. Needless to say that tractorisation has been regarded as the hall-mark of this

TABLE 10.4 : Working Cattle in Bihar

Characteristics	*1951*	*1961*	*1965-66*	*1966*	*1968-69*	*1977*	*1979-80*	*1982*	*1986-87*	*1987*	*1987-88*	*1989-90*	*1990-91*	*1991-92*
(1)	(2)	(3)	(4)	(5)	(6)	(7)	(8)	(9)	(10)	(11)	(12)	(13)	(14)	(15)
Number of working cattle (lakhs)	75.3 (672.6)	78.9 (779.8)						75.0		57.0 (1716.86)				
Above as percentage share of All-India	11.12	10.11						10.8		3.32				
Place in above	3rd/5th	3rd				3rd				4th				
As percentage of total cattle population	49.21	49.00						46.29		28.64				
Per ha. of NSA	0.88	0.98								0.75				
Per ha. of GCA	0.77	0.71								0.54				
Per capita	0.19	0.17								0.07				
Male working cattle (lakhs)										5.73 (512.70)				
Percentage share in above										1.11				
Rank in all-India										14th				
Density (per sq. km)	432	453								327				
Draught animals per ha. of NSA	0.14 (0.08)													
Place in above	3rd													
Other kinds of livestock *(in lakhs)*:														
Total		8.5						21.6						
Horses and ponies		1.3		1.15		1.10		1.07 (91.60)						

(Contd.)

TABLE 10.4 (*Contd.*)

(1)	(2)	(3)	(4)	(5)	(6)	(7)	(8)	(9)	(10)	(11)	(12)	(13)	(14)	(15)
Donkeys				32812										
Camels (No.)				122				118						
Mules				1519										
Number of registered tractors				2132		10500	9109				4639		258000 (cumulative)	
Percentage share in above							2.43			5.11	58.4 (51.2)			
Consumption of fertilisers per ha. of GCA (kgs.)		1.09				15.4 (25.0	15.9 (30.5)	58.4 (51.2)		57.9 (72.4)	54.1 (65.4)			
Tractors per 1000 ha. (No.)					9.0	0.52	80	1.3788		91				
Number of energised pumpsets		1930			49375			11966				233000		
Percentage share in above														2.75
Number of installed diesel pumpsets											211000			
Percentage share in above											4.63			
Consumption of power in agriculture as percentage of total power consumption in the State					1.5				16.72					21.72

mechanisation, and the process of mechanisation is a continuation of the process of modernisation of agriculture which commenced several years ago.

It is believed extensively in Bihar that farm mechanisation and increased consumption of chemical fertilisers have resulted in a fall in Bihar's shares in livestock and working cattle. Let us dispose of first the mechanisation part of the argument.

As Table 10.4 shows, between 1966 and 1991 the number of registered tractors shot up 121-fold in Bihar. The compound annual rate of growth of tractorisation was 13.17 per cent (all-India 13.31) during 1979-80 to 1984-85, 28.41 per cent (all-India 10.53) during 1984-85 to 1989-90 and 21.35 per cent (all-India 12.67) during 1979-80 to 1990-91 in Bihar. The districts of concentrated development were Rohtas, West Champaran, Purnea, Bhojpur, Patna, East Champaran, Monghyr and Gopalganj. Districts in which the pace was very low were Singhbhum, Santhal Parganas and Giridih. Between 1972 and 1982 the increase in the number of tractors registered was 2.5 times. The percentage share of Bihar went up more than twice during 1979 to 1991. So far as energised pumpsets were concerned, the growth in their number between 1968-69 and 1982 was 2.26 times, between 1968-69 and 1989, 4.71 times and between 1968-69 and 1993, 5.30 times. Bihar's percentage share in the number of energised tubewells and pumpsets was 2.75 per cent in 1991-92 and 2.62 per cent in 1993. Consumption of electricity in agriculture in Bihar as a percentage of total electricity consumption in the total State economy rose from 1.5 per cent in 1965-66 to 21.72 per cent in 1991-92 through 16.73 per cent in 1986-87.

We now come to the second part of the explanation. Consumption of chemical fertilisers per hectare of GCA increased from 1.09 kgs. in 1961 (average of 1959-62) to 56.8 kgs. in 1990-91—a 52-fold increase. Bihar's percentage share in total fertilisers consumption increased from 4.6 per cent in 1978-79 to 6.6 per cent in 1989-90. In the increased amount of fertilisers consumption during 1971-72 to 1989-90 Bihar's share was 5.11 per cent, which was slightly higher than that during 1971-72 to 1984-85 at 4.9 per cent. During 1968-69 to 1987-88 the growth rate of fertilisers consumption in Bihar was 11.6 per cent, which was above the national average rate of 6.6 per cent.

Working buffaloes (Table 10.5) in Bihar in 1982 as percentage of total number of buffaloes in that year in the State were 16.32 per cent (7.54 versus 46.21 lakh). Bihar's share in their all-India number was 10.60 per cent. As proportion to total livestock population in that year,

TABLE 10.5 : Buffaloes in Bihar

Characteristics	*1951*	*1961*	*1963*	*1966*	*1972*	*1977*	*1982*	*1987*	*1990 (Projected)*
Number of all buffaloes (in lakhs)	33.1 (433.5)	36.9 (512.0)		36.54	36.8	44.6	46.2	48.72 (759.67)	46.70
Percentage share in All-India	7.63		7.20				6.65	6.41	
Rank in All-India	3rd	6th						6th	
Number of working buffaloes (in lakhs)							7.54		
Percentage share in All-India							10.60		
Young stock				12.59					
Male buffaloes over 3 years (in lakhs)				7.32		7.94 (837.8)			
Female buffaloes over 3 years				16.62					
Number of female buffaloes (lakhs)	1.67								
Number of buffaloes in milk (lakhs)							8.21		
Above as percentage of all buffaloes							12.84		
Above as percentage of all-India							4.56		
Number of breeding buffaloes (lakhs)						20.42 (312.65)			
Buffaloes over 3 years (lakhs)				16		20			
Above as percentage of total cattle population				35.62		38.91			
Number of dry buffaloes (lakhs)							12.78		
Above as percentage of total number of buffaloes							10.60		
Above as percentage of all-India dry buffaloes							27.78		

they were a mere 2.10 per cent. Between 1951 and 1987 their population rose by 132 per cent in Bihar and by 148 per cent in all-India. The projected figure for 1990 is an indication of the decline which the buffalo population in Bihar had to suffer, compared to that in 1987. Between 1951 and 1987 the percentage share of Bihar in all-India buffalo population fell from 7.63 to 6.41 per cent. Bihar's rank in the country in the number of buffaloes was third in 1951, which slid down to the sixth by 1961, and this has continued up till now.

Working buffaloes are one component of working cattle. Generally, female cattle are not deployed for work. In 1987 working male cattle as percentage of working cattle were 9.07 per cent, the national average figure being 2.89 per cent. Bihar's share in male working cattle in 1987 was a measly 1.00 per cent but its share in working cattle was 3.32 per cent.

In 1982 the number of working buffaloes as percentage of total cattle was 4.65 per cent. The number of working cattle as percentage of total cattle was 46.29 per cent, while other kinds of cattle like the oxen were 41.64 per cent of total cattle.

Bovine Cattle

Bovine cattle in this study stands for milch cattle, that is, cows and buffaloes, in the main. During 1966-82 in Bihar its population increased by about 111 per cent, while the human population increased by about 138 per cent. Studies reveal that the growth of bovine cattle in Bihar has lagged behind the growth of population. For this the slaughter of the animals in an unregulated manner is alleged to be responsible. The number of bovine cattle equalled that of total cattle (including buffaloes). In the State in 1982 the number in each case was around 208/209 lakhs. In 1966 it had been around 188/189 lakhs. The increase was by about 110/111 per cent. As percentage of the livestock population the population of bovine cattle in Bihar fell from 65.18 to 58.61 per cent.

The female bovine cattle were either in milk or dry. So far as the female cattle were concerned, between 1951 and 1987 their number multiplied three-fold. The increase in the number of adult male bovine, i.e., oxen and bulls was disproportionate to net area sown, which meant that the strain/pressure caused on the land mounted.

As illustrated by Table 10.6, bovine cattle in milk in Bihar, as percentage of total bovine cattle in the State, was 6.71 per cent in 1982, and as percentage of total cattle population in the State, it was 8.64 per cent. Bovine cattle in milk in Bihar as percentage of that in all-India was

TABLE 10.6 : Bovine Cattle in Bihar

Characteristics	*1951*	*1956*	*1961*	*1966*	*1977*	*1982*	*1987*	*1990 Projected*
Total population of bovine cattle (lakhs)				188.10		208.54		219.77
Above as percentage of total livestock population				65.18		58.61		
Percentage share in all-India total		5.0						
Bovine density (per sq. mile)		267						
Rank in bovine population		3rd						
Rank in bovine density		3rd (1953)						
Land under fodder per 100 bovine stock (ha.)		1.14					0.97	
Female cattle (lakhs)	5.48							
Number of milch animals (lakhs)			56.0					
Above as percentage of total cattle			28.75					
Milch cows and buffaloes per 1000 persons		68 (136)						
Rank in above		14th						
Bovine cattle in milk (lakhs)						14.0		
Above as percentage of total cattle population						8.64		
Percentage share in bovine cattle in milk in all-India						5.58		
Dry bovine cattle (lakhs)						26.0		
Above as percentage of total cattle population						16.0		
Total breedable bovine (lakhs)						65.40		
Total breedable cows (lakhs)						42.99		
Above as percentage of total cattle population						26.51		
Cows over three years (lakhs)				38		39		
Total breedable buffaloes (lakhs)						22.41		
Above as percentage of total number of buffaloes						48.28		
Buffaloes over 3 years (lakhs)				16	20(312.42)			
Above as percentage of total cattle population				35.62	38.91			
Female buffaloes (lakhs)	1.67							
Buffaloes in milk (lakhs)						8.21		

Note : In 1982 Bihar had 208.54 lakhs total bovine cattle, of which breedable cows were 42.99 lakhs, other cows 119.4 lakhs, breedable buffaloes 22.41 lakhs and other buffaloes 24 lakhs.

5.58 per cent (Table 10.6). The ratio between bovine cattle dry and bovine cattle in milk was 1.85 to 1.

In 1982 the number of breedable cows as percentage of the number of breedable bovine in Bihar was 68.57 per cent. In 1977 the ratio between cows and buffaloes (both of over 3 years) was 1.95 : 1. In 1982 the ratio between cows and buffaloes (both breedable) was 1.91 : 1. In percentage terms this signified 65.73 *versus* 34.27 per cent.

In 1982 in Bihar the number of buffaloes in milk as percentage of total number of buffaloes was 12.8 per cent, and the number of buffaloes which were dry was 10.60 per cent of their total number. The latter had a very high share in the all-India total. In 1987 the number of breedable buffaloes was 45.78 per cent of their total number in the State, and 6.53 per cent of the national total. Compared to the position in 1951, when female buffaloes formed a measly 5.04 per cent of the aggregate number in the country, the position in 1987, or even in 1982, was far better.

Finally, in 1982 total breedable bovine as percentage of total bovine were 31.36 per cent in Bihar.

Dairy Farming

As pointed out before, dairy farming has been a self-supporting and economically viable activity, especially for small and marginal farmers and landless rural labourers in Bihar. Between 1950-51 and 1992-93 there was about 225 per cent increase in the production and sale of liquid milk. The increase in population was by 223 per cent during the same period. That is to say, the increase in milk output was neck-to-neck with the increase in population. Between 1950-51 and 1993-94 the increase in milk production (by about 215 per cent) fell short of that in population (over 223 per cent). During 1971-72 to 1992-93, whereas the increase in milk output was by 192 per cent, that in population was about 157 per cent. This was comparatively a more comfortable period from consumption point of view. Finally, during 1950-51 to 1971-72 the rise in milk supply was by 117 per cent, while that in growth of population was by 145 per cent. These figures, as presented in Table 10.7, confirm the opinion that the milk supply curve in Bihar has been a rising, though a slightly fluctuating, one. This remark is corroborated by the Compound Annual Growth Rate (CAGR) percentages. Whereas during 1971-72 to 1992-93 the rate was 3.2 per cent in Bihar, it was 4.6 per cent in all-India. During the supervening decade, 1981-82 to 1990-91, the corresponding rates were higher in either case, 4.8 and 5.1

per cent. In Bihar, as in India, the period 1947-70 was one of stagnation in the field of milk outturn. The degree of variance between the minimum and maximum percentage shares of the State in all-India was extremely high—5.8 *versus* 9.8 per cent (this is to be qualified by the gaps in the data). This fluctuation had little relationship with the State's share in the bovine population. The bovine population relied largely on natural factors, while its milk production relied on both natural and man-made factors. Bihar's rank in all-India milk production was third in 1961. This had fallen to the tenth place in 1989-90. In the following year it was the ninth. Bihar's rank in all-India from the standpoint of the bovine population was above that from that of milk production. Milk output per milch animal has improved in the course of time but even at present it remains very low, though above the all-India average figure. In all periods and years average milk yield per buffalo has been higher than average milk per cow. In 1951 it was 2.11 times; in 1987, 4.97 times. Cow milk production as a ratio of buffalo milk production was 1.55 to 1 in 1951, and 0.81 to 1 in 1989-90. The inference is clear : in milk supply the buffalo had become the number one and the cow the number two milch animal in Bihar. 11.8 per cent of the total milk supply in the State was from the goats, 39.6 per cent from the cows and 48.6 per cent from the buffaloes.

The 2.25-fold increase in milk production that has taken place during the plan period so far, which would be a shade higher than the increase that has taken place in the number of the milch cattle (for want of data we cannot give here the exact figure, but we would assert this on the basis of the fact that about 164 per cent rise in the number of the milch cattle caused about 177 per cent increase in the amount of milk supply in Bihar during 1951-87) is due to other factors, which, when taken into account, make the result/gain look less than what it should have been otherwise. But this is a different issue.

During the period the State Government set up a number of dairy plants for the supply of milk. Similarly, a number of *Gosadans* were established. Technical guidance and financial assistance were given to them so as to develop them. Subsidised financial assistance was given to the weaker sections of society under the Integrated Rural Development Programme (IRDP) in order to enable them to acquire good breed of milch cattle and poultry and also to provide for their medical care. The number of dairy cooperative societies multiplied. This stimulated dairying. The cooperatives were of great help in the procurement of milk. The milk unions, etc. were also given loans and grants. On the

TABLE 10.7 : Production and Consumption of Milk and Milk Products in Bihar

Characteristics	*1950-51*	*1951*	*1955-56*	*1956*	*1961*	*1966*	*1969*	*1970-71*	*1971-72*
(1)	(2)	(3)	(4)	(5)	(6)	(7)	(8)	(9)	(10)
Milk production (lakh metric tonnes)	14.95 (194.57)	17.56			20.5 (209.3)				17.5
CARG of milk production (per cent)									
Percentage share in milk production	7.68	9.02			9.79				7.7
Rank in milk production		5th			3rd				
Per capita per year milk production (kgs)								31.5	
Rank in above					3rd			9th	
Per milch animal milk production per day (kgs.)	0.78								
Per milch animal per year milk production (kgs.):									
A. Cow		19.48							
B. Buffalo		41.22							
C. Goat									
Rank in above :									
A. Cow				3rd					
B. Buffalo				5th					
C. Goat				1st					
Per capita availability of milk :									
A. Per day	133 (gms.)				2.76 (ounces)		2.64 (ounces)		
B. Per year									
Per capita availability of milk and milk products :									
A. Per year (kgs.)		23.40							
Per capita milk consumption:									
A. Per year (lbs)		46	57	57					
Per capita per day milk consumption norm (ounces)					10				

(*Contd.*)

TABLE 10.7 (*Contd.*)

Characteristics	*1971-72 to 1981-82*	*1971-72 to 1992-93*	*1972-73*	*1974-75*	*1977-78*	*1980-81*	*1981-82*	*1981-82 to 1990-91*	*1982-83*
(1)	(11)	(12)	(13)	(14)	(15)	(16)	(17)	(18)	(19)
Milk production (lakh metric tonnes)				18.1	18.28	19.42			21.33
CARG of milk production (per cent)	1.5	3.2						4.8	
	(4.3)	(4.6)						(5.1)	
Percentage share in milk production									
Rank in milk production									
Per capita per year milk production (kgs)			31.0				29.2		
			(41.0)				(50.2)		
Rank in above									
Per milch animal milk production per day (kgs.)							1.05		
Per milch animal per year milk production (kgs.):									
A. Cow									
B. Buffalo									
C. Goat									
Rank in above :									
A. Cow									
B. Buffalo									
C. Goat									
Per capita availability of milk :									
A. Per day						76 (gms)	99 (gms.)		
B. Per year									
Per capita availability of milk and milk products :									
A. Per year (kgs.)									
Per capita milk consumption:									
A. Per year (lbs)									
Per capita per day milk consumption norm (ounces)									

(*Contd.*)

TABLE 10.7 (*Contd.*)

Characteristics	*1984-85*	*1987*	*1987-88*	*1988-89*	*1989-90*	*1990-91*	*1992-93*	*1993-94*	*1995*
(1)	(20)	(21)	(22)	(23)	(24)	(25)	(26)	(27)	(28)
Milk production (lakh metric tonnes)			26.50	29.0	30.0 (514.0)	31.23	33.6	32.1	
CARG of milk production (per cent)									
Percentage share in milk production				6.0	5.8		5.8		
Rank in milk production					10th	9th			
Per capita per year milk production (kgs)	31.5					36.2 (63.7)	37.3 (65.9)		
Rank in above	14th								
Per milch animal milk production per day (kgs.)									1.17
Per milch animal per year milk production (kgs.):									
A. Cow		37.61 (Combined)							
B. Buffalo		61.42							
C. Goat		304.69							
Rank in above :									
A. Cow									
B. Buffalo									
C. Goat									
Per capita availability of milk :									
A. Per day	85 (gms)/						95 (gms.)		
B. Per year	(116)					36.75 (kgs.)			
Per capita availability of milk and milk products :									
A. Per year (kgs.)									
Per capita milk consumption:									
A. Per year (lbs)									
Per capita per day milk consumption norm (ounces)		220 (gms)							

Conversion factors :

One metric tonne = 0.98420 long tonne = 1016.05 kgs.
One lb (pound) = 0.4535924 kgs.
One maund (md) = 37.5202 kgs. = 0.037394 metric tonne.
One ounce (os) = 28.350 gms = 0.2825 kg.

belief shared popularly that proper feeding of the miclh animals could alone boost milk output by at least 50 per cent, advances were made in feeding and grazing techniques as well as new methods of making good quality hay and fodder, and, as a matter of fact, milk production made a rapid headway. Upgradation of the milch cattle by cross breeding too had a positively good effect on their productivity. An integrated dairy development programme, the Operation Flood Project/Programme, which was launched in 1970, made good progress, under the auspices of the National Dairy Development Board. The Technology Mission on Diary Development setup State and district-level coordination committees, which reviewed the existing statutes and policies related to dairy development, dovetailed the ongoing programmes to avert duplication and wastage as well as eliminated difficulties in implementing the programmes. The NAFED lent a hand in marketing the milk and milk products which the cooperatives, unions, etc., produced and assembled. Research was also a significant factor in the promotion of milk production. It was the responsibility of the National Dairy Development Board, the Indian Council of Agricultural Research (ICAR) and the Technology Mission on Dairy Development. Gradually the marketing problems faced by the producers of milk and milk products in the urban areas (these are perishable products and they must therefore be delivered to the ultimate consumers by the quickest means of transport and in a manner that they are safe and uncontaminated, unpolluted and unpoisoned to be consumed) have been solved more effectively than in the rural areas where the majority of the producers have even today to use slow-moving means of transport like bicycles, pack animals, bullock-carts, country boats, rickshaws or, in the worst case, carry the pails on their heads or tied to the two ends of a rod carried on their shoulders. But even in the latter case the speed is faster now than before. The suppliers on the outskirts of cities use their motor-bikes and scooters, or three wheelers for this purpose. They come of those rural households which by combining cultivation with cattle-rearing have moved up in the economic ladder in the last few decades.

The prime use of milk produced in Bihar continues to be for consumption. The secondary use of it is in making products, like curd, butter, ghee, ice-cream, cheese, milk-shake, etc. In 1961 consumption of fluid milk in Bihar was about one-third of the total production of milk in the State.+

+ In parenthesis, in the early 1950s Bihar had a few butter manufacturing units; one near Danapur/Patna was Polson's.

As Table 10.7 brings out, in spite of the little improvement in per capita milk availability, it is still extremely poor. Per capita per annum milk out-turn in 1992-93 was 37.3 kgs. in Bihar, as against 65.9 kgs. in all-India. Bihar's rank in per capita per annum milk production was third in 1961, which had declined to the fourteenth place by 1984-85.

Per capita milk consumption in Bihar continues to be much lower than the prescribed norm of 220 gms. a day. In 1955-56 the availability of milk and milk products was less than half of the standard requirements. Even at present it is lower than what is desirable according to the nutritional standards or as warranted by the number of the milch animals. Despite good milk supply milk processing has not so far been developed to the extent desirable. In surplus districts there still is plenty of scope for drying milk. Inadequate and unorganised milk marketing arrangements (as catalogued above), the low handling capacities of the agencies concerned, and the inefficiency of the dairy cooperatives or their defunctness are the chief reasons for the slow/non-growth of the dairy farming sector in Bihar, leave aside the corruption and nepotism factor, which is common to all public/Government departments and offices.

Notwithstanding what has been said in the preceding paragraphs, the brute fact remains that compared to the strides made by some other predominantly agricultural States, in Bihar the number of milch cattle has not kept pace with the population, particularly the good quality milch animals, with the result that their productivity has been low—the milk yield rates are abysmally low—be they dairy or non-dairy animals, and this is because the animals are not properly fed and maintained, nor properly bred. The composition of the bovine population is uneven. To illustrate, the number of good breeding bulls is in short supply. Next, the bovine density is similarly uneven, it is higher in the plains and lower in the hilly tracts. There is a sharp contrast in the distribution of highly potential bovine cattle as between the regions—the two plain regions are in the milk shed areas and the milk yield rates are higher there, but in the Chotanagpur plateau region the rates are lower as the bovine cattle are of an inferior quality there. Not only that but also extensive pasturing (which has since declined) in the hilly region imparts an impetus to scrub animals, lacking in dairy value. In contradistinction to the plain regions in the plateau region there still is an abundant scope for mixed arable farming, which, in turn, is suited for the maintenance of the milch bovine, which, in its own turn, can provide ample scope for dairy farming.

But the development of dairy industry presupposes, in the first instance, better breeding of the milch cattle, improved sanitary conditions, in the second place, development of transport and refrigeration facilities, in the third place; and an elastic supply of suitably trained labour for the industry, in the fourth and final instance.

Other Kinds of Livestock and their Products in Bihar

In Table 10.4, we have given statistics concerning the less known kinds of the livestock, such as horses, ponies, donkeys, camels and mules. In Table 10.8, we attempt a short account of the second order of the livestock, namely, goats, sheep, and swines/pigs. While considering meat and allied meat products we must bear in mind the whole kingdom of the livestock and poultry and the fowl world, for even in a highly religious, superstitious and orthodox country like India, nothing is spared, when it comes to eating—the rats and the other rodents and the reptiles all included; there are castes/tribes which relish them. Fishes are outlined separately.

Goats find a regular place in the farm livestock of the poorer families and provide some employment for their women and children. Goat-rearing has tended to be confined to certain castes and communities in Bihar. During 1951-90 (Table 10.8) the number of goats in the State went up by 267 per cent. Bihar's percentage share rose moderately from 12.62 per cent in 1951 to 13.64 per cent in 1987. In ranking Bihar remained second throughout the period. There is in operation the Buck/ Goat Development Programme which has improving the productivity of goats as its central goal. Measures are afoot to progressively replace traditional breeds by improved stall-fed breeds.

Sheep farming in Bihar is a specialised occupation. Like goat husbandry, sheep-keeping is the monopoly of particular castes and communities in the State. It flourishes in areas where mixed farming is popular, as, for example, in the Chotanagpur plateau region. But in South Bihar in certain tracts sheep farming used to be very popular and rough blankets were woven, but this occupation has declined over the ages. The Shahabadi breeds deserve special mention here. They were noted for their coarse wool which was suited for carpet-weaving. Likewise, the Chotanagpur breeds were favoured because of the same trade. During 1951-90 there was a 143 per cent rise in the sheep population in Bihar, but the State's relative share in the country in this respect remained more or less stable, at around 2.66 per cent. However, its rank fell from the seventh to the tenth between 1951 and 1987.

We do not have information on the quantity of meat furnished by the sheep rearers. As for wool output, during 1951 to 1993, the increase

TABLE 10.8 : Other Kinds of Livestock and their Products in Bihar

Sl.No. Characteristics	1951	1956	1961	1966	1972	1976-77	1977	1978-79	1980-81
(1)	(2)	(3)	(4)	(5)	(6)	(7)	(8)	(9)	(10)
Goat Husbandry									
1. Number of goats (lakhs)	59.4/60.0 (470.7)		86.4/86.7 470.7	78.01	73.6		99.25 (756.20)		
2. Percentage share in all-India	12.62	18.0	14.20				13.12		
3. Rank in all- India	1st/2nd								
Sheep Husbandry									
4. Number of sheep (lakhs)	10.3/10.5 (388.3)		11.6 (402.2)	12.46	9.8		11.5 (409.07)		
5. Percentage share in all-India	2.65/2.70		2.86		1.55		2.81		
6. Rank in all-India	7th		9th						
Swine/Pig Husbandry									
7. Number of pigs (lakhs)	6.5 (44.2)			5.45			9.2		
8. Percentage share in all-India	14.70								
9. Rank in all-India	3rd.								
Products									
10. Wool (lakh kgs.)	7.35 (367.67)		3.62 tonnes (32.55)		5.47/ 8.10				9.20
11. Percentage share in all-India	1.99		11.12						
12. Rank in all- India	12th				12th				
13. Meat+ and allied meat products (million tonnes)	0.32316 (4.61244)								
14. Percentage share of above in all-India	7.0								
15. Rank of (12) in all-India	5th								
16. Per capita per annum consumption of (12)	0.58 kg.211 b & 6 Ozs								

(Contd.)

TABLE 10.8 (*Contd.*)

Sl.No. Characteristics	*1982*	*1983-84*	*1987*	*1989-90*	*1990 Projected*	*1990-91*	*1992-93*	*1993-94*
(1)	(11)	(12)	(13)	(14)	(15)	(16)	(17)	(18)
Goat Husbandry								
1. Number of goats (lakhs)	122.21/ 123.0		150.32 (1102.07)		156.36			
2. Percentage share in all-India			13.64					
3. Rank in all- India			2nd					
Sheep Husbandry								
4. Number of sheep (lakhs)	13.27/ 13.4		15.20 (457.03)		14.70			
5. Percentage share in all-India			3.32			2.67		
6. Rank in all-India		10th	10th					
Swine/Pig Husbandry								
7. Number of pigs (lakhs)	10.11/10.43				11.35			
8. Percentage share in all-India								
9. Rank in all-India								
Products								
10. Wool (lakh kgs.)		10.10		11.00		11.03	11.50	
11. Percentage share in all-India								
12. Rank in all- India				12th		12th		
13. Meat+ and allied meat products (million tonnes)			1.92 (1987-88)	2.09				2.65
14. Percentage share of above in all-India								
15. Rank of (12) in all-India								
16. Per capita per annum consumption of (12)				2.46 kgs.				

+ The Hindus do not eat beef (cow or calf or oxen meat). The Muslims do not eat pork. But there are everywhere in the country slaughter houses which kill cows and calves and oxen, also buffaloes, horses, camels, goats, sheep, pigs, etc. The Indian Constitution desires protection of the cows and their offspring. The Muslims and the Christians in India are, in general, against this. Meat and meat products here include poultry meat and products.

was by 156 per cent. Average wool yield per sheep was much less than one kg a year. The main objective of sheep development under the public programmes is meat production. For this scientific breeding of the exotic or cross variety is emphasised. Simultaneously the status of the sheep-breeders and wool-producers is being raised in various ways. While grant-in-aid is given, marketing is sought to be improved through all possible means.

Piggery is the main occupation of certain castes and communities in Bihar. It has a significant impact on the economic condition of their members. It has palpably improved the earning power as well as health level of a sizable section of the rural community which is socially almost at the lowest rung of the ladder, so to say. During 1951-90 the number of pigs in Bihar registered a 174 per cent increase. It is the tribal areas which have led the State in piggery development. Meat is the chief attraction in the piggery trade, for self-consumption as well as for sale. Under the state auspices at certain state farms the Yorkshire pigs have been multiplied.

The production of meat and allied meat products poses a subject which encompasses the entire animal kingdom, but there we have to limit our stock-taking to the portion of it which has been quantitatively studied over a sufficient period, such as the livestock. Slaughtered for meat, etc. were breedable cows, oxen (he cows and bulls), breedable buffaloes and he buffaloes, the goats, the sheep and the pigs, and the chickens and the fowl belonging to the bigger fauna world.

Meat and allied meat products increased in production by 646 per cent during 1951-90, whereas the livestock population increased by 172 per cent and the poultry population by 161 per cent during that period and the human population by about 222 per cent. By deduction, the productivity of livestock and poultry per unit increased spectacularly. Emphasis on the milch cattle and poultry under the IRDP was a compelling factor in this achievement. Supposedly, Bihar, which was, by and large, a vegetarian State on the eve of Independence, became a non-vegetarian one in a big way by 1990, per capita per annum consumption of meat and allied meat products having risen by 424 per cent since 1951.* All the same, from all empirical evidence, the per person consumption of goat meat has fallen, consumption of other kinds

* A different source gives per head per year consumption of meat in Bihar at about 1.3 lb. The Government of Bihar in the Planning Department gives per capita per annum availability of meat (excluding beef and buffalo flesh) for the non-vegetarian population at 67 per cent of total population 1.92 lbs for 1966 and 2.30 lbs for 1969, the norm being 68 lbs (including fish).

of meat (but not fish either, because, compared to the past years, per person consumption of fish as well has fallen) has gone up, especially the chick meat (and that too, not of the countryside chickens, because that has also fallen, when observed closely). Every day in many places in Bihar, as of now, several people return empty-handed from the butcher's shop as their demand for mutton cannot be fulfilled. Supply has to increase by a substantial amount if the heavy local demand for mutton is to be met fully.

The by-products of the cattle slaughter houses like hides and skins, wool, bones, hoofs, hair, bristles, blood, fat and castings are used for manufacture of goods demanded by people and factories. Tanneries (Charmalayas) government and subsidised bunkers have come up. Also have come up other processing and manufacturing units which utilise these by-products economically. But even today not all the by-products are collected efficiently, for example, bones, animal blood (which is used to produce blood meal, an input in fertilisers-making). Were all bones collected, the bonemeal industry would be feasible economically to be set up. Bihar is a front-rank exporter of hides and skins to the neighbouring States, such as West Bengal and Uttar Pradesh. In 1956, 6281 thousand metric tonnes and 16250 metric tonnes of animal bones were contributed by Bihar's livestock.

The location of the slaughter houses has entailed difficulties in aviation safety in the cities which have airports. The ill-equipped and poorly maintained slaughter houses are a threat, a hazard to public health on account of the pollution they cause incessantly. The wastage in the butcheries is estimated at 15 per cent.

The slaughter houses/abattoirs call for immediate modernisation. The wastage in them of the by-products has to be curtailed. The transport and refrigeration facilities have to be developed as the development of the meat industry is essentially conditional upon that factor.

Poultry Husbandry

Poultry is one of the salient components of the farm economy in so far as it yields additional income and provides job opportunities to a material extent for all sections of rural people in the shortest possible time. Very easily is poultry keeping unified with the routine of the farmers, if conducted on a small scale. In Bihar poultry husbandry is the preserve of certain castes and communities that belong to the lower orders of the society, though the old-time inhibitions are fastly losing their hold on the rural folk and the educated young men, city-bred, who have developed a special liking for the non-vegetarian food and who are pretty exposed and have some family savings, are coming forward to run poultry farms generally on the outskirts of the big towns and cities with incentives and support of the Government in several forms, and they not inoften come of the higher castes.

As Table 10.9 brings forth, the number of birds in Bihar increased during 1951-90 by 183 per cent more or less continuously, except for the last year of the period, that is, 1989-90. Bihar's share in all-India number of the birds has kept fluctuating, and declined from 14.28 per cent in 1951 to 5.76 per cent in 1990. The State's rank also fell from the second in the country from the point of view of the number of birds in the earlier years to the seventh in the later years.

So far as the number of eggs laid is concerned, between 1976-77 and 1993-94, there occurred an increase of 257 per cent. Set against the percentage rise in the number of the birds and the percentage increase in the number of the eggs laid by them, there is ineluctable evidence of an improvement in the productivity of the birds.

From the limited data available, and that also for the recent period, Bihar's percentage share in egg production has consistently gone down, with other States forging ahead with faster speed. Andhra Pradesh sends eggs to Bihar in several trucks every day. As for Bihar's rank from this standpoint, it was seventh in 1990-91, coterminous with the State's rank in the number of the birds.

During 1951-87 per capita per year production recorded an increase from 3.6 to 16.17 eggs—about 450 per cent rise. During 1956-87 the number of eggs laid per bird more than doubled, from 40 to 82. During 1951-87 the number of birds per sq km rose from 448 to 908, i.e., more than twice. This is proof of the growing popularity of the poultry farms in the countryside. But as a result of the rapid growth of population and hence the percentage of egg-eaters in the population (just make a note of the mushrooming of egg-sellers and sellers of cooked eggs on the pavements and by the roadsides and near spots of massive public traffic and intercourse) the supply of the birds slightly lags behind the requirement, forcing per capita availability of the birds to almost stagnate, 0.20 in 1951 *versus* 0.19 in 1987. The Annual Plan 1995-96 of the Bihar Government admits honestly that the demand for eggs in the State is high but their production is low. (According to the document, the availability of eggs for the 67 per cent of the total population estimated to be non-vegetarian increased from 20.95 in 1961 to 28.85 in 1969, as against the accepted norm of 365 eggs a year—compare this with the

TABLE 10.9 : Poultry Husbandry in Bihar

Sl.No.	*Characteristics*	*1951*	*1956*	*1961*	*1966*	*1972*	*1976-77*	*1977*	*1977-78*	*1980-81*
	(1)	(2)	(3)	(4)	(5)	(6)	(7)	(8)	(9)	(10)
	Poultry									
1.	Number of birds (million)	7.8/8.26 (58.24)	8.7/12.24 (97.37/173.52)	12.36	10.85	12.56	12.9	12.91/14.07 (160.87)		14.98/ 11.45
2.	Percentage share in all-India	14.28	8.92	10.81	8.89	9.11		8.75		
3.	Rank in all-India	2nd	2nd	2nd						
4.	Number of eggs laid (million)						55.3		62.0	75.2
5.	Percentage share									
6.	Rank									
	Other Birds									
7.	Ducks (lakhs)	4.5								
8.	Per capita per year production of eggs (number)	3.6	3.6					8.7		
9.	Number of eggs per bird per year		40							
10.	Number of birds per capita	0.20		0.26		0.22	0.20			
11.	Number of birds per sq. km.	448		710		721				
12.	Number of poultry farms									

(*Contd.*)

TABLE 10.9 (*Contd.*)

Sl.No. Characteristics	*1982*	*1982-83*	*1983-84*	*1984-85*	*1987*	*1987-88*	*1989-90*	*1990-91*	*1993-94*
(1)	(11)	(12)	(13)	(14)	(15)	(16)	(17)	(18)	(19)
Poultry									
1. Number of birds (million)		3 (5.98)			15.88 (275.31)		14.70		
2. Percentage share in all-India							5.76		
3. Rank in all-India							7th		
4. Number of eggs laid (million)	83.7	83.7	93.1	100.0	131.1	131.1/ 121.0		1355	139.0/ 145.0
5. Percentage share						7.3	6.5		5.9
6. Rank								7th	
Other Birds									
7. Ducks (lakhs)									
8. Per capita per year production of eggs (number)	11.68				16.17				
9. Number of eggs per bird per year	55.87				82.55				
10. Number of birds per capita	0.21				0.19				
11. Number of birds per sq. km.	861				908				
12. Number of poultry farms							15		

adage. 'An apple a day keeps the doctor away', and, by the same token, an egg a day keeps the doctor away, an acknowledged health precept in Bihar, or a glass of milk a day which in the nutritive sense is as good as an egg, by all means its forerunner.)

The 1955-56 NCAER study had suggested that in Bihar the output of the poultry products required to be increased sixteen times to satisfy the nutritional standards. In 1987 sixteen eggs per head per year was the actual achievement. This boiled down to the prediction that were egg supply to go up by 23 times (the gap has, assuredly, widened later), could the norm of egg consumption be met. But would everybody be having the purchasing power to eat an egg a day? That is the question-mark.

A gamut of factors made the small advance in this area possible. First, control of the poultry diseases by way of prophylactic vaccination. Second, more extension work to educate the farmers on the importance of vaccinating the birds and preventing the diseases. Third, improvement of the general management practices. Fourth, making the poultry-keeping farmers conversant with the modern scientific management practices. Fifth, the NABARD has executed a myriad of schemes to support the poultry occupation. Sixth, subsidised financial assistance to the weaker sections of society to enable them to acquire good-breed poultry and to provide for its proper medical care.

The poultry trade is constrained by a host of factors: For one thing, the birds commit serious depredations after sowing is done by eating up the seeds sown in the fields and also by destroying the young and tender plants as they sprout from the soil. This necessitates the upkeep of the birds in expansive strips, walled and fenced, a costly affair. In a good many cases the wagon of the poultry enterprise has to be shunted for a while or even abandoned. For another, the recurring cost of poultry rearing on a large scale may be prohibitive if the feed has to be purchased for the flock. For a third, beyond a certain size of the flock, the work tends to become a whole-time job, and clashes sharply with the primary task of agriculture. The farmer is in a position identical with the Buridan Ass, facing a dilemma, which is fatal to rational choice, being suspended between two equally attractive blades of grass. Either employment maximisation or income optimisation, or a trade-off between the twin goals has to be the objective, for only decision-making is critical to the end of the dilemma.

Before the curtain is drawn on the subject, the present problems and difficulties bestting the poultry business must be thrashed out: Firstly, the modern poultry production techniques of using the hybrid birds are mostly concentrated in a few pockets. Secondly, the availability of the feed and health care is not adequate. Thirdly, the marketing is not well-organised. Fourthly, the system of breeding is faulty. Lastly, the inferior breed of the birds predominates.

Fishery

The fish industry in Bihar, which is part and parcel of the State's agriculture, in terms of contribution to the primary sector income excels forestry and logging, which is a vital fact, to be kept in mind while appraising employment-generation and poverty-elimination programmes.

The outstanding sources of fish production/supply/catch are the rivers and streams of North Bihar. In South Bihar it is the culture of fresh water fishes that has been practised traditionally, and mostly. In innumerable places fish is grown alongwith paddy.

Knowledgeable Biharis inform that prior to Independence only fish and mango grew at compound rates in their State, all the rest being either stagnant or growing at the simple, arithmetical rate. But after Independence both ceased to do so, and grew at the same simple arithmetical, or the Hindu, rate of growth. Nearest our time, the *Khatals* have come up at a breakneck speed, with a thrust, unknown in Bihar's history, though at the same time the State cattle farms administered by the Animal Husbandry Department of the Bihar Government have been denuded of their fodder, letting the cattle to fond for themselves, giving rise to one of the biggest scams of the country being probed into by the CBI, under direction from the Supreme Court, rejecting the arrangement made by the Chief Minister, a *gowala* by caste and an upholder of the medicinal value of the cowdung (thank God that when the roads of Patna were cleaned with the Ganga water, the cowdung was forgotten and not applied, thereby creating another history). But this is a digression, though not irrelevant, for the present chapter is about cattle as well as fish.

Bihar is coming up in fish production. It has on the credit side a 50-fold spurt in its fish catch (inland) between 1956-57 and 1991-92, not a mean achievement in any case. Its percentage share has moved up from 2.0 per cent in 1951 to 4.5 per cent in 1991-92, a 2.5-fold raise. The yield of fish per hectare has gone up from 680 kgs in 1980 to 2131 kgs in 1994, a three-fold increase. In the public farms the yields are higher, and the private ones higher still (Table 10.10).

TABLE 10.10 : Fisheries in Bihar

Sl.No.	Characteristics	1947	1951	1956	1956-57	1980	1980-81	1981	1981-82
	(1)	(2)	(3)	(4)	(5)	(6)	(7)	(8)	(9)
1.	Land area under fisheries (lakh ha)								
2.	Inland/fresh water fish catch/production/yield (lakh tonnes)				0.37		0.80	1.65	
3.	Value of above (Rs. lakhs)				560				
4.	Above as percentage of primary sector SDP								
5.	Share in all-India inland fish catch			2.0			3.3		
6.	Rank in all-India fish catch	2nd	5th	1st			8th	12th	9th
7.	Per ha. per annum fish yield (kgs.) :								
	A. General					680			
	B. Private sector+								
	C. Public sector++								
8.	Number of persons engaged in fish industry on a full-time basis		16505						
9.	Number of insured fishermen								
10.	Per capita per year fish intake (kgs.)								
11.	Norm as to above (kgs.)								
12.	Total number of tanks reserved for fishermen coming of the SCs & STs.								
13.	Seeds (*Jeera*) produced (number in million)								
14.	Number of mechanised boats							311	
15.	Number of non-mechanised boats							11510	
16.	Number of fishing gears							92906	

(*Contd.*)

TABLE 10.10 (*Contd.*)

Sl.No.	*Characteristics*	*1985*	*1987*	*1987-88*	*1989-90*	*1990-91*	*1991-92*	*1994*
	(1)	(10)	(11)	(12)	(13)	(14)	(15)	(16)
1.	Land area under fisheries (lakh ha)				1.62			
2.	Inland/fresh water fish catch/production/yield (lakh tonnes)				15.10/15.60	15.99	18.50	
3.	Value of above (Rs. lakhs)							
4.	Above as percentage of primary sector SDP			2.90				
5.	Share in all-India inland fish catch				4.2	4.1	4.5	
6.	Rank in all-India fish catch					8th		
7.	Per ha. per annum fish yield (kgs.) :							
	A. General	3,000			9,321			14.82 (= 563 Kgs.) to 98.80 (= 3714 kgs.)
	B. Private sector+							10,000
	C. Public sector++							3,000
8.	Number of persons engaged in fish industry on a full-time basis							
9.	Number of insured fishermen				33,333			
10.	Per capita per year fish intake (kgs.)							4 (4)
11.	Norm as to above (kgs.)							28
12.	Total number of tanks reserved for fishermen coming of the SCs & STs.				35			
13.	Seeds (*Jeera*) produced (number in million)					347.63		
14.	Number of mechanised boats							
15.	Number of non-mechanised boats							
16.	Number of fishing gears							

\+ In a private reservoir of two acres situated in Fatwah/Fatuaha.

++ On the authority of the Fisheries Department of the Government of Bihar.

Note : Fishing in Bihar grew at the rate of 2.2 per cent (all-India 7.8 per cent) during 1990-91 and 15.5 per cent (all-India 5.6 per cent) during 1992-92.

How do we explain the gains made? Let us try to answer this questions:

The meteoric rise in fish production in Bihar is the joint outcome of expansion of the area in which fishing is carried out, on the one hand and the improvement of yield per unit of the fishery land, on the other. In the last four decades and a half tanks and *jheels* and swamps have been resuscitated, renovated and developed under the Inland Fisheries Projects sponsored and assisted by the World Bank, which has led to definite gains in both production and productivity. We now have fishes raised in the waterlogged lands and lands immersed in water for any reason—the *tals*, the *chaurs*, the *dhars* and the *mans*. Even in the drains and water channels and courses connected with the irrigational canals and the catchment areas of the rivers concerned are fishes harvested. To substantiate, the DVC started systematic pisciculture on a large scale. This point can bear reassertion.

Around 1970, in Bihar 7 lakh acres of widespread included 2 lakh acres of tanks and ponds, 1 lakh acres of the natural *mans* and *chaurs*, 1 lakh acres of rivers and 2 lakh acres of canals. The fishing activity taken so far in the canals was a bare tinkering with the stupendous task. The tree stumps and bushes which outlive in large numbers and exist in the reservoirs make fishing operations extremely difficult and hazardous, and Bihar has not taken any lesson from either Uttar Pradesh or Andhra Pradesh or Tamil Nadu or Madhya Pradesh. It should be indicated here that the first few years of the life of the reservoirs after impoundment are most productive for pisciculture. Thereafter, the productivity curve declines for a certain while and again rises gradually. Therefore, fish culture in reservoirs should synchronise with the beginning of impoundment. The reservoirs would require regular stocking with the fry fingerlings. Fish seed farms of suitable size should at least be constructed near the bigger reservoirs. It is futile to inform here that a large number of reservoirs came up after Independence but fisheries received scant attention. By constructing docks at suitable distances in the network of irrigation canals considerable water area could not be made available, with the result that intensive fish culture at reasonable cost could not be developed as expected. This sheds light on why the rank of Bihar in the area of fish production in the country which was the second in 1951 and moved up to the first in 1956 out to be turned the lowest among the twelve fishing States in 1981, though improved to the eighth rank in 1990-91, also on why per capita per annum fish intake in Bihar was as low as 4 kgs., as against the accepted norm of 28 kgs. Another detractor was the non-development of the culture of mudfishes in the *chaurs* as expected. Yet another deterrent to the satisfactory development of the fish industry in the State was the fact that for want of proper attention, made wose by encroachment upon the existing fisheries, the large number of *dhars* in Saharsa and Purnes known for their rich fisheries got silted progressively. They were not desilted nor made deeper and hence not converted into good fisheries. A third dampener was the decline of the fish resources of the *mans* consequent upon the stoppage of autostocking, as also the choking of the waters of the *mans* with weeds, rendering fishing operations more and more difficult. Fish seed farms were not constructed near the *mans* for their regular stocks and deweeding operations were not undertaken. The net result was a sharp decline in the supply of fish gifted with rare dediciousness.

Having advanced some factors repugnant to the growth of fishing in Bihar above, we want now to resume listing of the influences favouring the growth of fishing in the State. Area extension and yield improvement would not have proved so very effective, had not the cold storage and the ice-making industries made long strides and thereby imparted a fillip to the fish industry in the State in its progress to the extent recorded during the period.

Another stimulus came from the growth of population (and hence the numbers of the catchers of fish as well as its consumers) and real incomes of the people (however limited) which culminated in the widening of the market, local and outside. The medical viewpoint stressing the nutritive value and relative harmlessness of fish, as compared with meat, in the case of certain groups of patients acted as a catalyst in raising the demand for fish.

Yet another spur to the fishing industry was provided by the advance made on the front of fry fingerlings collection and spawning. The Bihar rivers are said to be producing about 52 per cent of the entire riverine spawn of India, a commanding position indeed. The intensive spawn collection activity is concentrated in the Sone and Ganga. The fish spawn is collected from suitable stretches of river banks between July and September every year. The major varieties of fish breed in flooded rivers during the monsoon, and not in confined water. To conclude, the phenomenal rise in the amount of *jeera*/seeds inserted in the most fish production potential parts of the local rivers is one main factors that account for the march of the fishing industry in Bihar.

Next to be considered are the refashioning and introduction of new institutions, organisations and agencies as an adjunct to the development of fishing in Bihar, for instance, reform of the fishers' cooperatives and establishment of the Fish Farmers' Development Agencies. These have reorganised the production and distribution processes as well as, improved fish farming methods and field practices, transport, storage and salting.

Incentives and inducements provided have been in the shape of grant of free leasing right, that is, exemption from the levy called *jalkar* (water tax), insurance of the fishermen, reservation of tanks and ponds for fishing only by the members of the scheduled castes and scheduled tribes, provision of fishing equipment and implements on hire-and-purchase, with subsidy, extension of credit facility to the fishing community from the Department of Fisheries as well as the banks, provision of technical training to the fishing members of the agencies and societies. Of the 6,000 tanks in Bihar, 4,000 are private and loans are sanctioned by the State Government for their renovation. The cost of renovation of the Government/public tanks is borne by the State Government itself.

Young, enterprising and educated people of the capitalist bent of mind have made their debut in the fishing industry and trade, breaking the caste barrier, with a 18 days' training, given free by the Government, as also a Government tank up to the maximum of 1.5 ha. in area loaned on a 10-year contract, adjoining their residence, on payment of a rent equal to 3 per cent of the assessed annual produce having been pledged to the Government. With enterprise and ability to coordinate the implicit activities fish production has multiplied manifold in a good many cases. Where the maximum yield of foodgrains in one acre of land is 6 mds (= 226 kgs.), fish yield is from 188 to 564 kgs., and in exceptional cases 1504 kgs. And when adjusted by relative prices, the gain is amazing, mind-boggling. Joint pisciculture on a 100 per cent subsidy is also in vogue.

Let us have a look at the marketing of fish in Bihar at this juncture. In 1956-57 half of the fish produced in Bihar was marketable surplus. Today the local demand is so heavy everywhere that it is sizably unmet by the local supply. Even in places where this should not have been the situation, exports for higher prices is instrumental in giving rise to it. Were fish not to come from Andhra Pradesh, a sizable number of fish-eaters, especially the Bengalees, who are resident in the State in very high proportions, would feel miserable. Bihar's shortage is to the tune of 2.5 lakh tonnes a year (output 4.5 lakh tonnes minus catch 2.0 lakh tonnes). 50,000 kgs. of fish arrives in Bihar from Andhra Pradesh daily, covering two to three days' journey by road. This is iced fish. The consumers are content with even this fish, and the price is very high. Another 10,000 kgs. a day comes from other States. But, oddly, Bihar exports the same quantity of fish (50 to 60 thousand tonnes a year) as it imports owing to mismanagement. This two-way fish trade is to the disadvantage of the State. What is exported (chiefly to Calcutta) consists mostly of the larger varieties caught in the rivers, viz., Catla, Mringal and Hilsa. Districts of Bihar on the border of West Bengal or conviently linked by trains with Calcutta are the chief exporters of river fish, notable for its uncommon taste.

The fishing industry in Bihar is under several constraints :

One, indecision and laxity on the part of the State Government. In 1981 the Government underwrote the World Bank's assisted fisheries development project, operative in certain districts. Completion of the formalities alone took four years to be completed. The work on it commenced in 1988-89. The Government of India felt constrained to intervene because this related to an externally aided project. This was in 1989. The project was taken over by the Centre. But the financial support to it became erratic. As a result, the progress slowed down. Not all the then 49 districts could be brought within the purview of the project.

Two, in 1985 a World Bank Project was launched to develop 18,000 ha. of tank area within a span of five years. The banks were to advance credit. However, there was default on this account.

Three, the fry fingerlings called *jeera*, i.e., seeds, could not be collected in full. Where 800 million was the target, the achievement was 500 million. Not only the price factor but also the natural factors like flood and drought presented difficulties.

Four, credit was required by the fishing community for the purchase of inputs and tools and implements including the boats and the nets. The equipment claimed 15 per cent of the cost, to be covered by the price of fish. The banks were reluctant to advance funds to the members who lacked credibility. In consequence, the fish price failed to be influenced by the supply of bank credit, as expected. The externally-aided projects too had more or less the same sad experience. After the patronage of the NABARD was enlisted, the situation changed for the better, but financing continues to be the weakest point of the fishing business.

Five, the legal frame within which the fishing trade has to be plied is not quite helpful to it. The tanks and lakes—*jheels*—which were taken over from the erstwhile zamindars are not being looked after properly by the Revenue Department officials. Ownership disputes crop up in the old *zamindari* areas, which often results in an inefficient use of the fishery resources. Furthermore, the leasing rights are owned by the Government or the Gram Panchayats on its behalf. Previously the fishermen's cooperative societies were preferred for grant of the lease. But of late there has been a change in government policy, for the individual fishermen have been authorised by the State Government to fish free. This has sparked off a direct fight between the private owners of the tanks and ponds and the fishermen. This has been a boon to the Naxalite elements in the areas concerned. The whole situation is in a melting pot.

Because of its vast, abundant acquatic resources, such as reservoirs, tanks, ponds, *jheels, tals, mans, chaurs, dhars*, etc., outlined above, befitting the pursuit of fisheries in Bihar (the total area of land under water perennially is 3 lakh acres, another estimate of impounded water areas stands at 75,000 ha. and the area under deep water paddy cultivation is 5 lakh acres, plus 35,000 ha. of *tals . . . dhars*), Bihar's enormous potential for developing inland, fresh water fish industry is irrebuttable, and in this Bihar is next only to Tamil Nadu, West Bengal and Karnataka. As stated above, markets, internal and external, for fish and its allied products are existent. The fortunes of several thousands of fishermen, who represent the most backward communities socially and economically, are very intimately and inseparably bound up with the development of the fishery industry in the State.

Fishing/fish culture is very much akin to the Bihar type agrarian economy which is, intrinsically, a small-farmer-dominated economy. Its relevance as an ideally suited subsidiary occupation to such an economy is beyond question. Its pertinence to land cultivation and utilisation is ingrained in its capability to be integrated with the agrarian mechanism. It is employment-intensive since it is not one activity (say, fish harvesting) but a chain of activities (summated into fish culture), each potent with additional labour utilisation, apart from agriculture, as the prime occupation. Its wealth effect, income effect and consumption effect cannot be overemphasised. Allotment of a portion of the fishery to a fisherperson is resource-begetting. This is the wealth effect. The assets build-up is another example of the same effect. The income earned is another factor in improving a fisherperson's socio-economic condition. Part of the produce invariably enters his or her self-consumption (by and large, for in the distress cases, the whole produce may be for sale/ surrender to the moneylender or the *Bania* who advances the food articles on credit), which improves the nutritional standard of the food eaten. The welfare effect on all those connected with the fishing trade is substantive.

Last but not the least, the suggestions: Fishing, as of today, calls for reorganisation of production and distribution. The shortfall in the collection of fry during seasons other than the rainy must be optimised during the rainy season itself. The prevalent field practices need to be extended. The farming methods of, say, prawn, should be streamlined. The accent should rest on fish culture, not fish harvesting, if additional employment to a much larger number of people is the aim and object. Salting and canning of fish must be speeded up. Adequate provision should be made for cold-transport, cold-storage of fish, etc. More and more fisherpersons should have the opportunity to get trained on the state stipend. Credit and marketing sides of the trade should be paid greater attention than has been the practice so far. Through pre- and advance planning shortfalls in the development of tanks can be avoided. It is worth reiterating here that every rupee invested in the uplift of the fishing industry would be self-financing, and there is no reason why the specialised financial institutions should not come forward to meet the credit needs of this sector.

Animal Husbandry Revisited

The chief problem facing animal husbandry in Bihar is one of low productivity—low yield per animal, low draught capacity per working cattle and low efficiency of the working cattle per unit. Responsible for this is a myriad of factors as under:

Low-level technology, to be interpreted in a broad sense : The poor stock of knowledge and the narrowest mental horizon/ken of vision of the farmer with some livestock or other. The typical village bullock-cart is one burning example of the low-level technological morass. In addition, the low level of the technology is represented by the existing methods in the areas of feeding, breeding, maintaining, etc. of the livestock.

Another problem kindred of the chief one is the existence in a very high proportion (the popular estimate is 10 per cent) of the superfluous cattle—cattle which are totally unproductive and decrepit, useless and diseased, and hence uneconomic, an irrebuttable burden on the soil. This keeps the Man-Animal-Plant-Land combine/nexus in a state of perpetual disarray.

One compelling reason for the livestock's low productivity is its low genetical make-up. In Bihar the cattle breeds are: local Bihari. Bachhaur and Harian. The buffalo breeds are: local Bihari, Harian

Tharparkar, Red Sindhi and Bachhaur. But these compare less favourably with the breeds in Punjab and Haryana. Notwithstanding the progress made during the last four decades and a half, the breeding system remains poor and inferior. In Bihar in most areas farm breeding being far less common, private breeding has been more in evidence but generally this has been a side occupation pursued by certain cultivators.

In recent years the improvement of the quality of the livestock has been paid some increased attention. In 1961 cattle farms were established by the State Government to raise bulls of high potential. With a view to upgrading the breed of the local buffaloes approved buffalo bulls were kept in artificial insemination centres. Besides, sub-centres were opened in the community development blocks. The start was made in 1951, when per breeding bull the number of cows was 68. This number went up to 98 by 1956. In 1989-90 the number of intensive cattle development centres was 9 and that of artificial insemination of cattle centres 112 (which was also the number in 1987-88).

Among the important State sector schemes aimed at the development of the cattle we have, in the period under survey, first, the key village blocks; second, the intensive cattle development projects, under which the intersemination centres provided input and extension support in the rural areas, and the artificial insemination centres focused on the exotic bull semen. The extension staff spread/purveyed the results of the experimental breeding centres. Approved bulls were distributed over a wide expanse to facilitate cattle improvement.

One achievement is the general improvement in the breeding technique. The quality of the livestock (here we should include the poultry counterpart) has since improved. The contribution of the extensive cross-breeding programmes has been of a bigger magnitude.

Even now, there is a lot to be done in the direction of the improvement of the livestock, sheep and goats included, via the breed uplift. To give an example, there is the lacuna in the well-defined local breeds of the cattle as well as in the professional breeders of the livestock which has to be obviated. Even at present the number of breeding bulls per 100 of Bihar's population is ten, as against the all-India average of 15. Efforts to tone up the local breeds and introduce improved breeds often fail largely because of the lack of quality fodder at reasonable prices. This deficiency needs to be corrected. Genetic improvement is interconnected with the castration of all bulls not required for breeding as a mandatory provision.

From the foregoing we have the feeding/fodder problem as an accomplice in the genetical problem. By implication, we have to blame the fodder problem for the low productivity of the cattle. Cattle feeding is defective and insufficient. The cattle are underfed. As Independence dawned upon the country, the State Government realised that Bihar was deficient in cattle feeds and fodder. Seventy-eight per cent of the fodder needs was met from internal sources. People went without food. Animals were starved. Extreme shortage of the cattle feed compelled the owners to keep the majority of the animals on submaintenance ration, especially during the summer months. To combat the situation fodder development received increased private and public attention. Measures were on the anvil/underway/afoot/and what not, to overcome the deficiency by developing the State's fodder resources.

Hay of the traditional type has over the ages remained the basic feeding stuff. The average peasant has in deciding upon the cropping pattern to be adopted by him has assigned fodder production its due place. The density/intensity of cropping has had a determinant in the link-up/symbiosis/coupling of the food/cash crop raised with the raising of fodder and roots as an admixture or a by-product/an incidental/spill-over/fall-out. This has been accompanied by the conservation of the summer monsoon grasses and fodder crops for periods of drought and shortage.

In parts of Bihar with the forest cover pasture feeding has been customary for most cattle. But this has not inoften played havoc with the forests and their vegetation, a matter of grave significance and an astonishing dimension. In Bihar the Chotanagpur region's advantage in the pasture land has been the highest, no doubt, but it has persisted as the most backward region in respect of the livestock. In certain districts like Champaran and Purnea, the Kosi region and certain parts of the plateau region, and, lastly, some of the milk pockets (Monghyr and Saharsa, for instance) with appreciable moisture in the soil and atmosphere pasture feeding has existed in unison with stall-feeding, as an obligatory course of action in months beyond the wet monsoon season, which is limited only to a few months in the year.

By and large, Bihar has been suitable for stall feeding-cum-arable-animal farming. Stall-feeding underlines the possibility and desirability of mixed arable-animal husbandry and a natural integration of these two wings of land utilisation. But systematic stall-feeding requires appropriate supply of fodder and more nutritive feed.

Baled hay produced in the forest areas and sweet potato (also *suthani*) grown ubiquitously in Bihar are valuable cattle feeds.

At the Government level, the thrust of the drive/campaign has consisted in integrating/affiancing the animal husbandry programme with fodder development, in the direction of which good progress has been made. Compact areas for the special programmes for fodder production have been identified. Fodder nurseries have been set up in almost all community development and national extension blocks. Fodder banks (on the lines of the grains-lending banks) have been established.

Grasses and fodder crops available in certain seasons are tried to be conserved with enhanced attention and care. The wastage in the process of hay-making is sought to be reduced.

Purchase of fodder from other States to meet the deficit is an annual feature.*

Were the supply of good quality fodder and feeds to increase and be available evenly to all the owners of all stall-fed cattle, price of milk would fall, as twenty per cent of it is a mere reimbursement of the cost of the fodder and the feeds.

A third factor explaining the low productivity of the livestock in Bihar is their ill-health. The diseased cattle are unproductive. They are a threat to the undiseased cattle even. The cattle diseases are sometimes epidemic. So long as they are confined to the individual cattle, they are controllable, in cases uncomplicated and inserious, but isolation of one individual cattle from the others, that is, its segregation is not easily practicable, as the cattle move and prefer to herd together, joining their mouths or rubbing their bodies against those of the cattle nearby. In a word, the health cover and the disease control of the livestock in the poorest of all States in India have been its worst headache.

The State Government set out vigorously in the direction of disease control from the earliest years of five-year planning and some improvement was the result. The cattle, milch, draught, pack, working, and so on were the beneficiaries. Their weak and poor health found a remedy to the extent that their diseases were at the back of their weak and poor health but the fact that they were not properly fed, not properly housed, not properly managed, and hence they were weak and morbid, disease or no disease, had to be seriously reckoned with and abstracted/segregated from the cases afflicted with diseases, personal or group.

The investment in the cattle by a farmer of limited means is all wasted and fruitless when it falls a prey to some disease or other

* The multi-crore fodder scam under the regime of CM Laloo Prasad Yadav is an event of incalculable significance which may prove to be the Waterloo of the political heavy weights in Bihar, for it is being fought at the High Court level with the assistance of the CBI on direction from the Supreme Court. The deal under contest is a blot on the administration nay, on the humanity in Bihar itself, in so far as it snatched the very feed of the cattle from their mouths. And this during the term of some one supposed to be the Cow Protector.

suddenly without medical help. High death rate/low survival rate and hence a shorter productivity period is the common problem encountered by many an area even today in Bihar. Calf mortality is very high on account of lack of awareness among the farmers about the need for regularly vaccinating animals.

Since Independence animal health care centres, viz., veterinary hospitals and dispensaries (they numbered 1258 in 1989-90), mobile dispensaries, etc., have come up in the State, almost reaching the target of one veterinary dispensary in each community development and national extension block, though, owing to the paucity of contingency funds this infrastructure is failing to provide a type of effective health cover in the sphere of the livestock that had been the planners' concept in its very origin. But this cannot dissuade us from making the observation that through all these years improvements of animal husbandry are perceivable in the field of disease control. The major livestock diseases are now under control by way of prophylactic vaccination, the number of which had risen to 78.64 lakhs in 1989-90. To this we must add the progress that has been made in using the clean dairy farming methods and hygienic standards for equipment and buildings in milk production.

It is rather unfortunate that of late the susceptibility of the livestock has increased to various diseases, entailing increased morbidity and mortality. However, this is eliciting the requisite attention of the experts. It is hoped that this new development would be arrested soon.

To sum up, from the year 1961-62 which saw the establishment of the Animal Husbandry Information and Extension Service in Bihar with the purpose of educating the cultivator-cum-milk producer in modern methods and animal husbandry, through various communication media and organising cattle shows at the State, district and other levels, to the present day, the fact that cattle management has evidently made strides in the area of health, breeding, feeding, dairying, segregation of the unproductive and diseased cattle and their removal to the *Gosadans*, cannot be denied. The real breakthrough occurred during the 1980s under the IRDP, as narrated above, which was reinforced by special livestock production programmes and projects.

Throughout the Plan period so far, the outlay on the animal husbandry and poultry sectors has been on the low side, with the result that the problems posed concerning these sectors have not been tackled in the magnitudes targeted. The industrial areas in Bihar lacking in enterprise and response have failed to stimulate animal husbandry and horticultural activities in their surrounding areas. This is very disappointing.

Suggestions to tone up animal husbandry and poultry and fishery in Bihar have been made by us in passages devoted to them separately, but for the convenience of the readers, the cardinal ones are categorised here: Firstly, the animal husbandry programme should be integrated with the development of fodder. Secondly, the administrative infrastructure should be restructured and refashioned for a more effective implementation of the development programme. Thirdly, the special livestock production programmes and projects should have a focus on the small and marginal farmers and be based on the subsidy principle. Fourthly, these should be monitored as far as possible in the framework of the agricultural produce-oriented cooperative marketing system. Fifthly, agriculture should be balanced with reference to cultivation and animal husbandry within a scheme of controlled grazing in the forest areas. Sixthly, dairying and animal husbandry would continue to be household occupations based chiefly on stall-feeding instead of pasture-grazing owing to the climatic conditions. Seventhly, all agricultural development schemes should simultaneously concentrate on the provision of good bullock power through improved animal husbandry until agriculture is completely mechanised. Eighthly, sheep, goat and pig husbandries and poultry have great potentialities in rehabilitating the landless families. The post-zamindari abolition period has witnessed in Bihar uprooting and proletarization of the small peasantry. The livestock and poultry sectors provided more self-employment opportunities to the socially and economically disadvantaged strata of the rural community, including rural womenfolk, the unemployed youth, etc., compared to any other sector of the rural economy. If unemployment is to be brought down to negligible levels by the turn of the present century, then the State economy in Bihar must generate about 0.9 million additional job opportunities every year. Bulk of these must arise in the rural areas, proportionally less in agriculture and proportionally more in non-agriculture, activities allied to agriculture included. Ninthly and finally, the working cattle become functionally less productive and useful in the case of those household farms which have their size dwindling continuously under the pressure of family partition and in a premeditated bid to circumvent the legislation calculated to seize the landed property from the private hands, and hence it is economically justified that this policy should be brought to a halt but if this cannot be halted, then the remedy lies in paving the way for the switch-over of the working cattle to animal husbandry from agriculture, even if by sale and reinvestment, in order that its productivity looks up.

11

MODERN/NEW AGRARIAN TECHNOLOGY (NAT) IN BIHAR

By the modern/New Agrarian Technology (NAT) we understand the use and application of the bag/assortment/basket/combination/complex/ package comprising, by and large, modern inputs, such as water (for irrigation purpose)—seeds (improved/HYVs)—chemical fertilisers. This *package* may be further expanded to incorporate pesticides, weedicides, etc. Except for the first component input, i.e., irrigation water, which is common to the old, traditional technology, though not in an accentuated, pronounced form, the other component inputs are very much of recent origin and growth and all these component inputs constitute a complex or a package.

The modern inputs are said to be scale-neutral. By their scale-neutrality is implied the idea that individually the modern inputs are perfectly homogeneous and hence infinitely divisible. Collectively, the modern inputs are perfectly complementary and have to be used strictly in certain proportions.

The capability of each modern input to appreciably augment yield is indisputable. As a body or group, in a composite dose, the sumtotal of their capabilities is more than their simple arithmetical total, it is the simple arithmetical total multiplied by a factor analogous to the multiplicand, denoted by the hyphen in between two inputs.

Modern inputs have a certain usage, and central to that usage is a certain timing attribute or trait or characteristic. Only those who possess the two-fold knowledge, knowledge of the usage and knowledge of the timing, are effective in optimising the yield.

We do not have today in Bihar agriculture as many people with a deep knowledge of the NAT as in Punjab agriculture, for example.

So far as the productivity impact of the NAT has been quantified in terms of the yield of a crop per unit of land, not per unit of an individual modern input—irrigation water, seeds, fertilisers, etc.—or even per unit of capital/credit, so crucial to the adoption of the NAT, or per unit of manpower.

In so far as the modern inputs form a package, we can say, more precisely, that under the NAT, the old land-labour combine assumes a new, more expanded form, the land-modern inputs package-labour combine. In the alternative, the old labour and capital co-partnership in production has now reappeared in the parts of the co-partnership between capital subsuming land and other inputs and labour, remaining *in tact.*

Bihar had successively in the last six to seven years good monsoon. Understandably, even this bounty of nature as bestowed on Bihar's native or natural soil fertility could not, in the absence of an adequate supply of the modern inputs, make any salient difference to the yield of crops. Here we should keep in mind the necessary as well as the sufficient condition of the NAT. By so doing we would be in a position to reveal the true genesis of the NAT.

As it is, the NAT has not made any significant impression on Bihar agriculture uptill now. In other words, the NAT has only a limited application in Bihar agriculture. All in all, the NAT has not taken a firm root in Bihar agriculture.

The low productivity level at which Bihar agriculture operates at present is closely associated with the low technology it employs for its various operations.

It would be misleading on our part to remark that societies which cling to the old techniques of agricultural production are traditional, whereas societies which have opted for the new techniques of agricultural production are modern inasmuch as the distinction between the two types of societies is based on other considerations as well. A society which is essentially traditional may have an amalgam of the old and the new techniques, although, in the admixture, the proportion of the new techniques would be negligible. By the same token, we may have a modern society, in whose case the mixture has a far higher proportion of the new techniques and a lower one of the old techniques and that because it subscribes to the ideology of 'walking on both legs'.

The Government subsidies and facilities, price or non-price, credit or non-credit, are best regarded as stimulants to change, from the traditional to the modern society. In such a scenario, the change becomes guided, directed or managed.

Findings derived from field investigations testify to the fact that the rising ratio of farm harvest prices to prices of modern inputs or prices of household consumption goods in the farm sector, purchased from the non-farm sector acts as an inducement to the increased use of these modern inputs and vice-versa. But this is not to deny the existence of a body of studies which is at variance with these findings.

It is time we took a stock of the constraints checkmating the progress of the NAT, which enshrine the problems of supply of inputs, availability of capital/credit, institutional obstacles, etc. Not all areas possess the facilities which the adoption of the NAT presupposes. Here we are not insinuating that small, fragmented holdings cannot lend themselves to the adoption of the NAT with necessary readjustments. Instead we are accepting their ability to do so. The flexibility and adaptability qualities of the NAT make this possible. The NAT has a propensity to become more elastic in its application with the passage of time.

Higher productivity/yield rates, the hall-mark of the NAT, are an attribute not only of the NAT but also of suitable agricultural practices. On a very conservative calculation, a 10 per cent rise in the productivity/ yield rate can be expected from improved agricultural practices, which are equivalent to technological change in agriculture. Increased cropping intensity, which is a ratio between GCA and NSA, is one celebrated example of improved agricultural practices. Increased ratio of GIA to GCA and of GIA to NSA are the two other examples of improved agricultural practices. Yet a fourth form consists in how the enterprising farmers change the texture of the soil by carting earth of complementary type from elsewhere to their own plots to the purpose. The fifth one is the soil conservation measure carried out in the agricultural land. In the rainfed areas another improved agricultural practice relates with the choice of the proper sowing date, as also of the proper time for applying fertilisers. Another one lies in the adoption of inter-cropping and relay cropping methods to minimise the risks of the failure of the monsoon rains. The next one is selection of the short-duration crops which comprise mostly coarse cereals, the poor man's grain.

In 1954-55 the Japanese method of growing paddy/rice was experimented on certain plots in Bihar which showed that paddy yield often exceeded 123.5 mds per hectare for an additional cost of Rs. 247 per hectare. The rise in the value of yield per hectate was Rs. 741. Next year, that is, in 1955-56, the method was introduced in those plots of the State. In 1961-62 experiment in the cultivation of cotton in certain areas of the Chotanagpur region was made. In 1981-82 the cultivation of soyabean in Ranchi and of peanuts/groundnuts in the Kosi region was commenced. In 1985-86 sunflower was grown in the plateau region for the first time.

At present the rural economy in Bihar appears to be walking on both its legs—the old as well as the new techniques—in practically all its principal aspects. In the conditions that obtain in the rural economy of Bihar the old techniques cannot be scrapped and discarded all at once nor can the new techniques be assimilated and absorbed by the rural economy with immediate effect. In either alternative the programme has to be gone through with gradually but steadily. Any attempt to do either on a war footing would unsettle the rural economy in a most abrupt and violent manner. Therefore, for the sake of a smooth change-over, the old techniques must, for a time, stayput, alongwith the new ones.

Increased and sustained improvement in the productivity of Bihar agriculture would provide, firstly, more employment to the rural population and, secondly, maintain more people at a reasonable standard of living. But this prediction cannot be stretched to suggest that the increased productivity of Bihar agriculture and its sustained improvement would provide employment to all the rural people as well as maintain the ever-growing rural population at a reasonable level of living. This would be by all means unbelievable. For that would produce only a limited impact unless the rural people's dependence on agriculture for their living is drastically curtailed.

There was a time when Bihar was acclaimed as the 'garden of India', supplying food to most parts of the country and abroad. In order to regain that position Bihar has to plod for years with the NAT.

With this preliminary remark we now go on to discuss at length the first modern input, irrigation.

12

IRRIGATION IN BIHAR

As would be evident from Table 12.1, North Bihar is a high rainfall region, whereas the soil-moisture condition in South Bihar and Chotanagpur is inferior to that in North Bihar.

94 per cent of total net area sown in Bihar has a reasonably assured supply of rain water, as against the all-India average of 51 per cent only.

TABLE 12.1 : Rainfall in Bihar

(*in mm*)

Region	*South-West Monsoon 1.6.92 to 30.9.92*		*Post-Monsoon 1.10.93 to 31.12.93*		*Winter Monsoon 1.1.94 to 28.2.94*		*Pre-Monsoon 1.3.94 to 31.8.94*	
	Actual	*Normal*	*Actual*	*Normal*	*Actual*	*Normal*	*Actual*	*Normal*
Plains (North and South Bihar)	948	198	53	75	42	31	31	70
Plateau (Santhal Parganas and Chotanagpur)	895	1062	80	99	35	45	45	92

Note : Irrigation statistics of Bihar as contained in *Plan Statistics*, published by State Planning Board, start from the year 1960-61. For statistics preceding 1960-61 we had to depend on other sources, private as well as public publications.

Rainfall

The distribution of the monsoon rains is alleged to be often uneven week-wise, *Nakshatra-wise*. When the *Hathia* showers fail, the rainy season comes to an abrupt close.

Average annual rainfall in Bihar varies from less than 1000 mm around Patna and Gaya to above 1400 mm in the last and extreme south. The variability of rainfall is extremely high in the districts around Patna. For example, Saran and Muzaffarpur are in the low rainfall region. In the flat alluvial regions (North Bihar and South Bihar) the percentage of rainfall tending to infiltrate down to the ground water is about 20 to 22 per cent of annual rainfall. Rainfall is the source of both surface and ground water and hence it controls their interdependence. In the plateau region the percentage of rainfall tending to infiltrate down to the ground water may be between 5 to 9 per cent of annual rain fall.

Rain water is stored in tanks and reservoirs for irrigation. Among the reservoirs in Bihar we have the following :

Statement showing Reservoirs in Bihar

1. Auranga
2. Bal Paharhi
3. Barnar
4. Durgavati
5. Konar
6. Maithon
7. North Kosi
8. Panchet
9. Punsel
10. Tenughat
11. Tilaiya

Some irrigation works are dependent on such rivers as are adequately snow-fed. A few others are dependent partly on inadequately snow-fed rivers and partly on yearly rainfall. The yearly rainfall assumes significance in the case of those irrigation works which are not dependent or, if dependent, then only dependent, in part, on snow-fed rivers.

About 90 per cent of the annual total rainfall is received during the short period of four months (from mid-June to mid-October).

The Rivers

The rivers in Bihar contribute immensely to irrigation. Ganga is the key river. In addition to Ganga and its tributaries, other rivers are Sone, Punpun, Falgun, Barakar, Koel, Kiul, Harohar, Damodar and Subarnarekha. Among the tributaries of Ganga are Ghaghra, Gandak, Kosi (meaning the *River of Sorrow*) and Mahananda.

During the rainy season the subsoil water level rises along the beds of the tributaries of the rivers, which is helpful to the farmers in getting irrigation water for the crops. Use of river water has made possible a successful agriculture.

In North Bihar and South Bihar we have snow-fed-cum-rainfed rivers. The North Bihar rivers have their catchments in the perennial water source region. The South Bihar rivers do not have their catchments in perennial water source region, except Sone, extending upto Madhya Pradesh and Uttar Pradesh. They are all rainfed with smaller catchments. Except in the monsoon, they have very little water. All the rivers in the Chotanagpur region are rainfed. Storing their water is a difficult problem. At times it becomes very difficult to sink a well as the soil is very hard.

Flood

Perhaps the most impressive work carried out in Bihar during the Plan years is in the direction of flood control. In 1954 the strategy adopted to control flood was multi-pronged.

In 1954, 25 lakh ha. land was vulnerable to flood. In 1986, the area had risen to 61/65 lakh ha.; of which about 54 per cent remained to be protected. Nearly Rs. 1140 was the outlay per ha. and Rs. one crore per km. on embankment construction during 1954-86.

Maintenance of the embankments constructed to control flood siphons off four-fifths of the funds allotted to the head 'flood control', the remaining one-fifth being available for the construction of more embankments.

Let us at this juncture remind ourselves of some statistics : Nearly 16 per cent of total land area in Bihar is flood-prone. About 17 lakh ha. land in North Bihar is flood-prone. One-third of the cultivated land in some districts of North Bihar remains flooded during the Kharif season. 32.9 lakh ha. land is prone to acute waterlogging in North Bihar. Nearly one-fourth of South Bihar is flood-prone.

The catchment of the rivers like Ajay, Punpun and Sone are flood-prone. Flood is being fought at the Government level since 1954 as it is a recurrent phenomenon in Bihar.

National calamities take a toll of about twenty lakh tonnes of foodgrains every year, on the average, in Bihar.

The damage done in a year to a harvest by a flood or a drought in Bihar cannot fully be made good in another single year of good rainfall—arrears remain to be made up in the next year or years, provided the history is not repeated.

Water Resources

Bulk of Bihar floats on water. In the plains of Bihar water is available within 10 to 20 feet of the ground level.

The Gangetic plain contains 5.26 per cent of the annually utilisable ground water resources of the entire country.

Uses of Irrigation

The greatest use of water resources is for irrigation. Irrigation is the artificial application of water to crops.

Irrigation is a promotional input for agriculture. It has a production-augmenting effect. Other things being equal, the field levels under irrigated cropping are higher than those under non-irrigated cropping.

According to an estimate, one per cent increase in the irrigated area is capable of augmenting agricultural output by about 2.1 per cent.

Irrigation has a land-augmenting effect. As the use of water resources develops, the area of land resources put to production uses also increases.

Where the water resource conjuncts with the land resource, land productivity rises nearly six times and this gain is akin to the output from land, in area a multiple of the former land, denoting as if the land had, in effect, increased economically, if not physically.

Irrigation by bringing water to the waste and uncultivated land makes it cultivable.

It is water, and not the available land surface, which is the more limiting factor in land utilisation. The problem of conservation of water and its utilisation is, therefore, of paramount importance.

Irrigation has a production stabilising effect. It serves as an insurance against the vagaries of the monsoon rainfall. It insulates agricultural production from the impact of a poor monsoon. It helps to meet the challenge of an aberrant weather.

As only about 10 per cent of the annual total rainfall is received in the months from January to mid-June and after mid-October to December, irrigation with the help of surface and ground water is unavoidable for cropping intensity exceeding 100 per cent.

Over the rainy season irrigation rectifies the deficiency in the distribution of precipitation and helps the farmer to keep to the time-schedule as expected *Nakshatra*-wise.

Only on the basis of irrigation could a stable agricultural production base be built up.

Irrigation has an employment effect. It is an aid to agricultural intensity. It holds the key to the intensification of farming. It also contributes to the diversification of agriculture in its own way. During the dry season it increases the diversity of the cropping pattern.

A technological transition from rain-based agriculture to assured irrigation-based agriculture is replete with high employment potential. According to a calculation, one per cent increase in the irrigated area is capable of augmenting rural employment by about 0.8 per cent.

Irrigation-based agriculture is employment-intensive, provided irrigation is comprised not only of construction of the source of it but also of its utilisation and maintenance and thus combined with cultivation.

Water should be available in all agricultural seasons in a balanced manner if agriculture were to be a year-round occupation.

Availability or non-availability of irrigation facility to land in one and the same village makes a lot of difference to land values.

Irrigation development transforms itself into rural development. Extension of the means of irrigation to the countryside represents a new environmental factor which necessitates a structural or organisational change of some kind or other.

Water transport may be a potent factor in income propagation as was true of Bihar for long. Its decline has worsened Bihar's position *vis-a-vis* other States where water transport is still as robust todav as it was in the past.

Irrigation is an insurance against uncertain rainfall and during a drought. The drought-prone areas have, by and large, low water resources, for which reason they have to depend, in general, on rainfed agriculture. The years of drought in Bihar were 1966-67, 1972-73, 1977-78, 1979-80, 1992-93 and 1993-94. The 1966-67 drought-led *ahars* (i.e., artificial reservoirs or shallow catchment basins), *pynes* (i.e., channels or ditches), etc., fell into disuse after the drought and were neither renovated nor replaced and hence fell into disrepair.

We have listed above districts in the State which are drought-prone. Gaya is one such district. It is within the Sone Command Area. Despite this in it use of irrigation water is low. This may be due to low consumption of fertilisers.

In 1992, of the 91 drought-prone districts in India, five, viz., Monghyr, Nawadah (part of old Gaya), Palamau, Rohtas and Santhal Parganas were in Bihar. In July-August 1993 a drought—like situation obtained in the State. About 10.7 lakh ha. land could not be cultivated for Kharif.

Origins of Irrigation in Bihar

Irrigation was an old art in Bihar. References to it have been traced to many centuries prior to the commencement of the Christian era. Irrigation appears to have begun with agriculture itself. Some tanks had been in existence for ages.

The known history of public sector irrigation in Bihar commenced in 1853 with Lt. Col. Dicken's suggestion for the construction of the Sone canals. The Sone canals were completed in 1875 with a total capital outlay of Rs. 268 lakh. They irrigated 265 thousand ha. of land and yielded 7.3 per cent return on the capital outlay.

The Tribeni canal was taken up in 1903 and completed in 1914 with a total capital outlay of Rs. 82 lakhs. It took off from Gandak. It irrigated 46 thousand ha. of land and yielded a return of 3.1 per cent on the capital outlay. The vast amount of ground water had probably delayed the construction of the Tribeni canal till 1903 as surface water resource had not actually been needed. At present it irrigates lands in Champaran (both), Gopalganj, Siwan, Saran, Muzaffarpur and Vaishali.

The Tiar, Teur and Dhaka canals also take off from Gandak.

At Independence Bihar was one of the four States noted for irrigation, namely, Uttar Pradesh, Punjab, Madras (later Tamil Nadu) and Bihar. In spite of this Bihar's irrigation base was poor. Agricultural activities in the State were largely dependent on the timely rains.

Bihar's Ultimate Irrigation Potential

Surface water resource is that portion of the rainfall which is channelised into streams or rivers and utilised.

Ground water resource is that portion of the rainfall which is absorbed by seepages and fissures.

Bihar has inexhaustible sources of ground water. Upto 1960-61 there was no clear estimate of the water resources of North Bihar. South Bihar and Chotanagpur had about 3 per cent of the all-India water resources, with which they could irrigate 4.048 million ha. of land.

On the basis of information that became available subsequently, the total annual replenishable ground water resources in Bihar may be put at 3.3 m ha. metres.

The annually usable ground water resources in Bihar are estimated at 2.86 ha. metres.

Bihar is rich in hydro reserves. It ranks third, the first and second ranks going to Uttar Pradesh and Andhra Pradesh respectively.

The identified irrigation potential under major and medium irrigation projects in Bihar is 65 lakh ha. and under minor irrigation projects it is 59 lakh ha., which gives a sumtotal of 124 lakh ha. (Table 12.2).

TABLE 12.2 : Estimate of Ultimate Irrigation Potential of Bihar : 1993-94

(*Lakh ha.*)

Sources	*Area*	*As Percentage of All-India*
Major and Medium	65.00 (584.65)	11.11
Minor	59.00* (550.00)	10.72
Total	124.00 (1135.00)	10.92

* One estimate of Bihar's ultimate ground water resources potential is 71.917 lakh ha.

The ultimate potential, i.e., benefits to be derived, of the multipurpose and major irrigation projects in Bihar is summed up in Table 12.3.

The collective ultimate irrigation potential of the six major irrigation projects of Bihar viz., (1) Sone, (2) Kosi Eastern, (3) Rajpur, (4) Lower Kiul Valley, (5) Badua, and (6) Chandan is 24.78 lakh ha. The potential of the Subarnarekha project would be 2 lakh ha.

TABLE 12.3 : Ultimate Potential/Benefits of Multipurpose and Major Irrigation Projects in Bihar

Sl. No.	*Name of Project*	*Area ('000 ha.)*
1.	Western Kosi Canal	289.30
2.	Bagmati	101.40
3.	Subarnarekha (inter-State)	209.30
4.	North Kosi Reservoir	131.00
5.	Durgavati Reservoir	63.40
6.	Barnar Reservoir	22.40
7.	Konar Diversion	62.80
8.	Tilaiya Diversion	48.60
9.	Bateshwarasthan Punp Phase I-Banasagar (inter-State)	25.40
10.	Ajoy Barrage Sika	40.40
11.	Gandak Phase II	70.00
12.	Kosi Eastern Canal Phase I	(No direct benefit)
13.	Masan Dam	82.00
14.	Auranga Reservoir	55.40
15.	Punsel Reservoir	24.00

Progress of Irrigation

In 1951, as percentage of NSA, area irrigated in North Bihar was 9.8 per cent (equal to 3.56 lakh ha.), 5.4 per cent in South Bihar (equal to 13.84

lakh ha.) and 12.5 per cent in the Chotanagpur plateau (equal to 3.52 lakh ha.).

In 1951 canal irrigation was available in the Sone valley and Champaran district to a moderate extent.

At the 1951 Census, in Saran cultivation depended to a large extent on artificial irrigation; wells formed the chief source. Canals provided irrigation to a large area in Champaran. Elsewhere in the North Bihar plain irrigation was not practised to any large extent. It became necessary in years of deficit rainfall.

At 1951 the Tribeni, Dhaka and Teur Canals covered Champaran.

At the 1951 Census, in the South Bihar plain, the construction of small and medium irrigation works was facilitated by the slope of the country and the shallow channels of rivers. As a result, artificial irrigation was practised more extensively in this region than in the other two regions of Bihar and 54 per cent of the cultivated area was irrigated. The Sone Canal System served the greater part of Shahabad and small portions of Gaya and Patna. During some years preceding the census, lift irrigation was provided in parts of Patna and Shahabad. Elsewhere, irrigation was done mainly from *Ahars* and *Pynes* and to a small extent from wells.

In 1951 the Sone Canal covered Shahabad, Patna and part of Gaya.

In 1951 the Sakri Canal covered Gaya.

The rugged nature of the country did not facilitate the construction of extensive irrigation works at cheap cost in the plateau region. Irrigation was, therefore, practised only to a small extent.

Before the inception of the First Plan Bihar had four canal systems, namely, Sone, Tribeni, Dhaka and Teur—these provided assured irrigation facilities to 4.03 lakh ha. Besides this, the 180 State tubewells had been sunk in Shahabad and Patna districts which irrigated an area of 0.19 lakh ha.

In 1951, 18.21 lakh ha. under the command of the various minor irrigation works, i.e., built around diversion arrangements, were essentially temporary and were intended to make available the run-off of local rain water in the good years. They contributed at best to strengthen the.precarious cultivation in the command.

The economics of the canals during 1950-51 is given in Table 12.4.

During the First Plan none of the important river valley projects like Kosi, Gandak or Sone was taken up as part of the Plan.

Important schemes taken up were the Triveni Canal system, the Botave Reservoir Scheme, the Upper Morhar and the lower Kiul Irrigation Schemes.

TABLE 12.4 : Economics of Canals in Bihar : 1950-51

Name	*Mileage of Canal Operation including distributaries*	*Total Capital Outlay (Rs.)*	*Net Revenue (Rs.)*	*Net Profit (+) or Loss (–)*
Sone Canal	1588	26823344	1504918	(+) 640184
Tribeni Canal	247	8158407	1128443	(–) 1393188
Dhaka Canal	43	632773	21557	(+) 930
Teur Canal	13	066	—	—
Sakri Canal	44	2205	(-) 001	(-) 0,54

All in all, during 1951-65 the irrigation facility was extended even to the barren lands.

In the formative years of planning the rural development projects under the community development programme and the IADP accorded priority to areas possessing irrigation facility or assured rainfall and aimed at extending irrigation benefit to half of the cultivated area.

Farmers were stimulated to go in for irrigation faster on securing better prices for their produce and subsidies in different forms.

The CWC prepared in 1987 a perspective plan for the Ganga basin water resources development.

Recently the Sone River Commission completed a comprehensive plan for irrigation development.

Major Irrigation Works : The River Valley Projects

Irrigation projects are classified at present on the basis of the area cultivated within their commands or catchments as major, medium and minor.

That the fixation of the command area of an irrigation project has been done chiefly with reference to the requirements of kharif is proof of its relative importance in sharing the water supply.

Major irrigation projects are those projects which have a CCA of more than 10,000 ha.

Medium irrigation projects are those projects which have a CCA of more than 2000 ha. and upto 10,000 ha.

Minor irrigation projects are those projects which have a CCA of less than 2000 ha.

The major and medium irrigation projects are part of surface irrigation projects.

By 1994, 23 major and 163 medium irrigation projects had been completed in Bihar.

Most of the major and medium irrigation works simply distributed the rain water supply over space in keeping with the requirements of individual crops, as also over time in order to remedy the uneven distribution of rainfall from week to week or an abrupt and early close of the rainy season on account of the failure of the *Hathia* showers.

Between 1950-51 and 1988-89 the percentage share of major and medium works in irrigation GIA went up by 15.98 per cent, whereas that of minor works went down by the same percentage—the percentage of ground water minor works rising by 29.67 per cent and that of surface water minor works falling by 45.65 per cent (Table 12.5).

TABLE 12.5 : Percentage Distribution of Gross Irrigated Area in Bihar by Sources

Year	*Major and Medium Works : Surface Water Percentage Share*	*Minor Works*			*Total*	
		Ground Water Percentage Share	*Surface Water Percentage Share*	*Total of (3) and (4)*	*Coverage (Lakh Ha.)*	*Percentage*
1950-51	19.38	12.41	68.21	80.62	20.19	100.00
1960-61	25.94	12.65	61.41	74.06	20.63	100.00
1967-68	36.20	20.28	43.52	63.80	20.11	100.00
1988-89	35.36	42.08	22.56	64.64	42.43	100.00

Among the multipurpose river valley projects in Bihar were the Gandak project on the Gandak, the Kosi, the Banasagar (on the Sone), the Damodar Valley Project (DVC) on the Damodar, the Kiul-Badua-Chandan Subaranarekha (yet to commence), Mayurakshi and Rangali Mandira.

The river valley projects are to subserve a trinity of purposes : (1) to generate electricity, (2) to control flood, and (3) to irrigate lands. We may add navigation and horticulture and pisciculture as other, minor purposes. Hence, they are known as multipurpose projects.

The *Gandak Project* was perhaps the cheapest irrigation project in the country. The Gandak canal system irrigates the sugar belt.

The *Kosi Project* was included as part of the Second Plan and the barrage was under construction. The flow of Kosi was diverted through the barrage at Hanuman Nagar on March 31, 1963 against heavy odds. Kosi now flows through the barrage. The Kosi-Mahananda canal passes through Saharsa, Madhepura, Purnea and Katihar.

The Kosi canals have helped in the reclamation of vast tracts of land, about 1,40,000 ha., rendered waste by Kosi in the past. The Kosi canals provide assured irrigation. The two embankments of the Kosi Project afford direct protection against recurring flood. The Belka dam and the Kothar Dam have hydro-electricity potential.

The Sone Canal system caters to nine districts in the region. It irrigates substantial areas in Aurangabad, Gaya, Patna, Rohtas, Bhojpur and Buxar districts. In parts of its catchment the Sone Canal system decayed for almost three decades from 1951 to 1981.

The two high-level canals of the Sone Barrage Project irrigate about 1.2 lakh ha. more land.

The Damodar Valley Project was started in 1950 and completed in 1953. The Damodar Valley Corporation (DVC) was formed with the involvement of the Governments of Bihar and West Bengal. It was funded by a World Bank loan.

The multipurpose storage dams, e.g., Tilaiya, Konar, Maithon and Panchet Hill with hydro-electric plants have been constructed in the Damodar Valley Project with a view to irrigating vast tracts of land by constructing canals and ensuring effective flood control.

A small 12.5 mile-long canal from the Massanjore dam irrigates about 9 thousand ha. of land in Dumka district.

The steel city of Jamshedpur, the copper mines at. Ghatsila, the coalfields of Jharia, etc. have their power supply from the Bokaro Thermal Power Station and the hydel power stations at Tilaiya, Maithon and Panchet.

Certain parts of the DVC resulted in the submergence of many villages and a large forest area and uprooting of the people in the tribal belt of Bihar—an environmental damage. Had these costs been taken into account, the benefits from the project would have very much diminished.

All the same, there are a few small dams of late origin, such as Palana dam near Jamshedpur, Tajna Barrage and Buchaopa dam in Ranchi district, which provide irrigation to areas in the tribal belt of Bihar without uprooting people and submerging the forest area on a large scale.

On the whole, however, the irrigation benefit of the DVC accrued largely to the people outside the tribal belt for non-agricultural purposes.

The canal systems were primarily designed to provide protective irrigation, that is, insurance against crop failure.

With the progressively increasing intensity of cultivation and development of hybrids and the HYVs requiring five to six waterings for maturity, the canal system have proved inadequate to provide the optimum irrigation requirements.

The multipurpose major projects at present provide little irrigation within South Bihar and Chotanagpur.

Because of their deep levels the major rivers of Chotanagpur and Santhal Parganas cannot be used for canal irrigation.

All the same, the river valley projects are another instrument with which the irrigation potential has been developed.

Created Irrigation Potential

'Irrigation Potential' is interpreted with reference to the area which can be irrigated with the irrigation means water available at a channel outlet. Roughly speaking, in 1950-51 Bihar's share in all-India created irrigation potential was nearly 2.7 per cent. By 1992-93 it had risen to nearly 9.6 per cent (Table 12.6).

In 1993-94 the irrigation potential created in Bihar was 82 lakh ha., against the ultimate potential of 124 lakh ha., that is, 66 per cent—42.5 per cent in the case of major and medium projects and 91.5 per cent in the case of minor ones. In all-India the created irrigation potential was 75 per cent of the ultimate potential—54 per cent in the case of major and medium works and 97 per cent in that of minor ones. Thus, in making headway on the irrigation front, Bihar was below the all-India average. The ultimate irrigation potential had been inadequately harnessed in Bihar, specially in respect of the major and medium projects.

As Table 12.7 shows, in the case of three multipurpose major projects, which are presented here for the sake of illustration, the potential created is as low as 26.60 per cent but only as high as 59.84 per cent.

TABLE 12.7 : Multipurpose and Major Irrigation Projects

Sl. No.	*Name of the Project*	*Potential Created at the End of 1991-92 ('000 ha.)*	*(3) as Percentage of Ultimate Potential*
1.	Western Kosi Canal	62.50	26.60
2.	North Kosi Reservoir	78.40	59.84
3.	Gandak Phase II	24.50	35.00

While there is unanimity on the disclosure that the irrigation potential in the Kosi and Gandak systems has not been developed in full, opinions on the minor counterpart differ. An extreme view holds that only 25 per cent of the ground water resource in Bihar is exploited, as compared to 43 per cent in all-India. This makes our figures look too big.

TABLE 12.6 : Irrigation Potential as Created in Bihar

(Lakh ha.)

Sl. No.	*Sources*	*During First Plan*	*1982-83*	*1984-85*	*1985-86*	*1989-90*	*1990-91*	*1991-92*	*March 1992,*	*1992-93*	*1993-94*
1.	Major Projects	4.03				22.84					
2.	Medium Projects	1.87						13.65			
	(Surface Water)							(114.56)			
3.	Major & Medium	5.90	33.025	34.32+		27.75		24.25++			28.00
	Projects	(97 in	(291)	25.3++		27.15		25.25++			(321)
		1950-51)		28.3+++++		(329)		27.35		27.00	
				(300)		22.84		(307)		27.96	
								48.18			
								(503.48)		(313.57)	
								59+++			
								90++++			
4.	Minor Projects	0.19/0.20	(342)	(375)	35.92*	(468)	46.06*	(503)	48.74		54.00
	Ground Water	(129 in						35.12			(534)
	Schemes	1950-51)						(388.92)			
5.	All Sources	6.10	(633)	(675,		(797)		101.47			82.00
		(226 in						108.00			(855)
		1950-51)						(810)			

\+ CWC.

++ State Irrigation Department.

+++ After allowing annual decline at the rate of 5 per cent—State Government's figure.

++++ State Government's figure.

+++++ State Planning Board.

* As percentage of TCA/SCA 34.15 in 1985-86 and 43.93 in 1990-91.

Note : Irrigation potential created in Bihar during the Seventh Plan was 11.3 million ha., according to the State Government.

TABLE 12.8 : Utilisation of Created Irrigation Potential

(Lakh ha.)

Source	*During First Plan*	*1979-80 to 1983-84*	*1981-82*	*1982-83*	*1983-84*	*1984-85*	*1989-90*	*1990-91*	*1991-92*	*1992-93*	*1993-94*
Medium (Surface water)									12.22 (102.88)		
Major & Medium Project	1.07	17.00++		4.513		21.75+	19.0*			23.25 (268.71)	
Minor Ground water : Effective									43.58 (465.57) 31.35 (362.48)		16.94
All Sources						27.76**	14.79++ 21.48	14.11++ 20.08+	18.85+	33.44	

+ Irrigation Department.
++ Statistics Department.
* Azit Mazoomdar.
** State Planning Board.

Utilisation of Created Irrigation Potential

An absolute, area terms and all sources considered, during the First Plan, of the created potential of 5.90 lakh ha., only 1.07 lakh ha. was utilised, which gave a percentage of 18. In 1992-93, of the created potential of 28 lakh ha., utilised potential was 23.25 lakh ha., which yielded a percentage of 83 (Table 12.8). This apart, the vicious/faulty nature of the data cannot be overemphasised.

In recent years the created potential in the major projects appears to have been utilised upto 45 to 46 per cent, as revealed by Table 12.9.

TABLE 12.9 : Utilisation of Created Potential : 1991-92 End

(Percentage)

Name of Major Project	*Utilisation Percentage*
Western Kosi Canal	52.00
North Kosi Reservoir	38.26
Gandak Phase II	48.98

In 1985-86 the major irrigation works like Kosi, Gandak, Kamla and Sone etc., irrigated about 9.94 lakh ha. land (1.29, 6.04, 0.21, 2.40 lakh ha. respectively), as against the expected area of 21.37 lakh ha. This gave a figure of 46 to 47 per cent.

In some years the percentage in which the existing potential of the major and medium projects was tapped was as low as 13.14 per cent (Table 12.10).

TABLE 12.10 : Magnitudes of Utilisation of Created Irrigation Potential in Bihar

(In Percentage)

Type of Projects	*Period/Year*	*Utilisation as Percentage of Total Created*
(1)	(2)	(3)
Major	In the current years	75
Government Canals,	do	40
e.g., Kosi and Gandak	do	(less than) 55
Major & Medium	do	76 to 93
	First Plan	57
	1982-83	13.75
Minor	First Plan to Present Day	100.00

(Contd.)

TABLE 12.10 (*Contd.*)

(1)	(2)	(3)
Ground water Resource+	Current	23.56
	1978-79	18.10
	1982	25.00
All Sources	1978	24.09
	1981-82	77.00
	1982-83	13.75
	1984-85	76.91
	1989-90	53.09
		79.00
	1990-91	51.07
		73.00
	1991-92	69.00
	Current	30.00

+ The statistics given here are relevant more to the utilimate rather than to the created potential.

Utilisation of the irrigation potential of the Government canals has been reported to be as low as 40 per cent.

It is generally believed that the potential of the minor schemes of irrigation in the private sector, for instance, under tubewell irrigation, is exploited cent per cent.

All sources considered, since 1978 the lowest percentage of utilisation was 25 per cent in 1978 and the highest 79 per cent in 1989-90. Obviously, this might be the aftermath of the remarkable progress made by the minor sources, reducing the proportion of the major and medium ones to the minimum.

Faults of Irrigation Systems

Two evident weaknesses of the irrigation systems must be noted : One is that the whole of the created irrigation potential under the projects is not utilised at present. There is less than full utilisation of the created capacity. The other is that there is an inevitable lag between the construction of the storage and distribution schemes and the actual utilisation of the irrigation potential. To substantiate, in the case of major and medium schemes, the effective utilisation of the created potential has taken, on an average, 5 to 7 years.

We must distinguish between the estimated potential of a source of irrigation and its actual potential. The latter may fall short of the former. The actual potential turns on how well the source is maintained. If it is not in proper working condition, the actual potential may be considerably lower than the calculated. Secondly, it turns on the volume of water available per unit of time. If the volume falls, the actual potential may be significantly less than the estimated.

Generally, one cusec outlet is capable of irrigating about 40 ha. area under its command. The effectiveness of one cusec outlet turns on the type of soil and the crop raised.

The canals are not realigned or, if realigned, then they are realigned scantily, with the *ahars*, though water rates are charged to those farmers who fall within the jurisdiction of the *ahars*. This is another hindrance.

Less than full exploitation of the created irrigation potential is explained largely by the non-development so far of a satisfactory distribution-cum-drainage system.

Absence of a satisfactory distribution-drainage system is another factor accounting for a lower percentage utilisation of the created potential. The potential created under the major and medium irrigation projects is not used optimally due to certain critical gaps in field channels, *inter alia* other ones. The State Government has so far failed to construct field channels in an adequate number. According to one study, 25 per cent of the created potential of the major projects is not utilised owing to inadequacy of the field channels, etc. Where field channels exist, the State Government has failed to adequately maintain them. During the crucial periods of transplanting paddy saplings and irrigating the rabi crops the inadequacy of water channels and courses is most acutely experienced.

Also, assured irrigation cannot be guaranteed from the 40-hectare outlets.

Another reason for the underutilisation of the created irrigation potential is the ignorance on the part of the average peasant of the cropping pattern conducive to irrigated farming. The ordinary farmer lacks the knowledge basic to the change-over from a system of dry/rainfed farming to irrigated agriculture.

Certain critical gaps in the drainage system result in a suboptimal utilisation of the created potential. In North Bihar drainage and tube-well development are complementary. The State Government has so far failed to construct field drains in the requisite number. Waterlogging is hard hitting factor.

Where field drains exist, the Government has failed to properly maintain them.

Summing up, whether or not the created potential of the sources of irrigation would be utilised in full or less than full and in what degree is determined by a host of factors as follows :

1. Whether or not they are in good working condition.
2. Existence or absence of field channels.
3. Evenness or unevenness of the land surface.
4. Ownership, private or public or joint.
5. Water rates, high, low or economic.
6. Availability of alternative cheaper and easier to operate sources.
7. Sufficiency or insufficiency of rainfall in a particular season.
8. Whether there is some mechanical disorder or not.
9. Lack or no lack of lifting water, etc.

The Command Area Development Authorities (CADAs)

For the full and efficient utilisation of the irrigation potential the Government set up the CADAs for the major river systems.

The CADA is a Centrally-sponsored scheme. It aims at bridging the chasm between potential created and potential utilised so that the irrigation system optimises agricultural production.

The beginning of the CADA in 1974-75 acted as the harbinger of the birth of micro-planning in the area of irrigation.

Since 1974-75 the CADAs are striving to provide field channels in the whole of each command area as expeditiously as possible.

Conjunctive use of surface and groundwater is to be encouraged in the command areas of major and medium irrigation projects through a programme of sinking tube-wells so as to alleviate the waterlogging problem.

The cropping patterns in the command areas should be reworked in terms of the new zonal and sub-zonal agricultural priorities.

A number of the channels constructed by the CADAs have silted up for want of maintenance.

Neither the beneficiaries of the field channels nor the panchayats have been interested in paying towards the costs of their construction and their maintenance with the result that the CADAs are unable to recover the costs.

Underutilisation of capacity is one charge levelled against the Command Area Development Project.

Another charge against the CADA is the neglect of land levelling.

In those areas under the Command Area Development Agency where land levelling has constituted bulk of its total activity, the rate of return on the investment has been as high as 81.8 per cent. The agency has promoted a cropmix in which vegetables production has preponderated. In the growth of output extensive cultivation, i.e., area expansion has accounted for 19 per cent and yield improvement 9 per cent.

Gross and Net Irrigated Areas

Whereas GIA in Bihar nearly doubled during 1950-51 to 1990-91 (in all-India it increased by 264 per cent), the State's share in all-India aggregate GIA fell from 9.21 to about 6.91 per cent, as would appear from Table 12.11.

TABLE 12.11 : Gross Irrigated Area in Bihar

(Lakh ha.)

Year	*Area*	*Percentage Share in All-India*
1950-51	20.62 (225.6)	9.21
1958-59	20.61	
1959-60		6.59
1960-61	20.63 (274.8)	7.50
1961-62	21.87	
1965-66	27.34	
1970-71	33.62 (381.9)	8.80
1971-72		7.60
1975-76	33.62 (433.6)	7.75
1980-81	36.32 (497.8)	7.29
1984-85	38.00 (540.8)	7.02
1989-90	41.22 (596.4)	6.91
1990-91	41.92	

During 1950-51 to 1990-91 GCA in Bihar remained more or less unaltered (10450 *versus* 10485 thousand ha.). Foodgrains output increased by about 275 per cent during the period (from 44.52 to 122.5 lakh tonnes). Thus irrigation helped the same area to yield an increased food output more than proportionately to the increase in itself.

GIA as percentage of TRA in Bihar in 1956-57 was 22.9 per cent (all-India 17.3 per cent). In 1978-79 the percentage in Bihar was 32.57 (another estimate 34.69) per cent.

In 1989-90 GIA as percentage of total created irrigation potential in Bihar was 81.3 per cent (all-India 85.2).

GIA in Bihar as percentage of GCA in the State rose from 18.0 in 1950-51 to 39.6 per cent in 1989-90—a net gain of 21.6 per cent (as against a rise from 17.11 to 32.92 in all-India, a net gain of 15.81 per cent). Progress of GIA has been faster in Bihar as compared to all-India (Table 12.12).

TABLE 12.12 : Gross Irrigated Area as Percentage of Gross Cropped Area in Bihar

Year	*Percentage*
1950-51	18.0 (17.11)
1956-57	15.0 (15.30)
1960-61	18.6 (18.31)
1962-65	20.13 (19.00)
1965-66	20.9 (19.90)
1970-71	24.8 (23.04)
1975-76	29.8 (25.36)
1980-81	32.6 (28.32)
1980-82	33.67 (29.29)
1981-82	33.7 (29.15)
1982-83	34.7 (30.00)
1984-85	36.7 (30.72)
1987-88	39.8 (32.52)
1989-90	39.6 (32.92)
1992-95	43.18 (35.66)
1993-94	43.2 (36.50)

The ratio of GIA to GCA is a measure of technological change, that is, an indicator of improvement of agricultural practices.

From the data given above it is obvious that irrigation in Bihar has remained a shade above irrigation in all-India in relative terms.

On the eve of planning when the rainfall was scanty, area irrigated was around 24 per cent. As present the figure is about 40 per cent.

Another indicator of improvement in agricultural practices, i.e., technological change in agriculture is the percentage of GIA to NSA. This nearly doubled in Bihar during 1950-51 to 1990-91, as indicated by Table 12.13.

TABLE 12.13 : Percentage of Gross Irrigated Area to Net Sown Area in Bihar

Year	*Percentage*
1950-51	24.28
1958-59	—
1959-60	—
1960-61	25.70
1961-62	—
1965-66	27.0/32.77
1970-71	32.30/40.21
1971-72	—
1971-74 (Average)	25.5
1975-76	25.20/39.7
1980-81	43.68
1984-85	—
1989-90	—
1990-91	49.6

Between 1950-51 and 1990-91 NIA in Bihar went up by 162 per cent but the State's share in all-India aggregate NIA slid down from 10.0 to 7.05 per cent during the same period, that is, about 3 per cent (Table 12.14).

TABLE 12.14 : Net Irrigated Area in Bihar

(Lakh ha.)

Year	*Area*	*Percentage Share in All-India*
(1)	(2)	(3)
1950-51	20.6 (207.85)	10.08
1954-55	16.07 (218.9)	7.34
1959-60	18.07 (237.7)	7.60
1960-61	(246.6)	8.42
1961-62	19.43	—
1965-66	19.92	—
1970-71	21.55	6.93
1975-76	27.60	—
1980-81	29.53 (387.2)	7.62
1982-83	—	3.26+
1984-85	27.95 (417.2)	6.70
1989-90	31.24 (451.4)	6.92
1990-91	33.47 (474.3)	7.05
1992-93	33.44 (501.01)	6.67
1995	32.00	—

+ Appears to be absurd.

During the same period NSA in Bihar rose by nearly 122 per cent (8561 *versus* 10419 thousand ha.), whereas food production increased by 275 per cent. Thus 162 per cent increase in NIA brought about a 275 per cent increase in food outturn, much more than proportionally.

NIA in Bihar as percentage of NSA in the State increased from 18.9 in 1950-51 to 40.4 per cent in 1989-90—a net gain of 21.5 per cent (as against a rise of 14.4 per cent in all-India). Progress of NIA was faster in Bihar by comparison with that in all-India (Table 12.15).

Irrigation by Sources

Between 1951-52 and 1990-91, NIA by means of canals in Bihar increased by 270 per cent and its percentage share in the total increased by 10 per cent (in all-India the percentage share of canals declined by 4 per cent during the same period); NIA through tanks fell by 40 per cent and its percentage share fell by 12 per cent (in all-India too there was a fall, by 10 per cent); NIA by tubewells rose about 66-fold, the percentage share rising by over 40 per cent; NIA by other wells fell by 55 per cent, the percentage share falling by 10 per cent (in all-India the sumtotal of percentage shares of tube-wells and other wells declined by about 32 per cent); and, finally, NIA with the help of other sources diminished by 29 per cent, the relative share going down by nearly 30 per cent (in all-India this was by about 8 per cent only).

TABLE 12.15 : Net Irrigated Area as Percentage of Net Sown Area in Bihar

Year	*Percentage*
1950-51	18.9 (18.0)
1956-57	25.0
1959-60	22.6 (18.1)
1961-62	23.3
1965-66	23.9
1970-71	25.5
1975-76	32.6
1980-81	35.5
1981-82	38.6 (34.7)
1984-85	36.5 (29.7)
1985-86	36.5 (29.6)
1987-88	39.8 (32.52)
1989-90	40.4 (32.4)
1991-92	43.5 (34.5)
1992-93	46.7 (35.1)
1995	44.5

Thus in tank irrigation and irrigation by other sources decline occurred in both Bihar and all-India—in the former the magnitudes were more or less the same, but in the latter the decline in the case of Bihar was very severe, nearly four times as much as that in all-India. In respect of the remaining two sources of irrigation, whereas canal irrigation moved up in Bihar, it moved down in all-India and tubewell irrigation and irrigation by other wells taken together improved in Bihar but deteriorated in all-India, the change being in each case of more or less the same dimension.

In an extreme version, in 1951 in Bihar canals irrigated 2.38 lakh ha., which was 11.1 per cent of NIA, not 4.03 lakh ha. and 22.14 per cent as indicated by Table 12.16. According to the same version, in that year sources other than canals irrigated 18.58 lakh ha. which worked out to 89.9 per cent of NIA, and not 14.17 lakh ha. and 77.86 per cent, as displayed by Table 12.16.

TABLE 12.16 : Progress of Net Irrigated Area in Bihar by Sources

(Coverage in lakh ha.)

Year	*Canals*						*Tanks*	
	Total		*Government*		*Private*		*Coverage*	*Percentage*
	Coverage	*Percentage*	*Coverage*	*Percentage*	*Coverage*	*Percentage*		
(1)	(2)	(3)	(4)	(5)	(6)	(7)	(8)	(9)
1951-52	4.03	22.14	3.47	19.06	0.56	3.08	2.82	15.5
	(—)	(39.8)	(—)	(34.4)	(—)	(5.5)	(—)	(17.3)
1954-55	—	—	—	—	—	—	—	—
1959-60	—	—	—	—	—	—	—	—
1960-61	6.51	31.57	5.35	25.94	1.15	5.63	3.23	15.66
	(—)	(42.1)	(—)	(37.2)	(—)	(4.9)	(—)	(18.5)
1961-62	5.61	28.87	—	—	—	—	2.24	11.52
1965-66	6.32	31.72	—	—	—	—	1.76	8.83
1970-71	8.12	37.67	—	—	—	—	1.69	7.84
	(—)	(41.3)	(—)	(38.5)	(—)	(2.8)	(—)	(13.2)
1975-76	8.96	32.46	—	—	—	—	1.18	4.27
	(—)	(39.9)	(—)	(37.4)	(—)	(2.5)	(-)	(11.5)
1980-81	10.94/	37.04/	—/	—/	—/	—/	0.96/	3.25/
	13.97	38.46	—	—	—	—	1.18	3.24
	(—)	(39.5)	(—)	(37.3)	(—)	(2.2)	(—)	(8.2)
1988-89	15.00	35.35	—	—	—	—	1.14	2.68
1989-90	10.61	33.96	—	—	—	—	.87	2.78
	(—)	(36.1)	(—)	(35.0)	(—)	(1.1)	(—)	(7.1)
1990-91	10.90	32.56	—	—	—	—	1.15	3.43
	(—)	(35.5)	(—)	(34.5)	(—)	(1.0)	(—)	(6.9)
1992-93	9.34	27.93	—	—	—	—	1.28	3.83
	(—)	(34.10)	(—)	(—)	(—)	(—)	(—)	(6.47)

(Contd.)

TABLE 12.16 (*Contd.*)

Year	*Wells*				*Other Sources*		*Total*	
	Tube-wells		*Other wells*		*Coverage*	*Percentage*	*Coverage*	*Percentage*
	Coverage	*Percentage*	*Coverage*	*Percentage*				
(1)	(10)	(11)	(12)	(13)	(14)	(15)	(16)	(17)
1951-52	0.21	1.1	2.37	13.0	8.75	48.0	18.20	100.0
	(—)	(neg.)	(-)	(28.7)	(—)	(14.2)	(—)	(100.0)
1954-55							16.07	100.0
1959-60							18.07	100.0
1960-61	0.55	2.66	2.06	9.99	8.26	40.05	20.62	100.0
	(—)	(0.6)	(—)	(29.0)	(—)	(9.8)	(—)	(100.0)
1965-66	0.83	4.16	2.06	10.34	8.95	44.93	19.92	100.0
1970-71	3.65	16.93	1.84	8.53	6.25	29.00	21.55	100.0
	(—)	(14.3)	(—)	(23.9)	(—)	(7.3)	(—)	(100.0)
1975-76	8.46	30.65	2.25	8.15	6.75	24.45	27.60	100.0
	(—)	(19.8)	(—)	(21.9)	(—)	(6.9)	(—)	(100.0)
1980-81	7.93/	26.85/	2.63/	8.90/	7.67/	25.97/	29.53/	100.0/
	10.01	27.60	2.43	6.69	8.73	24.03	36.32	100.0
	(—)	(24.6)	(—)	(21.1)	(—)	(6.6)	(—)	(100.0)
1988-89	16.70	39.35	1.16	2.73	8.43	19.86	42.43	100.0
1989-90	12.54	40.14	1.12	3.58	6.10	19.52	31.24	100.0
	(—)	(30.8)	(—)	(19.6)	(—)	(6.4)	(—)	(100.0)
1990-91	13.88	41.47	1.31	3.19	6.23	18.61	23.47	100.0
	(—)	(50.8) (including 14)	(—)	(—)	(—)	96.5)	(—)	(100.0)
1992-93	17.01	50.87	—	—	5.81	17.37	33.44	100.0
	(—)	(52.97)	(—)	(—)	(—)	(6.46)	(501.01)	(100.)

A look at Table 12.17 would manifest that in Bihar the NIA movements, source-wise, have been larger as well as more perverse and violent than the GIA movements, source-wise.

The NIA movements in Bihar have been far less negatively inclined than the NIA movements in all-India.

In Bihar the overall decline in NIA has been a multiple of the overall decline in GIA.

Last but not the least, net decline in all-India NIA has been far in excess of the net decline in Bihar NIA.

TABLE 12.17 : A Comparative View of GIA and NIA in Bihar and All-India

(In Percentage)

Source	*Bihar*		*All-India*
	GIA (Difference between 1950-51 and 1988-89)	*NIA (Difference between 1951-52 and 1990-91)*	*NIA (As in 3)*
Canals (Government and Private)	(+) 4.0	(+) 10.0	(–) 4.0
Tanks	(–) 9.5 to 17.8 [Average (–) 13.6]	(–) 12.0	(–) 10.0
Tubewells	(+) 39.3 (approx.)	(+) 40.0	Both (–) 32.0
Other wells	(–) 8.7 to 9.9 [Average (–) 9.3]	(–) 55.0	
Other sources	(–) 18.8 to 35.6 [Average (–) 27.2]	(–) 30.0	(–) 8.0
	(+) 43.3 (–) 50.1	(+) 50.0 (–) 97.0	(–) 54.0
	Net (–) 6.8	Net (–) 47.0	

A glance at Table 12.18 would show that between 1950-51 and 1988-89 in Bihar the relative share of canals (government as well as private) in total GIA increased from 31.0 to 35 per cent, that is, by 4 per cent; that of tanks decreased by 9.5/17.8 per cent from 12.20/20.5 to 2.7/2.7 per cent; that of tubewells rose from a negligible percentage to 39.3 per cent; that of other wells diminished by 8.7/9.9 per cent from 11.4/12.6 to 2.7/2.7 per cent; and, finally, that of other sources moved down by 18.8/35.6 per cent from 38.6/55.4 to 19.8/19.8 per cent. In other words, during the period under review, in Bihar there was some improvement in the percentage share of canal irrigation; there was a deterioration in the percentage share of tank irrigation in Bihar, in

TABLE 12.18 : Gross Irrigated Area in Bihar by Sources

(Coverage in lakh ha.)

Year	*Surface Water Sources*					
	Major & Medium Works Canals				*Minor Works Tanks*	
	Government		*Private*			
	Coverage	*Percentage Share in Total*	*Coverage*	*Percentage Share in Total*	*Coverage*	*Percentage Share in Total*
(1)	(2)	(3)	(4)	(5)	(6)	(7)
1950-51	4.03	19.6	2.59	11.4	2.51	12.2
1954-55					4.61	20.51
1958-59 1959-60	4.33	21.0	1.47	7.1	4.14	20.1
1960-61	5.35 5.35 (4 included)	• 35.0 25.9 (5 included)	1.15 —	7.5 —	3.23 3.23	21.1 15.6
1961-62 1965-66	5.28	27.2	3.23	1.6	2.23	1.1
1967-68	9.58 (4 included)	38.89 (5 included)	—	—	1.94	7.8
1970-71	11.17 (4 included) 11.19 (Do)	38.4 (5 included) 40.9 (Do)	—	—	1.81 1.31	6.2 4.8
1975-76	11.30 (4 included)	34.3 (5 included)	—	—	1.34	4.0
1980-81	13.97 (4 included)	38.4 (5 included)	—	—	1.18	3.2
1988-89	15.00 (4 included)	35.36 (5 included)	—	—	1.14	2.7

(Contd.)

TABLE 12.18 (*Contd.*)

Year	*Ground Water Sources Minor Works*						*Total*	
	Tube-Wells		*Other Wells*		*Other Sources**		*Coverage*	*Percentage Share*
	Coverage	*Percentage Share in Total*	*Coverage*	*Percentage Share in Total*	*Coverage*	*Percentage Share in Total*		
(1)	(8)	(9)	(10)	(11)	(12)	(!3)	(14)	(15)
1950-51	—	—	2.59	12.6	11.35	55.42	20.48	100.0
			2.6	11.4	8.7	38.6	22.65	100.0
1954-55							16.07	100.0
1958-59	—	—	2.75	13.3	7.89	38.3	20.60	100.0
1959-60	—	—	—	—	—	—	18.14	100.0
1960-61	0.55	3.60	2.06	13.5	8.26	54.1	15.27	100.0
	0.55	2.66	2.08	10.0	9.41	45.6	20.62	100.0
1961-62	3.27	1.6	—	—	8.32	42.8	19.43	100.0
1965-66	—	—	—	—	—	—	22.52	100.0
1967-68	2.96	12.01	2.79	11.3	7.36	29.88	24.63	100.0
1970-71	5.16	17.7	2.22	7.6	8.73	30.0	29.09	100.0
	5.16	18.8	2.22	8.1	6.96	25.4	27.34	100.0
1975-76	10.33	31.3	2.67	8.1	7.28	22.1	32.92	100.0
1980-81	10.01	27.5	2.43	6.7	8.73	24.0	36.32	100.0
1988-89	16.70	39.3	1.16	2.7	8.42	19.8	42.43	100.0

* Such as *Ahars*, *Pynes*, etc. which are also surface works.

tubewell irrigation there was a gain in Bihar; there was a decline in the relative share of other wells in Bihar and, lastly, in the case of other sources, Bihar had the relative share reduced.

Tables 12.17 and 12.18 bring to light the transformation that has occurred in the composition of the irrigational instruments through and over time in terms of coverage and percentage share.

As Table 12.18 brings out, in 1950-51/1951-52 in Bihar 'other sources' of irrigation were more important than canals in terms of coverage as well as percentage share, enlisting the first rank, canals getting the second rank, whether we consider GIA or NIA. In 1989-90/1990-91 tubewell irrigation surpassed canal irrigation in both terms, capturing the first rank, canal irrigation remaining stuck up at the second rank.

In recent years, according to an estimate, canal irrigation in Bihar has progressed at the rate of 2.07 per cent per annum and well irrigation at that of 5.95 per cent per annum. On the contrary, tank irrigation has retrogressed at the rate of 4.00 per cent per year.

At present the canal system in Bihar is responsible for 32 to 36 per cent of total irrigation, which is suggestive of its progress since Independence, when it was 22 to 31 per cent. On the other hand, tubewell irrigation today accounts for 39 to 42 per cent.

A number of irrigation canals, taking off from the barrages have been constructed in the Kosi region. One canal takes out from Ganga near Danapur. Small river canals irrigate lands at Monghyr, Bhagalpur and Santhal Parganas.

We have two types of canals : one, inundation and the other, perennial. The inundation canals are taken out from rivers without any regulating system at their heads. They use the excess water of the rivers.

The perennial canals take off from the perennial rivers or reservoirs with a weir system to regulate the flow of water. The Tribeni and Sone canals are examples.

Tank irrigation is concentrated in Siwan, Santhal Parganas, Bhagalpur, Rohtas, Madhubani, Saharsa, Muzaffarpur, Monghyr, Gaya and Palamau.

Lands in the plains which do not align with the canal levels have to rely upon ground water irrigation.

Surface water irrigation is done also through canals, *Ahars* and *Pynes*.

South Bihar is suited for *Ahars*. *Hirs* and *Bandhs* account for the major part of irrigation in Chotanagpur and Santhal Parganas. Well irrigation is most common in the plains because the water level is fairly high. Wells are easier to dig. After the land has been irrigated the yield on it is far higher. Because of low water-table and abundance of small surface water sources well are rare in Chotanagpur and Santhal Parganas.

In 1951 the State (deep) tubewells had irrigated 0.14 lakh ha. By comparison with tank and open well-irrigation, tubewell irrigation is the cheapest. Tubewell and well-irrigation are more in use in the plains during the dry months. Open well-irrigation is popular in Chotanagpur, through declining.

Progress of tubewell irrigation has devalued the importance of open well irrigation.

Ahars have been popular in South Patna, Monghyr and Gaya districts.

About 30 per cent of the irrigated area in Bihar is still from 'other sources of irrigation'.

Irrigation by means of wells and other sources has been more popular with small farmers because they are more labour-intensive.

Some *Ahars* were constructed by the *Zamindars*, others through the collective effort of the community.

Pynes are come across in old Patna and Gaya districts.

GAI has increased marginally only where canals and tubewells were introduced which were well served previously by *Ahars* and *Pynes* (for example, in South Bihar).

Irrigation : Crop-wise

Crop-wise distribution pattern of GIA during 1950-51 to 1990-91 is presented in Table 12.19, from which it is evident that in Bihar during 1950-51 to 1990-91 GIA under rice/paddy increased by about 8 per cent from 1771 to 1910 thousand ha. (in all-India the increase was by about 195 per cent, from 9837 to 19213 thousand ha.) but the percentage share of rice/paddy in total GIA decreased from 78.1 to 45.5 per cent, i.e., by 32.6 per cent (in all-India the decrease was by 13 per cent, from 43.7 to 31.1 per cent).

During the above period in Bihar GIA under wheat rose by about 1300 per cent from 129 to 1681 thousand ha. (in all-India the rise was by 69 per cent from 3400 to 19347 thousand ha.) and the percentage share of wheat in total GIA rose by 34.5 from 5.6 to 40.1 per cent (in all-India the rise was by 16.2 per cent from 15.1 to 31.3 per cent).

In the case of maize during the same period in Bihar NIA went up by 717 per cent, from 405 ha. to 287000 ha. (in all-India the increase in

TABLE 12.19 : Crop-wise Percentage Distribution of Gross Irrigated Area in Bihar

Year	*Rice*	*Wheat*	*Barley*	*Maize*	*Gram*	*Total Cereals & Millets*	*Total Pulses*	*Other Cereals & Pulses*	*Other Food Crops*	*Total Food-grains*	*Sugar-cane*	*Other Non-food Crops*	*Total Non-food Crops*	*All Crops*
1950-51	78.1	5.6	2.6	neg.	—	—	—	5.9	5.1	—	2.1	0.2	—	100.0
	(43.7)	(15.1)	(6.1)	(1.6)				(11.0)	(3.8)		(5.2)	(7.3)		(100.0)
1954-55										94.6			5.4	100.0
										(90.0)			(10.0)	(100.0)
1959-60	82.3	4.9	2.2	0.1				1.6	5.3	99.6	2.8	0.3	9.4	100.0
	(44.2)	(15.4)	(5.0)	(1.6)				(9.7)	(4.8)	(89.7)	(5.3)	(6.7)	(10.3)	(100.0)
1972-73	59.4	29.9	—	1.3	0.3						1.3			100.0
	(37.7)	(25.9)									(5.0)			
1978-79	52.3	35.0		4.6	0.2					99.3	0.9		0.6	100.0
1982-82	45.2	39.2		7.4	0.1				1.1		0.9		0.9	100.0
	(32.9)	(31.3)									(4.6)			
1989-90	45.4	40.3		6.8)	0.1	92.8	0.3	—	—	93.2	0.4		6.8	100.0
	(31.7)	(30.9)		(2.0)	(2.1)	(68.4)	(3.7)	—	—	(72.1)	(5.0)		(27.9)	(100.0)
1990-91	45.5	40.1		6.8	0.1	92.82	0.5			93.3	0.5		6.7	100.0
	(31.1)	(31.3)		(1.8)	(2.3)	(50.8)	(3.9)			(71.6)	(5.1)		(28.4)	

Note : In 1992-93 irrigated area under food crops came to 38.54 lakh ha.

NIA was by 311 per cent, from 369 to 1149 thousand ha.), whereas the relative share of maize moved up by about 7 per cent (in all-India the increase was extremely small, by 0.2 per cent, from 1.6 to 1.8 per cent).

Coming to sugarcane, we discover that in the same period NIA under it diminished in Bihar by 58 per cent from 49 to 21 thousand ha. (in all-India there was instead increase by 267 per cent, from 1185 to 3172 thousand ha.), while its percentage share decreased by 1.6 per cent from 2.1 to 0.5 per cent (in all-India the percentage share fell marginally by 0.1 per cent, from 5.2 to 5.1 per cent).

From a broader point of view, the percentage share of NIA under total food crops in Bihar during 1954-55 to 1990-91 declined marginally by 1.3 per cent, from 94.6 to 93.3 per cent (in all-India the decline was by 18.4 per cent, from 90.0 to 71.6 per cent). And, conversely, so far as total non-food crops are concerned, in Bihar as well as all-India.

Conclusively speaking, from the broader point of view the pattern of distribution of GIA as between food and non-food crops in Bihar has remained more or less unchanged in the last three decades and a half. By comparison, in all-India there has taken place some transformation in this pattern, though not insignificantly.

In Bihar the best performance of wheat was due partially to the fall-out effect of the Green Revolution in the realm of wheat but more specifically because of the fact that rainfall was limited during the Rabi crop season.

In 1993-94, 85 per cent wheat area was irrigated, as against 35 per cent in the case of rice area.

In terms of rise in GIA the performance of maize was in rank second, next to wheat, and that because in developing new varieties of maize Bihar was perhaps the first State, we have now 2 to 3 crops instead of one before. In terms of percentage gain, rice was on close heels with wheat. The negative performance of sugarcane in both terms was largely owing to the deteriorating plight of the growers consequent upon accumulating arrears and adverse inputs supply position.

The irrigated area under food crops increased from 26 lakh ha. in 1971-72 to 36 lakh ha. (approx.) in 1986-87, i.e., by 138 per cent.

Between 1978-79 and 1990-91 GIA under total food crops increased by 6 per cent (from 3685 to 3912 thousand ha.) in Bihar and Bihar's percentage share of GIA under total food crops also fell by 6 per cent (from 99.3 to 93.3 per cent).

In Bihar only about one per cent of gram area was irrigated but the proportion of GIA under gram to total GIA was only 0.1 per cent.

Water requirement of each individual crop is different. The Kharif crop requires 100 cm depth of water in field. Of this, 50 cm is taken to be provided by timely rainfall. The remaining supply has to be met by irrigation. The Rabi crop requires a total depth of 25 cm water in the field—8 cm each for 3 waterings; or 6 cm each if 4 waterings are advised. Sugarcane requires 168.7 cm water depth in the field for maturity, paddy 19.43 cm., wheat 42.5 cm. and maize 75 cm. Sugarcane is a one-year crop. It requires maximum water in May, the driest month of its growing period. Being a hot weather crop sugarcane naturally requires a large quantity of water, it is water-intensive. Next to it are potato and onion which too require frequent, repeated watering. Except for certain parts of the State it is erroneous to opine that sugarcane has been a *prima donna* of Bihar agriculture, with far less acreage but far more irrigation. Very few would consider this to be a pampering of sugarcane in Bihar as in Maharashtra, for example. In Bihar sugarcane irrigational requirement is four to five times larger than that of any seasonal crop. Whereas three to four waterings are enough for sugarcane cultivation for a good yield in Bihar, in Maharashtra, Gujarat, Karnataka and Tamil Nadu it calls for twenty to twenty-five waterings. Income per unit of water for sugarcane may be lower than income per unit of water from a seasonal HYV crop but income per unit of land from sugarcane is very high. Nevertheless, there is not sufficient ground to insinuate that in Bihar subsidised irrigation has caused distortion in the cropping pattern by favouring the water-intensive crops like sugarcane.

Table 12.20 purports to confirm the extensively held view by the rural folk in Bihar that, by and by, the percentage of cultivated land which is irrigated has increased in the case of rice, wheat and maize. With regard to sugarcane the position appears to be one of constancy. But pulses which were not irrigated before have had since some time past the benefit of irrigation. Wheat is the most favoured crop so far as irrigation allocation is concerned. Maize and rice irrigation have more or less the same behaviour pattern. This remark holds good for wheat and gram irrigation as well.

Since Bihar is known outside itself as a Rice/Paddy State, it would be worthwhile noting how the three varieties of rice/paddy stood to one another with regard to sharing the GIA under it roughly during the last two decades for which data is available. Table 12.21 demonstrates that during the period there was a mild shift in favour of the Bhadai variety. This was at the expense of the Agahani variety. The relative share of the

Garma variety was more or less static during the period. In a word, there was nothing special about this phenomenon.

TABLE 12.20 : Irrigated Area as Proportion of Sown Area

(Percentage)

Crop	*1950-51*	*1959-60*	*1972-73*	*1978-79*	*1984-85*	*1986-87*
Rice	33.3 (32.9)	29.7 (36.8)	33.8	35.5	35.6 (42.9)	35.8 (43.8)
Wheat	23.12 (35.8)	13.7 (33.0)	42.1	71.4	78.6 (74.0)	79.0 (77.3)
Maize	0.06 (12.9)	0.27 (10.5)	4.5	19.1	29.2 (16.4)	29.7 (20.8)
Gram	—	—	—	—	4.0 (14.5)	3.8 (20.1)
Sugarcane	36.3 (61.1)	28.5 (70.2)	21.6	—	21.4 (85.2)	21.4 (82.1)
Total Pulses	—	—	—	—	—	1.3 (9.8)

TABLE 12.21 : Variety-wise Shift of Irrigated Land under Rice

Rice/Paddy (According to Variety)	*Percentage Share in Total Irrigated Area Under Rice/Paddy*				
	1972-73	*1978-79*	*1982-83*	*1986-87*	*1990-91*
Bhadai	2.1	3.6	Kharif : 97.2	4.6	4.8
Agahani	94.3	93.8		93.1	91.5
Garma	3.6	2.6	2.8	2.3	3.7
Total	100.0	100.0	100.0	100.0	100.0

Kharif remains the focal point of all thought directed towards irrigation in Bihar. However, the use of artificial irrigation in Kharif is low.

Ranchi, Dhanbad and Singhbhum encounter lack of water for Rabi cultivation.

For the uplift of agricultural productivity it is necessary that the relative share of Rabi in irrigation water distribution increases, even if it is beset with greater difficulty.

Minor Irrigation

'Minor Irrigation' incorporates both surface and underground irrigation.

Surface irrigation is carried out through lift irrigation, tanks and ponds, *Ahars* and *Pynes*.

Ground water occurs both under water-table and confined conditions.

The ground water resources are poorer in South Bihar and Chotanagpur by comparison with North Bihar.

During 1960-61 to 1988-89 the percentage share of ground water irrigation in total gross irrigated area increased from 12.6 to 42.0 per cent.

In 1992-93 the ratio between ground water and surface water irrigation was 28.4 to 1.

Tubewell Irrigation

We have supplied above a short account of tubewell irrigation. In the pages which follow we propose to outline its development in Bihar.

Palamau has comparatively a higher irrigation coverage due to investment in certain types of minor irrigation.

The private tubewells are shallow or open wells.

Tubewells are shallow or deep. Shallow tubewells cost less and are generally popular in the private sector, whereas deep tubewells costing an enormous investment are generally the monopoly of the State/public sector.

There was hardly any tubewell in Bihar in 1950-51, although on March 31, 1951, 110 tubewells were reported to be receiving energy, as per the NCAER report.

In the 1980s fixed capital investment required in a State tubewell was Rs. 5 lakh, with an irrigation potential of 13 ha., though the actual coverage was 10 ha. On the other hand, a private tubewell required fixed capital investment of Rs. 14,000 and provided irrigation to 3.4 ha.

In 1951 the minor irrigation schemes irrigated small areas from the local run-off water in the years of adequate rainfall. There was a large area under the command of various minor irrigation works, required to be maintained by the *Zamindars*. They had actually gone into disrepair and were not available for storage or diversion even of the local rain water in the years of normal rainfall.

After their take-over by the State Government some new schemes of renovation and re-excavation of the old minor works were formulated and executed.

In spite of this, the minor irrigation works like *Ahars, Pynes, Bandhs*, etc., which were the legacy of the old Zamindari regime/declined in their coverage in the years subsequent to their take-over by the State Government for lack of maintenance.

The public tubewell irrigation water rate was reduced by half during the first two Plans of Bihar. This aroused considerable response from the agriculturists.

The phenomenal progress made by tubewell irrigation in the private sector is explained also by another factor, a negative one, namely, the poor performance of Government-controlled surface irrigation (mainly canal and deep tubewell irrigation).

The quality of private sector tubewell irrigation excelled that of public sector tubewell irrigation.

In the areas having copious quantities of underground water supply, the tubewell programme captured the imagination of the cultivators as it enabled them to grow more than one crop on an assured basis.

A State-level Ground Water Organisation was set up to monitor the development of ground water resources.

Throughout the 1980s the operation of the State tubewells continued to deteriorate. Most of the sunk ones soon became worthless/defunct. The public tubewells declined most in Muzaffarpur and Darbhanga.

Between 1968-69 and 1986-87 the number of private tubewells rose by 33 times. In 1984-85 for every 18 open wells in the private sector, there was one electric pumpset in that sector.

In the mid-1980s only 30 per cent of the energised tubewells were actually operational.

By 1986-87 the State tubewells had become totally irrelevant. Private tubewells formed over 94 per cent of all tubewells, private or public, and irrigated 96 per cent of all land area irrigated by tubewells, private or public.

By 1988-89 the ratio between Private and State Tubewells had suffered a setback and stood at 70 to 30.

At this stage in our treatment of the subject it would be expedient to assemble all the available information on it in the form of a table (Table 12.22).

Between 1960-61 and 1985-86 the number of I.P. pumpsets/tubewells in Bihar fell by 36 per cent, from 32000 to 20500. In March 1992 Bihar's percentage share in all-India number of I.P. pumpsets/tubewells was 5.18 (Table 12.22).

In 1951-52 the ratio between electricity-energised and diesel-energised tubewells was 33 to 67. In 1986-87 the ratio was 46 to 54. Dieselisation had forged ahead.

TABLE 12.22 : Minor Irrigation : Tubewells in Bihar

Sl.No.	Characteristics	Pre-Plan Period	1950-51	1951-52	1951-56	1960-61	1962-65
(1)	(2)	(3)	(4)	(5)	(6)	(7)	(8)
1.	I.P. Pumpsets/Tubewells in private and public sectors (Number = No.)					32000	
2.	Their percentage share in total State Tubewell Irrigation						
	A. Private sector tubewells (No.)						
	B. Area irrigated by private sector wells						
	C. Total area irrigated by 1 (above)						
	D. Percentage share of private sector in irrigation						
	E. Percentage share of public sector in irrigation						
	F. Public sector Pumpsets/Tubewells (No.)	175			771		
	G. Area irrigated by 2F (above)		2.26 lakh ha.				
3.	Energised I.P. Pumpsets/Tubewells (No.)						
4.	Drill pumpsets (No.)						
5.	Percentage share of 2A (above) in All-India GIA						
6.	Division of 1 (above) into						
	A. Electric-operated (Percentage)			300 (24293)			
	B. Diesel-operated (Percentage)			600 (65934)			
	C. A (above) already achieved						
7.	Percentage share of 6A (above) in All-India Total			1.21			
8.	1 (above) as percentage of their estimated ultimate potential number						
	A. 6C (above) as percentage of 8 (above)						
9.	Percentage share of 6B (above) in total privately irrigated land						
10.	Percentage share of 6B (above) in All-India Total			0.91			
	A. Percentage share of 2 (above) in all-India						
11.	Other Minor Irrigation Sources						
	A. Tanks			27800			
	B. Wells			110700			
12.	Number of pumpsets per 1000 ha.						0.92 (4.58)

(Contd.)

TABLE 12.22 (*Contd.*)

Sl.No.	*Characteristics*	*1968-70*	*1973-74*	*1976-77*	*1980-83*	*1981*	*1981-82*
(1)	(2)	(9)	(10)	(11)	(12)	(13)	(14)
1.	I.P. Pumpsets/Tubewells in private and public sectors (Number = No.)						
2.	Their percentage share in total State Tubewell Irrigation						
	A. Private sector tubewells (No.)	90.4 (= 12000)					
	B. Area irrigated by private sector wells						
	C. Total area irrigated by 1 (above)						
	D. Percentage share of private sector in irrigation	90.40	82.16				
	E. Percentage share of public sector in irrigation	9.40					
	F. Public sector Pumpsets/Tubewells (No.)	1724					
	G. Area irrigated by 2F (above)			1.85 lakh ha.			
3.	Energised I.P. Pumpsets/Tubewells (No.)						
4.	Drill pumpsets (No.)						
5.	Percentage share of 2A (above) in All-India GIA						27 (all-India NIA)
6.	Division of 1 (above) into						
	A. Electric-operated (Percentage)						
	B. Diesel-operated (Percentage)						
	C. A (above) already achieved						
7.	Percentage share of 6A (above) in All-India Total						
8.	1 (above) as percentage of their estimated ultimate potential number						
	A. 6C above as percentage of 8 (above)						
9.	Percentage share of 6B (above) in total privately irrigated land						
10.	Percentage share of 6B (above) in All-India Total						
	A. Percentage share of 2 (above) in all-India						
11.	Other Minor Irrigation Sources						
	A. Tanks						
	B. Wells						
12.	Number of pumpsets per 1000 ha.				49.76 (49.16)		

(*Contd.*)

Sl.No.	Characteristics	1983-84	1984-85	1985-86	1986-87	1987	1988-89
(1)	(2)	(15)	(16)	(17)	(18)	(19)	(20)
1.	I.P. Pumpsets/Tubewells in private and public sectors (Number = No.)			205000			
2.	Their percentage share in total State Tubewell Irrigation						
	A. Private sector tubewells (No.)		95.9 (= 405000)				
	B. Area irrigated by private sector wells	11.68 lakh ha.					Tubewells 16.70 lakh ha. Open wells 1.16 lakh ha.
	C. Total area irrigated by 1 (above)	12.18 lakh ha.					17.86 lakh ha.
	D. Percentage share of private sector in irrigation	95.12					
	E. Percentage share of public sector in irrigation	4.88	98.78				
	F. Public sector Pumpsets/Tubewells (No.)	0.49 lakh ha.	50.93				
	G. Area irrigated by 2F (above)						0.59 lakh ha.
3.	Energised I.P. Pumpsets/Tubewells (No.)						
4.	Drill pumpsets (No.)						
5.	Percentage share of 2A (above) in All-India GIA	33 (all-Inida GIA)					
6.	Division of 1 (above) into						
	A. Electric-operated (Percentage)				46		
	B. Diesel-operated (Percentage)				54		
7.	Percentage share of 6A (above) in All-India Total						
8.	1 (above) as percentage of their estimated ultimate potential number						
	A. 6C (above) as percentage of 8 (above)						
9.	Percentage share of 6B (above) in total privately irrigated land				70		
10.	Percentage share of 6B (above) in All-India Total						
	A. Percentage share of 2 (above) in all-India						
11.	Other Minor Irrigation Sources						
	A. Tanks						
	B. Wells						
12.	Number of pumpsets per 1000 ha.					52.32 (64.94)	

(*Contd.*)

TABLE 12.22 (*Contd.*)

Sl.No.	*Characteristics*	*1992 (March 31)*	*1992-93*	*1993-94*	*1995 (May)*
(1)	(2)	(21)	(22)	(23)	(24)
1.	I.P. Pumpsets/Tubewells in private and public sectors (Number = No.)				
2.	Their percentage share in total State Tubewell Irrigation				
	A. Private sector tubewells (No.)				
	B. Area irrigated by private sector wells				
	C. Total area irrigated by 1 (above)				
	D. Percentage share of private sector in irrigation				
	E. Percentage share of public sector in irrigation				
	F. Public sector Pumpsets/Tubewells (No.)				
	G. Area irrigated by 2F (above)				
3.	Energised I.P. Pumpsets/Tubewells (No.)	486434			
4.	Drill pumpsets (No.)				1.59 lakh
5.	Percentage share of 2A (above) in All-India GIA				
6.	Division of 1 (above) into				
	A. Electric-operated (Percentage)				
	B. Diesel-operated (Percentage)				
	C. A (above) already achieved	258508 (9391108)			
7.	Percentage share of 6A (above) in All-India Total	10 lakhs (145 lakhs)			
8.	1 (above) as percentage of their estimated ultimate potential number				
	A. 6C (above) as percentage of 8 (above)	25.9 (64.8)			
9.	Percentage share of 6B (above) in total privately irrigated land				
10.	Percentage share of 6B (above) in All-India Total	5.18			
	A. Percentage share of 2 (above) in all-India				
11.	Other Minor Irrigation Sources				
	A. Tanks				
	B. Wells				
12.	Number of pumpsets per 1000 ha.			26.98 (55.11)	

The land area irrigated by deep tubewells in the State/public sector declined progressively from 2.26 lakh ha. in 1950-51 to 1.85 lakh ha. in 1976-77 and to 0.59 lakh ha. in 1988-89.

Commencing in 1981, the Government could achieve only 25.9 per cent of the target set on the basis of the total number of I.P. pumpsets/ tubewells to be drilled by 1992 March-end. The achievement in the country was 64.8 per cent, more than double of Bihar's.

By 1988-89, altogether 70 per cent of GIA in the private sector in Bihar was carried out with the help of the shallow tubewells.

Expenses incurred by the State Government on its tubewells were Rs. 258 lakh in 1975-76 and Rs. 2 lakh in 1985-86.

Loss on the State tubewells in 1983-84 was Rs. 4.8 crore—21 per cent on new works, 8.5 per cent on repair and maintenance and 70.5 per cent on salaries, etc. of the staff. In 1986-87 the loss borne by the State Government on account of the State tubewells was Rs. 11.82 crore (approximately).

At current prices, in 1986-87 total capital invested in the State tubewells was Rs. 400 crores.

The Jal Dhara Scheme introduced subsequently was concerned with sinking of tubewells, including shallow ones and bamboo borings, on a mass scale.

Contribution of tubewell irrigation in transforming Bihar's backward agriculture cannot be exaggerated : increase in foodgrains production has been maximum in those parts of the State where the progress made by tubewell irrigation also was maximum.

Tubewell irrigation has provided a fair margin of stability to agriculture in South Bihar.

Tubewell irrigation is control/controlled irrigation. The ground water mechanism provides the farmer with just the type of instant and control irrigation, which the new HYVs of seeds demand.

Surface water resources are subject to such limitations, as gravity flow irrigation, seasonal variation of flow, heavy transit losses, delayed creation of potential, etc.

Tubewells can meet the multiple watering needs of intensive cultivation and hybrids and the HYVs, though at higher costs. When combined with canal irrigation, the costs are lower.

The merit of ground water irrigation consists in its suitability to an economy characterised by fragmented and small holdings.

The result of excessive sinking of tubewells has been the lowering of the water-table in some parts of the plains, causing drying of open wells and their unusability.

Ground water utilisation by means of tubewells has fallen far short of the existing potential.

In 1976-77 the irrigating capacity of a private tubewell was estimated at 8.36 ha. In 1984-85 the estimate was 3.38 ha. In 1988-89 it was estimated at about 4 ha. Between 1977-78 and 1988-89 the fall was by 52 per cent.

In 1950-51 the irrigating capacity of a State/Public tubewell was estimated at 89.94 ha. In 1984-85 it was estimated at 10.08 ha. In 1988-89 it was estimated at 11.81 ha. The decline was by 87 per cent between 1950-51 and 1988-89.

During 1951-56 each deep public tubewell had provided assured irrigation to about 101.21 ha., according to one source.

In those years in which the rainfall is not normal, in total quantum as well as in distribution, the increase that is anticipated from expanded minor irrigation, in fact, falls short of that.

As said before, the pumpsets/tubewells are energised by electricity or diesel. On an average, a diesel-operated tubewell irrigated a lower area than an electricity-energised tubewell.

Dieselisation makes tubewell irrigation unnecessarily capital-intensive.

As the number of shallow tubewells has risen, supply of power has become increasingly erratic, with the result that both per tubewell irrigated area and total tubewell irrigated area have declined in extent, with the result that recourse had to be had to dieselisation in place of electrification of the pumping engines, which proved costlier. Underutilisation of capital has gone on hand in hand with overcapitalisation.

Of the total potential for setting up pumpsets, only 25 per cent could be energised upto March 1990.

One demerit of ground water irrigation is its higher cost, when compared to canal irrigation, which is due largely to water utilisation on a small scale by the private individuals.

The growth of tubewell irrigation, whether in the private or public sector, has been impeded by more or less one and the same set of factors, of course, in varying degrees. In the first place, the investment made was inadequate. Not many farmers have been willing to invest in installing tubewells, despite the presence of a high water-table in the plains. The pace of the limited investment made has been slow due to the inadequate flow of institutional credit.

Secondly, the progress of tubewell irrigation has been impeded by the absence of power supply—tubewells have remained unconnected with the power lines for months/years. In 1981 approximately 25 per cent of them remained idle for this reason. Where power supply has been available, it has been short and erratic. In 1981 nearly 11 per cent of all State tubewells were handicapped by the energy problem.

Thirdly, absence of field channels has been another impediment.

Fouthly, the smallness of the majority of the farmers has formed still another obstacle.

Fifthly, poor management is also to blame. Glaring has been lack of repair and maintenance. Of the State tubewells drilled till 1981, about 13 per cent suffered from mechanical faults/troubles. In May 1995, 4.3 per cent of all drilled pumpsets were defunct and derelict on account of lack of repair and maintenance. In a good many cases the burnt transformers had not been replaced.

The malfunctioning of tubewell irrigation has also infected the functioning of lift irrigation in the State.

Experts suggest that in view of Bihar's experience of the public tubewells, all new tubewells may be privately owned. Any capital subsidy on these tubewells could be linked to obligations to supply water to other farmers' lands within the tubewell command.

Private tubewell development need to have the highest priority in North Bihar districts over extension of canals.

So far as agriculture is concerned, the tribal belt is suited for small check dams and barrages, the weir irrigation schemes, the tanks and wells combined with mini hydroelectric projects associated with short technical training to the tribal and semi-tribal youth to man them.

In Chotanagpur and Santhal Parganas modernisation of minor irrigation works should have priority over new schemes.

Ahars, Pynes, etc., should be maintained by the Village Panchayats.

A Critical Estimate

Various criteria/tests have been employed to judge the performance of the irrigation systems :

1. By the ratio between the created and the ultimate irrigation potential;
2. By the ratio between the utilized and the created irrigation potential;
3. By the increase in GIA, rather than NIA;
4. By the quantity of water made available, both overall and in each principal crop season;
5. By the frequency and predictability of water supply; and

6. By the effect of (2) above on (a) cropping intensity, (b) cropping pattern, and (c) crop yield.

We have, earlier in this chapter already endeavoured as much as possible, in the face of the paucity and the dubious nature of the statistics available, to examine (1), (2), (3) and (4) at length. As for (5) and (6), we shall be discussing them presently.

The progress of irrigation in Bihar has been at a sluggish, slow pace.

The growth rate of GIA in Bihar was 2.22 per cent per annum during 1950-51 to 1970-71 and 2.54 per cent per annum during 1950-51 to 1986-87. That is to say, the pace became faster after 1970-71.

Generally, the experts judge the quality/intensity or irrigation :

(1) By its adequacy,
(2) By its timeliness, and
(3) By its equity.

Irrigation intensity is symmetrical with the quality of irrigation. Its measure is the twice or doubly irrigated area.

From Table 12.23, we find that the twice or doubly irrigated area in Bihar has increased continuously. In 1990-91 it was nearly one-fourth of GIA. Also, it was a shade above the national figure. It is at the same time the measure of the intensity or quality of irrigation.

TABLE 12.23 : Progress of Doubly/Twice Irrigated Area in Bihar*

(Percentage)

Year	*Percentage*
1950-51	100.0 (108.20)
1960-61	106.10
1961-62	112.55 (111.43 for 1960-61)
1965-66	137.24
1970-71	121.4/126.50 (122.79)
1975-76	121.81 (125.35)
1978-79	125.00 (127.00)
1980-81	121.1/122.99/123.00 (128.56)
1984-85	135.95 (128.83)
1986-87	128.00/128.20
1989-90	131.94 (131.66)
1990-91	125.24 (130.38)
1992-93	123

* This, i.e., irrigation intensity is equivalent to GIA as Percentage of NIA $= \frac{GIA}{NIA} \times 100$.

In 1984-85, 19.65 per cent of GIA was doubly irrigated. As percentage of all-India twice/doubly irrigated area, it was 7.37 per cent.

During 1950-51 to 1989-90, 8.45 lakh ha. land was irrigated more than once in Bihar. On the other hand, in all-India 1279 lakh ha. land was irrigated more than once. Bihar's share in the increase was 0.66 per cent (Table 12.24).

TABLE 12.24 : Area Irrigated More Than Once in Bihar

(Lakh ha.)

Year	*Bihar*	*All-India*
1950-51	0.00	171
1960-61	2.44	332
1965-66	7.42	—
1970-71	12.07	709
1975-76	6.03	887
1980-81	6.79	1106
1985-86	10.05 (1984-85)	1257
1989-90	8.45	1450

Coming to the criteria/tests, we find that in addition to being woefully slow, the progress of irrigation in Bihar has been grossly inadequate as well.

Supply of irrigation water to the *Rabi* crops has been deficient.

The irrigation system has failed to guarantee that the application of water is in right time and in right quantity, the twin pre-conditions of efficient agriculture, to which agriculture is extremely sensitive. The lapses from these norms have been serious in certain cases.

Given the irregularity of rainfall, the Kharif output in Bihar critically presupposes a stable, timely supply of water, which timeliness quality of a sound irrigation system has a question-mark before itself in the State.

The distribution system of the major and medium irrigation projects in Bihar is such as to make the supply of water uncertain with regard to the time when it is required.

Even today, to a notable extent, the irrigation sources other than canals turn largely on the adequacy of rainfall.

The rain water-based irrigation works distribute the rain water over space as well as over time in keeping with the requirements of the individual crops so as to remedy the uneven distribution of rainfall.

In a year in which the water supply from the snowfed rivers to them is not adequate their effectiveness is governed largely by total rainfall in that year.

Particularly in the plateau region in bad years coverage of protection irrigation is limited.

Use of the irrigation facility is deemed to be protective, if it is in Kharif and productive, if it is in Rabi.

It is the protective use of the irrigation facility, as for example in the kharif season, which accounts for the woefully low value of irrigation intensity or quality in Bihar.

What has been just said above is a potent reason why the irrigation service is not quite predictable or not predictable in the degree and manner prescribed by the experts.

'Distribution of water at the farm level is more particularly unreliable.

The 'legendary/legendaric myth' of dependence on surface irrigation was shattered and the vulnerability of these works exposed by the unprecedented drought conditions of 1965-67 in Bihar.

In 1992-93 only 21 lakh ha. land area got proper irrigation from the major and medium irrigation projects, 'proper' here signifying 'assured'.

The magnitude of assured irrigation has been low in Bihar. In 1951 the percentage of assured irrigation in Bihar was 32. Assured irrigation was available to 7.08 lakh ha., which worked out to 8 per cent of NSA. During the First Plan period only 3.4 per cent of the cultivated area was reported to be under assured irrigation. Around 1971 the percentage of assured irrigation was hardly 32. Other estimates are 12 and 12.5 per cent of NSA. On an average, during 1971-74, assured irrigation from the Government canals and tubewells was available to 14 per cent of NSA only. An estimate made in 1993-94 showed that whereas the increase in irrigation potential utilised in recent years in the State was of the order of 21.48 lakh ha. that in area of assured irrigation was to the extent of 0.275 lakh ha. only, that is, 1.28 per cent.

Tubewell irrigation comes under control irrigation.

The percentage of control irrigation to total irrigation is a measure of the quality or intensity of irrigation.

If the irrigation systems in Bihar are bereft of the qualities of adequacy and timeliness they have not the quality of equity either. As shown by irrigation according to the holdings size, they do not satisfy the equity criterion (Table 12.25).

Water is provided preferably to the large and medium farmers for irrigation.

To conclude, the irrigation systems in Bihar do not quite fulfil the triple tests, viz., adequacy, timeliness and equity.

Other shortcomings of the irrigation systems in Bihar are as follows : Firstly, the productivity per unit of land is low. Single-crop irrigation projects have predominated. Irrigation water is not utilised in a manner capable of maximising return per unit of its supply to the tilled land. For with the same amount of irrigation water more land could have been irrigated and more valuable crops produced. Owing to the inherent uncertainty of the monsoon and lack of study, the irrigation water distribution or control system in North Bihar is not in harmony with the erratic behaviour pattern of the monsoon.

TABLE 12.25 : Number and Area of Operational Holdings, Wholly and Partly Irrigated (by Sizes) and Their Respective Percentages in Bihar 1985-86

Sl. No.	*Size Class (in Hectares)*	*Wholly and Partly Irrigated Holdings*			
		Number ('000s)	*Percentage*	*Area ('000 ha.)*	*Percentage*
1.	0.02—0.5	2433	44.99	508	30.85
2.	0.5—1.0	1171	52.90	540	32.95
3.	1.0—2.0	737	55.53	573	30.66
4.	2.0—3.0	334	53.84	452	30.51
5.	3.0—4.0	177	53.66	310	27.93
6.	4.0—5.0	102	53.42	228	27.22
7.	5.0—7.0	76	52.60	204	23.26
8.	7.5—10.0	38	55.04	124	21.44
9.	10.0—20.0	23	53.40	102	17.88
10.	20.0—30.0	4	59.96	23	14.21
11.	30.0—40.0	1	62.54	11	22.51
12.	40.0—50.0	8.3	66.60	5	21.42
13.	50.0 and above	0.3	74.64	7	21.25
	All Sizes	5,097	49.21	3,087	28.38

Secondly, the efficiency of the irrigation systems is low and hence the service provided by them is of poor quality. Detectable is a leeway in the conjunctive use of ground and surface water in projects other than those of the CADAs. Not due attention has been paid to the complementary drainage and tubewell development programmes in North Bihar. Irrigation so far has had no significant impact on the cropping pattern in the State.

Thirdly, there are cost and time overruns in respect of the major irrigation projects. This is another, and an unfailing testimony to low executive efficiency.

Table 12.26 is illustrative of this.

In 1994 still under construction, in different stages of completion, were 50 major and medium projects. Already Rs. 1500 crores had been spent on them. To complete them Rs. 4000 crores more were required.

TABLE 12.26 : Multipurpose and Major Irrigation Projects in Bihar

Sl. No.	*Name of Project*	*Plan in which started*	*Estimated cost (Rs. Crores)*	*Expenditure upto 1991-92 (Rs. Crores)*
1.	Western Kosi Canal	3rd	357.44	196.95
2.	Bagmati	4th	314.67	35.58
3.	Subarnarekha (inter-State)	5th	1428.00	548.34
4.	North Kosi Reservoir	5th	475.00	342.82
5.	Durgavti Reservoir	5th	147.40	71.39
6.	Barnar Reservoir	5th	102.38	28.03
7.	Konar Diversion	5th	225.40	71.48
8.	Tilaiya Diversion	5th	121.33	11.99
9.	Bateshwarasthan Pump Phase-I Banasagar (inter-State)	5th	136.67	17.09
10.	Ajoy Barrage Sika	5th	133.11	64.84
11.	Gandak Phase II	7th	204.00	38.25
12.	Kosi Eastern Canal Phase I	7th	52.00	19.87
13.	Masan Dam	7th	58.00	8.36
14.	Auranga Reservoir	7th	257.00	13.87
15.	Punsel Reservoir	7th	145.00	32.30

The First Plan irrigation projects like the Kosi Barrage and Eastern canal had lingered on.

The Kosi project could not be completed by the end of 1987 as scheduled. By 1981 only a quarter of the project had been completed in Mithilanchal.

The Second Plan irrigation project like the Gandak canal too had lingered on.

In 1992 there were 40 ongoing irrigation projects, some of which had been started years ago; perhaps they might not be completed by the turn of the century. Of these, 14 were major projects (in India their number was 245), expected to benefit 8.76 lakh ha. (the all-India figure being 28.44 lakh ha.).

The Subarnarekha Irrigation Project could not take off so far because the State Government failed to adopt adequate steps for the rehabilitation and resettlement of the uprooted (*Outees*). Its original cost was Rs. 130 crores.

Choice of irrigation projects had not been based on an analysis of costs and benefits.

Inadequate investigations into the economics of the irrigation projects were, in part, responsible for the cost and time overruns.

The physical performance of the irrigation systems in Bihar has been marred further by investment shortfalls.

Impact of Irrigation

We have in Bihar in currency two diametrically opposed views on the services rendered by irrigation to agriculture and other segments of the economy. The votaries point to what is common knowledge in Bihar, i.e., that those districts of the State, e.g., Champaran, Shahabad and parts of Muzaffarpur, Gaya and Patna which have been endowed with irrigation facility for decades have unceasingly enjoyed immunity to famine because of the endowment. They further contend that increase in yield wherever it has taken place in the wake of irrigation has been of a self-sustaining nature, an event of far-reaching significance.

According to the champions, development of irrigation in Bihar has strengthened the capability of its agriculture to withstand the adverse effect of the natural calamities, even if partially. The supporters emphasise that irrigation has lowered the degree of instability of rice outturn.

The opponents severely play down the contribution made by irrigation in Bihar. In July, 1991 the then Irrigation Minister of Bihar is reported to have made a public statement that although Rs. 8000 crores had been spent in Bihar on irrigation, not an acre of addition land had been provided with irrigation facility.

In December, 1992 more or less a similar remark was made by the then Chief Secretary to the State Government at an official meeting.

Let us mention here how the antagonists make out a case against irrigation. One argument is that irrigation in Bihar has not so far made the agricultural production system sustainable. Besides, the contribution made by the advances of irrigation in Bihar in reducing the year-to-year instability of output due to the unevenness of the monsoon rains is not significant at all. Irrigation has acted more as a stand-by, used in times of failure of the monsoon, than as a promoter of agricultural production, apart from the monsoon rains. Finally, the progress of irrigation in Bihar has not had any perceptible impact on the sharp fall in the agricultural output in the years of drought.

Such being the mixed estimate, let us now critically enquire into the matter.

Candidly speaking, the acid-test of performance of the irrigation systems from the point of view of the peasantry is the benefit that accrues to it from them, be it in the form of water for irrigation or electricity for lighting or protection against the recurrent flood or a combination thereof.

The ratio of increased water utilisation to increased output therefrom provides one measuring-rod of the irrigational benefit.

Other things remaining the same, when a given land which was not irrigated before is now irrigated, then the extra yield minus the extra cost is the additional benefit to the cultivator and this is attributable to irrigation.

The advantage in terms of yield which a crop has when it is irrigated/ irrigated and sown with seeds that are the HYVs, compared to the yield it has without irrigation/irrigation plus the HYVs is illustrated in Table 12.27 with reference to rice, wheat and maize. Bihar's inferior position vis-a-vis all-India is self-manifest.

TABLE 12.27 : Irrigation Benefit in Bihar : 1984-85 and 1987-88

Crop	*Excess of Yield per ha. of Irrigated Crop over Yield per ha. of Unirrigated Crop (Per cent)*	*Excess of Yield per ha. of Irrigated Crop over Yield per ha. of Overall Crop (Irrigated and Unirrigated) (Per cent)*	*Excess of Yield per ha. of Irrigated Crop with HYVs over Yield per ha. of Unirrigated Crop (Per cent)*	*Excess of Yield per ha. of Irrigated and HYVs Crop over Yield per ha. of overall Crop*
Rice	40+ to 41+ (69) 41++ (59)	25+ (25)	50+ (94)	75+ (25)
Maize		4+ (9)		
Wheat	64++ (139)			

\+ They are for 1987-88.
\++ They are for 1984-85.

Estimates of irrigation benefit, return, excess/surplus, value/income gross, net and additional net, accruing to the growers of rice, wheat and sugarcane in the Sone Command Area for the year 1984-85 are contained in Table 12.28. In so far as the gains are much below those projected in theory the need of the hour is to remove the factors responsible for this. A point of immense interest is the relative advantage sugarcane derives from the irrigation service, larger in percentage, compared to rice and wheat.

So far as rice is concerned, we have to distinguish between its traditional and High Yielding Varieties. Taking the former, we find that compared to the unirrigated land, the irrigated land yields an output per ha. which varies by 4.64 per cent in the case of Bihar as a whole. The range is minimum, 0.17 per cent, in South Bihar and maximum, 13.08 per cent, in Chotanagpur. In the case of the HYVs, for the State as a whole the range is 13.03 per cent. North Bihar has the highest range of variation, 19.21 per cent and South Bihar the lowest, 8.06 per cent. The magnitudes of the range of variation in the case of the second HV

TABLE 12.28 : Irrigation Benefits in the Sone Command Area : 1984-85

Items	*As Percentage of gross Income of the Irrigated Land*	*As Percentage of Net Income of the Irrigated Land*	*As Percentage of Gross Return*	*Excess (Per cent)*				*Excess (In Quintals per ha.)*	
				Rice	*Wheat*	*Rice & Wheat*	*Sugarcane*	*Rice*	*Wheat*
Additional Net Benefit from Irrigation	29.7	43.4							
Net Value on the Irrigated Land	71.14								
Net Return :									
Rice			61.4						
Wheat			56.3						
Excess of Net Value on the Irrigated land over that on the unirrigated land				34 to 118	34	53	214	3.77	2.81

Note : The percentage of increase in the level of return per hectare for paddy, wheat and other crops was between 45 to 81 in the case of the East Gandak project.

variety in all regions as well the State as a whole exceed those of the range in the case of the first traditional variety.

Coming to wheat, we discover that the difference in yield as between the irrigated and the unirrigated land with regard to yield as between the regions in respect of its traditional variety is maximum in the case of Chotanagpur, 62.81 per cent, a very high figure and minimum in that of North Bihar, 0.53 per cent, a very low figure. The average for the State as a whole is 33 per cent, which is also a high figure, considering that in the case of rice, its both varieties, the range was not so wide.

As for the HY variety of wheat, the difference in yield between the irrigated and the unirrigated land is maximum, 39.75 per cent, again in the case of Chotanagpur and minimum, 14.08 per cent, again in that of North Bihar, the average for the State as a whole being 20.48 per cent. Table 12.29 indicates that when the differences in respect of the two varieties of wheat are compared region-wise, the difference is the least, 10.08 per cent, in the case of South Bihar and the highest, 23.06 per cent, in that of Chotanagpur. North Bihar stands in between the two regions with 13.55 per cent. For the State as a whole, the difference between the two varieties of wheat is 12.52 per cent.

Juxtaposing the traditional varieties of rice and wheat together, we discern that in the case of North Bihar the difference in yield as between the irrigated and the unirrigated land is exceptionally very low; in the case of the two other regions as well as Bihar as a whole the wheat differences are on the higher side compared to the rice differences.

Lastly, placing the yield differences in respect of irrigated and unirrigated lands side by side, when the HYVs are used, region-wise, we find that except for Chotanagpur, the differences are less pronounced in the case of wheat than in that of rice. That is to say, the differences are moderated in respect of the HYV rice and HYV wheat, while they are articulated in respect of the traditional rice and traditional wheat, of course, with the indicated exceptions.

To conclude, if we regard irrigation as a catalyst, then the gains reaped so far go to show only this that not the full leverage effect of this catalyst has been realised, and, therefore, efforts have to be tightened in order that this is achieved in the near future.

The rise in yield per unit of the irrigated land is extremely disappointing—as against the potential yield of 4 to 5 tonnes, the actual yield has been 1.7 tonnes. In other words, the difference should have been in perfect or ideai conditions 2.3 to 2.9 times more.

TABLE 12.29 : Region-wise Yield of Rice and Wheat in Bihar : 1990-91

(In quintals per hectare)

Region	Irrigated Rice		Unirrigated Rice		Difference between (In Percentage)		Irrigated Wheat		Unirrigated Wheat		Difference between (In Percentage)	
	Traditional Seeds	HYVs	Traditional Seeds	HYVs	(2) & (4)	(3) & (5)	Traditional Seeds	HYVs	Traditional Seeds	HYVs	(8) & (10)	(9) & (11)
(1)	(2)	(3)	(4)	(5)	(6)	(7)	(8)	(9)	(10)	(11)	(12)	(13)
North Bihar	15.73 to 21.17	21.83 to 33.19	14.45 to 19.39	17.39 to 22.93	8.85 to 9.18	25.53 to 44.74	20.33	25.44	17.82	24.25	0.53	14.08
South Bihar	20.91 to 24.78	27.34 to 35.25	17.08 to 20.27	21.43 to 25.99	22.25 to 22.42	27.57 to 35.63	19.63	24.57	14.63	19.80	34.17	24.09
Chotanagpur	18.37 to 20.01	23.55 to 36.63	16.08 to 19.78	20.15 to 28.16	1.16 to 14.24	16.87 to 30.07	17.47	22.36	10.73	16.00	62.81	39.75
Bihar as a whole	18.33 to 21.99	24.24 to 35.02	15.85 to 19.81	19.66 to 25.69	11.00 to 15.64	23.28 to 36.31	19.14	24.12	14.39	20.02	33.00	20.48

Because the reliance of the cultivators on the supply of irrigation water is less and on rainfall more, naturally the benefits from the irrigation schemes are lower in areas which receive high rainfall.

In South Bihar cost of production of canal irrigated rice varied between 32.6 and 47.2 per cent of gross income, and that of canal irrigated wheat between 41.6 and 48.3 per cent of it. the margin of surplus was above 50 per cent in both cases.

It is not only the size of holdings that makes a difference to the yield of one and the same crop under the alternative condition of irrigated or unirrigated cultivation but under the same irrigated condition, if the quantity of irrigation water provided is adequate in one case and inadequate in the other case, as also if water is supplied at the right time in one case but not supplied at the right time in the other case, quantity and time being of strategic importance in determining the yield, then also the yields would not be equal.

The unirrigated land is especially less attended to in larger farm holdings. The irrigation facility improves the degree of attention paid and hence the yield realised from them.

During 1950-51 to 1969-70 in Bihar for one per cent rise in the irrigated area there are 1.82 per cent rise in SDP (of which 1.05 per cent rise was in agriculture), whereas during 1970-71 to 1988-89 for one per cent rise in the irrigated area there was 1.34 per cent rise in SDP, of which 0.60 per cent rise was in agriculture.

It would be an oversimplification and an exaggeration to attribute the increase in agricultural output of the irrigation input alone, for the role of the other inputs cannot be overlooked.

In Bihar during 1978-79 to 1983-84 to produce one tonne more of foodgrains was needed 0.41 ha. more of irrigated land, 0.58 ha. more of land sown with the HYVs and 0.13 tonne more of fertilisers.

During the 1980s compared to irrigated wheat output, irrigated rice output showed a lower proportional rise in total foodgrains output.

Testing the proposition that irrigation improves the yield of land by basing the study on the data for one year or one triennium only may prove misleading and deceptive. Hence, it is suggested that the period chosen must be sufficiently long.

During 1950-51 to 1969-70, 1.0 per cent increase in irrigated area in Bihar was followed by 1.28 per cent increase in foodgrains production, whereas during 1970-71 to 1990-91 it was followed by 0.91 per cent increase in foodgrains production. The ratio had fallen.

To remind ourselves, the Third Plan had ascribed the increase in agricultural production during 1951-61 to the good performance of the planners in the direction of irrigation, particularly minor irrigation.

Lift irrigation has spearheaded the cultivation of short-duration crops and fertilisers-responsive strains in Bihar.

In most pockets of the major irrigation projects employment per hectare (for example, in respect of wheat) and the proportion of hired labour to family labour have both tended to increase. But this trend needs to be accentuated by combining the traditional techniques of multiple cropping with the addition of organic manure to restore the vitality of the soil.

If the past experience were any guide, the irrigation issue has demonstrated amply that it could be a cementing force socially. To illustrate, all the factions which were hostile to one another in the villages of South Bihar had stood united by sinking their differences at least on the issue of construction of irrigation works and cooperated with the authorities in parting with their lands needed by them for the purpose.

Identical was the experience of the social workers who mobilised all sections of the community in embanking the River of Sorrow, i.e., Kosi, in the formative years of planning in Bihar.

Strides made by irrigation in Bihar had a positive impact on the intensity of agriculture via increased double cropping.

Increase in double cropping is interchangeable with increase in the intensity of farming, which is expressive of and a measure of improved agricultural practice, i.e., technological revolution of agriculture.

Double cropping connotes in the present context 'Area Sown More than Once' (ASMO).

Cropping intensity is a function of doubly cropped area, that is, Area Sown More than Once (ASMO), i.e., Gross Cropped Area (GCA) divided by Net Sown Area (NSA).

Where water is available for the rabi cereals, double cropping has extended itself.

Roughly, the supply of the HYVs and the supply of irrigation water have between them determined the doubly cropped area in Bihar, though the influence of fertilisers or any other input is not denied. In other words, irrigation has been as much indispensable to cropping intensity as have been the HYVs or fertilisers or a combination of all three.

We arrive at the conclusion that the nexus between extension of irrigation and growth of double cropping cannot be denied.

Parenthetically stated, double cropping or ASMO may be regarded as a heroic, though a feeble, attempt on the part of the excessively populated areas in the river commands to catch up with their continuously growing burden.

Cropping intensity should have increased more to be proportionate to the increase in irrigation but this has not been so, not even in the command areas of the major irrigation projects. To exemplify, in spite of high coverage of irrigation in the Sone Command Area crop intensity is low at 1.50, which may be interpreted as suggesting that irrigation is a necessary condition but not the sufficient condition for the growth of cropping intensity; the HYVs or fertilisers or the entire package/complex may be more important than irrigation. To amplify, in four decades the net rise in cropping intensity in Bihar was by nearly 14 per cent, as compared to about 28 per cent in all-India (Table 12.30). On the other hand, the net increase in GIA was by 103 per cent in Bihar and by 164 per cent in all-India.

TABLE 12.30 : Cropping Intensity in Bihar

(Percentage)

Year	*Cropping Intensity*
1950-51	123.6 (113.1)
1955-56	113.4 (114.0)
1960-61	135.7 (119.6)
1962-65 (Av.)	1.41 (1.15)
1965-66	129.5
1966-67	123.0
1970-71	130.1 (125.5)
1976-77	136.0
1980-81	134.6 (132.6)
1980-82	1.33 (1.24)
1985-86	136.6
1990-91	137.5 (141.6 in 1989-90)
1992-95	1.31 (1.30)
1994-95	135 to 140

Note : Cropping intensity $= \frac{\text{GCA}}{\text{NAS}}$.

Between 1950-51 and 1986-87 ASMO in Bihar rose by 37.7 per cent, as compared to 35.2 per cent in all-India.

Area Sown More Than Once (ASMO), as percentage of Total Reporting Area (TRA) in Bihar, was 13.4 per cent in 1955-56 and 16.2 per cent in 1987-88. In 32 years the difference was of the order of 2.8 per cent only.

Between 1955-56 and 1987-88 ASMO in Bihar rose by about 12.45 lakh ha.

Between 1980-81 and 1990-91, i.e., one decade, ASMO in Bihar increased by 124 per cent (from 2.334 to 2.900 lakh ha.), as compared to 131 per cent in all-India (from 110.6 to 145.0 lakh ha.) during 1980-81 to 1989-90.

In 1984-85, of the land coming under irrigation facility, about 25/26 per cent was not doubly cropped, which was a great loss. On the other hand, 38.12 lakh ha. cultivated land had no irrigation facility. This prevented it from double cropping.

The Constraints

In the preceding pages we have discussed the absence/inadequacy of the channels/courses, which is perhaps the principal deterrent to the optimum utilisation of the created irrigation potential in Bihar.

The next constraint is the drainage problem. Kharif is affected adversely on account of failure to drain the excess water.

While considering yield, the damage done to the crops by waterlogging on account of over-irrigation, flood and poor drainage should be kept in mind.

The river projects are responsible for perennial waterlogging of 4 to 6 lakh ha. during the kharif season and 2.4 to 3.6 lakh ha. during the rabi season.

The major river projects such as Kosi and Gandak were designed without adequate consideration of drainage problems. This resulted in waterlogging and development of salinity in their command areas.

Under the Special Area Programme the drainage scheme was carried out in the Command Areas of Gandak and Kosi.

Drainage needs to have the highest priority in North Bihar districts. Eight lakh ha. in the Kosi and Gandak basins call for drainage. At 1994 prices Rs. 400 crores were needed. Maintenance would require Rs. 200 crores and flood control Rs. 100 crores.

The field channels and drains represent subsidiary irrigation works.

Draining of *chaurs, jheels* and depressions should be attempted with great caution, otherwise the water level and moisture of the air may be impaired.

The predominance of small and marginal farms is a third constraint, partly technical, partly economic and partly legal. Developing this point, we may note here how the government officials face resistance from farmers in their effort to construct field channels. They find it extremely difficult to convince them of the utility of the field channels. One farmer's field channel often passes over the plot of another farmer, which leads to frequent altercations/bickerings between the two. A farmer has to think twice before installing a shallow tubewell or a dug-well in his plot because he cannot irrigate all his fragmented plots with one such facility. Part of the capacity created would face idleness.

The small size of the operational holdings and their fragmentation is a physical, technical constraint. The existence of a very large number of marginal and small holdings obstructs the progress of construction of irrigation channels in the command areas of the major irrigation projects, particularly in North Bihar.

In 1985-86 the average size of operational holdings was 0.93 ha. in Bihar (all-India 1.69 ha.). In Bihar holdings with the scheduled castes had an average size of 0.42 ha. (all-India 1.05 ha.) and those with the scheduled tribes 1.91 ha. (all-India 2.25 ha.).

Tubewells and pumpsets are capital-intensive and hence their productivity is positively correlated with the size of the farms. This is an economic constraint. Below a particular threshold, the size is an economic constraint. Thus tubewells or wells cannot economically be sunk on small and fragmented plots. Wastage and underutilisation are typical of such plots.

Non-availability of the irrigation facility to land holdings having an area below 0.81 hectare prevents them from using the HYVs which need much watering.

The smaller cultivators do not receive water on an assured basis on account of interference by the bigger cultivators, who enjoy more power and influence. Even otherwise they are priced out.

The *Warabandi System* hardly works in the case of the small operational holdings.

The consolidation work involving the small operational holdings has made little progress.

A serious hindrance to the consolidation in the Eastern region is the wide difference in land values within one and the same village originating from differences in the availability of the irrigation facility.

But it is a fact that in the central parts of Bihar, the larger a farm is in size, the lesser irrigation it receives, and *vice-versa.*

There is then a legal snag to be reckoned with. The tenure in the case of small holders is insecure. Moreover, the prevailing tenancy laws render assignment of water rights, management of tubewells, etc. extremely difficult.

The ground water resource is an ill-defined common property.

Land disputes have multiplied with irrigation disputes in South Bihar.

A body of public opinion in Bihar maintains that had the loopholes in the enforcement of the land reform policy been removed before irrigation was emphasised, irrigation would have progressed more satisfactorily in the State

Without preventing encroachment in the flood-prone areas through legislation flood control cannot be effective.

The Power Constraint

Bulk of electricity consumed in agriculture in Bihar is for irrigation purpose. As Table 12.31 brings forth, between 1959-60 and 1990-91 the percentage share of this consumption had increased by 15 to 16 per cent, against 19 to 20 per cent in all-India.

TABLE 12.31 : Percentage Share of Agriculture in Power Consumption in Bihar

Year	*Percentage*
1959-60	3.0 (6.0)
1960-61	4.7 (Irrigation 2.0 : Punjab 12.6)
1965-66	1.5
1969-70	— (Irrigation 2.8 : Punjab 14.7)
1970-71	2.7
1975-76	12.1
1980-81	11.6
1985-86	14.2
1990-91	20.40 (26.44)

Power is an input or, better, a service of growing importance to irrigation. But its supply to the irrigation sector has never been in a position to meet the demand.

The lift irrigation schemes, well-suited to the hilly terrain of Chotanagpur and Santhal Parganas, failed due to the non-availability of power.

Around 1971 it was recognised by the State Government that assured irrigation had remained static at about 32 per cent of total cultivable land, primarily due to the inadequate availability of power. It was also realised that about 80 per cent of the public tubewells were inoperative for various reasons, the power supply position being Number One among them.

Bihar suffers chronically from power shortage. Rural power supply is inadequate, erratic and unreliable. Loadshedding is maximum in rural areas. Even when the monsoon is on time, 5 to 6 per cent of the land is planted late because of the inadequate and untimely supply of power.

Lack of proper dovetailing between rural electricity and irrigation planning has constrained the progress of irrigation.

Rural electrification in the plateau region is at a significantly lower level than in the plains, no doubt, because there is little tubewell irrigation in the region, ground water being scarce. Altogether the level of irrigation is extremely low in the tribal areas.

The public tubewells were affected by the power problem for long and had therefore to be abandoned.

Cultivation, specially, of the rabi crops, is hit hard by power shortage.

The Investment Muddle

As Table 12.32 would corroborate, upto the Seventh Plan the aggregate Plan outlay on irrigation and flood control in Bihar worked out to Rs. 3145.28 crores. As proportion to the total State Plan outlay, this expenditure varied from 15.16 per cent in the Second Plan to 33.80 per cent in the Seventh Plan. By comparison with all-India, the percentage was higher in all Plans except the First Plan. By 1991 the total expenditure on irrigation, according to Irrigation Minister quoted before, had gone up to Rs. 8000 crores (may be this includes the private sector investment

TABLE 12.32 : Plan Outlay (Public Sector) on Irrigation and Flood Control in Bihar

(Rs. crores)

Plan	*Bihar*		*India*		*Percentage Share of (2) and (4)*	*State Plan Provision for Irrigation as Percentage of All-India*
	Amount	*As Percentage of Total Plan (State)*	*Amount*	*As Percentage of Total Plan (All-India)*		
(1)	(2)	(3)	(4)	(5)	(6)	(7)
First Plan	12.94	17.66	434.0	22.2	2.98	8.8
Second Plan	26.98	15.16	430.0	9.2	6.27	10.2
Third Plan	81.97	24.70	675.0	7.8	12.14	8.0
Annual Plans	60.22	26.42	—	—	—	—
Fourth Plan	145.44	29.94	1354.1	7.4	10.74	7.2
Fifth Plan	270.57	29.57	3876.5	8.76	6.98	6.5
Sixth Plan	823.16	26.61	10925.10	9.96	7.53	9.9
Seventh Plan 1989-90	1724.00	33.80	16144.00	19.11	10.67	10.7
Annual Plan 1990-91	358.06	28.46	3830.17	15.79	9.34	—
Annual Plan	613.71	27.26	4432.25	15.55	13.84	—

during the Plan period, which was mostly on the minor works as well as the revenue expenditures for the entire period; otherwise this was an exaggeration). Our estimate is Rs. 3800 crores upto 1990-91.

Irrigation being a State subject, all the outlays on it have to be accommodated within the State Plan ceilings. But for capital expenditures the State Government can and does borrow from the Centre.

The flow of funds from the Centre to the State Government by way of loans and grants to be invested in irrigation has not been smooth. Unrelenting inflation has been another detractor.

The large irrigation works taken up by Bihar got bogged down in capital shortage from time to time because of the resource crunch encountered by the State Government. Irrigation investment faced substantial shortfalls.

Over and through time irrigation has become costlier. Delayed execution of the projects has entailed *cost overruns*. The average cost per ha. of constructing an irrigation scheme has gone up meteorically. In 1951, according to the 1951 Census, per ha. expenditure on irrigation through all types of means was Rs. 4090. This had shot up to Rs. 11743 during 1950-51 to 1989-90. Alternatively, in so far as during 1950-51 to 1990-91 by spending about Rs. 3800 crores irrigation potential equal to 17 lakh ha. was created, per hectare average investment came to Rs. 22,353. In 1993 it stood at Rs. 45,000. In 1993, it took an expenditure of Rs. 20,000 to create one ha. irrigation potential through the minor scheme and an expenditure of Rs. 1.10 lakh to create one ha. additional irrigation potential through the major and medium schemes.

Looked at this from a different angle, between 1950-51 and 1989-90, whereas the marginal expenditure on irrigation and flood control per tonne of foodgrains production in Bihar rose from Rs. 109.77 to Rs. 11215.14, 102 times (all-India figures being Rs. 283.03 and Rs. 6358.79 respectively, 23 times), the average expenditure on them per tonne of foodgrains production in the State rose from Rs. 23.02 to Rs. 1427.24, 62 times (all-India figures being Rs. 68.16 and Rs. 992.69 respectively, 15 times).

The State Government has been beset with an unprecedented resource crunch since 1989-90.

In recent years the annual expenditure on the upkeep of the major and medium irrigation projects has been from Rs. 5 to 10 crores (maximum Rs. 40 crores). The establishment cost of the Irrigation Department per year comes to Rs. 225 to 240 crores.

In 1992-93 all irrigation construction work had to come to a grinding halt. On the other hand, in order to complete the ongoing irrigation scheme at 1994 prices a sum of Rs. 3000 crores was required. In addition, the old canals, such as the Sone, called for remodelling on a priority basis.

There has been something basically amiss with irrigation investment planning in Bihar. In investing in irrigation the State Government took into consideration engineering feasibility only. Absence of agro-economic analysis in the selection and design of the irrigation projects was one reason why the benefits from them were low.

For benefits to be enduring and lasting the expenditures on irrigation have to be carried forward uninterruptedly, which has not been easy in recent years.

Investment in irrigation was assumed to build up the infrastructure basic to agriculture in its avowed bid to wipe out the lingering food deficit which made the State pitiably dependent on the Centre. That is to say, irrigation was no longer a commercial proposition in the post-independence period. The economic performance of the irrigation systems was to be evaluated in terms of their success in wiping out the food deficit, and not by the amount of the revenue they brought to the State coffers. Such a philosophy could be held responsible for why the irrigated systems could not be self-financing.

While new constructions have come in, the old ones have gone out of use for want of repair and other reasons. At places, extension of the canals has been at the expense of the existing ones.

There has been a proliferation of irrigation projects—more and more new projects have been started alongwith the ongoing, uncompleted projects. The resource crunch being there, this has resulted in resources being spread thinly over them all, an affront to the Big Push Maxim of growth. Intraregional pressures have had a hand in such an investment allocation in the irrigation sector.

Public opinion has averred that part of the investment made in major and medium projects should have gone into minor projects for the sake of quicker and surer results.

The erroneous belief that for reaping maximum benefits canal irrigation was the only alternative available had resulted in a fetish of it for the first 15 to 16 years of planning, which reduced total benefits accruing from irrigation.

In Bihar the Irrigation/Water Resource Department, one of the two departments—the other being the Power/Electricity Department with maximum budgetary revenue and capital allotments—has been also the most lucrative department for the politicians, bureaucrats and contractors.

The Ministers of these Departments came from that caste in Bihar which got its own members elected in the largest number of legislators to the State legislature. Reports have abounded exposing that funds meant to be invested in the irrigation works leaked out to private hands in a routine fashion.

Summarizing, we may assert that short of a Master Plan, irrigation development in Bihar has been planned only piecemeal. That there has been misplanning in this sector cannot be denied.

Futility of the Low Water Rates

Irrigation is heavily subsidised, implicitly as well as explicitly, especially minor irrigation, the rate ranging between 25 to 50 per cent, on all or selected schemes, e.g., distribution of pumpsets, supply of power, etc. In money terms, the irrigation projects have failed to recover even the working expenses, that is, the Operation and Maintenance (O&M) cost, leave aside the propriety of a reasonable return on investment. This is an aspect commented upon adversely by the CWC, the Planning Commission and the Finance Commissions. That is to say, inspite of the progress made by irrigation as a result of huge investment put in it, the revenue from the water rates charged has been extremely disappointing. Let us elucidate this :

Some years ago in the Sone Command Area irrigation cost was 5.6 per cent of total cost. Total cost was 28.8 per cent of gross value on the irrigated land and 44.5 per cent of gross value on the unirrigated land. But the water rate amounted to 2.27 per cent of net income in the case of rice and 1.48 per cent of net income in that of wheat. The water rate receipts as percentage of differential gross produce (defined as the difference between gross produce on the irrigated and gross produce on the unirrigated land) have amounted to 4.6 per cent in general, 2.3 per cent in the case of rice and 2.1 per cent in the case of sugarcane. Furthermore, irrigation cost as percentage of total cost of production came to 1.1 per cent in the case of rice and 1.5 per cent in that of wheat.

Nearer our time, that is, in 1990-91 so far as rice was concerned, the maximum water rate amounted to 12 per cent of gross value of the produce and the minimum to 5 per cent of it. On the other hand, consistent with the formula agreed upon the water rate was to be 20 to 50 per cent of net benefit, depending on the crops in question and other facts of the situation.

In fine, the loss sustained on account of the major and medium schemes has been a colossal figure.

Mismanagement of the Irrigation Systems : Poor Maintenance

More than low investment per farmer and per unit of cultivation mismanagement has been the hall-mark of the irrigation systems in Bihar. Irrigation management has suffered from *ad hocism* and lack of planning. Operation of the canal systems by engineers is alleged to be unproductive. An appreciable proportion of the created water potential goes to waste for want of sound management. Poor water management has held the key to why the benefits garnered from the projects have been far less than expected.

Part of the inefficiency of the canal irrigation system is owing to the defective irrigation scheduling and water delivery. The water year at present is from June to May. The most ineluctable proof of this management is the poor maintenance of the irrigation projects hailed as the catalysts of change on the eve of their launching. The single most important reason for low irrigation efficiency is inadequate maintenance. The irrigation facilities of the olden times faced destruction and obliteration, neglect and disrepair.

Especially in South Bihar the maintenance of the network of canals, *ahars* and *pynes* owned by the ertswhile landlords has been unsatisfactory. It was the State Government's responsibility to maintain the sources of irrigation taken over from the erstwhile *Zamindars* and preventing them from going out of use for lack of repair, etc. Less than due attention has been paid to modernisation and improvement of the existing systems. The canals suffer from sedimentation.

The century-old Sone canal system is paralysed by congealed mucus, which makes it unable to meet the emergency requirements of its catchment districts during a drought. Overdue is the renovation of the Sone canal. A few years ago a Rs. 238 crore plan had been submitted to the CWC for its modernisation.

The Kosi canal system has become defunct due to siltation and non-maintenance.

The Administration was apathetic to nursing community initiative and participation in the upkeep of the irrigation systems, which accounts for the lack of involvement of the irrigators in their management.

In view of the lacuna in the management of the irrigation systems the Third Plan of the Bihar Government proposed to entrust the maintenance of the earth work portion of the medium and minor *Ahars, pynes* and *bandhs* to the Village Panchayats.

Money meant for the maintenance of the irrigation works is alleged to have been spent on payment of salaries of the Government employees, with the result that the works have been poorly maintained.

A critical imbalance between construction and Operation and Maintenance (O&M) Programmes has ensued.

Funds for the maintenance of the main irrigation system from headworks to outlets are provided to the State Government under non-Plan on the recommendation of the Finance Commission every five years.

The limited renovation and re-excavation of the old minor sources of irrigation which was executed has amounted to mere tinkering with their maintenance.

Water erosion lowers the expected life of the projects. A proper maintenance of the irrigation works (and via this, of water and moisture) is not only directly necessary for the nutrition of the plant life (and forest cover) but is also required for the conservation of the integrity of the soil through an effective use of manures and fertilisers against erosion by air.

One facet of irrigation management has a very wide ramification : The State Government is required to get all its irrigation projects, major, medium or minor, cleared by the Central Government.

Where irrigation involves inter-State/Inter-country rivers, its progress in Bihar has turned on its progress in the other States/country(ies).

Public opinion in Bihar is highly critical of the fact that other States siphon off a good part of Bihar's precious gift of water.

The Gandak and Kosi Projects were constructed during the 1960s with the cooperation of Nepal.

The rivers originating in Nepal play havoc with the State economy. The State Government has to spend several crores every year to maintain the embankments to ward off flood, though most often in vain.

In a Nutshell

Since 1950-51 substantial irrigation potential has been created in North Bihar. However, South Bihar is more developed than North Bihar in respect of irrigation facility.

North and Central Bihar have rich potentials for irrigated crop husbandry with fertile alluvial soil, excellent surface and underground water and a fairly good amount of annual rainfall.

At present only 40 per cent of the cultivated land in Bihar is irrigated.

Only 24 per cent of the cultivated land area receives assured irrigation.

About 60 per cent of our agriculture is still a hostage to the vagaries of the monsoon rains, long drought spells or inadequate rainfall in the crucial months of transplantation and plant growth, which adversely affects agricultural production.

Uncertain rainfall still makes farming hazardous in a good many areas.

There are a good many parts in Bihar where great possibilities of intensive agriculture cannot be exploited because the supply of water is not assured and reliable throughout the year.

Even if all the ongoing schemes were to be completed by 2005 A.D., about 73 per cent of the cultivated land would be under irrigation and nearly 27 per cent of the total cultivated land would have to depend on the rains.

Suggestions

The benefits from irrigation can be optimised by the following methods :

1. By improving the level of utilisation—minimising the losses at the storage/diversion point and in the distribution system plus speedier and more efficient use of water in the fields—proper scheduling of irrigation to attain high efficiency in water use—rehabilitation and modernisation and maintenance—land improvement : levelling, bunding, provision and lining of field channels, drainage, more and better regulatory structures and communications combined with changes in the way water deliveries are regulated—introduction of *Warabandi* on rotational distribution system—remodelling and/or supplementing the existing canals and tubewells by constructing subsidiary irrigation works.
2. Due attention to be given to other related/connected aspects of agricultural development, such as supply of inputs, suitable extension facilities, intensive agricultural education and training programmes and demonstrations of the available technical expertise (let us remember that many pumping sets lie idle for want of it) and credit facilities. Given these, timely and adequate supply of irrigation water in a water year would optimise yield and result in increased agricultural income and hence public

revenue. In a word, there should be a polarisation of the crop-soil-water management priorities. But this would call for enhanced allocation of funds in the budget every year.

3. Whereas the location and design of the irrigation works is important in itself, close monitoring and periodic project evaluation is equally important for deriving maximum benefits from the irrigation system. The actual benefits should be compared with the proposed benefits and the factors responsible for the hiatus surmounted. This will necessitate analysis and identification of the problems in each project, existing and new.
4. The ultimate irrigation potential should be sought to be attained through the conjunctive use of ground and surface water.
5. Programmes of minor irrigation should be dovetailed with rural electrification schemes for energising clusters of wells or tubewells.
6. The farmers individually or preferably through their organisations and the public authorities of various departments in the command, catchment and watershed areas should participate in the scientific management of water and land resources with a view to optimising productivity, terrestrial and aquatic.
7. The National Plan for inter-basin transfer of water from the water-surplus areas to the water-deficit areas and an early solution to the inter-State and inter-country river disputes which at present hamper long-gestation irrigation projects would be imperative.

More Concretely

1. The old tanks have to be desilted.
2. The construction work should be balanced with the Operation & Maintenance Programmes.
3. The success of a Five-Year Plan has been linked with the most advantageous use of the land and labour resources engaged in agriculture in the State. But the land and labour resources have not proved helpful to the extent desired in the absence of their gearing to and integration with the water resources available in the State. This gearing and integration is considered fundamental to the prosperity of Bihar economy owing to the co-effects involved.

4. To be integrated with the use of river waters is also the exploitation of the subsoil water resources.
5. The care of water should be as much the concern of the farmer as the care of the land itself.
6. Water use can be optimised by means of land improvement, irrigation along the contours and a regulated discharge of water.
7. The watershed approach is pertinent to the rainfed areas. Watershed development would improve the productivity of the unirrigated tracts.
8. Authorities suggest that to make good the deficiencies in precipitation towards the latter part of the monsoon when the *Hathia* showers fail, it would be worthwhile for the farmer to set apart even a fraction of his holding for storing rain water.
9. The Drip Irrigation System is suited to areas having limited water resources.
10. Watershed development in South Bihar and Chotanagpur should be paid increased attention.
11. Water management in South Bihar and Chotanagpur would emphasise water conservation.
12. By means of quick-yield irrigation projects on a selective basis the regional imbalances in irrigation can be corrected.
13. Needed is not only an innovation in the pattern of farming but also in the attitudes and habits of the people.
14. By stimulating changes in the cropping pattern prevalent in the different regions, higher value outputs could be obtained.
15. The fact that a major constraint to agricultural development in Bihar is either too much of water or too little of it ought to be constantly kept in mind.
16. Enhanced supply of adequate water in a controlled manner and enhanced drainage facility should be the spearhead of agricultural development in Bihar.
17. Reduction of the 40 hectare outlets into 5 to 8 hectare ones would help the irrigation system reach individual holdings.

Abbreviations Used in this Chapter are as under :

Area Sown More Than One	= ASMO
Central Water Commission	= CWC
Command Area Development Authority	= CADA
Command Area Development Programme	= CADP
Cultural Command Area	= CCA

Gross Cropped Area	= GCA
Gross Irrigated Area	= GIA
Hectare	= Ha/ha
Million	= m
Net Cropped Area	= NCA
Net Irrigated Area	= NIA
Net Sown Area	= NSA
Operation and Maintenance	= O&M
Total Cropped Area	= TCA
Total Reporting Area	= TRA

13

FERTILISERS IN BIHAR AGRICULTURE

Use/consumption of fertilisers per hectare (ha) is taken as a surrogate for the progress of the Green Revolution (GR)/the New Agrarian Technology (NAT). In tracing the progress of fertilisers use/consumption in Bihar we shall keep this principle in mind. Table 13.1 depicts this growth. Between 1960-61 and 1991-92 there was a 35 to 36 times increase in Bihar, from 17 thousand tonnes to 607 thousand tonnes, according to one official, and to 610 thousand tonnes, according to another. In the case of India, during the same period there was a 38 to 62 times increase, sources being different.* The trend of growth of use/consumption of fertilisers in Bihar was continuously rising, except for the years 1979-80 and 1989-90, when the quantities fell in absolute terms.

Bihar's relative share in all-India fertilisers consumption which was 8.1 per cent in 1960-61 appears to have declined in the subsequent years through fluctuations. According to one source, the percentage of decline was 2.6 per cent; according to another, 3.5 per cent. This was not an event of mean importance. Gross cropped area in Bihar is at present around 6.0 per cent of the all-India total. So long as its share in all-India fertilisers consumption remained above 6.0 per cent, it was not a cause of concern but in the years in which it fell below that figure, the matter assumed seriousness. The number of such years has exceeded the number of years in which the contrary was the case.

An alternative method of assessing progress consists in estimating the percentage share of rise in fertilisers consumption in Bihar in comparison to the rise in it on all-India basis for periods in succession. Thus the figures for 1960-61 to 1970-71, 1970-71 to 1980-81 and

* One publication, *Indian Agriculture in Brief*, gives higher aggregates, while the other one, *Agricultural Statistics at a Glance*, gives lower totals, both being the publications of the Ministry of Agriculture.

1980-81 to 1990-91 were 6.5, 4.8 and 4.3 per cent respectively. In another estimate, for the period 1971-72 to 1984-85 it was 4.9 per cent and for the period 1971-72 to 1989-90, 5.1 per cent. The scenario was not promising for Bihar.

TABLE 13.1 : Consumption of Chemical Fertilisers (N+P+K) in Bihar

(in '000 tonnes)

Year	*Consumption*	*Bihar's Share in All-India Fertiliser Consumption (Per cent)*	*Bihar's Share in All-India GCA*
1960-61	17 (210)	8.1	7.2
1968-69	58	—	6.8
1970-71	100 (1487)	6.7	—
1971-72	108	—	—
1973-74	96.9 (2839.0)	3.4	6.3
1974-75	116.8 (2573.3)	4.5	6.6
1975-76	124.0 (2893.7)	4.2	6.6
1976-77	156 (2177/3411)	7.1/4.6	6.7
1977-78	173.2 (4285.8)	4.0	6.7
1978-79	194.7 (3116.9)	6.2	6.5
1979-80	184.3 193 (5255.8)	4.0	6.2
1980-81	205/204.5 (3678/5515.6)	5.5/3.5	6.4
1981-82	206 (6067.2)	3.4	6.7
1982-83	210.6 (6417.9)	3.2	6.5
1986-87	527 (8644)	6.1	5.9
1987-88	601 (9011)	6.6	—
1988-89	608 (11036)	5.5	—
1989-90	564/386 (12546)	7.6/4.5	6.0
1990-91	600/598 (7997/12546)	7.5/4.7	6.0
1991-92	610/607 (8046/12997)	7.5/4.6	

The data relating to fertilisers consumption in Bihar prior to 1960-61 is not available. The Budget Speeches of the Finance Ministers of the State contain very brief references to it for some years. Table 13.2 has been prepared on their basis. The amounts concerned were sold to the farmers by the State Government agencies. In 1951-52 the Credit Agricole Scheme had 1180 distribution centres throughout the State. In addition to chemical fertilisers, organic manure was produced and sold. Cooperation appears to have made its debut in the mid-1950s in the field of marketing of fertilisers. The BISCOMAUN came in later.

It cannot be denied that since 1960-61 there has occurred a phenomenal increase in per ha. Gross Cropped Area fertilisers consumption in

Bihar, over 36-fold, more than in respect of all-India, 22-fold. But even today, as in the beginning, nay, throughout the period, per ha. consumption of chemical fertilisers in Bihar is below that in all-India. In 1960-61, the difference was by 218 per cent. In 1995, it was by 131 per cent. The hiatus was narrower, however. Bihar was trying to catch up with all-India (Table 13.3). By comparison with other States like Punjab (162.23 kgs./ha.), Tamil Nadu (117.19 kgs./ha.), and Andhra Pradesh (114.20 kgs./ha.). Bihar's figure (year of comparison 1992-93 estimates) 57.18 kgs./ha. is by far small. Accepted on all hands is the fact that fertilisers consumption in Bihar is one of the lowest in the country. It has been so from the very beginning.

TABLE 13.2 : Consumption of Nutrients in Earlier Years in Bihar*

(In tonnes)

Year	*Total*	*Chemical Fertilisers*	*Bonemeal*	*Town Compost*	*Oil-cake*
1950-51		2000			
First Plan		12000 (Phosphate and bonemeal)*			
		67000 (ammonia)		2 lakh	
1955-56		22000 (sulphate excluding town compost)			
1956-57		40303			
1957-58		567 (phosphate and bonemeal)*		44161	2000
		22000 (ammonia sulphate)			
1959-60		50352 (37000 being ammonia)		43173	
		51000 sulphate and 12408 sulphate and bonemeal)			
1960-61		42000 (35000 ammonia sulphate)			
1977-78		1.73 lakh			
1978-79		1.95 lakh			
1979-80		191 lakh (1.47 N + 0.29 P +0.15 K)			

* Based on the Budget papers. Amounts sold by the Government agencies like Credit Agricole, Cooperative Marketing Union, BISCOMAUN, etc.

The Leading Events and Facts

In the raising of cash crops the neighbouring States of Bihar in the early years of the 1960s had resorted to a high level of organic manures and compared to them, Bihar was nowhere, take jute, Bihar's share in line sowing was not commensurate with the acreage under it. Bihar produced compost and used fertilisers and green manuring only in moderate doses.

TABLE 13.3 : Fertilisers Consumption in Bihar per Hectare of Gross Cropped Area

Year	*Consumption (Ha./Kgs.)*
1960-61	1.5 (3.27)
1962-63	2.43 (3.37)
1962-65	2.96 (4.33)
1968-69	4.1/7.3 (10.7)
1970-71	9.0/9.8 (13.6)
1973-74	9.11 (17.4)
1974-75	10.9 (15.8)
1975-76	12.5 (17.1)
1976-77	13.8/14.5/14.8 (20.0/20.1/20.4)
1977-78	15.4 (25.0)
1978-79	16.8 (29.7)
1979-80	15.9 (30.5)
1980-81	17.8/17.9/18.5 (31.83/31.9)
1980-83	27.46 (42.62)
1981-82	18.0 (34.6/34.99)
1982-83	18.5/20.2 (26.8/36.6/36.94)
1983-84	26.1 (44.5/44.66)
1984-85	35.9/37.20 (46.56/48.53)
1985-86	47.68/48.88 (47.39/48.44)
1986-87	50.57/51.42 (48.45/48.54)
1987-88	46.20/47.06/52.9/58.4/59.8 (47.1/49.00/50.81/51.13/51.2)
1988-89	57.80/57.82/58.88/60.8 (61.30/62.20/63.86)
1989-90	54.14/54.62 (63.86/65.4/66.91)
1990-91	56.8/56.91/57.44/57.95 (69.26/69.66/72.4/72.57)
1991-92	57.08/57.76/57.94/58.46 (67.64/70.27/72.17/73.62/83.74)
1992-93	57.18 /57.58(67.09/68.62)
1992-95	85.36 (89.08)
1993-94	56.82 (65.53)
1994-95	60/64.6 (75.7)
1995	51.7/58 (72)
1995-96	77.0 (74.8)
Triennium ending	
1959-62	1.09
1968-71	7.99
1970-71	9.42/9.8
1977-80	16.56

During the Second Plan period the rate of consumption of fertilisers in Bihar was about 2.5 lakh tonnes a year, which met but a very tiny part of the nutrient requirements of the soil. Rs. 8 crores was the budget provision a year for this. Added to this was nearly 44 thousand tonnes of compost, which cost Rs. 4 to 5 lakhs. All in all, in the triennium ending 1959-62 per ha. consumption of fertilisers was negligibly small.

Bihar witnessed an impressive growth of fertilisers consumption since the outset of the 1960s, starting from a scratch, so to say, though the pace was faster in the 1960s than in the 1970s, but when set against the rates during the two decades achieved by Punjab, Tamil Nadu and Andhra Pradesh, the pace in Bihar even in the 1960s pales into ignominy. The growth rate in Bihar of fertilisers consumption per ha. was 0.78 per cent per annum during 1959-62 to 1968-71, 0.28 per cent per annum during 1970-73 to 1979-82, and 11.6 per cent during 1968-69 to 1987-88 (in all-India it was 6.6 per cent).

During the 1960s and 1970s expansion of fertilisers consumption was much faster than the corresponding expansion of irrigated cropped area in Bihar. In 1976-77, for farms of all sizes, consumption of fertilisers was 57 per cent more in irrigated ones, as compared to the unirrigated, in the State (for all-India the figure was 30 per cent). In rain-based areas fertilisers were used, no doubt, but not with the same efficiency and effectiveness as they were used in areas based on irrigation or partly irrigation and partly rains (Table 13.4).

TABLE 13.4 : Fertilisers Consumption in Irrigated and Unirrigated Areas by Size-Group in Bihar : 1976-77

(Per ha. in kgs.)

Size-Group	*Irrigated*	*Unirrigated*	*Percentage Difference between (2) & (3)*
(1)	(2)	(3)	(4)
Marginal	135 (138)	57 (97)	237 (70)
Small	112 (125)	70 (110)	62 (13)
Semi-Medium	105 (125)	85 (91)	23 (37)
Medium	112 (121)	84 (99)	33 (22)
Large	99 (126)	85 (88)	16 (43)
All Sizes	115 (126)	73 (97)	57 (30)

Table 13.4 does not attest to the fact that certain disturbing causes, such as weather changes, supply conditions and euphoria waves for a modern input like fertilisers, cause year-to-year fluctuations in fertilisers consumption or further that the degree of variability in periods of higher growth has been higher than in those of lower growth, a subtle feature, more or less for the same set of factors, but a look at the district-wise figures, contained in *Plan Statistics* of the Bihar State Pianning Board, accords due confirmation to this.

In the improvement gained so far in the level of fertilisers consumption per ha. of GCA among the chief factors that have made notable contributions we have, firstly, the great interest taken by the State Government. It assumed the role of a trader/seller, and through its own media as well as the private parties it had the network spread all over the State, though not without certain glaring gaps and lacunae, which diluted the net effect of the exercise, but did not go without producing some salutary effect. The Grow More Food Campaign (GMFC) was the frame within which this exercise was undertaken, with renewed passion in 1952-53. The stress was dual, not only on chemical fertilisers but also on manures—green, compost and all the rest of it, of which the Government itself became a producer. Of course, the cooperative organisation was at the centre of all this, expanding its tentacles side by side. The second major influence originated with the introduction of the Japanese method of rice cultivation in Bihar during the First Plan, which emphasised fertilisers consumption. The farmers were amazed to see around them the yield rise twice to thrice, particularly where adequate moisture was present in the soil, and the irrigation water supply facility was handy.

The NCAER report, released in 1956, commented on the deficiency in organic and nitrogenous content of the soil in Bihar and prescribed green manuring on a large scale to be so organised as to cover at least one-third of the Net Sown Area (NSA). Popularisation was the most powerful method, according to it.

With the headway made in community development and extension blocks, demonstration at local places propagating knowledge about and the advantages of fertilisers, which were making their presence felt in such blocks, turned out to be the most effective tool. The early 1960s were marked all the more by this experiment.

The trend continued till 1972-73 when the State was hit hard by a severe drought, to which was imputed the loss of foodgrains of the order of approximately 28 lakhs. The State Government approached the Centre for aid in order to surmount the crisis. The Central aid was given for the purchase of more fertilisers and more pesticides—2 crores for the former and 0.50 crore for the latter. The State Government granted to the BISCOMAUN Rs. one crore for fertilisers. The 1973-74 Budget had a provision of Rs. 1.50 crores for fertilisers. In 1975-76, Rs 26 crores were obtained from the Government of India for providing fertilisers to the farmers.

Fertilisers are sold at lower prices to the users because they are the recipients of Government subsidy. Since 1980 the rate of subsidy was fixed at the rate of 10 per cent on N fertilisers, 25 per cent for P and K fertilisers and 25 per cent for pesticides. In 1980-81 the Bihar State budget had a provision of Rs. 10 crores for giving subsidy on fertilisers and pesticides. In 1984-85 the budget provision had increased slightly to Rs. 10.3 crores for paying subsidy on imported fertilisers. Irrigated farms were preferred in selling fertilisers.

Bihar has received from the Centre by way of subsidies on fertilisers and pesticides less than proportionately on account of the low level of consumption of these inputs.

Low intake of fertilisers in Bihar, despite the strides made, has been attributed, in the main, to (1) predominance of small, semi-marginal and marginal farms, (2) low credit availability, and (3) a low irrigation base. Let us appraise this in its historical perspective.

In the early 1960s a number of farmers had, in fact, a positive experience with fertilisers but were not fully convinced about the efficiency of continued use of fertilisers. Today, in 1998, such farmers remain, but in a reduced percentage.

In the early 1960s the existing information and bountiful agencies had not succeeded in bringing about any basic change in the attitude of most farmers towards fertilisers consumption. At present the situation is much better, thanks to the regular programmes on the topic on the radio and the TV, but the old habits die hard, and we must allow a lapse of some more years for total acceptance.

In the early 1960s the high prices of fertilisers had acted as a great disincentive, notwithstanding the offer of a 25 per cent subsidy on the price of superphosphate to the farmers. Prices of fertilisers have turned adverse to those of agricultural products in later years, and in spite of the subsidy, the farmers have complained of the increased burden, to what extent is not easy for us to answer without data, which are lacking. What can be said with a modicum of confidence on the basis of Table 13.5 is that whereas expenditure on fertilisers in all-India has gone up in respect of paddy and wheat, in Bihar it has gone down. Given the bottlenecks and malpractices characterising fertilisers supply the price which the farmer pays for fertilisers in his block of panchayat is far above the price which the Finance Minister wants him to pay for them, and hence the situation in this regard, though better than before, is still far from the desired.

In the early 1960s inadequate credit was a major impediment to fertilisers use. The prevalent terms of credit, both the rate of interest and the repayment procedures, did not take into account the special types of risks the users of fertilisers had to bear. The most common grievance was about the inflexible nature of the period of the repayment of the loans. Even when the harvest was poor, the repayment was insisted on by the credit agencies. After three decades no radical change in the mentality of the credit agencies can be claimed, though on paper the policies have become small man-friendly and the Government guarantee has become more broad-based.

TABLE 13.5 : Cost Aspect of Fertilisers Consumption in Bihar

(Rs./ha.)

Sl. No.	Item	1985-86			1986-87		
		Paddy	Wheat (All Irrigated)	Maize	Paddy	Wheat	Maize
1.	Total Cost of Production	3245 (4126)	3358 (3160)	1551 (2247)	4433 (4144)	3968 (3464)	—
2.	Expenditure on fertilisers	158 (141)	171 (159)	213 (146)	129 (172)	180 (182)	—
3.	2 as percentage of 1	4.87 (3.41)	5.09 (5.03)	13.73 (6.49)	2.91 (4.15)	4.53 (5.25)	—
4.	Return over cost	5132 (4894)	4326 (4775)	4494 (5526)	3426 (5335)	2805 (4126)	—
5.	4 as proportion of 1 (per cent)	158 (118)	129 (151)	290 (246)	77 (128)	70 (119)	—

In the early 1960s the cooperative societies were not in a position to provide for an adequate number of sale points, with the result that there was excessive and frequent accumulation of stocks, particularly attributable to the inability of administration to arrange supply in time. By and large, the market forces controlled the allocation of the stocks between areas and over time, and not inoften the allocative efficiency of the market forces was in serious doubt and irrational outcomes were perceived. Moreover, the cooperatives existed merely to fulfil a set target. The result was fertilisers distribution was not as effective or pervasive or timely as it should be. This was very much so because the cooperatives enjoyed a sort of monopoly position and as such were not charged/buoyed/informed with the requisite incentive to sell fertilisers. The motive was neither purely profit maximisation nor rendering maximum good to the farmer class. The result could not have been different. The BISCOMAUN which handled nearly half of the total supply of fertilisers to the users had been operating with the help of the same old cooperative structure in a large measure, and therefore the experiences were not far different. As reports go, the plight of the users was worse than before. We shall return to this point later on.

In the early 1960s the farms with the *Bataidars* either eschewed the use of fertilisers or were hesitant to use them because they knew that not only the investment made was risky but the increase in the yield was unlikely to rest with them, and their dilemma was unnecessarily prologned by the exasperating slowness with which the State Government was trying to implement the land reforms which adumbrated certain institutional reliefs to the *Bataidars*. The aura of uncertainty persists even today, though the pro-Bataidar organisations have come up during the last three decades, under the banner of which the battle is fought with success in some parts of the State and without it in others, the law and order authorities blowing hot and cold, as dictated by the shifting sands of their relative political clout and the ideological learnings of the ruling party.

A factor which has stood as a deterrent to the growth of fertilisers consumption in all decades so far is this that the farmer would not use fertilisers unless he has found a very favourable correlation between the cost of fertilisers and the additional returns ascribable to fertilisers. This is the rationality premise. The innate pragmatism of this premise could not be questioned. Put in another way, fertilisers consumption was a matter of basic motivations as well as the attitudes of farmers towards farming as a business.

The Fertilisers Consumption Norm

The present-day norm of fertilisers consumption per ha. in respect of rice is 40 kgs. in case of MYVs and 80 kgs. in case of HYVs, whereas the actual consumption is 3 kgs. per ha. (both varieties combined). In respect of wheat the corresponding figures are 40 and 80 kgs., whereas the actual figure is 3 kgs. only (combined) in the majority of cases. In the case of rabi wheat the norm laid down is 175 kgs. per ha. but in actual practice the average is around 15 kgs. per ha. For all crops put together, the average today at 54/55 kgs. a ha., is adjudged to be one-third of the norm, i.e., 162/165 kgs. a ha.

Inequalities in Fertilisers Consumption

During the 1960s and 1970s wheat and rice were fertilisers-intensive crops but a sizable proportion of the cropped area under them was not irrigated. In 1977-78, 57.84 per cent of the total supply of fertilisers went to rice, 25.74 per cent of it to wheat, 12.45 per cent to maize, 3.31 per cent to sugarcane and 0.66 per cent to jute. The corresponding all-India percentages were 34.72, 22.65, 1.23, 7.12 and 7.44. For Punjab the related figures were 15.31, 72.02, 2.16 and 6.29 per cent (jute and cotton) respectively. In Maharashtra sugarcane's percentage share was 23.10 and jute-cum-cotton's 12.79.

In the same year (1977-78) fertilisers consumption per ha. in kgs. in Bihar in the case of sugarcane was 46.22, in that of maize 27.02, in that of wheat 26.94, in that of rice 20.00 and in that of jute 7.69 (kgs./ha.). For Punjab the corresponding figures were 101.00, 40.29, 125.69, 131.00 (kgs./ha.) and (not available). In Maharashtra sugarcane had the maximum fertilisers consumption, 338.02 kgs./ha.

Between Kharif and Rabi crops (ignoring Garma crops as negligible) fertilisers consumption in Bihar is low in the former and high in the latter, the ratio between the two in this regard being 1 to 3 or 3.4 (more than 3 in 1980-81) and 1 to 1.15 in 1991-92 (in all-India the ratio was more or less the same). This shows a change for the better. In absolute terms, the consumption in the kharif season rose by a quantity (2.1 lakh tonnes) between the two years which coincided exactly with the quantity (2.1 lakh tonnes) by which the consumption in the rabi season rose. But in percentage terms the rise in the case of kharif crops was by 555 per cent, whereas the rise in the case of rabi crops was by 228 per cent, the sumtotal of the two quantities rising by 297 per cent (Table 13.6).

Fertilisers consumption in the kharif season was lower because water management during the season was frightfully difficult. In the absence of controlled water supply the returns were not good during the kharif season. In the kharif season fertilisers were used mostly in the cultivation of vegetables and other cash crops. Kharif rice is not provided the quantity of fertilisers which is the norm, as is wheat but the gap is by a higher percentage in respect of kharif rice than in that of rabi wheat. With the peasant's mental frontiers expanding and his ken of technical knowledge stretching, his prejudice against the use of fertilisers in kharif crops is diminishing. The Government-sponsored special programmes are casting their imprint on this practice.

Towards the end of the 1970s, the percentage of area securing fertilises to total cropped area in Bihar was extremely low among the marginal farms and only a shade better among the small farms. Although the general situation after the elapse of nearly two decades has definitely improved, the disparity is still there, and as we move from the bottom to the top of the hierarchy of farms, classified in the ascending order of

TABLE 13.6 : Relative Shares of Kharif and Rabi Crops in Fertilisers Consumption in Bihar

(Lakh tonnes)

Season	1980-81		1981-82		1986-87		1987-88		1988-89	
	Quantity	Percentage	Quantity	Percentage	Quantity	Percentage	Quantity	Percentage	Quantity	Percentage
(1)	(2)	(3)	(4)	(5)	(6)	(7)	(8)	(9)	(10)	(11)
Kharif	0.45	22.5	0.51	24.4	2.12 (39.5)	40.2 (45.7)	1.96 (38.9)	32.6 (43.1)	2.85 (52.0)	46.8 (47.2)
Rabi	1.58	77.5	1.55	75.6	3.15 (46.9)	59.8 (54.3)	4.05 (51.2)	67.4 (56.9)	3.43 (58.0)	53.2 (52.8)
Total	2.05	100.0	2.06	100.0	5.27 (86.4)	100.0 (100.0)	6.01 (90.1)	100.0 (100.0)	6.08 (110.0)	100.0 (100.0)

(Contd.)

TABLE 13.6 (Contd.)

Season	1989-90		1990-91		1991-92		Increase between 1980-81 and 1991-92	
	Quantity	Percentage	Quantity	Percentage	Quantity	Percentage	Quantity	Percentage
(1)	(12)	(13)	(14)	(15)	(16)	(17)	(18)	(19)
Kharif	2.5 (53.7)	44.6 (46.4)	2.6 (57.4)	43.3 (45.7)	2.5 (59.0)	40.9 (46.3)	2.1	555
Rabi	3.1 (62.0)	54.4 (53.6)	3.4 (48.1)	56.7 (54.3)	3.6 (68.3)	59.1 (53.7)	2.1	228
Total	5.6 (115.7)	100.0 (100.0)	6.0 (125.5)	100.0 (100.0)	6.1 (127.3)	100.0 (100.0)	4.2	297

size, the per ha. fertilisers consumption shows an unbroken increase upto a level, when the curve abruptly takes a downward slope, which, as suggested above, is a reflex of decline of interest of those who manage the farms by proxy in the absence of their real owners.

When viewed regionally, Central Bihar (this is a natural division, not administrative, composed of Patna, Shahbad, Gaya, Bhagalpur and Monghyr, and as such is distinct from South Bihar, which is comprised of Patna, Shahabad and Gaya districts) is the first in terms of fertilisers consumption per ha. During 1959-80 the rate of growth was the highest in North Bihar (24.6 times), followed by Central Bihar (12.58 times) and Chotanagpur (natural division : South Bihar) 12.33 times. For the State as a whole, the rate was 15.19 times (Table 13.7).

TABLE 13.7 : Region-wise Fertilisers Consumption in Bihar

(kgs./ha.)

Region	*1959-62*	*1968-71*	*1977-80*	*Increase during 1959-80 (Times)*
North Bihar	0.65	8.42	15.99	24.60
Central Bihar	2.03	11.09	25.55	12.58
South Bihar	0.42	2.36	5.18	12.33
Bihar State	1.09	7.90	16.56	15.19

During 1959-62 to 1968-71 annual compound rate of growth of fertilisers consumption was: North Bihar 28.8, Central Bihar 17.4 and South Bihar 18.7 per cent. For Bihar as a whole the rate was 21.8. per cent During 1970-73 to 1979-80 the rates were 7.1, 11.4 and 6.8 per cent respectively. For Bihar as a whole the rate was 7.8 per cent. By comparison, the rates were lower in the latter period than in the former (Table 13.8).

TABLE 13.8 : Growth Rate of Fertilisers Consumption in Bihar : Region-wise

(Annual compound/per cent)

Region	*1959-62 to 1968-71*	*1970-73 to 1979-80*
North Bihar	28.8	7.1
Central Bihar	17.4	11.4
South Bihar	18.7	6.8
Bihar	21.8	7.8

Tables 13.9 to 13.11 reveal considerable inter-district variations in fertilisers consumption. From them are obvious ups and downs in per ha.

consumption in some districts in the course of years. However, there are other districts which indicate unhindered growth of this consumption. Districts fall into two broad classes—one, with maximum rates, and

TABLE 13.9 : District-wise Fertilisers Consumption in Bihar

Districts (only illustrative)	*1959-62 to 1968-71 Range (kgs./ha. of GCA)*	*1978-79 (kgs./ha.)*	*1979-80 (kgs./ha.)*	*Triennium ending 1980-81 (kgs./ha.)*
Purnea	0.10 to 3.01	5.66	0.65	
Saharsa	0.10 to 5.04			
Saran	1.10 to 15.00	28.14		
Champaran	1.10 to 19.21			
Katihar			0.50	
Gopalganj			3.67	
Madhubani			0.75	
Monghyr		17.68		
Patna	0.16 to 17.87	32.09	3.45	
Nalanda			3.11	
Hazaribagh	0.61 to 2.20			
Dhanbad	0.49 to 2.25			
Ranchi		6.40		
Palamau	0.37 to 1.00	3.75		
3 districts (Patna, Muzaffarpur and Gopalganj)				35 to 38
12 districts				18 to 34
16 districts				Below 18

TABLE 13.10 : Maximum and Minimum Fertilisers Consumption Districts in Bihar

Year	*Maximum (only illustrative)*	*Minimum (only illustrative)*
1973-74	Patna Nalanda Rohtas	Dhanbad Giridih Hazaribagh
1975-76	Rohtas Bhojpur Patna	Same as above
1977-78	Bhojpur Rohtas Gaya	Dhanbad Giridih Katihar
1980-81	Rohtas Bhojpur Gaya	Dhanbad Giridih Hazaribagh

two, with minimum rates, but the latter class is far more numerous. Likewise, we have districts experiencing the highest rates of growth and districts experiencing the lowest. But at any rate the latter far outnumber the former.

TABLE 13.11 : Highest and Lowest Growth Rate Districts in Fertilisers Consumption in Bihar

(Compound Annual in Percentage)

Period	*Highest Growth Rate Districts (only illustrative)*	*Lowest Growth Rate Districts (only illustrative)*
1959-62 to 1968-69	28.2 to 48.7 Saharsa, Purnea, Champaran and Saran	9.3 to 12.9 Palamau, Patna, Hazaribagh and Dhanbad
1970-73 to 1979-80	14.7 to 17.9 Monghyr, Shahabad and Gaya	3.4 to 5.5 Saharsa, Champaran, Hazaribagh and Santhal Parganas

Bihar had a higher rank in 1962-63 among States in respect of fertilisers consumption per ha. but in the next ten years its rank deteriorated, and being in rank the seventh State in sharing the total foodgrains production of the country, Bihar is eleventh in rank in fertilisers consumption per ha. This is expressive of under consumption of fertilisers. Assessed alternatively in terms of percentage share in total fertilisers consumption in the country, Bihar's tenth rank was also unfavourable, considering that it was in rank seventh in foodgrains outturn in all-India. This was another measure of Bihar's under-consumption of fertilises. The almost static rank of Bihar is to be evaluated against the fact that the rate of increase of fertilisers consumption had accelerated after 1973-74. It is odd, nay, is an irony that Bihar which even at its existing low level of productivity contributes 6.9 per cent of total foodgrains output in all-India should have a 4.7 per cent share in the country's aggregate fertilises consumption. This is the outcome of the glaring discrimination which Bihar suffers at the hands of the Centre in the distribution of fertilisers. Underfeeding of the jute crop with fertilisers has crippled it in Bihar. On the contrary, Orissa, despite its worse relative position in the matter of fertilisers, has somehow or other managed to keep its jute cultivation sturdy and robust by applying relatively more fertilisers (Table 13.12).

TABLE 13.12 : Inter-State Imbalances in Fertilisers Consumption

(Kgs./ha.)

State	*1962-63*	*1973-74*	*1994-95*	*Relative share in Foodgrains outturn (Average of 1987-88 to 1989-90) Per cent*	*Increase between (2) & (3) (In Per cent)*	*Increase between (2) & (4) (In Per cent)*	*Percentage share in total fertilisrs consumed in all-India in 1990-91*
(1)	(2)	(3)	(4)	(5)	(6)	(7)	(8)
Andhra Pradesh	8.62 (3)	22.2 (5)	121.4 (4)	7.4 (4)	257 (15)	1408 (15)	12.9 (2)
Assam	0.31 (15)	2.8 (15)	9.5 (17)	1.8 (14)	903 (7)	3064 (10)	0.30 (16)
Bihar	2.43 (7)	9.1 (11)	64.6 (11)	6.9 (7)	374 (13)	2658 (11)	4.1 (10)
Gujarat	2.25 (8)	21.3 (6)	77.5 (7)	2.4 (13)	946 (3)	3444 (8)	5.6 (9)
Haryana	0.48 (14)	22.8 (4)	126.4 (3)	5.1 (8)	4750 (1)	26333 (1)	4.6 (11)
Himachal Pradesh	0.48 (14)	—	34.6 (15)	0.7 (16)	—	7208 (4)	0.27 (17)
Jammu & Kashmir	1.33 (11)	—	48.2 (12)	0.8 (15)	—	3604 (7)	0.34 (15)
Karnataka	3.05 (6)	17.8 (8)	64.9 (10)	4.2 (11)	583 (10)	2127 (!4)	6.6 (5)
Kerala	9.36 (2)	27.6 (3)	66.7 (9)	0.7 (17)	295 (14)	712 (7)	1.9 (13)
Madhya Pradesh	0.85 (13)	6.7 (13)	37.4 (13)	9.4 (3)	788 (8)	4400 (6)	6.4 (7)
Maharashtra	2.25 (8)	14.9 (9)	75.4 (8)	7.4 (4)	662 (9)	3351 (9)	10.5 (3)
Orissa	0.97 (12)	9.0 (12)	22.5 (16)	4.1 (12)	927 (4)	2319 (13)	0.73 (14)
Punjab	3.37 (4)	58.2 (1)	174.7 (1)	11.1 (2)	1727 (2)	5184 (5)	9.5 (4)
Rajasthan	0.48 (14)	4.4 (14)	34.8 (14)	5.0 (9)	916 (6)	7250 (3)	2.9 (12)
Tamil Nadu	10.9 (1)	44.6 (2)	136.6 (2)	4.8 (10)	409 (12)	1247 (16)	6.6 (5)
Uttar Pradesh	2.20 (10)	20.3 (7)	99.3 (5)	20.3 (1)	922 (5)	9968 (2)	17.8 (1)
West Bengal	3.33 (5)	14.6 (10)	86.2 (6)	7.0 (6)	438 (11)	2588 (12)	6.0 (8)
All-India	3.3	17.4	75.7	100.0	527	2294	100.0

Low Fertilisers Consumption and its Diagnosis

Despite the low figures of consumption our statistical investigation discloses rather startingly that in 1960-61 in Bihar approximately 101.60 per cent of GCA received fertilisers, which had risen to about 142.10 per cent of GCA in 1990-91. In the earlier years fertilisers use was extensive; in recent years it has become intensive. Crops have to be provided fertilisers more than once.

Axiomatically, it is the availability of irrigation facility rather than the price factor which governs the use of fertilisers. Empirically too, this is what has been influencing the fertilisers business. Subsidy has clipped the wings of the price spiral in the case of fertilisers. The price support policy has stimulated the value of the grain (Table 13.13). In spite of this, fertilisers use in Bihar continues to be low by comparison with several other States as well as the rate of growth of fertilisers use is poor by the same comparison. The price incentive seems to be subservient to the real factors, such as the irrigation facility. The extremely sluggish pace of the progress of irrigation has retarded and arrested the pace of growth of fertilisers consumption in Bihar. The relatively lower utilisation of ground water is to be equally blamed for this. Then comes the poor credit availability. The rural credit structure functions under the shadow of predilection and prejudice. Only about one-third of the total chemical fertilisers requirement of the medium and nearly one-fourth of that of the marginal farmers have been available on credit. The timing of the flow of the credit made available has been unjudicious and constrained for reasons like regional bias, intractability of the human factor, staff psychology, the Centre's step-motherly treatment, etc.

A third obstacle was the faulty supply/distribution/delivery system of fertilisers. The authories/agencies responsible were the cooperatives, especially the BISCOMAUN, the Bihar State Cooperative Marketing Organisation, and so on. The kingpin was the BISCOMAUN, which was the apex distributing agency of the State Government. It disposed of nearly half of the total quantum of the fertilisers. In 1980-81 the amount sold was 2.04 lakh tonnes, 57.2 per cent by the BISCOMAUN and 42.8 per cent by the private dealers/stockists. In 1981-82 the figures were 2.05 lakh tonnes, 47.9 per cent and 52.1 per cent respectively. In 1982-83 the corresponding figures were 2.04 lakh tonnes, 50.5 per cent and 49.5 per cent. Inroads into the relative share of the BISCOMAUN were visible. The BISCOMAUN had to tap the cooperatives for marketing the quota assigned to it by the State Government. The PACS were its number one apparatus of operation in this field. Nearly 500 sales depots/points were opened by it all over the State for handling the sales.

TABLE 13.13 : Quantity of Wheat required to buy one kg

Year	*Quantity of Wheat (in kg) for 1 kg of*				
	N	*P_2O*			*K_2O*
		As SSP	*As DAP*	*As Complex*	
1971-72	2.64	3.41 to 7.28	2.45	3.24 to 3.91	1.17
1980-81	3.72	4.03 to 4.80	4.21	4.97 to 5.97	1.56
1984	3.07	3.49			1.32
1985	2.97	3.38			1.27
1986	3.15	3.67			1.34
1987	3.08	3.58			1.31
1988	2.95	3.43			1.25
1989-90	2.79	3.25	3.19	3.67 to 4.51	1.19
1990-91	2.38	2.76	2.71	3.13 to 3.84	1.01
1991-92	2.27	2.64	2.59	2.99 to 3.67	0.96

The functioning of the BISCOMAUN came in for a good deal of criticism. It left much to be desired. Inefficiency was writ large on its face. Efficiency was quantified by the volume of sales of fertilisers. Supply was fraught with bottlenecks reflected in distribution as between areas and in distribution over periods of time. Fertilisers shortage was felt when many areas went without the supply and when most areas reported absence of supply at the same time. Untimely supply was made which upset the farming schedule. Black-market was the result whenever there occurred a shortage at a period fertilisers had the highest utility to contribute. Cases came to knowledge of the public that fertilisers were in the stock but had not been supplied owing to bad administration. Cases of wastage due to negligence or mismanagement were not unknown. In so far as the sales depots/points were not in an adequate number, i.e., not in proportion to the stocks to be handled, bottlenecks were a recurrent feature. Last but not the least, the quality of the fertilisers sold was low because adulteration was practised on a large scale to make money in a clandestine manner. Apart from the above, the fertilisers distribution network existed upto the block level. For there was usually no agency for selling fertilisers below the block level. The network of retail outlets, particularly in the interior and hilly areas, was unsatisfactory. To give an example, in tribal areas the LAMPS served the farflung areas. The margin on fertilisers was not adequate to meet the distribution costs. Fertilisers were delivered at the block level at fixed prices and sold in bags of 50 kgs each. Many small and marginal farmers did not need such a big bag, nor had money enough to buy it. Distance from village to the block headquarters varied and cost of transportation was high in the interior and hilly areas. Farmers were obliged to travel long distances for buying fertilisers. In many areas the cooperatives failed in the task of fertilisers distribution on account of financial and managerial weaknesses, also because of the storage constraint faced by them.

We had occasion to mention that the very physical condition of certain areas necessitated a low level of fertilisers consumption, besides a very cautious and restrained approach in the matter. To illustrate, in the flood-prone areas the level of fertilisers consumption had to be kept low for evident reasons. In dry farming and drought-prone areas pragmatism counselled low consumption, as the failure of the monsoon rendered resort to fertilisers a lost proposition. Finally, in many areas there was the general absence of fertilising practices to repeat, the old parrot could be taught a new song only through perseverence and persuasion over a period of time that was in duration long and annoying.

Fertilisers as a Yield Lever

Starting from the Third Plan the State Plans in Bihar set great store upon fertilisers use as a lever of agricultural, particularly foodgrains, output, subject to the proviso that the use was proper. It has been believed widely that other things being equal, for every tonne of fertilisers put in the soil, foodgrains output was enhanced by 7 to 8 tonnes.

In the early years of the 1960s average yield per ha. of paddy was 1106 kgs. without fertilisers use and 2028 kgs. with fertilisers use (a difference of 918 kgs., an increase by 183 per cent; in the case of wheat 627 *versus* 1290 kgs. a ha., a difference of 663 kgs. or an increase by 205 per cent; in the case of maize 1004 *versus* 1382 kgs a ha., a difference of 278 kgs. or an increase by 137 per cent; and lastly, in the case of sugarcane 23045 *versus* 59917 kgs. a ha., a difference of 6872 kgs. or an increase by 260 per cent. In the case of barley the percentage increase was 210 and in that of gram 138 per cent.

During 1970-71 to 1988, for every additional kg. of fertilisers used, increase in foodgrains outturn was 9.34 kgs. in Bihar.

It is held that chemical fertilisers, after a time, produce a residual effect, which can, of course, be amended. It is pointed out that artificial chemical matter constituting chemical fertilisers has neither the power nor the ability to instil life into the soil, instead they lock the soil by hardening it. They destroy the soil and its organic elements.

Case for Green Manuring

Green manuring and the use of compost hold the key to the maintenance of fertility and would be absolutely necessary if intensive farming with its added strain on the soil were intended. In the early years of the 1950s in Bihar beyond throwing of some untreated farm dung left over after utilising it as fuel, not much was done by the average Bihari farmer for improving and revitalising and thereby maintaining the fertility of the soil.

The usefulness of green manuring is fully established by analysis and experiment. The ICAR in its 1957-58 research paper noted that whereas the use of chemical fertilisers augmented the yield per hectare to 67.20 mds only, the yield of the fields under green manuring soared to as much as 78.47 mds per ha.

Green manuring is suited more to those soils which are highly deficient in organic and nitrogenous content than chemical fertilisers.

Composting had not been integrated with the farming routine of Bihar by 1956 when the Bihar Unemployment Committee completed its report. In 1962-63 in the State about 7 lakh acres of land were covered by green manuring, which was 2.55 per cent of total cropped area.

Hedge culture and arboriculture can provide the farmer with materials, both fuel and green manuring.

Composts are a proven route for recycling organic wastes. They are richer in nutrients than farmyard manure.

Green manuring is a renewable nutrient rich resource; it is a bio-fertiliser. It can be used directly and is of biological origin. It is added to the soil to provide organic matter and nutrients contained in its biomass.

The green manures are real nutrient integrators. They absorb mineral nutrients, convert them into organic forms, which are then changed to mineral forms when the green manure decomposes in the field. It is this fascinating nutrient cycle which operates in agricultural soils day and night which makes a mockery of the compartmentalisation of farming into organic and mineral.

The practice of green manuring has diminished in spite of its technical merits. The area under green manures has nearly stagnated. It has virtually disappeared from its old stronghold, namely, the sugarcane-based farming system. The economic competitiveness and practical feasibility are as important factors in reaching a decision in this regard as are technical merits of this scientific finding.

In a nutshell, the work of composting involves much thoughtful and painstaking routine work and would provide self-employment to the farmer for a considerable number of mandays in the year which would be equated in terms of money value saved from the purchase of fertilisers as well as the value added to the produce.

Suggestions and Conclusions

Fertilisers replenish and maintain the balance of plant nutrients in the soil. With a view to providing nutrition for the plant, the soil itself requires nutrition. This is provided, in part, by the application of the nutrients.

In the early 1960s it was said that fertilisers had a social benefit, that is, a long-term effect on social fertility. By replenishing and maintaining the balance of plant nutrients in the soil, the benefit was received for years.

Plants require sixteen different nutrients for the normal development of which nitrogen is perhaps the most crucial, though phosphorus and potassium are equally very essential. A general improvement in the fertilisers off-take would improve the production base in most parts of Bihar and hence the agricultural situation. Moreover, fertilisers use in increased doses/compounds would make agriculture all the more intensive.

Fertilisers consumption is contingent upon the nutrient status of the given soil and the uptake capacity of the different crops for different nutrients. Fertilisers doses of the HYVs of the different crops hinge on the same basis. Needed is a balanced and integrated use of fertilisers, the prerequisites of which are as follows :

Firstly, prior, proper soil analysis/testing, to make fertilisers use fully effective. Fertilisers use attains optimum efficiency only under favourable soil conditions. Arrangements for testing soil samples should be strengthened. Suitable soil amendment measures should be adopted.

Secondly, fertilisers use should be combined also with use of improved seeds/HYVs and pesticides and requisite irrigation, without which fertilisers would be misused, ineffective or wasted. To absorb the large doses/compounds of chemical fertilisers a sufficient and stable source of irrigation is required. Fertilisers are fully effective only with good rains or assured irrigation. In a lean year they are not in a position to ensure a known minimum level of production. By the same token, the irrigation base of fertilisers-using farms is significantly higher than that of non-fertilisers-using farms. Where irrigation is deficient, the Green Revolution (GR) is not to be observed. In a word, resembling irrigation, fertilisers use presupposes a package of practices.

Thirdly, needed are special extension services to generate and sustain the demand for fertilisers among small and marginal farmers. For this they have to be adequately motivated and taught to regard farming not as a self-sufficient occupation but as a business proposition. They should be helped to switch over to the use of fertilisers.

Fourthly, the State and district-level organisations should hold enough stocks of fertilisers for supply to the PACS. The rural godowns should be utilised for storage purposes. Supply of sealed packets of 10 to 20 kgs should be arranged for the benefit of the small and marginal farmers. In areas which grow vegetables as the primary product, small packets of 5 kgs should be made available to the small and marginal farmers.

Fifthly, certain villages in each tribal block may be declared as the block headquarters for the purpose of issue of fertilisers at the pool price.

Sixthly, for obtaining a good crop without having any deleterious effect on the physical conditions of the soil, care should be exercised in selecting the fertilisers to be applied in a particular plot as well as its doses, time and method of administration.

Lastly, a decisive step to improve Bihar agriculture would be to reduce the incidence of non-use of fertilisers.

14

IMPROVED SEEDS IN BIHAR AGRICULTURE

Seeds are the most significant primary/basic input in agriculture. The importance of availability of certified/standard/improved seeds/HYVs/ hybrids to agriculture cannot be overemphasised. For a quantum jump in outturn this is the fundamental requirement. To augment production by the easiest and cheapest means there is no substitute of good quality seeds of an improved variety. The mainspring of the Green Revolution/ New Agrarian Technology has been formed by the HYVs. And behind the appearance of the HYVs is the development of the science of genetics and plant breeding.

Acreage under the improved seeds/HYVs is on the increase. In 1960-61 only 15 per cent of the cultivated land was sown with improved seeds in Bihar (12.1 lakh ha. out of total GCA of 81 lakh ha.). The HYVs were released for the first time on a significant scale in Bihar in 1965-66. In 1967-68, in Bihar 3.87 lakh ha. cultivated acreage was under the HYVs (about 4.20 per cent of GCA—in Punjab 10.12 lakh ha., 19.46 per cent of GCA). In 1968-69 the acreage under HYVs paddy/rice, wheat, maize, jowar and bajra in Bihar was 8.252 lakh ha. which came to 10.1 per cent of GCA (in Punjab the figure was 16.61 lakh ha., 39 per cent of GCA). In 1969-70 HYVs rice acreage was 39 per cent of total HYVs foodgrains acreage, HYVs wheat 53 per cent and HYVs maize 8 per cent in Bihar (in Punjab the corresponding figures were 3.6, 8.5 and 5 per cent). In 1970-71, 21.3 per cent of GCA in Bihar was under the HYVs (in Maharashtra 4.4 per cent).

Let us turn to Table 14.1, which shows how between 1975-76 and 1991-92 the area under HYVs paddy/rice in Bihar increased by 208 per cent and how its share in all-India increased from 14.6 to 36.8 per cent (1990-91 in place of 1991-92). In all-India the increase was by 221 per cent in area, and increase in terms of percentage was from 31.4 to

TABLE 14.1 : Progress of HYVs Acreage in Bihar

(Area in lakh ha.)

Crop	*1975-76*		*1976-77*		*1977-78*		*1978-79*		*1979-80*		*1980-81*	
	Area	*Percentage*	*Area*	*Percentage*	*Area*	*Percentage*	*Area*	*Percentage*	*Area*	*Percentage*	*Area*	*Percentage*
(1)	(2)	(3)	(4)	(5)	(6)	(7)	(8)	(9)	(10)	(11)	(12)	(13)
Paddy/Rice	7.68 (124)	14.6/ 15.0 (31.4)	9.98	18.8	13.00	23.3	13.65	24.5	10.60	20.7	14.00 (182)	25.5 (45.3)
Wheat	12.29 (135)	42.0/ 67.7 (66.1)	14.17	72.9	14.18	76.8	14.40	76.7	14.00	82.3	18.00 (161)	99.8 (72.2)
Maize	3.57 (11)	7/38.2 (18.3)	—	—	—	—	—	—	3.70	44.6	4.50 (16)	50.6 (26.6)
All Foodgrains	— (319)	— (25.0)	—	—	—	—	—	—	—	—	— (431)	32.7 (34.0)

(Contd.)

TABLE 14.1 (*Contd.*)

Crop	*1984-85*		*1985-86*		*1986-87*		*1987-88*		*1988-89*		*1989-90*	
	Area	*Percentage*	*Area*	*Percentage*	*Area*	*Percentage*	*Area*	*Percentage*	*Area*	*Percentage*	*Area*	*Percentage*
(1)	(14)	(15)	(16)	(17)	(18)	(19)	(20)	(21)	(22)	(23)	(24)	(25)
Paddy/Rice	12.83	—	15.92 (235)	29.8 (57.1)	16.47	30.7	—	—	—	—	—	—
Wheat	14.8	—	12.91 (191)	70.3 (83.0)	13.15	71.4	—	—	—	—	—	—
Maize	2.16	—	3.29 (18)	49.1 (31.0)	3.09	47.6	—	—	—	—	—	—
All Foodgrains	—	—	— (612)	— (47.8)	—	—	—	—	—	—	—	—
All crops	—	—	47.18 (all-India : 554.20)		52.51	—	56.16	—	40.27	—	34.64	—

(*Contd.*)

TABLE 14.1 (*Contd.*)

Crop	*1990-91*		*1991-92*		*1992-93*	
	Area	*Percentage*	*Area*	*Percentage*	*Area*	*Percentage*
(1)	(26)	(27)	(28)	(29)	(30)	(31)
Paddy/Rice	16.88	36.8	16.00	—	—	—
	(274)	(64.1)	(280)	(65.5)	(275)	(65.7)
Wheat	14.64	74.5	16.00	—	—	—
	(210)	(89.3)	(205)	(87.9)	(217)	(87.5)
Maize	3.66	—	5.00	—	—	—
	(26)	(44.0)	(28)	(47.4)	(26)	(43.3)
All Foodgrains	—	—	—	—	—	—
	(650)	(50.8)	(647)	(53.0)	(654)	(53.1)
All crops	35.40 (all-India : 649.84)					

Note : Percentage is percentage of HYVs acreage to Total GCA in the State/All-India.

65.7 per cent. There were fluctuations in area as well as relative share at times in Bihar, as also in all-India, though less, by comparison.

So far as HYVs wheat acreage is concerned, the increase during the same period was by 130 per cent in Bihar and by 217 per cent in all-India between 1975-76 and 1992-93. In terms of percentage share, the rise was from 67.7 to 74.5 per cent (another estimate is from 42 to 74.5 per cent) in Bihar, and from 66.1 to 87.5 per cent in all-India. There were fluctuations also in HYVs wheat acreage in certain years in Bihar but extraordinarily the percentage share of the State manifested a continuous rise. The Bihar farmer was enamoured of the wheat revolution.

Lastly, we have maize. During the same period Bihar had a 140 per cent increase in HYVs maize acreage, as against a 236 rise in all-India. There were fluctuations in the acreage in some years. But the general trend was one of a rising curve on a percentage share graph, faster in all-India and slower in Bihar.

During 1975-76 to 1992-93, the sumtotal HYVs acreage under rice, wheat and maize in Bihar, as percentage of GCA in the State, increased from 20.8 to 35.7 per cent, a gain of about 15 per cent (Table 14.2).

TABLE 14.2 : HYVs Acreage under Rice, Wheat and Maize (Combined) in Bihar as Percentage of GCA in Bihar

Year	*Percentage*
1975-76	20.8
1976-77	24.0
1977-78	26.5
1978-79	27.8
1979-80	26.9
1980-81	25.5
1985-86	30.5
1986-87	31.3
1988-89	32.5
1990-91	33.8
1992-93	35.7

Over the period (1975-76 to 1991-92) Bihar's shares in all-India in respect of HYVs rice, wheat and maize declined, most in maize and least in rice, wheat coming in between (Table 14.3).

In 1980-81 the HYVs acreage as percentage of GCA in Bihar was 32.7 per cent (in Maharashtra it was 26.3 per cent). In 1981-82 nearly 39.10 lakh ha. cultivated land was covered by the HYVs. Wheat, maize and potato benefited more than paddy. The growth rate of HYVs acreage in Bihar during 1974-76 to 1985-87 (average) was 7.9 per cent per annum, in all-India it was 6.3 per cent per annum (in Punjab the figure was 5.9 and in Maharashtra 9.4 per cent per annum). In 1988-89 the HYVs acreage in terms of percentage of GCA was 28 per cent in the case of rice, 73 per cent in the case of maize and 53 per cent in the case of maize. During 1988-90, on an average, the HYVs acreage under foodgrains was 75 per cent in Bihar (in Punjab 91 per cent and all-India 64 per cent). On the whole, the HYVs have been used more for the rabi rather than the kharif crops. The wide variations in local conditions in rice cultivation have been the chief factor retarding the use of the HYVs in the case of rice. There is unanimity of opinion in Bihar that in hybrid maize cultivation the State has done quite well. That the total coverage of the HYVs in Bihar would not exceed 25 per cent is the popular belief. This may be for the aggregate of all crops, food and non-food. In the most recent years the HYVs have an unusual success in consequence of the farmer's endeavour to raise a second rice harvest during February to June.

TABLE 14.3 : HYVs Acreage in Bihar as Percentage to All-India HYVs Acreage

Crop	*1975-76*	*1980-81*	*1985-86*	*1990-91*	*1991-92*
Paddy/Rice	6.2	7.7	6.7	6.1	5.7
Wheat	9.1	6.2	6.7	6.9	7.7
Maize	32.4	28.1	18.2	14.9	17.9
All Foodgrains			8.2		

In so far as the part played by the State Government in popularising the improved seeds/HYVs has been paramount, it would be more advisable to discuss the topic in the context of the Government effort. In the First Plan of Bihar there were a couple of schemes for the distribution of improved seeds, namely, paddy seed multiplication and distribution of disease-free potato seeds. The 1954-55 Budget mentioned arrangements for multiplying seeds of new varieties for distribution among cultivators, which were forging ahead. It informed that agricultural research had been intensified and certain flood-resistant varieties of paddy and quicker maturing varieties of paddy and wheat had been evolved. During the First Plan, five pilot projects distributed 529268 mds of improved seeds and 1330007 mds of fertilisers amongst the cultivators.

The Second Plan for Bihar envigaged a coverage of 61 lakh ha. of the gross sown area with improved seeds and Rs. 2.4 crores had been provided towards the cost of this scheme. But due to the widespread drought and flood conditions, the scheme was unlikely to succeed fully during that Plan.

The 1963-64 Budget referred to the multilateral researches that were being made in Bihar and the attempts which being made to grow new varieties of crops that promised better yields under the given conditions of soil and climate.

The Third Plan of Bihar visualised additional food output to the extent of 14.2 per cent, additional non-food output to the extent of 14.7 per cent and, finally, additional production of agricultural output to the extent of 14.3 per cent from the application of improved seeds. The contribution from improved seeds was to be equivalent to that from nutrients and major irrigation combined. If fertilisers and manures contributed one rupee worth of real agricultural outturn, improved seeds contributed 0.82 rupee worth of it. Of the total Plan outlay on agriculture, 5.85 per cent was to be spent on improved seeds.

The Seeds Act passed in India in 1966 and effective from October 1, 1969 had the objective of ensuring the supply of good quality seeds to farmers and to enable them to harvest a bumper crop as well as to protect the seeds dealers. This Act is now due for amendment on account of the developments which have taken place in the area in the last five years or so.

The certified seeds distribution has been the concern of the Government through its agencies from the very beginning. The seeds were purchased by the Government from outside. In 1975-76 for the first time a subsidy of Rs. 45 per quintal on standard seeds and another of Rs. 40 per quintal on certified seeds were allowed by the Government.

The State Seeds Corporation was established in 1980-81. It had its offices and godowns in different parts of the State. It were they which procured and supplied seeds to the farmers. This task was shared also by the Bihar State Marketing Union. The State farms too produced seeds of the different crops.

It would not be out of place to mention here that in Bihar from the very outset the Government put due emphasis on obtaining and distributing certified seeds of potato. In the Government's scheme of things potato seeds improvement claimed as much importance as did rice, wheat and maize seeds improvement.

In 1979-80 certified seeds distributed were : Paddy 34 thousand quintals, wheat 91 thousand quintals and maize 19 thousand quintals. Production of certified seeds in Government farms in the first three years of the 1980s is summarised in Table 14.4.

TABLE 14.4 : Production of Certified Seeds in Government Farms in Bihar

(In kgs.)

Crop	*1980-81*	*1981-82*	*1982-83*	*Increase in Three years (Per cent)*
Rice	4870	30813	35264	724
Wheat	1309	11718	14313	1093
Maize	178	4800	634	356
Gram	191	1326	1404	735
Pulses	—	286	562	—
Oilseeds	—	369	435	—
Others (e.g., Jute, potato, etc.)	1162	17253	24001	2065

The demand for the certified seeds for maize does not appear to be steady, as is clear from the table, whereas that for the certified seeds of the other crops is not only steady but constantly growing. That Bihar is a predominantly rice-producing State is patent from the quantity of its certified seeds produced on the Government farms, which was in the ratio of 1:1.17 to the quantities of all other certified seeds put together.

From 1981-82 the Government revised the subsidy on standard seeds at the rate of Rs. 30 per quintal in the case of paddy and subsidy on certified seeds at the rate of Rs. 20 per quintal. Subsidy on composite seeds of maize and Shankar brand of maize was fixed at Rs. 100 per quintal. Sales tax on inputs used by farmers was scaled down (included in them was organic manure).

Bihar is dependent on outside sources for most of its quality/improved seeds—of wheat, jute, pulses, oilseeds, vegetables as well as the seeds certified by its Government (i.e., the State Seeds Corporation and the State farms). The demand for the improved/certified/HYVs seeds is more than their supply, and increasing. This inadequacy of demand in relation to supply is a great disqualification of the State machinery. The foundation and breeder seeds of the suitable varieties (say, wheat, for instance) which have been identified are not available in the State, with the result that seed replacement has been replete with long time-lags and continues to be less than the norm defined. This low-key replacement or renewal is reflected in the rate of 5 per cent in respect of rice and 10 per cent in respect of wheat, against the formulated norm of 20 per cent. This is so after taking into account the fact that due mainly to shortfall in the availability of certified seeds many farmers produce their own seeds, besides exchanging seeds with other farmers. Timeliness is indispensable to the agricultural operations schedule and if for reason of non-availability of seeds or any other input on time it is upset, the net effect is perilous/ disastrous.

For some years past the State Government has claimed to have evolved rice varieties for different climatic situations, except low lands and land affected by waterlogging. The agricultural universities in Bihar have contributed richly in this direction. Similarly, suitable wheat varieties have been identified. But regrettably paddy seeds suitable for deep water conditions are not even now available.

In addition, the HYVs are now available for varied water regimes. However, the country has not so far recognised that the agricultural universities in Bihar have achieved anything remarkable in the realm of seed technology.

In the Eighth Plan Bihar has a target to bring 72 lakh ha. cultivated land under the HYVs, which would amount to 9.27 per cent of the all-India acreage under the HYVs. Of this, rice HYVs acreage would be 34.72 per cent of the State total and 10.48 per cent of the all-India rice HYVs acreage. For wheat the corresponding figures would be 48.61 and 10.38 per cent, and for maize 16.66 and 31.45 per cent.

From the 1994-95 Annual Plan of Bihar onwards the distribution of wheat seeds to farmers which used to be a Centrally Sponsored Scheme would be an absolutely State programme.

The 1994-95 proposed to set up a seed testing laboratory under production and distribution of quality seeds. Seed inspection and quality control would be stepped up. The subsidy on seeds of paddy would continue.

This brings us back to the economic implications of use of improved/ HYVs seeds. First, take what difference this has made to yield. Table 14.5 depicts this. On the average, the HYVs have an advantage in yield over Lower Variety (L/V) of the order of 151 per cent in respect of paddy/rice, of the order of 140 per cent in respect of wheat and of the order of 185 per cent in respect of maize.

These statistics furnish to us a rosier picture, in that while it is maintained, in general, that the HYVs use causes an increase of the order of 10 to 20 per cent in productivity, the finding we just have on the basis of our statistics gives a 40 to 85 per cent increase in yield, depending on which crop is being studied.

Between 1985-86 and 1992-93 the HYVs acreage has made intrusions into the L/V acreage—maximum in the case of maize and minimum in that of wheat, rice coming in between (Table 14.6). Production on the HYVs land as proportion to total production of the

TABLE 14.5 : Yield Rate with or without HYVs in Bihar

(Kgs. ha.)

Crop	1985-86				1986-87				1988-89			
	HYVs	L/V	Com-bined	Excess of HYVs over L/V (Per cent)	HYVs	L/V	Com-bined	Excess of HYVs over L/V (Per cent)	HYVs	L/V	Com-bined	Excess of HYVs over L/V (Per cent)
(1)	(2)	(3)	(4)	(5)	(6)	(7)	(8)	(9)	(10)	(11)	(12)	(13)
Rice	1294	1057	1128	122	1394	1008	1126	138	1553	975	1140	159
Wheat	1727	1300	1600	133	1706	1177	1555	145	1804	1360	1684	132
Maize	1693	941	1311	180	1822	1074	1420	169	2087/ 2090	892/ 898	1526	232/ 234

(Contd.)

TABLE 14.5 (*Contd.*)

Crop	1992-93				Excess of HYVs over L/V : Average of all Years (Per cent)
	HYVs	L/V	Com-bined	Excess of HYVs over L/V (Per cent)	
(1)	(14)	(15)	(16)	(17)	(18)
Rice	1172	632	802	185	151
Wheat	1896	1249	1747	152	140
Maize	1946	1238	1882	157	185

Note : L/V is the local variety seed.

crop in question has shown maximum increase (in percentage terms) in the case of rice, and minimum increase in that of maize, the position of wheat being in between the two (Table 14.7).

TABLE 14.6 : Ratio between HYVs and L/V Acreage in Bihar

Crop	*1985-86*	*1986-87*	*1988-89*	*1992-93*
Rice	1 : 2.35	1 : 2.25	1 : 2.52	1 : 2.12
Wheat	1 : 0.42	1 : 0.40	1 : 0.36	1 : 0.29
Maize	1 : 1.03	1 : 1.10	1 : 0.88	1 : 0.77

TABLE 14.7 : Production on HYVs Land as Percentage of Total Production of the Crop in Bihar

Crop	*1985-86*	*1986-87*	*1988-89*	*1992-93*
Rice	34.2	38.01	38.7	46.2
Wheat	76.01	78.4	78.2	83.6
Maize	63.5	60.6	72.5	67.0

From Table 14.8 it can be deduced that in recent years rice acreage under HYVs has been irrigated proportionally more and more. On the other hand, rice acreage under L/V has been irrigated proportionally less and less. This deduction applies to the case of maize as well. But the case of wheat seems to be of a different nature. In its case the acreage under both HYVs and L/V seeds has tended to increase proportionally, decidedly as a result of the encroachment made on rice and maize acreage under the L/V seeds. Let us not forget while interpreting the data that whereas wheat represents a mono-harvest crop, both rice and maize are double or triple-harvest crops.

As are, and can, be the L/V seeds either irrigated or not irrigated, so are the HYV seeds. The HYVs are and can be sown on both irrigated and unirrigated land, no doubt, but the average and maximum yields are much higher when they are sown on the irrigated than the unirrigated land. The HYVs perform best under conditions of controlled and timely irrigation. Thus, as disclosed by Table 14.9, HYVs yield with irrigation is 123 per cent higher in respect of rice and 118 per cent higher in respect of wheat than HYVs yield without irrigation. Rain water cannot be a perfect substitute of artificial irrigation water when agriculture is a matter of chemical fertilisers or HYVs. Observations reveal that maximum yield with irrigated HYVs is 136 per cent higher in the case

TABLE 14.8 : Irrigation of HYVs and L/V Acreage

(In percentage)

Crop	*Irrigated HYVs Acreage*				*Irrigated L/V Acreage*				*Irrigated HYVs & L/V Acreages Combined*			
	1985-86	*1986-87*	*1988-89*	*1992-93*	*1985-86*	*1986-87*	*1988-89*	*1992-93*	*1985-86*	*1986-87*	*1988-89*	*1992-93*
Rice	63.3	64.7	72.3	—	24.1	23.0	22.0	—	35.8	35.8	36.3	37.4
Wheat	90.4	90.4	93.0	94.2	51.1	50.2	59.0	64.3	78.8	79.0	83.7	87.3
Maize	55.9	57.6	—	—	5.3	4.4	—	—	30.2	29.7	—	42.0

of rice and 120 per cent higher in that of wheat, compared to unirrigated HYVs.

TABLE 14.9 : Yield Comparison between Irrigated and Unirrigated HYVs and L/V of Rice and Wheat in Bihar : 1990-91

(Kg./ha.)

	L/V		*HYVs*	
	Rice	*Wheat*	*Rice*	*Wheat*
Yield				
Irrigated	1833	1433	2424	1850
Unirrigated	1585	1159	1966	1567
Difference	248	274	458	283
Difference in percentage	116	124	123	118
Maximum Yield				
Irrigated	1433	1914	3502	2412
Unirrigated	1159	1439	2569	2002
Difference	274	475	933	410
Difference in percentage	124	133	136	120

Lower Variety seeds can be used under both conditions—irrigated and unirrigated, though yield is 116 per cent higher in respect of rice and 124 per cent higher in that of wheat under irrigated condition, as compared with those under unirrigated condition. Observations on maximum yield with L/V seeds demonstrate that the yield is 124 per cent higher in respect of rice and 133 per cent higher in that of wheat under irrigation condition, as compared to unirrigated condition.

We have stated above that the major agencies handling seeds distribution in Bihar are the cooperative organisations such as the BISCOMAUN, the BSCMU, the BRBN (Bihar Rajya Beej Nigam), and private dealers—also in charge of the distribution of fertilisers (as already discussed), pesticides, etc. The National Seeds Corporation (NSC) and the TDC too have their dealers' network/paraphernalia in Bihar. The PACS and the Vyapar Mandals procure seeds from the BISCOMAUN on commission basis for sale to the farmers. The BRBN has its contract growers in the project areas. The BISCOMAUN is the district agency for the State Government. Its members, principally the PACS, have 500-odd depots/sale points for the distribution of seeds (as also fertilisers, pesticides, etc.). The percentage share of the BISCOMAUN in the distribution of wheat and paddy seeds is around 70 and 30 per cent respectively. The

BSCB is blamed for selling low-quality seeds, as for rigging and untimely supply of seeds (and other agricultural inputs). Private dealers sell mostly potato, paddy and maize seeds.

There is usually no agency for supply of seeds below the block level. Most of the private dealers are located at the block level. The BISCOMAUN's network of godowns is spread upto the block level only.

In sum, the use of improved seeds has not been diversified so far in Bihar, with the result that the rate of seed replacement is low-key, which is suggestive of the slow pace of adoption of the improved varieties. The inordinate delay in the establishment of seed multiplication farms, inadequate systematic multiplication of the improved seeds, alleged adulteration of the new seeds with the old, deficiencies of storage and distribution of the newly released seeds, the bottleneck created by the inadequate supply of institutional credit, and so forth explain this failure of the State Government in this sphere.

The seeds production and distribution are constrained by a number of inhibitors and detractors. In the first place, the functionings of the twin arms of the State Government in this field, viz., the State Agricultural Department and the Agricultural Universities of the State have not been effectively coordinated, with the result that the foundation and breeder seeds are either not available or not in adequate supply. Secondly, there arises considerable time-lag in producing adequate quantities of the certified seeds of the newly released varieties. Thirdly, the seeds are not accorded high enough priority in the allotment of the railway wagons. The inherent delay causes serious losses in production. Fourthly, in the rainfed areas of the State the improved seeds are looked upon as a fairweather craft since they perform well only in a good year of rains, not in a lean year. Floods destroy the HYVs, so do droughts. Should the rains be deficient, the investment in the HYVs and other inputs would not be as productive as expected, and sticking to the traditional seeds would have been far more sensible, for the improved seeds could not have ensured even the known minimum level of yield. Lastly, as substantiated by the experiences of rice growers in the State, variations in soil and moisture conditions are of such a wide range, even within a district, that the switch-over to the more expensive improved seeds technology becomes a highly risky venture. This risk element is further aggravated by the inadequacy of area-specific input packages and extension services and uncongenial tenurial conditions.

In the light of the preceding observations what suggestions could be make? The answer is: One, the State Government should take steps to enhance the production capacities of the Seeds Corporation and government farms with regard to certified seeds. Secondly, the agricultural universities and research institutes should increase the output of foundation and breeder seeds. These steps should be taken in areas suitable from the climatic point of view. Thirdly, the management of the Seeds Corporation should be restructured through appropriate measures. Fourthly, necessary arrangements for distribution of the seeds should be made by the State Government. If required, the seeds should be bought from the farmers. Facilities should be provided to the farmers for exchange of certified seeds with grains produced by them by laying down appropriate barter terms for such exchange. This would provide new and improved varieties of seeds are distributed should be increased. Sixthly, at the same time, the State Government should tone up the retail network by installing more distribution points through the cooperatives or licensed private dealers. It is worth considering if every panchayat could have at least one sale point. Seventhly, the quality of the seeds sold must be controlled by the State Government. Eighthly, the practice of usings the FCI stocks for seed purposes by farmers should be discouraged through effective extension. Instead the State Government may consider stocking seeds in selected areas where the demand for them is very high. For contingency planning in areas prone to natural calamities, seeds of suitable alternative varieties/crops should be stocked. Ninthly, the entire area must be saturated with the HYVs within the minimum possible time. The annual rate of replacement should be 20 per cent in the case of self-pollinated crops like rice and wheat. Tenthly, the Seed Certification Agency should issue the necessary certificate to seeds produced by registered growers and contract farmers after making sure that they conform strictly to the minimum standards of quality laid down. Eleventhly, the railways should give priority in wagon allotment to the seeds transporters. Finally, seeds-fertilisers-pesticides-weedicides together with credit should be supplied as a composite package to the farmers under the single-window scheme so that all inputs are obtained conveniently used in a balanced and integrated fashion.

15

PESTICIDES IN BIHAR AGRICULTURE

The pesticides include insecticides, fungicides, rodenticides, etc. They compose the chemical technology. During 1969-77, 34 per cent of the increase in agricultural output in India was attributable to their use.

Plant protection is part and parcel of the Green Revolution technology. It consists in (1) seed treatment, (2) weed control, and (3) post-sowing prophylactic treatment, in addition to the aerial spray of pesticides.

Cereals (particularly paddy/rice), cotton, oilseeds (particularly groundnut), pulses and sugarcane are the crops most prone/susceptible/vulnerable to the pest attack.

In our country the scientific use of pesticides in plant protection began in 1947.

Some areas in Bihar are endemic sufferers from loss of crops due to pests and diseases and weeds, which is 15 to 20 per cent of the produce. Areas affected by insects, pests and bacteria or afflicted with diseases have poor yields.

In the 1950s the State Government embarked on the plant protection survey by trained staff which was equipped with the necessary inputs and implements and was maintained at different posts and centres in the State. During 1954-55 the plant protection scheme successfully controlled the spread of *Gandi bug* and other plant diseases. The most prominent step was spraying of pesticides on mango trees. The present-day surveillance units maintained at selected places like Patna and Ranchi are sophisticated forms of the earliest venture. Crop protection from the ravages of pests, diseases and obnoxious weeds has spread to several parts of Bihar. But they are not adequate in number and quality of service to meet the needs of all areas, whether chronic or not. In 1976-77, 19.8 per cent of the cropped area suffered from pests and diseases but the area treated with pesticides was only 7.2 per cent. Consumption of pesticides in Bihar was proportionally lower than its share in total

GCA of the country. In 1985-86 it was 1750 tonnes, 2.60 per cent; in 1986-87, 2000 tonnes, 0.29 per cent only; in 1987-88, 3010 tonnes, 4.50 per cent. Per hectare of GCA consumption of pesticides in 1987-88 was 0.28 kg., as against the all-India average of 0.37 kg.

Roughly speaking, as the size of a holding increased, application of pesticides also increased. An irrigated holding of a given used more pesticides than an unirrigated one of the same size. This would be evident from the statistics contained in Table 15.1.

The State Government's Agricultural Department is involved in the procurement and distribution of pesticides but its involvement is not total. Pesticides are usually procured by the apex cooperative organisations in bulk and distributed through cooperatives. The BISCOMAUN is the sole agency for sale and purchase of pesticides. Private licence-holders are also there. In 1982, 590 depots of the BISCOMAUN, 466 plant protection centres at the block level and nearly 4000 private licence-holders sold and purchased pesticides in Bihar.

TABLE 15.1 : Application of Pesticides by different Size-groups of Holdings : 1976-77

(in kg/ha)

Size-groups of Holdings	*Irrigated*	*Unirrigated*
Marginal	0.49 (0.17)	0.18 (0.09)
Small	0.37 (0.17)	0.27 (0.10)
Semi-Medium	1.57 (0.23)	0.28 (0.11)
Medium	0.61 (0.19)	0.30 (0.13)
Large	0.84 (0.17)	0.13 (0.14)
All Sizes	0.73 (0.19)	0.23 (0.12)

The pesticides market is marked by a number of drawbacks: One, price-tags are not attached to the packets and containers by the dealers. Two, there is no periodic checking of stocks maintained by the dealers. Three, there are reports of adulteration of the pesticides. Fourth, pesticides are used as poison or proved poisonous in numerous cases because they are not handled carefully/safely.

Paucity of credit is a serious factor in maintaining stocks of the implements and equipment required in the spraying of the pesticides, e.g., sprayers at the depots and units. Unless the surveillance units are fully equipped with quick transport facilities and necessary materials and apparatuses, they cannot serve large areas at short notices, with the result that considerable damage may be caused by pests and diseases, particularly to the HYV crops. Where pests are not detected timely and pesticides are not applied properly crop losses are aggravated.

It is necessary that adequate stocks of pesticides are kept for distribution to the PACS. Adulteration of pesticides by the licensed dealers must be curbed. The unlicensed dealers should be punished. Requisite knowledge about the pesticides, their uses and abuses should be given to the dealers. The existing lack of coordination between the apex cooperative organisations and the State Government's Agricultural Department, on the one hand and the State Government's Agricultural Department and its surveillance units in the procurement of the pesticides, on the other, must be made good.

The danger posed by chemical poisons to human and animal life and their environmental pollution and persistence of residues in air, water, soil and food material besides the loss of the natural flavour and taste of the grains, vegetables, fruits, milk, etc. have become a global phenomenon. There is thus a great need for adequate training on the safe use of pesticides for which a scientific approach has been lacking.

16

FARM MECHANISATION IN BIHAR

Even before Independence farmers in Bihar had begun adopting improved implements and Bihar agriculture had a smattering of the improved agricultural implements. The state farms were the first recipients of them, and they held demonstrations for the enlightened and educated and well-to-do private farmers in different places. Steel ploughs, barrows, hoes, fodder cutters, sugarcane crushers, etc., were known to these farmers and through them to others prior to August 1947. After August 1947 other improved agricultural instruments became known to the farming community by and by. These were tractors, pumping sets, water lifts, threshers, harvesters, plant protection machinery, diesel and electric sprayers, seed-cum-fertilisers drills, drip irrigation sets, etc.

During the Second Plan period 40776 improved agricultural implements were sold in Bihar. They included the plant protection equipment. Table 16.1 encapsules the progress of agricultural implements and machinery in Bihar.

Modernisation of agriculture is generally equated with tractorisation. The tractor ensures tillage of a better quality. Table 16.2 epitomises the progress of tractorisation in Bihar.

Bihar's share in tractors declined from 6.05 per cent in 1951 to 5.11 per cent in 1990-91, although in absolute terms their number multiplied 124.6 times during the same period. The increasing application of tractors had not made any dent in the number of the bullock-carts, which had risen 14.8 times, as against a 28.8 times increase in that of tractors during 1951-87. Bihar's share in bullock-carts increased from 5.17 per cent to 5.26 per cent during this period, but its share in tractors fell from 6.05 per cent to 1.97 per cent during the same period. In Bihar in 1951 there were 1008 bullock-carts per tractor; in 1987 per tractor the number of bullock-carts was 517. Obviously, the growth in the number of tractors had affected the number of bullock-carts in Bihar. At the same time, the number of ploughs, both wooden and iron, had increased

TABLE 16.1 : Agricultural Implements and Machinery in Bihar

Items	*1951*	*1961*	*1977*	*1982*	*1987*	*1987-88*
Agricultural Implements						
Wooden ploughs	24,18,000 (31,780)	58,62,000 (3,83,72,000)		46,85,158 (including iron ploughs)	4,60,24,000 (including iron ploughs) (51,88,85,000)	
Iron ploughs	30,000 (9,31,000)	1,48,000 (1,20,72,000)				
Carts	5,10,000 (98,63,000)	6,92,000 (1,20,72,000)		7,51,225	75,52,000 (14,35,04,000)	
Percentage Share			5.63	5.8		
Agricultural Machinery						
Oil/diesel engine pumps	630 (95,140)	3,187 (2,29,972)		2,63,804	26,37,000 (11,66,56,000)	(upto) 2,11,000
Electric pumps	278 (29,834)	1,930 (1,60,168)		1,11,966	11,10,000 (4,51,78,000) thousand)	4,48,797/ (4,55,549
Sugarcane Crushers Worked by:				42,734 (all)		
Bullocks	30,823 (5,19,509)	37,852 (5,90,210)				
Percentage Share			3.94	4.9		
Power	1,083 (21,228)	3,748 (3,33,000)			36,700 (7,17,600)	
Percentage Share			6.59	5.3		
Ghanis with Crushing capacity:						
Less than 5 seers/kgs.		32,480 (1,72,032)	8.99 (per cent share)			
5 seers or more/kgs.		5,110 (77,691)	5.85 (per cent share)			

TABLE 16.2 : Tractorisation in Bihar

Items	*1951*	*1956*	*1961*	*1962-65*	*1966*	*1972*	*1977*	*1979-80*
(1)	(2)	(3)	(4)	(5)	(6)	(7)	(8)	(9)
Number of tractors	506 (8354)	1,227	1,520 (1016)	—	2,132	—	10,500	9,109 (373889)
Above as percentage of all-India	6.05	5.8	4.90	—	2.4	—	3.7	2.43
Above per 1000 ha.	—	—	—	0.21 (0.30)	—	0.52	2.0	—

TABLE 16.2 (*Contd.*) (*Contd.*)

Items	*1980-83*	*1981*	*1982*	*1987*	*1989-90*	*1990*	*1992-93*
(1)	(10)	(11)	(12)	(13)	(14)	(15)	(16)
Number of tractors	—	15,283 (271032)	4600/ 14639	14,600 (738400)	59,105 (1152138)	63,091 (1232896)	—
Above as percentage of all-India	—	3.7/5.63	—	1.97	5.13	5.11	—
Above per 1000 ha.	1.94 (3.68)	1.7	1.37	8.88 (11.73)	—	—	617 (8.13)

Note : Between 1977 and 1983 the number of draught cattle and buffaloes per ha. of NAS was 0.97 in Bihar (all-India : 0.57).

18.8 times during 1951-87. Per cart, which was drawn by a pair of oxen, or even one ox if it was a small one, there were 4.8 ploughs, wooden and iron, in 1951; in 1987, the number of ploughs had risen to 6.1 per cart. Which plough would be used turned on the size and stamina of the oxen, the condition of the soil to be tilled, wages charged, etc. One thing was evident: both the old and the new technologies coexisted in the case of ploughs, wooden and iron, as well as carts and tractors, the economy walked on both its legs.

The proposition that other things being equal, certain advantages/economies/savings in cost of production attend increase in the size/scale of business/operation, whatever the field of economic activity we may consider, is confirmed by Table 16.3.

TABLE 16.3 : Ploughs According to Size-Groups of Land Holdings in Bihar : 1977 (15 April)

Size-Groups of Land Holdings	*Number of Ploughs*
Marginal	2355 (1555)
Small	777 (661)
Semi-Medium	476 (436)
Medium	304 (252)
Large	159 (115)

That rural electrification has had a slow and halting career would be clear from the fact that whereas the number of oil/diesel engine pumps increased 4185 times, that of electric pumps 3992 times (they were in addition), whereas Bihar's share increased from 0.66 per cent to 2.26 per cent in the case of the former, in that of the latter from 0.93 per cent to 2.45 per cent during the same period, that is, during 1951-87. Sugarcane crushers operated by power increased 33 times, while cane-crushers worked by both power and bullocks 1.33 times during 1951-82. Bihar's share in the total number of power-operated cane-crushers in India increased from 5.10 to 5.11 per cent only. This is attributable to the slow and tardy progress made by rural electrification in Bihar.

In the progress made up till now by farm mechanisation in Bihar the part played by the State Government cannot be belittled.

Among the institutional arrangements made for agricultural implements and machinery, the most significant element is represented by the Bihar State Agro-Industries Development Corporation. It is a joint venture of the Central and State Governments. It sells the equipment and machinery on hire-purchase basis. In some places its activities are supplemented by co-operatives organised by trained technicians as well as agricultural marketing cooperatives.

The Bihar State Agro-Industries Development Corporation, established in April 1966, ran service centres at a number of places through which service and maintenance of tractors was ensured after they were sold. Mobile servicing vans at all places were provided. Valuable information on care and maintenance of agricultural implements was supplied to the farmers regularly through the All-India Radio and the Television under the Farm Consultancy Service. During the Fifth Plan the State Government sanctioned a big scheme under which at least one set of improved agricultural implements was given to every village.

Out of a variety of factors arresting the progress of farm machanisation in Bihar, the general peasantry's poverty, the paucity of institutional credit and the preponderance of small and fragmented holdings are the most important. The old-fashioned ploughs, spades and sickles still survive in large numbers.

In those parts of Bihar where farm mechanisation has made long strides, and such parts are in the River Command Areas, hordes of migrants have left their villages and moved to distant places in search of employment and livelihood. An opposite view holds the shortage of labour supply in those parts accountable for precipitating farm mechanisation there. This is the old hen-and-egg conundrum.

17

AGRICULTURAL/RURAL CREDIT/ FINANCE AND COOPERATIVE MOVEMENT

We propose to first outline the problem prior to the Plan Holiday of 1966-69.

In 1947 the *zamindars* in Bihar numbering over 4.5 lakhs indulged, allegedly, in conspicuous consumption rather than capital formation, but they were strongly attached to their lands.

In 1950s farmers having land below average size had hardly any surplus of farm receipts left over for further investment towards capital formation after payment of labour (including family labour) and raw material charges for the maintenance of the farmers and their families at the subsistence level at least after incurring the minimum input costs.

Government Loans

In the early 1950s the State Government advanced loans to farmers under the provision of three Acts : (1) Agriculturists' Loans Act (to enable farmers to overcome the distress occasioned by scarcity and natural calamities causing failure of crops), (2) Land Improvement Loans Act and (3) Embankment Act. In 1950-51 the Government gave Rs. 25,89,295 and in 1951-52 it gave Rs. 28,04,286 under (2). In 1950-51, it gave Rs. 86,35,062 under (1). In 1952-53 the Government loans totalled Rs. 5.05 crores. In 1953-54 the volume of rural credit increased because the Government wanted its expansion.

The State Unemployment Committee set up in 1954, noted in its report that the pursuit of good, efficient farming was vitally dependent on adequate availability of credit, besides inputs, its wherewithals. It assessed the short-term and medium-term credit requirements at the rate of Rs. 2 lakhs per block, arriving at an aggregate of Rs. 12 crores. 25 per cent of it, that is, Rs. 3 crores was to be raised locally, out of savings. The Government loans met about 20 per cent of the total rural credit requirements.

In 1954 the amount distributed under the Government loans was Rs. 1.3 crores in Bihar. During 1954-55 the Government distributed loans for the new development projects in the community project areas. The natural calamities loans advanced in that year came to Rs. 17 crores. Irrigation, power and roads were allotted higher loans. At the beginning of 1955-56 arrears/dues outstanding with the agriculturists amounted to Rs. 21.41 crores, of which short-term agricultural credit was Rs. 14.52 crores, that is, 68 per cent. Recovery of the dues entailed a veritable problem. The situation improved slightly in the next two years, so much so that at the commencement of 1957-58, loans of various kinds outstanding with the cultivators amounted to Rs. 17 crores, of which Rs. 10 crores, i.e., 59 per cent was overdue for recovery. Arrears of water rate of canals amounted to Rs. 95 lakhs, and those of public tubewells Rs. 16 lakhs. The 1957-58 budget of the State commented on the slow progress of recoveries of loans and advances outstanding with the cultivators made by the Government staff, which undermined the recycling of the Government loan money. The 1958-59 budget provided for Rs. 1.58 crores for agricultural loans, Rs. 20 lakhs for land improvement, and some money for natural calamities loans, which suggested that the crop conditions were more or less normal, and recoveries of the money due from the cultivators had improved. Most of all, loss of crops affected the repaying capacity of the agriculturists. Only if the money lying with the agriculturists as loans were recovered from them could the Government plough it back into lending. Credit overdues had been accumulating for another reason (other than loss or failure of crops), namely, that public men had misguided farmers about the true nature of the Government loans, that they were not meant to be returned (and because cooperative and bank credits were available to farmers through the patronage of the Government which had partnership in these twin institutions, in course of time these credits became coterminous with the Government credit). The report of the State Unemployment Committee which appeared in 1959 recommended that the problem of default and non-recovery of dues, to whichever sector it belonged, had to be remedied as a matter of public demand. At the same time the quality of assessment of dues with the agriculturists and the amounts to be recovered should be improved.

Let us now try to see what for agriculturist/cultivators took loans from the Government and what they did with them as well as with the moneys they borrowed from other sources, as they existed in those years.

The agriculturists needed money/credit to meet their short-term, medium-term and long-term needs. During the short term, it was working capital which was needed—to purchase the required inputs, to pay wages, to meet modest expenses on other variable factors, and the like. In numerous cases consumption loans became unavoidable. Long-term farm expenditure was identical with investment or capital formation. This assumed the form of livestock, land improvement like land reclamation and soil conservation, construction of farm buildings, approach roads, fencing, etc., irrigation sources, implements and equipments, machinery, etc. Medium-term needs were those which came in-between the short-term and long-term needs.

Upto 1969 the farmers' own past savings and current income were the principal sources of their meeting their various needs. The second source was sale of assets, that is, disinvestment. The third source was borrowing from private agencies, government agencies and cooperative agencies. The fourth and last source was gifts, prizes, etc.

By and large, the farmers who borrowed credit from any source or more than one source used it to meet the same need as had made them incur the loan, but cases were not unknown where the borrowed money was diverted to some other purpose, even if unproductive, which implied either spending it for consumption purpose, or on observing social rites and rituals, bulk of which was sheer wastage.

Our calculations show that capital-output ratio in agriculture and activities allied to it was 8.7 during the First Plan, 5.6 during the Second Plan and 4.6 during the Third Plan.

We have said above that during the First Plan the short-term and medium-term credit requirements of cultivators were estimated at Rs. 12 crores. For the Second Plan the long-term credit requirement was estimated at Rs. 1.00 crore. At the end of the Second Plan estimate of overall credit requirement for agriculture, short-term and medium-term, was at Rs. 18 crores. Out of this, the Reserve Bank of India was to contribute Rs. 4 crores, the cooperative system Rs. 3 crores, and the rest, Rs. 11 crores, was to be provided by the State Government. During the Third Plan the total credit need of Bihar agriculture was put at Rs. 38.40 crores—Rs. 22.70 crores short-term, Rs. 10.70 crores medium-term and Rs. 5.00 crores long-term.

Rural Indebtedness

Debt rather than profit was the normal fate of the average farmer in Bihar. Around 1950 total outstanding loan from private agencies in the rural sector was estimated at Rs. 100 crores. This came to Rs. 23 to 25 per capita.

In 1951-52, according to the RBI survey, percentage of indebted rural households to total rural households, both cultivating and non-cultivating, was higher in Bihar than in all-India (Table 17.1). The cultivating households were relatively more indebted than the non-cultivating ones. In either case the figure for Bihar was above that for all-India. The Table 17.2 would show that debt per rural household, cultivating and non-cultivating combined, in Bihar was lower than the all-India figure, which was compatible with the fact that per capita income in Bihar was lower than per capita income in all-India. The amount borrowed by the cultivating household was higher than that borrowed by the non-cultivating one.

TABLE 17.1 : Rural Indebtedness : 1951-52 and 1961-62

	Bihar	*All-India*
Percentage of indebted rural households to total rural households (cultivating and non-cultivating)		
RBI		
1951-52	76	63
1961-62	63	63
NSS		
1953-54	34	36
1960-61	56	54
Percentage of indebted rural households to total rural households		
(RBI) Cultivating		
1951-52	79	69
1961-62	65	67
(RBI) Non-Cultivating		
1951-52	70	52
1961-62	55	52

In 1953-54, as the NSS survey brought out, percentage of indebted rural households to total rural households, cultivating and non-cultivating pooled together, in Bihar was lower than that in all-India. That within two years the position had undergone a U-turn in Bihar *vis-a-vis* all-India does not convince us. Similarly, according to the NSS data, debt per household in Bihar was less than the all-India figure, which is a finding not quite convincing to us.

TABLE 17.2 : Rural Indebtedness : 1951-52 and 1961-62

(Rupees)

	Bihar	*All-India*
Debt per Indebted Rural Household (cultivating and non-cultivating)		
RBI		
1951-52	296	447
1961-62	554	647
NSS		
1953-54	206	370
1960-61	330	469
Debt per Indebted Cultivator		
RBI		
1951-52	354	526
1961-62	605	708
Debt Per Non-Cultivator		
RBI		
1951-52	163	249
1961-62	335	430

In 1950-51 in Bihar the amount of guaranteed debt was Rs. 15,30,90,492, and that of unguaranteed Rs. 47,92,081. On Mach 31, 1952 the number of licensed money-lenders in Bihar was 29,984.

In 1961-62, according to the RBI data, the relative position of Bihar in all-India had definitely improved, in the case of both cultivating and non-cultivating rural households, though more so in the case of the latter. The relative improvement conclusion did not hold good in respect of debt per indebted household. The amount of debt had risen proportionally more in the case of Bihar than in that of all-India, between 1951-52 and 1961-62. The cultivating households were worse-off by comparison with the non-cultivating, but when compared to the all-India changes in the same (upward) direction, the cultivating households had suffered more in Bihar than in all-India, whereas the non-cultivating ones in Bihar had suffered slightly less than their all-India counterparts. All the same, we should bear in mind the fact of rising prices during the period throughout the country, which had occasioned a heightened burden of debt everywhere in monetary terms.

Coming to the percentage of indebted rural households, we find that between 1951-52 and 1961-62 whereas there was no change in it at the national level, the change in it in Bihar was appreciable; it was more impressive in the case of the non-cultivating households. The cultivating households in Bihar had their debts repaid/written off in a larger percentage than their counterparts in all-India.

Turning to the NSS data, we find that between 1953-54 and 1960-61 the percentage of indebted rural households increased more sharply in Bihar than in all-India, but still more sharp was the increase in the average amount of debt per household in the case of Bihar than in that of all-India, by comparison.

The NCAER study released in 1959 brought to light certain striking facts about the subject-matter: That the credit requirements of Bihar agriculture were still met by the agricultural money-lender who charged unconscionable rates of interest, that grain-lending at *sawai* interest (one-fourth of the principal) had lately increased to 50 to 100 per cent, due to increasing need for subsistence credit in times of underemployment, that the richer landlords, in general, lent on mortgages at 12 to 18 per cent rate of interest, that the largest amounts of mortgage loans by private money-lenders were in the prosperous districts of Shahabad, Muzaffarpur, Saran and Champaran, that the ways in which the usurious rates of interest were charged by the money-lenders were innumerable, that even the existing rates of interest permitted under the Bihar Money Lenders' Act were practically double of those prevailing in cooperative societies, and that a very large number of debtors with uneconomic holdings were almost insolvent.

The very small farmers, who had little surplus left with which they could repay the debts incurred, even if advanced by the public/institutional agencies, had always hanging over their heads the sword of a debt trap.

At 1948-49 prices, per capita income in Bihar in 1955-56 was Rs. 156 (Rs. 268 all-India), which rose to Rs. 189 in 1960-61 (all-India Rs. 293). On the other hand, at the same prices, annual gross value of output per hectare in Bihar was Rs. 269, which rose to Rs. 341 in 1955-56 and Rs. 400 in 1960-61. In 1959-60 loans per hectare of cropped area were Rs. 1.16, and per member of a cooperative society Rs. 20.8 in Bihar. In 1960-61 in Bihar the percentage of debt to per capita income was 11.00 per cent and the percentage of debt per ha. was 5.2 per cent of the gross income per ha.

At the end of June 1962 the proportion of households reporting outstanding loans was 62.9 per cent. It was higher among cultivators and lower among non-cultivators in Bihar.

Capital Formation/Investment

In 1955-56 the proportion of annual capital formation in Bihar agriculture was only 1.0 per cent of total gross income from agriculture, which amounted to around Rs. 7.16 crores, as estimated by us. In 1960-61 this amounted to 1.6 per cent, that is, Rs. 11.56 crores.

In the late 1950s the scope of investment in Bihar agriculture by the private sector was limited to the three-fifths of all agriculturists possessing land only. Holders of farms above 2.02 ha. in size were 21.8 per cent of all. They possessed 65.4 per cent of total cultivated area. It is they who contributed to capital formation. According to our own estimate, during the Second Plan the private sector in Bihar invested less than one-tenth of the amount invested by the public sector.

In 1959-60 capital formation per rural household in Bihar was Rs. 5, according to the NSS data, out of total expenditure of Rs. 156.02, i.e., 3.20 per cent. In 1961-62, according to the RBI data, fixed capital formation in farm business was Rs. 6.0. Other data were as follows: Average per rural household in 1961: value of assets Rs. 5556 (all-India Rs. 5358); net outstanding debt (1962) Rs. 345 (Rs. 406 all-India); borrowing (1961-62) Rs. 93 (all-India Rs. 180); repayment (1961-62) Rs. 44 (all-India Rs. 90); fixed capital formation in non-farm business (1961-62) Rs. 3 (all-India Rs. 4); and residential housing (1961-62) Rs. 21 (all-India Rs. 22). The all-India average for capital formation in 1961-62 was Rs. 24. This was four-fold of the Bihar figure.

In 1959-60 in Bihar cultivators (60 per cent) possessing land invested. Cultivators without land (40 per cent of the total agriculturists) did not contribute to capital formation. 21.8 per cent of farm holdings with more than 2.02 ha. in size possessing 65.4 per cent of total cultivated land offered scope for making saving after meeting labour and material charges and contributed to capital formation.

A study (by Sastri) made for the year 1963-64 disclosed that a larger farm made a higher investment in Bihar. Investment per holding in large size group was three times that in small size groups; investment per holding in medium size group was 12 per cent more. Increase in investment was not proportional to increase in size of holdings. That is to say, investment per ha. tended to decrease with increase in size of the holdings. Investment varied from Rs. 33 to 54 as between different size groups. As for the regions, the variation was between Rs. 182 and Rs. 423, the average for Bihar as a whole being Rs. 311 (Table 17.3). Investment per holding was more than twice in North Bihar, as compared to that in Chotanagpur, while it was 28 per cent higher in North Bihar than that in South Bihar. At any rate, the rate of investment was too low to raise the rate of productivity of Bihar agriculture. On an average, investment per ha. was Rs. 150.60.

TABLE 17.3 : Investment/Disinvestment (Per hectare) in Bihar Agriculture : 1963-64

(Rupees)

Size Groups (In ha.)	*Average Size of (Holdings) (ha.)*	*Investment*	*Disinvest-ment*	*Net Investment*	*Investment Per Farm*
Below 0.81	0.57	125	71	54	
0.81—2.02	1.39	60	27	33	
2.02 & above	4.28	50	14	36	
All Holdings	2.06	61	23	38	
Regions					
North Bihar					423
South Bihar					329
Chotanagpur					182
All Bihar					311

Investment on account of construction and repair of the farm house in the case of smaller size holdings was twice that in the larger size ones. On the whole, it was 43.2 per cent of total investment. Per farm it was 16.7 per cent. As between the regions it varied from 10.3 per cent in the case of South Bihar to 21.1 per cent in that of North Bihar, Chotanagpur occupying the middling position with 19.2 per cent of total investment.

Investment in livestock was 43.6 per cent of total investment. It was maximum in the case of medium-size holdings, 64 per cent. Next to come were large-size holdings, 44 per cent. Last were the small-size holdings, 19.2 per cent of the total. Per farm this investment was 43.4 per cent of the aggregate. Its percentage was the highest in North Bihar, 56 per cent. In South Bihar it was 32.0 per cent. It was the lowest in Chotanagpur, 17.6 per cent of the total.

Investment in purchase of implements, machinery and equipment claimed 2.6 per cent of total investment. Percentage varied from 1.8 per cent in respect of large-size holdings to 3.8 per cent in that of medium-size, the small-size holdings occupying the middle position with 2.8 per cent of the total investment. Per farm investment in this item was 2.6 per cent of the aggregate, North Bihar topping the list with 2.6 per cent and the remaining two regions bracketed with 2.2 per cent each.

Lastly, on development of the irrigation facility the private sector investment was 3.0 per cent of all. It was the largest percentage in the case of the large-size farms with 6.0 per cent. The percentage in the case of medium-size holdings was 1.7 per cent of the total. The small-size holdings lacked the capability to make any such investment. Per farm this head claimed just one per cent of total investment, and region-wise, North Bihar and South Bihar were conspicuous for any investment in this head, only Chotanagpur made an investment, the percentage share of which in total investment was only 1.0 per cent. In the public sector the share of Plan expenditure on irrigation and flood control was 17.66 per cent of total of Rs. 7327.61 lakhs in the First Plan (total investment in the rural sector was not less than 31.55 per cent which amounted to Rs. 2311.8 lakhs). Plan outlay on the rural sector was Rs. 7327 lakhs. In the Second Plan investment in irrigation and flood control was 15.16 per cent of the total, equal to Rs. 7763 lakhs, i.e., Rs. 7763 lakhs. In the Third Plan the investment in irrigation and flood control was to the extent of Rs. 14891 lakhs, 24.70 per cent of total outlay on the rural sector, equal to Rs. 32852 lakhs. During 1966-69 the total Plan outlay on irrigation and flood control was Rs. 112911 lakhs, 26.42 per cent of total Plan outlay. Thus Rs. 137878 lakhs were spent on irrigation and flood control head during 1951-69. The total Plan outlay in the rural sector during the period was Rs. 628089 lakhs. This gives a 21.95 per cent of total Plan outlay on the rural sector in 18 years. On the eve of the Third Plan the authors pointed out in no uncertain terms that unless savings through private investment in the rural sector increased considerably, any addition of investment in the public sector alone would hardly be in a position to enhance the agricultural produce considerably.

Disinvestment or capital consumption was one means whereby new investment was made by the farmers in Bihar. The average amount of disinvestment was Rs. 23, which had a range of Rs. 14 to Rs. 71, relying on the size-group of holdings. Sale of land and sale of livestock were the two components of disinvestment, the former was 16 per cent (for the purposes of old debt repayment and land repurchase) and the latter 84 per cent. Region-wise, North Bihar was first in the latter component and Chotanagpur the last, South Bihar occupying the middle position.

Table 17.4 brings out that in 1963-64 in Bihar upto 63.0 per cent of investment the agriculturists were dependent on their own past savings and current incomes. Disinvestment, i.e., capital consumption afforded the wherewithal to the extent of about 28 per cent. Only nearly 9 per cent of the resource for investment was supplied by sources from outside. This was proof of the peripheral part the outside sources played in financing investment in Bihar agriculture; the central part was played by sources other than borrowing. A look at the table would show that the source-wise distribution of investment credit in the case of farmers with holdings below the size of 0.81 ha. was the closest approximation to the overall picture presented immediately above. About 7 per cent of the investment made by them came from outside, the private agencies. Those with holdings in size 2.02 ha. and more had a pattern of investment corresponding more or less to that the lowest size-group had, except for the obvious difference that their percentage of borrowing was higher, and this because they had access to the institutional agencies whose funds they manipulated to their advantage as members or otherwise. The size-group coming in between the two, described above, had to depend more on their own resources as well as indulge in sale of assets to a fault, their borrowings being practically nil.

TABLE 17.4 : Sources of Supply of Farm Investment Credit in Bihar in 1963-64

(In percentage)

Sources	*Size Groups (Hectares)*			
	Below 0.81	*0.81—2.02*	*2.02 & above*	*All*
1. Own, readily available sources				
(i) Past Savings	17.1	17.1	33.8	27.1
(ii) Current Income	46.3	53.7	26.5	35.9
Total	63.4	70.8	60.3	63.0
2. Sale of Assets	29.7	29.2	26.5	27.8
3. Borrowings	6.9	—	13.5	9.2
Total	100.0	100.0	100.0	100.0

Cooperative Finance

The origin of cooperative societies in Bihar is to be traced to the pre-independence era. The aim and object of these societies was all-round economic and social advancement of the farming community, with special emphasis on the marginal and small farmers, stricken, most of all, by poverty and un- and under-employment.

In the early 1950s cooperative societies supplied short-term credit to agriculturists in the shape of fertilisers, seeds, oil-cake, bone-meal, etc., also credit at the appropriate time.

In 1951-52 cooperatives in Bihar met about 3 per cent of total credit needs of agriculturists. Under the Agricole Scheme the number of depots in the State was 198, which distributed fertilisers, oil-cake, etc. Approximately 1.63 per cent of total population constituted the membership of all coopererative societies in Bihar. Upto 1952 there was for every five villages and for every five sq. miles one cooperative society in the State. In 1959-60 loans per ha. of GCA from cooperative societies worked out to Rs. 11.61, and per member Rs. 20.81. Cooperative credit had hardly touched the fringe of the problem in Bihar. In 1960-61 cooperative societies served 10 per cent of the total agricultural population in the State. One-third of all cooperative societies were, in fact, incurring loss. In 1961-62 (triennial average) net cooperative bank flow was minus 0.18, which measured the credit received by agricultural households (the figures for Maharashtra was minus 6.26 and that for Punjab minus 0.63). On 30 June, 1963 of all members of cooperative societies only 33 members had been advanced loans (all-India number was 48). Of all rural households, only 4 could receive loans from cooperative societies (all-India figure was 14). In June 1964, 30 per cent of all cooperative societies were non-viable. In 1963-64 these societies provided about 14 per cent of the credit needs of agriculturists in Bihar. The cooperative societies supplied short-term and medium-term loans amounting to Rs. 8.00 crores during the Third Plan period.

The cooperative system in Bihar was a three-tier structure—at the bottom were PACS, in the middle Central Cooperative Banks (CCBs) and at the apex the State Cooperative Bank. Table 17.5 furnishes information on the progress made by the Primary Agricultural Credit Societies (PACS) in Bihar during the period 1950-51 to 1961-62. The number of PACS increased 2.84 times, their membership rose 10.30 times and average working capital per head 4.68 times.

TABLE 17.5 : Primary Agricultural Credit Societies (PACS) in Bihar

Characteristics	*1950-51*	*1955-56*	*1960-61*	*1961*	*1961-62*
(1)	(2)	(3)	(4)	(5)	(6)
Number of PACS	6468	12606	29739	28000	18394
Above as percentage of all-India	5.62		8.94		
No. of PACS per lakh inhabitants	36.2/36.7 (50.6)	52.8 (62.2)	65.70		65.7
Membership of PACS	103428		1719498	3558000	1066000
Above as percentage of all-India	2.02		5.02		

(*Contd.*)

TABLE 17.5 (*Contd.*)

(1)	(2)	(3)	(4)	(5)	(6)
Membership per 1000 inhabitants	15.8 (38.3)	21.8 (45.6)	39.10		39.1
Average membership per society	16 (45)	33 (49)	127 (80)		
Average working capital per head (Rs.)	1.28 (7.7)	3.90 (8.0	6.00		6.00
Loans advanced per member (Rs.)			74		41 (64)
Loans repaid as percentage of loans advanced					96
Loans outstanding as percentage of loans advanced (cumulative)					116
Loans overdue as percentage of loans outstanding (cumulative)					23
Loans advanced by Central Cooperative Banks to PACS (Rs. crores)	87		380		449

Note : Data differ as given in different sources. Alternative data are as follows:

	1950-51	*1959*	*1960-61*
PACS			
Number of Member	115748/13802	10593	17086
Membership	5369000/509717	3.62 lakhs	961 (thousand)
Working capital (Rs. crores)	1.23		
Reserve fund (Rs. crores)	0.27		
Average per Society			
Membership	45		56 (Do)
Share capital (Rs.)	1000		592 (Do)
Loans outstanding (Rs.)	2000		
Deposits (Rs.)			328 (Do)
Loans advanced (Rs.)			1077 (Do)
Other Particulars			
Number of villages			38822

(*Contd.*)

TABLE 17.5 (*Contd.*)

	1950-51	*1959*	*1960-61*
PACS			
Percentage of dormant societies of total societies			22.1
Percentage of borrowing members of total membership			25.9
Owned funds (Rs. lakhs)			120
Deposits (Rs. Lakhs)			56
Loans issued (Do) Total			184
Loans outstanding (Rs. lakhs)			255

Primary cooperative societies were both agricultural and non-agricultural, credit and non-credit, and assumed forms, many and varied (service societies, grain banks), single-purpose or multipurpose. Land mortgage banks also came under the umbrella of cooperation, and later graduated into land development banks. Examples of credit societies were State and Central Cooperative Banks, Cooperative Banking Unions and PACS which were credit societies.

On 30 June, 1951 for every 32 unlimited liability primary cooperative credit societies there was one limited liability primary cooperative credit society. In 1962-63 percentage of PACS not earning profit was 46.5 (all-India 32.0). At the end of June 1963 a little less than one-third of all PACS were dormant. The PACS depended on funds borrowed from the CCBs for making advances to their members.

Considering cooperative societies of all types/hues, we find that between 1950-51 and 1960-61 their number increased 2.51 times, membership 2.75 times and working capital 5.56 to 14.77 times (Table 17.6). Bihar was lower than all-India averages in almost all indicators, be it number of cooperative societies per one lakh population or membership per 1000 inhabitants or working capital per head.

By 1952 different professional/occupational groups of the rural inhabitants had come within the corpus of the cooperative movement in Bihar, as would be evident from Table 17.7. Sugarcane societies were most popular among the agricultural credit societies. During the First Plan period alone 12268 multipurpose cooperative societies were set up. During the Second Plan the position of the farming societies was better in Bihar than in several other States. There were several hundreds of

TABLE 17.6 : Progress of Cooperative Societies (All) in Bihar

Characteristics	*1950-51*	*Oct-end 1952*	*1954*	*1955-56*	*1959-60*	*1960-61*	*1961-62*
Number of societies	13618/ 181000 (8.7)	14710	10593	240000	313000/ 24142	332000	342000
Membership	504082/ 13715000 (5.7)	657206	362000	17622000	30321000/ 1086441	30321000	37836000
Total share capital (Rs. Crores)	56.13 (1.93)	93.83			220.56		
Deposits by Members (Rs. Crores)	29.58 (3.96)						
Loans from other societies (Rs. Crores)	22.66 (0.97)						
Share Aid (Rs. Crores)	0.22 (0.14)				140.72		
Reserves (Rs. Crores)	25.32 (2.03)						
Total working capital (Rs. Crores)	103.91 276 (0.01)	5.30		4.69	1083	1312	1535
Loans issued to members (Rs. Crores)	27.10 (0.77)						
Outstanding (Rs. Crores)			6.13				loans

Note : Data differ as contained in alternative sources. The following data are for 1950-51 :

(*Contd.*)

TABLE 17.6 (*Contd.*)

Cooperative Credit Societies	
Number	
State-Level Societies	20
District-Level Central Societies	505
Primary Non-Agricultural Credit Societies, etc.(FNACS)	7810
All	124083
Membership	
State Societies	31000
Central Societies	207000
PNACS, etc.	2178000
All	7785000
Working Capital	
All (Rs. Crores)	202.88
Loan Transactions (Rs. Crores)	
Advancement	71.48
Repayment	58.85
Outstanding	75.90
Overdue	7.98

village service cooperative societies in 1960-61. In 1964-65 they numbered 23 thousand (previously they had numbered 16 thousand), of which 11300 were viable. In addition to providing credit these societies supplied inputs (largely controlled) and provided marketing facilities.

TABLE 17.7 : Names and Numbers of Agricultural Cooperative Societies in Bihar

Names	*1950-51*	*1951*	*1952*	*1956*
Credit Depots		197	198	
Grain Golas	22			
Multipurpose		4717	5880 (6258 October-end)	7400
Higher Living & Rural Uplift		28		
Farming Milk Supply		22		
Fishermen's				
Harijan		8		
Housing				
Primary Teachers' Stock		382		
Cooperative Stores		188		
Producers' and Consumers'				
Vegetable Growers'			65 (76 October-end)	
Vishwakarmas'		28		
Cane Development		59		
Cane Growers'/Producers'		3468		
Cane Marketing		49		
Weavers'			140 (October-end)	
Oilmen's			64 (Do)	

Note : Agricultural Credit Societies were, by and large, service and multipurpose. Non-agricultural Cooperative Societies numbered 866 during July 1, 1950—June 30, 1951.

Examples of non-credit cooperative societies—service societies (not the concern of the present chapter)—are: working societies, sugarcane supply societies, milk supply societies, farming societies, processing societies, weavers' societies, consumers' societies, housing societies, fishermen's societies, etc.

The break-even institution in the three-tier cooperative system is the Central Cooperative Bank (CCB). By October-end 1952 there were in the districts of Bihar altogether 53 Central Cooperative Banks. In June 1963 their deposits totalled Rs. 1.76 crores (1.20 per cent of all-India) and working capital Rs. 5.64 crores (1.41 per cent of all-India).

In 1958-59 Bihar had no land mortgage bank and no irrigation society. The Central Cooperative Land Mortagage Bank was set up with the State Government as a partner during the Second Plan (which later was redesignated as Bihar State Land Development Bank). From the very start this bank suffered from paucity of funds and hence it could not spread its organisation over the State.

An Overview

The Primary Agricultural Credit Societies (PACS) were graded according to the quality of their performance, proportion of their own funds, their deposits, their overdues, the standard of their management, and so on. They borrowed from the CCBs at the rate of 5 per cent and lent at the rate of $6^1/_2$ per cent. During the Third Plan period in rural areas the rate of interest had gone up by 50 to 100 per cent. The cooperative credit reached the real farm holder at the rate of 8 to 9 per cent.

In June 1962 the number of agricultural credit societies was 18394 (8.55 per cent of all-India), their deposits Rs. 99.30 lakhs (5.62 per cent of all-India), and working capital Rs. 5,09,40 thousand (1.56 per cent of all-India).

The position of overdues was not happy in the cooperative world. Overdues formed about half of the outstandings on 30 June, 1959. In June 1963 about two-fifths of loans outstanding were overdue.

The Bihar State Unemployment Committee in its Report (1959) observed that the cooperative organisation was the most versatile social institution which could take on any kind of function, so much so that the original enthusiasts had dreamt of even neutralising the coercive authority of the state itself through cooperation. Even though the initial efforts for fostering cooperation might have to come from outside, the ultimate objective should be to make the people take to cooperation of their own choice. The credit needs of the cultivator were best known to the local cooperative society, which is supposed to keep a watch on how he utilises his loan. In so far as the Bihar economy was expected to grow and diversify itself as well as improve its health, so to speak, the rural credit system was to be put on sound lines to operate smoothly in consonance with the needs of such an economy.

Around 1954 the features of agricultural credit and multipurpose cooperative societies were as follows: small membership, poor share capital, multifarious objectives, smallness of transactions under short-term and medium-term loans, crop loans advances being less than medium-term loans for fear that they would be used for unproductive purposes, excessive caution exercised in the issuance of loans, medium- and large-size landholders receiving loans for purchase of land or for getting lands of the poor classes on mortgages which were in proportion higher than loans small and marginal holders got (they were deprived of even fertilisers loan), there being no identity of interests between two classes, lax administration, supervision and control, lack of trained staff and hence poor accounts keeping, improperly done audit work, abuses perpetrated by office-bearers, non-official leadership not built up, etc.

The PACS were criticised on various grounds: pursuit of a restrictive and flawsome loan policy, which made the service rendered limited, offering of credit facilities to farmers on traditional lines in the form of assets-based credit, which resulted in the flow of credit mainly to the owner-cultivator-type farmers, who offered the mortgage of their lands as collateral/security for the credit availed of by them, absence of real help to the tenant-cultivators, who had to furnish two good sureties, and so on.

All in all, the rural people had not come to regard cooperation as the repository of their hard-earned savings. This was an undeniable proof of the failure of cooperation to attain its desideratum in Bihar. The malpractice reflected in the non-maintenance of books/accounts in a satisfactory manner was the chief villain of the piece. Rural savings found alternative avenues in unproductive expenditures in which the rural savers canalised them or remained with them as inactive, idle balances, or got immobilised in the shape of coins, gold and land.

By the mid-1960s the cooperative movement in Bihar was steeped in a quagmire, a stalemate. It was virtually in the throes of stagnation. It lacked financial strength. It was plagued by a plethora of professional policies and procedures. These made the State Government adopt ways and means to strengthen the owned funds of the PACS as well as their week deposit base, as also of the institutions at the other two levels of the cooperative credit structure.

Another problem which afflicted the cooperative edifice was the entanglement at all levels of management with political dimensions of rural life, dominance of vested interests and caste lobbies, large-scale embezzlements, defalcations and frauds, and so forth. In 1961-62 alone cases of embezzlement numbered 852, involving Rs. 33.90 lakhs.

In a nutshell, the system was in dire need of arresting stagnation, beginning from the PACS' level onwards. The State Government's partnership percentage was fairly high, at 91 to 92 per cent of all societies. The Government contributed to share capital. It allowed a margin to the PACS on the loans taken from it through the CCBs via the State Cooperative Bank. It provided a certain safeguard to the PACS against bad and doubtful debts. A rebate at the rate of 1.5 per cent was paid to such of the PACS as repaid their dues in time to the CCBs.

The State Government intensified its attempts to free the genuine cooperative societies from the vested interests founded on caste or other lines at the same time that it endeavoured to make them viable. Viability was defined in June 1964 at the all-India level in concrete terms as having sufficient business turnover so as to enable a society to have: (1) its own full-time paid secretary, (2) its own office building, (3) adequate profits to contribute to reserves, and (4) adequate profits to pay the members a reasonable dividend.

For years the Reserve Bank of India (RBI) had a separate department which dealt with rural development, with the result that the activities of the three-tier cooperative system with full details and data were published by it periodically. Rural credit flowed from the bank as the mainspring. If cooperative societies were saved from insolvency, responsible for this was the bank's generosity and liberal attitude, which found vent in release of ever-increasing funds at concessional rates. Under the stewardship of the State Government the State Cooperative Bank received the RBI's advances at interest rates 2 per cent below its Bank Rate, which seeped down to the PACS through the CCBs.*

In the mid-1960s a mistake was made by the officials at the lowest rung of the ladder when some of the well-functioning large societies were converted into service cooperatives despite instructions to the contrary, an instance of unnecessary witch-hunting, confirming the saying 'the courtiers are more kingly than the king himself'.

Furthermore, frequent changes in the policy towards the size of a cooperative society during the 1960s in a way destabilised the base of the cooperative superstructure.

Around 1963 a suggestion was made that an alternative agency be set up to look after the credit problems of the farm sector. During 1963-64 the Union Government suggested to the State Government to introduce the crop loan system for financing agriculture by the rural cooperative societies. Short-term production finance was to be provided

* During 1961-63 the State Cooperative Bank advanced loans to the CCBs at 3 to 4 per cent rate of interest, and the CCBs to the PACS at 5 per cent and the PACS to individual members at 7.5 per cent rate of interest.

to all credit-worthy agriculturists by cooperative societies; loans were to be advanced on the basis of anticipated crops, not land security. This was a shift from the asset nexus to the production nexus. The credit-worthiness of the borrower was to be linked to his production and repaying capacities. Acreage and time of repayment as linked to the harvesting season became the chief tests in due course.

1969 to 1979

There occurred a breakthrough in rural savings from 1969 onwards, with a change in the outlook of the rural people towards the future, also because their fields produced more than before, though no less because the channels for investment increased in number, and proved more attractive than had been the case before (we must not forget here the great services rendered by term deposits in post offices).

In 1971-72 agricultural savings in Bihar amounted to Rs. 156.83 crores (11.96 per cent of agricultural income), and rural Rs. 167.55 crores (11.47 per cent of rural income). In the same year rural informal savings (meaning financial assets with counterpart financial liabilities—examples being purchase land) as a ratio of gross formal financial savings were 0.96, and for most part were balanced by disinvestment; expenditure on purchase of land as a proportion of gross formal financial savings was 0.10; total informal savings as a proportion of gross financial savings were 0.16; and the Gini Coefficient for asset holdings was 0.672. Net financial savings, rural, were Rs. 37.55 crores—agricultural Rs. 32.63 crores and non-agricultural Rs. 4.92 crores. Net financial savings and gross physical investment, rural, totalled Rs. 0.29 crore—0.26 agricultural and 0.85 non-agricultural.

Table 17.8 is a witness to what happened to financial savings of agricultural households in Bihar in 1971-72/1971-82. Cash-mindedness of the agriculturists was uppermost, followed by commercial bank deposits which had started with a bang, so to say, and life insurance premia and provident funds and small savings invested mostly in the purchase of certificates and papers available in post offices, when lumped, formed the next important item. Cooperative credit came first, followed by government loans. Commercial Bank credit had become a component worthy of reckoning. The C-D ratio was low at 6.76/7.68 per cent. The multi-form Drain had sown its seeds in the very beginning.

In 1971 rural households in Bihar held shares in select financial stocks as follows : Commercial Bank deposits 14, life insurance fund 7, provident fund 10, post office deposits 7, Commercial Bank credit 1.23 and government credit 5.66 per cent.

TABLE 17.8 : Financial Savings of Agricultural Households in Bihar : 1971-72

Items	*Amount (Rs. crores)*		*Percentage Distribution*			
	1971-72	*1971-82*	*Gross*		*Net*	
			1971-72	*1971-82*	*1971-72*	*1971-82*
Currency	18.33	18.70	32.27	34.34	56.17	19.80
Life insurance premia	3.24	4.0	6.58	7.34	9.93	10.65
Provident fund	8.59	11.93	17.46	21.91	26.32	31.77
Small savings	2.22	2.69	4.51	4.94	6.80	7.16
Cooperative shares and deposits	1.13	1.13	2.29	2.07	3.46	3.01
Commercial bank deposits	15.67	16.00	31.86	29.38	48.02	42.60
A. Gross formal financial savings (Total)	49.18	54.45	100.00	100.00	100.00	100.00
					Percentage Distribution	
Commercial bank credit	1.06	1.23		6.40	7.27	
Cooperative credit	9.83	9.83			59.40	58.16
Government credit	5.66	5.84			34.20	34.57
B. Total credit	16.55	16.90			100.00	100.00
C. (A - B) Net financial savings	32.63	37.55				
Informal financial savings		3.4				
Net financial savings as percentage of gross financial savings					66.34	68.96

In June 1971-end per capita formal financial assets and liabilities in rural and agricultural households in Bihar were as follows: gross assets—rural Rs. 10.74 and agricultural Rs. 10.89; gross liabilities—rural Rs. 3.33 and agricultural Rs. 3.66; and net assets—rural Rs. 7.40 and agricultural Rs. 7.22. Share of cultivator households in rural financial assets and liabilities was as follows: commercial bank deposits 0.98, life insurance fund 81.13, provident fund 72.24, post office deposits 84.85, commercial bank credit 0.98 and government credit 0.95 per cent.

During 1961-62 to 1971-72 annual growth rate of gross capital expenditure undertaken by cultivators in Bihar was: farm business 2.6 per cent, non-farm business 24.5 per cent, and total 5.1 per cent.

Compared to 1960-61, in 1971 (confining to the RBI data) percentage of indebted rural households had slid down from 63 to 38.4, whereas debt per indebted rural household had slid down from Rs. 554 to Rs. 288 (Table 17.9).

TABLE 17.9 : Rural Indebtedness : 1971

Indebted Rural Households	*Bihar*	*All-India*
Beginning of the RBI 1971 Survey Period :		
(a) As percentage of total rural households	38.4	41.3
(b) Debt per household (Rs.)	28.8	487
(c) Average assets (Rs.)	12828	11311
(d) Percentage share of land in (c)	74.3	66.3
(e) Debt: land asset ratio (per cent)	3.0	6.5
End of the RBI 1971 Survey Period :		
(a) As percentage of total households	37.2	44.0
(b) Debt per household (Rs.)	310	552

Source : Gothoskar, S.P., RBI Occasional Papers, December 1988.

Membership of the PACS in Bihar in 1970-71 was 28 lakhs. In 1978-79 it had risen to 587 lakhs (Table 17.10). Between 1950-51 and 1978-79 the increase in it was of the order of 1092 per cent. But their number had fallen to the extent of 12 per cent during the period. Except for a slight decline in number, cooperative credit societies recorded increase in each and every item, as indicated by the Table 17.10

In 1979-80 there were in Bihar 418 PACS concerned with marketing, 17 PACS concerned worth processing and 420 PACS concerned with distribution, their transaction was valued at Rs. 1,16,51 thousand in the case of the first and Rs. 1,04,15 thousand in that of the last (no figure is available for the second). Between 1970-71 and 1978-79 there was improvement in a number of items, and the number of the PACS had fallen.

The Land Development Bank was established in Bihar during 1958-59. Upto 1970-71 loans issued by it were small in amount. After that loans disbursement made long strides which continued till 1976-77. In the next years a setback had to be faced by the bank in its activity.

TABLE 17.10 : Progress of Cooperative Credit Societies in Bihar

	1950-51	*1970-71*	*1978-79*	*Percentage Increase*	
				1950-51 vs 1978-79	*1950-51 vs 1970-71*
Number of Credit Societies					
State Society	20		48	240	
Central Society	505		345	(–) 32	
PACS	115748	17171	6605/ 101679	(–) 12	(–) 62
PNACs	7810		21797	279	
Total	124083		123869	(–) 1.2	
Number of Members ('000)					
State Society	31		2582	8329	
Central Society	207		333	160	
PACs	5369	2750 thousand	58671/ 4600 thousand	1092	167
PNACs	2178		13183	605	
Total	7785		74769	960	
Owned funds of PACS (Rs. lakhs)		578	1161		201
Deposits of PACS (Rs. lakhs)		298	239		(–) 10
Working Capital (Rs. Lakhs)	20288		1344224	6625	
Percentage of borrowing members to total membership of PACS		33.1	36.1		109
Loan Transactions (Rs. Lakhs)					
Advances+	7148		290063	4058	
Repayment	5885		251048	4265	
Outstanding++	7590		387682	5107	
Overdues	798		110559	138	
Average per PAC Society					
Membership	45	160	969	1220	435
Share capital (Rs.)	1000	2912	16033	4900	550
Deposits (Do)		1735	3618		208
Loans advanced (Do)	2000	7256	37613	10700	518

\+ Advance loans by PACS Rs. 1246 lakhs—Rs. 1152 lakhs short-term and Rs. 94 lakhs medium-term in 1970-71. In 1978-79 the corresponding figures were: Rs. 2485 lakhs, Rs. 2096 lakhs and Rs. 389 lakhs respectively.

++ By PACS : Rs. 1992 lakhs in 1970-71 and Rs. 5345 lakhs in 1978-79.

Loans advanced per borrower member in the PACS increased from Rs. 20.81 in 1959-60 to Rs. 137 in 1970-71 to Rs. 150 in 1979-80. In the terminal year of the period under review PACS loan per ha. of GCA was a measly amount, Re. 0.19.

During the 1970s short-term credit advanced by the PACS rose by about 182 per cent, and medium-term by 433 per cent, whereas the sumtotal of the two by about 200 per cent. Credit advanced by the LDB, which was of a long-term nature, rose by about 124 per cent.

The apex of the cooperative system, the Bihar State Cooperative Bank at the end of the decade in question had advanced short-term and long-term loans to the CCBs, which were only 3 per cent of the total credit advanced by it to them (Table 17.11).

TABLE 17.11 : Supply of Cooperative Credit to Agriculture in Bihar

(Rs. Crores)

Year	*PACS*			*Total*	
	Short-term	*Medium-term*	*LDB*	*Bihar State Coop. Bank*	
1970-71	11.5	0.9	6.9		
1974-75	13.0		11.3		
1978-79	21.0		5.2	2900.63	
1979-80	21.0	3.9	8.6	*Short-term*	*Medium term*
				11.58	63.70

Note : Short-term cooperative credit was given for seasonal agricultural operations, purchase of agricultural implements, marketing crops, processing of agricultural produce, other agricultural purposes, pisciculture, consumption loans, etc.

Medium-term cooperative credit was given for sinking or repairing wells, purchase of machinery, purchase of cattle, animal husbandry activities, minor improvement in land, pisciculture, other agricultural purposes, replacement agriculture, consumption loans, gobar gas plants, purchase of store line, etc.

Long-term cooperative credit was given for time-consuming activities, with yield/return in periods longer than those covered under the above two kinds.

During 1974-75 to 1979-80 short-term credit in Bihar increased by 186 per cent, whereas term (medium and long) credit by 171 per cent and total credit by 190 per cent. As proportion of total credit short-term credit increased from 43.3 to 45.2 per cent, while term credit decreased from 56.7 to 54.8 per cent (Table 17.12).

Within five years of reform ushered in the banking system, in 1973-74, the cooperative credit sector had suffered a setback, about 20 per cent in measurement. In the cooperative credit sector CCBs controlled

43 per cent of total credit, short-term and medium-term, while the PACS handled 57 per cent of it (Table 17.13).

TABLE 17.12 : Disbursement of Institutional Credit in Bihar

(Rs. crores)

Year	*Total Loans*	*Short-Term*	*(3) as Per-centaged or (2)*	*Term loans Medium-cum-Long-Term*	*(5) as Per-centage of (2)*	*(5) as Per-centage of (3)*
(1)	(2)	(3)	(4)	(5)	(6)	(7)
1974-75	3.28	1.42	43.29	1.86	56.71	131
1975-76	4.77	2.22	46.54	2.54	53.46	114
1976-77	5.71	2.32	40.63	3.39	59.39	146
1977-78	4.44	2.39	53.82	2.05	46.18	86
1978-79	5.38	2.58	47.95	2.80	53.05	108
1979-80	5.84	2.64	45.20	3.19	54.80	121

TABLE 17.13 : Institutional Credit : Source-wise in Bihar : 1973-74

(Percentage)

Short-Term Credit		*Short-Term & Medium-term*		*Total Institutional Credit*		
Cooperative including LDB	*Scheduled Commercial Bank*	*Coopera-tive*	*Com. Bks*	*Cooperative Through*		*As Percentage of All-India*
				PACs	*CCBs*	
80.4 (1.8)	19.6 (2.1)	6.1	5.1	57.1	42.9	5.6

Note: Figures in brackets are shares in all-India totals.

Between 1973-74 and 1979-80 cooperation suffered a serious decline in its relative share in the country, becoming static in the last three years. Bank credit had ups and downs in its relative position, the decline being persistent in the last three years. In terms of total institutional credit, Bihar's percentage share fell from 5.6 to 3.1 per cent during the period (Table 17.14).

In 1978-79 the PACS credit to farmers in Bihar, having less than one ha. was Rs. 69, having 1 to 2 ha. Rs. 81, having 2 to 4 ha. Rs. 183, having 4 to 8 ha. Rs. 225, and having above 8 ha. Rs. 238 per ha. credit diminished as size of holding rose, though a larger size holding was paid more credit in absolute terms.

In 1979-80, farmholders having 2 to 4 ha. formed 28 per cent of all borrowers in Bihar and received 34.5 (maximum) per cent of total disbursement (Table 17.15). Farmholders of 0 to 4 ha. constituted 72 per cent of all borrowers but were recipients of 57 per cent of all disbursement; the remaining 28 per cent got 43 per cent—this was inequitous, but the state of affairs had naturally improved in a decade.

TABLE 17.14 : Bihar's Relative Shares in all-India Loans (Medium-term and Long-term)

Year	*Cooperative (including LDB)*	*Sch. Com. Bks.*	*Total Institutional Credit*
1973-74	6.1	5.1	5.6
1974-75	5.0	3.3	4.5
1975-76	6.3	4.1	5.5
1976-77	4.7	5.6	5.1
1977-78	2.1	4.9	3.3
1978-79	2.1	4.8	3.4
1979-80	2.1	4.3	3.1

TABLE 17.15 : Rural Credit at Primary Level of Cooperation in Bihar : 1979-80

Holdings according to Size-class (ha.)	*Number of Borrowers ('000s)*	*Percentage of Borrowers*	*Amount Borrowed ('000s)*	*As Percentage of Total*
Upto 1	249	15	17174	6.9
1—2	482	29	38956	15.6
2—4	465	28	85214	34.5
4—8	282	17	63302	25.4
Above 8	184	11	43825	17.6
Total	1661	100	248471	100.0

From the cooperative sector to the scheduled commercial banks sector, time-frame mid-1969 onwards, we find the nationalisation of 14 scheduled commercial banks in 1969 gave an impetus to agricultural credit (part of the priority sector in rural areas) with these banks opening more and more branches in rural areas and expanding their deposit-advance business there, of course, against the background of added significance to advances, which, when plotted on graph paper, show a continuously rising curve. It is chiefly the bank sector which has specialised in long-term credit to the agriculturists for purchase of tractors, agricultural implements and machinery, minor irrigation—items which have accounted for the bulk of the bank loans disbursed. With the banks penetrating agriculture financially, focussing on long-term finance, the cooperative sector has centred its effort on meeting the short-term and medium-term needs of its members. both sectors have vied with each other for rural deposits, and gradually the bank sector has achieved an increasing business, which has meant an inroad into the business so far monopolised by the cooperative sector, though an expanding rural economy has partly neutralised the brunt of this encroachment.

In June 1969 the banks had 29 branch offices in rural areas 10.6 per cent of all their offices in Bihar (2.01 per cent of all-India rural offices). In 1970 the rural branches numbered 123, population per branch being 412 thousands (all-India average 116 thousand), 30.8 per cent of all branches in the State.

In June 1969 rural deposits of banks totalled Rs. 468 lakhs (2.47 per cent of all deposits in Bihar, and rural advances Rs. 431 lakhs (2.48 per cent of all advances in the State). The C-D ratio was 91.2 (for the State as a whole 36.9). Direct bank credit to farmers was 0.93 crore (0.80 per cent of the State-wide direct credit) in 1969 and 3.36 crores (1.39 per cent of the State-level direct credit) in 1970. As total of advances to the priority sector public sector bank advances in June 1969 amounted to 9.6 per cent.

Table 17.16 provides information on disbursement of short-term, medium-term and long-term loans (the latter two being term loans) to agriculture in Bihar during 1974-75 to 1979-80. During this period short-term disbursement rose by 458 per cent, while medium-term and long-term disbursements by 513 per cent. The old rubicon had been crossed. A thrust was dealt to the emergent sector. As percentage of total bank credit disbursement, term credit disbursement had increased from 316. to 354 per cent. As proportion of all-India term credit disbursement by banks, term bank credit disbursement in Bihar comprised 3.3 per cent in 1974-75, which rose to 4.3 per cent in 1979-80.

First of all, in 1968-69 the State Bank of India (SBI) decided to provide direct finance to agriculturists and to give them assistance indirectly. Crop loans were granted to agriculturists to enable them to meet their working capital requirements, including costs of seeds, fertilisers, insecticides, etc., and payment of wages, etc. These loans were expected to be repaid in about two months after harvesting of the crop. In 1973-74 total crop loans given in Bihar were 2.7 per cent of the all-India total. In consumption of fertilisers in that year Bihar's share was 3.4 per cent. This was proof of underdisbursement to Bihar. 1979-80 short-term advances made for seasonal agricultural operations aggregated to Rs. 2074.14 lakhs (1.69 per cent of all-India). Of this,

Rs. 1078 lakhs was for paddy (52 per cent), Rs. 533.17 lakhs for wheat (25.70 per cent), and Rs. 270.96 lakhs for sugarcane (13.06 per cent).

TABLE 17.16 : Disbursement of Credit by Commercial Banks in Bihar

(Rs. crores)

Year	*Short-term Loans*	*Term Loans Medium and Long-term*	*(3) as percentage of All-India*	*(3) as percentage of (2)*
(1)	(2)	(3)	(4)	(5)
1974-75	1.2	3.8	3.3	316
1975-76	4.3	5.2	4.1	121
1976-77	5.4	13.7	5.6	253
1977-78	6.1	11.9	4.9	195
1978-79	4.9	18.9	4.8	385
1979-80	5.5	19.5	4.3	354

Since 1969 the SBI has advanced medium-term loans to farmers for purchase of agricultural machinery, levelling of land, provision of irrigation facilities, construction of godowns, etc. These loans are to be repaid in 5 to 10 years. Direct finance is granted for plantation, horticulture, transportation of agricultural produce, construction and management of special farming activities, such as poultry, fishery, dairy, piggery, etc. Agriculturists are indirectly financed in stocking agricultural implements or similar other purposes that help in achieving agricultural growth through cooperative societies, cooperative banks, etc.

To conclude, the 1970s witnessed expansion of institutional credit at a steady rate. The institutional agencies took into account actual requirements of the borrowers, expected crop yields and repaying capacity. With increasing supply of working capital and assurance of a reasonable price for the produce risk-bearing by the farmer had increased. The net inflow of commercial bank credit in Bihar's rural sector was to the extent of Rs. 2.08 crores in 1977-78. Three years prior to 1977-78 there was an outflow of Rs. 2.21 crores through commercial banks from rural households. Net flow of cooperative finance into agricultural households of Bihar which had been Rs. 0.18 crore in 1961-62 increased to Rs. 8.70 crores in 1971-72 and Rs. 12.28 crores in 1977-78.

Around 1973 a farmer in Bihar with a family of five members was economically viable if he had one ha. of irrigated land and resorted to multiple-cropping and used the HYVs, and was assisted by the

Government financially and technically, with an annual earning of Rs. 3,000.

Modern Period : 1980-81 Onwards

In 1981-82, according to a RBI study, in Bihar 62.8 per cent of all rural households reported capital expenditure, which amounted to Rs. 348 per such rural household. Only 0.4 per cent of rural households reporting capital expenditure reported borrowings.

Compared to the 1971 position, the 1981 position with respect to indebted rural households percentage in Bihar was certainly superior, the percentage had come down from 38.4 to 12.2, and debt per indebted rural household had declined from Rs. 288 to Rs. 202. The ratio of debt to land asset too had fallen from 3 (per cent) to 1 (per cent). The data remained the same : the RBI survey (Table 17.17) is illustrative of this.

TABLE 17.17 : Rural Indebtedness : 1981 (at its beginning)

Item	*Bihar*	*All-India*
Percentage of indebted rural households	12.2	19.4
Average debt (Rs.)	202	653
Average assets (value in Rs.)	32347	36090
Percentage share of land in assets	65.6	62.1
Debt to Land Assets Ratio (per cent)	1.0	2.9

Authors like Azit Mazoomdar still report heavy indebtedness of the rural households in Bihar to the traditional sources at high rates of interest. Over 30 per cent of agricultural labourers are bonded as a result of their indebtedness to their masters. This is one reason for social tension in the farmer-moneylender-trader-agricultural labourer nexus, and in the tribal areas for the anti-moneylending agrarian struggle.

We are here concerned with a period which has seen the maximum growth of institutions entrusted with the task of meeting the credit needs of the agriculturists, forming the crest of a sector designated as the primary sector. The institutional credit structure for agriculture consists of cooperatives, scheduled commercial banks (hereinafter written as SCBs) and regional rural banks (hereinafter written as RRBs). Direct institutional loans are issued for agriculture by cooperatives, the State

Government, SCBs and RRBs. Direct short-term loans are disbursed by the PACS including LAMPs (large-sized Adivasi multi-purpose societies) and FSSs (Farmers's Service Societies). Direct medium-term and long-term loans are issued by the PACS and CLDBs (Central Land Development Banks). Cooperative loans are direct; whereas RRBs and SCBs loans are indirect.

The position of co-operation in Bihar (*vis-a-vis* India) was as follows : Percentage share in total number of Cooperative Credit Societies in June 1980 5.43 per cent; percentage share in total number of members of Cooperative Credit Societies in June 1980 6.26 per cent; percentage in all-India investment in cooperative institutions at the end of 1983-84 3.99 per cent; percentage share in all-India cooperative overdues in June 1980 3.44 per cent; percentage share in total employment in Cooperative Credit Societies in June 1980 0.63 per cent; percentage share in total loans issued by Cooperative Credit Societies in 1981-82 1.24 per cent; and value of agricultural produce marketed by cooperatives per ha. in 1982-83 Rs. 38.34 (Rs. 131.13).

Upto 1984-85 in Bihar the number of rural families brought under the cooperative fold was 59 lakhs. This was 54 per cent of the total number of rural families. In 1985 average number of members per cooperative society in Bihar was 106 (all-India 412).

In 1983 the cooperative credit structure in Bihar was composed of the State Cooperative Bank at the apex level, 34 Central Cooperative Banks at the district level, 6182 PACS, 101 FSS and 474 LAMPs.

In 1982-83 the amount of short-term loans advanced per hectare by the cooperative credit structure in Bihar was Rs. 25.8 (all-India Rs. 113.2), which the cooperative support to agriculture was of the order of Rs. 85.4 (all-India Rs. 47.0).

In 1989-90 cooperative societies of all types were over 2.5 thousand in number, 0.16 per cent of all-India 1.17 thousand (0.22 per cent of all-India) credit and 1.4 thousand non-credit (0.13 per cent of all-India).

Membership in 1989-90 exceeded 80 lakhs, 6.4 lakh (80 per cent) in credit and 16 lakh (20 per cent) in non-credit societies. Paid-up share capital exceeded Rs. 112,100 lakhs and working capital Rs. 101,900 lakhs.

Total cooperative credit advanced in 1989-90 in Bihar was Rs. 365 crores (6.63 per cent of all-India)—Rs. 275 crores short-term (6.51 per cent of all-India), Rs. 50 crores medium-term (12.04 per cent of all-India) and Rs. 40 crores long-term (37.73 per cent of all-India). Short-term credit in Bihar was nearly 75 per cent of total cooperative credit, term credit being about 25 per cent.

Term cooperative credit in Bihar as percentage of total all-India term cooperative credit was 2.7 per cent in 1980-81 and 2.3 per cent in 1984-85. In 1981-82 it had been 4.6 per cent. The decline was to the disadvantage of Bihar.

Short-term credit for kharif and rabi seasons is provided to the farmers at a low rate of interest by the cooperative societies, whereas long-term credit is provided by the land development banks—the former being under the jurisdiction of the Bihar State Cooperative Bank and the latter under that of the Bihar State Cooperative Land Development Bank Ltd. Processing and marketing of agricultural produce and inputs comes under the ambit of the BISCOMAUN.

The PACS constituted the backbone of the cooperative credit structure. Besides credit, they have distributed agricultural prerequisites to their members, even consumer goods. In 1980 they numbered about 6.60 lakhs; in 1983-84, 6.75 lakhs (2.06 per cent of all-India number); and in 1990-91, 6.95 lakhs (excluding grain goals, 8.40 per cent of all-India). In 1982-83, 54 per cent of all rural households in Bihar was covered by the PACS.

As for the membership of the PACS, in 1980 it was 46 lakhs, in June 1983, 57.78 lakhs (8.4 per cent of all-India membership), in 1987-88, 60.57 lakhs, and in 1990-91, 61.76 lakhs (7.70 per cent of all-India). As percentage of population, in 1989-90 membership of the PACS was 7.0 per cent (all-India 9.1 per cent). In 1984-85 average number of members per society was 106 (all-India 412) and per thousand of population there were 9 societies.

The total share capital of the PACS in Bihar was Rs. 1325 lakhs, which increased to Rs. 2797 lakhs by 1990-91 (2.28 per cent of all-India). In 1983-84 their reserves totalled Rs. 127 lakhs, which rose to Rs. 420 lakhs in 1990-91 (1.01 per cent of all-India). Their total loans amounted to Rs. 5466 lakhs in 1982-83 (of this Rs. 132 lakhs was from the State Government) and to Rs. 31262 lakhs in 1990-91 (4.01 per cent of all-India). Their total deposits were Rs. 41 lakhs in 1983-84 (0.09 per cent of all-India) and Rs. 163 lakhs in 1990-91 (0.12 per cent of all-India). Their working capital worked out to Rs. 10266 lakhs in 1982-83 and Rs. 31642 lakhs in 1990-91.

Details of credit provided by the PACS are given in Table 17.18. Between 1980-81 and 1992-93 disbursement by the PACS increased by 533 per cent (total credit), by 521 per cent (short-term credit) and by 250 per cent (medium-term credit). Short-term credit, as proportion of total credit purveyed by the PACS, increased from 88 to 94 per cent during the period.

Of total loans advanced to agriculture and activities allied to agriculture in Bihar, loans advanced by the PACS comprised 66 per cent (0.9 per cent of all-India total), 34 per cent coming from other agencies, in 1980-81. In 1984-85, this figure was 61.2 per cent (1.2 per cent of the all-India total), the rest coming from other sources.

TABLE 17.18 : Credit Disbursement by the PACS in Bihar

(Rs. crores)

Year	*Short-term*	*Medium-term*	*Total*	*Short-term Credit as percentage of Total*
1980-81	14.6	2.0	16.6	87.95
1981-82	25.4	2.3	27.7	91.69
1982-83	26.9	2.2	29.1	92.43
1989-90	85.60/245.91 (2.34/6.15)	22.34/50.00 (3.87/12.02)	26.8	91.79
1990-91	36.50 (1.29)	20.00 (5.46)	38.5	94.80
1991-92	86.67 (2.19)	50.00 (12.78)	61.6	91.88
1992-93	83.55 (1.62)	50.00 (27.44)	88.5	94.35

Note : Figures in brackets are percentage shares of Bihar in all-India.

Percentage of borrowing members to total members of the PACS rose from 26.2 in 1976-77 to 39.9 per cent in 1980-81, 48 in 1982-83 and 24.9 per cent in 1987-88, showing a declining trend.

Loans advanced by the PACS amounted to Rs. 150 per borrowing member, which fell to Rs. 77 in 1980-81, rose to Rs. 102 in 1981-82, and to Rs. 104 in 1982-83.

Loans per ha. of GCA amounted to Rs. 24 in 1981-82. According to class-distribution of holdings, size-wise, the picture in 1981-82 was as given in Table 17.19. Maximum credit was enjoyed by the holdings of size 2 to 4 ha. in an absolute sense, but per ha. the maximum amount was enlisted by the holders of land upto one ha. in area (Table 17.19).

TABLE 17.19 : PACS Credit according to Size of Holdings : 1981-82

Size-classification of Holdings (ha.)	*Amount of PACS Credit (Rs.)*	*Amount of PACS Credit Per ha. (Rs.)*
Upto 1	33	66
1—2	47	31
2—4	169	56
4—8	46	8
Above 8	90	9

The PACS advanced Rs. 36.47 crores short-term loans in 1990-91, which was 0.84 per cent of all-India total. 578 thousand borrowers (3.33 per cent of all-India total) benefited. Per borrower credit amounted to Rs. 631. Of the borrowers, about 16 per cent came from the tenant, cultivator and agricultural classes, etc. Per head credit advanced was Rs. 745.

Table 17.20A depicts the state of affairs characterising cooperation in Bihar during 1990-91.

TABLE 17.20A : Cooperation in Bihar : 1990-91

Items		*Number*	
Number of Cooperative Societies :			
Credit		7640 (6.92)	
Non-credit		19917 (10.06)	
Total		27557 (5.40)	
Membership ('000) :			
Credit		7317 (6.38)	
Non-credit		1092 (2.63)	
Total		8409 (5.40)	
Institutional Credit Advanced through Cooperative Banks (Rs. lakh):	*Short-Term*	*Medium- and Long-Term*	*Total*
1992-93	8185 (1.14)	2781 (1.25)	10886 (1.16)
1993-94	5786 (0.07)	850 (0.37)	6636 (0.65)
1994-95	24300 (2.51)	1830 (0.74)	26130 (2.15)
Of which Primary Agricultural Credit Societies (PACS):			
Number		6957 (8.39)	
Membership ('000)		6176 (7.71)	
Share Capital (Rs. lakh)		2797 (2.28)	
Reserves (Ditto)		254 (0.61)	
Deposits (Ditto)		48 (0.03)	
Total Working Capital (Ditto)		5365 (0.45)	
Loans borrowed during the year (Ditto)		3647 (0.77)	

Note : Figures in brackets are percentage shares of Bihar in all-India.

In 1990-91 the position of PACS short-term credit according to the size of holdings was as given in Table 17.20B.

TABLE 17.20B : PACS Short-term Credit to Holders according to Size

Ownership Holdings	*Number of Borrowers ('000s)*	*Amount Advanced*	
		Total (Rs. Lakhs)	*Per Borrower (Rs.)*
Upto 2 ha.	217	1248	575
	(2.51)	(0.83)	(1740)
Above 2 ha.	269	1713	637
	(5.01)	(0.78)	(4053)
All	578	3647	631
	(3.33)	(0.84)	(2485)

Table 17.20B indicates Bihar's relatively adverse position in relation to all-India in percentage shares in number of borrowers, amount advanced and credit per borrower. The holders of lands in size above 2 ha. were in a better condition, when compared with those of lands in size upto 2 ha.

In the three-tier federal structure of cooperation the CCBs (Central Cooperative Banks) occupy the most strategic position and can be rightly described as the kingpin of the structure. They form the link between the PACS and the SCB (State Cooperative Bank)—the PACS are federated into the CCBs, which, in turn, are federated into the BSCB (Bihar State Cooperative Bank). All the PACS and all the CCBs are members of the BSCB Ltd. at Patna.

In 1971 the CCBs were 28 in number in Bihar and had 132 branches. The figures for 1979 were 28 and 226 respectively, and for 1980, 28 and 241 respectively. In 1987-88 the number of CCBs was 34, and in 1990-91, 34 (9.63 per cent of all-India), located in 34 districts.

In 1987-88 the membership of the CCBs was 28718 and in 1990-91, 1929 individuals and 25263 PACS, that is, 27292. In the former year paid-up capital was Rs. 76.74 crores, deposits Rs. 147.88 crores; and in the latter year share capital was Rs. 83.42 crores, reserves Rs. 18.75 crores, and deposits Rs. 242.82 crores. Outside borrowings accounted for Rs. 316.85 crores. Total working capital was Rs. 749.99 crores. Loans issued during the year were Rs. 56.26 crores. In 1990-91 the relative shares of CCBs in all-India were : membership 3.19 per cent, share capital 8.93 per cent, reserves 2.32 per cent, deposits 2.34 per cent, total working capital 4.06 per cent and outside borrowings 5.84 per cent.

The CCBs are sanctioned credit limits flowing from the RBI. On their part they allocate funds received from the SCB among the PACS.

The apex of the cooperative structure in Bihar is the Bihar State Cooperative Bank (BSCB) Ltd., with its Head Office in Patna. In 1993 it had 15 branches in the State. Its membership was 139 (0.12 per cent of all-India). Also, 9 individuals were its members (0.01 per cent of all-India). In 1971 the number of branches was 9. In 1987-88 the membership was 147. Among its members were apex cooperative bodies like the BISCOMAUN, BSC, LDB, Bihar State Consumer Cooperative Federation Ltd., Bihar State Housing Cooperative Federation Ltd., Bihar State Warehousing Corporation Ltd., Bihar State Rural Housing Cooperative Federation Ltd., Bihar Cooperative Federation Ltd., Bihar State Cooperative Sugar Federation Ltd., Bihar State Industrial Cooperative Federation Ltd., and Bihar State Labour Cooperative Federation Ltd. (BS is abbreviation of Bihar State). The jurisdiction of the BSCB Ltd. extends to the whole State.

In 1987-88 the BSCB Ltd.'s paid-up share capital was Rs. 13.34 crores. In 1990-91 too the share capital was the same. In 1987-88 the deposits were Rs. 151.98 crores. In 1990-91 they had gone up to Rs. 210.75 crores. In that year its reserves amounted to Rs. 33.93 crores. Its relative shares in share capital, reserves and deposits in 1990-91 all-India totals were 6.00, 6.68 and 3.14 per cent respectively. Outstanding borrowing amounted to Rs. 57.36 crores, 1.60 per cent of all-India; and total working capital Rs. 582.74, 4.72 per cent of all-India. Loans issued by it came to Rs. 56.36 crores during that year, 0.90 per cent of the all-India figure.

Loan credit to the cooperative sector towards short-term seasonal agricultural operations was furnished by the RBI (Table 17.21 gives the statistics for three years 1979-80 to 1981-82). Development finance is provided to cooperation by the National Cooperative Development Corporation through the BSCB Ltd. The NABARD is another institution which provides financial support to cooperation. We shall presently discuss this.

TABLE 17.21 : Reserve Bank of India Credit

(Rs. crores)

Items	*1979-80*	*1980-81*	*1981-82*
Limit sanctioned	13.20	10.90	14.90 (1.67 per cent of all-India)
Drawals	8.26	5.09	12.31 (0.86 Do)
Repayment	14.98	7.64	7.10 (0.59 Do)
Outstanding	4.43	1.89	7.10 (1.34 Do)

To meet the long-term credit needs of the agriculturists the Bihar Government set up in 1958-59 the Bihar State Land Development Bank

(BSLDB) as part of the cooperative credit structure. It provided credit of duration upto 20 years against the mortgage of their lands by the agriculturists for the loans. In 1983 it had 164 branches in the State. In 1971 the number of branches had been 58. In 1979 it had risen to 130. It had a federal structure, with itself as the Central LDB. There was no primary LDB in Bihar during 1970-80. In 1990-91 too there was no primary LDB. There were 9 member LDBs of the Central LDB. Other than them, there was one bank/society affiliated to the Central LDB. 7 lakh individuals were members of these LDBs. Total share capital was Rs. 31.52 crores (11.24 per cent of all-India). Total reserves equalled Rs. 1.91 crores (0.03 per cent of all-India), and deposits Rs. 11.31 crores (0.28 per cent of all-India). Loans issued during 1980-81 to 1990-91 were as shown in Table 17.22. Due to the improved eligibility of branches after the adoption of a rehabilitation programme lending had picked up from 1980-81 onwards.

TABLE 17.22 : Loans Operation of Land Development Bank (LDB)

(Rs. crores)

Year	*Loans Issued*
1980-81	14.3
1981-82	29.1
1982-83	20.2
1986-87	31.1
1988-89	51.9 (1.93)
1989-90	0.39/2.23 (0.05/0.29)
1990-91	53.8 (6.85)
1991-92	2.49 (0.24)
1992-93	8.67 (0.71)

Note : Figures in brackets are per cent of all-India.

In 1981 per ha. of GCA amount advanced by the LDB was Rs. 63, as against Rs. 93 for all-India. In 1988-89 per borrower the amount loaned was Rs. 9230 (all-India Rs. 1.22 lakhs). Upto 2 ha. landholdings the amount per borrower was Rs. 8564. Above 2 ha. landholdings loan per borrower was Rs. 14732. Total number of borrowers was 56237, of which 89 per cent were in the first category and 11 per cent in the second category.

Commercial Bank Credit

In 1983 there were in rural areas of Bihar 2217 branches of commercial banks, 72 per cent of total number of their branches in rural, semi-urban and urban areas. This worked out to 9.8 per cent of all-India. Rural population covered per branch was around 29,000, as compared to 24,000 in all-India. In 1988 rural branches of scheduled commercial banks claimed 73.6 per cent of all, the all-India figure being 55.2 per cent. In 1993-94 their branches in rural areas were 75.5 per cent of all, as against 57.6 per cent in all-India. During 1983-93 the growth rate of rural branches of commercial banks was 17.5 per cent in Bihar, as against 15.7 per cen in all-India. In March 1994, the number of branches had risen to 3710, 75 per cent of total number of branches.

In 1983 total rural deposits in the rural branches of scheduled commercial banks in Bihar was 24.8 per cent of all deposits (all-India 14.6 per cent). In 1993 the figure was 31.7 per cent in Bihar (all-India 14.8 per cent). In March 1994 total deposits amounted to Rs. 4048.25 lakhs, 32.37 per cent of total deposits. The SBI branches contributed Rs. 1043.36 lakhs, 25.77 per cent. The growth rate of deposits during 1988-93 was 140.9 per cent, as against 134.0 per cent for all-India.

In 1980-81 bank advances to agriculture in Bihar totalled Rs. 20.37 crores—Rs. 5.67 crores short-term and Rs. 14.70 crores medium-term and long-term. They formed 25.7 per cent of total bank advances. In 1979-80 they were Rs. 25.32 crores—Rs. 5.49 crores short-term and Rs. 19.83 crores medium- and long-term. In December 1981 bank credit in Bihar agriculture was about 5 per cent of total bank credit to agriculture in India. This was 29.4 per cent of all bank credit in Bihar in 1984-85. As percentage of all-India bank credit to agriculture, it was 3.1 per cent. In March 1992, bank credit to agriculture and allied activities was Rs. 83.2 crores (4.78 per cent of all-India). As proportion to total bank credit in Bihar this came to 23.62 per cent (all-India figure being 12.59 per cent). In March 1994, rural bank credit came to Rs. 1915.45 crores, 42.24 per cent of total bank credit.

The priority sector bank advances in Bihar, as percentage of the national figure, were 9.6 per cent in June 1969, which rose to 56.7 per cent of total bank credit in Bihar by December 1983. In March 1990 this had further increased to 63.10 per cent, in March 1991 to 60.82 per cent, and in March 1992 to 61.22 per cent, as against the all-India averages of 37.70, 34.56 and 34.24 per cent respectively.

Total rural bank credit in Bihar as percentage of total bank credit for the combined rural, semi-urban and urban sectors was 35.4 per cent in 1988 (all-India 15.0 per cent). By 1993 this had escalated to 41.5 per cent in Bihar (all-India 14.10 per cent).

Percentage share of bank term credit (medium-term and long-term), credit from the RRBs included, in Bihar to the national figure was 3.7

per cent in 1980-81, 4.5 per cent in 1981-82, 5.7 per cent in 1982-83, 4.1 per cent in 1983-84 and 5.7 per cent in 1984-85.

Growth rate of rural bank credit in Bihar during 1988-93 was 118.9 per cent (all-India 106.7 per cent).

The data adduced above are arranged in Table 17.23.

Table 17.23 portrays how between 1969 and 1994 the number of rural branches of banks increased 128 times, rural deposits of banks 8.65 times and rural advances by banks 444 times. During the same period scheduled commercial banks had their percentage share in total rural bank deposits increased from 2.58 to 32.3 per cent, and their advances in rural areas increased from 8.2 to 48.1 per cent.

Between 1969 and 1983 percentage of rural families in Bihar which received loans was 25. Percentage of total loans which went to the weaker sections was 40 (total loan disbursement on 31 March 1984 was Rs. 171.73 crores, of which 50.7 per cent was short-term, 6.5 per cent medium-term and 42.8 per cent long-term).

In December 1981 the number of borrowers' accounts in scheduled commercial banks in the names of persons occupied in agriculture in Bihar was 575900 (5.52 per cent of all-India and 72.83 per cent of all bank borrowers' accounts in the State).

The rural C-D ratio which was 54.9 in 1988 (all-India 64.4 per cent) was 50.9 per cent in 1993 in Bihar (all-India 56.9 per cent).

Table 17.24 would show that there was under way a positive scheme to reduce the degree of inequality in the allocation of bank credit. In 1979-80, 5.9 per cent account holders managed to obtain 33.2 per cent bank credit (all types), while 94.1 account holders had to content themselves with 66.8 per cent bank credit—the ratio being 0.17 and 1.40 respectively in the following year. 5.4 per cent account holders obtained 25.4 per cent bank credit, while 94.6 per cent account holders obtained 74.6 per cent of it—the ratio being 0.21 and 1.26 respectively. The relatively more favoured class had in it those who had holdings above 4 ha. Those in the previous three classes were collectively provided bank credit in a lower percentage. Put in an alternative fashion, in 1979-80 the holders with land above 4 ha. got bank credit 8.23 times more than the three classes combined get; in 1980-81, they got 6.03 times more. The imbalance was getting corrected. Moreover, per account holder the average bank credit in the fourth class (Rs. 32821) was 2.7 times more than the sumtotal of bank credit in the first three classes (Rs. 11849) in 1979-80. In 1980-81 it was 1.59 times more (Rs. 24145 *versus* Rs. 15163). A brake over the disparity was being exercised. Lastly, the average bank credit received by the first two classes was

TABLE 17.23 : Progress of Rural Banking and Credit in Bihar

Characteristics	*1969 June*	*1970 Dec.*	*1979-80*	*1980-81*	*1981 Dec.*	*1981-82*	*1982 March*	*1982 June*	*1982 Sept.*	*1982-83*	*1983 Dec.*	*1983-84*	*1984-85*
(1)	(2)	(3)	(4)	(5)	(6)	(7)	(8)	(9)	(10)	(11)	(12)	(13)	(14)
1. Number of rural branches of sch. com. banks	29 (1443)										22618		
2. SBI's share in (1)													
3. (1) as percentage of total branches in the state											72		
4. (1) as percentage of total in the country													
5. Number of bank branches per 1 lakh of rural population	0.1 (0.4) (Sept. 1968)								3.2 (3.8) (Offices)				3.5 (4.5) (June 1984)
6. Number of bank branches per 1000 km. of rural areas													
7. Rural population per branch											29000 (24000)		
8. Rural deposits of all banks (Rs. Lakh)	468				38487				47248				
9. Deposits of Nationalised Com. Banks in (8) (Rs. Lakhs)													
10. Percentage of SBI in (8)									31.67				
11. (8) as percentage of total bank deposits in the State	2.58										24.8		
12. Percentage share of Nationalised Com. Banks									52.4				
13. (8) as percentage of all-India											1.46		

(*Contd.*)

TABLE 17.23 (*Contd.*)

(1)	(2)	(3)	(4)	(5)	(6)	(7)	(8)	(9)	(10)	(11)	(12)	(13)	(14)
14. Rural credit/ advances by all banks (Rs. lakhs)	431			17475				22538					
15. Amount advanced by nationalised com. banks (Rs. lakhs)			25.32	20.37					8195				
16. Percentage of SBI in (14)									41.0				
17. (14) as percentage of total bank credit in the State				25.7	29.4				92.46				
18. (15) as percentage of (14)									36.36				
19. (14) as percentage of all-India					5.0								3.1
20. Term bank credit to rural sector (Rs. crores)			25.32	20.37									
21. Short-term component (Rs. crores)			5.49	5.67									
22. Medium- and Long-term component (Rs. crores)			19.83	14.70	14.70								
23. (20) as percentage of all-India				3.7		4.5				5.7			15.7
24. Priority sector bank credit as percentage of total bank credit in the State	9.1 (14.9)			57.0 (35.3)							56.7		
25. Percentage share of (24) in all-India	9.9												
26. Growth Rate													
27. Per capita rural deposits (Rs.)		41							70 (123)				
28. Per capita rural credit (Rs.)								34 (72)					
29. Per hectare credit support by all agencies (Rs.)													

(*Contd.*)

TABLE 17.23 (*Contd.*)

Characteristics	*1985-86 Sept.*	*1986 Dec.*	*1987*	*1988*	*1988-93 Dec.*	*1989 March*	*1990 March*	*1991 March*	*1992 March*	*1993*	*1993-94 March*	*1994*
(1)	(15)	(16)	(17)	(18)	(19)	(20)	(21)	(22)	(23)	(24)	(25)	(26)
1. Number of rural branches of sch. com. banks		3181				3388						37.1
2. SBI's share in (1)						58.5						14.6
3. (1) as percentage of total branches in the state		75.1				65.7					75.5	75.5
4. (1) as percentage of total in the country		9.8		5.5							5.7	7.5
5. Number of bank branches per 1 lakh of rural population			5					5				
6. Number of bank branches per 1000 km. of rural areas			18					22				
7. Rural population per branch												
8. Rural deposits of all banks (Rs. Lakh)		1037.59				2133.67						4048.25
9. Deposits of Nationalised Com. Banks in (8) (Rs. Lakhs)		594.61										2218.17
10. Percentage of SBI in (8)		26.32										25.7
11. (8) as percentage of total bank deposits in the State		24.02				27.7					31.7	32.3
12. Percentage share of Nationalised Com. Banks		23.30										54.8
13. (8) as percentage of all-India												

(*Contd.*)

TABLE 17.23 (*Conctd.*)

(1)	(15)	(16)	(17)	(18)	(19)	(20)	(21)	(22)	(23)	(24)	(25)	(26)
14. Rural credit/ advances by all banks (Rs. lakhs)		540.93				1159.73						1915.45
15. Amount advanced by nationalised com. banks (Rs. lakhs)		222.38				528.28						922.30
16. Percentage of SBI in (14)		147.94				26.5						27.8
17. (14) as percentage of total bank credit in the State		32.30		35.4		38.1/42.2			23.6 (12.6			42.2
18. (15) as percentage of (14)		41.11				45.5						48.1
19. (14) as percentage of all-India				1.5								
20. Term bank credit to rural sector (Rs. crores)												
21. Short-term component (Rs. crores)												
22. Medium- and Long-term component (Rs. crores)												
23. (20) as percentage of all-India												
24. Priority sector bank credit as percentage of total bank credit in the State							63.1/63.7 (37.7/40.4)	60.8	61.2 (34.2)	61.1 (33.9)		
25. Percentage share of (24) in all-India												
26. Growth Rate												
(1)				17.5 (15.7)								
(8)				140.9 (134.0)								
(14)				118.9 (106.7)								
27. Per capita rural deposits (Rs.)												
28. Per capita rural credit (Rs.)												
29. Per hectare credit support by all agencies (Rs.)	59											

Note : In March 1994, 48 per cent of all rural bank branches were in Bihar, with a total deposit of Rs. 1099 crore, outstanding credit of Rs. 557crore and a C-D ratio of 51 per cent.

TABLE 17.24 : Direct Finance to Agriculturists in Bihar advanced by Scheduled Commercial Banks

Size-class of Holdings (Ha.)	Number of Accounts		As Percentage of Total Accounts		Amount (Rs. Lakhs)		As Percentage of Total Amount		Amount Per Account (Rs.)				Total (Rs.)	
									1979-80		1980-81		(10) + (11)	(12)+ (13)
	1979-80	1980-81	1979-80	1980-81	1979-80	1980-81	1979-80	1980-81	ST	MT & LT	ST	MT & LT		
(1)	(2)	(3)	(4)	(5)	(6)	(7)	(8)	(9)	(10)	(11)	(12)	(13)	(14)	(15)
Upto 1	49154	39902	47.9	49.0	554	616	22.1	30.2	494	2066	795	2501	2560	3296
1 to 2	33865	26246	33.0	32.2	651	580	26.0	28.4	1085	2742	1244	3715	3827	4959
2 to 4	13636	10967	13.2	13.4	344	323	13.7	15.8	1556	3906	1776	5132	5462	6908
Above 4	5663	4168	5.9	5.4	953	518	33.2	25.4	3151	29670	2975	21570	32821	24145
All Holdings	102618	81313	100.0	100.0	2502	2037	100.0	100.0	959	4360	1191	4360	5319	5551

Note : Number of Accounts as well as Amount of Direct Finance advanced is the sumtotal of short-term and term (medium-term and long-term) accounts loans. The ratio between short-term and term advances was as under :

Size-Class of Holdings (ha.)	*Ratio*	
	1979-80	*1980-81*
Class I	0.35	0.40
Class II	0.38	0.52
Class III	0.57	0.64
Class IV	0.11	0.13
All classes	0.27	0.38

lower than the overall average, whereas that received by the last two classes of holders was higher in both years but the inequality for which the system was blamed was being lowered. In 1979-80 the average per account holder was Rs. 5319; in 1980-81 it had risen to Rs. 5551—more bank credit was being pumped into the rural economy.

By interpreting the data contained in columns (12) to (15) of Table 17.24, we can discover as to what is happening to investment in agriculture. Term loans are meant for the investment purpose. Table 17.25 brings out that only the last class of landholders (those with land above 4 ha.) invested more than the average percentage; all the three classes with land below 4 ha. invested below the average percentage. That even the landholders with land upto 1 ha. invested, and invested proportionally more than the next two classes of landholders, provided they got bank credit, is a finding of immense significance, for it refutes the accusation made hitherto that they were desirous of the modern technology. Another notable finding is that the investment in agriculture is open to fluctuations even yearly, depending upon a host of factors, natural playing a key part, and the lag which arises between investments is of a longer duration than common in the manufacturing business. The rigid factors in agriculture outnumber those in industry.

TABLE 17.25 : Investment in Agriculture in Bihar

Size-class of Holdings	*Investment (Term Loans as Percentage of Total Loans)*	
	1979-80	*1980-81*
Upto 1 ha.	80.7	76.0
1 to 2 ha.	71.6	74.9
2 to 4 ha.	71.5	74.3
Above 4 ha.	90.4	89.3
All Holdings	81.9	78.5

Note : This table ought to be interpreted in relation to the figures given in the footnote to Table 17.24.

That the smallest landholders take term loans for investment in a proportion higher than all other landholders, except those with lands above 5 ha. in area, who invest in the highest percentage, would be clear from Table 17.26, which is for the year 1980-81. From this table also would be evident the fact that the working capital requirements, met by short-term bank loans, are in proportion above the investment made in the case of all classes, except that of the largest landholders, in whose case the converse holds good.

In 1980-81 bank credit per borrower as advanced by the commercial banks was Rs. 1191 (this is much lower than that given above) in Bihar. Only those with lands less than one ha. were given bank credit per borrower less than this average, and the maximum went to the landholders with lands above 4 ha. (Table 17.27). In 1980-81 borrowers of short-term loans from commercial banks as percentage of borrowers of short-term loans from the PACS were 2.2 per cent. On the other hand, borrowers of term loans from commercial banks as percentage of total number of landholders were 0.30 per cent.

TABLE 17.26 : Direct Advances to Agriculture in Bihar by Scheduled Commercial Banks in 1980-81

(As percentage of total)

Size-class of Holdings	*Short-term Loans*	*Term Loans (Medium & Long-term)*
1 ha. and less	31.4	29.8
1 to 2 ha.	35.2	25.9
2 to 5 ha.	22.4	13.3
5 ha. and above	11.0	31.0
	100.0	100.0

TABLE 17.27 : Credit Advanced by Commercial Banks in Bihar

(Rs.)

Size-Distribution of Holdings (ha.)	*1980-81*	*1983-84*
Upto 1	795	—
1 to 2	1245	—
Upto 2.5	—	1023
2 to 4	1777	—
2.5 to 5	—	886
Above 4	2975	—
Above 5	—	1482
Average Per borrower	1191	1035

In 1981 the loan advanced per ha. of GCA by the scheduled commercial banks was Rs. 155 (all-India Rs. 240).

In 1983-84 the amount of bank credit advanced by commercial banks per borrower had fallen to Rs. 1035 from Rs. 1191 in 1980-81 (Table 17.28). The landholders with lands above 5 ha. in area obtained bank credit which was both in excess of the average and the highest among all other landholders.

TABLE 17.28 : Short-term Direct Finance Advanced to Farmers by Scheduled Commercial Banks in Bihar : As on last Friday of June 1991

(Number of accounts in '000s and Amount of credit in Rs. Crores)

Characters	*Upto 1.01 ha.*	*1.01 to 2.02 ha.*	*Above 2.02 ha.*	*Total*
Number of Accounts	20.9	19.6	9.9	50.3
As percentage of total number of accounts	41.5	39.0	19.5	100.0
Amount of S.T. Bank credit	7.5	8.2	6.9	22.6
As percentage of total ST Bank credit amount	33.1	36.2	30.7	100.0
Bihar's share in All-India :				
Accounts	3.75	2.06	1.54	1.61
Amount	0.98	1.31	1.04	1.10
ST Bank Credit per Borrower (Rs.)	35.88	41.83	69.69	44.93

In so far as different sources give different figures for one and the same economic subject great confusion prevails. An instance readily available is furnished by the data on short-term bank credit advanced to agriculturists for the year 1980-81. The confusion is further confounded when we try to correlate data on a subject over a period of years. Here, we are concerned with short-term bank credit advanced to agriculturists in 1980-81, as compared with that in June 1991. For the year 1980-81 the figures were : Rs. 795 for holders with lands upto 1 ha., Rs. 1244 for those in size-class upto 2 ha., Rs. 1777 for those in size-class 2 to 4 ha. and Rs. 2975 for those in size-class above 4 ha. For 1991 these figures were : Rs. 35.88 for size-class upto 1 ha., Rs. 41.83 of size-class upto 2 ha. and Rs. 69.69 for all the rest, average for all holdings being Rs. 44.93. These figures are very low, and reconciling them with the very high figures for 1980-81 seems an uphill, if not, an impossible task.

The above apart, the thesis that there is concentration of bank credit in the highest landholdings cannot be denied, and is borne out by a look at Table 17.28 as well. 9.9 per cent of account holders in size-classes above 2.02 ha. had got 30.7 per cent of short-term bank credit (ratio being 3.10), whereas 90.1 per cent of account holders had 69.3 per cent short-term bank credit (ratio being 0.77). Ratio of Bihar's share in accounts vis-a-vis its share in amount of bank credit was 0.26 for size-class upto 1.01 ha., 0.63 for that upto 2.02 ha. and 0.67 for that above 2.02 ha. average ratio being 0.68.

Regional Rural Bank Credit

Regional Rural Banks (RRBs) were introduced in 1995 throughout the country with one nationalised bank opening two offices/branches in rural areas of two districts in Bihar. In conception, the RRBs aimed at supplementing rural credit provided by cooperative societies and commercial banks in rural areas, particularly to the weaker sections of the community; they were to combine the rural culture property of the cooperative system with the urban work style property of the commercial banking system; they were to be established in rural areas that were totally unbanked; they were to serve the poor people as if they were their own bank by paying specific attention to their credit needs; even amongst the rural poor their target groups were defined; they were to play their part in promoting bank-led rural growth, so to say; they were to become an apparatus of income distribution in rural areas; and so on.

As Table 17.29 would narrate, of course, statistically that in the first year of the birth of the RRBs Bihar had the credit of enlisting 15.38 per cent of all their branches in the whole country, their number rising to 622 in 1980 (19.26 per cent of all-India total), to 1892 in 1992 (13.04 per cent of all-India total)—a retrogression in percentage terms.

As for deposits, between 1982 and 1994 they increased over 16 times; and credit advanced about 11 times during the same period.

The RRBs' percentage share in all branches of all types of banks in the State reached its peak, 39.64 per cent, in 1989, which suffered a decline, the percentage falling to 35.56 per cent in 1994.

In mobilising rural deposits the RRBs through their rural branches managed in 1992, 69.23 per cent of their aggregate resource-mobilisation through all their branches, which increased to 77.28 per cent in 1994. As their relative share in all deposits by all types of banks in Bihar, the RRBs claimed 3.93 per cent in 1986, which rose to 6.26 per cent in 1994.

Credit advances attained their height in the case of the RRBs in 1987, 89.12 per cent of their total credit advances in the State as a whole, in all its areas. In 1982 this had been 87.90 per cent. But their contribution in this respect took a poor turn in the beginning of the 1990s, as evidenced by the figures for 1992 and 1994. So far as the relative share of the RRBs in total rural credit advanced by all types of banks in the State is concerned, the maximum was reached in 1983, whereafter a decline appears to have set in the trend. In 1994 this percentage was 12.28 only.

TABLE 17.29 : Progress of Regional Rural Banks (RRBs) in Bihar

Characteristics	*1975*	*1980 Dec.*	*1980-81*	*1982 Sept.*	*1983 June*	*1984-85*	*1986 Sept.*
(1)	(2)	(3)	(4)	(5)	(6)	(7)	(8)
1. Number of Banks	1 (6)	14 (85)			17 (150)		
2. Number of their offices/branches	2 (13)	622 (3229)			1298 (7795)		1663 (1775)
3. Number of districts covered	2 (11)	22 (144)			27 (265)		
4. Deposits (Rs. lakhs)				4818	11073		16981
5. Credit/Advances (Rs. lakhs)				5096			17061
6. (2) as percentage of all offices/ branches of all types of banks in the State							39.30 (only in rural areas)
7. (2) as percentage of all-India total							0.38
8. (4) as percentage of total deposits of RRBs				69.23			72.28
9. (4) as percentage of deposits of all types of banks							3.93
10. (5) as percentage of all advances by RRBs				87.90			88.66
11. (5) as percentage of advances by all types of banks					16.33		10.18
12. Short-term credit advanced by RRBs as percentage of total short-credit to rural sector			8.3			9.4	
13. Long-term credit advanced by RRBs as percentage of total loan-term rural credit			25.7			24.7	
14. (12) as percentage of all-India total			3.2			1.2	
15. (13) as percentage of all-India total						7.3	

(*Contd.*)

TABLE 17.29 (*Contd.*)

Characteristics	*1987 June*	*1987 Sept.*	*1989 Dec.*	*1990 March*	*1992 Sept.*	*1993-94*	*1994 March*
(1)	(9)	(10)	(11)	(12)	(13)	(14)	(15)
1. Number of Banks					22 (196)		22
2. Number of their offices/branches		1665 (1778)	1680 (1824)		1892 (14500)	1892	1746/1885
3. Number of districts covered					47 (397)		(All districts except Dhanbad)
4. Deposits (Rs. lakhs)	24600	25484	38874	58600	78770	101905	78671
5. Credit/Advances (Rs. lakhs)	18600	23273	32418	40600	44880	53138	55948
6. (2) as percentage of all offices/ branches of all types of banks in the State		39.05 (only in rural areas)	39.64				35.56/38.43
7. (2) as percentage of all-India total					13.04		
8. (4) as percentage of total deposits of RRBs		73.70	73.60				77.28
9. (4) as percentage of deposits of all types of banks		4.43	5.05				6.26
10. (5) as percentage of all advances by RRBs		89.12			10.71		10.57
11. (5) as percentage of advances by all types of banks		10.85	10.67				12.28
12. Short-term credit advanced by RRBs as percentage of total short-credit to rural sector							
13. Long-term credit advanced by RRBs as percentage of total loan-term rural credit							
14. (12) as percentage of all-India total							
15. (13) as percentage of all-India total							

What do these facts add up to? The answer is that there has taken place a commendable expansion of the RRBs in Bihar so far as their coverage and operations are concerned. The RRBs have delivered the goods, no doubt, by mobilising rural savings. They have foregathered under their umbrella all the rural folk who have plied tertiary activities and carried on production in their households of a diverse, varied nature. They have enacted an important role in rural lending, covering crop finance, integrated rural development programmes and agriculture and allied activities.

But on the debit side the RRBs have faced problems of recovery of loans. Mounting losses have made them non-viable entities. Their delivery system has been under constant attack. Their management has been ill-equipped with resource-raising capabilities, for example, staff that is suitably trained and motivated, and, in consequence, the transaction cost has been higher than in other areas, and the like. Most of them could not function effectively owing to the resource barrier.

To get over these deficiencies and infirmities it has been suggested that the RRBs should close down their separate identities and merge with the rural branches of their sponsors in order that they improve their viability. Simplification of procedures and a close rapport with the local borrowers are considered the means to that.

The National Bank for taking specialised interest in agricultural development through meeting its financial needs, known as NABARD, came into existence in July 1980 on the national scale. The NABARD extends financial support to a broad spectrum of production activities in the rural sector. It focuses attention on the underbanked States like Bihar, and the less developed areas in Bihar are treated on a priority basis.

The NABARD provides short-term credit (upto 18 months) to Bihar State Cooperative Bank for seasonal agricultural operations, e.g., crop loans, purchase and distribution of fertilisers, working capital requirements of cooperative sugar mills, etc.

The NABARD provides medium-term credit (for 18 months to 7 years) to the RRBs and cooperative societies through the State Cooperative Bank for approved agricultural purposes.

The NABARD provides long-term credit (for a period upto 25 years) to the State Cooperative Bank, Land Development Bank and RRBs for investment in agriculture like minor irrigation, farm mechanisation, land development, plantation, horticulture, fishery, animal husbandry, etc.

Refinance assistance is provided by the NABARD also to the IRDP, a major poverty-alleviation programme, launched on October 2, 1980, and is routed through the scheduled commercial banks, State-level Land Development Bank and RRBs.

Bihar's share in agricultural finance advanced by the NABARD in 1990 was 7 per cent. At the end of March 1990 the NABARD had disbursed Rs. 87 per capita in Bihar, as against Rs. 502 in all-India.

Table 17.30 relates statistically the refinance assistance provided by the NABARD in Bihar in select years. The figures given are cumulative.

TABLE 17.30 : Refinance Disbursed by NABARD in Bihar

(Rs. lakhs)

Purposes	*1977-78*	*1980-81*	*1982-83*
Land-based investments	1159	2236	1604
Others	705	210	3136
Total	1864	2446	4740

In 1991-92 the amount of refinance to Bihar was Rs. 8900 lakhs (4.33 per cent of all-India). In 1992-93 it was Rs. 8700 lakhs (3.68 per cent of all-India). In 1990 the percentage share of Bihar was, as mentioned above, 7 per cent, while in the succeeding two years it was 4.3 and 3.6 respectively, which epitomised a declining trend.

The NABARD oversees the functioning of the cooperative sector. It inspects the working of the CCBs and RRBs.

The lending institutions, whether cooperative or commercial or regional rural or land development, are all beset with the problem of outstanding loans and loans overdue, a problem which has become worse as time has passed, with the overdues mounting (Table 17.31). The outstanding loans of the PACS in Bihar in 1959 amounted to Rs. 61.34 lakhs, which increased to Rs. 13652 lakhs, that is, 222 times, by 1990-91; in the case of the LDBs the increase was from Rs. 6970 lakhs to Rs. 21989 lakhs, i.e., a little over three times between 1982 and 1990-91. In 1983 the outstanding loans of commercial banks in Bihar were about 13 per cent of the national total. In 1992 the outstanding loans of the RRBs formed 11.6 per cent of the all-India total.

The overdue loans of the PACS were Rs. 3747.40 lakhs in 1978-79, which rose to Rs. 5864 lakhs by 1983, that is, by 156 per cent.

Overdue loans as percentage of annual demand increased in the case of the PACS from 56 per cent in 1970-71 to 74.8 per cent in

TABLE 17.31 : Rural Credit Overdues in Bihar

Characteristics	*1959*	*1970-71*	*1974-75*	*1977*	*1978-79*	*1979-80*	*1980*	*1980-81*	*1981*	*1981-82*
(1)	(2)	(3)	(4)	(5)	(6)	(7)	(8)	(9)	(10)	(11)
1. *Loans/Advances outstanding (Rs. lakhs) :*										
A. PACS	61.34				3876.82	2178				
B. BSCB Ltd.										
C. CCBs										
D. LDBs										
E. CBs										
F. RRBs										
G. Total					110559					
2. *Loans Overdue (Rs. Lakhs) :*										
A. PACS						3747.40		3241 (2.94%)		4982 (4.11%)
B. BSCB Ltd.								215 (13.29%)		2176 (12.43%)
C. CCBs								4155 (4.42%)		4642 (4.28%)
D. RRBs										
3. *(2) as percentage of (1) :*										
A. PACS										
B. RRBs										

(*Contd.*)

TABLE 17.31 (*Contd.*)

(1)	(2)	(3)	(4)	(5)	(6)	(7)	(8)	(9)	(10)	(11)
4. *(2) as percentage of demand :*										
A. PACS		56	33.6		59.4	63/76.4		45.5/46.0		66.4
								(41.4)		(43.0)
B. BSCB Ltd.								51.6		48.3
								(9.8)		(10.0)
C. CCBs								60.3		67.4
								(37.0)		(35.3)
D. LDBs (at primary level)								18.9		45.9
E. CBs										60.5
F. RRBs										
5. *Loans recovered as percentage of demand :*										
A. CBs				40.6			53.5			
				(50.0)			(52.0)			
6. *Overdues per ha. of GCA (Rs.) :*										
A. LDBs									63	
B. CBs									232	
7. *Overdues per borrower (Rs.) :*										
A. CBs										

(*Contd.*)

TABLE 17.31 (*Contd.*)

Characteristics	*1982*	*1982-83*	*193*	*1983-84*	*1984-85*	*1986*	*1987-88*	*1990-91*	*1991*	*1992*
(1)	(12)	(13)	(14)	(15)	(16)	(17)	(18)	(19)	(20)	(21)
1. *Loans/Advances outstanding (Rs. lakhs) :*										
A. PACS			6295				12919	13652 (2.10%)		
B. BSCB Ltd.							25785			
C. CCBs							28416	31685 (5.84%)		
D. LDBs	6970					11030		21989 (5.61%)		
E. CBs			8048 (12.9)							
F. RRBs										16660 (11.59%)
G. Total										
2. *Loans Overdue (Rs. Lakhs) :*										
A. PACS		5864 (4.44%)	5864				11920			
B. BSCB Ltd.		3286 (17.97%)								
C. CCBs		5417 (4.39%)								
D. RRBs			1724 (10.8)							

(*Contd.*)

TABLE 17.31 (*Contd.*)

(1)	(12)	(13)	(14)	(15)	(16)	(17)	(18)	(19)	(20)	(21)
3. *(2) as percentage of (1) :*										
A. PACS			93.2				92.3			
B. RRBs			21.4							
			(25.4)							
4. *(2) as percentage of demand :*	(All Types)				ST 67.6					
					Term 60.9					
A. PACS		74.8			63.2					
		(40.9)								
B. BSCB Ltd.		51.4								
		(8.2)								
C. CCBs		80.3								
		(38.5)								
D. LDBs		59.6			44.9					
E. CBs										
F. RRBs										52.6
5. *Loans recovered as percentage of demand :*										
A. CBs	51.5									
	(52.3)									
6. *Overdues per ha. of GCA (Rs.) :*										
A. LDBs						105				
B. CBs						448				
7. *Overdues per borrower (Rs.) :*										
A. CBs	5870					47120		9300		

1982-83. In the latter year the percentage in Bihar was very much higher than that in the country, about 41 per cent. In the case of the CBs the percentage had moved down from 60.5 to 50.0 per cent during 1981-92.

Loans recovered as percentage of demand in respect to the CBs had registered an improvement from 40.6 to 51.6 per cent during 1977-82, which was a better performance in the case of Bihar, compared to all-India where the improvement was by about 2.3 per cent, from 50.0 to 52.3 per cent. In 1982-83 percentage of loan recovery was 37.5, which improved to 41.6 per cent in the following year (1983-84).

Finally, overdues per ha. of GCA of the LDBs had increased from Rs. 63 in 1981 to Rs. 105 in 1987-88, whereas those of the CBS had risen from Rs. 232 to Rs. 448 during the same period.

In 1979-80 ownership holders of the size-group 2 to 4 ha. had the maximum percentage share of outstanding loans, 45.22 per cent, and it was this class which had the minimum percentage of loans overdue. Those with holdings of 4 ha. and above in size had the minimum sum total of loans outstanding, about 9.2 per cent but it was their class that had the highest percentage of, about 66 per cent, loans overdue. The small landholders had nearly 44 per cent of loans outstanding and nearly 30 per cent of loans overdue. In 1990-91 the small landowners and the landless sections had between them around 47 per cent loans outstanding with them, the rest, 53 per cent, lay with those who owned landholdings of size above 2 ha. In 1991 per borrower rural loans outstanding were maximum in the case of landholders with landholdings in excess of 2.02 ha.; they were minimum in the case of landholders of landholdings between 1.01 and 2.02 ha. in area, the class of borrowers with landholdings upto 1.01 ha. had, on an average, a loan which in amount was in between the twin amounts stated above (Table 17.32). The situation facing overdues was better in the case of the CBs, and worse in that of the PACS and the RRBs.

How nagging the issue of overdues has been in Bihar is best illustrated with the State Government's experience with regard to the LDB during 1979-82. In 1979-80 the State Government was called upon to embark upon a rehabilitation programme of the LDB so as to enable it to participate in the fourth ARDC credit project. The Government contributed Rs. 25 crores towards the share capital of LDB and further contributed Rs. 1.2 crores each towards share capital and a short-term loan to the federal units during 1980-81. Overdues arising from natural calamities amounting to Rs. 8.2 crores in 1980-81 and Rs. 5.1 crores in 1981-82 were rephased by the LDB. In addition, the LDB was permitted

TABLE 17.32 : Ownership/Borrowers' Holdings Size-Class-wise Outstanding and Overdue Loans in Bihar

Size-class of Holdings (ha.)	*PACS*			*Scheduled Commercial Banks 1991 June Outstanding Loans*	
	1979-80 (Percentage Distribution)		*1990-91 (Percentage Distribution) Outstanding Loans*	*Amount (Rs.)*	*Percentage Share in All-India*
	Outstanding Loans	*Overdue Loans*			
Ownership/Borrowers'					
Upto 1	14.59	11.99			
Upto 1.01				3050	2.13
1—2	30.00	17.99			
1.01—2.02				2890	2.26
Upto 2			37.7		
Above 2			12.5		
Above 2.02				3360	2.19
2—4	45.22	3.17			
4—8	3.70	34.99			
Above 8	5.49	31.86			
Tenant cultivators, agricultural labourers and others			9.4		

to block overdues over 3 years amounting to Rs. 11.8 crores, subject to a firm commitment from the State Government that it would meet the shortfall in the recoveries upto 20 per cent of the blocked amount every year. An amount of Rs. 6.7 crores in 1980-81 and another of Rs. 4.0 in 1981 was blocked by the LDB. As a result of the aforementioned steps, overdues of the LDB were brought down substantially in 1980-81. However, the overdues issue reappeared in the very next year. And it is still dogging the authorities.

Our outline of progress made by rural finance in the preceding pages had been interspersed with references to the part which the State Government has played in it. This is one aspect of the subject which merits further details. During the Plan period it has been the Government endeavour to increase the number of cooperative societies, to diversify their funds in order that they discharge their functions like supplying inputs and raw materials and making suitable arrangements for the marketing of the agricultural produce, to the satisfaction of the people and the superior authorities, which necessitated that the Government took steps to strengthen their managerial staff by stepping up personnel training, as also to persuade the uneconomic cooperative societies to merge with the viable ones, and so forth.

It was during the First Plan period that the State Government enacted a legislation with a view to revamping the cooperative movement in the State in keeping with the viewpoints expressed by Mahatma Gandhi. What worried the Government most was that the base of the grass-root level PACS was thoroughly weak, for the simple reason that the cooperative structure in the State was primarily constrained by lack of resources, which dissuaded it from underwriting the losses and bad debts of the weak CCBs (through which funds seeped down to the PACS) and to make them viable.

Whether it was mere lip-sympathy or the polemics of politics which caused concern in the minds (not hearts) of the elected leaders holding the reins of the Government in their hands over the failure of the cooperative institutions to cover the small and marginal farmers scattered over the State, many living in the remote and inaccessible rural areas to the extent desirable. This was a sad comment on the delivery system of the cooperative sector. Neither the supply of inputs and credit was adequate nor was if timely, which incapacitated even the advantaged farmers to benefit from the opportunity. The NAT had rendered agriculture more capital-using in the sense of both long-term investment in capacity-building and working capital to meet the current needs of an ever-recurring character. Rising prices of inputs and wages apart, at any time per unit of cultivated land and per unit of agricultural produce capital needed, fixed and working, under the NAT was higher, which was, in itself and by itself, an ostensible factor justifying the increased demand.

We would like to advert here to the turning-point in the Government approach towards the best mechanism to be chosen for making rural development an ongoing process—credit-led rural growth, credit becoming the engine or agent of growth of the rural economy. Suddenly it occurred to our social engineers that the missing component in rural growth was the glaring inadequacy of working capital, in particular, and of real investment, in general. It was also realised by them that in the case of the poor peasants inadequacy of demand for consumption goods during the slack period of agriculture due to non-employment was a dampening influence on the functioning of the rural sector, and working capital in the case of these sections of the rural society signified consumption loans. In this turning-point we had a confluence of the classical and Keynesian ideas on the practical plane.

Initiatives were taken by the State Government for strengthening the cooperative structure and making non-solvent banks viable units. These consisted in a *package deal*—(1) Revitalisation of the PACS, (2) Firming up components and guidelines, (3) Providing administrative support (by the State Government, officialisation of the cooperative system) and financial assistance (by the State Government and the RBI), (4) Expanding and diversifying the loan portfolio, (5) Rationalising the loan policies and procedures, (6) Mobilising resources, (7) Redeploying resources, including manpower, and (8) Reducing management costs.

A fall-out of the above was the advancing of consumption credit to those cultivating land upto 0.20 ha., agricultural labourers and rural artisans—all representing the weaker sections of the rural community, by fortifying the PACS and the LAMPs.

The Fourth Plan saw in Bihar the setting up of the Small Farmers Agency in three districts, namely, Purnea, Patna and Champaran and the Marginal Farmers and Agricultural Labourers Agency in tribal districts and districts inhabited chiefly by the scheduled castes, both aiming at meeting the credit needs of the target groups concerned, a task that had the utmost urgency, considering the fact that these sections were contemplating recourse to the NAT in the hope of producing more and acquiring increased income thereby, a coupling/lumping of the dual goals, but at times they were awed and irked by the thought that were the crop to fail or to fall below the expected amount, the venture would throw them into a bebt trap, a spectre haunting them day and night, which found a belated remedy in the form of the crop insurance scheme introduced in 1985 and limited to Kharif, as implemented by the General Insurance Corporation of India, having a very poor beginning—in 1985-86 area covered was 1.1 lakh ha. and claims paid amounting to Rs. 1.1 lakhs; in 1986-87, area 0.8 lakh ha. and claims not known; and in 1987-88, area 10.6 lakh ha. and claims Rs. 386.7 lakhs. It was during 1992-93 that the scheme was extended to Rabi. Funds were allotted crop-wise. This was not sufficient. Under it area differences were ignored.

Here we must keep in mind the distinction between crop loans advanced by commercial banks and crop insurance. Bihar's share in the former was 1.0 per cent in 1980-81, while its share in fertilisers consumption was 3.7 per cent; in 1984-85 its share in crop loans stagnated at 1.0 per cent, in spite of the increase in its fertilisers consumption to 4.6 per cent. The Centre's step-fatherly/mothsly treatment to Bihar persisted.

In passing, we may point out here that investment in the cooperative institutions in Bihar in June 1984 was estimated at 4.00 per cent of total investment in the country in them.

Bihar's share in institutional term credit (all kinds) of the country, which was 3.3 per cent in 1980-81, rose to 4.6 per cent in 1981-82, fell to 4.2 per cent in 1982-83, further to 3:3 per cent in 1983-84, and again rose to 4.5 per cent in 1984-85.

Plan expenditure during 1969-90 on agriculture and allied activities, rural development, special agricultural programmes and irrigation and flood control in Bihar totalled Rs. 4905 crores, 47.57 per cent (average) of total Plan expenditure in the State during the period (Table 17.33). The ICOR in agriculture and allied activities increased from 1.04 (total economy 3.22) in the Fourth Plan to 2.22 (total economy 4.80) in the Seventh Plan.

The total investment in the rural sector of Bihar during 1969-90 would not have amounted to Rs. 4905.59 crores because part of the expenditure was not on real capital formation. There were also leakages because of the corruption prevalent in the system. Even if 40 per cent of this amount resulted in capital formation the investment must have added up to Rs. 2500 crores.

TABLE 17.33 : Plan Expenditure on Agriculture and Allied Activities and ICOR in them in Bihar

Plan	*Expenditure (Rs. crores)*	*As Percentage of Total Expenditure*	*ICOR*
Fourth (1969-74)	235.15	48.41	1.04 (3.22)
Fifth (1974-78)	409.66	44.78	1.87 (3.23)
Annual (1978-79)	322.30	48.08	—
Sixth (1979-84)	1468.48	47.47	1.67 (4.20)
Seventh (1985-90)	2470.00	48.43	2.22 (4.80)

Note : ICOR in brackets are for Bihar's total economy.

The Upshot

Divergences in the data* on the same item cause trepidation, which stands in the way of highlighting the main points identified in our detailed account of agricultural/rural credit and cooperative movement in Bihar since 1950-51, which incorporates in it discussions of savings and investment in Bihar agriculture during the period. Steering past this obstacle, we would like to underline the following, which are menaced the least by the data disparity : Firstly, in its totality, institutional rural credit increased tremendously (Rs. 615 *versus* Rs. 256723 lakhs) between 1960-61 and 1992-93—cooperative and LDB rural credit 50.1 times (Rs. 184 *versus* Rs. 9230 lakhs), and bank credit (commercial banks and RRBs combined) 574.2 times (Rs. 431 *versus* Rs. 247493 lakhs, Rs. 191545 lakhs of the latter being from commercial banks) during 1969 to 1994. During 1950-51 to 1994 SDP ensuring from the primary sector in Bihar increased approximately 35.65 times (Rs. 43270 *versus* Rs. 1542725 lakhs). On the other hand, in India the quantum of increase in GDP arising from the primary sector was 44-fold approximately during 1950-51 to 1993-94, whereas during 1950-51 to 1992-93 the increase in cooperative sector rural credit (including LDBs) was 884.6 times approx. (from Rs. 2428 lakhs to Rs. 22 thousand lakhs), that in the bank sector (RRBs included) was 11364.4 (from Rs. 59 lakhs to

* In several cases we have the data on cooperative credit mixed up with the data of bank credit, and *vice-versa*. Also, in several cases it has not been made clear whether the bank data were inclusive or exclusive of the RRB data and referred to the CBs data alone, and conversely.

Rs. 670500 lakhs), or, in its sumtotal rural credit in India increased approximately 1127.4 times (Rs. 2546 *versus* Rs. 2870500 lakhs) during that period. At present in Bihar institutional rural credit is approximately 8.94 per cent of the aggregate in the country. Bihar had an edge over the national average in enlisting institutional rural credit for its primary sector when the percentage changes are compared in the two cases. Needless to add here that part of the institutional rural credit in Bihar was put to unproductive uses, proportionally more than in other parts of India.

During the period the dominance of the private agencies in the provision of rural credit was supplanted by the dominance of the institutional sources in practically all parts of the State, which were interlinked with the urban areas, more so in the tribal belt. Cooperative banks meet at present a fair proportion of the rural people's short-term requirements. The land development banks meet their long-term needs. The commercial banks and regional rural banks have also made their presence felt in all types of loans, thanks to the epoch-making policy-change in 1969. It is the middle-level farmers who drive the highest social profitability out of institutional rural credit. Brokers have emerged in rural areas whose job is to take needy farmer, illiterate or semi-literate, to the office of the bank and get paid to him the bank loan, out of which he deducts his commission, which is exorbitant, but even then the farmer is happy, and he may be a small or marginal farmer. In 1969 share of commercial banks in rural credit was around 4.2 per cent; in 1994 it was around 74.6 per cent. In 1994 the share of the RRBs was around 21.8 per cent. this meant that the relative share of the cooperative sector was marginalised to a figure around 3.6 per cent in 1994; in 1960-61 it had been around 30 per cent. Average loan per member of the PACS was Rs. 45 in 1950-51. In 1959-60 it was Rs. 20.81 in 1960-61, Rs. 119 in 1970-71, Rs. 137 in 1979-80, Rs. 150 and Rs. 631 in 1990-91 (all-India Rs. 2485). Let us not forget that prices had been rising all the while. This loan was mostly short-term.

The base of the PACS is stronger today, but compared to the banks, it is weak. The cooperative organisation has now a better representation of the people of the area having different sizes of holdings. The entrenched, vested groups, coming of the upper castes, imbued with the feudal mentality, are important even at present but not so important as to monopolise all opportunity to themselves. The opportunity is now shared with other sections as well. Control has become deconcentrated. The capital structure of the PACS has been partially refashioned.

The effectiveness or success of the PACS is determined by applying a dual measuring-rod, namely, availability of credit at a reasonable rate of interest and a suitable repayment schedule. Where the PACS stands the test, the credit flow is unhindered and the unit is viable, and the risk involved in any choice made by the farmer is taken into account. Repayment is not insisted on by the society in bad times, and time allowed voluntarily. Attention is paid to deposit mobilisation, which is the touch-stone of the development of its business by a society. An insurance cover is provided in the deposit mobilisation scheme. This has given a fillip to the scheme. On its success would turn the viability of the society. The entry of the commercial and regional rural banks has militated against the cooperative movement by making competition tougher for the PACS. This is good in an open economy but would call for coordination, which would enable the cooperative societies to put up with the competition without sustaining any harm.

Short-term commercial bank credit per account holder in 1979-80 in Bihar was Rs. 5319. Term credit advanced by commercial banks in 1980-81 was Rs. 5551. Per capita short-term bank credit in 1991 was Rs. 44.43. All rural credit per capita was Rs. 34 (all-India Rs. 72) in 1982. In 1981-82 per borrower it had been Rs. 1191, which had fallen to Rs. 1035 by 1983-84.*

Priority sector bank credit as percentage of total bank credit in Bihar was in 1969, 9.1 per cent (all-India 14.9 per cent) which had moved up to 61.1 per cent by 1993-94 (all-India 33.9 per cent). The existing tenancy laws created difficulties in the distribution of bank credit in the earlier years, which hurdle was offset to an appreciable extent in the subsequent years. The rates at which agricultural output grew and the local demand for consumption and production rose set limits to the rate at which bank credit expanded in the rural sector. The commercial banks operating in the rural areas were assigned a staff whose efficiency was lower and a defective motivation. They were overburdened with the obligation of funding the IRDP, and in 1989-90 the huge writing-off of the past loans had a crippling, stunning effect on their rural business. The management costs of rural branches were higher. In the foregoing pages we have already offered certain suggestions for solving these problems.

The RRBs are conceived of as the bridge between the cooperative system and the commercial bank system of rural credit, imparting as

* Here we come across another discrepancy, hard to reconcile—Is the lower figure for one year only? Are the higher figures cumulative? Nothing can be said with confidence.

they do an urban touch to an otherwise rural setting. As percentage of total bank credit earmarked for the rural sector, the RRBs rural credit formed 16.33 per cent in 1983, which slid to 10.57 per cent in 1994. The RRBs are bedevilled by problems distinguishable in character from problems that besmirched the CBs.

Another measure of the progress made by institutional rural credit is the availability of credit per hectare of gross cropped area (GCA). In 1959-60 the cooperative loan per ha. was Rs. 1.16. Twenty years after it was even less, Re. 0.19 per ha. In 1981 the LDB credit (of a long-term nature) was Rs. 63 per ha. (all-India Rs. 93). In 1985-86 credit per ha., as provided by all institutional agencies was Rs. 59. At 1983-84 prices the RBI Committee had estimated per ha. credit requirement at Rs. 1200 in the case of the irrigated land and Rs. 800 in the case of the unirrigated. An average farmer was supposed to save 30 per cent of this amount, and borrow the remaining 70 per cent from the institutional sources. This is proof of the insinuation made by the average politician and government official that the all-India institutions had starved Bihar of rural credit, which was the most important reason why Bihar had lagged behind in adopting the NAT on a scale on which some oft-quoted States had.

In Bihar there has been since long a general public complaint that the banks, commercial or regional rural, have by maintaining a low credit-to-deposits (C-D) ratio/profile drained resources out of the rural areas and also out of the State. In June 1969, the first year of nationalisation of the commercial banks, numbering fourteen, the C-D ratio in Bihar (rural areas) was exceptionally high, 92.09 (all-India 30.86). In 1982 it was 47.70 (all-India 40.29), in 1988, 54.6 (all-India 64.4) and in 1993, 50.9 (56.9)—higher than the national average in the earlier years but lower than that in the later years. In respect of the RRBs the C-D ratio was 83.31 in 1982, 75.6 in 1987, 69.2 in 1990 and 52.1 in 1993-94. Of course, the C-D ratio was higher, by comparison, in the case of the RRBs, because of their basically rural orientation, but as the time has elapsed, the resources the banks have mobilised in rural areas have been diverted to either urban areas in the State itself or areas outside the State. The rural branches have become deposit mobilisation centres for deploying the resources elsewhere, not so much as centres for credit dispensation—giving rise to what has been called Reverse Resource Transfer, stimulated by the Risk-Aversion Mentality and the Security-Consciousness Factor. That spread of banking to rural areas would lead to balanced development of both rural and urban areas and remove/plug the economic gap that exists between them and thereby generate equity. The banks argue apologetically that the poor, low bankability of the projects proposed for the rural areas, the low credit absorption capacity of the rural areas, the inadequacy of infrastructural facilities, etc. are factors that deter attempts at stepping up the C-D ratio there.

In July 1995 the commercial banks, the regional rural banks and the cooperative banks collectively drew up an annual action plan, known as the Bihar State Credit Plan, of over Rs. 1500 crores for 55 districts, ensuring the institutional credit flow in the State in the priority sector. This plan was expected to ensure a five-fold spurt in the actual credit flow over the years.

Low recovery of outstanding loans, be they from the cooperative societies or land development banks or commercial banks or, finally, the regional rural banks, as characterised the Government loans of the earlier days, whose recipients regarded them as Government gifts, not to be repaid, the periodic writing-off thereof consolidating the notion (the latest was in the case of bank loans exceeding Rs. 10,000 crores during 1989-90), is a formidable impediment to the smooth flow of the institutional credit for want of recycling or reprocessing or regenerating. To give examples from the past, in 1950-51 percentage of overdues to outstanding loans in Bihar was 210. In 1955-56, 68 per cent of Government loans were outstanding. In 1957-58, 59 per cent of Government loans were overdue for recovery. In 1961-62 loans outstanding as percentage of loans advanced were 116, and loans overdue as percentage of loans outstanding 23. In 1970-71, overdue loans as percentage of annual demand were 56. In 1982-83 this percentage had risen to 74.8. Overdues per ha. of GCA amounted to Rs. 63 in 1981 and Rs. 105 in 1987-88 in respect of the LDB loans, and Rs. 232 in 1981 and Rs. 448 in 1988 in respect of the CBs loans. This is therefore an endemic problem and must be remedied energetically.

18

RESTRUCTURING OF THE AGRARIAN SYSTEM

Before the abolition of zamindari in Bihar, the State had four types of estates: (1) permanently settled revenue-paying estates numbering 205977, with a total revenue demand of Rs. 1,08,09,085; (2) permanently settled revenue-free estates, numbering 11295; (3) temporarily settled estates, numbering 739; and (4) Government estates, numbering 421.

Through the Bihar State Management of Estates Act (the earliest title) Bihar launched upon the first stage of social revolution of a tremendous import, a revolution which was supposed to culminate in the complete disappearance of the *zamindari* system.

Land reforms are structural and organisational changes: They imply refashioning and remodelling of the existing institutions and the ushering in of new ones. They signify restructuring of the agrarian relations. They make an impact on land utilisation and cropping pattern. Their incentive effect is on the farmer's ability and willingness to work and save and invest. By removing the sense of insecurity as to the prevalent tenure and tenancy they eliminate the all-round barrier to the on-farm development works programme, and install security in its place, which brings forth an access to credit, and to undertake risk, to adopt the new agrarian technology and to choose crops. These alternatives to development are not open to the farmer where tenancy and share-cropping rights over land are not clearly and properly defined.

Land reforms comprise abolition of the intermediaries/zamindars, fixation of ceiling on holdings, consolidation of holdings, development of cooperative village management, tenancy reform, updating of land records, etc.

In essence, land reforms address themselves to the problems which originate from the land system in vogue as well as the very change of the land system in operation. The first is executed with the help of the triple reform of the land system—by means of the Three F's, viz., fair rent, fixation of the tenure and free transfer. This is palliatory. The second is attempted through the removal of the intermediaries. This is curative.

Those who considered the zamindari system a fraud perpetrated on the peasants, those to whom the zamindars were a redundant institution between the State and the real tillers of the soil, those who wanted the real tillers of the soil to become the full-fledged owners of the land and have a direct relationship with the state emphasised the change of the perpetuating land system. By difference, those who stressed the reform of the existing land system did not foresee any striking improvement in the economic and social lot of the real tillers of the soil from the break-up of the erstwhile *zamindaris* into a number of holdings on paper within the legally prescribed limits and the relief brought to a very limited percentage of the tillers, who came to be vested with the occupancy rights. Among the opponents of the proposed change of the land system were such stalwarts as Dr. Rajendra Prasad, Maharaja Dhiraj of Darbhanga, Sir C.P.N. Sinha, Raja of Ramgarh, etc., on different fronts—political, legislative, judicial and administrative. On economic criteria Bihar's need was, as put by the report on the Techno-Economic Survey of Bihar, better utilisation of the available land through consolidation, ample credit, better marketing facilities, multipurpose cooperatives, etc.

The 1956-57 budget admitted that the abolition of the intermediary, rentier class was not the be-all and the end-all of the establishment of a socialistic community of landowners, based on cooperation and with the rights of the share-croppers and *Bataidars* delineated, efficient cultivation carried out within the corpus of the ceiling legislation and provisions of consolidation, by averting subdivision and fragmentation of the existing holdings and by taking measures to update the land records and survey, which would be the main planks of land reforms in a regime in which the tillers of the soil land the other people who own the lands are bound together by an indissoluble bound of mutual interests, being the architects of their own destiny. The earliest political leadership was totally opposed to class hatred and disapproved of methods which were apt to play upon it or work it up. But this did not connote that they were lukewarm towards the necessity of lowering the degree of inequality in society. What this really meant was that in an economy experiencing rapidly growing population partition of the assets possessed by a family, whatever its economic status, being unavoidable, the redistribution of all the given land equally among the families could not provide a solution to the problems of poverty and unemployment for all time to come. But if a clay-footed economy such as the Bihar economy (because its agriculture was in the throes of near stagnation) was so reconstructed by focussing on a comprehensive and well-integrated agricultural development programme, which encompassed the essential land reforms, that agricultural productivity in it was optimum, the level of well-being enjoyed by all sections of people would be higher than that which would be attained in an alternative situation in which the intermediaries were eliminated and large holdings were split into smaller ones, but efforts were slack in forthcoming in the direction of the degree of security enjoyed by the tenants so that the rent continued to be grabbed from them by the real owners of their land, the inputs which augmented the yield could not be had by them because credit was hard to come by or for other reasons, etc.—that is, the agrarian structure had been transformed but the organisation of production and marketing remained very much unchanged and hence the agrarian system was placed in a different gear. In other words the little gain which the award of occupancy right or security of tenure and hence the stimulus to work it generated would pale into insignificance on being confronted with unmitigated usury, rackrenting and exploitation which are at the root of the low produce. Abolition of zamindari and fixation of ceiling on holdings were only the two main planks in a multi-plank agrarian reform, popularly known as land reform, which had tenancy reform, cooperation, village panchayat, consolidation, up-to-date records, agricultural productivity maximisation, etc., etc., as its other, no less important, planks. The final goal was a total/holistic solution to the peasant's problem, which was sought to be achieved through a series of partial solutions.

Zamindari Abolition

The enactment of the legislation for the abolition of the intermediaries in Bihar was not achieved without the State Government facing litigation appertaining to the validity of the legislation disputed by the intermediaries in the courts of law. First to be introduced was the Bihar State Acquisition of Zamindaris Bill by the Congress Government that came to power in 1946, passed in November 1947 and assented to by the Governor-General in July 1949. To replace it Bihar had the Bihar State Management of Estates and Tenures Act, 1949, which was purported to enable the State Government to learn how to manage the estates by taking them over for a period. In its place came the Bihar Land Reforms

Bill in 1949, passed in 1950, which provided for the liquidation of the zamindari system in Bihar. It was enforced in September 1950. The validity of this act too was challenged and it was not until May 1952, when Article 31 of the Constitution of the Republic of India was amended and the Supreme Court upheld the validity of the constitutional amendment that the abolition of the intermediaries could actually be proceeded with. All the intermediaries between the Government and the cultivators *Raiyats* were removed. The *Raiyats* were brought in direct touch with the State Government. On payment compensation the *zamindaris* were abolished. By 1956-57 the process of abolition of the zamindari system was accomplished.

In the first phase of the abolition programme, which ended in September, 1952, the State Government abolished, under the Bihar Land Reforms Act, 1950, all intermediaries, having gross annual incomes exceeding Rs.50,000. The number of intermediaries so abolished was 155. In the second phase, commencing from September, 1952, it was decided to abolish all intermediary interests in the districts of Gaya, Hazaribagh, Palamanu and Darbhanga and necessary steps were taken in that direction in 1953-54 all intermediary interests, having gross annual income between Rs.50,000 and Rs. 10,000, were abolished.

Under the Bihar Land Reforms Act, 1950 as it stood before the enactment of the Bihar Land Reforms (Amendment) Act, 1954, it was necessary to issue a separate notification in respect of each individual intermediary giving details of all intermediary interests held by him in the estate proposed to be acquired. This made the progress of abolition somewhat slow.

The State Government, therefore, got the provisions of the law amended in this regard through the aforesaid amending Act which came into force on May 17, 1954. It empowered the State Government to take over all intermediary interests, situated within a particular area or throughout the State, by a general notification after giving at least a 3 months' notice by means of a proclamation. After this, it became possible to proceed faster with the abolition of intermediaries and on January 26, 1955 all intermediary interests in eight districts of the State, comprising approximately half the area and population, were acquired by the issue of area notification.

The eight districts, which were included in this programme were Gaya, Hazaribagh, Palamau, Monghyr, Purnea, Saharsa, Darbhanga and Champaran. The intermediary interests in the remaining nine districts of the State, viz., Patna, Shahabad, Muzaffarpur, Saran, Bhagalpur, Santhal Parganas, Ranchi, Sighbhum and Manbhum (excluding

Manbhum Sadar) were abolished with effect from January 1, 1956. With this the process of acquisition of intermediary interests in the State was completed.

In a trinity of respects the Land Reforms Act had a clear advantage over the Zamindari Abolition Act, namely, (1) in associating village panchayats with rent collection, (2) in assigning supervision work of the estates and tenures to village panchayats and (3) in appointing a Land Commission.

The Government of Bihar laid down a sliding scale for the assessment of the compensation and made provision for *ad infinitum* payment. The rate of compensation was 3 to 20 times the net annual income. 42 per cent of the arrear rent was to be paid alongwith the compensation. The preceding year's figures of net income ranging from Rs.500 to Rs. 1 lakh and above were taken. The full amount of compensation was estimated at about Rs.158 to 160 crores (Table 18.1). Half of the

TABLE 18.1 : Number of Zamindars (Intermediaries) to be Compensated and the Amount of Compensation to be Paid in Bihar

Income-Group	*Number of Zamindars*	*Approved Amount of Compensation (Rs.)*
Rs. 5000 or less	353650	431238000
Between Rs. 5000 and Rs. 20000	70560	528259000
Between Rs. 20000 and Rs. 100000	20600	416225000
Between Rs. 100000 and Rs. 250000	1390	44109000
Between Rs. 250000 and Rs. 500000	35	10196000
Between Rs. 500000 and Rs. 1000000	7	4477000
Rs. 1000000 and above	3	8841000
Total	446245	1443345000
Alternatively,		Rs. 158.00 crores (413.00)
Add Interest		Rs. 80.98 crores (150.07)
Total		Rs. 238.98 crores (664.66)
Number of years in which compensation is payable		40
Acreage (million)		30.64
Per acre compensation		Rs. 39*

* Compensation was provided at specified amounts for different classes of land value. The amounts was varying between Rs. 50 and Rs. 900 per acre.

compensation had to be paid by March 31, 1958. Those entitled to compensation of not more than Rs.50 were to be paid in cash, others in bonds, which were to be negotiable and transferable. The amount of bonds to be issued was estimated at Rs.110 crores.

Bihar's net resources before compensation (1950-51 to 1960-61) amounted to Rs. 840 lakhs. Compensation paid in cash or partly in cash amounted to Rs. 1095 lakhs, The net impact of zamindari abolition was minus Rs. 255 lakhs.

The NCAER team had advised the State Government to pay compensation to the zamindars in terms of shares in enterprises instead of bonds and cash (thank God that this advice was not acted upon by the State Government, otherwise the zamindars would have been ruined because the State undertakings which were set up got into the red within a very short time).

Ceiling Legislation

The land ceiling act of Bihar imposed a ceiling on the quantum of land to be held by a landowner. Land was classified under different classes according to their respective productivities and the ceiling fixed. Any land that was surplus, that is, in excess of the ceiling, had to be acquired and redistributed to landless persons for cultivation. The ceiling was fixed on the holdings of 30 acres in the plain areas and at 50 acres in the plateau regions for a family of 5 persons or less. On irrigated holdings with two crops the ceiling was 6.07 to 7.28 ha. (as against that suggested in National Guides, which was 4.05 to 7.28 ha.), irrigated land with one crop 10.12 ha. (as against 10.93 ha.) and dry land 12.14 to 18.21 ha (as against 21.85 ha.). A sugar mill was entitled to possess 100 acres of land (though 40 to 50 thousand acres of surplus land were under the possession of 28 sugarcane farms).

As Table 18.2 would disclose in 1950-51, 31 per cent of all land holdings in Bihar were in size 0.40 ha. or less in size and comprised 3.6 per cent of total cultivated area (all-India figure also 3.6 per cent), 77 per cent were in size 2.02 ha. or less and comprised 31.8 per cent of total cultivated area (all-India figure 44 per cent), 8.7 per cent were in size above 4.04 ha. and comprised 44.0 per cent of total cultivated area, and 2 per cent were in size 10.12 ha. or more and comprised 19.1 per cent of total cultivated area (all-India figure 20 per cent). The total number of holdings was estimated at 49 lakhs.

Size distribution of land holdings in Bihar in the early 1950s displayed an undoubtedly skewed, unequal distribution, which was at once a factor in agricultural inefficiency and an impediment to agrarian transformation. Not only that but it was also amongst the highest in India. A look at Table 18.3 manifests that the bottom 65's percentage share, 8.71 in total operated area in Bihar was less than the top one per cent's, 9.90, in it.

TABLE 18.2 : Size Distribution of Holdings in Bihar : 1950-51

Size of Holdings (ha.)	*Number (Percentage)*	*Area (Percentage)*
0.40 and below	31.0	3.6
Above 0.40 but less than 1.02	25.5	10.3
Above 1.02 but not above 2.02	20.5	17.9
Above 2.02 but not above 4.04	14.3	24.2
Above 4.04 but not above 10.12	7.1	24.9
Above 10.12 but not above 20.24	1.1	8.6
Above 20.24	0.5	10.5

TABLE 18.3 : Area Operated by Various Segments of Holdings in Rural Bihar : 1953-54

(In Percentage)

Indicators	*Percentage*
Share of Bottom	
25 per cent	2.08 (1.97)
40 per cent	6.63 (5.77)
50 per cent	11.19 (9.71)
Share of Middle	
40 to 80 per cent	33.25 (28.92)
50 to 80 per cent	29.69 (24.98)
Share of Top	
20 per cent	60.72 (65.35)
10 per cent	46.65 (47.88)
5 per cent	27.59 (33.24)
1 per cent	9.90 (10.97)

The next Table 18.4 reveals that whereas 81.5 per cent of all families claimed 87.5 per cent of all holdings and 93.6 per cent of all area, 18.5 per cent of all families claimed 12.5 per cent of all holdings and 6.4 per cent of all area in Bihar in 1950-51. 11.2 per cent of all land was with the landowners' families, 68.8 per cent with the tenants' families and 13.6 per cent with the agricultural labour families. 3.8 per cent of all holdings were the direct concern of the landowners' families. 49.6 per cent of them that of the tenants' families and 34.1 per cent of them the concern of the agricultural labourers' families with land. The landlords' families had the largest number of persons to support per family and the agricultural labourers' families without the smallest number of them. The average size was the largest in the case of landowners' families and the smallest in respect of the agricultural labourers' families without land. 26.4 per cent of the rural population with land requisitioned agricultural labour on wages during the peak season of agriculture; others made do with their own family labour.

TABLE 18.4 : Land Ownership Pattern in Bihar in 1950-51

Indicators	*All Agricultural Families*					*Non-Agricultural Families*
	All	*Land Owners*	*Tenants*	*Labour*		
				With Land	*Without Land*	
Percentage of families	81.5	3.0	38.8	25.5	14.2	18.5
Average size of families	5.6	6.8	6.2	5.4	4.3	5.5
Percentage of holdings held	87.5	3.8	49.6	34.1	—	12.5
Percentage of area held	93.6	11.2	68.8	13.6	—	6.4
Average size of holdings (ha.)	2.38	4.85	2.26	0.64	—	0.85

A comparison between Table 18.4, for 1950-51 and Table 18.5, for 1954-55 would show that the Zamindari Abolition Act, already implemented, and the ceiling legislation on the anvil, had their impact as well as reverberations/echoes on the size distribution of ownership and operational holdings, though to some inarticulate extent in particular classes of holdings and to some highly accentuated extent in other particular classes of holdings. To illustrate, in the case of the marginal holdings while their percentage share in area decreased slightly, their percentage share in number increased perceptively. In the case of the small holdings the change in the percentage share in area was as substantial as the change in the percentage share in number. So far the medium class of holdings was concerned, the percentage change in area was a decrease of a very immaterial magnitude, but the decrease in the percentage share in number was not insubstantial. Lastly, in the class of large holdings the percentage share in area went up significantly, whereas the percentage share in number went down meagrely.

TABLE 18.5 : Size Distribution of Ownership Holdings : July 1954 to April 1955 in Bihar

Classes of Holdings/ Class-Distribution of Holdings (ha.)	*Number of Households ('000)*	*Area Owned ('000 ha.)*	*As Percentage of Total No. of Holdings*	*As Percentage of Toal Area Owned*	*Average Size of Ownership Households (No. of Persons)*
Marginal					
0.000 to 0.002	1177	—	16.56	—	1.06
0.002 to 0.40	2463	299	34.67	3.54	4.81
0.40 to 1.02	1140	771	16.04	9.12	5.10
Small					
1.02 to 2.02	1056	1524	14.86	18.04	5.89
2.02 to 3.03	509	1259	7.16	14.90	6.06
3.03 to 4.04	272	959	3.83	11.35	6.72
Medium					
4.04 to 6.06	268	1321	3.77	15.62	7.58
6.06 to 8.05	110	760	1.55	8.99	8.25
8.05 to 10.12	45	760	0.63	8.99	8.23
Large					
10.12 to 12.14	28	401	0.35	4.74	9.61
12.14 to 20.24	28	424	0.35	5.01	12.11
20.24 & above	11	418	0.15	4.94	13.36
Total	7107	8453	100.00	100.00	5.30

Were we to keep the comparison confined to the two broad classes, one, the marginal-small and two, the medium-large, then we would find that in the latter period, as set off against the former, an increased percentage of 22.3 households in the former could net in an increased percentage of 16.8 area, while in the latter a reduced percentage of the order of 2.9 households could net in an increased percentage of 15.1 area—the institutional change that had already happend and that yet to come about, had, by causing a reshuffle, made for further concentration, and hence aggravated the inequality in land ownership and operation. The goal that was sought had been stalled and dealt a blow. Anticipations/ expectations gave rise to subterfuges/sabotages.

The recommendations of the Planning Commission on land ceiling were as follows:

(1) There should be an absolute limit to the future acquisition of land.

(2) As an interim solution each State should enact land management legislation, prescribing standards of cultivation and management and setting up the necessary machinery for land management. Farms, above a limit (to be fixed), should be divided into two groups, namely, those which were so efficiently managed that their break-up led to a fall in production, and those which did not meet this test. In the case of the second group, the Government should take over the management for settling landless cultivators in co-operation groups and otherwise.

(3) There should be an absolute limit to the extent of land which any individual might hold.

With a view to implementing the above recommendations of the Planning Commission, the Bihar Government drafted and introduced the Bihar Agricultural Land (Ceiling and Management) Bill, 1955.

The salient provisions of the Bill may briefly be described as under :

(1) The ceiling area of a land-holding having a family of 5 persons, including himself, would not exceed 30 acres in the plains and 50 acres in plateau areas or in areas with poor quality of land.

(2) A family would be taken as consisting of the landholder, his wife, his sons, and his sons' sons, their wives, dependent parents of the landholder, unmarried daughters and sisters of the landholder and his sons and his sons' sons.

(3) If the number of persons in a landholder family exceeded 5, an area of 5 acres in the plains and 8.5 acres in other areas would be added to the ceiling area for each such additional person, provided that the total area did not exceed 300 acres.

(4) Where the total area held by a landholder exceeded the ceiling area, he would have the right to decide which of the land held by his *under-raiyats* would be included in the ceiling area.

(5) The incidence of the land of an *under-raiyat*, included in the ceiling area, would be laid down in the tenancy law for the time being in force.

(6) An *under-raiyat* holding land, not included in the ceiling area of the *raiyat*, would acquire occupancy rights therein on deposit, in the Treasury, of compensation equal to fifteen times the rent of the land.

(7) A landholder would be bound to farm his lands in excess of the ceiling area in accordance with the principles of good husbandry to be laid down.

(8) The prescribed authority would be entitled to issue direction to any landholder or a body of landholders for the purpose of regulating the standard of efficient cultivation and management crop-planning and due observance of the principles of good husbandry.

(9) If a landholder to whom any direction was issued by the prescribed authority was unable to carry out the same, he might voluntarily make/turn over the land to the authority issuing the direction or join a registered co-operative farming society.

(10) If a landholder failed within the prescribed time to comply with the direction issued to him by the prescribed authority, he might, under orders of the latter, be dispossessed of the land if he did not voluntarily surrender the same or joined a registered co-operative farming society.

(11) Where a landholder was dispossessed of his land for his failure to comply with the direction, the land would be managed by the prescribed authority directly or through a registered co-operative farming society or through other landholders or the landless agricultural labourers.

(12) The dispossession of a landholder of his land, in the circumstances stated above, would remain in force for a period not exceeding 5 years and that, during this period, the landholder would be entitled to such annual payments, not less than the rent which he was required to pay for the land, as might be determined by the prescribed authority.

(13) The land of a landholder in excess of 300 acres, to be selected by him, would be acquired by the Government on payment to him of compensation at the rate of ten times the rent thereof.

(14) The land so acquired by the Government would be settled with the landless agricultural workers on such terms and conditions as might be prescribed.

The Bihar Legislative Assembly in its monsoon session of 1961, passed the Bihar Land Reforms (Fixation of Ceiling On Land) Bill, 1959 after introducing necessary changes. Diverse opinions had been expressed in the Bihar Legislative Assembly on the Bill. The ceiling for class I agricultural land, originally fixed at 30 acres and subsequently reduced to 24 acres by the Joint Select Committee, was further cut down to 20 acres on the recommendation of the Planning Commission. There was a corresponding reduction in the four other categories of land, 60 acres being the highest individual holding. Further scaling down of the ceiling, it was argued, might result in the migration of the agricultural labourers to the industrial areas with danger to production. The maximum quantum of land that a family could hold was fixed. In Section 4 of the Act Ceilings were fixed on the following basis:

(a) Twenty acres of the land irrigated by flow irrigation work, constructed or maintained, improved or controlled by the Central or the State Government or by a corporate body constituted under any law.
(b) Thirty acres of the land irrigated by lift irrigation work or tube-well, constructed or maintained by the Central or the State Government or by a corporate body constituted under any law.
(c) Forty acres of the land on which there is an orchard or which is used for other horticultural purposes or any land other than the land referred to in Clauses (a) to (d).
(d) Sixty acres of land which is hilly and sandy, surplus homestead land or other land, none of which yields paddy, rabi or cash crops.

In the Second Five-Year Plan fixation of the ceiling on land was included as one of the important programmes for the agrarian development of the country. So much importance was attached to this by the Government of India that a special panel (which came to be known as Land Reforms Panel) was set up in the Planning Commission to advise and assist the States in their land reform measures.

The importance attached to *land reforms* as part of the national development programme was particularly tow-fold : Firstly, land reforms were favoured for removing such impediments to increase in agricultural production as arise from the agrarian structure inherited from the past. Secondly, they were favoured for eliminating all elements of exploitation and injustice within the agrarian system in order to provide security for the tillers of the soil and to assure equality of status and opportunity to all sections of the rural population. It is obvious, therefore, that the fundamental problem in any land reform measure is to strike a balance between these two objectives.

The size of a household operational holding is affected by: (a) the number of households operating upon the total arable land and (b) the distribution pattern of the cultivated area among the cultivating households. The first factor can be studied by working out the average size of a household operational holding for a particular area by overriding the pattern of land distribution. The average size of holding is generally small in areas where the yielding capacity of land is more by way of assured rainfall, irrigation facilities, better quality of soil, etc., and the density of population is high. It is not correct to say that in areas where yield per acre is more, it is so because the average size of holding is small.

The First Five-Year Plan of India had recommended that the ceiling limit should be equal to three times of the family holding. A family holding was defined as an area which was equal to a plough unit or a work unit for a family of an average size depending on local conditions.

The level of ceiling in different States broadly followed the recommendations of the Planning Commission as embodied in the Second Five-Year Plan of India (reproduced above). The ceiling limits were fixed in terms of acreage depending on the class of land (in the case of Bihar they were 20 to 60 acres).

The Land Reforms (Fixation of Ceiling Area and Acquisition of Surplus Land) Act/ceiling legistation was passed in 1961 and became effective from April 1962. The level of ceiling was between 6.07 ha. and 18.21 ha. It was amended on different occasions with a view to providing ceiling on agricultural land and to acquire surplus land and to redistribute it among the landless people.

A major thrust was imparted to the ceiling legislation implementation when it received sufficient emphasis as one of the points in the 20-Point (Economic) Programme of 1975, retained with the same fervour in the revised, new 20-Point Programme of 1982.

The Land Ceiling Act was a fairly comprehensive piece of legislation. Sections 29,37 and 45 (b) of it were amended by the State Government as part of the land reforms measures. In other words, to be included in the Ninth Schedule of the Constitution the land legislation had to be reviewed and reformulated, for the laws in this schedule were beyond any challenge in the courts of law on grounds of infringement of the Fundamental Rights.

To begin with the area of land to be acquired under the Ceiling legislation was estimated at 1.3 million acres. Added to this was 0.5 million acres of land under reclamation land 0.5 million undistributed *Bhoodan* land, giving a total of 2.3 million acres, reckoned to be enough to allow about 1.5 acres to each of the 1.7 million families of landless agricultural labourers. The data furnished in Table 18.6 led to a lower estimate of 19,89,000 acres as surplus, which amounted to 9.52 per cent of the total owned area of 208,81,000 acres. But the State Government's target was fixed at a lower figure of 9 lakh acres only, amounting to 4.31 per cent of total owned area.

TABLE 18.6 : Estimate of Surplus Land in Bihar

Class of Land	*Estimated Owned Area ('000 acres)*	*Ceiling as Per Legislation (acres)*	*Area above ceiling Level (per cent)*	*Estimated Surplus Area ('000 acres)*
Class I	4272	20	18.43	787
Class II	212	30	9.97	21
Class III	14804	40	7.63	1130
Class IV	573	50	4.95	28
Class V	924	60	2.49	23
Total	20,785			1989

Difficulties Besetting Zamindari Abolition

Owing to a number of difficulties besetting Zamindari Abolition in Bihar, the Bihar Land Reforms Act had to be implemented by stages, by selecting a set of districts one by one. This made the implementation tardy, slow and unsatisfactory. A couple of technical difficulties plagued the implementation from the right outset: One, absence of an adequate administrative machinery in rural areas and two, absence of reliable and uptodate land records. A third factor that marred the implementation was the lack of follow-up measures in most cases for the very nature of the change brought about. To compound the problem was an atmosphere, a climate which did not favour it, namely, the poor political will and the dominance of vested interests. While the implementation was, by and large, ineffective, the repercussions on the socio-economic framework of the epoch-making legislation were not reviewed, and not reviewed continuously, in consonance with the agricultural development programmes adopted under the Five-Year Plans.

In the pre-1965 period the feudal forces in rural Bihar were on the defensive in the wake of the limited land reform measures that were put through. By the mid-1960s these forces were in a position to reassert their grip and consolidate their position.

As acknowledged by some of the Chief Ministers of Bihar the provision for the writ petitions was the most formidable hurdle in the effective implementation of the land reform measures. At one stage, total land under dispute was 70766 acres and stay granted by the applleate courts covered 20292 acres. On March 31, 1989, 79600 ha. land was locked in litigation. In 1995, cases involving 162469 acres of land were pending in the law courts, as also in the court of the Member, Revenue Board 14855 acres, in the High Court 851 pending cases involving 65240 acres, the courts of the SDO's 342 cases involving 36142 acres, the courts of the DM's 25876 acres, and in the Supreme Court (-cum-High Court) 884 cases involving 68435 acres.

Among the fifty-six districts, the maximum number of cases related to West Champaran involving 28111 acres. Next to come were Purnea 19334 acres, Samastipur 9994 acres, East Champaran 6000 acres, Gaya 2341 acres, Chatra 800 acres, Vaishali 318 acres and Jehanabad 373 acres.

In Bihar Zamindari Abolition was spontaneously accompanied by the advent of a bureaucratic superstructure and hierarchy of administration which retarded rural development and speeded up exploitation. Compared to the neighbouring State, West Bengal, Bihar's performance was utterly disappointing.

All in all, the zamindari system had gone from Bihar but the zamindars survived in the State, as is the common belief.

Problems Facing Ceiling Legislation

The level of ceiling varied from region to region in Bihar itself, differing according to the type of soil, type of crops grown, method of irrigation, or, finally, a combination of these factors. Under the circumstances, an element of arbitrariness in the fixation of the level of ceiling was inevitable because no account was taken of the extent of the surplus land likely to be available or the extent of requirement of land for redistribution among the landless agricultural labourers and the marginal and small holders. A large section of the enlightened mass doubted if this could satisfy the land hunger of all the landless agricultural families. The legislation was opposed by many people on the score that it would result in further fragmentation of holdings, thereby telling upon agricultural productivity. Bringing the fresh land recipients within the cooperative fold would have a good psychological effect, besides ensuring the advantages of large-scale farming, but in the case of Bihar this was not feasible because the peasants were scared of joining cooperative farming—the experience and record of cooperation in Bihar had been disappointing.

It was further argued by the critics of the legislation that not only the holdings shared with the landless agricultural families would become too uneconomic for cultivation but also they would be legally vested in the hands of such people as would not be as good as the average cultivators and, in consequence, the transferred holdings would be cultivated less efficiently (but an opposite view was expressed by the exponents of the legislation that ownership when endowed on the labourers would turn the soil into gold). It was also contended that the Government's slogan "land to the landless people" was a political stunt, meant to win over votes in the elections, and as a measure it was bound to weaken the village economy and breed insecurity. Those who had anticipated loss on account of the legislation had already contrived arrangements to circumvent the legislation, for example, by *Benami* (bogus) transfer among the members of their families and their relations and even fictitious institutions of the land in excess of the ceiling or in the worst cases by selling it to others.

A snag that hit the eye most was the failure of the State Government to institute a study into the effects the legislation would have on the surplus-producing farmers, for it was publicised by them that their total produce would be considerably lowered in the wake of the legislation. Their propaganda was countered by the enthusiasts of the legislation, who maintained that its implementation would release the latent productive forces of Bihar agriculture, so far enmeshed in a pernicious land tenure system. Even today no expert study exists that can be consulted by us for obtaining a picture of the balance of the affirmative over the negative account, and *vice-versa.*

Many people have opined that the delay in taking action with regard to the ceiling legislation was deliberate. The Government was reluctant to enforce it in right earnest. Besides, there were certain loopholes in the legislation. There was resistance to the legislation even outside the Government at all levels. As said above, anticipatory/pre-emptive action through nominal/bogus partitions, fictitious transfers and other dishonest devices excessively diluted and distorted and vitiated the intended impact of the ceiling legislation.

A body of public opinion found fault with the legislation on the ground that it was discriminatory—it was against the agriculturists in rural areas, for the non-agriculturists were left untouched.*

---

* While the author was studying in Patna College, the two English dailies, the *Searchlight* and the *Indian Nation*, were continuously engaged in the land reforms legislation debate, the former supporting it and the latter decrying it. At a public meeting held at Gandhi Maidan, Patna, Sardar Patel had indicated the move to acquire *zamindari* without paying compensation as *Dakaiti* (robbery).

A serious hurdle emanated from the lack of complete and accurate records of rights and well-defined titles to land. This was aggrandised by the ignorance of the tenants, share-croppers and oral lesses as to their rights. Even those who were sure of them made no attempt to get them enforced. Next was the in-fighting amongst the landless agricultural labourers—the landlords' policy of 'divide and rule', an imitation of the erstwhile British policy towards the two major communities in India—if any old tenant protested came part on the moment a new one to take his place on the terms dictated by the landlord, who had always with him muscle-men to teach the rebel a lesson. Above all, the interests of the tenants were prejudiced by the ineffective implementation of the ceiling legislation. Again, the propagandist overtones of the ceiling legslation only diverted attention from the more urgent goal of effectively guaranteeing the rights and interests of the actual tillers of the land. Lastly, loose terminology, dilatory procedures and vested interests conspired to defeat the ceiling legislation.

The Land Tenure System in Bihar has been governed by: (1) The Bihar Tenancy Act, 1885; (2) The Chotanagpur Tenancy Act, 1908; (3) The Bihar Bakast Dispute Settlement Act, 1947; (4) The Ranchi District Tana Bhagat Raiyats Agricultural Land Restoration Act, 1947; (5) The Bihar Privileged Persons Homestead Tenancy Act, 1948; (6) The Bihar Restriction of Uses of Land Bill, 1948; (7) The Santhal Parganas Tenancy (Supplementary Provisions) Act, 1949; (8) The Bihar Hindu Women's Rights to Property; (9) The Kosi Area Restoration of Lands to Raiyats Act, 1951; (10) The Bihar Consolidation and Prevention of Fragmentation Act, 1958; (11) The Bihar Land Reforms (Fixation of Ceiling Area and Acquisition of Surplus Land) Act, 1961; and (12) The Bihar Tenancy Act (Amendment) Act, 1953 and 1955. Nos. 3 and 4 protected the raiyats against eviction. They also ensured special privileges to the scheduled castes and scheduled tribes against alienation. No. 12 gave security to the tenants including the under-raiyats and share-croppers from eviction from their tenancies. The Collectors were empowered, and empowered fully, not only to restore possession to the tenants unlawfully evicted but to take steps to prevent eviction even when it was threatened. This protection was necessary to enable the tenants to take to settled farming and get loans for investment on seeds, fertilisers, plant protection, etc. During 1954-64 a series of legislation was enacted in the country for the reform of the land tenure system. This inevitably implied extensive transfers of legal rights and title to land ownership.

Tenancy Reform

Under the existing provisions of the Bihar Tenancy Act, the Chotanagpur Tenancy Act and the Santhal Parganas Regulations, the occupancy raiyats have permanent and heritable rights in the agricultural lands held by them. They enjoy adequate security against eviction and against enhancement of rent. Their status is hardly distinguishable from that of the proprietors in this regard, particularly as the Government is not the only landlord after the abolition of the *Zamindari.* This class of tenants does not perhaps require any strengthening of their existing rights.

Under the Bihar Tenancy Act of 1885, an under-raiyat, who held land continuously for a period of 12 years, acquired rights of occupancy therein and could not be evicted therefrom, except when the holding was sold for arrears of rent. An under-raiyat, who had not acquired the right of occupancy, could not also be ejected from his land held by him, except in execution of decrees obtained on one or more of the following grounds:

(1) Failure to pay arrears or rent;
(2) Using the land in a manner so as to render it unfit for the purpose of the tenancy; and
(3) Where he had been admitted to the occupation of the land by a registered lease on the ground that the terms and conditions of the lease had expired.

Until recently an under-raiyat, ejected by his landlord illegally from the land held by him, did not have any remedy other than to go to the Civil Court. But as litigation in a Civil Court involved heavy expenses and considerable harassment in other ways, most of the poor under-raiyats were unable to obtain any relief. The ejected under-raiyats were further handicapped in this regard because of the fact that the raiyats did not either execute any lease in their favour or grant any receipt with the result that the former did not have any documentary evidence in their possession to support their case. Therefore, in order to protect the under-raiyats from illegal ejectments, the Bihar Tenancy Act was amended through the Bihar Tenancy (Second Amendment) Act, 1955. The amending Act empowered the Collectors to take action either on their own initiative or on application for restorations of possession to under-raiyats ejected unlawfully from their lands, since February1, 1953. This amending Act came into force on December 1, 1955.

Occupancy *raiyats* and under-raiyats already enjoy adequate protection against eviction from their homestead lands. Where the homestead forms part of the *raiyat's* agricultural holdings, the same incidence governs his homestead too. Elsewhere, the incidence is regulated by local custom or usage. The Bihar Privileged Persons Homestead Tenancy Act enacted in February, 1948, confers right for permanent tenancy in their homesteads on all persons (other than proprietors, tenure holders, under-tenure holders and Mahajans) who, besides their homestead, hold either no land or hold any such land not exceeding one acre in the area. Such persons are termed in the Act as "Privileged Tenants". The conferment of permanent tenancy on such persons is, of course subject to the payment of such rent as is agreed upon between them and their landlords, provided it is not unfair or inequitable or such fair and equitable rent as is fixed therefore by the Collector on application or on his own initiative.

The Bihar Tenancy (Second Amendment) Act of 1955 reduced rent to the five-twentieth of the gross produce. Subsequently, the Bihar Land Reforms (Fixation of Ceiling Area and Acquisition of Surplus Land) Act of 1961, provided for fixation of maximum rent at 25 per cent of the gross produce. Under the existing provisions of the Bihar Tenancy Act, an under-raiyat paying produce rent was not entitled to get his rent commuted to cash rent. The State Government decided to amend the provisions in this regard so as to entitle such an under-raiyat to commute the kind rent, payable by him, to cash rent so that the money-rent determined after commutation, as payable by him, did not exceed the maximum cash rent prescribed as payable by an under-raiyat.

The landlords of the occupancy raiyats did not have, under the old tenancy laws in force in the State, any right of resumption for personal cultivation. So far as an under-raiyat was concerned, his landlord was entitled to resume the land only on the expiry of the lease where the land was sublet by a written lease. The tenancy law did not contain any provision for enabling the landlord of an under-raiyat to resume the land for personal cultivation before the expiry of the written lease. The State Government decided to give the raiyats the right to resume land for personal cultivation, subject to the following conditions:

(1) The maximum area to be resumed would not exceed half the ceiling area proposed to be fixed under the Bihar Agricultural Lands (Ceiling and Management) Bill, 1955. This would be exclusive of the land already held in the possession of the raiyat.

(2) The right of resumption would not be exercised in a manner so as to leave less than two acres of land in possession of the under-raiyat (including the land held by the under-raiyat as a raiyat or occupancy or non-occupancy under-raiyat) in each case except where the land owned by the raiyat himself did not exceed five acres, the raiyat would be entitled to resume the entire land leased out by him to his under-raiyats.

(3) The area for resumption would be indicated within six months of enactment of the proposed legislation, but the final selection of land for resumption would be made with the approval of the Collector.

(4) The raiyat's right of resumption would be exercised within three years of the enactment of the proposed legislation.

(5) If, after resumption, the raiyat failed to bring the land under personal cultivation within one year or ceased to do so within next four years, the Collector would have the right to restore the land to the under-raiyats on the same terms and conditions as at the time of the resumption.

(6) For this purpose "personal cultivation" would include cultivation by any member of the joint family of the raiyats or by servants or hired labour. Steps were taken to enact a legislation in this regard.

The question of right of purchase of lands of tenants does not arise in Bihar so far as occupancy tenants are concerned. With regard to the under-raiyats holding lands under landlords, who had lands in excess of the ceiling proposed to be fixed under the Bihar Agricultural Lands (Ceiling and Management) Bill, 1955, the State Government decided to give right to the undertenants to purchase the raiyat's interests therein on payment of compensation to him of fifteen times the rent. This right was proposed to be given to the under-raiyats irrespective of any consideration for the period for which they had held the land.

With regard to the subletting of lands by raiyats in future, the State Government decided as follows, and took steps to enact necessary legislation at an early date:

(1) Subletting of land should, as a rule, be prohibited in future.

(2) Relaxation might be allowed in the matter of subletting of land in cases where the raiyat was an unmarried, divorced or separated woman, or a widow, or a minor or a person subject to

physical, legal or mental disability or a member of the Armed Forces of the Union in active service.

(3) In case of persons of the categories mentioned above, the subletting might be permitted through a registered lease, only and for a minimum period of five years. The lease might, however, be determined earlier on service of a notice of one year if it was required by the raiyat for personal cultivation. The under-raiyat might be made liable to be evicted before expiry of the lease on his failure to pay rent or on his using the land in a manner so as to render it until for the purpose of tenancy.

(4) In respect of lands which had already been sublet, the under-raiyats should be conferred rights of occupancy in the land irrespective of the period for which they had already held the same and without any payment, except in case of persons of the category referred to under sub-para (2) above, and subject to the right of the raiyats to resume for personal cultivation.

Under the existing provisions of the tenancy law, there was no restriction on the transfer of agricultural lands (where such transfer was permissible) by the agriculturists to the non-agriculturists by sale, lease or otherwise. This had been responsible to a great extent for concentration of agricultural lands in the hands of the non-agriculturists in certain areas. The holding of large areas of agricultural lands by the non-cultivating interests was incompatible with any satisfactory pattern of the agrarian economy and was also not conductive to the utilization of such lands for maximum production.

In view of the above, the State Government decided that the existing tenancy law should be amended in order to provide that no transfer or sale of agricultural lands would be regarded as valid or be permitted except where the transferee was an agriculturist and needed the land for personal cultivation, or, if he was not an agriculturist, he undertook to take to cultivation or wanted the land for construction of any building or for setting up an orchard.

The right given to the landowners to resume land from their tenants, subject to certain conditions, for making farming their profession land developing agriculture was, in fact, abused. Land was resumed in most cases not for personal cultivation and agricultural development but to add to the leased agricultural properties. This fact was disguised by all sorts of artifices. This right had to be exercised within the ceiling limit, but as the ceiling can be and has been an instrument of dispossessing the tenant for increasing exploitation, a means for enforcing submission on the tenants, even if it is not exercised, and when it is, it generally means that the rentiers have more land which is cultivated by the tenants-at-will or share-croppers though nominally by the cultivating owner with the help of the hired labourers. The entire scheme is based on an unrealistic assumption that the rent-receiving landowners can be converted into progressive farmers within the ceiling limit and will be a leaven in the countryside, for they, as a class, cannot by tradition be thus converted. This right is a source of great insecurity in the countryside and has done more harm than good by cowing down the peasantry, by enabling the rentier class—a functionless class-to prolong its existence and continue its exploitation and by impeding the process of its change-over to a more productive role.

The Share-cropping/Bataidari System and Agricultural Labour

At Independence the widespread system of share-cropping/*Bataidari* was branded as the bane of Bihar agriculture. In 1950-51 about 18.97 per cent of casual agricultural labourers also took land on lease on the share-cropping basis from their masters. 8.8 millions of agricultural population were agricultural labourers either with *Bataidari* land or without any land. The under-raiyats, i.e., the tenants were 3.3 million. 22.5 millions of the agricultural population were occupancy raiyats. The aggregate agricultural population was 34.6 millions. So 60 per cent of the population composed by the occupancy raiyats/ryots had acquired permanent and heritable security in land. In 1954-55 the number of families of landless agricultural labourers was 17 lakh. In 1956, 94 per cent of the owner and tenant families cultivated all their holdings. In 1980-81 the agricultural labourers with or without land numbered 73.5 lakhs. This amounts to saying that in about thirty years the population of agricultural labour (all members of the families considered) had risen by 14.5 lakhs. Of these, 291441 families in 1982-83 were landless as well as homeless.

From the point of view of gross produce per unit of land the owner cultivators were the best. Next were the cultivators of leased-in land on rent in terms of either fixed cash or in kind. The worst were the share-croppers.

A field study launched in 1981-82 by the A.N.S. Institute, Patna brought to light a number of interesting facts about the share-croppers in the two plain regions of Bihar, where the share-cropping type tenancy was a widespread practice/phenomenon. Nearly 59.04 per cent of the cultivating households and 43.19 per cent of the rural households leased-in land on share-cropping terms or on labour service terms, the two standing to each other in the ration of 6.5 to 1.0. The number of rural households reporting this was 19.1 lakh and the area involved was 9.2 lakh ha. 17.22 per cent of all rural farm holders and 7.44 per cent of large farm holders were in the vanguard of leasing. For every one resident owner who leasedout, there were more than two resident owners who leasedin . The leased-out area as percentage of the owned area by marginal workers was 6.85 per cent in 1971-72, which had fallen to 4.32 per cent in 1982. The area leased-in per sharecropper was one acre or less, reminiscent of the traditions in tenancy handed down from the feudal days.

The share-croppers paid rent to their landlords out of the produce. The rent was exorbitant. It was half of the produce. This was applicable to practically all share-croppers. In addition to this, they paid exactions of other kinds/in other forms, such as produce rent, *Begar* (free services), presents (Nevta/Neg) on the eve of social functions held in the families of their landlords, etc. The actual terms and conditions of this varied between districts, as also in the various parts of one and the same district. The above-mentioned study showed that the terms of the lease were as follows: (1) 1.07 per cent of all leases were on cash rent, (2) 10.16 per cent of them were on kind rent, and (3) 11.76 per cent on labour service. As a rule, the landlords did not supply inputs to their share-croppers. But in the exceptional cases where they shared the costs thereof, that equalled half of the cost. The by-product generally remained with the share-croppers.

Where the landlords did not share the cost and took away half of the produce or even more than it, the share-croppers surrendered part of the surplus value that was created by their labour. But there was a second surrender of surplus value to the landlords where usury was combined with rackrenting. According to the study under reference, about 32.14 per cent of the attached agricultural labourers borrowed from their landlords. About 17.86 per cent of the bonded agricultural labourers were bonded on both accounts—indebtedness and tenancy. Often agricultural labourers needed consumption loans, which paved the way for their usurious exploitation by their masters.

One notable finding of the study alluded to here was that share-cropping tenancy decreased where the area under irrigation was on the increase.

In 1987-88 the number of tillers of the soil and their dependents in Bihar was 75.3 per cent of the total population of the State. A very large proportion of the land in the State was cultivated by the occupancy rayots with permanent and inheritable right in their land, who also constituted the majority of the agricultural classes in terms of number. With their dependents they were 48.9 per cent of the total population in Bihar and they did not, in general, hire labour. Bihar was still steeped/ embedded in semi-feudal production relations. Share-cropping was still in vogue. Tenancy was prohibited on paper but existed in a concealed/ covert form. The share-cropping held tenuous oral leases (about one-third of the total land under share-cropping was under this). The oral lease-holders were liable to be moved from field to field. They were discouraged or even dissuaded from joining the cooperative societies for fear that their membership of the institution might indirectly vest them with occupancy rights. They were made to pay a rent which was half of the produce or even more. The result of this was that even if they could find the necessary credit for the purchase of inputs for carrying on their cultivation on the lines of modern technology they lacked the incentive to do so. They lacked in the motivation to introduce permanent improvements in their land and thereby increase its productivity because of their precarious tenurial status and the inequitous share in the increased produce which would be left eventually with them by their parasitic landlords.

The much-maligned share-cropping system cut at the very root of better farming since it deprived the actual tiller of the basic motivation as well as the resources for switching over from subsistence farming to modern farming. It was oblivious of the necessity of properly maintaining the existing community irrigation works in the case of absentee landlordism. Especially in respect of the large holdings, the adverse effect of the share-cropping was more in evidence. All told, the share-cropping system acted as a drag on the refashioning bid in the sphere of agrarian relations and institutions, and hence the drive for a richer and fuller life in rural Bihar.

The ceiling legislation permitted the individual, as against the family ceiling but it was soon watered down, with the result that share-cropping got a fresh lease of life. The enforcement of the minimum agricultural wages by the Government and insistence shown by the agricultural labourers' sympathisers who have organised armies for the purpose and the increased volume of migration from Bihar to other States are the recent developments which have rekindled the old share-cropping practice. The semi-feudal production relations persist, the lion's share of the produce goes to the people who are on top of the economic ladder in the countryside, which throws a douche of cold water on the incentive to work hard in the case of the ordinary agricultural labourer, who is condemned perpetually to a life of hardship and penury.

To conclude, the data support the hypothesis that it is, by and large, on account of the infirmities of the land system that an average tenant's unending plight in Bihar is forced to anyhow survive, the concentration of land area under share-croppiong is the highest in the State and leasing-in is proportionally outpacing leasing-out.

Implementation of Land Reform Measures

The Bihar Government declared that upto 1981-82 land that was surplus was 98380 ha. On March 31, 1989 that land which was surplus in accordance with the ceiling legislation in Bihar was 1,92,100 ha. in area. On November 11, 1989 the figure remained unaltered. In September 1990 there was a very small increase and the figure was 1,92,154 ha. In 1993 the figure stood at 1,92,307 ha.

Under the ceiling law between 16 July, 1977 and February, 1979 the area of land acquired was 2406 ha. Upto December 31, 1981, the area of land acquired was 11174 ha. Till March 1982, the State Government had acquired 96,315 ha. of the surplus land. Upto 1983-84 the area acquired as revised was 107685 ha. On November 11, 1987 the acquired land totalled 14,051 ha., upto 1988, 145717 ha., on March 31, 1989, 148100 ha., in September 1990, 151853 ha. (79.03 per cent of the area declared surplus) and in 1993-94, 162960 ha. Upto 1994, the figure was 163575 ha.

Accepting that there was confusion of redistributed ceiling surplus land with redistributed *Bhoodan* land and/or Government *Gairmazrua* land, we note that between 16 July, 1977 and February, 1979 the area of redistributed land was 6668 ha., but the figure for the period upto 31 December, 1981 was substantially higher, 56989 ha. Upto the end of 1981-82 the area of land redistributed was significantly higher, as per the data available, 12.14 lakh ha. According to one estimate, the State Government had distributed over 57,060 ha. of the acquired land among 0.16 million families upto March 1982, which incorporated 85,088 families of the scheduled castes and 16,816 families of the scheduled tribes. However, the data given for the period upto 1983-84 was surprisingly lower, 67,996 ha. Had part of the land acquired gone into dispute or what? As on November 11,1987 total land redistributed was

1,03,462 ha. But, then, the figure given for the period upto 1988 was 110995 ha., higher than before. Next, till September1990, 1,02,030 ha. land was reported to have been distributed. This was 53.10 per cent of all land taken possession of upto then. There was an improvement during 1988-90 but even then the figure was below that we had for the period upto 1987. For 1993-94 the figure was 118814 ha. Till 1994-end, in 26 years since the implementation of the ceiling legislation, the total land redistributed was 119437 ha. Account is not taken of 7822 ha. land which was not fit for distribution. Let us note that in redistributing the acquired land the Government first kept in mind the dire needs of the weaker sections of our society, viz., scheduled castes which were preponderant in North Bihar, scheduled tribes which were predominant in the plateau region and other backward sections, which were scattered all over the State. Other inhabitants came in for consideration after the requirements of these three categories of the population had been attended to. A family which was devoid of land as well as a roof over its head was the norm.

As for the number of families benefited, between July, 1977 and February, 1979, it was 16736. But the figure given of the benefited families upto 31 December 1981, is lower, it is 1,51,510. Upto 1981-82, the figure was still lower, 118771. The position on 31 March, 1989 was 286100 families (of the landless people). Per beneficiary family the distributed land was 0.4 ha. Upto the end of 1994 in 26 years after the ceiling legislation was enforced the total number of families benefited came to 358952.

The ceiling surplus land was settled with the scheduled castes and scheduled tribes upto 1981-82 : 70742 families of the former and 18421 families of the latter (plus 29608 families of the other sections, which were without land). This gives the following percentages 59.5, 15.5 and 25.0 respectively. Upto November 11,1987,176446 families of the scheduled castes (60.6 per cent) and 33975 families of the scheduled tribes (11.1 per cent) benefited from redistribution, besides other weaker sections 28.3 per cent. Their shares in area settled were scheduled castes 58 per cent 59661 ha. and scheduled tribes 29.3 per cent 29933 ha. The area allotted to all the three categories upto 1988 amounted to 10005 ha.; upto 1989-90, 102686 ha.; and upto 1993-94, 118582 ha. The State Government arranged for financial assistance to the beneficiaries of the land allotment policy.

It was soon realised by the well-wishers of the scheduled tribes in Bihar that their welfare depended a great deal on agricultural development, which called for a three-pronged attack—first, tenurial reform , second introduction of the NAT with restraint, adopting the policy of 'walking on both legs' for a time, and three, provision of irrigation by means of renovating the old ponds and wells in the first instance, and by installing pumping-sets and tubewells in the second instance, subject to the provision of power supply. Here we are concerned with the first measure. Under the Chotanagpur Tenancy Act, as amended, the tribals were protected against alienation from their lands and the power to sell and purchase land was withdrawn from the Deputy Commissioners and reinvested in the tribals themselves. Between 1969 and 1982, 24432 cases of usurpation of land from the tribals were disposed of and 11692 ha. of land returned to them. Upto 1988, more than 16.19 lakh ha. land was returned to the tribals. Upto June 1988, 437114 ha., and upto June 1994, 160230 ha. land illegally alienated was restored to the tribal families in question. Financial and legal assistances were respectively arranged for by the State Government for the tribal families which were returned their land and tribal families which suffered alienation.

The *Gairmazrua* lands (uncultivated lands) held previously by the *zamindars* were taken over by the State Government and settled with the landless agricultural labourers. Till 1967 there were 18.62 lakh ha. of such lands. Upto 1972, about 1.62 lakh ha. of these lands were settled with these labourers. From July 1977 to February 1978, 18064 families were benefited and 4772 ha. land settled. Upto 1981-82 the State Government had allotted 175426 ha. land to 504728 landless families.*

One main plank or adjunct of the land reform programme was the *Bhoodan Movement* launched by Acharya Vinoba Bhave, Mahatma Gandhi's most trusted disciple. It was his movement which led to the land ceiling legislation and redistribution of the ceiling surplus and donated lands. The Bihar Government passed the Bihar Bhoodan Yagyna Act in 1954. Under this act 8.63 lakh ha. lands were donated by the State Government, zamindars, and other landowners.

During the 1950s Vinoba received 857391 ha. of land from the donors, which he distributed among 395637families, including 14981 ha. given to 804119 persons for housesites.

Upto 31 March 1964, under the Bhoodan Movement, land collected was 863470 ha., 50.4 per cent of total land donated to Vinoba in all-

---

* The reader would bear in mind the likelihood of confusion between families-benefited under various methods, already hinted at above, overlapping and duplication being the reasons.

India. In Bihar about 13 per cent of the donated land was distributed. The all-India average was 25.3 per cent. The number of villages donated was 121 in Bihar, 1.77 per cent of the all-India figure.

Upto 1967 the State Government received through the Bhoodan Movement 8.50 lakh ha. of land. The *Gairmazrua* lands donated by the State Government to Acharya Vinoba were 0.80 lakh ha. and were settled with landless agricultural labourers till 1972.

Between July 1977 and February 1979, 16108 ha. land, received through the Bhoodan Movement, was distributed, benefiting 51419 families.

Upto March 31, 1989 the position of the Movement was as follows: Land collected 857391 ha., land distributed 272782 ha., number of beneficiaries 526029, land unfit for distribution 495679 ha., land pending for distribution 88928 ha. and wasteland and disputed lands were 57,81 per cent.

Upto November 1995, 291302 ha. of the Bhoodan land was redistributed among the landless families. But in 1994 cases of more than 3.06 lakh farmers, among whom the *Bhoodan* lands had been distributed were pending with the Circle Officers all over the State for the fixation of their revenues and collection thereof after the fixation.

When estimated critically, in all-India perspective, it appears that Bihar's performance, compared to those of West Bengal, Orissa and Uttar Pradesh, was the poorest.

One method of tenancy reform relates to homestead and usufruct mortgage. Homestead rights were given to the privileged persons of the weaker sections of society under the Bihar Privileged Persons Homestead Tenancy Act, 1969. Developed housesites were also provided to the rural landless labourers. The following table (Table 18.7) summarises the progress made so far in this direction.

In implementing this measure (allotment of housesites, developed houses, etc.) of the land reform programme Bihar did slightly better.

During 1937-39 when the Congress Ministry was formed and was in power in Bihar, tenancy laws were passed and palliatives were introduced to mitigate rural indebtedness, which, though not radical in themselves in the existing context, yet had a real political and social import. Upto 1981-82, 59 to 60 per cent of the agricultural households were indebted to the traditional sources of rural finance. Upto 1981-82 bondage of agricultural labourers was a widespread phenomenon in Bihar. In 1982 the number of bonded labourers identified and freed was 4958. The number of bonded labourers to be identified and freed under

TABLE 18.7 : Distribution of Housesites in Bihar

Year/ Period	*Allotment to Landless (No. of housesites)*	*Slips given to Persons for Housesites (No.)*	*Housesites given to Persons (No.)*	*Allotment of developed housesites to families (No.)*	*Allotment of houses to economically weaker sections families (No.)*	*Allotment of houses to lower income groups (No. of houses)*	*Allotment of house sites to landless agricultural workers (No.)*
July 1997 to February 1979		55845					
Upto 1981-82			75706				32684
1981-85	45000						
1985-86	36110						
11986-87	22571						
Position on 11 November 1987							150075
Upto 15 November 1987				151940			150075
1987-88	23682						
1985-89				108449	50750	1866	
Upto 1988				168113/ 169177/ 168113			
1989-90				25000	10000	866	
1993-94				16558			32684

other ongoing schemes was 952. With the inauguration of the 20-Point Programme during the 1975-77 Emergency, the programme directed at the rehabilitation of bonded labourers got a further momentum, as a result of which the number of bonded labourers rehabilitated during 1978-79 to 1981-82 was 4615. For some of the subsequent years the figures were : 15 November 1987 (cumulative?) : 12102, 1988-89 : 468, 1989-90 : 494, 1993-94 : 364 and 1994-95 : 12180 (cumulative?)

The Bihar Debt Redemption Act, passed in the early 1950s proved effective and within a short duration over half the indebted households received permanent relief.

We now come to *Village Panchayat* as an apparatus of management of land as legislation conceived of under the ceiling. Chapter IX of the Bihar Land Reforms (Fixation of Ceiling On Land) Act envisages the manner in which the surplus land would be disposed of. Under Section 27 it was laid down that all lands acquired or deemed to be acquired by the State Government under this Act might be entrusted to the management of village panchayats within whose jurisdiction the acquired lands are situated.* If 1,989 thousand acres of the surplus land was distributed among about 14 thousand village panchayats. Each panchayat, on an average, would be required to manage about 142 acres, a farm of which size would be large enough under the conditions prevailing in our country to be managed economically by a village panchayat. A snag which lay in the fact was that 142 acres of land could not be one consolidated piece of land but a very large number of fragments. This would obviously be a very uneconomic proposition and may ultimately affect agricultural production adversely. As a matter of fact, there was great likelihood of futher fragmentation as the landholder, on fixation of the ceiling, would have the option to select the land he wanted to retain within the permissible limit and to part with the rest. It was, therefore, necessary that in order that both the objectives of land reforms could be fulfilled, a serious and strenuous drive had to be made for the consolidation of holdings. It was also necessary to make some provision in law such that a village panchayat, when asked to manage the surplus land on behalf of the State Government, was able to operate a compact and consolidated block of the surplus land thus acquired. This should be extended also to the co-operatives of the landless agriculturists as an alternative technique of management.

---

* During the First Plan an increasing number of village panchayats had been entrusted with the task of collection of land revenue.

The advocates of the land reforms were of the opinion that it was possible to organise *cooperative farming* in Bihar with the clear objectives of: (i) eliminating the wasteful features of the small land fragmented holdings, (ii) imparting progressiveness to Bihar agriculture, (iii) providing local leadership, (iv) securing the advantages of large-scale purchase and sale, and (v) owning jointly such mechanical appliances as are beyond the reach of the individual farmers. The preponderance of dwarfish holdings was a compelling reason for making cooperative farming, the most effective measure for the expansion of production, improvement of techniques of rational utilization of land and the most desirable allocation of manpower. But that would have necessarily involved a fundamental change in the rural economy itself. The strongest objection to this change was the attachment of the peasants to land and their unwillingness to put their best into it until the right of ownership had been vested in them. In any well-conceieved and well-operated socialist society this had to be duly considered and provided for. However, one could not gloss over the fact that individually farming was incompatible with such a society as it produced oligarchy, bred acquisitiveness and vitiated the community life at its very base. However, the introduction of cooperative farming had to be preceded by long and careful preparation involving the development of all other types of cooperatives. Cooperative farming had to be the highest stage in the development of the cooperative superstructure. It had to develop as a voluntary mass movement under genuine local leadership and as a logical growth of community development and cooperation at the village level. This was not practicable in Bihar in the conditions that obtained in it.

With a view to remedying the problems faced by the medium and small owners of land, the Planning Commission recommended to the State Governments to take up in their respective States the programme of *consolidation* of holdings and to pursue it with vigour. In order to implement this recommendation of the Planning Commission the Bihar Government drafted and introduced the Bihar Consolidation of Holding and Prevention of Fragmentation Bill in 1955. The Bill sought to enact a comprehensive legislation for the consolidation of holdings and prevention of fragmentation. The salient features of the Bill were as given below:

(1) Undertaking the consolidation of holdings in any area of publication of a notification in this behalf by the State

Government on its own initiative or on applications of the holders of land, having the right of the occupancy therein.

(2) Setting up of the requisite machinery (e,g, Consolidation Officers, Settlement Officers, Settlement Commissioners, etc.) for purposes of the consolidation work.

(3) Setting up of an Advisory Committee, where village panchayats did not exist, to advise the Consolidation Officers in preparation of the schemes of consolidation.

(4) Empowering the consolidation authorities to amalgamate the public roads, etc., with private holdings for purposes of drawing up schemes for consolidation and to divert the public roads, etc., on other lands and also to direct that any land specifically assigned for any public purpose should cease to be assigned and to assign any other land in its place.

(5) Barring of the jurisdiction of the Civil Courts in matters arising out of the consolidation proceedings.

(6) Preparation of maps and records of rights incorporating the changes consequent upon the consolidation work.

(7) Payment of compensation to the landholders receiving holdings of lesser valuation than their original holdings and realisation of compensation from the landholders receiving holdings of higher valuation than their original holdings.

(8) Assessment, apportionment and realisation, in part or in whole, of the cost of the consolidation work.

(9) Granting land improvement loans and agricultural loans to the landholders for payment of cost or compensation in connection with the consolidation proceedings.

(10) Exemption of transfers, exchanges, etc., involved in consolidation from execution of instruments in writing.

(11) Exemption of all instruments, if executed, in this behalf from registration.

(12) Determination and declaration by the State Government to any local area and the class of land, the laying down of restrictions, as aforesaid on transfer, sale, etc. to fragments and prohibition of creation of fragments in future. The ideal way of preventing fragmentation of holdings in future would be to amend the existing personal laws of inheritance so as to introduce the Law of Primogeniture but perhaps such a course was fraught with difficulties in the existing conditions of things and hence its adoption was not generally favoured.

The Bill became an Act in 1958 and in accordance with this Act, four pilot projects, one in each division, were started. The State Government constituted a committee to go into the various aspects of the question of the introduction of cooperative farming in the State. The report of the committee was received and its recommendations were considered by the State Government.

The State Government decided to embark upon the consolidation of holdings work, which started in 1958 itself. To begin with, it was begun in a few selected districts, with decision to extend its scope to other districts in the successive stages.

Upto 1960-61, landholdings of the area of 9716 ha. were consolidated. Upto 1966-67, 2 per cent of all holdings had been consolidated. By 1974, 2.6 per cent of all cultivated land was brought under consolidation. Till 1989 consolidation had extended to 17.18 lakh ha. Till July 3,1992, 188 *Anchals*/blocks of 25 districts had been covered by consolidation.

Meanwhile, Chief Minister Laloo Prasad Yadav found fault with the very basis of the programme and ordered that until the weaknesses of the same were removed the programme would remain suspended. So the work came to a halt with effect from July 4, 1992. The staff engaged in the programme were shifted to survey work-cum-updating of the land records.

The consolidation of holdings programme was calculated to help the poor cultivators who were below the very basic standards of cultivation on account of the extreme subdivision of their holdings, and most of them in spite of their knowledge and application of the advanced, modern technology failed to develop the potential of their land more fully, as also failed to make a living from their occupation anywhere near the social minimum. This rendered the creation of much larger units of cultivation an absolute necessity. The singular success of the Green Revolution in Punjab was attributed by many to the consolidation of holdings in the State prior to the arrival of the Green Revolution. A fundamental change in the shape of consolidation of holdings in the prevalent structure of lands of the kind that took place in Punjab was indispensable if Bihar too desired its agriculture to be vibrant and dynamic and prosperous like Punjab's.

Let us here categorise the hindrances to consolidation in Bihar. The presence of a considerable number of marginal and small holdings is the first that comes to our mind. This characteristic adds to the difficulty at the practical level and is time-consuming. Secondly, the landholdings that are consolidated are liable to be divided as and when partitions arise. Thirdly, it was soon realised that whenever a team connected with the consolidation work reached a village, the villagers unduly got worked up. Fourthly, the local traditional customs were sometimes an obstacle. Fifthly, the average area per parcel of land was relatively much smaller in Bihar, compared to what was in Punjab's lot on the eve of the consolidation programme. Finally, the bureaucratic staff lacked the amount of tact and patience which was an essential prerequisite of consolidation, and hence Bihar had to face the inscrutable opposition of the small landholders which became aggravated with the sabotage planned by the official staff.

In fine, with the passage of time, the initial difficulties had been overcome to a large extent, but the stand taken by the Chief Minister in 1992 was almost fatal. The remarkable changes in the life and economy of the villages which the programme intended to usher in became, as a result, uncertain between the twin stools of the limited progress made till 1992 and the doubts cast on the necessity of the programme by the Chief Minister in 1992.

One reason why the land reforms implementation was ineffective was the absence of proper and uptodate land records as well as revision of the land records periodically. At the time *zamindaris* were abolished the outgoing zamindars did not hand over all the papers of their zamindaris to the State Government available with themselves. Also, those who had the papers with them did not like to part with them on the ground that they required them in connection with the collection of rent arrears. A large body of the erstwhile zamindars did not have in their possession full details of their own occupant tenants and share-croppers. The land records which existed were nearly 30 years old at the time the zamindaris were abolished, or even more than 30 years old, and in some cases over 50 years old. The Survey and Settlement Operations had been conducted many years precedent to the abolition of the zamindari system. It was in the light of the old entries recorded in the last Survey and Settlement Operations that the Field Bujharat had reconstructed the village records.

Ever since the take-over of the zamindaris, updating of the land records has been the most important task before the Land Reforms Department of the State Government. Even then the land survey work could not be completed uptill now in all districts because the State has been badly constrained by the paucity of funds and manpower required for the uphill task. Land records are now being computerised district and block-wise.

Another factor responsible for the slow and tardy progress of the land reforms programme in Bihar has been the weak revenue administration. Strengthening of revenue administration has been a prime task before the Government ever since the zamindaris had passed into its control and ownership. Upto 1956 there was total absence of any revenue administration below the district level. After the zamindaris were abolished, the revenue agencies in the village had to be built up from a scratch, so to say. There was great dearth of the subordinate personnel, of the ranks of Tahsildars in Bihar, as this class of revenue officials did not exist in the State. Therefore, the recruitment programme to the junior civil service had to be greatly geared up. As of the present, land revenue is collected by the Block-level officers. It is a concern of the Block-level administration. Even so, serious lapses are discerned on the part of the revenue staff of the development blocks. The tenants are required to pay rent in cash.

Another major event of the recent times is the conversion of the concealed tenancy into written settlement by the State Government. In 1981-82 the decision to provide to every farmer a pass-book with details of his land, ownership, khasra number, etc., was made. As of today, in many districts the individual landowners have their *Khata Pustaks* with those details. Contained in them are the names of the share-croppers, who could now borrow agricultural credit by showing the pass-book. Those who are landless and are provided land are given *Lal Parchas*, although we cannot disregard the fact that a vast number of the possessors of these *Lal Parchas* (documentary proofs of having been provided which strips of land) have not so far been able to establish their possession rights over the land.

Unequal Distribution of Land : Once Again*

In the earlier period of post-independence in Bihar the glaring inequality in the distribution of land was taken as representative/symbolic of glaring social inequality and hence one chief plank in the land reforms policy was redistribution of land through the ceiling legislation. What incidence this had on the relationship between number of operational holdings and their areas by size-class can be sampled from a comparison of the bottom size classes (upto 2 ha.) with the top size classes (10 ha. and above) in 1985-86, as compared with the same in 1970-71(Tables 18.8 and 18.9).

* The question of population in relation to land in Bihar during the last fifty years has been examined at length, in its various ramifications, in our earlier publication, *Population Pressure and Economic Backwardness*, Anamika, Delhi-52.

TABLE 18.8 : Number, Area and Average Size of Operational Holdings by Size-class in Bihar, 1970-71, 1976-77 and 1980-81

Category	*Size-Class (ha.)*	*Number of Operational Holdings ('000)*					
		1970-71	*1976-77*	*1980-81*	*Percentage Variation*		
					During 1976-77 W.R. to 1970-71	*During 1980-81 W.R. to 1970-71*	*During 1980-81 W.R. to 1976-77*
(1)	(2)	(3)	(4)	(5)	(6)	(7)	(8)
	Below 0.3	3527	5445	6585	(+) 54.4	(+) 86.7	(+) 20.9
	0.5—1.0	1349	1771	1935	(+) 31.4	(+) 43.6	(+) 9.7
1. *Marginal*	Below 1.0	4874	7215	8521	(+) 48.0	(+) 74.8	(+) 18.1
2. *Small*	1.0—2.0	1109	1191	1218	(+) 7.4	(+) 9.8	(+) 2.3
	2.0—3.0	575	593	612	(+) 3.3	(+) 6.5	(+) 3.1
	3.0—4.0	346	324	339	(–) 1.8	(–) 0.4	(+) 1,5
3. *Semi-Medium*	2.0—4.0	915	928	951	(+) 1.4	(+) 3.9	(+) 2.5
	4.0—5.0	223	217	214	(–) 2.9	(–) 4.3	(–) 1.4
	5.0—7.5	320	205	175	(–) 13.7	(–) 19.5	(–) 14.4
	7.5—10.0		97	82			(–) 15.1
4. *Medium*	4.0—10.0	54	519	472	(–) 4.5	(–) 13.2	(–) 9.1
	10.0—20.0	105	64	53	(–) 38.9	(–) 49.6	(–) 17.8
	20.0—30.0	19	13	10	(–) 33.4	(–) 45.4	(–) 18.1
	30.0—40.0	6	4	3	(–) 39.2	(–) 53.1	(–) 22.8
	40.0—50.0	2	1	1	(–) 47.9	(–) 55.9	(–) 15.5
	50.0 and above	3	1	1	(–) 12.0	(–) 65.1	(–) 39.9
5. *Large*	10.0 and above	135	83	68	(–) 38.3	(–) 49.6	(–) 18.2
	Total	7577	9936	11230	(+) 31.1	(+) 48.2	(–) 13.2

(*Contd.*)

TABLE 10.8 (Contd.)

Category	Size-Class (ha.)	Area of Operational Holdings ('000 hectares)						Average Size (hectares)		
		1970-71	1976-77	1980-81	Percentage Variation			1970-71	1976-77	1980-81
					During 1976-77 W.R. to 1970-71	During 1980-81 W.R. to 1970-71	During 1980-81 W.R. to 1976-77			
(1)	(2)	(9)	(10)	(11)	(12)	(13)	(14)	(15)	(16)	(17)
	Below 0.3	865	1351	1560	(+) 56.1	(+) 80.3	(+) 15.5	0.2	0.2	0.2
	0.5—1.0	280	1227	1392	(+) 25.2	(+) 42.1	(+) 13.4	0.7	0.7	0.7
1. *Marginal*	Below 1.0	1845	2578	2952	(+) 39.7	(+) 60.0	(+) 14.5	0.4	0.4	0.3
2. *Small*	1.0—2.0	1568	1592	1648	(+) 1.9	(+) 5.4	(+) 3.5	1.4	1.3	1.3
	2.0—3.0	1379	1386	1453	(+) 0.5	(+) 5.3	(+) 4.8	2.4	2.3	2.3
	3.0—4.0	1153	1110	1141	(–) 4.1	(–) 1.4	(+) 2.8	3.4	3.3	3.3
3. *Semi-Medium*	2.0—4.0	2537	2496	2594	(–) 1.6	(–) 0.1	(+) 3.9	2.8	2.7	2.7
	4.0—5.0	989	939	976	(–) 5.9	(–) 5.3	(+) 0.7	4.4	4.3	4.3
	5.0—7.5	2187	1201	1066	(–) 8.1	(–) 18.9	(–) 11.2	6.8	6.7	6.0
	7.5—10.0	8175	808	707			(–) 12.5		8.3	8.0
4. *Medium*	4.0—10.0	3175	2939	2709	(–) 7.4	(–) 14.7	(–) 7.8	5.8	5.7	5.7
	10.0—20.0	1392	868	709	(–) 37.7	(–) 49.1	(–) 18.3	13.2	13.5	13.8
	20.0—30.0	447	290	246	(–) 35.0	(–) 45.0	(–) 15.3	23.4	22.9	23.6
	30.0—40.0	195	123	92	(–) 37.0	(–) 52.8	(–) 25.0	33.7	34.9	33.9
	40.0—50.0	102	53	44	(–) 47.6	(–) 56.5	(–) 17.0	44.3	44.5	43.7
	50.0 and above	225	134	74	(–) 40.4	(–) 67.1	(–) 44.7	87.3	89.8	82.4
5. *Large*	10.0 and above	2360	1468	1165	(–) 37.8	(–) 50.6	(–) 20.6	17.5	17.6	17.9
	Total	11480	11073	11068	(–) 3.5	(–) 3.6	9.0	1.5	1.1	0.9

Source : Agricultural Census, 1980-81.

Note : W.R. = With Reference.

TABLE 18.9 : Number and Area of Operational Holdings by Size Class in Bihar 1985-86

Size-class (in ha.)	*Total Holdings*				*Average Area Per Holding (ha.)*
	Number ('000)	*Percentage*	*Area ('000 ha.)*	*Percentage*	
Marginal					
1. Below 0.02	1354	11.56	21	0.19	0.01
2. 0.02—0.5	5409	46.19	1645	15.09	0.31
3. 0.5—1.0	2213	18.90	1637	15.02	0.74
Total (1+2+3)	8976	76.65	3303	30.30	0.37
Small					
4. 1.0—2.0	1327	11.33	1869	17.15	1.41
Total (4)	1327	11.33	1869	17.15	1.41
Semi-Medium					
5. 2.0—3.0	621	5.30	1482	13.60	2.39
6. 3.0—4.0	330	2.82	1111	10.20	3.37
Total (5+6)	951	8.12	2593	23.80	2.73
Medium					
7. 4.0—5.0	191	1.63	836	7.67	4.37
8. 5.0—7.5	144	1.23	877	8.05	6.11
9. 7.5—10.0	69	0.59	580	5.33	8.35
Total (7+8+9)	404	3.45	2293	21.05	5.67
Large					
10. 10.0—20.0	43	0.37	568	5.21	13.25
11. 20.0—30.0	7	0.06	165	1.52	23.33
12. 30.0—40.0	2	0.01	49	0.45	32.58
13. 40.0—50.0	1	0.01	23	0.21	44.08
14. 50.0 and above			34	0.31	69.82
Total (10+11+12+13+14)	53	0.45	839	7.70	15.99
All Sizes	11,711	100.00	10,898	100.00	0.93

Source : Agricultural Census, 1985-86.

Table 18.10 shows that between 1970-71 and 1985-86 at the bottom of size distribution of holdings the number of holdings below 2 ha. increased by 172 per cent, whereas the area under them increased by 113 per cent, which denoted a decrease in the average size. As percentage of total number, the holdings of size upto 2 ha. were 9.0 per cent up but

TABLE 18.10 : Impact of Land Ceiling Legislation on Number and Area Relations of Operational Holdings in Bihar

Size-class (ha.)	*Number ('000)*		*Percentage*	*Area ('000 ha.)*		*Percentage Change*	*Average Size (ha.)*		*Percentage Change*
	1970-71	*1985-86*		*1970-71*	*1985-86*		*1970-71*	*1985-86*	
Bottom									
Below 2.0 ha.	59.83	10303	(+) 172	4553	5172	(+) 113	0.76	0.50	(–) 34.3
As percentage of Total	78.9	87.9	(+) 9.0	39.6	47.4	(–) 7.8			
Top									
10 ha. and above	135	53	(–) 61.0	2360	839	(–) 65.0	17.48	15.83	(–) 9.5
As percentage of Total	1.78	0.45	(–) 1.33	20.5	7.7	(–) 12.8			
All	7577	11711	(+) 154.0	11480	10898	(–) 5.0	1.51	0.93	(–) 38.5

Note : The figures in this table are derived from Table's 18.8 and 18.9.

as percentage of area they were only 7.8 per cent up, which also denoted a dent in the average size. By comparison, during the same period the number of holdings at the top, 10 ha. and above,fell by 61.0 per cent, while their area fell more sharply by 65.0 per cent, thereby signifying a decline in the average size. As percentage of total, the share of the top land holdings fell by a far higher percentage in area than in number. Interpreted, this meant that owners with holdings exceeding the ceiling limit had taken steps to reduce their number, which impringed heavily on total area under them, with the result that as percentage of the aggregate, the share diminished more sharply in terms of area than in those of number, the average size of holdings being reduced, though less than proportionally than area. Lastly, taking the total number and total area of holdings into consideration, we discover that the percentage rise in their number share was several times higher than the percentage fall in their area share (154 per cent *versus* 5 per cent). The decline in the average size was to the extent of 38.5 per cent. The land reforms programme had ended in the break-up of the bigger into the smaller holdings. The number of holdings had gone up spectacularly, whereas part of the old total area had passed into non-agricultural uses. The number of men operating the holdings had increased, but the total area operated had decreased.

The trend towards subdivision and fragmentation of holdings had become more entrenched than before with the passage of time under the influence of socio-economic factors, of which the law of inheritance was the king-pin, given the inborn fascination of an average rural inhabitant for the landed property, no matter even if it is miniscule. In numerous cases the plot cultivated by the average family is so small that it cannot fully occupy all the time all the members of the family. Farm and approach roads cannot be constructed ; irrigation and drainage channels cannot be provided in areas where the holdings are small because costs involved far outrun the benefits envisaged. In many cases the fields are mere plots of land. The holding is very much fragmented. Its layout is so scattered in some cases that there are 17 to 20 fragments per holding. Only about two decades ago there were five parcels per holding and the average area per parcel came out to be barely 0.22 ha.; among the holdings below one ha. each, it was 0.10 ha. The more fertile the land is, the more fragmented is the holding. The only rational reason behind fragmentation is that for the sake of protection against a natural calamity which is a more frequent visitor in Bihar than elsewhere a farmer prefers to have a plot in each tract/segment. On the whole, however, fragmentation of holdings is an impediment to agrarian transformation.

When we try to have a look into the share of area operated by the various segments of holdings in rural area over a fairly long period, here from 1953-54 to 1982, 27 to 28 years (Table 18.11), we find maximum percentage rise in the case of top 5 per cent, and minimum in that of top one per cent, the two figures being 1.18 and 0.29 per cent respectively. Likewise, the maximum fall occurred in the of top 10 per cent, 3.41 per cent and the minimum in that of the middle 50 to 80 per cent, 0.86 per cent.

TABLE 18.11 : Share of Area Operated by Various Segments of Holdings (Rural) in Bihar : 1953-54 *Versus* 1982

Indicators		*Bihar*	*All-India*
Share of Bottom			
25 per cent	1953-54	2.08	1.97
	1982	2.44	1.21
40 per cent	1953-54	6.63	5.77
	1982	4.84	4.91
50 per cent	1953-54	11.19	9.71
	1982	9.78	8.74
Share of Middle			
40 to 80 per cent	1953-54	33.25	28.92
	1982	33.77	29.77
50 to 80 per cent	1953-54	29.69	24.98
	1982	28.83	25.94
Share of Top			
20 per cent	1953-54	60.72	65.35
	1982	61.39	65.32
10 per cent	1953-54	46.65	47.88
	1982	43.24	46.71
5 per cent	1953-54	27.59	33.24
	1982	28.77	32.16
1 per cent	1953-54	9.90	10.97
	1982	10.19	12.68

The marginal holdings have each an area under one ha. Table 18.12 illuminates how between 1970-71 and 1985-86 there has been further marginalisation of holdings and the average area of the marginal farms has further shrunk. The number of marginal farms increased by 184 per cent, whereas the area under them increased by 179 per cent. 76 per cent landholders cultivated 30 per cent of total land area.

TABLE 18.12 : Position of Marginal Holdings

Characters	1950-51	1953-54	1954-55	1956	1970-71	1976-77	1980-81	1982	1985-86
Ownership Holdings as percentage of total number of holdings of all size-classes			68.09						
Ownership Holdings Area as Percentage of total area			13.97						
Operational Holdings:									
As percentage of total number of holdings in the State:									
Sub-marginal	31.0	29.46 (19.71)		61.0	64.32	72.61	75.88	42.32 (32.30)	
Marginal	25.5/ ('0000)	21.77 (19.44)					75.87	26.30 (23.21)	76.6
Number					4874	7215	852		8976
As percentage of all-India total number									13.5
Percentage share in total area :									
		3.02 (1.07)						5.49 (2.42)	
Submarginal	3.6								
Marginal	10.3 ('000 ha.)	8.82 (4.36)			16.07	23.28	26.67	16.92 (9.08)	30.3
Area					1845	2578	2952	—	3303
Percentage share in all-India area									7.6
Average size (ha.)									
Sub-marginal		0.17 (0.16)						0.13 (0.16)	
Marginal		0.68 (0.68)			0.4	0.4	0.3	0.64 (0.66)	0.37 (0.39)

Note : Sub-marginal holdings are less than 0.40 ha., and marginal less than 1.0 ha.

The small holdings (ownership) in Bihar, as percentage of total holdings in the State, in 1953-54 were 22.77 per cent (all-India 20.85 per cent), with 19.73 per cent of total land area (all-India 10.01 per cent). In 1954-55 the small farms (ownership) in Bihar were 25.85 per cent of total number of all farms and had 18.67 per cent of total land area. In 1961-62 farms below 2.02 ha. in size were 77.27 per cent of all holdings in Bihar. Table 18.13 reveals how between 1970-71 and 1985-86, whereas the number of small holdings in Bihar rose by about 118 per cent, their area rose by nearly 119 per cent, which is proof of the average size of small holdings remaining static, unchanged during the period. The percentage share of the number of small holdings increased by about 3 per cent, while the percentage share of the area of these holdings increased by about 5 per cent. These changes attested to the impact of the Government's policy on the redistribution of land among the landless by acquiring it from those who owned land in excess of the prescribed ceiling limits.

TABLE 18.13 : Position of Small Holdings

Characters	*1950-51*	*1953-54*	*1970-71*	*1976-77*	*1980-81*	*1982*	*1985-86*
Number of Operational marginal holdings ('000)			1109	1191	1218		1327
Percentage share in total number of holdings	20.5	22.77 (20.85)	14.63	11.98	10.84	17.66 (19.53)	11.3
Area ('000 ha.)			1563	15.92	1648	18.69	
Percentage share in total area	17.3	19.73 (10.01)	12.01	14.37	14.89	25.85 (16.59)	17.1
Bihar's share in all-India in:							
Number							7.4
Area							6.1
Average size (ha.)		1.45 (1.46)	1.4	1.3	1.3	1.46 (1.44)	1.41 (1.43)

Note : Small holdings are those with size between 1 ha. and 2 ha.

Taking into account the marginal and small farms together, we find that on the eve of zamindari abolition they were 44.54 per cent of all farms in Bihar and cultivated land under them was 28.55 per cent of the total, the ratio between the two being l:0.64. In 1985-86 the corresponding figures were 87.9 and 47.4 per cent, and the ratio between them was

1:0.54. The ratio had been eroded by about 16 per cent during 32 to 33 years. The predominance of these two types of holdings which was typical of the agrarian system in the pre-zamindari abolition days has persisted even after the abolition of the zamindari system, and is insinuated to be a formidable hindrance to agrarian restructuring in the State. As for the explanation for this predominance, the propounders urge that this is not so much due to the maldistribution of land as to the excessive pressure of the population on the soil. Between 1952 and 1986 the subtotal of the two size-classes of holdings increased from about 49 lakhs in number to 89 lakhs in number, their percentage share in number rose from 44 to 88 per cent, while during 1970-86 the area increased by about 141 per cent. In 1980-81 42 per cent of GCA was claimed by them.

Remorse and anguish has marked works dealing with the marginal-small farms/holdings combine. The curve depicting their output used, in general, upward-rising continuously untill the farm management studies in the mid-1950s pointed out that absolute size was not the key determinant of farm efficiency, since in isolated cases even small farms could make do economically. This theory had a shot in its arms with the revelation that the NAT was scale-neutral. After the playing/watering-down of the conventional, orthodox thinking, which was contained at the practical level when the policy-making diverted their attention to the importance of the supply of inputs and institutional assistance and incentives, price and non-price, to the small producers, by imperceptibly reconciling themselves with the deemphasis of the redistribution of land route to the uplift of the teeming members of the marginal-small farmers combine, the final picture which we have at present of this big chunk of the agrarian system in Bihar may be briefly drawn in the following words:

To the extent that the action on the ceiling legislation has been taken according to the spirit and letter of it, the interests of the landless labourers in rural areas have been well served in the sense that a certain fraction of their total number has been provided with land, which has made them owners/occupants of the marginal-small holdings. But to the extent that the action on the legislation was forestalled or nipped in the bud or impounded in the legal warfare, pending judgment, quite a number of tenants/Bataidars were dispossessed of their strips of land and evicted by the outgoing zamindars.

As of now, the economic viability of the marginal-small units is seriously in doubt: this was so even on the eve of zamindari abolition.

No piece is enough to go around. This makes the pursuit of petty agriculture incumbent upon the holders. The plots are of an uneconomic size. They cannot keep the members of a family occupied with farm work all the year round. Labour efficiency is therefore low. The scanty investment in cattle, tools and implements, and other assets is not utilised productively owing to the small size of the plot, and this becomes a reason against introducing improved modern appliances, e.g. , tractors, pumpsets, threshers, etc. Underutilisation of labour and capital and adherence to the old technology together cause the yield to be low, earning to be extremely low and the accrual of the surplus a rare phenomenon. All these combine to condemn the small farmer to bare subsistence/survival, and lack of staying power, thereby compelling him to look for secondary means of livelihood, and so on. The set-up in which he has to operate poses the problem of proper management and organisation of the whole gamut of functions, which his scale of operation and his material position make extremely difficult, and the outcome is a suboptimal management and organisation. He is obliged to fall into the trap laid by the semi-monopolistic private and public organisations, with unwholesome consequences, socially as well as economically.

Mention of non-acceptance of the NAT by marginal-small farmers merits more discussion than firnished above. According to one school, the marginal-small farmers lack the capacity to invest in the high-cost modern inputs as well the motivation to do so. According to another, they may lack the capacity but assuredly not the motivation, and are found suffused with the desire and initiative for modernisation, and this in a larger measure than even the bigger farm-holders are, but because of the institutional flaws and the underlying difficulty of obtaining the necessary credit, they have to eschew the desire and the initiative. In areas where these hindrances have been surmounted, the marginal-small farmers vie passionately with their superior counterparts in striving to raise two blades of corn where only one has been raised so far.

To cut the long story short, a bright future lies in speeding up the institutional reforms in the agrarian system, while trying to push through the NAT. Only this double-pronged policy approach would break the present concentration of poverty and unemployment in the marginal-small combine of the farm households and thereby release them for being brought into the mainstream of growth and development in an increased degree, provided the progress made so far since independence is not denied.

Between 1970-71 and 1985-86 the number of semi-medium farms rose by 4 per cent, whereas their area did so by 2.2 per cent, and, as a result, the average size fell from 2.8 ha. to 2.7 ha. As percentage of total number of holdings, the number of semi-medium holdings declined from 12.07 per cent to 8.1 per cent. As percentage of total area, the area under semi-medium farms increased nominally from 22.53 to 23.8 per cent (Table 18.14). Tenants and *Bataidars* had been evicted in the process during the period.

TABLE 18.14 : Position of Semi-Medium Holdings

Characters	*1950-51*	*1954-55*	*1970-71*	*1976-77*	*1980-81*	*1985-86*
Number ('000)		781	915	928	951	951
Percentage share in number	14.3	10.99	12.07	9.34	8.46	8.1
Area ('000 ha.)		2218	2537	2496	2594	2593
Percentage share in area	24.2	12.78	22.53	22.54	23.43	23.8
Average size (ha.)			2.8	2.7	2.7	2.73

Note : Semi-medium holdings have an area between 2.0 and 4.0 ha. each.

In 1980-81, 19.30 per cent of all farms were in the small and semi-medium size-classes and operated 38.24 per cent of total area. In 1985-86 the two percentages were 19.4 and 40.9 respectively. Evidently, more lands had passed into the hands of their owners from those of the tenants and Bataidars. Those size-classes of holdings were the gainers.

So far as the medium holdings are concerned, Table 18.15 unravels that their number diminished by 21.4 per cent between 1970-71 and 1985-86, while the area under them had diminished by 19.3 per cent. The axe of the ceiling legislation had fallen on the owners of these holdings. Their percentage share in number had declined from 5.7 to 3.4 per cent, and that in area from 27.65 to 21.05 per cent during the same period. Their average size too had suffered a setback (from 5.8 to 5.6 ha.).

According to an estimate,in 1961-62 holdings in Bihar above 4.04 ha. in size were 8.12 per cent of the total number. Every thirteenth holding was in that group of holdings. Holdings over 6.07 ha. in size claimed 3.3 per cent of the aggregate number. Every thirtieth holding was of this size. Holdings which were in size 6.07 ha. and above were 3.4 per cent of all holdings and their owners were well-to-do.

In 1985-86 the semi-medium and medium holdings were 11.5 per cent of the total number of holdings and had under them 44.8 per cent of the aggregate area.

The ceiling legislation affected the large holdings most, lowering their number by 61 per cent and land area by 64.5 per cent during 1970-86. In percentage terms, the share in number fell from 1.78 to 0.45 per cent, and that in area from 20.5 to 7.7 per cent. The latter was very steep indeed. The average size of the large holdings got slashed from 17.5 to 16 ha. (Table 18.16).

Critics after critics have attacked the large holdings in Bihar on ground of mismanagement and inefficient operation. In 1956 the proportion of uncultivated area was as high as 78 per cent in holdings above 20.24 ha. Studies in 1970-71 brought out that large holdings were actually cultivated by share-croppers. Enquiries made in 1980-81 reiterated that finding. They also disclosed that absentee management had grown.

Even at present Bihar has a good percentage of large farmholders as is apparent from Bihar's percentage shares in both number and area (Table 18.16). Feudalism lingers on in its attenuated form of semi-feudal relations, as described earlier.

The medium- and large-size holdings in Bihar in 1980-81 had 4.80 per cent share in total number of holdings in the State and 34.99 per cent share in total area. In 1985-86 the two figures were 3.85 and 28.75 per cent, which meant a slight improvement in the number : area ratio—7.46 *versus* 7.29. Investigations extended the allegation of unsatisfactory management and operation of large farms to medium farms as well. In both hired labour added much less to total product.

Bihar was the pioneer State in liquidating the age-old zamindari system and taking over land in excess of the defined ceilings, at least on paper, though also in regard to the implementation of the land reforms measures, if not without being marked by hesitation, diffidence, inaction, trepidation, indecision,and stumbling through anyhow. That the concentration of land into holdings has got relaxed is evident from the growth of the total number of holdings—between 1950-51 and 1985-86, of the order of 239 per cent, and between 1970-71 and 1985-86, 154 per cent, on the one hand, and between 1970-71 and 1985-86 the decline in area under the holdings was to the extent of 92 per cent (may be due to increased non-agricultural uses of land, water-cum-wind erosion of the soil, etc.). The rise in percentage share of Bihar in the number of holdings was accompanied by a fall its percentage share in area (1.31 *versus* 0.76 per cent) (Table 18.17).

TABLE 18.15 : Position of Medium Holdings

Characters	*1950-51*	*1953-54*	*1954-55*	*1970-71*	*1976-77*	*1980-81*	*1982*	*1985-86*
Number ('000)			423	514	519	472		404
Percentage share in number	7.1	21.78 (27.48)	5.95 (ownership)	5.71	5.22	4.20	12.17 (19.71)	3.4
Area ('000 ha.)			2041	3175	2939	2709		2293
Percentage share in area	24.9	43.19 (31.15)	33.60 (ownership)	27.65	26.54	24.47	37.68 (38.75)	21.05
Bihar's share in all-India number (per cent)								5.1
Bihar's share in total area under medium holdings (per cent)								8.7
Average Size (ha.)	—	3.32 (3.45)	—	5.8	5.7	5.7	3.09 (3.31)	5.67 (5.96)

Note : Medium holdings are those which have each an area between 4.0 and 10.0 ha.

TABLE 18.16 : Position of Large Holdings

Characters	*1950-51*	*1953-54*	*1954-55*	*1956*	*1970-71*	*1976-77*	*1980-81*	*1982*	*1985-86*
Number ('000)			67		135	83	68		53
As percentage of total holdings	1.6 (ownership)	4.28 (12.52)	(ownership) 0.85 (ownership)	0.5	1.78	0.83	0.60	1.55 (5.25)	0.45
Area ('000 ha.)			1243		2360	1468	1165		839
As percentage of total area	19.1 (ownership)	25.24 (25.41)	14.69 (ownership)	32.0 (ownership)	20.55	13.25	10.52	14.06 (33.16)	7.7
Bihar's share in total number of large holdings (per cent)									12.1
Bihar's share in total area of large holdings (per cent)									6.2
Average size (ha.)		9.87	(13.0)		17.5	17.6	17.9	9.09 (10.66)	15.99

Note : Large holdings are those which fall in the size-class 10 ha. and above.

TABLE 18.17 : Total Holdings in Number and Area

Year	*Total Number of Holdings ('000)*	*Percentage Share in Number*	*Total Number of Area ('000 ha.)*	*Percentage Share in Area*
1950-51	49.00	—	—	—
1961-62	65.03	—	—	—
1970-71	75.77	10.67	114.80	7.08
1976-77	99.36	—	110.73	—
1980-81	112.30	—	110.68	—
1985-86	117.11	11.98	108.98/	—
	—	—	102.40	6.24
1995	150.00	—	—	—

In consequence, the average size of the holdings crashed from about 1.65 ha. in 1950-51 to 0.90 ha. in 1985-86, or, from 1.51 ha. to 0.90 ha. between 1970-71 and 1985-86 (Table 18.18). The moral to be drawn from this is that there has been marginalisation of the holdings, both real and fictitious. Between 1951 and 1986 the average size of holdings declined by 33 to 37 per cent. Bihar has had all along perhaps the lowest average size among all States. This was so even when Bihar has had proportionately less cultivable waste land than most other States. Cooperative farming as a mode of organising the institutional transformation was rejected by almost all sections of the people. Consolidation of holdings was given cold shoulders by the potential beneficiaries, and about four years ago by its very sponsor, the Government. The recipients of very small plots of land have faced all sorts of odds in establishing their ownership thereof. When the penchant of the champions of the land reforms (such as the first Revenue Minister of Bihar, Krishna Ballabh Sahay, who piloted the zamindari abolition bill, etc. till they became Acts and who was the sworn enemy of the Ramgarh estate in Hazaribagh district on account of the humiliation he had suffered at the hands of the zamindars of the estate) and the exuberance and euphoria of the potential gainers were weighed up against the resulting frustrations and disillusionment of the long-drawn-out exercise the exponents' hearts were filled with unalloyed disgust, nay, ennui. The fervour with which the politicians had embarked upon the course of action without first having coolly gone into its legal infirmities was at the root of the enormous amount of time that had to be unnecessarily dissipated over it, during which period the air was suck out of the politicians' balloon, much to the dismay or amusement of the onlookers, depending upon the group to which they belonged.

TABLE 18.18 : Average Size of Holdings

Year	*Average Size (ha.)*
1950-51	1.66/1.64/1.38 (3.03)
1952	1.38/1.64
1953-54	1.76/1.67 (3.04)/(3.03)
1955-56	1.21 (2.83)
1956	1.21 (2.83)
1960-61	1.57/1.61 (2.65)
1961	1.17
1960-62 (Average)	1.57 (1.69)
1970-71	1.51 (2.28/2.30)
1976-77	1.37/1.11 (2.00)
1980-81	0.99/1.01 (1.82/1.84)
1982	1.00 (1.68)
1985-86	0.93/0.87 (1.68/1.69/1.37)

Note : The holdings analysed in the tables are operational holdings, unless indicated otherwise, i.e., ownership.

The average sizes of the holdings as held by the different categories of agricultural clsses interests differed—in 1951 the landowners' holdings were, on an average, 4.85 ha. in size; the tenants' 2.26 ha. (54/55 per cent smaller), the agricultural labourers', having land, 0.42 ha. (one-eleventh to one-twelvth), and, finally, the non-agricultural families' 0.85 ha. (one-fifth or one-sixth). We do not have recent data to say, by comparison, whether or not the hiatus between one and another category has narrowed or widened, but it can be stated safely that in some cases there has been narrowing, while in other cases widening, of the hiatus. Polarisation has forged ahead, covertly or overtly, side by side with depolarisation in this sphere.

In 1956 the Government of Bihar had acknowledged that the average size of holdings in the State was 1.21 ha., and it was fragmented into a dozen plots. That being so, even if all agricultural families, including the landless labourers, had been provided with land equally, per family the land allotted would have been 1.41 ha. In 1996 that would not have been above 0.62 ha., other things being equal. Not all families which are agricultural would like to be bothered with a parcel of land of this limited size, supposing it is not fragmented into pieces, and if it is fragmented, it would be still less desirous to be bothered with it, and, in all probability, it would like the small strip to be rented, which, when it materialises, would destory the very essence and material substance of the land reforms. However, if this land is earmarked for growing some highly profitable commercial/money crop, or alternatively, for horticulture or fishery, and the Govenment adopts a holistic approach in the matter of supporting the activity, then even this small land could be economically viable, provided the number of people depended on the unit from a nuclear family. But a much more expedient alternative would be to work for the increase of the average size of holdings in Bihar upto the economic, if, as predicted by the authors of the Third Plan of Bihar, the Bihar economy had to be improved to a level consistent with jobs for all and minimum subsistence to the poorest of the poor. But this would call for a fresh thought on the right to heredity, short of which a minimum size of operational holdings cannot be prescribed and insisted upon in practical application, nor can further subdivision of the given agricultural land in Bihar be given a final quietus burial, In a word, the declared surplus land, even if acquired and redistributed among the landless agricultural families *in toto*, would not be sufficient for the purpose of removing poverty and unemployment and would not make any material difference to the agrarian structure, except that it would provide some succour/relief to the benefiting families, but in no case would it be a step towards the socialist transformation of society. However, in the equalisation programmc, in particular cases the provision of relief too has a critical part to play. Because it has been misconceived in certain respects and because a lot has been amiss with its implementation, the change brought about by the ceiling legislation has not been of any great moment/import in the prevalent land system—it has not reduced inequalities appreciably, has not provided for the settlement of landless labourers and has not led to the promotion of farming cooperatives.

A Final Stock-Taking

Abolition of the zamindari land system in Bihar aimed at eliminating the non-cultivating agricultural classes/interests like the rent-receivers (the rentier class) from it and at improving the status of the cultivators-cum-tenants who were the *bona fide/de jure/*legal owners of the land by conferring on them the virtual proprietary rights and thereby making their position secure. It was neutral to the occupancy raiyats whose rights were pretty well secure under a series of tenancy laws. Another aim, incidental, was to raise the amount of land revenue received by the State Government.

In the formative years of land reforms in Bihar the real tillers of land breathed a whiff of fresh air and felt elated at the new agrarian relations that were about to dawn upon the production mechanism which had existed for many decades and become outomded, that is, the noose of semi-feudalism around their necks was about to loosen. Some landlords came forward and tried to patch up their differences with their tenants and share-croppers by promising help in procuring modern inputs and credit from the Government and its affiliates. Zamindari abolition had prepared the ground for providing basic security for agricultural prosperity. It favoured the hardworking castes in Bihar like the Kurmis, the Koeris and the Yadavas, which had the arts of cultivation in their very blood. Those who actually tilled the soil developed a sense of attachment and belongingness to their lands, which, in turn, made them dedicated to their work, in response partly to land reforms and partly to the various incentives and assistances given both directly and indirectly.

The land ceiling legislation (1961) was inoperative from 1970 onwards to 1992, during which in different parts of Bihar, *Benami* transfers of land above the ceiling were made in numerous cases and large numbers of tenants were voluntarily evicted in the process and their lands resumed by the landlords for personal cultivation. The State Government had to detect the violation and acquire the surplus lands and redistribute them among the landless agricultural labourers. In 1990, 390 landlords possessed land in excess of the ceiling limit. In 1992 the list was revised—529 landlords possessed more than 81 ha. land each. The alliance of zamindars, bureaucrats and politicians was avowedly pitted against the success of the tenancy laws and, as a result, Bihar's record was poor and slow.

All talks of guarantee of security of tenure proved hollow. Tenancy reforms continued to be the most neglected aspect of land reforms. Looseness, laxity and lukewarmness in their implementation apart, they were very time-consuming both at the ground level and outside it, if fought in a court of law. The share-cropper in Bihar, the equivalent of Bargadar in West Bengal, were shorn of the right of ownership of the land. Sharecropping may be today bad in law but it is alive in its tacit/ concealed form in Bihar, with the result that Bihar's prformance compares poorly with the performance of West Bengal, Orissa and Uttar Pradesh. The share-croppers are btter-off and their farms are well poised to growth in these States.

No Government, Congress or Janata, so far in Bihar has ever endeavoured to stop *Benami* transanctions of lands above the ceiling for fear of antagonising the landed gentry. The Bataidars did work up their agitation at a number of places. The police opened fire on them at those places. This has gone on for years. Chief Minister Laloo Prasad Yadav asked the police verbally not to open fire on the land-grabbers. But the police defied his verbal orders.

In the last few decades Bihar has seen the origin and growth of a number of groups of people subscribing to violence. Some of these hold the view that the village could become the nuclei of a socialist economy only through the working of the revolutionary forces.

The violence enveloping many parts of rural Bihar is primarily due partly to the land question and partly to the wages question. During the regime of Chief Minister Laloo Prasad Yadav there has been a steep rise in the number of killings—in 1990, 120; in 1991, 128; in 1993, 112; in 1994, 163 and in 1996 (upto November) 228. Most of the land dispute incidents were reported from such districts as suffered from the extremes of poverty and wealth, such as Gaya, Bhojpur, Aurangabad, Palamau, Nalanda, Jehanabad, Madhubani, Purnea, Darbhanga, Champaran (East and West), Vaishali, Garwa and Patna. Agriculture in Bihar remains mostly imprisoned in a state of ferment, turmoil and commotion because of the tug-of-war being waged between the protagonists and antagonists of land reforms.

There are thinkers in Bihar who are of the opinion that giving the *Bataidars* rights in land and protecting them against eviction would unsettle the entire village economy, as well as the whole system of the existing social relationships and social security. The slowing down of the pace of growth of agriculture is in their view the outcome of the breakdown of law and order in several rural areas. The underdogs are determined to establish a power-base of their own, by letting loose such activities as harvest-looting and land-grabbing. The left parties and extremist and Naxalite outfits have taken advantage of the land disputes and influenced the poor farmers. Under the umbrella of land reforms a war is being waged by them against the landlords by mobilising the landless farmers who earn their bread by working in their fields. *Dharnas*, rallies, etc. are organised by them at different places. These create a law and order problem.

Stagnation or slackening of the pace of development in agriculture consequent upon the falling volume of investment and public sector outlay or on account of the disincentive/negative effects of curtailment of the incentives given by the Government in various forms and hence the increases in the prices of the inputs used by the farmers in cultivating their lands and the consequential deterioration in their economic conditions has forced the farmers to organise *Senas*/armies/*Sabhas*/ associations to agitate against their neglect or victimisation by the Government and to cow their rebellious *Mazoors*/labourers who have joined the parallel *senas*. When anti-social elements get mixed up with the *senas*, they do not remain peaceful but instead turn unpeaceful.

A totally different kind of situation is developing in areas not normally accessible, where the criminals can live without being easily vulnerable to the police action, say, in marginal lands in the plateau region, in the forest areas in the north-western corner of the State, the flood-prone or temporarily waterlogged tracts of the trans-Kosi-Purnea or in pockets where we have the robber barons, who are the brothers-in-arms of the politicians, ruling or unruling, who have among their muscle-men the erstwhile share-croppers or *mazoors* of the big landlords now on the war path, who amass limitless wealth by plundering the rich around them (kidnapping is one of the methods employed) while keeping the poor peasantry in their catchment areas completely ingratiated with themselves by meeting their marriage and similar other heavy expenses. All these outlaws have, however, upset normal agricultural activity in their belts.

Conclusively speaking, disparites in the villages have not ben reduced significantly by the ceiling legislation. Despite the ceiling legislation the agrarian structure in Bihar has remained resistant to the advance of socialism in the State.

19

RURAL ROADS IN BIHAR

Available for the year 1977, we have statistics dealing with the basic amenities in the villages of Bihar (*vis-a-vis* India), as published in *Economic and Political Weekly*, dated 6 April, 1985, which we feel tempted to reproduce in the form of Table 19.1.

TABLE 19.1 : Basic Amenities in Villages of Bihar : 1977

(*As Percentage of Villages*)

Sl. No.	*Basic Amenities*	*Bihar*	*All-India*	*Bihar's Rank*
1.	Number of villages for which data were processed	62404	558519	3rd (total number)
2.	Railway station (with 5 km.)	23.03	18.34	7th
3.	Metalled road (with 2 km.)	43.21	45.26	2nd
4.	Bus stop (Do)	34.29	40.26	6th
5.	Post office (Do)	57.22	53.29	10th
6.	Primary or junior basic school (Do)	92.02	90.12	11th
7.	Middle school (Do)	55.86	48.76	5th
8.	High/Higher Secondary school (within 5 km.)	62.87	20.92	7th
9.	Dispensary (within 2 km.)	25.32	24.59	12th
10.	Helath centre (Do)	31.04	11.98	2nd
11.	Hospital (within 5 km.)	45.93	35.48	6th
12.	Fertiliser depot (Do)	32.99	43.39	15th
13.	Seeds store (within 5 km.)	29.28	40.33	15th
14.	Agricultural pump repair (Do)	19.65	18.76	11th
15.	Storage and ware-houseing (Do)	20.67	20.72	15th
16.	Veterinary dispensary (Do)	40.67	45.19	15th
17.	Credit cooperative (Do)	67.71	60.75	11th
18.	Bank (Do)	35.52	39.88	12th
19.	Daily market (within 2 km.)	17.16	14.81	9th
20.	Hat (Do)	37.98	26.84	6th
21.	Fair price shop for grocery (Do)	49.11	35.05	5th
22.	Electricity	17.41	33.36	17th
23.	Drinking water within the village	92.39	92.61	11th

Having the second rank in populaton, the ninth in area and the third in the number of villages, Bihar was a back-bencher and a slow coach (just imagine the lapse of 26 years of planned development) in all respects, except two, No, 2 and No. 10 of the basic amenities.

The effectiveness of productive efforts made even in rural areas is dependent largely on the presence there of infrastructure like rural roads and rural electricity supply in adequate quantity and quality. Supply bottlenecks are fewer in number and less injurious in periods during which the progress made by rural roads and rural electricity supply is faster, and conversely. The supply and demand gap in respect of these two leading components of the rural infrastructure is critical to the development of the rural sector on the pattern set by the Five-Year Plans, as also the economy as a whole. All developed countries at one stage or another had experiences similar to what developing countries subsequently had.

Of the three primary components of the rural infrastructure, rural roads are one, the other two being water and electricity. Rural roads are the most essential ingredient of rural development in so far as about 85 (1991 census and 87.5, 1981 census) per cent of the population of Bihar lives in rural areas. They are indispensable for achieving the objective of integrated rural development. All sectors of development in rural areas are dependent on good roads. All programmes of rural development have been crucially contingent upon the provision of accessibility to rural areas by means of roads. Effective and quick transport has been the topmost precondition of rural marketing, especially of horticultural and livestock products, but also of no less importance in the transport of other agricultural commodities. Sugarcane has been popular among those farmers who have enjoyed the facilities of irrigation water and transport and the relative advantage of the existence of a sugar mill/ factory accessible within eight to ten hours of haulage of sugarcane by the bullock-cart from the field to the factory. Where rural roads have not been helpful from that standpoint, sugarcane has been transported to the sugar mills situated on the borders of the contiguous State, say, Uttar Pradesh. Perishable commodities are best produced and marketed in compact areas, within a radius of 50 to 70 kms. from the centres of demand. The areas which grew indigo in the years preceding the Non-Violent Satyagraha launched by Gandhiji in Champaran had better rural roads, and the so-called indentured labour possessing the knowledge of planting indigo was sent from those areas to South Africa by the Britishers and when sugarcane replaced indigo, with the advent of sugar mills, labour from the same belt was sent to some of the islands in the Indian ocean which were under their occupation and in both cases the existence of good rural roads linking the rural areas with the railway stations in the nearby towns proved to be a great boon. It is these areas that are even today predominant in terms of the number of migrants going from Bihar to other States. They are nearer to the towns having railway stations, and comparatively better rural roads facilitate this kind of migration.

In our study *Rural Roads* by definition comprise other district roads and village roads.

Table 19.2 encapsules the progress made so far. The countryside was opened up gradually to the outside world. Comparing in terms of length, we find that there took place a 4.88* times increase in the length of village roads in Bihar during 1956 to 1992. Bihar's share in all-India length of village roads fell from 15.5 per cent in 1956 to 11.8 per cent in 1982. The share of length of village roads in length of all roads in the State itself rose from 65.9 per cent in 1956 to 95.2 per cent in 1991-92. Percentage of the number of villages in Bihar connected by all-weather roads to total number of villages in the State improved slightly from 32.0 per cent in 1980-81 to 34.4 per cent in 1987-88 (Table 19.2). Assuming that the total length of all manner of rural roads in Bihar upto 1992 was 26215 kms, the road density came to 23 kms per 100 kms. of land area, or, 47 kms. per one lakh of population.

The bullock-carts (or simply carts) in Bihar are at the centre-stage of the rural transport system. In 1954 they carried traffic equivalent to the entire volume of traffic carried by the railways. Although this was not true in 1996, yet it cannot be gainsaid that the bullock-carts even today render an important service in the nature of feeder services to the railways and other modes of transport. Carts are used also for carrying the PVC pipes for water supply. They bring together the primary and secondary sectors and thereby integrate the whole rural economy. But for them, it would not have been feasible for the public authorities to meet the expenses on road construction, a highly capital-intensive activity on account of the resource crunch faced by them, which the motor-energised vehicles make unavoidable, and in the absence of which they could not have been introduced. The bullock-carts are best equipped to face the given situation characterising the rural roads, such is their adaptability.

---

* Other estimates are 6.74 and 6.95 times.

TABLE 19.2 : Progress of Rural Roads in Bihar

Characteristics	*1956*	*1962*	*1968-69*	*1977-78*	*1980-81*	*1981*	*1982*	*1984*
(1)	(2)	(3)	(4)	(5)	(6)	(7)	(8)	(9)
Total number of villages						67546 (only non-revenue)		
Above as percentage of all-India total						11.66		11.41
Length of rural roads* (kms)	3770	4550					12450	
Level of connectivity to villages by all kinds of roads (kms.)								
Percentage share in all-India length of rural roads	15.5	11.4					11.8	
Percentage share of length of rural roads in total length of roads in the State	65.9	56.2						
Number of villages connected by all-weather roads							19543	
Percentage of all-weather roads to that of main roads			16.6					
Villages connected by all-weather roads as percentage of all villages					32.0		28.9 (27.9)	
Proportion of all villages without any road connection								
Number of villages unconnected by all-weather roads								
All-weather non-accessible villages as percentage of aggregate number of villages in the State								68 (70)
Above as percentage of all-India total								11.41
Number of villages with population more than 1500 connected with *pucca* roads						4948		
Percentage of villages with a population of 1500 and above connected by roads				19.5				
Number of villages connected by roads of all kinds							67566	
Percentage of rural population having access to all-weather road				10.4				

(*Contd.*)

TABLE 19.2 (*Contd.*)

Characteristics	*1985-86*	*1986-87*	*1987-88*	*1989-90*	*1991*	*1991-92*	*1993-94*
(1)	(10)	(11)	(12)	(13)	(14)	(15)	(16)
Total number of villages						67503/77694/ 77848 (including revenue ones also)	
Above as percentage of all-India total							
Length of rural roads* (kms)	17900			14150		18430	
Level of connectivity to villages by all kinds of roads (kms.)				24721		25433/ 26215	
Percentage share in all-India length of rural roads							
Percentage share of length of rural roads in total length of roads in the State	97.2	97.2				95.2	96.7
Number of villages connected by all-weather roads			23600+ (240700)				
Percentage of all-weather roads to that of main roads							
Villages connected by all-weather roads as percentage of all villages			34.9 (40.7)				
Proportion of all villages without any road connection			33.3				
Number of villages unconnected by all-weather roads			13181				
All-weather non-accessible villages as percentage of aggregate number of villages in the State							
Above as percentage of all-India total	11.16						
Number of villages with population more than 1500 connected with *pucca* roads							
Percentage of villages with a population of 1500 and above connected by roads							
Number of villages connected by roads of all kinds							
Percentage of rural population hving access to all-weather road							

One km of the rural road is capable of yielding an economic return of Rs. 77,423 per year by way of saving in operation costs, economic cost of the passenger time saved and valuation of incremental load from the time saved, let alone the social and economic benefits bestowed by it. The bullock-carts which have improved tyres suitable for the draft power and size of local traffic give 30 per cent return on investment, as compared to about 7 per cent done by the conventional bullock-carts.

Construction of rural roads has been on top in the agenda of relief works executed by the Government during the pre-independence days for providing transient employment to the rural work-force, rendered workless by natural calamities and hence forced to face famine-like conditions. No other rural work programme has been replete/buoyed with so much employment potential, susceptible of starting and stopping with maximum elasticity and resilience.

Solid achievements have been made in extending rural roads in certain parts of Bihar, though not without increased corruption. In this the highest share of credit should go to the MNP. In the MNP the rural roads construction has had the pivotal place. During 1969-92, 12830 kms. of black topped roads, of which 2417 kms. were in the tribal areas; 1761 kms of hard crust roads, of which 1022 kms. were in the tribal areas—both giving a total of 14591 kms., 3439 kms. being in the tribal areas, were constructed.

During the Fourth Plan (1969-74) Rs. 5.44 crores, 15.0 per cent of total allocation to the roads head, was set apart for the construction of the rural roads in Bihar.

The Rural Engineering Organisation looked after the construction of the rural roads, besides the roads owned and maintained by the Zila Parishad. It was under the Rural Development Department of the State Government. Upto 1992 it had constructed 13764 kms. of black topped and 6739 kms. of hard crust roads. The Road Construction Department had constructed 3120 kms. of other district roads. The district boards had constructed 2000 kms. Lastly, the other agencies had constructed 592 kms. of the rural roads. These gave a grand total of 26215 kms. of the rural roads.

During the 1980s much emphasis was laid on the construction of the rural roads under the MNP, the RLEGP and the NREP. Under the RLEGP and the NREP during 1985-92 the achievement was construction of 5912 kms. of rural roads, of which 1211 kms. were in the tribal areas. Construction of rural roads has been one of the planks of the Bihar Plateau Development Project.

As a result of the headway made in this direction, the inter-State disparity in infrastructural facilities has diminished, and Bihar's relative position is better than before. But this should not make us forget that the pace of progress in this field in Bihar is slower than in several other States.

The World Bank gives aid to the State Government through the Centre in its road construction projects. A minimum of 10.4 per cent of the total plan outlay is on the rural roads. This is the norm. In recent years construction of the missing links and bridges has been emphasised.

The obtaining position of the rural roads may be summed up as follows: Not all villages are connected through link roads with the nearest motorable roads. In a number of villages motorable roads are accessible through the link roads. In fewer villages the motorable roads are connected with the marketing points in the urban areas, but these are scarcer in the interior areas. The middle-level conveyances, such as bicycles and autorickshaws, as also jeeps, tempos and mini-trucks, besides lorries and buses, in far exceptional cases, have penetrated the rural areas. Even tractors are turned into trucks for traffic, passenger and goods, by attaching trolleys into them. But the non-all-weather roads alongwith a large number of all-weather roads become unserviceable during the rainy season. The condition of rural roads in the flood-prone, waterlogged areas of the plains and the hilly terrain of the plateau region is awful. The poor drainage system is to blame most for this. The maintenance of the rural roads today is at an extremely low level. The fund provided for it is far from being adequate and, to add insult to injury, is often diverted to pay salaries, etc., of the staff. Moreover, the fund is fraught with leakages owing to corrupt practices. True, in recent years the rural roads head has claimed a huge amount of investment but despite this the general feeling is of discontentment with the amount spent. That part of the investment has been unbalanced and lopsided is another criticism levelled against the Department of Road Development. All in all, Bihar compares unfavourably with some other States in this matter. The net result is that the rural roads in Bihar are deficient in the sense that they cannot subserve the requirements of the developing Bihar agriculture. This aggravates the supply-side constraints. Bad rural roads and poor warehousing prevent the farmers from taking advantage of better prices for their products in distant markets. By comparison, Punjab and Andhra Pradesh have very vibrant and prosperous agriculture and allied activities respectively because these two assets are available to the peasants there in an ideal combination. In a word, the existing rural roads are not useful for any major traffic. Even the black topped roads are not quite reliable. Over 22 per cent of total fuel consumption is due to the poor quality of the rural roads. Last but not the least, lack of coordination between the Government and the semi-Government departments connected with the rural roads subject is also responsible for the malaise in its own way.

What would we suggest to improve the situation? One, more investment should be allocated to rural roads. For maintenance in addition to the regular fund, special funds should be placed at the disposal of the local authorities for meeting the maintenance and contingent needs. The remaining unconnected villages should be connected by all-weather roads. Stregthening and augmentation should be the watch-words. The part which the village panchayat can play in this field cannot be underscordered. Two, the benefits from the given rural roads should be maximised. Three, the ongoing projects should be speedily completed, at least the core ones. Four, the old roads should be strengthened by exploiting the new knowledge and techniques. Five, more bridges and culverts should be constructed. Six, there is an imperative case for reprioritisation of the investment made between different modes of road transport so that rural roads are at once augmented and consolidated. Between the twin inescapable needs of the rural people—rural roads and rural electricity supply—the former should come first. By the turn of the present century the average distance of any village from the nearest road should not be more than 1.6 kms. which requires a record 60.65 km. density per 100 sq. km.

20

RURAL ELECTRIFICATION IN BIHAR

Table 20.1 depicts progress made in Bihar in the field of rural electrification. In 1955-56 the number of electrified villages was 2043. By 1994-95 the number had risen to 47715, that is, 23 to 24 times. During a shorter period, 1960-61 to 1994-95 the number increased 16 times, from 3000 to 47715. The second indicator of progress of rural electrification, namely, percentage of electrified villages to total number of villages increased in Bihar from 4.43 to 70.6 per cent during 1960-61 to 1994-95. In all-India in 1994-95 this percentage was 85.5. In other words, the rate of rural electrification was slown in Bihar, when compared to all-India. The third measure of progress of rural electrification in Bihar is the State's share in the all-India total number, which was 9.17 per cent in 1965-66, which had gone up to 9.68 per cent in1993-94.

From the figures adduced in the table we find that during the first three Plans every year 500 more villages were electrified. The purpose of electrifying rural areas was to energise the irrigation pumpsets/ tubewells, for lighting houses, powering fans, operating small machines dehusking paddy, expelling oil from groundnut, working flour/village oil mills, playing radio and electrifying the *Harijan Bastees*—a multi-pronged programme.

Rural electrification was extended speedily during July 1966 to June 1967, a period of severe drought, under a programme, carried on in terms of the series of schemes cleared, one after another, by the Rural Electrification Corporation of India (REC). Subsequently, rural electrification became one of the minimum needs to be met for the rural people. It was part and parcel of the MNP. It was also stressed in the 20-Point Programme. The Integrated Rural Energy Programme (IREP) was another latter-day development influencing rural electrification.

Finance has been the weakest point of the rural electrification programme. This has been caused by default on the part of the State Government to reimburse the outlays incurred on rural electrification by the Bihar State Electricity Board (BSEB) or those incurred under the MNP schemes. The State Rural Electrification Corporation (SREC) has not been in a position to pay the interest charges on the loans incurred by it on account of the resource-constraint.

TABLE 20.1 : Rural Electrification in Bihar

Year	*Total Number of Villages*	*Number of Villages Electrified*	*(3) as Percentage of (2)*	*Bihar's Percentage Share in All-India Total Number of Villages Electrified*
(1)	(2)	(3)	(4)	(5)
1951	71358+ (Approx. 10.1 per cent of all-India)	4 (3061)		0.13
1955-56		2043		
1960-61	67665 (11.98 per cent of all-India)	3000	4.43 (3.8)	
1965-66		3080 (during)/ 16301 (Upto)		9.17
1981 Census	67546 (11.72 per cent of all-India)	21269	31.48 (47.3)	
1982-83			51.8 (56.2)	
1984 March-end				9.55
1985 March-end		33397	49.44 (63.5/64.0)	
1985-86	67566			
1986-87		38125/38135		7.68
1987		38729/38129	49.0 (69.9)	
1987-88		41036	51.9/57.3	9.85
1988		41038	63.0/64.8 (77.6)	
1989 March-end		42527/43746	63.0/64.8 (77.1/78.7)	9.52
1989-90		43152	63.89	
1991	77697 (12.37 per cent of all-India)			
1991-92		47240	69.9 (83.8)	9.67/9.50
1992 March-end		47240		
1993 October-end		47510/47551	70.0 (84.0)	9.70/9.66
1993-94		47068	61.0/69.7	
1994-95		47715	70.6 (85.5)	

\+ 1951 Census Report.
* Provisional.

Note : All percentages are based on the 1981 census figures.

Table 20.2 contains data on amounts of money disbursed in Bihar by the REC in some years of the 1980s.

TABLE 20.2 : Amount Disbursed to Bihar by Rural Electrification Corporation (REC)

Year	*Amount (Rs. Crores)*	*As percentage of All-India*
1987	211.8	7.7
1988	241.9	7.1
1989	284.0	6.7
1990	329.4	7.0

The mere installation of poles at some points together with the transformer and the wiring has been taken to imply that a particular village has been electrified. Even if the supply has been for an hour or less, the village has acquired the epithet/appellation 'electrified'. Reports showed that soon after the installation, the wires were stolen away, so were the transformers, and the unit concerned became defunct. But on paper the village continued as 'electrified'. This created problems instead of solving them.

Turning now to consumption of electricity in agriculture in Bihar, we find that in quantity it rose from 22 gWh in 1959-60 to 1694 gWh in 1991-92, 77 times, as against 72 to 73 times in the case of all-India, from 833 gWh to 60492 gWh during the same period. So far as the share of electricity consumption in Bihar agriculture in total electricity consumption in the State economy as a whole is concerned, it was 3.0 per cent in 1959-60, which moved up to 21.7 per cent by 1991-92. On the other hand, the increase in the all-India average was from 6.0 per cent to 24.2 per cent during the same period. That is to say, the improvement in Bihar was below that in all-India. Finally, Bihar's percentage share in all-India electricity consumption in agriculture recorded a very small increase during the period, from 2.64 per cent to 2.80 per cent. Judging modernisation of agriculture by the magnitude of use of electricity in it, it can be stated here that modernisation of agriculture in Bihar was slow and fluctuating, though the common trend was upwards, showing an improvement. Shortages in power in the State crippled not only industry but also affected the scale of activities in its agriculture, and rendered them more expensive owing to the recourse the agriculturalists were obliged to have to diesel/oil as the source of energisation. The Government had allowed power shortage to become a severe constraint on the development process in all three sectors of the

State economy. Table 20.3 furnishes a statistical resume of consumption of electricity in agriculture in Bihar during the Plan period.

TABLE 20.3 : Consumption of Electricity in Agriculture in Bihar

Year	*Consumption of Electricity in Agriculture in Bihar (In Quantity MkWh-gWh)*	*(2) as Percentage of total Consumption of Electricity in Bihar*	*Percentage Share of (2) in all-India*	*Irrigation and Dewatering Percentage Share in Electricity distribution by Bihar State Electricity Board*
(1)	(2)	(3)	(4)	(5)
1953		4.5		
1959-60	22	3.0 (less than) (6.0)	2.64	
1960-61		2.04		
1961		1.04		
1962-63	20	1.56	1.81	
1965-66	29.33	1.51	1.55	
1967-68		1.13		
1969-70		2.84		
1970-71	69.13	2.7		
1971		5.34		
1975-76		12.1		
1978		12.56		
1978-79				6.43
1979-80				15.50
1980-81	434.63	11.6 (17.59)	2.99	14.91
1981-82	493.73	10.9 (16.84)	3.24	15.58
1982-83	618.05	13.1 (18.64)	3.46	18.59
1983-84	646.28	13.0 (17.81)	3.55	12.64
1984-85	603.65	11.9 (18.38)	2.88	
1985-86	799.51	14.2 (19.04)	3.41	
1986-87	791.61	16.17/16.8 (21.66)	3.29	
1987-88	1149	17.22 (24.22)	3.25	
1988-89	1373	19.14 (24.27)	3.53	
1989-90	1459	20.75 (25.12)	3.25	
1990-91	1341.7/ 1463	19.3/ (20.40) (26.44)	2.71/ 2.95	
1991-92	1694	21.72 (28.20)	2.80	

Note : In 1993-94 in Bihar power consumption in agriculture amounted to 142 kWh per one thousand ha., as compared to the national average of 379 kWh per thousand ha.

Lastly, we have energisation of pumpsets/tubewells in Bihar, a subject coming under minor irrigation. As Table 20.4 would disclose, between 1951 and 1994-95 the number of energised pumpsets/tubewells

TABLE 20.4 : Energisation of Pumpsets/Tubewells in Bihar

Year/Period	*Energised Pumpsets/Tubewells*		*Electric Pumps*		*Percentage Share in Diesel/oil Pumpsets/ Tubewells*	*Installed Pumpsets/ Tubewells Number*	*Number of diesel pumpsets installed*	*(8) as Percentage of All-India*
	Number	*As Percentage of All-India*	*No.*	*As Percentage of All-India*				
(1)	(2)	(3)	(4)	(5)	(6)	(7)	(8)	(9)
1950-51							600	0.09
1950-51 to 1965-66	10556							
1951	444	2.11	278	0.93				
1961			1930	1.20				
1965-66	11000	2.07/2.14						
1966-67 (During)	39000 (more than)							
1968-69 (Upto)	49329/49375/50000	4.59						
1977		3.8						
1979-80 (Upto)					4.82	128000		
1980-81	157000/160000	3.61/3.69						
1982 (Upto)			111966 (of which irrigation : 16225)					
1984-85 (Upto)							173000	4.8
1985 (In)	12000	0.21						
1985 (Upto March-end)	192000 (19.2 of potential number to be sunk)	3.36						

(*Contd.*)

TABLE 20.4 (*Contd.*)

(1)	(2)	(3)	(4)	(5)	(6)	(7)	(8)	(9)
1987 (March-end)	159732	(47.5 per cent of the potential number to be sunk)						
1987-88					4.63	210836/ 211000		
1988-89 (Upto)	233000	2.62						
1989 (March-end)	233000	3.05						
1989-90 (Upto)			243229 (all irrigation)					
1990-91	257000	2.82						
1991 (November-end)	257632	2.83						
1991-92 (Upto)	258000	2.75						
1992 (Upto March-end)	258508	2.75						
1993 (October-end)	262000	2.62						
1993-94			265051 (all irrigation)					
1994-95	264000	2.52						

Note : Bihar's percentage share in oil diesel engine pumpsets/tubewells for minor irrigation purposes in 1977 was 5.59 per cent. Consumption of electricity in agriculture per 100 ha. of irrigated area through minor irrigation schemes in 1980-81 in Bihar was 17.6 gWh (all-India : 46.1 gWh). In 1981-82 the number of pumpsets/tubewells in Bihar per 100 ha. of irrigated area by minor irrigation schemes was 16 (all-India : 14).

in Bihar, meant mostly for irrigation, multiplied 594/595 times, from 444 to 264000. In India the increase was 498-fold, somewhat less, from 21041 to 10475520. Bihar's percentage share in all-India total number of tubewells/pumpsets increased slightly from 2.11 per cent in 1951 to 2.52 per cent in 1994-95. The number of installed pumpsets/tubewells exceeded the number of energised pumpsets/tubewells in most years. To exemplify, around 1980-81, the former numbered 128000, whereas the latter 50,000, either by electricity or diesel/oil. In other words, only 39 per cent of the installed pumpsets/tubewells received electricity supply. In 1987 the situation was better, for about 75 per cent could get electricity supply (210918 *versus* 159732). Around 1989, out of 243229 electric pumps, only 233000 could be energised. This amounted to 95.7 per cent. The situation was still better. Around 98.8 per cent of electric pumps got power supply (265051 *versus* 262000). The situation had further improved. Here, it is necessary that we should make our statement clearer by adding that even if the power supply were just for one hour or less, it was equated with electricity supply for the requisite hours of the day. Those units which did not receive electricity supply, they were worked by diesel/oil. Energisation was by either source. Therefore, it is important to bear in mind what this improvement curve really signified. Lastly, Bihar's share in energised pumpsets/tubewells was maximum in 1968-69, which was during the Plan Holiday. That period marked the beginning of the best chapter in the history of minor irrigation in Bihar—4.59 per cent in all-India. Upto now, the minimum relative share of Bihar, 2.52 per cent was in 1994-95. The maximum relative share of the State in respect of the diesel-run tubewells/pumpsets was 4.82 per cent in 1979-80. In a word, dieselisation had a better performance in Bihar than electrification so far as minor irrigation by means of pumpsets/ tubewells was concerned. This is a subject-matter which we have discussed at length in the chapter on irrigation.

There has been in Bihar from the very first years of planning distribution of pumping sets/tubewells on subsidy basis. It was tried for some years, then called off, and again resumed in 1957-58. The inducement dragged its feet, when, in 1966-67, an unprecedented drought hit the State hard in its face, thereby actuating the authorities to emphasise energisation of pumpsets/tubewells on a war footing, and in this they were indoctrinated by the team which came from the Centre, for it is institctive in the habits of mind of the ruling Biharis that if they do not have their own caste-men who are experts, no matter of what quality their expertise is, who can be made advisers/consultants, they would invariably prefer non-Biharis, and these invariably from outside the

State, for tendering to them the required advice, which becomes for them the gospel word/counsel in the matter worrying them. The interest taken by the Centre and the facilities extended by it enabled the State Government to forge ahead with the programme. Subsidies went a long way in the development of shallow tubewells in the private sector.

The cumulative effect of the advance made in the area of tubewells/pumpsets in Bihar was increased crop security. The amplitude of fluctuations of agricultural outturn diminished. Agricultural produce became more resilient, more stable. The period 1967-68 to 1975-76 witnessed increased allotment of electricity to agriculture in the State. After 1975-76 the quantum of electricity sold for irrigation purpose steadily declined. The sale crashed from 454 gWh in 1975-76 to 197 gWh in 1978-79. In 1981-82 the number of pumpsets/tubewells per 100 ha. of irrigated GCA was 6, as against 14 in all-India. The public sector tubewells got power supply for about 2 to 2.5 hrs only per day in 1983-84, as against the norm of 16 hrs. per day during the peak irrigation period and 6 hrs. per day during the lean irrigation period. Even the 2 to 2.5 hrs. a day supply was erratic. Experiences of the private sector tubewells were far worse. Supply of power being reduced and uncertain, the small and marginal farmers found it far more difficult to tap that source, and their groundwater stock was of no good to them. A sizable fraction of the budget set apart for minor irrigation, inclusive of subsidy and loans, was diverted to other, rather unproductive, expenses, to tide over the financial constraint.

Table 20.5 furnishes an important piece of information on the use of pumpsets for purposes of minor irrigation by the land holders size-group-wise : The marginal land holders made the highest use of the pumpsets, followed by the medium ones. That scale economies characterised the use is evident from the figures in the table. Bihar lagged/behind all-India in the use of pumpsets. The position remains unaltered even today.

TABLE 20.5 : Installation of Pumps in Bihar : Size-wise of Land Holdings as on 15 April 1997

Size-Groups of Land Holdings	*Number of Pumps Per 1000 ha. of Area*
Marginal	50 (64)
Small	37 (59)
Semi-Medium	32 (53)
Medium	40 (42)
Large	23 (20)
All	38 (43)

21

AGRICULTURAL MARKETING IN BIHAR

The market performs several functions: assembling, storing, financing, insuring, grading, standardisation, selling (disposal of the agricultural produce), transporting (movement/haulage), etc. A number of functions call for technical skill and specialised knowledge as well as adequate resources. They aim at ensuring that the farmer gets the best possible return on his produce, the consumer gets an adequate supply of the articles he requires in appropriate quality and the trader gets a reasonable margin of profit. Needless to say that only an efficient marketing system can deliver these goods.

The local rural market is the primary market, which is the *hat* held on particular days in the week, weekly or bi-weekly, or the periodically held fairs connected with the religious celebrations or organised by certain residents in which livestock, apart from the surplus agricultural produce, sells. At the crest is the nearby town *mandi*, which is a wholesale assembly market, a powerful nodal/focal point, an important link between the producer and the ultimate consumer.

The country towns have strong links with the villages. Large towns serve as distribution centres for seeds, fertilisers and credit for farmers as well as for organised markets for their produce. The bigger cities provide services and facilities to both the smaller towns and the rural areas in their hinterland.

The chief trade centre in each district is the principal (headquarters) town which has a network of subsidiary trade centers, i.e., subdivisional headquarters towns and other smaller ones to serve it. These channels are largely unregulated but the number of the regulated ones is constantly on the increase.

Most markets, whatever is their radius, are not modern and well-laid-out. They are not properly organised and managed. The rural market does not serve as a centre to provide various services and activities for the rural folk. Even the wholesale assembly markets are least developed.

Quantitative and Qualitative Inadequacies of Infrastructural Facilities

Bihar's agricultural marketing structure bristles with a number of gaps. It is imperfect and poorly organised. It is poorly equipped with the basic amenities/infrastructural facilities. It lacks full and free competition. The interior areas are more conspicuous in this respect. The tribal areas are in glaring arrears. Let us develop this:

Storage is bad and deficient. We know that agricultural produce has to be protected against damage and deterioration caused by moisture, rodents, insects, pests, etc. The rural warehouses, godowns and cold-storages are few and far between. There is neither grading nor standardisation. The processing facility is also rare. Transportation is unsatisfactory. It is both inadequate and unreliable. The road network outside the urban limits leaves much to be desired. Most roads are *Kachcha* (unmetalled) and unusable in the rainy season. On March 31, 1990 total road length per lakh of population in Bihar was 124 kms., as against 211 kms. in all-India. Length of surfaced roads per lakh of population in Bihar was 49 kms. as against 101 kms. in all-India. Inadequate transport facilities constrained the width of the rural market. This was rendered far worse on account of the lack of storage facilities and the mushroom growth of agricultural marketing and service cooperatives, content with an inefficient working, kept alive through aids and writing-off of debts. The outcome of all this was that the farmers in the areas could not take advantage of better prices. Next to be considered are the communications—post offices, telegraph offices, telephone facility—which were more inadequate in number and far more inferior in the quality of service. The market intelligence/information was the most lacking input. The weights and measures in use were unfair. The sugar mills had their weighing booths overcrowded, so much so that in many bullock-carts the loaded sugarcane had almost perished. When the farmer was courageous enough to carry his surplus produce to the town *mandi*, the unwarranted deductions and delayed settlements taught him such a lesson that he never came there a second time. Even in the town *mandi*, there was seldom any proper arrangement for assembling and exhibiting of the agricultural produce. Similarly, market information was fitful and intermittent. All in all, the deficient marketing facilities depressed the prices which the farmers could get for their produce.

Marketing of perishable commodities is generally controlled by private trade. Facilities enjoyed by the growers are grossly unsatisfactory.

Fruits, vegetables, animal husbandry products, sugarcane, etc. are of a perishable nature. Mango, *lichi* and banana gardens are sold through auction. In these cases the producers obtain a very small share of the price paid by the ultimate consumers and, therefore, have no incentive to grow these crops. Above we have adverted to the plight of the bullock-cartmen waiting in the impasse for long hours at the weighing booths,, sometimes reaching the stage in which the sugarcane is rejected by the *mill-clerk* there. Jute, oilseeds and sugarcane are marketed immediately as the farmers are in urgent need of cash. At the beginning of the planning period approximately 85 per cent of oilseeds and 90 per cent of jute were sold and the rest in each case retained for self-consumption, the sale market varying. In the mid-1950s about 30 per cent of all agricultural produce was sold in the town *mandis*. The marketable surplus of foodgrains varied by crops and by regions. But more of this later.

The sugar, rice dal, oil, flour, etc. mills in Bihar drew their raw materials from their hinterlands as well as from outside them and outside the State. Raw jute normally went to the mills in West Bengal. In Chotanagpur the minor forest produce was sold under inadequate marketing conditions. Examples were lac and silk. As for lac, the packers themselves sold it.

While enumerating the infrastructural hindrances to agricultural marketing, it is incumbent on our part that we take into account those difficulties, adverse and disabling factors which directly or indirectly interacted with them. Lack of staying power or lower staying power of the peasants who were obliged to sell their produce on the farm itself or at the farm gate, that is, who rushed into selling it soon after the harvest, what is known as distress sale, fetching a very low price is traceable to their abject poverty, their indebtedness to the money-lenders (a bondage that was pronounced in the tribal areas), their illiteracy and their ignorance. In other words, lack of working capital/credit facility was the most critical, crucial factor in the great disadvantage they suffered. Next in oppressiveness/rigour was the unfamiliarity factor when the produce was brought to the *mandi* for disposal. The middleman who managed to win over the farmer in the first instance by instilling confidence in him was the person who succeeded in laying a trap for him into which he fell, allowing himself to be fleeced by him, allowing his milk to be skimmed off its cream, such being the malpractice of the trader/dealer/merchant/middleman, exploiters of the highest order. We may, in passing, emphasise that the prevalent agricultural marketing system was interlinked with the system of land relations, both of more or less the same age. Another genuine factor to bear in mind is the precarious state of the existing transport which costs, on an average. 20 to 30 per cent of the price, if the *mandi*, that is *Barha Bazar* is distant.

Of all farmers, the small and marginal ones are the worst sufferers of the traders' exploitation. The existing facilities are not available to them. They are scared away from the wholesale markets, with the result that they have no alternative other than selling bulk of their produce in the village market itself.

In most rural markets the movement of the agricultural produce from the field to the consumers does not guarantee to the farmer the best possible return and the final consumer adequate quality of the foodgrains and to the trader a just and reasonable margin of profit. Among the post-harvest problems, lack of marketing facilities has a prominent place, as also a significant negative effect on production and hence on the welfare of the cultivator—a negative, that is, a disincentive effect on the productivity of the land and the psychology of the man behind the plough.

Classification of Agricultural/Rural Markets

The wholesale markets dealing in the agricultural produce may be assembling or non-assembling. Among both types we have the regulated markets. Not all wholesale markets are important. The assembling wholesale markets are divided into three classes: regulated, principal and sub-market.

In 1982 Bihar has nearly 7,000 weekly and biweekly markets. Between 1963 and 1982 the number of wholesale markets rose from 314 to 672, that is, by 214 per cent. Of these, regulated markets increased by 190 per cent, from 63 to 120 per cent during the same period. As for the wholesale assembling markets, the number remained almost fixed, at 443 in Bihar, though as percentage of all-India, it was 6.78 per cent in 1963, which had fallen to 6.67 per cent by 1990. During 1976-92 the number of regulated markets rose from 76 to 82, i.e., by 10.89 times. The percentage share of Bihar in the all-India total number of regulated markets was 12.46 per cent in 1992. During the same period the number of principal markets increased from 107 to 122, i.e., by 114 per cent. In percentage terms as well, the increase was from 5.40 per cent in 1976 to 5.55 per cent in 1992. Lastly, during the same period the number of sub-markets increased from 76 to 706, that is, 9.36 times; so did the relative share of the State in the aggregate number of sub-markets in the country, from 4.60 per cent to 15.89 per cent. Let us note here that in 1982 only 40 per cent of the regulated markets had market yards (Table 21.1).

The Intermediaries/Middlemen

A large number of intermediaries/middlemen are present in the agricultural marketing system. The number of middlemen is determined by the structure of the market; so also their fees. The middlemen are not mere marionettes of the market forces but instead they are capable of successfully manipulating them. Their subjective attitudes preeminently based on mature experiences are an independent factor in the market. They have to work more on behalf of the farmers in the task of marketing and hence they are larger in number than should be and also earn more profit than they should.

Advance at the time of sowing for the purchase of inputs is given to the farmers by the middlemen, after fixing the price in advance (a speculative price) at which the finished produce would be purchased. The Advance System is in vogue in the sale and purchase of the commercial crops, say, oilseeds, pulses, jute, cotton, tobacco, lac, ghee, paddy, mangoes, banana, etc.

As said above, farmers usually sell their surplus produce to local traders, who are often money-lenders, at the farm-gate, and who buy it either on their own or as agents of bigger merchants of the neighbouring *mandis*. Local money-lenders and big landowners take part of the produce in lieu of the loans, which they haul to towns where they sell in the *Galla* markets at higher prices. In the process they exploit the farmers who lack information on prices of agricultural commodities.

Then we have a group of dealers and traders who reach the village *hats* and *melas* on the days they are held from outside the village concerned and enlist supplies.

There are itinerant traders who deal in cash crops like jute, *haldi* (turmeric), tobacco and chillies.

Most of the above-mentioned merchants are members of a professional class and have great hold on the marketing of agricultural produce from village to town.

Next we have the commission agents, who invariably and the traders, who exceptionally, do their business by maintaining shops in the town markets but not necessarily are they located in one and the same part of the market; most often they are scattered without any adequate space for

TABLE 21.1 : Agricultural/Rural Marketing System in Bihar

Item	*1963-64*	*1976 December 31*	*1982 December 31*	*1987 December 31*	*1988 March 31*	*1990 March 31*	*1992 March 31*
Number in each case							
Rural markets (weekly and bi-weekly)			7000				
Agricultural Produce Wholesale Markets	314		672				
Of which:							
Regulated	63		120				
Considered important	150						
Wholesale Assembling Markets:		427 (4248)		443 (6095)	443 (6528)	443 (6633)	
Of which:							
Regulated		76 (612)		797 (5942)	798 (6052)	598 (6217)	828 (6640)
Principal		107 (1981)		122 (2136)	123 (2149)	123 (2193)	122 (2198)
Sub-markets		76 (1650)		175 (3806)	675 (3903)	375 (4024)	706 (4442)
Cold-storage capacity of the above (tonnes)			212 (341000)				

the market yard, if there is one, to function properly. The condition of storage provided by them is outmoded and unscientific.

The grain traders work either independently or in partnership, depending upon the local supply and other cognate factors. The big traders use the services of the small traders on a commission basis.

Brokers/*Arhatiyas/Dalals* are a class by themselves. The *Arhatiyas* divide themselves into two categories, *Pucca* and *Kachcha*. The former buy and sell through the latter. The *Dalals* in *mandis* help the farmers in disposing of their surplus produce to the *Arhatiyas* (wholesalers), who, in turn, sell to retailers or mills and processing units.

There is no dearth of brokers. They are everywhere, in the village and in the town. They are always available to the farmers to lend to them a hand in getting their produce sold. For the services they render they charge a brokerage.

We have been speaking of the malpractices of the middlemen in the foregoing paragraphs without giving concreteness to our statement. It is time that we removed this lacuna. Before we elaborate this, it would be advisable for us to add that the malpractices we have in our mind are more to be met with in the markets that are not regulated, compared to those which are regulated. The malpractices, whether more in degree or less, are indulged in to exploit the farmers, who are gullible and distraught, in all ways possible. Transparency is completely absent. There is no level playing. The *Dalals* and *Arhatiyas* bargain through a code language. The deals are not fair and above board. On the contrary, they are underdeals, fraudulent and dubious. So organised are the traders and such powers do they wield that they get their individual brokerages from both parties, the selling and the buying, which is vicious. Nearly 40 per cent of the price is grabbed/siphoned off by them. A product is sold four to five times as it moves from the lower to the higher rung in the ladder of the traders. In weight and measurement the farmers are duped. Their credulity is the cause of the deceit they suffer. Illegal deductions, such as *dharmadan, dhalta, namoona, lawa-gholi,* etc. as well as other irrational market charges, are made from the price to be paid. A number of fees, e.g., octori, terminal fee, toll, etc. are realised from those farmers who take their produce to the *Galla* bazar in towns. The actual trading practices and the various deductions and charges that a farmer has to pay while selling his produce continue to be in practice in a large number of markets, even the regulated.

The fact that the farmers bringing their produce to the town *mandis* face additional difficulties inherent in overnight stay for themselves and their animals actuates them to seek the help of the traders who exploit their helpness by raising their fee for the greater exertion they make, a make-believe in most cases, which the entrapped/ensnared farmers have to pay through their noses.

We would like to conclude this section with a quotation from our earlier work (Foundations of Modern Economics) which gives an outline of the classic model of the middleman trader. In different industries the middleman is a trader, a merchant, a dealer, an agent, a broker, a wholesaler or a retailer. He is the member of a distinct, differentiated social class or group. He is a specialist. He completes the work of production. He is an intermediary, a link between the producer and the consumer, undertaking for profit the task of distribution. He intervenes in the process of purchase and sale either between the primary producer and the manufacturer or, alternatively, the manufacturer and the ultimate consumer. He has to preoccupy himself with the distribution of goods between their place of production and the manufacturer in the case of raw materials or the retailer in the case of foodstuffs and manufactured goods. In buying from the producer in anticipation of a sale and in carrying stocks of goods from place to place or through time, the middleman takes important marketing risks, thus easing the burden on the manufacturer. He flattens the spatial price differences. He integrates the otherwise isolated sections of the market. He interprets the wishes of the consumer as well as the producer.

But the middleman is not a term of endearment. Starting as an agent or fiduciary of consumers and other economic functionaries, he tends to become a dictator. As 'the unloader of what has already been produced'; also, to some extent, as 'an arbiter of what has already been produced'; he, like other human beings, is 'apt to lose his head both when things go well and when things go ill'.

In our present case the link considered is one-way, from the producer of the agricultural produce to a very high level of the marketing/distributive system; the other functions of the middleman trader are not taken into account here.

The biologists tell us that there are three distinct circumstances, competitive (corn-weeds), parasitic (mistletoe-oak) and symbiotic (bee-clover)—within which different species exist together, and the third far outnumbers the sumtotal of the first two. So also in economics the relationship between the consumer and the producer, or between the producer/consumer and the trader is neither wholly competitive nor wholly parasitic but rather symbiotic.

The Changing Market Structure

The agricultural market system in Bihar today is not the same as at the time of Independence. Both quantitatively and qualitatively a great change has taken place. In 1947 food supply was administered by the Government through rationing and price control in selected urban areas. The size of the market was less wide because the population was smaller and the purchasing power of the people was less. The agricultural output was lower. Some commodities which we find today were not known then. Similarly, some commodities which were more popular then are less so now. The agricultural market was more inward-looking then; today it is far more outward-looking. The role of the Government in sale and purchase of the agricultural produce has multiplied. A vast machinery is involved in it. The Government fixes prices of a number of agricultural products. These act as sign-posts to the growers. The influence exercised by the Government is to be reckoned with, and not to be trifled with. The grain is pumped in and pumped out of the market. The rural landscape has had a face-lift with the expanded infrastructure during the last 50 years. The agricultural marketing system which has come out in the wash is not such as can be condensed/compressed into this summary, for the details are more interesting than the cut-and-dried resume given here.

Coming to the details, we have first the market arrivals of foodgrains from villages to the assembling markets (Table 21.2). The percentage of population dependent on the market for the purchase of its food requirements has tremendously increased since Independence. Only a very small proportion of the rural population has not to rely upon the market for the purchase of its food requirements. During 1984-85 to 1988-89 in the case of increased output in rice, the market arrivals of rice increased, proportionally more in two years, and proportionally less in one year, whereas in the event of decrease in the outturn of rice, its market arrivals also decreased, proportionally more, in the year concerned. In four consecutive years the increase was in two years in succession, accompanied by a decrease, and thereafter in the fourth year again an increase. On the whole, the elasticity of the market arrivals to the output was evident; it was consistent/symmetrical as between increase and decrease, and hence reversible. Table 21.3 portrays the relationship between production changes and market arrival changes.

The figures for wheat demonstrate that in two cases with a rise in its production, the rise in the market arrivals was more than proportionate. Two years of good wheat harvest were followed by two years of bad

TABLE 21.2 : Market Arrivals[+] of Foodgrains in Bihar

Foodgrain	*As Percentage of Production*							*Relative Share of Bihar in All-India*		
	1980-81	*1982-83*	*1984-85*	*1985-86*	*1986-87*	*1987-88*	*1988-89*	*1984-85*	*1986-87*	*1988-89*
Rice	15.8	—	16.3 (31.6)	16.6 (31.2)	16.8 (32.3)	16.7 (32.9)	14.4 (29.7)	9.15	—	9.01
Wheat	12.2	12.3 (26.7)	12.3 (26.7)	10.3 (24.7)	11.2 (28.2)	11.3 (28.7)	12.6 (26.2)	5.67	6.45	—
Gram	16.9	28.3 (30.7)	38.3 (30.7)	39.7 (30.0)	37.1 (29.5)	41.9 (30.3)	43.3 (31.2)	2.66	3.31	—

\+ From villages to assembling markets, *mandis*.

wheat harvest, but the market arrivals decreased in one year only and the decrease was less than proportionate, while in the other year the market arrivals instead increased, and increased proportionally more. This was not a normal but a perverse behaviour.

TABLE 21.3 : Relationship between Grain Production and its Market Arrivals in Bihar

Given Year over Previous Year	*Percentage Increase (+)/Decrease (-)*					
	In Production			*In Market Arrivals*		
	Rice	*Wheat*	*Gram*	*Rice*	*Wheat*	*Gram*
1985-86/1984-85	+112.0	+121.0	+118.0	+114.0	+101.0	+122.0
1986-87/1985-86	+100.4	+103.0	–13.8	+101.6	+112.0	–19.5
1987-88/1986-87	–22.6	–03.3	+111.8	–23.1	–02.3	+126.3
1988-89/1987-88	+135.8	–02.5	–6.2	+117.1	+108.6	–3.1

Finally, in the four years under consideration, gram production increased in one year, attended by decreased production in the following year. In the twin cases of increased gram production, the increased market arrivals were proportionally more, whereas in the two cases of decreased production, the decrease in the market arrivals was proportionally more in one year and proportionally less in the other year.

TABLE 21.4 : Production *Versus* Market Arrivals of Grain in Bihar: A qualitative Analysis

Given Year/ Previous Year	*Production*			*Market Arrivals*			*Quantity of Foodgrains in PDS*
	R	*W*	*G*	*R*	*W*	*G*	
1985-86/ 1984-85	+	+	+	+	+	+	+
1986-87/ 1985-86	+	+	–	+	+	–	+
1987-88/ 1986-87	–	–	+	–	–	+	–
1988-89/ 1987-88	+	–	–	+	+	–	–

R = Rice, W = Wheat, G = Gram, PDS = Public Distribution System.
+ is Increase.
– is Decrease.

In the qualitative analysis (Table 21.4) we have attempted we notice that in the first three years production changes stood in corresponding relationship with market arrival changes in the case of all the three grains, namely rice, wheat and gram. Only in the last year the mutuality of relationship between production and market arrivals of wheat was upset, and it assumed the form of contrariness/inverse relationship.

When we juxtapose the above account with the releases of foodgrains through the Public Distribution System (PDS) to the market, we discover that these releases are interconnected with the position of the market arrivals of rice and wheat; they rose when the market arrivals of rice and wheat rose in two out of three years and fell when their market arrivals fell in the remaining year. If in a year the PDS behaved erratically, its releases were in tune with the market arrivals of gram.

Continuing the part assigned to the PDS, we find from the statistics contained in Table 21.5, that during 1980-92 supply of foodgrains to the PDS in Bihar had fallen by about 129 per cent, (while population of Bihar had grown by about 129 per cent), foodgrains production had increased by about 126 per cent, (rice by 120, wheat 140 and gram by 114 per cent), market arrivals of rice, wheat and gram had increased by 104,121 and 120 per cent respectively, assuming that the past trend persisted. Bihar's relative share in all-India total PDS releases had fluctuated between 2.85 and 6.71 per cent during the period and the general trend was towards a decline. The proportion of wheat in the buffer stock and hence the PDS was 87 per cent in 1980, which had come down to 80 per cent by 1992. The maximum proportion of wheat in the PDS in Bihar was 95.5 per cent in 1987 and the minimum, 94 per cent, in 1990. As percentage of all-India, the share of wheat supply in

TABLE 21.5 : Public Distribution of Foodgrains in Bihar

(In thousand tonnes)

Year	*Foodgrains*		*Wheat*	
	Quantity	*As Percentage of All-India*	*Quantity*	*As Percentage of All-India*
1980	1006	6.71	877	9.94
1985	633	4.00	586	6.91
1986	788	4.55	716	8.41
1987	1020	5.58	974	11.08
1988	905	4.87	848	9.72
1989	707	4.30	648	7.43
1990	457	2.85	429	6.22
1991	594	2.94	524	5.67
1992	713	3.75	569	6.74

the PDS of Bihar was maximum, 11.08 per cent, in 1987, and minimum, 5.67 per cent, in 1991. In 1993-94 the number of the fair price shops in Bihar was 53518. Procurement of grain in Bihar was never a matter of pride. In the last few years it had been held in abeyance by the State Government. This was necessitated by the controversy that the system touched off, namely, that the block officers implemented the regulation by discriminating between individual growers because that helped them to amass wealth illegally, which entailed widespread resentment among the people who were victimised.

The PDS is a stable and permanent feature of the planning strategy in India addressed to the control of prices, reduction of fluctuations in them and achievement of an equitable distribution of foodgrains. It helps in operating dual pricing in respect of certain commodities, i.e., supplying them at lower prices to the vulnerable sections of society and at higher prices to other sections who buy from the open market. The issue prices of rice and wheat sold to the individual consumers on the basis of the ration card are lower but when sold to the mills for processing them are slightly higher. Here we have the combined role of the Government—as a purchaser (one method being procurement and another, purchase from the open market) and as a seller (the Government as a trader).

The Government needed a certain regulatory mechanism to reach a modicum of succor to the large mass of the unfortunate poor people suffering in silence in the countryside. The PDS became that mechanism and has since performed its major function of ensuring supplies of foodgrains to the people at reasonable prices, particularly to the weaker sections of the community. Such distribution of foodgrains through the public channels has like a shield protected the poor, particularly in times critical, supplying to them foodgrains at reasonable prices. But even in this Bihar was at a disadvantage, per person per year the amount of grain provided by the PDS was far less in Bihar than what was provided in some other States. In 1992-93 the figure was 7.8 kg. for Bihar, as against 28.6 kg. in Andhra Pradesh and 92.4 kg in Delhi. The total amount distributed in Bihar was 6.93 lakh tonnes. In 1993-94 only 14 districts in Bihar had been covered under the RPDS area.

The 1995-96 Annual Plan of Bihar wrote that the Civil Supplies Department of the State Government considered the primary responsibility of the State to ensure availability of essential goods at reasonable rates to all consumers and to protect them from exploitation and the unhealthy market forces. Depending on the degree of competition among the sellers, the grain market witnessed conditions of occasional glut and scarcity. Being agriculture-based the prices of foodgrains were subject to large seasonal variations. On the other hand, the demand for foodgrains was largely inelastic, with the result that a marginal fall in their output and availability often led to a disproportionate increase in their prices. An efficient management of the supplies was therefore of decisive significance from the point of view of maintaining stable price conditions. This is exactly what the Government sought to attain through the instrumentality of the PDS, which maintained a network of nexuses between production, procurement, transport, storage and distribution of the foodgrains in question, besides maintaining a linkage between the Centre and the State. The success of the PDS was governed by the degree of efficiency with which the supply-line of the foodgrains was maintained. In Bihar the conditions of roads were in a deplorable state. The attitude of the Centre towards the State in all matters was unhelpful, including the release of the quota of grain required to fill the food gap, because the intentions of the administration were suspect. The infrastructural inadequacies in Bihar incapacitated the PDS in covering the remote areas and areas which were impenetrable and uncommonly backward, and these were come across mostly in rural areas.

From the preceding account it follows that the State Government would naturally develop and strengthen the existing infrastructure for storage, movement and distribution of the essential commodities on a priority basis. Construction of godowns is of pivotal importance for gearing up the PDS to the task of making available foodgrains to the consumers from the nearest point. Incidentally, it is essential to reduce the cost of distribution by taking advantage of the economies of bulk transaction/handling, avoiding cross movements of goods, building up a chain of rural godowns, using non-mechanised means of transport from the godowns to the *mandis,* etc.

A little while ago we referred to the role of the Government in extending price support to the producers of certain agricultural crops. This has constituted a new dimension in the state policy towards agriculture. Among the food crops, paddy, coarse cereals, maize, wheat, barley, gram, arhar, moong and urad, and among cash crops, sugarcane, cotton, jute, groundnut, soyabean, sunflower, tobacco, sesame, rapeseed mustard and tori enjoy procurement/minimum support prices. The initiative comes from the Centre. However, the State Government is competent to announce a revised price, invaraibly higher, say, as in the case of sugarcane, which is an area of keen politics in Bihar. The Jute

Corporation of India purchases raw jute in Bihar. The quantity purchased has varied violently from 22.1 thousand bales of 180 kgs. each in 1989-90 to 383.2 thousand bales in 1985-86. As proportion of all-India purchases by the Corporation, Bihar's share was as low as 1.67 per cent in 1988-89 and as high as 30.57 per cent in 1980-81. We cannot say with confidence if this has obeyed the Cobweb Theorem or not; in several instances the sugarcane outturn has obeyed the theorem (Table 21.6).

TABLE 21.6 : Purchases of Raw Jute in Bihar by the Jute Corporation of India

(In '000 bales of 180 kgs. each)

Year	*Quantity*	*As percentage of All-India*
1980-81	324.7	30.57
1981-82	275.4	15.63
1982-83	69.3	8.06
1983-84	53.8	6.39
1984-85	98.7	9.73
1985-86	383.2	13.56
1986-87	277.8	12.48
1987-88	53.7	9.93
1988-89	11.4	1.67
1989-90	22.1	4.35
1990-91	71.7	8.41
1991-92	160.4	25.95
1992-93	80.3	8.75

Trade, in the sense of imports and exports, internal, i.e. within Bihar and external, outside the State, which is a vital part of the economic activity and involves sale and purchase at multiple points, with a cascading effect produced by any factor inserted into the process, forms a dimension which cannot be disregarded without being provided an important thought in any study concerned with marketing.

A large quantity of trade is carried out by country-boats, trucks, buses, bullock-carts, pack animals, etc. The country-boats used in inland water transport are licensed, as also the employment in road transport by the bullock-carts. The volume of rural trade in Bihar is on the increase. Trade is on a wider scale in towns. The products involved are both local and those imported from other parts of the State and other States. Considering this, it cannot be denied that Bihar's countryside is vested with a physical potential which can enable the State to have its economic intercourse with the outside world by tapping its potential water navigation. Table 21.7 presents an account during September, 1991-August, 1992.

TABLE 21.7 : Inter-State Movements/Flows of Goods in Bihar

Sl.No.	*Goods*	*From Outside: To Outside Ratio*
1.	Rice	9.00 (:1)
2.	Wheat	6.46
3.	Flour	1.48
4.	Maize	3.10
5.	Gram and products	56.13
6.	Other pulses	0.14
7.	Coarse grains	0.00
8.	Oilseeds (Rape and mustard)	156.00
9.	Raw jute (in bales)	0.01
10.	Cotton (indigenous and imported)	468.43
11.	Fruits and vegetables	40.10
12.	Raw tobacco	0.01
13.	Coal and cooking	0.10
14.	Iron ore	3.95
15.	Kerosene oil	162.94
16.	Sugar	19.06
17.	Khandsari Sugar	0.03
18.	Gur and Shakkar	0.81
19.	Salt	2822.20
20.	cement	5.48
21.	Iron and Steel	0.06

From Table 21.7, it appears that Bihar's dependence on the outside sources is the maximum in the case of good No.8, that is, oilseeds, when we confine our observation to the agricultural commodities, followed by gram and gram products, fruits and vegetables; rice, wheat and maize are also imported, besides sugar. Bihar sends out raw jute, raw tobacco, khandsari sugar, gur-and-shakkar, and other pulses. Bihar is a deficit State in respect of food and raw materials to its own industry. During the period few jute mills in Bihar were in operation, jute bags and jute cloth manufactured by them were among the exports from Bihar. It is not true that no amount of pulses, oilseeds, rice, wheat and maize was exported from the State. What is true is that the amounts of such exports were small, compared to those of their imports. Bihar produced vanaspati but its share in all-India vanaspati production was insignificant, I.07 per cent in 1988, 0.24 per cent in 1991 and 0.61 per cent in 1993. Articles like lac and shellac were imported by traders from Chotanagpur for being exported outside Bihar, what is called as 'resale'. *Sabai* grass and catechu were forest products, found mostly in Chotanagpur and moved to other parts of the State. Chotanagpur received sugar, gur, pulses, tobacco, etc., in plenty from other parts of Bihar. Raw silk was produced in Chotanagpur and Bhagalpur and was used within the State as well as exported from it. In 1989-90 raw silk output in Bihar was 2.77 per cent of all-India production; in 1992-93, it was 2.39 per cent. As we have written in the chapter on forests, stick lac production was on the decline in Bihar. As proportion of all-India, the output was 60.74 per cent in 1986-87 and 56.56 per cent in 1991-92.

It would be proper to point out here that the poor quality of the agricultural produce in Bihar has acted as a handicap/drag in export markets in respect of turmeric, wool, lac and sheep and goat skins. Grading of food products like milk, ghee and oil in internal trade has contributed richly towards the superior general health of the people in Bihar.

Reports say that Pusa Basmati rice, honey, *lichi* and *makhana* from Bihar sell in foreign countries. Bihar can strike a gold-mine in fruit-processing, also processing of patato and tomato, besides growing specific herbal and medicinal plants, such as *Sarpgandha, Sataavar,* lemon grass and *Pudina.*

Lastly, the goat skin of Tirhut and hides from Sitamarhi, Madhubani and Darbhanga are recognised in the world market for their quality. We are not mentioning here the manufactures of industry, factory and non-factory sector, which are in demand outside Bihar, as also outside India.

Administered Pricing

Price formation of agricultural commodities is not totally, nor perfectly competitively determined inasmuch as the preconditions of a full and perfectly competitive market do not obtain. The personal factors remain as important as impersonal, turning on the commodity and the State in question. We have noted above that even precedent to Independence, the Government used to fix the price of sugarcane and insist on the sugar mills that that price was paid. The introduction of rationing and price control in the pre-Independence years was not compatible with the competitive market solution. The big farmers' lobby influenced the market prices of such commodities as sugarcane, onion, red pepper, coconut, tobacco, cotton, and so on. In 1964 food zones were fixed by the Central Government in order to control the inter-zonal movement of grain (like rice, wheat, etc.), which was an aberration/departure from the perfectly competitive model.

Prices of agricultural commodities/crops have increased steeply more or less continuously since 1950-51. Upto 1991-93 the index of wholesale prices of agricultural commodities had risen from 100 in 1950-51 to 1282.3, that is, by almost thirteen times till 1992-93. Increase in a given year was 20 per cent or about 20 per cent over the previous period during this long period. This spelled a disaster to the poorer sections of the community as the PDS at best met their minimum needs and for the rest of their requirements they had to look up to the free, open market for either coarse cereals or more quantities of rice, as also wheat, their demand responding to the purchasing power they commanded and the prevalent market prices. The subsidised issue prices charged under the PDS enjoyed stability and rose only at intervals.

The farm (harvest) prices of rice, wheat and maize alongwith their minimum support/procurement prices (in brackets) are given in Table 21.8, which purports to saying that except in 1983-84 when the Government announced minimum support/procurement prices were lower than even the harvest prices, which are generally throw-away prices because of the distress sales, the former remained the latter in all other years, and benefited only the big farmers.

TABLE 21.8 : Fluctuations of Harvest Prices in Bihar

Crop	*1983-84 (Price per quintal in in Rs. = 100)*	*1987-88 Index*	*1988-89 Index*	*1989-90 Index*	*1990-91 Index*	*1991-92 Index*	*1992-93 Index*
Paddy/Rice:	(132.00)	(150.00)	(160.00)	(185.00)	(205.00)	(230.00)	(270.00)
Autumn	153 = 100	122.8	126.1	139.2	139.8	167.3	194.1
Winter	167 = 100	131.1	116.7	152.7	128.7	184.4	186.2
Wheat	216 = 100	107.8	113.9	110.6	143.5	176.4	—
	(152.00)	(173.00)	(183.00)	(215.00)	(225.00)	(250.00)	(330.00)
Maize	172 = 100	118.0	115.7	119.2	137.2	175.5	186.6
	(124.00)	(135.00)	(145.00)	(165.00)	(180.00)	(210.00)	(245.00)

Note : Figures in brackets indicate the minimum support prices/procurement prices announced by the Government.

Of deep concern have been the yearly rapid and violent fluctuations in the prices of agricultural commodities/crops such as wheat, pulses, sugar and gur and raw jute, wrighting disastrous consequences on their growers. This and with passage of time the political pressure for including more and more items together occasioned the adoption of an agricultural prices policy by the Government at the Centre. This step had its basis in the assumption that a positive relation existed between the price incentive (a booster) and agricultural production. In consonance with this decision the buffer-stock of foodgrains was built up from 1964-65 onwards at the Centre through the Government procurement/purchases at predetermined prices and the gaps between supply and demand in different States bridged/plugged by releasing quotas to them through the PDS which was maintained extensively, the two arms of the Government in its role a State Trader, which task was assumed by the Food Corporation of India (FCI). The aim and object of the measure was to keep the prices of agricultural commodities within reasonable limits. This in its turn was part of wider goal of price and income stabilisation consistent with the growth of the economy which was the capstone/king-pin of the planning strategy.

There are certain significant implications of this policy-mix. The buffer-stock has far exceeded the annual release to the PDS. The open market is left with a grain stock which is smaller to the extent of the proportion procured/purchased by the Government at the minimum procurement/support prices. The total annual release is lower than the annual food requirement of the poor people (the percentage of those below the Poverty Line in Bihar is the highest). The PDS in Bihar meets only 10 per cent of their requirement. Only one per cent of their rice requirement is met by the PDS. They have to rely upon the open market for their unmet requirement. In Bihar foodgrains production has been increasing at a rate slower than the demand for food has been rising. The percentage share of Bihar in the number of ration shops is 13.2 and its offtake is 5.52 per cent of the national figure. The urban bias in the opening of the ration shops has been a plain/patent fact, a blunt truth. The disequilibrium between demand and supply in the food market whips up the speculative activity, which is to the disadvantage of the poor.

The employment generation for the poor today is better than it was before but with an increased number of inmates/members the earning of an average poor family from its employment is not adequate. Besides, the price-hike consequent upon falling supply and/or increased issue prices (consequent upon the hefty hike in administered prices under pressure of the big farmers' organisations) erodes the real worth of their money income.

Cooperative Agricultural Marketing in Bihar in Historical Retrospect

Cooperative agricultural marketing aims at transforming the marketing structure with it attendant factors, such as the middlemen and the costs of marketing. By forming cooperative agricultural marketing societies the farmers bargain collectively. Also, the available land is better utilised when togetherwith other preconditions, the precondition of better agricultural marketing facility is also fulfilled. Towards this end the cooperative agricultural societies, when strengthened and refurbished, aid and assist agriculture in marketing, as also in production and processing. In its final analysis, cooperative agricultural marketing is a device among other devices to break the shackles of poverty and hunger disease and squalor, with which scourges the poor peasantry has to put up in their absence.

Cooperative agricultural marketing societies were known even during the pre-independence days. The sugarcane marketing societies were amongst the earliest ones established in Bihar. While direct selling of their sugarcane produce by many growers was in vogue, selling it to the nearby sugar-mills through their cooperative societies by other sugarcane growers was also in practice in a good many segments of the sugarcane belt. Insofar as the sugarcane price has a long history of being fixed by the Government of the day. But due to low consumption of sugar in the earlier years when per capital income was low, compared to the position now, coupled with the fact of declining demand for Indian sugar in foreign markets owing to the presence of formidable competitors in several years the sugar-mills were ill put to it to pay the price fixed by the Government for sugarcane. Besides sugar has been under Government control since pre-independence days with regard to its price—it has been one case of dual pricing—as well as the partitioning of total sugar output between controlled and open markets, with the result that the sugar mills have often fallen into heavy arrears to the cooperative sugarcane societies, which were forced, as a result, to employ contractors on heavy charges for raising funds for payment. Their incapacity, genuine or feigned, has compounded with the politicisation of sugarcane and sugar, given the fact that the food issue has been a great leveller of politics in our country from the very beginning of its independence. The sugarcane belt has concentration of the vote-banks.

In 1954 in Bihar 7161 PACS with a membership of 2.64 lakhs marketed the produce of their members valued at Rs.23 lakhs. Upto 1960-61 in the State 220 primary marketing societies had been organised.

In June 1963 their number stood at 218, which was 7.0 per cent of the national aggregate. Value of agricultural produce marketed by the marketing cooperative societies in 1968-69 was Rs.7.36 crores, just 1.3 per cent of all-India, which went up to Rs.18.23 crores, 1.5 per cent of all-India by 1976-77. In 1985-86 the number of agricultural marketing societies was 441, 1.74 per cent of all Cooperative Societies in Bihar. In 1988-89 the number had moved up to 473, 1.69 per cent of all cooperative societies in the State. In addition to sugarcane cooperative marketing societies the other leading cooperative marketing societies were related to dairy products, milk, fish, fruits and vegetables.

From the short account presented above the conclusion which is patent in this that in Bihar so far there has not emerged a clear breakthrough in the area of cooperative agricultural marketing.

In Bihar the use of improved agricultural inputs has risen, no doubt, but very slowly only. The Bihar State Cooperative Bank was the earliest institutional agency to distribute chemical fertilisers in the State on behalf of the State Government. From the mid-1950s onwards the Bihar Cooperative Marketing Union supplied fertilisers. The BISCOMAUN is the sole distributor of fertilisers in Bihar, as also the sole Government agency for the marketing of the agricultural produce.

By 1982-83 per hectare value of the marketed agricultural produce was Rs.38.34, as against the all-India figure of Rs.131.13. Per hectare godown capacity of the agricultural marketing societies was 19.59 kgs., as compared to the national average of 37.07 kgs.

The Government agencies, like the Bihar State Cooperative Bank and the BISCOMAUN, have been accused by the farmers of supplying low-quality seeds and inferior, adulterated fertilisers, besides indulging in other corrupt practices. The malfunctioning of the agricultural cooperative societies has been discussed in Chapter 17, which is common with that of the cooperative societies of other kinds. In a word, the existing cooperative agricultural societies are, structure-wise and function-wise, not in harmony with the socialist pattern of society envisaged as long ago as in the Second Five-Year Plan period.

Government Regulation of Agricultural Marketing

The Government has since long been interested in upgrading agricultural marketing. Cooperative marketing was, therefore, emphasised. Sugarcane sale and purchase societies were first to be formed and promoted. Subsequent to Independence, the speed of effort gathered momentum. The Bihar State Warehousing Corporation was set up in 1956-57. In

1965-66 it had two central warehouses and twenty-one other Warehousing Corporations. Stocks of agricultural commodities, consumer goods and inputs were held in order to meet situations of seasonal glut and scarcity. Storage facilities were provided to farmers and advancing of loans from commercial banks on the basis of receipts arranged for. The All-India Warehousing Corporation with the help of the State-level corporation set up and managed a whole network of warehouses in several towns and *mandis*. Rural godowns were constructed by paying subsidies.

Upto 1958-59 the State Government had not contributed any money towards the share capital of the non-credit central marketing societies. Of late, financial assistance, mostly working capital, was granted to the scheduled castes fair price shops dealers for ensuring a smooth running of the shops.

In 1960 the Bihar Agricultural Produce Market Act was passed. The rules of business were framed and got ready by 1962.

Upto 1960-61 a couple of jute baling plants had made their debut in the cooperative sector.

Around 1964 a market secretary for each agricultural produce marketing committee (the number had risen to 63) was posted by the Government to look after the development of the markets and to help the producers and traders in their daily business transactions. The State Agricultural Marketing Board exercised a general control over the market committee of the State. The Board was funded by the State Government for taking up the stupendous marketing development programme. It imparted a new life to the marketing project by the Government.

Later in the day rural markets were developed, each market costing Rs.6.05 lakhs. The Government provided the basic facilities for storing, movement, grading and disposal of the agricultural produce as well as strengthened the existing infrastructure of the market in question so as to make sure that the farmers secured the best possible return on their produce, the consumers received adequate supplies of good-quality food and the traders realised a reasonable margin of profit.

The rural areas inhabited by the Scheduled Castes and Scheduled Tribes are now-a-days served better through the mobile vans operated by the State Food Corporation.

In the 1995-96 Annual Plan the State Government has a programme to construct a 100 metric tonnes capacity godown at each block headquarters. After 1993-94, 292 godowns were completed and handed over to the State Food Corporation by the Bihar State Food and Civil Supplies Corporation.

Another, quite effective medium by which the Government provides impetus to agricultural marketing is by giving publicity to market information on the radio and television daily and weekly in their programmes meant for the farmers. Included in the market information is information on market price trends of the agricultural commodities. A weekly bulletin on prices is published. Very useful talks are broadcast/ televised by experts on various aspects of agricultural marketing in Hindi and other recognised languages from the stations concerned. The market prices with their trends are published in the newspapers and periodicals as well as government bulletins.

The 1995-96 Annual Plan of Bihar recognised the urgent need for revamping the existing infrastructural facilities meant for agricultural marketing.

The State Government is keen on implementing with religious zest and resoluteness the Standards of Weights and Measures (Enforcement) Act, 1985, effective from 1 July 1988 because much leeway remains to be made good in the matter of standard weights and measures.

Grading has made strides in Bihar in recent years under the stewardship of the Marketing Department of the Union and the State Government. Tests in the laboratories in this connection are made for the benefit of the producers of vegetable oil, ghee, spices, honey, etc., Gur is graded and sold under the auspices of a number of unions. In grading an agricultural product, its size, colour, weight, etc. are taken into consideration.

It is regrettable that the Agricultural Produce Markets Act is not enforced properly and evenly across all parts of the State.

As indicated above, among the principal markets we have the wholesale markets and the regulated markets. The presence of a marketing yard is a cardinal feature of these markets. As a result of the Government effort made in the last few years in this direction regulated markets are coming up and the marketing structure is getting streamlined. Table 21.1 contains some information on them.

The regulated markets are directed at improving the existing facilities and practices in the marketing system . A regulated market yard is a composite market for the growers of the agricultural products. In a regulated market the charges of brokers and weighmen are under Government control. In it unauthorised deductions are prohibited.

As a matter of fact, the regulated market yard is supposed to become the nucleus for the growth of a modern township around itself. The facilities provided by it are as follows:

1. Sale platforms—traders' shops.
2. Storage—godowns and warehouses.
3. Rest houses for farmers.
4. Parking space for the carts and vehicles alongwith rest-houses for the cattle carrying the agricultural produce to the marketing yard.
5. Arrangement for clearing and grading of the produce.
6. Posts and banks.
7. Prompt and up-to-date marketing information.

A regulated market yard provides the following facilities to the cultivators:

1. Inputs, e.g., seeds, fertilisers, pesticides, improved implements.
2. A workshop where tractors, pumping sets, threshers, dryers and sprayers are repaired.

Every regulated market has a network of link roads and approach roads in the radius of about 10 miles around each market yard. On an average, every market yard has a *pucca* road of the length of about 50 kms. and as such 50 market yards have a total length of about 2500 kms. road, which cater to the felt needs of the cultivators. The link roads and the feeder roads facilitate the agriculturists in their task of bringing their produce to the market yard through *pucca* roads by the quickest means possible. One per cent of the value of the agricultural produce brought and disposed of in the regulated market yards is set apart for meeting the cost of the approach and the feeder roads.

With the assistance of the World Bank, Bihar has constructed a large number of well-developed marketing yards (Table 21.1) The rural roads feeding these yards have to bear extra vehicular traffic, and call for regular attending, as also improvement and upgrading, which the State can ill afford because of resource stringency.

Extension officers are available at the regulated market yard to impart training to the cultivators in the yard itself at intervals, where the latest development of agricultural techniques is explained threadbare to the cultivators.

Despite the distinct achievement in this field, the fact remains that the benefits of the regulated markets have flown mostly to the big farmers who had marketable surpluses to sell. Secondly, in the market yards the roads and lanes are congested, narrow and underdeveloped, without an adequate space for the carts to be parked. Thirdly, on account of the inadequacy of the requisite machinery for market development and regulation, the age-old disabilities of the farmers such as underpaying of prices, cheating through unfair weights and harassment through delayed settlements, exploitation through unwarranted deductions continue to be suffered by them.

The Changing Rural Scenario

It is needless to point out that modern agriculture is commercialised. Commercialisation of agriculture is a great integrating agent, for development radiates from it. The existing economy is diversified to some extent. Development of transport and communications, storage and processing, provision of other economic overheads, e.g., rural electrification, besides the social overheads, etc. has worked out towards this change. Extension of irrigation and improved crop husbandry have had a similar effect. The interlinking of agriculture, off/non-farm rural activities and industry effected by the transport system was a leading factor in giving rise to commercialised agriculture. The headway made by monetisation of the rural markets was another influence in altering the ground realities of agriculture. Since the people engaged in the sick village industries have no other avenue of employment open to them, they keep them alive so that they eke out a living and anyhow survive. Where agro-based processing units have been in existence for long, concentrated labour nuclei have sprung up. Growth of refrigeration has made possible putting to different and more profitable uses the agricultural products. The big industries have brought about a reorientation in the volume and direction of trade within the State and without it. But because of the glaring disparity in the power wielded by the agriculturists and manufacturers, distortions arise which unsettle the allocative and pricing processes.

In short, modern agriculture has external linkages: (i) Procurement of necessary inputs from the market; (ii) Storage of products; (iii) Marketing of products; and (iv) Use of specialised knowledge disseminated by the agricultural experts. These activities are more economical on a large scale.

As things stand today, indications get an affirmative support that agricultural marketing which for ages limited itself to the handling of the agricultural produce would extend its frontiers further and become coterminous with rural marketing, enshrining thereby all the goods which the rural inhabitants require, which would not be far different from what the urban ones require, and already the hardness and sharpness which distinguished the want systems in the two different areas has become fainter due to their interpenetration.

22

AGRICULTURAL ADMINISTRATION AND PLANNING IN BIHAR

The Agricultural Extension Agencies are either Community Development Blocks or National Extension Services. Launched by the State Government in Bihar on 2 October 1952, the Community Development Blocks (CDBs) were acclaimed by it as a unit of planning and development, or more specifically, a unit of village planning in alliance/alignment/collaboration with Village Panchayats, with the family as its nerve-knot/keystone, as also a unit of welfare administration. The Community Development Programme (CDP) was visualised as a cooperative partnership between the Government and the rural people. It was intended to harness popular initiative and participation in the development process/mechanism. It was designed to provide a sound basis for microplanning (decentralised planning) and thereby create the proper outlook among the villagers on the development programmes, so that they took more than casual interest in them. It was meant to foster an interest in the people for improving their economic conditions through self-help as well as bring about the uplift of the economy largely through community effort. It is a manifestation of the Government's commitment to protect the interests of the rural peasantry.

Community Development Programme (CDP)

During the First Five-Year Plan of Bihar, 98 community development and national extension blocks were set up, covering 11750 villages, with an area of 11564 sq. miles and a population of 6.4 million. In 1984 there were in 38 districts of the State 587 Community Development Blocks (CDBs) encompassing 78027 villages. In 1994 Bihar had 55 districts, 727 CDBs, 1097 civil thanas and 59 railway thanas. On 31 December, 1992 the village panchayats numbered 11969 in Bihar.

In the incipient years the CDP dealt with three important subjects, viz., minor irrigation, cottage and small-scale industries and training artisans by giving them loans and organising them into cooperatives. The CDBs established training-cum-productive centres for artisans, mostly landless like most of their agricultural labourers brethren, replaced later by the cluster-type institutions during the Third Plan. The rural industrial centres comprised service and maintenance workshops and training centres. The pilot projects were established "to act as laboratories for controlled observations to find possible solutions to problems that had come up in the field of cottage and small-scale industries". Much later, when women development/empowerment became an unavoidable object of development, Mahila Mandals were formed by the CDBs and managed by them, with a view to organising women and training them in better home management. But lack of proper guidance and follow-up constrained this novel experiment.

All agricultural developmental and rural welfare schemes of the State Government were executed and coordinated by the Circle Officers and the Block Development Officers (BDOs), who stood for the executive authority at the bottom, and represented the base of the pyramid of the administration. We shall enumerate the schemes in the section on agricultural planning.

As the CDP entered the third decade of its career, it suffered a serious setback, and reached a stage resembling disbanding. This lasted for quite some years. A number of developmental agencies appeared at the village level land contributed towards the relegation of the CDP to the background—the SFDA, the FWP, the IRDP, the RYSEM, etc. More concretely, in blocks where the Government funds were lacking, activities languished and the staff remained supernumerary.

Not all was well with the CDP. For it failed to develop local leadership which was presupposed to assume in part its responsibility. The people's participation in the programme was neither spontaneous nor adequate. As a result, the programme did not become self-reliant and locally rooted, it remained assisted and schematic. Some of the tasks fell into arrears, e.g., provision of drinking water, latrines, multiplication and distribution of improved seeds. As for the industrial training centres, many artisans joined them for the sake of the stipend only and did not follow the trade or craft later on. The most prosperous farmers preferred the superior products of the factory industries to the articles manufactured by the village artisans.

The CDP had an effect repugnant to the community with the widening of its coverage, increased inefficiency and corruption. That its establishment cost clustered around 36 per cent of the total budget was proof of its inefficiency and hence lack of popular support and participation. It turned out to be a corrupting influence on the people's morals. It developed into a huge racket. There were frequent reports of great misuse of the public funds. It killed the local initiative when people noticed that proportionally larger benefits ensued to the better-off sections of rural society and individual interests were served at the cost of the collective.

Balances were conspicuously absent in certain matters. For example, most of the staff was engaged in the programme of assistance and guidance to the rural people. Whereas the agricultural improvements were underemphasised, the building up of social capital assets, such as roads, wells, schools and dispensaries was overemphasised.

Lack of coordination was revealed in a number of respects : Between the Development Officers at the different levels—village, block and district. Between different Government Departments involved in the block work, since they failed to evolve the practice of thinking together as a team/tank so as to ensure that the local projects which were designed met the local problems. Between industrial and non-industrial programmes or rural development.

The aforementioned weaknesses of the CDP compelled Vinoba Bhave to remark that the CDBs had served no useful purposes and should therefore be abolished. Let us go into the Block Agency/ Administration in detail at this stage.

The Community Development Blocks (CDBs)

The CDB commenced as the normal agency of administration in the countryside. It generally had more than one police station, with one police station located at the block headquarters. It was generally under the charge of the Junior Civil Service Officer or Officers of the State Agricultural Service, designated as the Block Development Officer (BDO). The Anchal Adhikari was also an officer of the Junior Civil Service. Each worker in the block considered himself to be a multipurpose man. Formulation, execution and supervision of the entire CDP was left to the Block Development Committee (previously called Block Advisory Committee), subject to the overall supervision of the State Government. The Committee had non-official members, the representatives of the people were associated with it, for example, the *Mukhiya* of the village panchayat, representatives of cooperative societies, women and other special interests. In the earlier years the block officers functionaries were saddled with several/multifarious functions. With the advent of the new agencies and the special programmes implemented by various Government Departments their burden was lowered. Even at present the Block Agency is the chief agency for implementing or assisting in the implementation of the different agricultural programmes.

The fault found with the Block Administration dissolves itself into the criticism levied on the bureaucracy/the civil servants, in this case, at the three-tier system—the village (this is discussed in the section on the Village Panchayat, to follow), the block (which is the theme of the present section) and the district level (though, in passing, only). In the block the bureaucracy has so far remained aloof and authoritarian, unimaginative and unresponsive to the felt needs of the people. The pride and prejudice of the block administrators has deterred them from interacting with the rural folk. The common man has been exploited by the staff of the Revenue Department. The character and integrity of the block staff has been in doubt. The block officers have been averse to mix freely with the villagers among whom they have had to work. They have failed to readjust their relations with the common man in the village. They have failed to convince the rural people of the desirability of the departmental schemes. They have lacked the capacity to win the confidence of the rural people and their active cooperation. At the district level the administrative set-up was reorganised to harmonise with the needs of the development plan, assuming that the revenue administration was perfect and left ample time for attending to development activity in the block (a frivolous assumption, in the opinion of the commentators), but with the mounting size of the plan outlay at the district level, which meant, by implication, plan outlay at the block and the village level, by allocation of funds by the district-level committee, it was increasingly realised that the district administration was not ideally equipped for that purpose.

A gamut of factors gave rise to the dissatisfaction which attended the CDBs. On top of all was the paucity and non-availability of trained and experienced technical personnel and engineering staff, on the one hand, and raw materials, tools and equipment, etc., on the other, which constrained the functioning of the CDBs. Another hindrance was the overlapping that was a regular feature of the schemes , having more or less the same scope and goal, implemented under the auspices of the different departments of the State Government, which never met round the table to thrash out the interconnections between the schemes and thereby to avoid duplication (duplication of the costs was an end-result of the failure to do so). To amplify, in the early 1950s the minor irrigation schemes were conducted by the Grow More Food Programme (GMFP) as well as CDP. Lastly, inability to utilise all the sanctioned funds for want of either preparedness or smooth flow thereof from top to bottom was also an accomplice in this malperformance of the CDBs/ CDP.

In Favour of the CDP

The CDP was not a total flop. It had some good, positive impact on the agricultural sector. This was physical or material and reflected in increased agricultural production and improved social amenities of the villages. It contributed its mite towards rural awakening, in a modest degree, all the same. The rural people were made conscious of the practice of intensive agriculture. This indirectly strengthened the cooperative societies. Improved agricultural practices spread, though slowly. The pilot projects for the artisans and craftmen were partially successful, judging by the satisfaction expressed by the trainees with the training imparted.

National Extension Services (NES)

The National Extension Services (NES) was born of the recognition that successful agricultural effort would turn, to a large extent, on the strength of an extension movement and popular participation, fortified at the base by an integrated irrigation system. This was during the Second Plan period. In its essence, the NES sought to sprearhead a process of transformation of the socio-economic structure of the agrarian economy. Under it the farmers were given training about the latest technology. Their problems were discussed. Endeavour was made to sort them out. The improved techniques were disseminated amongst the farmers, who were taught judicious land-water-soil management.

The NES is the concern of a number of agencies in addition to the State machinery, namely, the Indian Council of Agricultural Research (ICAR)—the State Agricultural Universities research combine, progressive farms, voluntary organisations, industry, etc. The orientation courses for the key block personnel are organised periodically by the NES.

While The CDP had to face an odd time, the NES was lucky to receive the Government's attention uninterruptedly. Its machinery was augmented and strengthened continuously. Its T&V system, with its functionaries at the village and higher levels, advised the farmer on what to do, step by step, and at every stage of crop growth so that crop productivity was optimised. Between 1980-81 and 1987-88 the number of agricultural extension workers rose from 2187 to 6220, that is, by 284 per cent, in Bihar.

An important offshoot of the agricultural extension is meant for such women as head farm families. The women extension workers try to meet their requirements. For their improvement agricultural extension services obtain external aids.

The Extension Services suffered from three drawbacks—three I's : inadequacy, inefficiency and ineffectiveness. They were alleged to be unable to meet the felt and emerging needs of the farming community. The critics went to the extent of alleging stagnation overtaking the extension services/custom service facilities. The delivery system of the needed inputs was full of defects. The modern inputs were not available in the composite package. Despite the recent progress, much difficulty was experienced in obtaining improved tools and implements. Moreover, the supply of pesticides and weedicides was not adequate.

The Agricultural Engineering Officers were reported to be not concentrating on agricultural development because they were made to perform several other functions by the BDOs. Supervision by them was poor in the non-tribal areas; in the tribal areas it was poorer still.

The Extension Services failed to make any meaningful impact on the transfer of technology to the farmers. The field visits by the VAWs were inadequate (as the time spent in the villages was limited) as well as irregular. Staffing was below the sanctioned strength. The quality was inferior. The VAWs too were used for non-extension work. They were deployed by the local, ruling politicians for purposes other than those for which they had been appointed.

The orientation courses themselves were tedious and unexciting and called for reorientation and improvement.

The grass-root technocrats did not fruitfully interact with the pride and prejudices of the peasantry and the busybodies who were capable of fishing in the troubled waters facing the villages. This has become quite rife in late years.

Constraints to the Extension Services at the local levels were not identified and appropriate steps were neither afoot nor in the offing or on the anvil to tide over them inasmuch as the administration was far from being efficient. Needed were action programmes to overcome this.

The Extension system should work and work, well and appear to be working well in the opinion of those who are genuinely interested in the uplift of the villages.

Agricultural Education and Research

In Bihar agricultural science is taught in schools, agricultural colleges and agricultural universities. Every agricultural teacher and research worker has to do some extension education work in addition to teaching and research.

The Indian Agricultural Research Institute was established at Pusa in Bihar in 1903 but later, after the earthquake of 1934, shifted to Delhi.

In the early 1950s within the Government in Bihar development of sugarcane research *versus* cultivation of sugarcane was the topic of debate, and the verdict was in favour of the former.

Bihar has two agricultural universities: one, the Rajendra Agricultural University (RAU), established in 1971 and the other, the Birsa Agricultural University (BAU), established in 1981. The RAU organises and coordinates extension educational activities for the transfer of well-proven technology in the field of agriculture, veterinary, fisheries, etc., to extension functionaries, farmers and farm women. The BAU renders research and extension support to farmers, particularly transfer in the area of technology. The latter has its jurisdiction in Chotanagpur, whereas the former has its in the plains. The two universities are directly linked with the State Government and have also their academic linkage with the ICAR. So far they have carried out research in crops like rice, cereals, oilseeds, sugarcane and jute as well as fruits. They maintain a field experimentation service and preoccupy themselves with research also in soil and pests and diseases. New problems faced by farmers are referred to the twin universities.

The two Agricultural Universities in Bihar are, reportedly, starved of research funds because of the financial stringency faced by the State Government. Their research so far has been beset with a number of gaps—soil analysis, waster management, drought-resistant varieties of sugarcane, the needed varieties of rape and mustard and pulses, and so forth, have not been evolved uptill now. Expenditure on irrigated rice research has hitherto equalled a mere 0.035 per cent of the value of the rice crop.

The results of agricultural research are germane to intensive farming, subject to the provision that they are conscientiously applied. In the earlier years both vertical and horizontal linkages between research and agricultural extension service were lacking. In recent years this disability has been surmounted but to an extent only; a lot remains to be overcome.

In the north-west alluvial plains zone the absence of rough and resistant varieties of wheat for unirrigated lands, redrot resistant varieties of sugarcane, rapeseed and mustard seeds resistant to aphid attack and pulses suited to the soils of the zone, such as gram and peas, is too obvious to be overlooked.

Varieties of rabi crops that can fit into the double-cropping system in the low lands of the plateau zone under late sowing and rainfed conditions have not as yet been discovered. Also, there is a glaring lack of suitable drought-resistant varieties of rice and ragi.

The above-mentioned gaps need immediate attention.

The Village Panchayat (VP)

The Bihar Panchayati Raj Act was passed in 1947. It was under this Act that the First Plan of Bihar saw the establishment on an extensive scale of the Gram Panchayats. At the end of the First Plan, there were in Bihar 7392 Gram Panchayats, covering 46,989 villages with a population of 24.76 million people. On 31 December, 1992 the number of village panchayats had risen to 11,969.

The First Plan envisaged that a new administrative culture would be introduced by the CDP and the VPs would develop not only as a means but also as an end in itself. Both institutions were expected to act as nurseries and training ground for leadership. In the planners' conception, the Block Administration and the Panchayati Raj are wedded to each other. Both institutions are funded exclusively by the State Plan. The consensus seems to be veering round the view that saddling the existing total responsibility of the Block on the Village Panchayat may turnout to be a great mistake.

In summary, the Village Panchayat is meant to change the centre of social activity of our polical economy and transform it into an organisation in which small autonomous living communities become the most creative centres and the base for the whole federalised superstructure.

Every Village Panchayat has a Panchayat Samiti which is headed by a *Pramukh*. Among its members are the *Mukhiyas*, the BDO who is its Secretary, and all officers of the State Government in different Departments who have truck with the village(s) concerned in the block in question. Every village is to have its own Panchayat.

The Zila Parishad comprises all the Panchayat Samities of a district. It is headed by the Chairman and the Deputy Development Commissioner. A senior scale IAS officer is its Secretary.

The VP is, in theory/principle, entrusted with all responsibilities of local development. It is the nucleus/the nodal agency for the execution of the various schemes of the State Government, developmental or relief. The development plan of the village is formulated by it. All schemes are to be approved by it prior to their implementation. All this is in complete unison with the demoractic decentralisation of administration and its programmes. That power must be delegated absolutely to the people at large.

The Village Panchayat development plan is discussed in the Zila Parishad at the district level. The State-level schemes have to be approved by the concerned district-level agencies.

In further, more concrete terms, from the very First Plan days the compulsory duties imposed on the Village Panchayat (VP) have been for the maintenance of the works of irrigation, public drainage, water supply and construction of field channels. Among the optional functions of the VP we have had certain primary judicial powers entrusted to the Sarpanches, certain specified offences the sole control of which vested in the VP, raising of a village voluntary force for self-defence and assistance to the law and order authorities, etc. The VP was empowered to levy a labour tax for purposes of construction of community works.

The Janata Government in Bihar (since March 1990) has not been keen on conducting the Panchayat elections. However, it set up in 1994 the State Panchayati Raj Finance Commission for recommending measures for making the economic base of the Panchayati Raj institutions strong. Delay in holding the Panchayat elections consistent with the amended provisions amounted to a constitutional breakdown.

Until quite recently, the intervention of the law courts in a good many cases of the Panchayat elections resulted in the putting-off of the formation of the Village Panchayats and the Zila Parishad according to the former Act. As a corollary, the original enthusiasm had cooled down. The fear that the elections, if held in accordance with the modified provisions, would in all probability result in the unsettling of the existing caste equations which favour the present Janta Government is the main factor which accounts for the unreasonable delay in conducting the elections.

The JRZ is under the management of the VPs.

The caste idea has got aggrandised ever since the introduction of the VP system in Bihar. Elections conducted for the formation of the VPs were followed by caste feuds and squabbles of the worst type, dashing to ground the hopes of the people pinned on this institution for the execution of genuine constructive activity in the countryside. As has been peculiar to Bihar, the election-period bickerings and in-fightings in the villages have tended to become permanent enmities among the villagers divided along caste lines. The village factions and cliques on caste lines have for long disrupted and ravaged the community life in the villages. The observation made by the correspondents of the national dailies who visited Bihar during the elections that the last thing which could be looked for in the villages of the State was 'peace and quiet' proves the point.

Agricultural Planning

In the State Plan of BIhar given are the major and minor heads of development in the sphere of agriculture and allied activities, such as under:

1. *Crop Husbandry :*
   (a) Crop husbandry—its main thrust is on (i) improving the production of breeder, foundation and certified seeds and (ii) sound arrangements for inputs supply—the HYV seeds, fertilizers, pesticides, micronutrients, etc. Included in it is the Integrated Programme for Rice Development (introduced in the Seventh Plan), also the development projects for pulses, jute, tobacco, sugarcane, lac, horticulture, etc. Shifting of land from rainfed wheat to maize and upland paddy and rainfed wheat to pulses is also among the planks of agricultural planning.
   (b) Sugarcane development.
   (c) Lac development.
2. *Food Storage and Warehouses* : Included are the special foodgrains production programmes incorporating rice, wheat, rabi maize and gram.
3. *Soil and Water Conservation :* Its main thrust are on :
   (a) Soil amendments. Some districts in Bihar have got soil testing labs. The area of alkaline and saline soil in the State is 2 to 6 lakh ha. Soil amendment/treatment is demonstrated to the public.
   (b) Diversification and intensification of agriculture by better land-water management, with special reference to small and marginal farmers.

   These would involve the forest department alongwith the agricultural department.

4. *Animal Husbandry* and
5. *Dairy Development*
   Not only animal husbandry and dairy are to be encouraged but also poultry farming and agro-processing.
6. *Fisheries.*
7. *Forests and Wild Life.*
8. *Agricultural Education and Research* : This aims at strengthening the infrastructural facilities for transfer of technology to farmers.
9. *Investment in Agricultural Finance Institutions* :
   (a) The cooperative department.
   (b) Institutional finance.
10. *Marketing and Quality Control.*
11. *Cooperation* : 9 to 11 are intended to ensure adequate credit and marketing support to agricultural production and distribution.
12. *Irrigation and Flood Control* : This is to be read togetherwith 3 above. Included are :
    (a) Major and medium irrigation.
    (b) Minor irrigation.
    (c) Command Area Development.
    (d) Flood Control.
    (e) Energy/Power supply, including non-conventional sources. The main thrust here is on additional creation of irrigation potential and increased utilisation of the created irrigation potential. Included are the Tal area and Diara land development schemes.
13. *Special Area Programmes* : These involve agriculture, welfare, rural development and irrigation departments of the State Government.
14. *Community Development.*
15. *Panchayati Raj.*
16. *Land Reforms Incorporated are* : The main thrust is on their effective implementation.
    (a) Ceiling and distribution of the surplus land.
    (b) Consolidation of holdings.
    (c) Updating of the land records.
17. *Rural Development* : The Special Programmes are the IRDP, DPAP, IREP, NREP, JRZ, etc.

The objects of agricultural planning by the State Government through its own and the Centrally sponsored schemes are to boost agricultural production, protect the farmers' incomes as well as stabilise them and, finally, to iron out the wide gap that exists between rich and poor in rural society. For every rupee spent by the private sector on the development of agriculture, the State sector has spent nearly four rupees, directly and indirectly, during the Plan period. One rupee spent on labour engaged in agriculture has yielded about Re. 0.56 in the shape of additional value added to agricultural output.

Table 22.1 contains, Plan-wise, figures of expenditures by the State Government (in the public sector) on agriculture and allied activities in Bihar.

Criticism of State planning of agriculture in Bihar is related with the organisational set-up, to a great extent, in the sense of its failure to deliver the goods, its bad delivery. It is the Extension machinery which implements the agricultural programmes/schemes. But the involvement of the departmental staff above the SD level in extension work in fields is limited. In consequence, the quality of the extension service is poor. Credit and other facilities are not provided satisfactorily due to the flaws of the organisational superedifice/superstructure.

Another criticism hurled at the organisation outfit of agricultural planning is the loose coordination between different Government departments which have truck with it at practically all levels : Agricultural Department, Irrigation Departments (Major, Medium and Minor), Rural Development Department,Revenue and Land Reform Department, Cooperative Department, Institutional Finance Department, Sugar and Cane Department, Planning, Statistics and Evaluation Department, Rural Engineering Organisation, Rural Energy Organisation, Education (included in it is technical education) Department, Welfare Department, Housing Department, etc. Lack of coordination results in ineffective management of the various agricultural programmes and unnecessary duplication and overlapping, and hence wastage.

As said above, research support for extension work is weak. The outcome is that the contribution of research to agricultural productivity is much below the potential. It is imperative that the linkages between research and extension are restored and tightened.

Barriers to agricultural planning are wide and varied as we move down the district to the village level but their nature and degree have not so far been identified. It is high time that agricultural planning became region-specific, down to the block level and based on the foundations of the farming systems and not crop-wise.

TABLE 22.1 : State Expenditures on Agriculture and Allied Activities in Bihar : Plan-wise

(*As percentage of Total State Expenditure*)

Heads	*First Plan*	*Second Plan*	*Third Plan*	*Annual Plans (Three)*	*Fourth Plan*	*Fifth Plan*	*Annual Plans (Two)*	*Sixth Plan*	*Seventh Plan*
1. Agricultural programmes	11.67	14.06	11.72	19.55	14.84	14.21	41.41	20.00	5.27 0.10 (special programme)
2. Cooperation, community development and village panchayats	2.41	14.40	8.91	4.71	3.63	1.00	1.24	0.86	8.80 (rural development)
3. Irrigation and flood control	18.67	15.16	24.70	26.42	29.94	29.57	32.44	26.61	33.15
Total	32.75 (2399.59)	43.62 (7763.05)	45.33 (14891.81)	50.68 (11551.49)	48.41 (23515.64)	44.78 (40971.90)	74.09 (49656.59)	47.47 (146824.71)	47.40 (246500.00)

Note : Figures in brackets are amounts in lakhs of rupees.

One criticism, rather universal, is that planning at the decentralised levels—district, block land village—existed in name but not in fact. For years the targets for local development had been thrust on the different levels. Besides, the programmes and policies were often of an *ad hoc* and piecemeal nature.

The end-result of the defects stated above is waste of resources and efforts.

We suggest that the responsibility be fixed for inadequate coordination and monitoring, starving blocks of funds and non-involvement of the field functionaries in the formulation of the Government policies and programmes.

We further suggest that at the block level a compact multi-disciplinary apparatus be provided because with the launching of the IRDP, the NREP/JRZ, the Panchayati Raj, etc. this has assumed an unavoidable urgency. Let us underline here that the developmental process in rural areas is very much dependent on the initiatives stimulated by the support systems, most of which are poorly equipped.

In a nutshell, the impact of agricultural planning is discernible in the improvement in agricultural production and incomes, increased employment opportunities to the rural poor and enlarged flow of purchasing power to the rural poor.

The Eighth Plan of Bihar had the following focal points in its agricultural programmes : Integrated cereal development, pulses development, oilseeds development, horticultural development, distribution of certified seeds, distribution of minikits to the small and marginal farmers, agricultural engineering, laboratory development, seeds and soil testing, quality control, plant protection, *Diara* development, dry land farming, and extension and training. The foodgrains production strategy is addressed chiefly to irrigation, watershed development, and wasteland development. The Government has proposed recourse to adoption of scientific agro-techniques, better management of inputs and expansion of infrastructural facilities.

The Human Factor in the Villages of Bihar*

One broad aspect of the CDP and the Panchayati Raj (PR) was psychological which was presumed to consist in the change in the

* Projecting on a wider canvas and enunciating the problem more critically we have examined agricultural classes and agrarian interests/relations in Bihar (*vis-a-vis* all-India) in our earlier publication, *Four Decades of Indian Agriculture*, Manas, Delhi-52, Vol. I (Chapter 5) and Vol. II.

attitudes of the rural folk so that they desired a better life. But unfortunately the common man in the village, even after the lapse of 45 years, has not been made interested in what the Government was doing and proposed to do. The passivity of the popular mind and the apathy of the people were writ large and loomed large. An average Bihari peasant was psychologically inhibited. He suffered from the fear of the public servant. He had not risen above his distrust of the people who had an urban base. He could not inculcate/cultivate a proper outlook on the developmental programmes and most ostensibly took casual interest in them. The villages abounded with people who did not know whether it was the State Government, and if so, the Government of which political party or a combination of which political parties, or the Central Government, and if so, the Government of which political party or a combination of political parties, which implemented this or that policy or measure, causing good or harm to them. Quite often something corresponding to a smoke-screen was created and the villagers were left bewildered when the politicians preached on every available occasion such ideas as were very far from realisation in a vocabulary which was uncustomary/unfamiliar.

Still in parts of the State and among certain sections of the people there are farmers with particular attitudes and habits which cannot be deemed helpful to agricultural progress. To substantiate, the extremes of credulity and suspicion which they exhibit are not in keeping with the principles of agricultural prosperity. Although conventions and customs rooted in ignorance, illiteracy and superstition are not rigidly adhered to now by the villagers, yet they are many farmers who are steeped in the primitive ideas and practices. 'Pure obscurantism', a false sense of pride over being born in the upper caste Hindu families, to cite Kusum Nair's report, prohibits them from touching the plough, though these communities are full-time agriculturists and often own, except in the predominantly tribal regions, most of the best cultivated land. Extravagance in observing social rites and rituals, beyond means, by incurring huge debts, just to keep the reputation of the family as high as before (in Bihar there was in the ancient time a philosopher of the name of Charvak, who preached in favour of consuming *ghee* even by incurring loans, in case a family lacked the capacity, perhaps in the hope that the greater physical/brawn power generated by so doing would lead to increased production—this was a forerunner of Keynes' deficit financing remedy) is still in vogue, although this was being frowned upon and the same money was being put to improving the land under cultivation.

To an extent, the alleged attitude is explained with reference to the farmer's real, matter-of-fact, experience. In so far as an average farmer in Bihar is liable to face near starvation in bad years, bare physical survival defines the concept of his life even today, but even that is rendered difficult for him by his four real fears—fear of the natural calamities like flood, drought and earthquake, fear of the landlord, fear of the money-lender and fear of the public servant, But added to his real fears are some false ones, fear that multiple cropping is injurious to soil fertility, that the use of chemical fertilisers depletes the natural powers and properties of the soil which cannot be replenished. The typical farmer is comparable to the old parrot who cannot easily be taught a new song.

Furtheron, given the equality of resources and opportunities, in one and the same region or locality, the peasant community differs, caste-wise, not only in attitude towards manual work but also in other traits and aptitudes, such as thrift, diligence, mobility and readiness to exploit an existing economic opportunity. By implication, in the absence of common values, a uniform response to common incentives and stimuli cannot be expected. Variations in the value system make all the difference to the degree of success or unsuccess of the development scheme, independent of the material and physical resources. They also defeat the basic purpose of many of the reforms, policies and programmes which were Centrally framed for uniform and universal application to all rural communities and castes.

That being so, the incentive of the cultivator has got to be fortified by fostering the conditions under which the farmer could appraise a proper correlation between his effort and its fruit. That alone would sustain self-confidence and a spirit of enterprise.

The grim experience of the past, which made the common man desperate with the vision of a bleak future in his mind, has been instrumental in defining his static but stable equilibrium symbolised by the production of the staple foodgrain, say, rice, as the crux of his entire effort. Natural calamities make his farming future precarious, uncertain, and thereby inhibit his effort, thrift and prudence. There are in his agricultural produce sharp seasonal variations, at times violent, sporadic ups and downs, the psychological imprint on his mind of which is distressing, engineering as they do a permanent sense of impending disaster, besides giving rise to apathy and fatalism, an attitude of passive resignation, scarcely conducive to the building up of a stable economic climate for agricultural growth and development.

The statements made above about the human factor found in Bihar agriculture are amenable to be construed to imply that the poverty of Bihar is, in final analysis, the product of the low productivity of the human resource that inhabits the State, lower than even the productivities of the material resources. The human abilities, faculties, skills have not properly been developed. Human investment, capital formation has not been undertaken in proper measure. Pitting of rapidly growing population against the slowly increasing material resource base has proved to be a poverty-aggravating factor. In general, the question of poverty of Bihar is fundamentally a question of low productivity. Let us devote a moment of our time to find out how growth is related with productivity, more human and less material. Increase in human productivity is not the outcome of working longer and still longer hours. It is the result of the human effort being suitably equipped with abstract and concrete knowledge, man equipped with machine, human energy dovetailed with material energy. Hard work is expressive of work ethic or culture, which is perpetually under eclipse in Bihar as in most other parts of India. The average peasant/agriculturist in Bihar is more hardworking than his counterpart in either Haryana or Punjab but his work is not so productive as theirs. Per hour of work increased real output is coterminous with increased productivity, and growth is coordinate with increased productivity. Increased productivity is determined by allocative efficiency, scale economies and technological progress. Economic activity is defined as effort directed at increasing productivity. That is to say, growing productivity is the engine of growth and development. Not only increased output per hour, which gives a more reliable result, but also increased output per man, which may be sometimes misleading, is on all fours with growth and development. Other than these two variants of real output there is no indexing measurement to which the quality of people be reduced.

Low productivity is a ubiquitous phenomenon in Bihar. Per capita output in all sectors and their sub-sectors is low. Total output-total population ratio is abysmally low. Per capita income disparity, as it exists between States, is ascribable to availability of skill equipment and capital (fixed and working) equipment per man in one State, as against another State. Not only replacement and modernisation but also accumulation and maintenance can raise capital productivity of the resources, human and material, and bring the low-productivity States to the level of the high-productivity ones.

It can be argued that the average/ordinary Bihar farmer is not irrational, if he is not innovative and ploughs his lone furrow with the help of the arts inherited from his forebears, for he is deeply interested in maximising his income, even if he is bereft of the right outlook, training or experience to exploit the available opportunities. What prevents him from improving his productivity is the social framework which lays premium on the status-maintaining use of resources. This is an institutional factor. But another institutional factor is favourable to agricultural production in Bihar. This is the inter-caste differential in the skills. Certain castes in Bihar (e.g., Koeri, Kurmi, Yadav, etc.) hold agricultural work in great esteem. which has been handed down the generations in their families, as owner-cultivators, tenants or even landless agricultural labourers, and who have given proof of their inherited superiority in crop husbandry over the upper castes which have been, in the main, non-cultivating, through generations, and hence shown utter want of the arts of cultivation. By contrast, the arts of cultivation have been in the blood of the members of the middle castes, confirming excellence on their part, most of which now stand under the banner of the Other Backward Classes (OBCs), in contradistinction to the forward castes, in Bihar, since while the OBCs may or may not depend on the field help of the people of the scheduled castes, the latter invariably depend on it, for cultivation is rough work to them and their dependence on the help of the scheduled caste members makes up the deficiency in their own knowledge of how the agricultural operations are to be conducted.

The preceding piece of information can be reset in a different caveat. We have in the villages the rural rich composed of the small old *zamindar class*. They dislike physical work, nay, hate it. Their empire rests on the backs of the agricultural labourers, with land or without it, the rural poor. The agricultural labourers' class is, population-wise, the largest class, the vote bank has its concentration in it. In so far as the large-size farm holdings belong largely to the rural rich, their management is largely dependent on the help and cooperation of the agricultural labourers,whom the rural rich keep in their control in several ways. Devoid of the brain-power, but gifted with enormous brawn-power, provided they are well-fed, the agricultural labourers, the poorest of the poor in the villages, toil ceaselessly, and in work ethic they are on competing terms with the small and marginal farmers coming largely of the OBCs. Among them we have a slightly better-off section, which consists of the share-croppers, tied in varying degrees to the rural rich. The exploitation attributed to share-cropping tenancy and usury until quite recently has diminished appreciably as a concomitant of the changes initiated and stimulated by the Government through the installation of new, preparatory institutions, on a wider scale, but more as a sequel to the sense of social awareness created in the villages in greater proportion by those groups of people who have been non-believers in non-violence and enthusiasts of violence and lawlessness. Although it cannot be maintained even now that agriculture in Bihar is no longer embedded in semi-feudal production relations, which have acted as a powerful drag on agricultural advancement, yet the apathy and fatalism which it bred are "remnants of a feudal past", for they have been largely blighted on account of the agricultural labourers' organised onslaughts on the landed propertied classes. The villages too had their spells of unruly and wayward agricultural labour, threatening to destroy the very foundations on which agriculture has rested for ages. When these spells have arisen or the rural rich have reacted with lock-outs at their farms, and moved, for a time, to the cities, agricultural production has suffered a setback owing to absentee landlordism. This part of the agrarian system has been creaking and groaning under the weight of its own inner excesses and the distortions and dilutions forced upon it by external agents and agencies in the last four decades and a half.

The *cultivators* who are a class of owners of their own plots, of varying sizes, previously were used to rely upon the help of hired agricultural labour but now mostly bank upon their own labour, which includes the family labour, to the maximum extent, enlisting outside help during the peak season. Unlike the rural rich, they do not suffer from any inhibitions or compunctions, obliging them to desist from touching the soil or tilling it with a plough. Being conversant with the secrets/tricks/arts of cultivation imbibed from their forefathers, they have had definite advantages over the other two classes, one richer than themselves but incapable of self-exertion and hence trying to wriggle out of what is irksome to them, and the other, capable of harder work but divested of land and skill. As migration of agricultural workers from many parts of Bihar has been on the rise, there have arisen, and there still arise spells during the peak days of sowing and harvesting when the requisite supply of agricultural labour has not been forthcoming or not forthcoming at the right time. But this has not held up work because the families have curtailed their leisure and plodded without any sense of remorse or social criticism. That in the central parts of the State these families have not had land in any sense above the ceiling has been a great help in 'Creamy Layer' meeting the eventuality. The economically well-off we have among the OAC families is the spearhead of modern, scientific, capitalist farming in Bihar.

Agricultural labourers as a class have amongst them a tiny section of small and marginal farmers, who are, by and large, the creation of the land reforms and welfare measures. Their work sense is exemplary but whereas the OBC small and marginal farmers wield some social clout and a modicum of credibility with the outside world, the SC ones are socially excluded and bare of credibility, with the result that they have the same will to improve the yield of their land, but less opportunity to translate their will into action. There is no lacking in patience, self-denial and thrift in either group, qualities which enable the members to face the most trying circumstances and, more often than not, come safely out of the dangers that surround them. A life of hardship has stood them in good stead, compared to the old zamindar class which has partly perished because its members were habituated to lead a life of ease which was under constant attack from their critics since the gain of Independence. Had the agricultural labourer class the benefit of knowledge and capital instruments, they could earn more even if they worked less hard and for shorter hours because then they could work more productively. By the same token, they could invest more in the improvement of their existing land instead of running after more land, thereby making the best of a bad job, as is characteristic of their OBC counterparts. The rates of illiteracy and unskill must be brought down if the small and marginal farmers, no matter from which section they came, were to effectively improve their economic lot and social status.

There was a time when only field labourers were mobilised by contractors and taken to other parts of the country to work in the mills of West Bengal and tea gardens of Assam, to other parts of the State to work in road building and other construction works in Chotanagpur and outlying areas as well as were sent by sea to the adjoining islands and even to South Africa for doing various kinds of work. But for the last two decades or so it is largely the young lads with a smattering of middle school or high school education, drop-out cases predominating, who work as guards/gate-keepers, night watchmen, peons or domestic servants, besides the artisans cobblers, hawkers/vendors or *panwallas* who do not have viable employment in their own places or neighbouring towns, or, alternatively, who earn more or get higher wages elsewhere, who have been migrating in larger numbers. One comes across these migrants as employed in brick kilns, rickshaw-pullers, repairers, *coolies*, etc. The village labour has become more mobile, more desirous of earning fair wages, more alike the Economic Man. This invites the comment that population explosion in Bihar has shaken the Bihar society out of its conservatism, and withdrawal of the excess labour from agriculture through outmigration has lowered the strain on the soil marginally, not structurally, and thereby contributed towards an improvement in the productivity of those engaged in agriculture and of the land allocated to cultivation. In addition, when the migrants are back to their villages during the festivals or the sowing/harvesting seasons, they have an educative impact on their neighbours, also a demonstrative effect, with their altered habits and tenor/tone of life, exuding catholicity and tolerance towards communities and castes other than their own, with their improved apparel/attire and possession of articles of daily use, which were marks of urban life until quite recently, and wares like the transistor, the cassette player, the wrist watch, a pair of terelyne trousers and shirt, and their acquired knowledge of the first-aid medicines. Their exposure to the bigger world arouses admiration for them in the hearts of those who have not as yet gone out of their village homes even for once.

The villagers have become more knowledgeable with the inauguration of planning. Under the CDP a social education programme was executed from the First Plan onwards, its principal adjuncts being drama, *kirtan* and cultural activities. The villagers were desirous/hungry of knowledge. They were educated to/urged upon to abandon the costly customs. They were educated to loosen the shackles of the age-old bondage of superstitions and fatalism. The radio and the TV and the small reading centers which provided newspapers and magazines and Government hand-outs were the means whereby knowledge and information was imparted/purveyed to the village people. The Adult Education and Basic Education programmes of the firstever Congress Government in Bihar during the late 1930s worked in the direction of illiteracy removal and enlightening the large mass of the rural illiterates. The village school teachers were associated with the extension work. But inadequacy of funds was the chief difficulty in the progress of the Adult Literacy Programmes, which were continued after certain revisions, e.g., Adult Education, Vocational Training, etc. even during the Plan Period which followed.

During the Laloo regime (1990-96) the school was taken to the fields, to provide basic education to the village lads while they were grazing their cattle. *Charwaha* Schools were established throughout the State. This became a big news. Foreign correspondents commented favourably on this. But the hollowness/futility of such a crazy/funny notion became exposed in no time and the schools became *khatals/*

cattle-sheds for the members of the ruling caste, and all the money spent on the project was a sheer waste.

Good higher education is a main source of social innovation. Most ideas for social change emerge from the campuses of colleges and universities. Changes are initiated also by enterprising individuals using uptodate teachings. The young men from villages who studied in cities during long vacations disseminated ideas for change among their co-villagers but they soon fell preys to the rabid caste feeling, which had been making heavy inroads into the organic wholeness of rural life, and in a short time the poor quality of college and university education and the vicious atmosphere prevailing in the colleges and universities of Bihar, which milled the caste venom in the highest quantity, threw most of them on the scrapheap of the unemployables, in the number of which Bihar was perhaps unequalled in India; selection, though competitive on paper, having been made more on the basis of caste considerations, (the lion's share going to the candidates of the ruling caste, or the ruling caste axis) than on that of merit—resort to corrupt methods being the common practice. So very wretched was the higher education system in the State that the students knew less and less as they studied more and more, and swapped their power of discrimination between good and bad in lieu of the art of manipulating adegrees and diplomas by means which were highly objectionable, nay, criminal. Timely examinations, and not proper teaching, was the sole official fiat.

In sum, however, the rural people, even if they have not gone to any school, today know, on an average, more about agriculture than was the case with them on the eve of the First Plan, and in this the quantitative explosion of the educational institutions and the increased circulation of newspapers and periodicals and the expanded coverage of the radio and the TV had their respective roles to play. And knowing more has caused social change to take place, to the liking of some sections and to the disliking of other sections, as disclosed in the formation of the Government by this or that party or a united front of parties, with regard to the path or form or substance or even the extent of that social change. There are more people who want the social change to subserve their interests than there are people who want it to get consolidated and stabilised.

We now propose to divert our study to the affinity between technological advance and productivity growth. The level of productivity is a function of the level of technological advance. Time management, experience analysis and research point of view are among the major determinants of productivity. Productivity involves a certain attitude of the mind, which unfolds itself in the scale and the speed with which the complex tasks are tackled. Lower technology is identifiable with lower productivity. Lower wages are commensurate with lower productivity because with lower wages the worker cannot eat a balanced diet, cannot live under hygienic conditions, and cannot have a sound body and a sound mind. So his productivity is lower. The average farmer's existing techniques are rationally scaled/adapted to his level of disposable capital. He is a risk-averter more than a risk-taker. He prefers a technology that combines a low mean yield per hectare with a low variance to alternative technologies and crops that may promise a higher mean yield but also avert the risk of a great variance. Where such a technology is not available, his hankering/quest for the remains.

Where an appropriate technology does not exist, there certainly is no question of the farmer's failure to adopt it and the productivity being lower, Examples are given above (section captioned 'Agricultural Education and Research').

But where an appropriate technology exists, it is not adopted by the farmer because of the market failure on other counts or other reasons. This can be elaborated: The farmers may be ignorant of the existence of the appropriate technology. Many farmers in several areas are not familiar with the potentialities of their own areas. Also, they do not know in what proportions the various components of the modern agrarian technology have to be used so as to derive optimum benefits from them. The flow of knowledge from the lab/experts to the field/farmers may be constrained. Both agricultural education and agricultural research which contribute to agricultural production and productivity may be at fault. The Extension Services are also to blame. The benefits of the new technology are not broadbased. The farmers are not convinced of the superiority of the improved techniques. Those who are convinced are unable to obtain them. The mass communications and training which are instrumental in the transfer of technology are slow to act. Inordinate delay occurs. In the earlier years of planning demonstration on local places proved to be the most effective method of propagating knowledge about the merits of new technologies, for instance, the fertilisers, the HYVs, etc. By their nature people believe only when they see the results with their own eyes. The World Bank in its project (1978-79) had emphasised motivation of the farmers in Bihar through the dissemination of information needed in an effective manner. In Bihar the dearth of R&D funds was a retarder in the spread of the known technologies.

Out of a host of factors highlighted above, we would like to treat the Extension Services factor with an added dose of amplification, considering its far-reaching importance. As we have shown in our study above, the patience and capacity of some top-level officials to listening to the villagers was wanting in the lower-rank officials. The lines of communication for facilitating free flow of ideas from the top-level to the low-level officials and from the village level to the top were not fully open. Consultation with the local farmers was thought to be essential for avoiding errors as well as for enlisting the enthusiasm of the people. It is not that the individual farmers are totally innocent of innovativeness. There are among them intelligent ones who are given to experimenting and hitting upon valuable innovations. To illustrate, the cultivation of the rainy season potato in Ranchi or of winter paddy in the Kosi belt resulted from this. The cultivation of many of the crops undertaken since the past few decades was originally popularised by the missionaries and their primary schools. The Japanese method of paddy cultivation required that the fertiliser was spread between the lines of plants and thereafter was puddled by hand spade or with a wheeled puddler. In the alternative, the fertiliser was mixed with earth and made into balls. The story goes that a resourceful family in Ranchi district with a large number of children adopted the system of mixing the fertiliser with clay, and making small balls out of the mixture and then inserting one ball by hand under the root system of each growing plant separately. As a result of this device, not only was there a saving in the quantity of the fertiliser consumed but the produce also was higher compared to that when the strip of land was cultivated by the standard Japanese method *per se*.

In those cases where land reform measures produced situations which were simulations of the models that influenced the legislative Acts and the rent-paying tenants acquired ownership rights in the concerned lands or redistribution of the surplus lands benefited certain families which came to have parcels of land for cultivation on payment of token rent to the Government or free of rent or the rack-rented tenants were protected by fixation of fair rent payable to the landowners, the impact of this series of steps was, in the aggregate, a net increment of investment of labour and modern inputs in the cultivation of the lands in question, with their outputs rising, bringing in its train contentment to the people involved, and a changed scenario in the villages concerned.

At, the same time, the landlords of the yesterdays, cut to size and chastened by the zamindari abolition law, who had called off their farm business and trekked to the cities, returned to their ancestral homes, setting up modern, capitalist farms, profiting from the facilities and incentives (say, in purchase of machines and implements and other accessories at concessional rates, with bulk of the price paid coming from the land mortgage banks) extended by the Government. In their case we have had entrepreneurship parallel to that displayed by those in manufacturing industry. A less unfree market in agriculture, with no liability to pay any tax, these capitalist farmers soon became ideal farmers, overlapping with the progressive farmers, turning to good account the lesson preached by the demonstration farms of the Government/agricultural universities, a sort of surrogates/proxies of the modern, capitalist farms. Their demonstrable operational success had a mighty impression on the minds of the villagers, thoroughly wholesome, generating a kind of order/symmetry in motivations of the farmers of diverse/different categories—the Maximisation of Profit hypothesis. The partnership of the Government with the farming capitalists, the various special grain/cash commodity production programmes commencing from the Sixth Plan, the crop insurance safeguards, the creation of a single window/delivery agency for supply of credit and modern inputs, the continuance of price and non-price incentives, etc., all of which go to support the emerging agrarian system, at the heart of which is a farmer different from the traditional.

We have attempted to correlate the agriculturist's productivity with his general education and special knowledge of agricultural operations/ technologies. It would be in the fitness of things if we introduced in our study the health dimension, considering that in Bihar, which has the highest incidence of poverty in the country, the maximum proportion of the poor is to be met within agriculture in the families of the agricultural labourers and those of the small and marginal farmers, which have, on an average, a larger number of mouths to feed. We would not be mistaken were we to urge that in a larger number of cases low productivity was poverty-borne. We cannot hope to find high productivity in a person with ill or poor health. His brawn power, his physical stamina is a function of his health. Poor health connotes disease, it signifies morbidity. Good health is a worker's best asset, best ally and its maintenance is obligatory on his part, for on it hinges his welfare and the welfare of those in his family whose fortunes are entirely bound up with his being in a proper working condition, and it is precisely in this sense that he is a machine. The machine has to be kept in proper order, otherwise the factory cannot work. This calls for advance funding. The human body, a machine,has to be energised. And it is the food which the worker eats which supplies that energy to his body. The human body burns food as energy, that is, derives energy from the food. The harder the physical work, the greater the need for energy and the more the food needed. The human body asks for clothing as for shelter, but its demand for food is the uppermost need, and has to be met, even at the cost of his other bodily requirements. Given adequate food, keeping the worker in good, working health becomes easier.

Both education (rather knowledge of agriculture) and health which are the worker's assets are also the elements/ingredients of what is termed 'the quality of life', which strictly denotes the rate of literacy, rate of infant mortality and the expectation of life, inasmuch as short of education and health, these measures/indicators of the quality of life are not so articulate. The Minimum Needs Programme (MNP), the 20-point Programme, the Adult Education Programme, the maternity and child care and protection, the mass vaccination and immunisation programmes, etc., which are Government sponsored, all have bearing on the quality of life and their incidence on health and education of those engaged in agriculture cannot be overestimated. These are in the direction of and are addressed to productivity-augmentation.

The term 'health' envelops sanitation and hygienic conditions as well as adequate supply of potable, safe drinking water. Houses, neat and clean and well-ventilated, free from squalor, having separate accommodation for the human beings and their cattle, which are behind the concept of the Indira Awas Yojana (IAY), multiply the energy which the worker derives from his food intake.

The common/ordinary agriculturist raises the food himself for his and his family's consumption, to the extent possible, and avoids dependence on the market. He is the key factor/agent in the production of his material needs, food being their capstone. He must be satisfied with his material needs, which comprise his material life, failing which he would cease to exist. Man is what he eats, said Marx. It is also true that he becomes what he eats. He is an animal to the extent that he suffers from the needs like food, clothing and shelter. But he is a conscious animal, a social animal. He is a tool-maker notless than a tool-user. He is a pleasure machine, though imperfect. The farm or field is not the factory which provides perfection by wiping out imperfection. He is a viewer of the material world around himself. He is an aspect of nature —he is included in nature and nature is included in him. He labours in a material world of nature physically as well as mentally. He is a self-seeker only to the point where it does not clash with his innate passion for social alignment. Above all, he is not a static model, a standardised product; on the contrary, he is a differentiated product.

In India the States which have had a better performance in human capital/resource development, compared to that in economic overheads development,for example, Kerala, have registered a faster rate of growth. Bihar's performance has been unsatisfactory in both areas. The explosion in educational institutions which Bihar had since Independence has caused frustration to many. Treating public health with lesser favour has resulted in the recall of the diseases which had been banished from the State with considerable endeavour. The lack of capacity which the public sector has shown in rising equal to the task (let us bear in mind the scams to which education and public health also have been subjected in Bihar) has not been made good by the private sector, for the simple fact that the private sector educational and public health facilities are subsidyless, market-sold goods, which only those with resources afford, with a balance of disutility over utility in an infinite number of cases, for the quality of the goods has been intrinsically inferior. Those who have lacked resources have either not afforded them or if they have done so, had their hopes dashed, for their wards had great difficulty in securing employment, which had developed caste orientation and/or had to be purchased by paying a fabulous price, in some cases by disposing of land and ornaments or by insisting on heavy dowry, and in the case of public health, the net benefit has been beneath expectation.

We, therefore, conclude with a question: Will more investment in education or in public health increase the people's productivity further in Bihar? On the right answer to this question would turn a right allocation of the Plan resources in the State,. All in all, the rural people place health before education, for to them health is wealth, it is through a healthy body that they can hope to earn their bread. Bad health forces them to remain absent from employment, or inflicts upon them the painful realisation that thier contribution to output is impaired due to ill-health. They fail to exert to the full, and if they make the mistake of exerting despite bad health, they quicken their end. Poor health is one of the host of factors which drives them to the money-lender. Loss of health to an ordinary agriculturist is more distressing than the loss of some wealth, and hence he leaves no stone unturned to regain his health. The medical revolution and the interest of the State Government, Central Government and world bodies evinced in public heath in the countryside in recent years in Bihar has certainly, in consonance with an improved level of living as a result of the economic progress made during the period, given rise to a situation in which we have everyone in the rural areas now enjoying better general health than before. The death rate has fallen. The expectation of life has risen. The rural medical centres have removed the helpness of the people in the matter of first aid and first attendance to their illnesses and accidents in most parts of the State. While supply of safe drinking water to all villages has been engaging the attention of the Government for some years, the provision of hygienic latrines in the villages has for some time past become an important programme. The combined effect of all these measures on the general health and psychology of the rural people and hence their productivity has been laudable/praiseworthy.*

* For data on these the reader is advised to consult our book *Population Pressure and Economic Backwardness*, Anamika, Delhi-52

23

AN OVERVIEW/AN OVER-ALL ESTIMATE

On The Eve of Independence

Area of Bihar State	:	21,141 sq. miles
Estimated population	:	1946 — 3,29,29,000
		1946-47 — 3,86,67,412
		Less than 12 years of age — 1,28,95,860
		Above 12 years of age — 2,50,33,140
Percentage of population dependent on agriculture and activities allied to agriculture	:	86
Total land area	:	44330 thousand acres
Cultivated land area	:	40 per cent/17653 thousand acres

Acreage : 1946-47

(in thousand acres)

TCA	28991
ASMO	6698 (132 per cent of NSA)
Paddy	13154 (66 per cent of TCA)
Maize	1832
Gram	1762
Wheat	2017
Barley	1189

Pulses

('000 acress)

Khesari	2408
Arhar	677
Peas	303

Cash Crops

Sugar-cane	363
Jute	122
Tobacco	54

Note : An attempt is made in this chapter to supplement and update, as far as possible, given the constraint of time taken by the press, the information provided by us in the previous chapters. The last volume in this series, *Resources : Human and Financial (State Finances, Budgetary and Plan)* would try to update the data again.

Season/Harvest-wise

	('000 acres)
Bhadai	6307
Aghani	808
Rabi	8329

Yield : Average of 1942-43 to 1945-46

	(Pounds per acre)
Paddy	627 (1045)
Barley	717
Wheat	787
Maize	672
Gram	644

Production : 1946-47

	('000 tonnes)
Paddy	6156
Maize	441
Gram	279
Wheat	430
Barley	244
Khesari	380
Arhar	147
Peas	58
Sugar-cane	2423
Jute	327
Tobacco	22

Per capita/per day rice production : 1946-47 — 9 ounces

Total irrigated area : 1946-47 — 5326/4879 (thousand acres)

Irrigation : Source-wise

	('000 acres)
Canals	
Government	683
Private	971
Tanks	1513
Wells	889
Others	1270

73 per cent land dependent on the monsoon.

Gross Income per Acre : 1945-46

	(Rs.)
Paddy	88
Wheat	124
Barley	82
Maize	60
Gram	82
Mustard	82
Linseed	30
Sugar-cane	273
Tobacco	860

Food Supply : 1946-47

Production (rice, wheat, gram, maize and barley)	5498 thousand tonnes
Imports	301548 tonnes
Total	6799548 tonnes
Per capita per day availability (including seeds)	One pound
Total food requirement	6300717 tonnes
Deficit/Gap	501169 tonnes
Food intake criterion per consumption unit : 1946	20 chhataks of grain or 13.8 chhataks of ready food
Number of adult consumption units	3,14,81,070

On the above criterion, no district was self-sufficient.

Food diet deficiency 40 to 45 per cent

Basis 2400 to 2800 calories per capita per day

Percentage of population dependent on the market for food : 1945 75

Food deficit

(*Percentage of families*)

Group	
With no land	29 (faced semi-starvation)
With less than 5 acres	49 (on margin of starvation)
With 5 to 15 acres	16.6
With above 15 acres	5.6

Note : The third group in Saran and the fourth group in Muzaffarpur, Darbhanga and Hazaribagh saved part of their food produce.

Grain was loaned on kind rate of interest, 125 to 150 per cent.

Bihar's food crisis started in 1943.

The communal riot in 1946-end : result : refugees had to be fed by the Government.

6 seers of toddy equalled one seer of grain in nutritive value.

The Food Levy Order imposed in 1946

Total State Income : 1946-47 Rs. 3449 lakh

Net income from livestock Rs. 4553 lakh

Contribution of agriculture to State Income 67 per cent

Per capita land area : 1946-47 About 0.5 acre (All-India : 0.71 acre)

Per Capital Income

(*Rs.*)

Annual	90 to 100
Monthly	8

Activities Allied to Agriculture : Production

Milk 45749 mds. (value : Rs. 3659.84 lakh)

Milk output (Annual) :

Per cow	620 pounds
Per buffalo	1526 pounds
Per goat	340 pounds

Eggs Produced

Number 1,28,420 (Value: Rs. 120.40 lakh)

Fish Production

1009 thousand mds.
10 lakh tonnes in 1946
(Value : Rs. 400 lakh)

Value of skins, hides and wool Rs. 5,387.27 lakh

Landless Labourers' Families as Percentage of All Rural Families : 1946-47

Maximum	11.16 in Ranchi district
Minimum	45.36 in Monghyr district

Agricultural labourers :

Number	87.95 lakh
Earning (number)	34.29 lakh
Average size of family	5.5 members

Earning members (number) per family	2.13
Percentage of casual labour	78
Percentage of attached labour	22
Employment (Number of days) in a year (average available)	150

Wages

	(Rs.)
Daily	
Male	18 annas.
Female	14 annas.
Child	9/10 annas.

Annual Earning

Per worker (Rs.)	66
Per family (Rs.)	363
Total annual incomes of families	Rs. 5,802.09 lakh
Total rural indebtedness	Rs. 100 crores

Rural Loans Granted by Government

Under the Land Reforms Act	Rs. 1,31,000
Under the Peasants' Lands Act	Rs. 4,35,852

First Congress Government formed in Bihar in 1937

Next Congress Government formed in Bihar in 1946.

Primary Agricultural Cooperative Societies (PACS) : 1946

Limited liability : Number 88

	Agricultural Cooperative Societies : 1946	*Non-agricultural Cooperative Societies : 1946*
Number	9442	355
Membership	231728	46776
Reserve Fund (Rs.)	1720348	2398370
Working Capital (Rs.)	6471347	923359
Profit (Rs.)	490817	314354

Number of multi-purpose cooperative societies	247
Depots under the Credit Agricultural Scheme (number)	81

Central Cooperative Banks : 1946

Number	45
Membership	1605
Number of societies	6306
Working capital (Rs.)	4011764

II

Land utilisation in Bihar in 1993-94 was as shown in Table 23.1 :

TABLE 23.1 : Land Utilisation in Bihar in 1993-94

Sl.No.	*Land Uses*	*Area ('000 ha.)*	*As Percentage of Sl. No. 1*	*As Percentage of All-India*
1.	Reporting area	17330	100.00	5.69
2.	Land under forests	2949	17.01	4.31
3.	Land not available for cultivation	3236	18.67	7.89
4.	Land not cultivated	813	4.69	2.77
5.	Fallow land	3065	17.68	12.75
6.	*Area sown*			
	A. Net area sown	7267	41.93	5.11
	B. Area sown more than once	2481	14.32	5.60
	C. Gross area cropped	9748	56.25	5.23

Under area sown is included the *Tal* area under which fall 494 villages and 26 blocks and which is extended in the districts of Patna, Nalanda, Munger, Bhagalpur and, to an extent, to Begusarai and Khagaria districts. Pulses are the major crops taken in the *Tal* area during the Rabi season, e.g., gram, lentil and peas. Water accumulates during the rainy season. Moisture is available for a short duration only after the rain-water has receded from the area. The cultivation of pulses has potential for being promoted in this area.

The growth rate of GCA and NAS during 1962-95 is given in Table 23.2 :

TABLE 23.2 : Growth Rate of GCA and NAS in Bihar

(*Per cent per annum compound*)

Period	*GCA*	*NAS*
1970-73 over 1962-65	0.04 (0.43)	(-)0.32 (0.19)
1980-83 over 1970-73	(-)0.50 (0.56)	(-)0.44 (0.14)
1992-95 over 1980-83	(-)0.76 (0.24)	(-)0.60 (0.07)
1992-95 over 1962-65	(-)0.46 (0.40)	(-)0.44 (0.12)

That both GCA and NAS during 1962-95 displayed negative growth rates in Bihar (as against the positive rates in all-India) is a matter of grave concern to us all. While there are certain ostensible factors that go to explain this, it has to be probed further if agriculture is becoming less remunerative and hence less attractive, as contended by many farmers, and for what reasons. Has the land reforms device gone astray? Has it belied the hopes pinned on it, and for what reasons? Or has the flight of labour and capital as well as the exodus of the landowners to urban areas anything to do with this upturn of events? How far are the mounting rural tensions in the comparatively better situated agricultural regions responsible for this unhappy trend?

During 1995-96 the monsoon was erratic. This stalled transplantation of an area of about 3.77 lakh ha. of paddy in the State.

III

In 1994-95 in Bihar almost 63 per cent of total area was under the Kharif and 37 per cent under the Rabi food crops. Compared to the all-India position, the former had some dominance over the latter. Table 23.3 would bear this out:

TABLE 23.3 : Division of GCA between Kharif and Rabi Food Crops in Bihar: 1994-95

Type of Crops	*Area under (Lakh ha.)*	*As Percentage of GCA*	*Percentage share in all-India*
Kharif	54.6	62.83	7.20
Rabi	32.2	37.17	6.64
Total	86.8	100.00	7.03

Keeping Tables 23.3 and 23.4 in mind, we find that the acreage under both Kharif and Rabi crops is unstable as are those under total cereals and millets (wheat and maize being more involved) and total pulses, either slight rise, as in the case of the former group or an evident fall, as in the case of the latter group. Rabi is looking up (including wheat and maize, as compared to the all-India situation in respect of them). That by comparison with all-India the acreage in Bihar is tilted towards Kharif and that Bihar is a densely rice-growing State by comparison with all-India are findings which cannot easily be underestimated.

TABLE 23.4 : Land Area under Certain Food Crops and their Groups in Bihar during 1989-91

Crops	*Area ('000 ha.)*		*Percentage Share in Total Land Area under Foodgrains*	
	1989-90	*1990-91*	*1989-90*	*1990-91*
Total Foodgrains	9413	9428	100.0	100.0
Kharif			67.4	67.9 (62.4)
Rabi			32.6	32.1 (37.4)
Total cereals and millets	8205	8252	87.2	87.5 (80.9)
Total Pulses	1258	1176	12.8	12.5 (19.5)
Rice				
Total	5268	5391	56.0	57.2 (33.2)
Autumn	735			
Winter	4452			
Summer	81			
Wheat	1988	1965	21.1	20.8 (18.9)
Maize	703	665	7.5	7.1 (4.6)

IV

The Bihar State Forest Development Corporation Ltd. collects and markets the non-wood forest products. Other programmes/schemes relating to forestry in Bihar are as follows :

1. Forest conservation and development : Regeneration of the sal forests, social and farm forestry; extension forestry; fuei wood and fodder projects.
2. Road-side plants including urban forestry and planting of the school premises.
3. Rehabilitation of the degraded forests.
4. Afforestation of the already mined areas.
5. Development of minor forest products.
6. Promotion of training facilities.
7. Forest publicity and public relations.
8. Wild life preservation.
9. Development of sanctuaries.
10. Development of the National Parks at Patna, Ranchi, Palamau and Valmikinagar.
11. Control of poaching and other illegal trade practices.
12. Soil conservation afforestation (forestry).

The following extract from *Statesman*, an English daily published from Calcutta and Delhi, dated 2 November, 1995, concerning the World Bank aided forestry project in Bihar would be of instant interest.

"IBRD May Wind Up Bihar Project

That the Bihar Chief Minister, Mr. Laloo Prasad Yadav's recent endeavour to attract foreign investors to the State seems to have failed to bear much fruit is apparent by the reported decision of the World Bank to wind up the prestigious Rs. 293.22 crore Bihar forestry project. The State Government's low credibility in execution of other World Bank projects is reported to have forced the international organisation to take an adverse decision against the forestry project.

According to informed sources the World Bank has to review its earlier decision to grant the Bihar forestry project to the State Government and wind it up if possible in the wake of the State Government's poor performance with regard particularly to the Bihar Plateau Development Project (BPDP) and the Integrated Child Development Scheme (ICDS), both of which are World Bank aided projects. The sources said that the Bank officials had been quite concerned over tardy progress made by the State Government in the plateau project meant for the Jharkhand region and the child development scheme to be executed throughout the State. The World Bank teams sent to the State to review the progress in these two schemes have reportedly made adverse comments against the Government agencies responsible for their execution.

It were these adverse reports which made the World Bank take a decision not to give direct funding to the Bihar Government for the Forestry Project. The Bank instead proposed that a separate agency be created for the purpose in the shape of both the State Government and the World Bank to execute the Forestry Project in the State from October 1994. The project was to be implemented for toning up the forest management plans in the State in two phases and to last for nine-and-a-half years. The State Government agreed to create such an organisation and persuaded the World Bank to have 77 per cent of the share in the proposed set-up.

Though the project could not be started in time on account of procedural wrangling, it appeared at one stage that the unique organisation to implement the prestigious World Bank (WB) project in Bihar was almost a reality. The WB too was optimistic about the project's viability and it seemed that the State which had faced the .argest devastation of flora and fauna in the south-east Asian region would be able to overcome the problem with the help of the proposed World Bank project. The Bank appeared sanguine that forest protection through the people's participation as well as biodiversity conservation, as envisaged in the Bihar Forestry Project, would save the forests in Bihar.

But the hopes of the World Bank were belied the moment the proposal consented to by the State Government started gathering dust in the offices of the Union Government. The Bihar Government sought the approval of the Centre over the proposal to have a separate agency to receive the funds from the World Bank to implement the prestigious forestry project. For quite sometime the file could not be traced and it reportedly kept on travelling from different departments of the Union Government Ministries. With the World Bank officials appearing in a hurry to get the green signal of the State to release funds to the proposed agency, the State Government officials continued their pressure on the Centre to clear the proposal so that it could be implemented in time.

Ultimately, the Centre decided to examine the matter with the help of the Department of Economic Affairs of the Ministry of Finance. The bureaucratic wranglings at this stage came in the way of the proposal and the department turned down the same pleading the absence of any precedence to have an agency to receive foreign funds to execute any international project in a State.

The department maintained that the loans by the World Bank had to come to the State Government so that there could be an accountability for its repayment and the guarantee could be furnished by the State Government itself. It said that in case of a separate organisation having a very nominal share of the State Government such guarantee might not work.

However, the World Bank kept on maintaining that it would not give funding to the State Government directly in view of its bitter experience with regard to the BPDP and the ICDS. Meanwhile, the State Government, which kept on maintaining it contact and liason with the World Bank over the proposal, promised to improve its performance.

The meeting is scheduled to take place on Saturday in Patna where the World Bank team is likely to put certain stringent conditions sot that the forestry project does not meet the fate of the BPDP or the ICDS. The State Government officials seem apprehensive to meet these conditions putting a question mark over the very proposal by the forestry project itself."

V

Production of foodgrains in Bihar during 1990-91 to 1995-96(P) is presented in Table 23.5 :

TABLE 23.5: Foodgrains Production in Bihar during 1990-91 to 1995-96

('000 tonnes)

Items	*1990-91*	*1991-92*	*1992-93*	*1993-94*	*1994-95*	*1995-96 (P)*
Total foodgrains	12258.9	10638.4	9082.4	12776.1	12971.0	13069
Rice	5663.5	4753.2	3641.2	6108.5	6297.9	6910.9
Wheat	3560.4	3594.3	3449.5	4356.7	4275.0	4180.5
Coarse cereals	1219.2	1440.5	1298.4	1575.4	1608.5	1405.6
All Cereals	11343.1	9788.0	8389.1	12040.6	12181.4	12497.0
All Pulses	915.8	850.4	693.3	735.5	789.6	572.3

Note: (P) is Provisional.

Harvest-wise foodgrains production in Bihar in 1994-95 was as brought out in Table 23.6 below :

TABLE 23.6: Harvest-wise Foodgrains Output in Bihar in 1994-95

Harvest	*Quantity (Lakh tonnes)*	*As percentage of*	
		Total Output	*All-India Total*
Kharif	68.7	53.46	6.84
Rabi	59.8	46.54	6.61
Total Foodgrains Output	128.5	100.0	6.72

There was a little improvement in Bihar's relative position in all-India from the standpoint of food output in 1994-95, compared to the period from 1991-92 to 1993-94.

The target of paddy production in Bihar during 1995-96 was not achieved.

In 1996-97 total foodgrains production in Bihar was sought to be achieved by assigning percentage targets to individual and group of crops, as shown in Table 23.7.

Bihar's percentage share in all-India production of food and non-food crops during 1990-91 to 1994-95 was as given in Table 23.8.

TABLE 23.7 : Foodgrains Production Targets in Bihar in 1996-97

Items	*As Percentage of Total Foodgrains Production*
Total Foodgrains output target	194.50 lakh tonnes + 100.00
Rice	43.30
Wheat	35.99
Maize	11.31
Coarse cereals	1.28
Total pulses	8.22

TABLE 23.8: Bihar's Share in Agricultural Production during 1989-90 to 1994-95

Production of Crop(s)	*As Percentage of All-India Average of Period :*		
	1989-90 to 1990-91	*1990-91 to 1993-94*	*1991-92 to 1994-95*
Total foodgrains production			6.3
Rice production			6.7
Wheat production			6.6
Gram production	3.05		
Cash/Non-food crops :			
Oilseeds		0.7	
Sugar-cane		2.7	

The quality of soil (which is synonymous with its fertility or productivity) determines, first of all, which crop would grow best on which soil. Districts in Bihar (e.g., the north-western part of West Champaran—remember the joke "Strange is the tract Majhauwa in Bihar, where even the crow does not care a fig/two hoots for rice/paddy," or, "Spread a handful of paddy seeds over any field in Majhauwa and you have a bagful of rice") having medium to good fertility soil have a good rice crop. The northern part of Bihar's fertile soil grows paddy, sugarcane, jute and oil-seeds, in addition to the millet crops/contingent/catch crops.

Whereas food production/supply in Bihar has increased, food demand has increased in consequence of more consumption on the part of the people, in general, residing in both rural and urban areas, made possible by the increase in their real income, (even if the productivity of agricultural workers, mainly male ones, has fallen), caused by increased production in the economy, execution of programmes aimed at providing more employment to the people as well as reducing the incidence of unemployment, besides implementation of policies addressed to liquidating poverty, lumped with the centring of attention on the sale prices of the food articles supplied through the public distribution system, which in practice is akin to the open market operations method of credit control by the Central Bank/compensatory spending or pump-priming by the Government in a free-enterprise economy facing falling effective demand. All in all, Bihar's food problem is an organic/integral part of the wider problem of agriculture.*

VI

Working more productively is not, of necessity, working harder or for longer hours; it is using more knowledge, more capital instruments. (1) Hard/patient work/enterprise, (2) abstinence/self-denial/thrift and (3) invention/innovation are the means to prosperity, though the first one is the most important of all. Malthus had maintained that a community's attitude to work could be a more decisive determinant for stepping up productivity than its material resources, including technology. Increased productivity of the agriculturists/their increased quality is coterminous/coordinate with technological progress. A progressive farmer, as compared to an average one, by handling the available resources and reacting to situations more efficiently and intelligently attains a higher level of yield than does an average farmer. In other words, the personality/character of the farmer is central/germane to yield. Similarly, areas not affected by floods/droughts have higher productivity in the current year.

Table 23.9 furnishes figures of average yields of certain crops/crop groups during 1990-95 :

TABLE 23.9: Average Yields in Bihar

(ha./kgs.)

Principal Crops	*1990-91*	*1991-92*	*1992-93*	*1994-95*
(1)	(2)	(3)	(4)	(5)
Foodgrains		1173 (1382)	1113 (1445)	
Kharif				1260 (1340)
Rabi				1460 (1860)

(Contd.)

* The reader is advised to go through the author's another publication called *Population Pressure and Economic Backwardness : A Comparative Study of Bihar and All-India*, Anamika, Delhi-52, for more data illumining these remarks.

TABLE 23.9 (*Contd.*)

(1)	(2)	(3)	(4)	(5)
Total cereals	1375 (1571)	1226 (1574)	1164 (1650)	
Coarse cereals	1360 (900)	1596 (778)	1592 (1065)	
Rice		932 (1741)	814 (1744)	
Wheat		1811 (2394)	1748 (2394)	
Total pulses		785 (533)	733 (573)	
Gram	941 (712)	821 (739)	693 (673)	
Total Oilseeds		578 (601)	476 (601)	
Sugarcane		48838 (66069)	45384 (63810)	1480 (1547)
Jute	1306 (1634)	1415 (1662)	1383 (1058)	

It is clear from Table 23.9 that except in respect of coarse cereals, total pulses and total oil-seeds yields in Bihar continue to be below the all-India averages.

Table 23.10, which follows, illustrates the finding that in Bihar during the last three decades growth rate of agricultural output/average value of crop yield was lower than that in all-India both absolutely and relatively:

TABLE 23.10: Growth Rate of Agricultural Output/Average Value of Yield in Bihar

(*Per cent per annum compound*)

Period	*Growth Rate of Agricultural Output Average Value of Crop Yield*
1962-65	1.08 (1.64)
1970-73	0.10 (1.80)
1980-83	2.86 (3.15)
1992-95	1.46 (2.30)
1970-73 over 1962-65	1.12 (2.08)
1980-83 over 1970-73	– 0.41 (2.38)
1992-95 over 1980-83	2.08 (3.40)
1992-95 over 1962-65	0.99 (2.71)

It is distressing to note that in the last three decades the rate growth of average productivity per male agricultural worker in Bihar has continuously declined at changing percentages, productivity having been measured by money value of his product at 1990-93 prices in Bihar, whereas the rate has been positive, though altering, in the case of all-India, as depicted by Table 23.11 :

TABLE 23.11: Growth of Productivity of Agricultural Workers in Bihar

Characteristic	*1962-65*	*1970-73*	*1980-83*	*1992-95*
Productivity (Rs):				
Bihar	3860	3500	2965	2934
All-India	6414	6552	7215	8961
	1970-73 over 1962-65	*1980-83 over 1970-73*	*1992-95 over 1980-83*	*1992-95 over 1962-65*
Growth rate of productivity (Per cent per annum) :				
Bihar	–1.22	–1.64	–0.09	–0.91
All-India	0.27	0.97	1.82	1.12

The State planners assign this to a triad of bottlenecks, viz., (1) poor irrigation, (2) a low rate of application of fertilisers, and (3) uneconomic size of holdings for the low rate of yield and assert that Bihar's agriculture would not develop unless steps were taken to remove them.

Substantiating their theory with reference to the low yield of sugar-cane (50 tonnes per ha., all-India average 70 tonnes per ha.), they impute it to the low coverage of the HYVs, low input consumption and lack of knowledge of the new techniques. The Government took a few measures to improve the yield: (1) Quality seed production, (2) Seed transportation, and (3) Encouragement of the use of the recommended quality of inputs. In 1995-96, 22 districts, noted for sugar-cane cultivation, were selected for the purpose. The Government of India introduced a Centrally-sponsored scheme, namely, the Sustainable Development of Sugarcane based Cropping System directed towards the same goal.

At the State Government level, we have the vegetable sub-sector plan, the potato and tuber development scheme and the kitchen garden scheme.

The entry of the Government in agriculture in a number of ways has facilitated the integrated growth of agriculture in keeping with the pre-conditions of the NAT. This has accelerated the pace of adoption of the NAT. But the pace has been slow and unsmooth, proving mill's observation to the hilt that between agriculture and industry, the adoption of a new technology is far more difficult in the former.

It would be useful to have here some information on cost of cultivation, cost of production and value of output of agricultural commodities. This is available for one food crop, paddy and three commercial cash crops, viz., sugarcane, jute and potato. We have supplied it in Tables 23.12 to 23.17 below.

Except for one year, cost of production of paddy in Bihar has been higher than that in Punjab. Between 1981-82 and 1990-91 the cost rose by 215 per cent in Bihar and by 225 per cent in Punjab. It has been cheaper to produce sugarcane in Bihar than in Maharashtra. Between 1982-83 and 1990-91 cost rose by 172 per cent in Bihar and by 143 per cent in Maharasthra. Except for one year, cost of producing jute has remained higher in West Bengal than that in Bihar. During 1981-82 to 1988-89, on one estimate, the cost rose by 161 per cent in Bihar and on another, by 174 per cent. On the other hand, the rise in West Bengal was by 171 per cent. As for the rise in cost of production of potato in Bihar in one single year it was by 127 per cent. This deduction calls for a qualification, namely, that here we have not considered the difference in the quality of the product.

TABLE 23.12: Cost of Production of Paddy

(*Rs. per quintal*)

Year	*Bihar*	*Punjab*
1981-82	103.06	102.31
1982-83	114.64	103.87
1983-84	133.76	122.32
1986-87	158.31	129.23
1987-88	175.77	149.19
1990-91	221.36	230.54

TABLE 23.13: Cost of Production of Sugarcane

(*Rs. per quintal*)

Year	*Bihar*	*Maharasthra*
1981-82	11.82	
1982-83	11.77	14.71
1983-84	13.25	15.91
1986-87	12.60/12.77 (47.53)	17.10
1987-88	13.99/14.20 (25.84)	16.89
1990-91	20.31	21.12
1991-92	18.33	

Note: Figures in brackets are percentages of cash and kind expenses to total cost.

TABLE 23.14 : Cost of Production of Jute

(*Rs. per quential*)

Year	*Bihar*	*West Bengal*
1981-82	151.55	181.32
1982-83	135.91	183.15
1983-84	183.80	198.45
1986-87	188.39 (46.04)	200.67
1987-88	276.11/302.13 (41.59)	268.59
1988-89	244.81/263.51 (41.74)	310.38

Note: Figures in brackets are percentages of cash and kind expenses to total cost.

TABLE 23.15 : Cost of Production of Potato

(*Rs. per quintal*)

Year	*Bihar*
1985-86	61.29 (60.56)
1986-87	78.09 (62.90)

Note: Figures in brackets indicate percentages of cash and kind expenses to total cost.

TABLE 23.16: Value of Output of Principal Cash Crops in Bihar

(*Rs. per ha.*)

Year	*Main Product*			*By-Product*		
	Sugarcane	*Jute*	*Potato*	*Sugarcane*	*Jute*	*Potato*
1985-86	—	—	16047.66	—	—	8.06
1986-87	6154.85	2784.71	12941.52	663.47	260.02	48.67
1987-88	11595.00	3489.04	—	100.06	263.15	—
1988-89	—	3953.86	—	—	213.24	—

TABLE 23.17: Cost of Cultivation of Principal Cash Crops in Bihar

(*Rs. per ha.*)

Year	*Cash and kind expenses*			*Total Cost*		
	Sugarcane	*Jute*	*Potato*	*Sugarcane*	*Jute*	*Potato*
1985-86	—	—	4928.61 (61.35)	—	—	8032.12
1986-87	1668.55 (44.62)	1225.51 (46.04)	5730.30 (71.34)	3739.03	2661.42	9512.01
1987-88	1627.49 (25.26)	1375.47 (41.39)	—	6440.81	3323.08	—
1988-89	—	1460.49 (41.81)	—	—	3492.99	—

Note: Figures in brackets indicate the percentages of cash and kind expenses to total cost.

In Bihar per ha. income from sugarcane far exceeds that from both jute and potato. Total cost of production per ha. of potato is far higher than that in the case of both jute and sugarcane. Limiting to the year 1986-87 for which figures are available for all the three crops, we have the following results (Table 23.18) :

TABLE 23.18: Profitability Rate of Producing Certain Commercial Crops in Bihar: 1986-87

Commodity	*Income per ha. (Rs.)*	*Cost per ha. (Rs.)*	*Difference (Rs.) (2) - (3)*	*(4) as percentage of (2)*
(1)	(2)	(3)	(4)	(5)
Sugarcane	6818.32	3739.03	3079.29	45.16
Jute	3044.73	2661.42	383.31	12.59
Potato	12990.19	9512.01	3478.18	26.77

We find from above the table that the rate of profitability as percentage of income per ha. is the highest in the case of sugarcane. Between jute and potato, the latter is more remunerative than the former.

The farmers everywhere in India have expressed their resentment over the fact that whereas their revenue from sale of their agricultural produce rose by 577 per cent between 1970-71 and 1993-94, the expenses on producing it which they incurred rose by 659 to 1123 per cent, with the result that they were hit hard by the losses suffered by them on this account. The data presented in Table 23.19 confirm this :

TABLE 23.19: Price Problem facing Farmers in India during 1970-71 to 1993-94

Item	*Percentage Rise in Prices*
Government purchase price:	
Wheat	434
Rice (ordinary)	574
All agricultural products in the open market	577
Articles needed by farmers	659
Capital assets needed by farmers	930
Fuel, energy, lighting and lubricants	1123
All articles: Wholesale prices	697

Let us remind ourselves here of the fact that prices of manufactures as percentage of prices of agricultural products were 92.5 in 1950-51, which had moved up to 105.4 by 1984-85.

Table 23.20 derived from the Kharif Report of 1994-95 published by the Agricultural Costs and Prices Commission of India gives the needed information :

TABLE 23.20: Index of Prices Paid and Received by Farmers in India during 1983-84 to 1993-94

Year (April to June)	*Index Number of Prices received by Farmers for their Products*	*Index Number of Prices paid by Farmers for all Products/ Inputs needed by them*
1983-84	261.1	302.6
1984-85	276.8	321.8
1985-86	278.0	337.4
1986-87	308.0	361.2
1987-88	348.2	400.5
1988-89	364.0	422.2
1989-90	393.5	455.1
1990-91	454.6	505.1
1991-92	516.9	570.1
1992-93	529.1	623.0
1993-94	576.8	658.9

From Table 23.20, it is obvious that the farmers' outgoings increased by higher percentage points, i.e., 356.3 than their incomings, which increased by 315.8 percentage points between 1983-84 and 1993-94, that is, in one decade.

We know that the terms of trade were against agriculture in the years preceding Independence. For the first ten years of the planned development era there was a short supply of chemical fertilisers everywhere; there occurred delay in the establishment of seed multiplication farms; also there was for long lack of a suitable agency to ensure the distribution and exchange of the improved seeds among the different classes of the registered growers; the per capita Plan outlay on agriculture and rural development was meagre; the funds to be spent on agricultural R&D were marked by dearth; working capital needed by the farmers was not forthcoming in the amount desired and, of course, not at the rate of interest and on terms and conditions within the capacity of and convenient to them respectively, and, finally, at the Extension level apathy of the officials disheartened them most of the time. The disincentive effect of these could not be overemphasised.

Costs of cultivation have escalated as the supply of the HYVs and fertilisers as well as diesel has been far from adequate and the supply in the pipeline has been, not inoften, rigged as well as untimely, while the farmers have competed for purchasing and storing them.

The petty farmers have been in the habit of over-exploiting the soil fertility, without striving to continuously replenish its depleted fertility.

Quite a proportion of the urban population has retained its nexus with the primary sector in degree high and low, according to the number of days in the year spent in their original village homes. In 1991 in 124 towns out of 211 in Bihar (58 to 59 per cent, as compared to the all-India average of 47.5 per cent) 113.5 lakh people out of 215.7 lakh people, that is, 36.3 per cent comprised this category of people.

As mentioned before, in those districts of Bihar where caste/class war has been on/on-going, vast strips of land have lain fallow because their owners could not be sure of reaping the harvest, even if they had mobilised the required workforce to get their lands cultivated and sown, the first hurdle which had to be surmounted. The real cultivators in large percentages have been without any entitlement to the ownership of the lands they have cultivated for years, down the generations, mixing the sweat of their brow with the soil tilled, while their present owners have not associated themselves physically with the task of cultivation because they had no need to do so or because they considered this beneath their dignity in society. The former have not put in their labour their heart to the extent and in the manner they did in the past. The share of the produce that fell to their lot has failed to enthuse them now. On the contrary, those whose material happiness in its entirety has turned on the size of the produce from their fields cultivated by others, have failed to involve themselves bodily in the task and have got infuriated over the change in the attitude of their yesterdays' servers and taken recourse to awarding corporal punishment to the non-cooperators, which has at times ended in fatal injuries. This unlawful measure has been lately answered by the other class with an equally unlawful measure. In the meantime, agriculture in those districts has almost stood still with stagnation-like conditions.

As far as the commercial crops are concerned, we would like to suggest that their production being trade/export-oriented, is an indisolvable part of the State's economic base, and as such it deserves Government backing primarily on economic considerations.

VII

A glance at Table 23.21 would demonstrate how Bihar's agricultural produce has been fluctuating from year to year. During the last decade and a half its share in the State product has declined at both current and constant prices, which is consistent with the growth theory, but even at present it remains quite substantial :

TABLE 23.21: Place of Agriculture Income in State Income of Bihar

Year	*Agricultural Produce (Rs. Lakhs)*			
	At current prices	*At constant prices (1980-81)*	*As percentage of NSDP at*	
			Current prices	*Constant prices*
1980-81	302911	302911	47.73	47.73
1984-85	491529	362691	43.22	44.68
1985-86	529357	363868	42.80	43.87
1989-90	764481	332107	39.39	35.46
1990-91	953790	396613	41.78	38.45
1993-94	945840	309551	30.81	30.50
1994-95 (P)	1520392	351344	23.45	23.10
1995-96 (Q)	1618349	392109	41.41	35.76

P = Provisional. Q = Quick.

From the national point of view agricultural output did the best during the 1970s. The 1980s were disappointing from this standpoint. In the last thirty years Bihar's share in the incremental value of the nation's agricultural output has been a mere 1.94 per cent, as is evident from Table 23.22 :

TABLE 23.22: Bihar's Share in all-India Incremental Value of Agriculture Output

Period	*Amount (Rs. crores)*	*As Percentage of all-India*
1970s over 1960s	366.06	3.62
1980s over 1970s	(–) 171.69	(–) 0.97
1990s over 1980s	1155.73	2.77
1990s over 1960s	1350.10	1.94

That with about 6.03 per cent share in GCA and about 6.9 per cent share in total foodgrains output of the country Bihar should have a share between (–)0.97 to 3.62 per cent in the incremental value of agriculture output in India could only mean that it was affected by the Green Revolution only peripherally/tangentially, deriving merely fringe gains from it, less than proportionally than its due share. Not only this, the second decade which bore the imprint of the GR as a carry-over from the first decade stood as the best among the four decades covered by our study. However, it was followed by the third decade which wore the scar of being the worst of all from this angle of view. The fourth decade was a positive gain, no doubt, but it was again below the gain that the second decade had bestowed on the state. In sum, the impact of the GR was dwindling through time, may be for reasons catalogued above.*

VIII

As Table 23.23 brings out, during the last fifteen years, the contribution made by forestry and logging to agricultural income in Bihar has fallen, whereas that made by fishery has risen. Although their joint contribution had slightly improved, the improvement had not produced an impression of any meaningful brunt/depth. From 7.01 per cent to 7.14 per cent share of the two activities allied to agriculture in total income from it was not of any great moment, considering the credit accorded to them for it by the Government during the Plan period.

TABLE 23.23: Place of Forestry and Fishery in Bihar's Agriculture

Year	*Value of Product(s) from (Rs. lakhs)*		*As Proportion of Value of Agricultural Produce (per cent)*	
	Foretry and Logging	*Fishery*	*(2)*	*(3)*
(1)	(2)	(3)	(4)	(5)
1980-81	15196	6075	5.01	2.00
1981-82	18241	6240	6.03	2.06
1982-83	18572	6745	5.52	2.00
1983-84	21425	9202	5.33	2.29
1984-85	22560	11209	4.59	2.28
1985-86	23017	14006	4.34	2.64
1986-87	22962	14929	3.63	2.36
1987-88	22766	20670	3.60	3.32
1988-89	43803	24569	5.64	3.16
1989-90	36933	29759	4.83	3.89
1990-91	37282	29957	3.90	3.14
1991-92	45956	37827	3.85	3.14
1992-93	42471	34696	4.52	3.72
1993-94	51352	44800	4.06	3.54
1994-95(P)	54787	45376	3.60	2.98
1995-96(Q)	58451	57232	3.61	3.53

* See *Appendix I* at the end. Bihar agriculture should take a lesson from Punjab. We said this thirtyfive years ago and we are saying this again.

Animal production is an integral part of the agriculture dominated rural economy of Bihar and is firmly interwoven with the socio-economic fabric/matrix of the rural population.

Bihar possesses one-tenth of the total livestock and poultry population of the country but their genetical make-up is poor.

In spite of what is said above, animal husbandry acts as an agency for agricultural production, provides the source for nutrition, food materials and raw materials for industry, though inadequately, and thereby forms an arm of the agricultural sector, or rather the primary sector.

A number of schemes have been launched by the Government for the uplift of animal husbandry:

1. Scheme for the control of the foot-and-mouth disease.
2. Scheme for the systematic control of the animal disease and livestock disease of national importance and other related aspects.
3. Scheme for a sample survey of estimating milk, eggs, wool and meat output, etc.
4. Scheme for the establishment of the State Veterinary Council.
5. Scheme for the reorganisation of the administrative machinery.
6. Expansion of the veterinary services and animal health infrastructure.

Horticulture is another area in which there is a chain of Centrally assisted schemes (ten in number). At the State level, under the *Diara* Development Project horticulture receives the Government's attention.

IX

We now turn to the NAT. As said above, technical progress is quality improvements in human beings in their role as economic agents/actors. Technical improvement, when sufficient, releases agricultural workers and generates agricultural surpluses. In bringing about this improvement price and non-price (e.g., subsides) policies play their parts. The contribution made by the Agricultural Extension Programme cannot be underestimated, for under it farmers are given training about the latest technology; their problems are discussed and efforts are made to remedy them, and if any new problems crop up, they are referred to the two State agricultural universities for research. By 1966 the programme was extended to 31 districts. Steps were also under way/afort for reorganising the programme.

There is another programme at work. This relates to the integrated development of cereals. It is an on-going programme, a Centrally sponsored scheme on a 75:25 basis. It is designed to augment/boost/buttress the production as well as the productivity of rice, wheat and maize. Farmers are given the needed training. The new technology is demonstrated to the growers of these crops. Under the Prime Minister's Special Programme there is a minikit scheme for paddy. A biological Central lab has been set up.

The Village Level Workers (VLWs) are trained in the training centres meant for them. There are also the *Kisan Vidyapeeths* (Farmers' Schools). The Secondary School students are acquainted with knowledge about agricultural extension. The local farmers are acquainted with the modern technologies which are being practised in different States by taking them to those places in batches from Bihar at short intervals. Another method by which the farmers are helped to acquaint themselves with the new technologies lies in holding periodic public exhibits. Agricultural workshops are maintained in selected districts. Under the Special Programme for Rural Development is conducted the Drought Promotion Area Programme, also a centrally-sponsored scheme.

According to the latest estimate, the ultimate irrigation potential of Bihar works out to 122.98 lakh ha., out of which 66.295 lakh ha. (i.e., about 54 per cent) has been reached through the major and medium irrigation schemes, and the balance, 56.685 lakh ha. (i.e., about 46 per cent), has been attained through the medium, surface and groundwater irrigation programmes.

At the end of the Seventh Plan, so far as the major and medium schemes were concerned, the potential created as percentage of the ultimate potential came to 53.90 per cent, as compared to the national average of 40.99 per cent. Of the potential created, 86.40 per cent was utilised in Bihar, as against 89.53 per cent in all-India.

During the Eighth Plan (1992-97) the Bihar Government accorded the top most priority to the completion of the spilled-over schemes of the pre-Sixth Plan, 17 major (four from the Seventh Plan and 13 pre-Sixth Plan), of which six were scheduled to be completed during the Eighth Plan; of the six, five belonged to the pre-Sixth and one to the Seventh Plan period), 26 medium (15 of the pre-Sixth and 11 of the Seventh Plan) 29 medium (15 of the Seventh Plan and 14 of the pre-

Sixth Plan) which were to be completed during the Eighth Plan. The Kaduan and Jamania schemes are the post-Seventh Plan ones.

Under the Bihar Plateau Development Project there is focus on agricultural development and to speed it up there is minor irrigation which is to be made an important instrument.

Under minor irrigation during the Eighth Plan the NABARD aided the surface water and State tubewell projects. In developing shallow tubewells in the private sector subsidies have played a significant part. In May, 1995, 97582 out of 5.63 lakh tubewells sunk for supplying drinking water, that is, 17.33 per cent, were defunct for want of repair and maintenance.

In the tribal areas the available water is to be most meticulously shared between drinking water for the people and irrigation, on the one hand and between drinking and irrigation, on the other. The problem is common to the plains but less stringently/rigorously. But everywhere, particularly in the urban areas and the drought-prone pockets water resources have to be conserved because the water reserves are likely to be at a low ebb in some years, when water availability would become the centre-piece in the determination of new settlements and new sites for businesses and industrial units in consequence of the inter-State rivalry in picking up momentum in water gathering.

One adjunct of the Integrated Central Development Programme concerns giving of incentive on recently (i.e., in the last ten years) released varieties of seed in the form of subsidy to farmers (as also the seed growing agencies), distribution of certified seeds of rice, wheat and maize by giving subsidy by the State Government, the aim being to cover the entire cultivable area with the HYVs seeds. Each district is to have a seed-testing lab. The quality of seeds is to be tested and maintained by the Inspecting machinery. Besides, each administrative division is to have one seed-processing plant. At present there is one such plant at the State level. The traditional varieties produced by farmers are exchanged for the certified HYVs.

There is also in force the Oilseeds Production Programme and the Scheme for Vegetables Hybrid Seeds Distribution.

Between 1986 and 1996 there occurred a three-fold increase in fertilisers consumption in terms of nutrients in Bihar from 2.05 lakh tonnes in 1981-82 to 6.90 lakh tonnes in 1995-96. The Government keeps vigilance on the quality of fertilisers being made available to farmers. Labs have been set up for testing their quality.

Table 23.24 furnishes some interesting statistics on the use of nutrients and production of paddy and wheat :

TABLE 23.24: Economics of Nutrients as Used in Bihar: 1986-87

Crop	*Yield (kgs./ha.)*		*Return (Rs./ha.)*			*Nutrients (kgs./ha.)*			*Percentage of cases exceeding the target*	*Number of demons-trations*
	Mean	*Highest*	*Gross*	*Cost of production*	*Return over operating costs*	*N*	P_2O	K_2O		
(1)	(2)	(3)	(4)	(5)	(6)	(7)	(8)	(9)	(10)	(11)
Paddy	39.81 (47.49)	52.60 (89.32)	7858 (9479)	4433 (4144)	3426 (5335)	81 (85)	32 (44)	16 (43)	8 (61)	45 (792)
Wheat	35.38 (35.00)	45.00 (52.60)	6863 (7590)	3968 (3464)	2895 (4126)	91 (107)	57 (49)	32 (26)	4 (426)	29 (426)

Under the Integrated Cereal Development Programme subsidy is given to those farmers who purchase improved kinds of agricultural implements. There is another programme under which the farmers residing in the tribal areas are provided with improved agricultural implements on a subsidy basis. Finally, under the Prime Minister's Special Programme farmers are supplied with small tractors. This is a step in the direction of evolving and promoting an Appropriate Technology.

Plant protection works are carried out by the plant protection offices throughout the State from the block upto the State level. There is, what is called Integrated Pest Management, a Centrally-sponsored programme at work in Bihar. During Kharif the squads have to fight the high incidence of the gall fly, a pest of paddy in the Chotanagpur plateau area and the BPH in the Sone Command Area. Attempts are made to keep the pest incidence under check. A surveillance unit keeps watch on dynamics of growth of different insects, pest and pathogens of the major crops. Added to this is a scheme for monitoring and forewarning of the pests and the threatened diseases, also for advising the farmers to adopt on time the needed plant protection measures.

X

The co-operative movement in Bihar aims at the all-round economic and social development of the small and marginal farmers, artisans and other poverty-stricken and weaker sections of society through co-operation.

The Eighth Plan proposed to bring nearly 90 per cent of the rural families under the co-operative fold through a variety of schemes. This was expected to maximise employment generation and hence to bring about a special transformation and uplift of the people belonging to the weaker sections of society. Also, this was expected to contribute to rural development, which alongwith agriculture claimed half of the total Plan resources in the public sector. Farmers were to obtain short-term credit and fertilisers from a single-window delivery system/agency. The weaker sections were to be advanced consumption credit (cultivators with land upto 0.5 acre and rural artisans were the constituents of these sections, by definition). The PACS and LAMPs were to be strengthened by providing them with adequate share capital and managerial subsidy so as to enable them to divert a portion of their resources to consumption credit. Financial assistance was made available to the allottees of the ceiling surplus land by the Government through their co-operative society or a Government bank or its rural branch.

Farms and farm houses built on the outer farming of cities jostling with vast tracts of virgin lands have become a medium vehicle of absorbing/containing sizable chunks of unacquainted money, representating at the same time growth of rural investment.

XI

Supply of land being fixed, growth of population and an average Bihari's love of possessing land as well as other cognate factors (this is the theme of chapter 3 of our other publication *Population Pressure and Economic Backwardness: A Comparative Study of Bihar and India*) has caused per capita availability of land to fall with time. Thus in 1951 per capita land area in Bihar was 0.45 ha. (all-India 0.24 ha.); in 1991 it had become 0.20 ha. (all-India: 0.38 ha.). In 1951 per capita NCA was 0.22/0.23 ha. (all-India: 0.30 ha.); in 1991 it had fallen to 0.20 ha. (all-India: 0.38 ha.). The declined average size of operational holdings in Bihar during 1951-86 and 1971-91 is another proof of this, as shown respectively in Tables 23.25 and 23.26 :

TABLE 23.25: Decline in Average Size of Land and Operational Land Holdings in Bihar

Item	*1951*	*1970-71*	*1976-77*	*1980-81*	*1985-86*	*Between 1970 and 1986*
(1)	(2)	(3)	(4)	(5)	(6)	(7)
Average size of land holdings (ha.)	1.41/ 1.64	—	—	—	—	—
Change in above (per cent)	—	—	—		—	(-)42.00
Average size of operational land holdings (ha.)	—	1.5 (2.3)	1.1	0.91 (1.83)	0.11	—
Area of operational land holdings (lakh ha.)	—	—	—	—	102.4	—
Number of operational holdings (lakhs)	—	—	—	—	911	—

Between 1985-86 and 1990-91, whereas the land area of operational holdings increased by 106 per cent, their number increased by 128 per cent. Partly, acquisition of rented land by its real owners after evicting the tenants and, partly, consolidation of holdings could be the reasons for the resultant rise in the average size.

TABLE 23.26: Decline in Average Size of Operational Holdings in Bihar

Characters	*1970-71*		*1990-91*	
	Bihar	*All-India*	*Bihar*	*All-India*
Number of operational holdings ('000)	7577	710116	11711	105278
Area operated ('000 ha.)	11480	482335	10898	165619
Average size of holding (ha.)	1.52	0.68	0.93	1.57

Distribution of the cultivated land in Bihar, when plotted on the graph paper, gives a pyramid. This skewness/unevenness/inequality is an evidence of concentration of landholdings in Bihar, as disclosed by Table 23.27 :

TABLE 23.27: Concentration of Landholdings in Bihar

Type of holding	*Land size*		*Percentage share in*		
				Total area	
	1954-55 (acres)	*1985-86 (ha.)*	*Number of holdings 1985-86*	*Owned 1954-55*	*Operated 1985-86*
Marginal	Below 2.49	Below 1	76.65	12.66	30.30
Small	5.00	Between 1 and 1.99	11.33	18.06	17.15
Semi-Medium	10	2-3.99	8.12	26.25	23.80
Medium	24.99	4-9.99	3.45	29.36	21.65
Large	Above 25	10 and above	0.45	13.69	7.70
Marginal and small					42.00
Medium and large					30.00

Note: Some estimates for 1951—operated land area percentages, class-wise, were as under:
Marginal: 36
Small: 44
Large: 20

Table 23.28 presents the operational holdings by the major size groups in Bihar in 1990-91.

That nearly 88 per cent of the marginal and small operational holdings claims 47 per cent of land area, whereas 0.44 per cent of the large holdings claims 7.70 per cent of land area. (that is, medium and large holdings 4 per cent in number claim almost 29 per cent of total land area) is indicative of concentration of land. Average size of holdings increases with increasing size, from 0.37 ha. to 15.43 ha.

TABLE 23.28: Operational Holdings by Major Size Groups in 1990-91

Size Groups of operational holdings	*Number ('000)*	*Percentage distribution*	*Area ('000)*	*Percentage distribution*	*Average size (ha.)*
Marginal	8976	76.64	3303	30.30	0.37
Small	1327	11.33	1869	17.15	1.41
Semi-medium	951	8.12	2593	23.80	2.73
Medium	404	3.45	2293	21.04	5.67
Large	52	0.44	839	7.70	15.43
All holdings	11711 (105278)	100.00	10898 (165619)	100.00	0.93 (1.57)

In Chapter 2 of our other publication cited above we have gone into details of the agricultural classes in which the rural population is divided over a period of forty years (1951 to 1991). Here we give the bare bones (Table 23.29);

TABLE 23.29: Growth of Agricultural Labouring Class in Bihar

Year	*Number (lakhs)*		*Percentage Distribution of Agricultural Population*			*Growth rate of Male Agricultural Labourers (Per cent per annum)*
	Cultivators	*Agricultural Labourers*	*Cultivators*	*Agricultural Labourers*	*Others*	
1951	76.78	36.02	55..1/55.3	23.5/25.8	19.2/20.9	
1991	120.48	102.76	43.5/43.6	37.1	19.3/19.4	
1970-73 over 1962-65						2.36 (1.81
1980-83 over 1970-73						1.26 (1.40)
1992-95 over 1980-83						2.17 (1.55)
1992-95 over 1962-65						1.92 (1.57)

Between 1951 and 1991, while the percentage of agricultural labourers rose by 1.3/3.3 per cent and that of cultivators fell by 11.6/ 11.7 per cent, the number of the former increased by 66.74 lakhs and that of the latter increased by 43.70 lakhs (dependents being included in both cases and in both years). The number of male agricultural labourers increased at the rate of 1.92 per cent per annum during 1962-65/1992-95 in Bihar, as compared to 1.57 per cent per annum in all-India during the same period.

Zamindary abolition in Bihar was followed by the immiserisation of a class of servile labour in the plains (North and South Bihar). The Chotanagpur plateau had a more coherent social hierarchy and a different land tenure system. Accordingly, there was no such social upheaval in that region. There the problem arose in the guise of fraudulent practices like indebtedness/eviction/displacement/deprivation of the hereditary avenues of livelihood that became the order of the day.

Even today the condition of agricultural labourers in Bihar has not changed materially, rather in certain pockets it has deteriorated in spite of the land reforms. The three-tier pyramid of backwardness, economic, social and educational, still characterises this class. The educational counterpart of the pyramid suggests that the agricultural labourers are still condemned to the levels of education and are deficient in skills. This obstructs their mobility/marketability/employability. Fortunately, upto a certain age, health is not a counterpart of the multi-faceted pyramid. It is his health which is an average agricultural labourer's real asset/wealth.

Between the landlords/landowners and landless agricultural workers there are other layers/gradations in Bihar, depending on whether agrarian relations are sharp and clearly defined or not. The layer/region signified by the semi-feudal production relations is derived from class inequality in land distribution, migration of agricultural labourers, existence of bonded agricultural labourers, etc. A layer/region marked off by mixed semi-capitalist and semi-feudal production relations (as for example, in Purnea) is also there.

The institutional milieu in rural society is changing slowly and with it is changing the spectrum/hierarchy of production relations amongst the different layers/regions. We have in conflict the tendency to accept the socially determined position/status by some sections of rural society, the tendency to accept the same on sufferance by other sections of it and to strive continually for self-betterment by comparing their own position with that enjoyed by the other better-off sections and the tendency to ward off further setback to their traditionally given position/status by yet other sections of society, perhaps the most well-to-do. The first group is identified by a sort of physical strain, while the rest by some kind of psychological stress.

The zamindars in Bihar have constantly fought against the enforcement of land legislations which have intended to divest them of their rights and thereby affect their hierarchical position. "Successive governments have also invariably adopted a pro-zamindar stance, though mouthing pro-tenant slogans" (P.S. Ramu, *Searchlight*, 22 November, 1981). The zamindars still hold most of the land pronounced surplus under the ceiling Act as *Benami*. Furthermore, large tracts of their land were shown in records as fisheries so that they were removed from the purview of the Act.

The use of hired labour is 'a status symbol' for the big landlord in Bihar, as is renting part of his land to others. In both respects he exercises a very high degree of monopoly power. He is disinclined to spend money on the improvement of the profitability of his farm activity. He is apt to optimise his net revenue by resort to alternative methods—sale of canal or tubewell irrigation water, foodgrains trading, fetching commodities from the town market to the village market, money-lending, etc., often employing them by turn in different agricultural seasons.

The existing class of landlords harbours the recruiting base for the intelligentsia. The surplus-earning zamindars disburse their surplus on conspicuous consumption, luxury purchase of more lands, etc. The benefit from the inflated value of land (caused by provision of irrigation or public merit goods under the aegis of the State Government) which flows to this class is spent on purchase of more rent-yielding land or is dessipated on ostentatious consumption. This class does not pay any income-tax. Land revenue and cess(es) paid to the State Government by them are minimal.

The landlords wield considerable political influence/clout. They control the vote banks in their respective localities. They finance the election and other expenses of the political parties with which they have recognisable affiliation. They inculcate affiliations with the Government officials on caste lines. They manipulate the affairs in order to hog/gobble up agricultural finance and other incentives extended to the peasantry class. They corner/rig the supply of the inputs made through the institutional agencies.

In our rural society the power equation conforms to the area of land possessed by a person and exploitation of those persons whose survival and subsistence is dependent on the whim of their landlord is facilitated by the possession of power, which also guarantees exemption from immunity to the punishment prescribed under the laws.

The landed class has been unwilling to relinquish its privileged position, being capable of 'a sustained rear-guard action' against the actual implementation of the legislative measures. In consequence, land reforms have got bogged down in legal tangles.

From the mid-1960s onwards in the State and from the mid-1970s onwards at the Centre the writ of a single party became irregular, with the result that no ideology but the self-interest of the political party in power, or of a political party which was anally of the government, the support of which was indispensable to its survival, became the deciding factor in the amount of interest with which land reforms were pursued. The outcome so far has not been gratifying.

In a nutshell, the members of the weaker sections have had great difficulty in securing the physical possession of the bits of surplus land allotted to them. Cases of influential persons like civil servants and public figures belonging to the Scheduled Castes who got plots of land for extremely low prices and had them sold to people not belonging to the Scheduled Castes at exorbitant prices, have not been unknown in a large number.

Even today there are tenants who have not acquired the occupancy right to their plots in spite of possessing them for over 12 years. The *under-raiyats* do not enjoy any security of tenancy as special squads were not created and land records not updated, the twin tools by which land reforms were intended to be intensified, and hence insecurity of tenancy not eliminated.

Where even marginal security was given, by converting the *tied* share-croppers into the *rotational* ones, self-cultivation became possible, as for example in sugarcane (a cash crop with high returns) cultivation, where it has taken a firm root.

That rent would be one-fifth to one-fourth of the gross produce was a decision taken at the national level. In Bihar it was fixed at one-fourth. But this was only on paper; in actual practice the rent was much higher.

The lingering tenancy system fractionalises society into hierarchical strata with unequal economic and political powers. This generates apathy and distrust among the major sections of the rural community and impairs the intensity of their participation. Neither has land been redistributed nor have the pre-requisites of efficient cultivation, as visualised by the NAT, been provided on an equitable basis.

The share-croppers of those landowners (belonging to castes like Bhumihars who do not themselves cultivate their fields) even do not have either the necessary motivation or the resources required for land development and modernisation of agriculture. They are still the victims of social oppression and economic bondage. The semi-feudal, i.e., semi-slave-master relations in the production of agricultural commodities persist. These production relations are part and parcel of the entire array/complex of social relations, and so the latter have to be revolutionised first before the former are sought to be revolutionised.

To sum up, land reforms so far could not provide 'the real burst of enthusiasm' nor release a genuine fund of energy among the working peasantry. All in all, they did not become a pre-condition to increased agricultural production. The landless still lack that dose of confidence which is basic to efficient production. Less than 10 per cent of the cultivable land only could so far be consolidated.

Land reforms could not become part of a comprehensive and well-integrated agricultural development programme. The socio-economic landscape of the countryside is still far from being transformed beyond recognition even in the last fifty years as had been stipulated on the eve of planning. In a word, land reforms could not pave the ground for the reorientation of values, sensibilities and responses.

XII

In the year 1997, the caste-war toll (number of killings) in Bihar, according to the *Sunday*, 14-20 December, 1997, totalled 206, spread over 11 districts—the highest in Jehanabad 96, followed by Palamau 29 and Patna 20—in 22 attacks, the maximum being in August, 1997, 5 times.

There are 11 private armies in Bihar. Castes having affiliation with them are Bhumihar, Rajput, Yadav and Kurmi. Bhumihars have the largest number of armies 4, Yadav 3, Rajput 3, and Kurmi 1. One Rajput army has Muslim members too. Eight armies operate in Jehanabad, seven in Patna and four in Bhojpur.

There are three guerrilla groups in Bihar—Lal Dasta backed by the MCC operating in 22 districts; Red Squad backed by the CPI Party Unity operating in 12 districts, and Red Army backed by the CPI(ML) Liberation operating in 15 districts.

The upper-caste groups and intermediaries seek the help of a particular *sena* to counter the Naxalite forces. Naxalism flourishes in Bihar as it does in Andhra Pradesh. Where the feudal inequities still govern the relations between landowners and their labourers, the naxalites establish their hold through a familiar admixture of terror tactics and expressions of sympathy for the poor.

Caste, land and violence are inextricably mixed up in Bihar. Caste, family status, orthodox customs, etc. are those institutions which are considered to be the remnants of feudalism and semi-feudalism but they persist in Bihar's rural community. The village economy remains entrenched in a scheme of stratification largely on the lines of caste and occupation. These malaises have not been eradicated uptill now.

Central Bihar, in particular, has been turned into an 'Armageddon' by caste polarisation and agrarian tension for the Ultra-Lefts and a particular Bhumihar-dominated *sena*. The sympathisers of the Ultra-Lefts Naxalite activists are the *sena's* target.

The Naxalite forces in Bihar are divided in a number of groups, which are on the war path, one against the other. After the largest ever carnage in Jehanabad in 1997 they were thinking of sinking their mutual differences and giving a befitting reply to the upper-caste *senas*.

The BJP was reported to be a supporter of the private army of the landlords. The groups led by Yadavas were reported to have proximity to the ruling party in the State. The Amnesty International held that functioning of the State administration has broken down totally.

Killing of Harijans commenced in 1977 in Belchi in Patna district. Between 1977 and 1997, killing took place five times in Jehanabad district, four times in Bhojpur district, twice in Patna district, and once in each of Aurangabad and Palamau districts. People killed were the Harijans. Among the killed were women also, some of whom were raped before being killed. The total number of the Harijans killed was 243—Jehanabad 121, Bhojpur 69, Patna 28 and Aurangabad 12. Between 1987 and 1992 the number of upper-caste people killed was 81—once in each of Aurangabad 42 and Gaya 39.

The Kisan stir/movement was not unknown during the pre-Independence years in a number of States, Bihar included (Swami Sahajanand was a great leader of the peasantry at the State level) and top leaders of the National Congress provided leadership to the peasant class in its war against exploitation by the intermediaries and others. The past history remains an undying source of inspiration to the peasants in Bihar even today.

In Bihar the 1980s* commenced with incidents of open confrontation between the landless agricultural labourers and their landlords, ending in numerous killings of members of both classes. The landless agricultural labourers organised themselves under the banner of the Kisan Sabha, aided and abetted by the political activists like the Naxalites and the communists. On the other hand, the landlords organised themselves under that of the Kisan Sangh, aided and abetted by the ruling politicians.

---

* We are reproducing here this portion from our other publication ***Problems of Indian Economic Development***, chapter 3 entitled "The Political Economy of India's Retarded Growth" and chapter 23 captioned "Indian Drama of Democratic Planning: An Institutional cum-Sociological Approach," Sterling, New Delhi-16.

Both parties constantly equipped themselves with firearms. The police was neutral and acted in collusion with the stronger of the two groups and hence failed to arrest the situation in the rural areas of Bihar from worsening. The rural workers insisted on having their minimum wages fixed at 3 kgs. of rice and 750 gms. of *sattu* as their daily wage per worker. Their employers instead paid 5 kgs of rice and 500 gms of *sattu* (which in money terms equalled Rs. 7.50 in April 1982). Since the majority of the landlords owned either small or medium farms, they were hard put to it to pay more. The statutory minimum daily wage for agricultural labourers was between Rs. 8 and 9. In many villages farmers faced acute shortages of the supply of agricultural labourers. The working class in the rural areas had become acutely conscious of its rights and was fighting for them. By contrast, in the urban areas even semi-literate hands were available for menial work on the daily wage of Rs. 5 in any number.

Throughout the 1980s Bihar was the centre of peasant activism in India. The 1997 Jehanabad carnage was explained (*Sunday*, quoted above) with reference to providing shelter by some Harijan families to the CPI(M-L) activists and a land dispute (for details see the journal). Our President was constrained to express his sense of revulsion at the unchecked growth of caste and economic wars against the rural poor.

Experts like Cassen are emphatically of the view that explanations of agrarian unrest/tensions should take into account the conditions of work of life, the consciousness of these conditions, and the political organisation of the consciousness. Besides, the rural sociology and the balance of political forces in the country-side form the very nerve-knot of it. A simplistic theory is no good. Needed is an all-inclusive, unover-simplified explanation.

The political pressures and social tensions in rural society emanate from the relative power equations of the peasants and landlords in the existing property and production framework.

Except for the 1970s, agriculture in Bihar has faced stagnation-like situations, which has been disquieting. The economic lot of the weaker sections dependent on agriculture has deteriorated in many parts of the State.

The growing militancy among the economically weaker sections of rural society has served as an index of their growing relative poverty as well as growing political awareness.

The laws protecting the lands of the weaker sections from alienation have not been implemented effectively. Their dispossession has gone on, though to a lesser extent. Land has been the most time-honoured form of property in Bihar. Its owners have considered it an inseparable part of their own being and defended it to the bitter end of laying down their life. This has accounted for the growing number of clashes and killings even for small plots of land. The tenants and the agricultural labourers have taken recourse increasingly to riot, violence and onslaught against their landlords and employers respectively. They have found their patience wearing thin. They have objected to being left out in the cold. Therefore, they have preferred to flock to the camp of the Naxalites, who have launched a crusade against poverty and exploitation.

What has distinguished Bihar from other States is that the poor in the State have been in distress but not in despair. They have had an inexhaustible capacity for forbearance. They have surpassed others in both love and hate. Out of their absolute ignorance of the truth/reality, they have been the worshippers, on caste lines, of the black sheep, the outlaws, the corrupt and the chargesheeted. They have hoped that the government of their own caste brethren only would put things right, for it is they who have been their real friends, well-wishers and saviours. They have set great store upon parliamentary democracy, which during the elections has meant, by and large, sheer capture of the voting booths by the goons and bogus voting knowing no bounds.

The above is the explanation of why during the last twenty years or so agrarian unrest in Bihar has boiled down to stray cases of lawlessness and the agrarian movement has borne a semblance to "fire sweeping over stubble rather then a steady blaze." It has been localised and transient, diffuse and fragmentary. In the areas vulnerable to the duopolistic warfare, the landlords/uppercastes have perpetrated carnages on their under-ryots and agricultural labourers coming largely of the Harijan families and extremely backward communities respectively to protect their possessions and privileges and the latter have acted in utter desperation and, in consequence, agrarian relations have become wholly anarchical, showing signs of considerable strain; the various interests forming a hierarchy have been at loggerheads with one another, while violence has loomed large on the horizon, and Bihar has invited comments from foreign authorities like W. Hauser: Bihar continues to hold the centre-stage in agrarian terms, that is, peasant activism. And the casual, cursory remarks and suggestions made by the foreign commentators and non-Bihari outsiders on Bihar's contemporary ills carry a weight ninety-nine times higher with the government of the day than those made by the Bihari insiders who still afford to think and write, even if they are based on deep and sustained analyses, unless they happen to emanate from those who belong to the caste in power or its axis, who are deemed by the rulers as the real *pandits* of the subject.

XIII

The Panchayati Raj, an instrument of democratic decentralisation, has assumed more relevance after the 73rd amendment of the Indian Constitution. This is summarised below:

> "Independence must begin at the bottom. . . . It follows, therefore, that every village has to be self-sustained and capable of managing its affairs. . . . The Government of the village will be conducted by the Panchayat. . . . These will have all the authority and jurisdiction required. . . . The greater the power of the Panchayats the better for the people. . . . It is the function of the Panchayats to revive honesty and industry. . . . It is the function of the Panchayats to teach the villagers to avoid disputes, if they have to settle them. . . . If we would see our dream of the Panchayati Raj, i.e., true democracy realised, we would regard the humblest and lowest Indian as being equally the ruler of India with the tallest in the land. . . . This presupposes that all are pure or will become pure if they are not. And purity must go hand-in-hand with wisdom."
>
> — Mahatma Gandhi

The Panchayati Raj Institutions have been in existence since long in India. But, for various reasons, they could not acquire the status of viable and responsive people's bodies. Therefore, there was an imperative need to enshrine the basic features of the Panchayati Raj Institutions in the Constitution itself to provide them certainty, continuity and strength.

The Constitution (73rd Amendment) Act, 1992

The Constitution (73rd Amendment) Act, 1992 came into force with effect from 24th April, 1993. By this amendment, Part IX relating to Panchayats has been inserted in the Constitution. It lays the foundation for strong and vibrant Panchayati Raj Institutions in the country.

Salient Features

* Almost all the States/UTs where provisions of Part IX of the Constitution are applicable have taken steps to constitute Panchayats in accordance with these provisions.
* Panchayats to be established at village, intermediate and district level.

* Panchayati Raj Institutions to function as institutions of self-governance and to be endowed with power and authority to formulate and implement schemes for economic development and social justice.
* Regular elections to Panchayats every five years.
* Direct election of members of Panchayats at village, intermediate and district levels. Indirect election of Chairpersons (except at village level).
* Reservation of seats in Panchayats for Scheduled Castes/ Scheduled Tribes in proportion to their population.
* Reservation of one-third seats for women.
* Similar reservation in respect of the office of Chairpersons of Panchayats.
* States empowered to provide for reservation in favour of the backward class of citizens.
* Almost all the States/UTs have constituted State Election Commissions for the conduct of Panchayat Elections and Finance Commissions for reviewing the financial position of Panchayats.

Adequate Powers

After the Panchayati Raj Institutions come into position through due electoral process, the States will endow these institutions with adequate powers, autonomy and authority:

1. To enable them to effectively function as institutions of local self-governance.
2. To discharge their constitutional responsibilities regarding preparation and implementation of programmes for economic development and social justice.

Schedule XI of the Constitution enumerates 29 subjects which could be entrusted with the Panchayati Raj Institutions.

Bihar is one of those States which could not conduct the Panchayati Raj elections for years on account of the bitter experiences of the past. These elections created bickerings and feuds of such vehemence and virulence that they became permanent enmities among the rural folk. The rural community was split into warring groups along caste lines, which stalled all developmental work for long. The present Government with its caste bias has deliberately avoided the ordeal, fearing its debacle.

In its 28 March, 1997 issue the *Times of India* remarked that CM Laloo had neither faced the gigantic problem of agrarian reforms nor prepared Bihar for facing the Panchayat election. However, this failure of his has not taken any toll of his mass popularity. One has not to delve/dig deep to find an explanation for this. In a State stuck up in the quagmire of maximum poverty in the country, the struggle for survival has largely eclipsed the slogan for social justice, nay emasculated it. The backward classes' euphoria over their politically cornering the forward classes which tyrannised over them for ages is also partly responsible for this.

The administration in Bihar has left much to be desired in the last several years, unlike the early 1950s when some administrators in the State were eulogised by foreign assessors as persons of outstanding merit by any standards. The quality of the government services has been poor and inferior. The law and order situation has been far from satisfactory, it has further deteriorated. A nexus between politicians, police and criminals has developed, which has played a havoc.

As a complement to other instruments, the administrative machinery has not played its part in institutional reform conscientiously. The planning mechanism has been creaking and groaning.

The delivery system has totally collapsed. On this point even foreign commentators like William Hauser who have visited Bihar periodically in the last five decades are agreed—that there has occurred a lot of deterioration in the fields of education, health care and other similar areas.

The administration has not been clean. The decision-making process has not been transparent. The employees holding public offices or responsibilities have been found to be amenable to corrupt practices in the discharge of their official duties for illegal gratification. A number of civil servants have been chargesheeted in the 900-crore fodder scam by the CBI alongwith the politicians and others.

A number of the public servants have been loyal to particular governments or ministers, and not to the law. The High Court chastised some of the civil servants by summoning them and observing that they have not done their job properly, that they have been sluggish and unjust and therefore, they had to be disciplined and prodded into action by the judiciary. This happened in a number of cases.

The *Times of India*, dated 6 August, 1997 carried a report that the High Court observed that there was "no government worth the name in Bihar as a handful of corrupt bureaucrats ran the administration." It went on to say that this was worse than the "Jungle Raj" as there was "no regard to court directions and public interest."

Of course, the non-functioning Government of Bihar (an accusation made several times by the High Court/Supreme Court in the last twenty years or so against the Bihar Government) has disappointed many but Biharis have the skin of the rhinocerous. Lacking work culture/ethic and being ease-loving, they have preferred an equally ease-loving government.

The reader must have formed some opinion of the law and order situation obtaining in Bihar on the basis of what has been said about agrarian tensions above. In urban areas in recent years murders out of personal or domestic enmity, kidnappings of businessmen, doctors, etc. and political assassinations have risen in number and frequency. On 2 April, 1997 *TOI* wrote that Bihar represented an "uncivilised part of the country," that Bihar observed law and order only in breach, that it was engulfed in a complete breakdown of law and order, that it faced a near-anarchist situation, that law had been hijacked by the private *senas* (armies), and so on. The largest number of killings is reported from Bihar during the elections. The maximum percentage of sensitive polling booths is reported from Bihar. The crime curve is upward rising in Bihar. Among those killed are senior civil and police officials. People have great fear in expressing their views on public issues freely—that they would be roughed up by the ruling politicians. The situation has gone from bad to worse as time has passed. The observation of the High Court (worse than the "Jungle Raj") is most apt. Recent political leadership, ruling and unruling, is alleged to have contributed to the criminalisation of life in all fields, inclusive of politics (the percentage of persons with criminal records who are members of the State legislature and Parliament is high, and the Election Commission has appealed to all political parties not to give tickets to such persons in the next election). The phrase 'Reign of Terror' has often been identified with the ruling political leadership.

Recent political leadership is criticised for its misrule/maladministration, its dominant personalised style of government, its total control and demoralisation of the administration, its encouragement of incompetent people who are mere cycophants—all this for temporary political gains at the cost of permanent values (*Sunday*, 7-13 April, 1997). Among the top ruling political leaders in recent years we have had leaders who were notable for their inclination to sense in every friend of theirs a hidden foe eager to grab their *gaddi* (*TIO*, 1 June, 1997) and, therefore, they have decided in favour of grooming their own kith and kin as their political successors, thereby giving an impetus to the continuation of the family rule. This was nothing short of naked opportunism. For till yesterday these leaders were highly critical of the family rule. Being turn-coats they were capable of saying and doing anything to enjoy the fruits of power. In politics there were no permanent friends or foes. The Rashtriya Janata Dal (RJD) leaders blamed the Congress for Bihar's backwardness/impeded growth till March 1997; from April, 1997 onwards they were full of praise for the Congress (*TIO*, 18 January, 1998). They were thus capable of doing what they themselves decried. Their single slogan was that there was only one family in Bihar (as there was only one family in Delhi) which was the true ally/Messiah of the poor and hence justified to rule Bihar (India in the other case). The history of a man/family was sought to be made into the history of a state/Nation—an impossible task according to us.

In political corruption Bihar is at the top. Among the chargesheeted by the CBI are two past CMs (one was the first ever CM to be chargesheeted in a criminal case of financial offence while in office (*TIO*, dated 23 June, 1997), Ministers (State/Central), bureaucrats/civil servants (in service or superannuated), Members of Parliament/State Legislature, etc. People believe that the corrupt elements have been enjoying the patronage of the ruling politicians. The High Court referred to the handful of corrupt bureaucrats who ran the administration in Bihar (see above). The illegal exactions/payments prevalent every where in Bihar were a relic of the feudal system. They were in vogue during the days of the East India Company. They were prevalent in the judiciary at its lower levels before Independence. They are still there. They pervade all government departments, public offices.

Those chargesheeted by the CBI tell that they have been falsely implicated by their enemies. Some of the chargesheeted political leaders have made 'Fight Against Corruption' part of their party election manifesto.

Some of the political leaders facing charges contend that they are victims of the rigid caste system (as of the lingering feudal system) in Bihar. Whereas parliamentary democracy helped the son of a landless labourer, and a member of a backward class/caste to assume the leadership of Bihar, the upper-castes and the feudal lords could not reconcile themselves with this situation and what has happened is the outcome of that hatred and animosity (*TIO*, 7 May, 1997). There is in Bihar a class war as well as a caste war. Members of one caste distrust those of another caste. It cannot be denied that for many years in the past the so-called foreward classes in Bihar rode roughshod over the so-called backward classes and in a good many cases even those of the latter classes who had most loyally aligned themselves with those of the former classes for long time were sacrificed unceremoniously by them when they realised that because of them the interests of their own brethren were at stake. Likewise, caste consideration was extolled to an unusual height in the last few years by the political leadership of a particular backward class/caste, in the main. The list of candidates released by this leadership for the 1998 Lok Sabha election had 14 seats out of 38 (nearly 37 per cent) allotted to the caste it represented (population-wise, it was 11 per cent only).

What defies all explanation is this that the unique mass popularity and security of leadership enjoyed by the above-mentioned political leadership in Bihar does not appear to have suffered any setback on account of the charges levelled against it. It continues to draw loud cheers from the crowd. Even today it is capable of exhorting the crowd as it was before. It does not seem to have lost its old prestige or public standing (*TIO*, 19 March, 1997).

Of course, there are critics of this leadership, who hold that everything has gone wrong in Bihar after 1989. There are leaders of other political parties in Bihar who agitate against it by urging that both economic and social frustration have multiplied and Bihar is at present in an awful mess. The aggrandisement of the caste factor and the rapid growth of corruption enveloping all walks of life coupled with the non-functioning character of the present government ("inviting such strictures as unending infancy" and "retarded childhood"), having one-point programme before itself of going on holding the reins of the government in its own hands by bequiling the illiterate and gullible masses in the State, nay, even by confusing and misleading them and stuffing their mind with all manner of untruth and tall promises, never to be fulfilled. The enthusiasts of this leadership argue that those who think that replacement of this leadership by another leadership to be provided by another backward class/caste would be better are totally mistaken, for the simple reason that in essence they are of no different character and not made of any intrinsically different stuff, also because what would be good for Bihar could be delivered only by the existing leadership, for it is the ruling leadership which had provided political stability to the State after 30 years, and no other leadership would be in a position to do this, and even if it succeeded in its present game, it would force Bihar to relapse before long into the same dark period of instability which was its sad lot in the past.

We have in Bihar votaries of casteism. To them, equality of opportunity of social justice has no meaning. All that is relevant to them is the fact that for several years the forward classes/castes, by turn, ruled the State and distributed the maximum of opportunities to their own caste-men. In the last seven to eight years a particular backward class/caste having the maximum political representation in the State (even if disproportionately to its percentage share in total population of the State) has ruled the State and grabbed the maximum number of opportunities for its own members by violating all norms, in league with some communally motivated constitutional heads equally eager to bargain, and thus excelling the politically most represented forward class/caste of the past in this bid. Leaders of other backward classes/castes in Bihar are also not made of a different clay. Today they are highly critical of the rank casteism practised by the ruling political leadership and the loot of public money by it. Suppose they come into power next time. What is the guarantee that they would not indulge in the same misdeeds? This is the question which keeps nagging people in Bihar. They too have a commitment to their own caste-men in the same manner. They have not as yet handled public funds of that magnitude. They are not known defenders of merit. They are not persons who would do good to others for nothing. They have also amongst them people who would grab public property at the earliest opportunity, that is, enrich themselves by improverishing society. In a word, it is not difference of kind but difference of degree which is implicit in this matter. The caste feeling is so very sinister and viriluent, rife and rampant that a really honest and capable man coming of a socially and politically weak section of society may be era long falsely framed by his rivals coming of the ruling or a politically strong section of it in order that their chances to move up in their professions remain safe and secure, this reaching its destination finally in his flight from or being hounded out of the State.

William Hauser is strongly of the opinion that the political history of India cannot be written without reference to caste. Casteism is not specific to Bihar; it is to be come across in a number of other States. However, casteism manifests itself in Bihar in an acute form, not seen in other States. Casteism is synonymous with an ethnic identity. The ethnic factor is capable of becoming a determinant of the political system and an instrument of government formation. Caste wars have strengthened the foundations of democracy. At present Bihar is passing through a transitional phase. According to Hauser, the post-1989 political leadership in Bihar struck a rapport with the masses. It contributed to social churning in the State, which cannot be underestimated. Hauser hopes that the attempt to pluralise politics and society would first succeed in Bihar. And Bihar would emerge as a stronger and freer State in the years to come.

Regrettably, we do not find ourselves in agreement with Hauser's prediction, and would like to conclude that unless casteism and corruption are weeded out from Bihar and the regime of merit and equality of opportunity is rehabilitated in the State, the future of the people in Bihar would remain as gloomy and bleak as their present.

XIV

Lord Buddha, the Light of Asia, is reported to have once remarked that Magadh (now Bihar) would never be immune to the three F's, namely, Fires, Floods and Feuds (we are not sure if he also included serpents). This we are noticing even today. The Chinese travellers (like Hsuan-tsang and Ts'ung), the 16th century European and English travellers like Barbosa (Portugese), Master Singer Frederick (from Venice), Master Gulph Fitch (English), Doctor Bernier (French), Varthewa (Italian), Manooclo (from Venice) and Tavernier, as well as the 19th century English traveller Doctor Buchanan who visited Magadh/Bihar spoke very eloquently of its rich agriculture, its agricultural products, such as grain, sugarcane, spices, fruits, flowers, etc., unique in their quality, aroma, scent and taste, and its farmers, noted for their ability, knowledge and arts of cultivation (see the present author's book *Bihar's Resources, Agriculture and Industry*, in Hindi, published in 1954 for details). A folder circulated on the eve of a seminar, held in March, 1997, by an organisation called Cheetee of Keshav Saraswati Vidya Mandir, Patna recounts such revered names associated with Bihar as Chanakya/Kautilya, Chandragupta, King Janak, Vidyapati, Swami Vivekananda, Birsa Munda, Vanbhatta, Guru Govind Singh, Babu Kunwar Singh, Yajnavalkya, Bhagwan Mahavir, Bhagwan Buddha, Patanjali, Jeewak, Khudi Ram Bose, Mahatma Gandhi, JP, Aryabhatt and Bharati (wife of Pandit Madan Mishra) and world-renowned universities like Nalanda and Vikramshila, etc. Let us hope that good senses prevail on Bihar's political leadership, and communalism, casteism and corruption practised, right and left, by the political leaders and civil/public servants and others come to an early end so that economic development in the State picks up in tempo and poverty and social injustice and unemployment which plague the State today are surmounted effectively and successfully and Bihar regains its past glory before long.

APPENDIX-I

AN EXTRACT : CASE OF PUNJAB

We quote below certain portions from V.S. Mahajan's review of Pritam Singh's book *Political Economy of the Punjab*, published in *the Political Economy Journal of India*, Vol. 6, No. 1 since they would be useful to the Bihar planners.

"It was the Punjab's hard and self-reliant peasantry that had migrated from Pakistan's Punjab after partition who through their sheer labour and innovative spirit were soon able to transform this traditional food deficit area of the Indian Punjab into surplus one and also played a unique role in the present Haryana's economy which in the pre-November 1966 period was an integral part of Punjab.

The author brings out how area under HYV in wheat and rice which was mere 3.5 and 1.4 per cent respectively in 1966 (at the time of reorganisation) is today 100 per cent covered under wheat and 92 per cent in case of rice, the same is the state in the use of chemical fertilisers and irrigation facilities. The situation is as well equally comfortable in the use of farm machinery and other inputs. The impact of these steps is reflected in the steady rise in yield per hectare in case of wheat from 1236 kg. in 1965-66 to 4040 kg. in 1993-94 and in case of rice from 1490 kg. in 1969-70 to 3493 kg. in 1993-94—indeed a remarkable achievement within a quarter of century.

Thus with limited land area this state has been able to achieve almost super status in the production and productivity of these two crops and has thus become the principal supplier to the Central pool of both wheat and rice.

Notwithstanding such outstanding performance in agriculture, which has been acknowledged the world over the state has to pay a high price for such revolution. First, financial gains from farm prosperity is only partially shared by local agriculturists while the major share is siphoned away by intermediaries mostly from outside the Punjab as well by the Centre in one shape or the other. Second, intensive use of land for raising two in some cases even three crops a year has had its adverse impact on the ecology and life of local people.

This has been highlighted in the chapter on ecology in the book. With intensive agriculture a number of deficiencies have occurred in essential elements in the soil causing deficiency diseases to the crops which are posing problems. Further, because of wheat-paddy cycle the land never gets dry leading to high scourge of malaria in the region. For instance, the total number of malaria cases reported between 1975 and 1986 have averaged annually around 10 per cent of total cases in the country, against Punjab total population of around 2 per cent in the country. Thus there are five times malaria cases compared to its national share in population which is a sad fall-out from green revolution. While the current data is not given, it appears the situation would not have improved meanwhile, rather it might have further deteriorated in view of growing farm cropping intensity.

Equally such wheat-paddy crop cycle is also causing high pollution in another way for after harvesting paddy fields have to be prepared immediately for wheat sowing. "As the cost of clearing the fields of the roots of harvested paddy plants is very high and there is not time to allow the roots to decompose into humus, therefore, the paddy chaff is burnt. It causes so much smoke that breathing becomes a problem during the season. It has resulted in allergy problems and diseases of respiratory system for a large number of people. With the burning of chaff eco-friendly earth-worms that convert the agricultural waste into farmyard manure also get burnt, thus aggravating the ecological crisis." (p. 188).

As well such wheat-paddy cycle has resulted in overuse of ground water. With the maximum use of tubewell irrigation the underground water potential is gradually getting exhausted and poor rainfall in the region is not in a position to replinish it. This situation coupled with excessive and careless use of fertilisers and insecticides is also resulting in the pollution of ground water, making it unfit for drinking purposes.

Also the draining of effluents and sullage water mixed with chemicals into the rivers is raising another alarm bell of fast infecting of river water.

There is as well fall out on the forest area. The State's green cover has been steadily declining and is currently said to be below 10 per cent while it should be around 20 per cent minimum.

Thus Punjab has to pay a high price in the wake of green revolution or wheat-paddy revolution. The situation is indeed alarming and calls for heart searching by administrators, farmers, farm scientists and politicians. Having once been in such vicious circle and that too for several years it would not be an easy job to emerge out of it, unless the State could create alternative employment avenues.

The book contains chapter on employment (rather unemployment) which brings out the hard reality that employment potential in agriculture is almost zero, as well in existing industries (there is also chapter on industry) both textile mills and sugar factories—the two dominant industries based on agriculture, the manpower planning has not been done (in terms of providing necessary training to local people) with the result that between 80 to 85 per cent of labour employed in spinning mills is from outside the state and almost similar situation is found in sugar mills. This brings out the need for proper planning of training programmes in our technical institutes to suit local conditions.

Interestingly even the existing agro-based industries are not doing well. For instance majority of coopérative sugar units are in deep red. The situation in spinning units is not better either. Further Punjab's long score over small engineering units appears to be now spent up.

On the other hand, the state does not have any large industry—the basic type to be found in other parts of the country which not only provide sustained industrial development as well employment, these as well help the emergence of a large number of units functioning as ancillaries or independently and thus help to widen the scope of employment and income.

This has unfortunately failed to happen in Punjab where even the Central Government's investment has been meagre, rather gone down from 1.95 per cent in 1978-79 to 0.61 per cent in 1991-92. Further because of the lack of appropriate industrial climate the state has been suffering in another way. Credit deposit ratio in this state has been persistently low even compared with backward states like Orissa and Madhya Pradesh. Thus savings made by local population find investment outside the state, thereby depriving this state of the benefit which could have accrued to it in case it had appropriate industrial climate with some leading industries in the forefront.

The author says: "To acquire an industrial licence to set up industry in the Punjab by a private party becomes as difficult as bearding a lion in his den. Even the State Government and its public undertakings find the experience extremely frustrating." (p. 270)

This should make a frustrating reading and little surprise that large-scale private investors—many Punjabi entrepreneurs are running major industries in other states—are hesitant to invest in Punjab. Certainly with improved political climate and support from the government it should not be difficult with good infrastructure which could be even further improved in accordance with the requirement of private sector.

There is also a chapter on 'cultural dimensions' which brings out distinctive cultural character of Punjabis, like progress loving, forward looking and less conservative, open minded, innovative and hard working. They occupy top positions both within the country as well abroad. A large number of them have emigrated to practically every part of the world, even to areas where western people would be cautious to adventure. With their adventurous spirit coupled with hard work they changed the landscape of a country like Canada at a time when few Europeans dared to tame its vast and harsh wilderness.

With this background it is ironic that we have not been able to tap the talent, enterprise, spirit of globalisation of these Punjabi nationals who are doing so remarkably well in other parts of India as well world."

SOURCES OF DATA

In so far as the period covered in this book ranges over half a century, the data furnished in it have been taken from a large number of sources, official as well as private. The author has himself produced a number of books dealing with the subject. Most of them are comparative : Bihar *versus* other States/Bihar *versus* All-India. They were published from time to time. They are the chief sources of the data used in this treatise. However, the old data needed up-dating. This was done with the help of the Government of India, Government of Bihar and Governments of other States publications, mostly statistical. Some statistical hand-books on India published by the private institutions were also consulted. The CMIE publications were of immense help in bridging the gaps. At places all the data which were available were presented, but the most reliable ones were used for substantiating a point/remark. This has been indicated there. The author would submit that knowing the nature of the data which are generally available, the data given by him in this book can be relied upon, ruling out scrutiny.

The following works of the author contain comparative chapters, Bihar *versus* All-India and other States:

1. *Economics of A Backward Region in A Backward Economy*, a two-volume set, Scientific Book Agency, Calcutta-1.
2. *Problems of Indian Economic Development,* Sterling, New Delhi-16.
3. *India's Rural Problems*, Concept, New Delhi-59.
4. *Poverty, Inequality and Unemployment in India*, Concept, New Delhi-59.
5. *Indian Economy Since 1951*, Intellectual, New Delhi-2.
6. *Four Decades of Indian Agriculture*, Manas, Delhi-52.
7. *Bihar Economy through the Plans*, Northern, New Delhi-2.
8. *Indian Economy Since Independence*, a two-volume set, National, New Delhi-2.
9. *Population Pressure and Economic Backwardness*, Anamika, Delhi-52.

10. *India's Economic Problems*, M.D. Publications, New Delhi-2.

Each of the above works has a different theme and a different mould in which the facts and the figures are cast.

For the analytical parts of the present book, the following theoretical publications of the author were used:

1. *Technological Choice under Developmental Planning*, Popular, Mumbai-34WB.
2. *Economic Development in the Third World*, Sterling, New Delhi-16.
3. *Studies in Economic Analysis and Policy*, Sterling, New Delhi-16.
4. *Foundations of Modern Economics*, Sterling, New Delhi-16.
5. *Development of Philosophical Thought in Economics* (in relation to those in other social sciences), Himalaya, Mumbai-4.
6. *Lectures on Micro-Economic Theory*, Himalaya, Mumbai-4.
7. *Growth, Development and Planning*, Himalaya, Mumbai-4.

The following titles deal with Bihar alone:

1. *Strategy of Industrial Dispersal and Decentralised Development*, R. Chand & Co., New Delhi.
2. *Bihar Ke Sadhan, Krishi Aur Udyog* (Bihar's Resources, Agriculture and Industry), R. Lal, Allahabad.

The other forthcoming volumes/titles in the present series *Dimensions of Development* are :

1. *Industry.*
2. *Mining, Decentralised Industry and Infrastructure.*
3. *Resources : Human and Financial* (i.e., State Finances).

Note: The author published a dozen books (in addition to No. 2 above) on his discipline in Hindi during 1952-61, of which five were recipients of awards. They are not listed here for want of space.

BIBLIOGRAPHY

ADRI, *Bihar Economy : A Reconnoissance*, ed. by V.K. Kantha, Patna.
Ahmad, E., *Bihar*, Ranchi.
Bose, S.R., *Economy of Bihar,* Calcutta.
Cassen, R.H., *India : Population, Economy, Society.*
Hajra, S., *Bihar and Punjab : A Study in Contrast.*
Houlton, S., *Bihar : The Heart of India.*
Jannuzi, F.T., *Agrarian Crisis in India.*
Mazoomdar, A., *Bihar : Problem of Development.*
Nair, K., *Blossoms in the Dust,* London.
Nair, K., *Transforming Traditionally*, New Delhi.
NCAER, *Techno-economic Survey of Bihar.*
Prasad, R.C., *Bihar.*
Sharma, A.N. and Gupta, S., *Bihar : Stagnation or Growth,* Patna.
Singh, A., *Planning for Developing a Backward Economy.*
Sinha, G., *Food Economics.*
Sinha, S., *Bitter Harvest.*
Srivastava, K.C., *The Cooperative Movement in Bihar.*

Government of Bihar

Department of Labour & Employment, Report of the Bihar Unemployment Committee, 1960.
Planning Department, Five-Year Plan, from First to Eighth; also, approach papers, draft plans, annual plans, technical notes, documents, etc.
Directorate of Economics and Statistics/Statistics and Evaluation, Statistical Handbook on Bihar, Bihar through Figures, Bihar at a Glance, etc. (annual).
Department of Finance, Memoranda submitted to the Finance Commissions.
Land Commission, Bihar, Status papers (the author was a member for several years).
State Planning Board, Statistical Pocket Book, Selected Plan Statistics, Status papers, etc. (the author was associated with the Board from

the very outset; was Member for three years after his superannuation from the university service).

Department of Water Resource Development, Status Papers, etc. (the author was Member, Irrigation Commission for three years).

Office of Census Superintendent. Census Reports and related publications.

Private Sources

Bihar Chamber of Commerce, various annual reports, etc.

Bihar Industries Association, various annual reports, etc.

Government of India

Central Statistical Organisation, Statistical Abstract of India, Statistical Pocket-Book on India.

Central Water Commission, Pocket-Book on Water Data.

Ministry of Agriculture, Agricultural Situation in India, Indian Agriculture in Brief (various editions).

Ministry of Food and Agriculture, Agricultural Statistics, Agricultural Censuses.

Ministry of Finance, Economic Survey, etc. (annual), Reports of finance Commissions, India : Pocket-Book, etc.

Ministry of Information & Broadcasting, India (annual).

Planning Commission, Five-Year Plan, from First to Eighth, approach papers, draft plans, annual plans, mid-term appraisals, etc.

Reserve Bank of India

Bulletin, Currency & Finance, Annual Report, Occasional Papers, Sen Committee Report, etc.

NABARD

Annual reports and other publications.

Miscellaneous

Agarwal *et al.*, *India*, National, New Delhi (annual).

Jagran's *India at a Glance* 1998.

Observer Research Foundation, Statistical Handbook of India (annual).

Tata Series Ltd., Statistical Outline of India (annual).

Periodicals

Agricultural Situation.
Business Standard.
Bihar Journal of Agricultural Marketing.
Business.
Business Today.
Business India.
Economic & Political Weekly.
Economic Times.
Financial Express.
Frontline.
Hindu.
Hindustan Times.
Illustrated Weekly of India.
Indian Economic Journal.
Indian Economic Review.
Indian Express.
Indian Journal of Agricultural Economics.
Indian Journal of Economics.
Indian Journal of Political Economy
Indian Nation.
India Today.
Journal of Indian Institute of Bankers.
Journal of Indian School of Political Economy.
Journal of Rural Development.
Mainstream.
Observer.
Outlook.
Pioneer.
Sahara.
Searchlight.
Southern Economist.
Span.
Spark.
Statesman.
Sun.
Sunday.
Telegraph.
Times of India.
Tribune.
Week.
Yojana.

CONVERSION TABLE

Area :

1 acre	=	0.4047 hectare.
1 hectare	=	2.471 acres.
	=	10000 sq. metres.
1 mile	=	1.6095 km.
1 square mile	=	2.590 square kilometres.
	=	640 acres.
	=	259 hectares.
1 square kilometre	=	0.3861 square mile.
	=	100 hectares.

Distance :

1 passenger km.	=	0.62137 passenger mile.
1 metric tonne km.	=	0.61558 long tonne mile.

Weight :

1 ounce (oz.)	=	28.3495 grams.
1 gram	=	0.03527 ounce.
1 pound	=	0.4536 kilogram.
1 kilogram	=	2.2046 pounds.
	=	1.072 seer.
	=	34.28 ounces.
100 kilogram	=	1 quintal.
10 quintal	=	1 tonne.
1 metric tonne	=	0.98420 long ton.
	=	1000 kilograms.
	=	2204.63 pounds
1 maund (standard)	=	82.2857 pounds.
	=	27.32 kilograms.
	=	0.0373 metric tonne.
1 seer	=	0.933 kilogram.
	=	933 grams.
1 long tonne	=	1.01605 metric tonne.
	=	1.10231 short tonne.

	=	2240 pounds.
	=	1016.05 kilograms.
1 metric tonne	=	26.792 maunds (standard).
	=	0.98420 long tonne.
	=	1000 kilograms.
1 short tonne	=	0.90718 metric tonne.
	=	2000 pounds.
1 tonne	=	1.016 tons.
	=	1016 kilograms.
	=	2240 pounds.

Volume :

1 cubic foot	=	0.02832 cubic metre.
1 cubic metre	=	35.31 cubic feet.
1 gallon	=	4.536 litres.
1 litre	=	0.2205 gallon.
	=	1.7598 pints
1 pint	=	0.568 litre.

Length :

1 inch	=	2.54 cms.
1 cm.	=	0.3937 inch.
1 km.	=	1,000 metres.
	=	0.6214 miles.
1 mile	=	8 furlongs.
	=	1.609 kilometres.
1 yard	=	3 feet.
	=	0.9144 metre.
1 foot	=	12 inches.
	=	0.3048 metre.
1 metre	=	3.281 feet.
	=	1.094 yards.

Power :

1 kilowatt	=	1.359 horse power.
1 horse power	=	0.7457 kilowatt.

Yield :

1 metric tonne	=	5.5116 bales of Jute (400 lbs.)
1 bale of jute (400 lbs.)	=	0.181436 metric tonne.

INDEX